TERRORISM

Documents of International and Local Control

VOLUME 91

TERRORISM

Documents of International and Local Control

VOLUME 91

TERRORISM INTELLIGENCE: WHAT WE KNOW AND HOW WE KNOW IT

Douglas C. Lovelace Jr., Esquire
Senior National Security Strategist

Oceana®
NEW YORK

OXFORD
UNIVERSITY PRESS

Oxford University Press, Inc., publishes works that further Oxford University's objective of excellence in research, scholarship, and education.

Published by Oxford University Press, Inc.
198 Madison Avenue, New York, New York 10016

Cataloging-in-Publication information is available from the Library of Congress.

ISSN 1062-4007
Terrorism: Documents of International and Local Control

ISBN: 978-0-19-538101-6 (v. 91)

Note to Readers:
This publication is designed to provide accurate and authoritative information in regard to the subject matter covered. It is based upon sources believed to be accurate and reliable and is intended to be current as of the time it was written. It is sold with the understanding that the publisher is not engaged in rendering legal, accounting, or other professional services. If legal advice or other expert assistance is required, the services of a competent professional person should be sought. Also, to confirm that the information has not been affected or changed by recent developments, traditional legal research techniques should be used, including checking primary sources where appropriate.

(Based on the Declaration of Principles jointly adopted by a Committee of the American Bar Association and a Committee of Publishers and Associations.)

TABLE OF CONTENTS

VOLUME 91

TERRORISM INTELLIGENCE: WHAT WE KNOW AND HOW WE KNOW IT

DOCUMENTS

J. INTELLIGENCE ESTIMATES FOR CONGRESS

PREFACE

TERRORISM INTELLIGENCE: WHAT WE KNOW AND HOW WE KNOW IT

In reviewing the key documents that bear on terrorism, one should periodically survey the authoritative publications that describe what is known about the threat posed by terrorists, how it is evolving, and what should be done to increase the nation's capability and capacity for understanding it, in its many variegated aspects. This volume of *Terrorism: Documents of International and Local Control* serves that purpose from a U.S. perspective. It presents and comments on key documents that explain the U.S. Government's understanding of global terrorism, points out the more salient concerns, and suggests ways to increase U.S. security. Due to space constraints, the volume presents only enough key documents to bring the reader up to date on the major issues that shape contemporary perceptions of the threat, current actions to reduce it, and future plans to thwart it.

The volume appropriately begins with a discussion of the 2006 and 2007 *Country Reports on Global Terrorism,* produced by the U.S. Department of State's Office of the Coordinator for Counterterrorism. These reports are directly relevant to the volume's discussion of intelligence on terrorists. Volume 70 of this series presented the 2006 *Country Reports on Global Terrorism*; therefore, this volume resumes discussion of the topic with *Trends in Terrorism: 2006,* a report for Congress prepared by the Congressional Research Service in 2006, that assessed the 2006 *Country Reports on Global Terrorism. Trends in Terrorism: 2006* paves the way for presentation and analysis of the 2007 *Country Reports on Global Terrorism* provided in this volume. The astute reader will note several significant differences between the observations reported in the 2006 and the 2007 reports. *Trends in Terrorism: 2006* assists in understanding some of those differences. The three documents provide an excellent foundational suite for updating our understanding of the terrorism threat to U.S. national security.

After presenting *Trends in Terrorism: 2006* and the 2007 *Country Reports on Global Terrorism,* the volume presents *Terrorist Precursor Crimes: Issues and*

Options for Congress. This document is an excellent overview of an issue set that has received far too little attention. The report points out that terrorist groups all require funding, operations security, and coercive power. To meet those fundamental needs, terrorist organizations engage in criminal activity; therefore, they commit an array of "precursor crimes" to facilitate their ultimate acts of terror. The key question posed by the report is what can be done, at all levels of government, to identify and thwart such precursor crimes, and where prevention fails, to bring the perpetrators to justice, thus eliminating terrorism capacity over time.

Next, the volume presents, in its unclassified form, what is arguably the most prominent terrorism intelligence document of 2007. A presentation of the intelligence of terrorism would be incomplete absent the inclusion of the *National Intelligence Estimate of the Terrorist Threat to the US Homeland*. National intelligence estimates (NIEs) are the most important intelligence judgments by what is referred to as the Intelligence Community (IC). They provide policy makers and strategists key judgments about the likely course of future events and identify implications for U.S. policy. The *National Intelligence Estimate of the Terrorist Threat to the US Homeland* offers several key judgments on the Global War Against Terrorists. NIEs are collaborative products, in that they are produced and vetted among many different organizations comprising the IC. The DNI or his representative briefs the NIEs to the President or his representative and senior policy makers. Of late, the U.S. Congress has developed a healthy appetite for NIEs.

The statements for the record provided in this volume add texture to the July 2007 NIE discussed above. The Director of National Intelligence (DNI), J. Michael McConnell, begins his statement with a discussion of the findings of the NIE, reminding the committee that an NIE is the most authoritative written judgment of the IC on a particular subject. He then uses the quality of the NIE to suggest that many improvements to the Intelligence Community (IC) have been made since September 11, 2001. In that regard, he first discusses intelligence reforms that moved the IC away from its lingering Cold War structure. The DNI's statement is accompanied by that of John Scott Redd, Director of the National Counterterrorism Center. Vice Admiral (Ret) Redd begins by addressing the role the National Counterterrorism Center (NCTC) plays in detecting, disrupting, and deterring the threat of terrorism against U.S. interests both at home and abroad.

The volume next presents the Federal Bureau of Investigation's (FBI) report on publicly acknowledged terrorist incidents and preventions that occurred on U.S. territory during the years 2002 through 2005. It omits criminal incidents not designated as terrorism by the FBI, but discusses major FBI investigations overseas and identifies significant events and program developments relevant to U.S. counterterrorism efforts. The report concludes with a summary of the history of the FBI's counterterrorism program. The report is not intended to be a comprehensive annual review of worldwide terrorist activity.

Cyberterrorism has become a prominent topic in national security circles. In the spring of 2007, Estonian government computers suffered debilitating attacks by what many believe were political protestors. The protestors may have hired the expertise of cybercriminals to execute the attack. U.S. Department of Defense (DOD) experts opine that similar cyberattacks from individuals, groups, and countries will increasingly target economic, political, and military organizations in the future. This volume presents *Botnets, Cybercrime, and Cyberterrorism: Vulnerabilities and Policy Issues for Congress,* to provide a more complete picture of the terrorist threat the United States and other advanced countries will face in the future.

The extraordinary expansion of the worldwide web and the attendant information explosion have made an enormous amount of information available from what the IC refers to as open sources. Unclassified, open source information now figures prominently in intelligence analysis and policy making. *Open Source Intelligence (OSINT): Issues for Congress* provides an up to date assessment of open source information and its use in gathering intelligence on terrorist suspects.

This volume presents the *Intelligence Authorization Act of 2008* to help inform the reader of the intelligence priorities of the U.S. Congress and to alert the reader as to how they support the Global War Against Terrorists. Although the bill was vetoed by the President and returned to Congress unsigned, it still is a must read, if one is to understand the sense of Congress with respect to intelligence support for the War. The volume also presents and discusses the President's veto.

The final document this volume presents, *Intelligence Estimates: How Useful to Congress?*, provides an interesting discussion of the pros and cons of Congress' increased appetite for such assessments. In this report the Congressional Research Service questions the actual utility of NIEs to Congress. It acknowledges Congress' ever-increasing interest in NIEs, as the U.S. government's formal intelligence assessments of various critical issues affecting U.S. national security. However, the CRS report prudently cautions that formulation of an NIE is time consuming and not an exact science. It also reminds us that any NIE is only as good as the information upon which it is based.

Together, the documents presented in this volume should edify even seasoned intelligence analysts and national security policy makers. Although they may raise as many questions as they answer, the documents are offered to prepare readers to participate in a more informed way in ongoing debates concerning intelligence collection and use for diminishing the threat of terrorism. Moreover, the documents help inform strategy formulation that will lead to greater national security. The publishers of *Terrorism: Documents of International and Local Control* are pleased to present them.

A. TRENDS IN TERRORISM

TRENDS IN TERRORISM: 2006

CRS Report for Congress

July 21, 2006

Commentary

The 2006 and 2007 *Country Reports on Global Terrorism*, produced by the U.S. Department of State's Office of the Coordinator for Counterterrorism are relevant to this volume's discussion of intelligence on terrorists. Volume 70 of this series presented the 2006 report; so, it is not included here. Instead, this volume presents *Trends in Terrorism: 2006*, a report for Congress prepared by the Congressional Research Service. *Trends in Terrorism: 2006*, published to the U.S. Congress on July 21, 2006, references the 2005 report and assesses the 2006 *Country Reports on Global Terrorism*. In doing so, it serves as a bridge to the 2007 *Country Reports on Global Terrorism* provided in this volume, with appropriate commentary. The Country Reports are immensely valuable to scholars, policymakers, and researchers alike. The astute reader will note several significant differences between the observations reported in the 2006 and 2007 reports. *Trends in Terrorism: 2006* assists in understanding some of those differences. The three documents provide an excellent foundational suite for updating our understanding of the terrorism threat to U.S. national security.

The Department of State (DOS) provided the 2006 countries report to Congress on April 28, 2006. The comprehensive report provided Congress the annual strategic assessment it required of trends in terrorism and multinational efforts to curb it. In many instances it provided very detailed information. Buttressed by extensive data, the report describes a radical Jihadist threat that is becoming increasingly diffused and locally originated. The report correctly observes that many of the global terrorist threat organizations, cells, or individuals have no linkage or affiliation with al-Qaeda, as some argue. For good reason, the report presents no convincing evidence to suggest that al-Qaeda's leaders and leaders of other terrorist organizations collaborate or even coordinate their terrorist activities.

The report describes three trends in terrorism, which an expert analyst could accept readily. First, the report describes the emergence of "micro-actors," or small cells or individuals who are unable to forge alliances with large organizations like al-Qaeda, because of the United States' and other's effectiveness at eliminating or intimidating their leadership. Those successes have cause al-Qaeda leadership and the leaders of other high-visibility terrorist organizations to "go to ground" in the interest of self-preservation. The resultant inhibition on activity makes it difficult for them to reach out to potential allies and increases their suspicion of those who seek access to them.

The second trend is one toward more sophistication. Terrorists have turned more toward exploiting the global flow of information, finance, and ideas to their benefit, often through the Internet. This byproduct of increasing and irreversible globalization comes as no great surprise. An open Internet is necessary for global commerce but presents many opportunities for terrorists. That said, the U.S. and other governments are becoming more adept at protecting their networks from attack, misuse, and abuse, while at the same time constantly acquiring more effective capabilities for tracking down terrorists through their Internet usage. Additionally, the public is becoming more Internet savvy and more difficult to exploit. The time may soon come when cyberspace is no longer a safe maneuvering space for terrorists.

The third trend the report astutely presents is that much of what is being described as politically motivated terrorism is violence administered for other purposes, such as economic gain or revenge. Those genres of violence, though terrible in nature, are more appropriately viewed as criminal activity to be addressed by law enforcement means and judicial processes. Some respected analysts report, for example, that much of the "terrorism" in Iraq is criminal activity carried out by Mafia-type organizations interested mostly in economic gain. The same observation could be made for acts of terrorism elsewhere in the world. Nonetheless, the report legitimately suggests a nexus between terrorism and criminal activity that clearly exists, to the extent that true terrorists finance their efforts through robberies, kidnappings, drug dealing, and the like.

The CRS report obliquely criticizes the 2006 countries report for not recognizing that the increase in some dimensions of terrorism in Iraq are actually insurgent activity, as well as criminal activity. Terrorism, however, is a tactic, not a form of warfare and not the continuation of politics by other means. It is merely a tactic that can serve political, criminal, and insurgent efforts.

The countries report suggests that state sponsorship of terrorism is on the decline, except in the case of Iran and Syria—two very notable exceptions. One should be slow to embrace this observation, however, since it is likely explained by a reduced propensity of states to openly admit support for terrorist acts and an increased difficulty in tracing an attack back to a nation state, as states and terrorists become more sophisticated in their approaches. Still, it is likely that the most important factor preventing a weapons-of-mass-destruction attack on the United States is the counter-proliferation effect that results from the probability of being able to attribute a nuclear or biological weapon to a particular nation state.

The countries report foresees a larger number of smaller attacks in the immediate future. Many analysts disagree with that assessment. They posit that since opportunities for attacks are significantly limited by more effective offensive and defensive security measures, terrorist organizations such as al-Qaeda will bide their time, until they believe that they can mount a devastating attack. The CRS report suggests that a shift in anti-terror tactics toward law enforcement measures and away from military approaches may be appropriate. In a sense, that is a false dichotomy, since both efforts may and do occur simultaneously.

Specifically, the CRS report asks that if terrorist acts are becoming more the product of localized micro-actors, should the U.S. anti-terror strategy and tactics reflect a more international law-enforcement oriented approach. The CRS report suggests that such an approach was envisioned in the February 2003 *National Strategy for Combating Terrorism*. A careful reading of that document, however, leaves one with the impression that it contemplates a whole-of-government approach. Still, the CRS report's recommendations that policymakers should consider expanding programs that support foreign law enforcement training and educational exchanges, joint and multilateral training exercises, the creation of bilateral or multilateral law enforcement task forces, staff exchanges among foreign and domestic law enforcement agencies, and expansion of "rule of law" programs have great merit.

The CRS report also notes that many are calling for more effective public diplomacy, to counter terrorists' efforts to gain the support of vulnerable populations, in order to recruit soldiers. Additionally, the CRS report calls for better collection, analysis, fusion, and sharing of intelligence across government agencies domestically and multilaterally. It sees benefit in greater participation in the intelligence process by industry, state and local governments, and academia, as well. Those are all good thoughts, but implementation will be difficult, given the distinctly different cultures and motivations of the disparate entities. In total, however, the CRS report makes many important points and is worthy of a careful read.

DOCUMENT NO. 1

TRENDS IN TERRORISM: 2006

CRS Report
RL33555

July 21, 2006

Raphael Perl
Specialist in International Affairs
Foreign Affairs, Defense, and Trade Division

Summary

On April 28, 2006, the Department of State sent to Congress its annual report on global terrorism: *Country Reports on Global Terrorism 2005*. The 262-page report provides an annual strategic assessment of trends in terrorism and the evolving nature of the terrorist threat, coupled with detailed information on anti-terror cooperation by nations worldwide. The report and underlying data portray a threat from radical Jihadists that is becoming more widespread, diffuse, and increasingly homegrown, often with a lack of formal operational connection with al Qaeda ideological leaders such as Osama Bin Laden or Ayman al Zawahiri.

Three trends in terrorism are identified in the Department of State report which are independently reflected in the work of analysts elsewhere. First is the emergence of so called "micro actors," in part spurred by U.S. successes in isolating or killing much of al Qaeda's leadership. The result is an al Qaeda with a more subdued, although arguably still significant, operational role, but assuming more of an ideological, motivational, and propaganda role. Second is the trend toward "sophistication"; i.e. terrorists exploiting the global flow of information, finance, and ideas to their benefit, often through the internet. Third is an increasing overlap of terrorist activity with international crime, which may expose the terrorists to a broad range of law enforcement countermeasures.

The report notes an overall increase in suicide bombings, especially in Iraq, where terror incidents accounted for almost a third of all terror incidents globally in 2005 and more than half of terror related deaths worldwide. However, some observers suggest that much of what the report characterizes as terrorist incidents in Iraq would be better categorized as insurgent activity and also to some degree as criminal activity. The report suggests that active, direct, state sponsorship of terror is declining, with the notable exceptions of Iran and perhaps to some degree Syria.

Emerging trends that may require enhanced policy focus are (1) attacks that aim to cause economic damage such as attacks on transportation infrastructure, tourism, and oil installations, (2) the growing number of unattributed terrorist attacks, and (3) the growing power and influence of radical Islamist political parties in foreign nations. Recent suggestions that al Qaeda remains operationally active are of growing concern as well.

The State Department report suggests an immediate future with a larger number of "smaller attacks, less meticulously planned, and local rather than transnational in scope." If so, some adjustment in implementation of United States anti-terror strategy and tactics to reflect a more international law enforcement oriented approach, such as that envisioned in the February 2003 *National Strategy for Combating Terrorism*, may be warranted. As the global economic, political, and technological landscapes evolve, data being collected to identify and track terrorism may need to change.

This report will not be updated.

Background

Purpose and Scope of Report

This report summarizes and discusses trends in terrorism as identified in recent analyses by the State Department, the National Counter Terrorism Center (NCTC), and independent analysts. Potential issues for Congress arising out of these analyses are identified and discussed as well.

This report is one of several related CRS reports discussing issues related to trends in terrorism.[1] A selection of additional CRS reports addressing terrorism is found at the conclusion of this report

Definition of Trends

For the purposes of this report, trends in terrorism can be defined as changes in the type, number, and lethality of terrorist attacks (*modus operandi*), attitudes of terrorist groups, and other factors, over time. Changes in terrorist infrastructure such as those related to command and control,

[1] CRS Report RL33160, *Combating Terrorism: The Challenge of Measuring Effectiveness* and CRS Report RL32417, *The Department of State's Patterns of Global Terrorism Report: Trends, State Sponsors, and Related Issues*, both by Raphael Perl.

capabilities, recruiting, and financing are often considered particularly meaningful. What are the capabilities of a terrorist group to inflict serious damage? Are they increasing or decreasing? For example, a large number of terrorist groups might be seeking to acquire a nuclear, chemical, or biological explosive device but may lack the resources or capability to achieve this objective and the technical expertise to employ such technology.[2] In what ways are terrorist capabilities and expertise changing?

Relevant as well is whether the leadership of a particular terrorist group or network is being weakened; is its recruitment base, network, or target list growing; and is the number of defectors from its ranks increasing or decreasing? To what degree may an organization be changing its role from an operational one to an ideological/inspirational one? Have the intentions or ideology of a movement or group changed and if so are they more or less radical—more or less focused on causing widespread damage? Are they becoming increasingly involved in criminal activities or seeking to cause violence for its own sake? Also relevant are changes in levels of popular and government support for specific terrorist organizations.

Importance of Trends

Identifying trends as indicators of terrorist activity can assist policymakers in a number of areas including (1) prioritizing counter-terror resources; (2) targeting terrorists and terrorist activity with the intention of preventing attacks; and (3) showing anti-terror progress where it has been achieved.

In addition to trends influencing government responses, government anti-terrorism strategies and tactics may also affect terrorism trends.[3] For example, hardening U.S. government physical infrastructure overseas or in the United States might cause terrorists to shift the focus of attacks to softer non-government targets, or to employ new explosion delivery methods such as improvised explosive devices (IEDs), or to deploy suicide bombers. Likewise, better systems to evaluate the authenticity and content of travel entry documents at lawful U.S. ports of entry might prompt terrorists to switch from the legal entry tactics employed by the 9/11 hijackers to crossing the U.S. border at unsecured locations.

---

[2] For a discussion of issues involved in measuring terrorist capabilities and government countermeasures, see CRS Report RL33160.

[3] Insight into this phenomenon comes from a media report of a document reportedly contained on a computer chip found June 7, 2006, on the body of Abu Musab Zarqawi, the Jordanian born al Qaeda leader in Iraq. The document is said to list a number of allied successes against terrorist activity including massive arrests, tightening financial outlets, confiscating weapons and ammunition, and a media campaign successful in portraying terrorism as harmful to the population and in magnifying the terrorist's mistakes. A need is cited for counteractions designed to improve the image of the terrorist "resistance," increase its number of supporters, and exploit social, ethnic and class divisions within the society and between it and the allies. Building the group's own armaments industry is cited as a revised goal as well. See "Papers Reveal Weakening Terror Group," by Rowan Scarborough, *The Washington Times*, June 16, 2006, p.1.

Trends in terrorism may also be influenced by responses perceived by terrorists as directly related to advancing their cause or detracting from it—such as the number of governments that embrace appeasement policies—and the amount of media coverage the terrorists receive. A related issue is how U.S. policies and actions affect trends in terrorists' popular support and recruiting. Has the U.S. intervention in Iraq, for example, led to the demotivation, detention, or killing of more terrorists than the number of individuals it may have radicalized in areas important to U.S. interests around the world?

Some analysts question whether the diverse nature of individual terrorists and terrorist networks—which often seek to cultivate surprise—allows for meaningful trend analysis. Others point out the potential pitfall of using past trends as predictors of future activity, such as assuming that because a particular activity has not been observed for a long period of time, there is no concomitant threat. The absence of violent conflict or even decreases in terrorist activity may simply mean that terrorists are focusing attention on economic, political, or social spheres, or just that they are in a planning or "waiting period."[4] Another potential pitfall is to project trends in a linear fashion. Such projections can miss qualitative changes in modus operandi, particularly those that move to new types of terror.

Trends are usually identified by the executive branch and independent analysts on the basis of empirical data collected by public and private sources. As the global economic, political, and technological landscape evolves, and as terrorists may seek to surprise and attack through more fluid organizational structures and in innovative ways, data being collected to identify and track terrorism may need to change. Hence, one challenge facing the counter-terrorism community is how to facilitate incorporation of new data indicative of new trends while maintaining the continuity of earlier data where relevant.[5] Another challenge is how to

---

[4] For example, in *The One Percent Doctrine: Deep Inside America's Pursuit of Its Enemies Since 9/11*, Ron Suskind reports that al Qaeda's leadership called off a planned gas attack on the New York subway system in 2003, speculation being that it was not deemed spectacular enough. See "Book Argues al Qaeda Planned NYC Gas Attack," Reuters dispatch of June 17, 2006, and book excerpt in *Time*, p. 27–35, June 26, 2006. Calling off a planned attack, if true, may suggest the presence of a trend of avoiding small-to-medium incidents in the United States—or conversely—concentrating on a mega-attack that would dwarf the incidents of 9/11 in terms of horror, casualties and economic damage. A common pitfall of those seeking to identify or enumerate trends is an overreliance on *quantitative* indicators at the expense of their *qualitative* significance. For example, a single large scale attack causing many casualties could have a major impact, far more than a dozen relatively small attacks.

Moreover, a single qualitatively creative/different incident may prove to be the beginning of a trend by triggering a wave of copycat follow-on terror incidents with a resultant change in terrorists' strategy, weapons, tactics, and targets. See for example: "Hamas Trying to Add Toxic Chemicals to Bombs," by Amos Harel, [http://www.haaretz.com], (Israeli Daily), June 6, 2006, citing Israeli security sources.

[5] An example of such efforts is the recent upgrading by the National Counter Terrorism Center (NCTC) of its collection methodologies to support the State Department's annual report on terrorism and the changes in format and content of the report [currently titled: *Country Reports on Terrorism, 2005*].

anticipate sinister trends and prevent them before they materialize. Such anticipation, supported by accurate intelligence, is widely regarded as central to an effective policy of deterrence and preemption.

Markedly different pictures can be presented depending on what one chooses to include in data relating to terrorism. For example, some would argue that the Iraq casualties—which are largely the product of sectarian violence, rampant criminal activity, and home grown insurgency—grossly distort the global terrorism picture and perhaps should not be attributed to terrorist activity. According to NCTC data, outside of Iraq, the total number of incidents with ten or more deaths remained at approximately the 2003-2004 level—70 per year. This suggests that, excluding Iraq, the number of higher casualty terror attacks remains relatively stable.

Reported Trends in Terrorism

2006 State Department Report

On April 28, 2006, the Department of State sent to Congress its annual report on global terrorism: *Country Reports on Global Terrorism 2005.*[6] Statistical data on terrorist incidents, which form the basis for the report's analysis, are provided by the newly created National Counter Terrorism Center (NCTC).[7] The 262-page report provides an annual strategic assessment of trends in terrorism and the evolving nature of the terrorist threat, coupled with detailed information on anti-terror cooperation by nations worldwide. The report focuses on trends related to: (1) state sponsors of terrorism; (2) foreign terrorist organizations; (3) the terrorist situation in individual countries (including those that provide safe haven for terrorists); (4) potential terrorist acquisition of weapons of mass destruction (WMD); and (5) U.S. antiterrorism coalition building efforts and cooperative endeavors. Within its discussion of policies intended to shape trends in a desired direction, the report emphasizes building international will and capacity for counterterrorism, including the issue of countering terrorism on the economic front.

The report and underlying data portray a threat from radical Jihadists which is becoming more widespread, diffuse, possibly more deadly, and increasingly homegrown, often with a lack of apparent formal operational connection with al Qaeda ideological leaders although perhaps inspired by

---

See CRS Report RL32417, *The Department of State's Patterns of Global Terrorism Report: Trends, State Sponsors, and Related Issues,* by Raphael Perl.

[6] [http://www.state.gov/s/ct/rls/crt/c17689.htm] See also: testimony of John Scott Redd, Director, National Counterterrorism Center, and testimony of Henry A. Crumpton, Coordinator for Counterterrorism before the Senate Foreign Relations Committee in a hearing on "Counterterrorism: The Changing Face of Terror," June 13, 2006.

[7] [http://www.nctc.gov]

them or assisted through training. This homegrown phenomenon of looser, and more local, networks was manifest in the May 2003 restaurant, hotel, and Jewish cultural center bombings in Morocco; the 2004 attacks on Madrid's trains; the July 7 and July 21, 2005 terrorist attacks on London's transit system; and more recently—after the report's release—in the June 2, 2006, arrests of 12 men and 5 juveniles in Ontario, Canada on bombing conspiracy-related charges.[8] This emergence of a global-homegrown terror movement has lent itself to the characterization of terrorism as a "glocal" phenomenon.

Five major trends in the evolution of terrorism are included in the State Department report:

More Micro-Actors

The report depicts the emergence of micro-actors as having been spurred by the widespread use of the internet, militant preachers and the impact of Arabic language television, coupled with U.S. and allied successes in capturing, isolating, and killing much of al Qaeda's leadership in Afghanistan, thereby reducing its centralized command and control capability. The result, according to the report, is an al Qaeda seen to be assuming more of an ideological, motivational, propaganda role, and a reduced operational role.[9]

The report views the operational component of the movement as increasingly being assumed by small autonomous cells and individuals—often homegrown with a resultant diversity in identity profiles, structures, motives, and tactics. Such operational cells may be new to the terrorism landscape, may be technologically savvy and small, decentralized, and without regular communication with other groups or cells.[10] These characteristics make their actions extremely difficult to detect or counter. As a result, according to the report, a growing percentage of future terrorist attacks may be carried out by micro-actors using traditional bombs and bullets rather than more lethal weapons.

Increased Sophistication

Increasingly, according to the report, terrorists are seen as exploiting the global movement of information, finance, and ideas to their benefit. They are

[8] Canadian officials have stated that the majority of those arrested in the June 2nd operation were native born Canadians. Note, however, that some experts, such as Peter Bergen and Alexis Debat, think there was some Ayman Al Zawahari involvement in the London train attacks—such as training of the bomb makers and perhaps in the Madrid attacks as well. See Bergen article cited in note 27 below. See also: "Al Qaeda Video Emerges on Eve of Anniversary" by Alan Cowell, *New York Times*, July 6, 2006, suggesting al Qaeda sought to be associated with the July 2005 train and bus bombings.

[9] See CRS Report RL32759, *Al Qaeda: Statements and Evolving Ideology* by Christopher M. Blanchard.

[10] This lack of regular communication should not be construed as implying that such relationships are necessarily casual.

also seen as improving their technological sophistication across many areas of operational planning, communications, targeting, and propaganda.[11] According to some observers, terrorism has become a "web directed" phenomenon.[12]

Overlap with International Crime

The report describes a growing overlap between terrorism and international crime. Such a trend, to the extent that terrorists do indeed use the same supply, transport, and money-moving networks used by criminal groups, creates a major vulnerability that can be exploited by law enforcement authorities: the more terrorists engage in non-terror forms of criminal activity, the more likely they are to show up on the law enforcement radar screen and the more likely they are to be subject to arrest and prosecution under a far reaching umbrella of general criminal statutes and more specific terror related laws as well.[13]

Increase in Suicide Bombings/Links between U.S. Iraqi Operations and Global Terror

Also cited in the report are an increase in suicide bombings,[14] and a strong connection between the ongoing unrest in Iraq and the broader war on terrorism. Terror incidents in Iraq, according to the report, accounted for almost a third of all terror incidents globally in 2005 and more than half of all the terror related deaths worldwide. There is concern that Iraq will become an exporter of seasoned terrorists, weapons, and shared tactics—especially the use of improvised explosive devices (IEDs) with "spillover" not only into the neighboring Gulf nations, but to Europe and other regions as well.[15]

[11] Many experts are concerned about the vulnerability of global infrastructures to attacks by cyber-terrorists. See CRS Report RL32114, *Computer Attack and Cyberterrorism: Vulnerabilities and Policy Issues for Congress*, by Clay Wilson. Some speculate that al Qaeda-linked terrorists attach numerological significance to the selection of dates for terror attacks. For example, some suggest one possibility would be that a massive cyber-attack might occur on the date 4/11, the phone number commonly dialed for information. For a discussion of the overall issue of technology and terrorism, see "The Future of Terrorism" by the editors of *Discover*, v. 27, No.7, July 2006, p. 32–42, 76.

[12] See for example: "Terrorists Turn to the Web as Base of Operations" by Steve Coll and Susan B. Glasser, *Washington Post*, Aug.7, 2005, p. A1 and *Terror on the Internet: The New Arena, the New Challenges* by Gabriel Weimann, United States Institute for Peace (Washington, D.C.) 2006, 309 p.

[13] Reportedly, criminal activity financed, in part, the 2004 Madrid bombings (drug trafficking) and the 2005 London bombings (credit card fraud).

[14] Although the total number of suicide bombings increased in 2005, is not fully clear that the ratio of suicide bombings to other forms of attacks has increased concomitantly.

[15] NCTC data indicate that Iraq accounted for almost 30% of worldwide terrorist attacks in 2005, and 55% of the fatalities. Moreover, attacks on non-combatants in Iraq also increased significantly last year.

Decline in State-Sponsored Terrorism and Increased State Antiterrorism Cooperation[16]

Aside from **Iran**, and perhaps to some degree **Syria**, the report suggests that, with a few notable exceptions, active state sponsorship of terror is declining. The report continues to list **Iran** as the most active state sponsor of terrorism.[17] As in previous years, **Syria** is cited for providing political and material support (presumably weapons) to both Hizballah and Palestinian terrorist groups, which also enjoy sanctuary in Syria. **Cuba** and **North Korea** are primarily cited for lack of anti-terror cooperation and past involvement in terrorist incidents thereby possibly suggesting a trend of less active support for terrorism than in previous decades.

The report says that the **Saudi Government** "carried out numerous operations resulting in the capture or killing of all 26 wanted terrorists publicized in a December 2003 state announcement." The report cites close cooperation with **Pakistan's** security services and notes that Pakistan "captured or killed hundreds of terrorists, significantly increasing the effectiveness of its counterterrorism operation," and stresses that President Musharraf has declared a "Jihad on extremism" and promised to close down extremist institutions. Some observers might argue, however, that the report tends to mute criticism of nations of strategic importance to the United States, such as **Pakistan** and **Saudi Arabia,** that arguably could do much more to curb terror.

Echoing language of previous years' versions of the report, the 2006 edition states that **Libya** and **Sudan** "continued to take significant steps to cooperate in the global war on terror." Although specific examples of cooperation are cited for each of the two nations, the report—which was drafted and went to press early in 2006—otherwise contained little to

---

[16] Nations on the State Department's legislatively mandated list of state sponsors of terrorism are Cuba, Iran, North Korea, Sudan, and Syria. Libya was certified by the Secretary of State as being eligible for removal from the list on May 12, 2006. See Presidential Determination No. 2006-14, May 12, 2006, which went into effect June 28, 2006. [http://www.whitehouse.gov/news/releases/2006/05/20060515-5.html]

[17] As in preceding years, the report cites Iran as the most active state supporter of terrorism and states that its Islamic Revolutionary Guard Corps and Ministry of Intelligence and Security were directly involved in the planning and execution of terrorist acts. That included providing Lebanese Hizballah and Palestinian terrorist groups with extensive funding, training and weapons. The Revolutionary Guard, it is asserted, was increasingly involved in supplying "lethal assistance" to Iraqi militant groups with the effect of destabilizing Iraq. Also addressed was Iran's continued development of a nuclear program and that Iran is "also capable of producing biological and chemical agents or weapons." Iran, the report states, "could support terrorist organizations seeking to acquire WMD." The report does not specifically address growing concerns among some experts that Iran might use surrogate organizations with broad networks, e.g. Hizballah, as delivery vehicles for dirty bombs for the enriched radioactive material generated by its "nuclear research." The report also does not discuss Iran's allegedly active role in training and equipping insurgents in Iraq. See June 22, 2006, Press Conference of Defense Secretary Donald Rumsfeld.

support speculation that Libya would be subsequently proposed for removal from the U.S. list of state sponsors of international terrorism.

2005 NCTC Statistical Data

Beginning with data collected in 2005, the NCTC substantially revised its methodology for reporting incidents and increased the priority and number of personnel assigned to compiling data on terrorism incidents and trends, leading to what Administration officials characterize as more accurate and comprehensive reporting. These methodological changes contributed to a significant increase in the reported number of terrorism incidents.[18]

Data released by the NCTC concurrently with the Department of State's 2006 terror report indicate the following:

In 2005, the NCTC lists roughly 40,000 individuals wounded or killed in terrorist incidents as compared to 9,300 the previous year and 4,271 in 2003. Reported terror-related deaths in 2005 numbered 14,602 as compared to 1,907 deaths in 2004 and 625 in 2003. The report placed the number of total reported terrorist attacks in 2005 at 11,111 as compared to 3,168 in 2004 and 208 in 2003. Foiled attacks are not included in the data reported.

Other highlights of the NCTC's data include:

- armed attacks and bombings accounted for the vast majority of fatalities in 2005.
- of the 11,111 attacks reported, 6,000 or roughly 54%, were against facilities and resulted in no casualties.
- of the approximately 40,000 persons worldwide killed or wounded—at least 10 to 15 thousand were Muslim with approximately 80 mosques being attacked, in most cases by Muslim extremists, with a high percentage of these incidents occurring in Iraq.
- approximately 6,600 police, 1000 children, 300 government officials, 170 clergy/religious figures, 140 teachers, and 100 journalists were killed or wounded by terrorists in 2005.

Trends Reported by Other Sources

Trends in terrorist activity have been the subject of analysis by many other organizations and analysts. In many instances, such independent analysis

[18] See for example: "Terrorists Killed More than 14,500 People in 2005, Report Says," *Bloomberg*, April 28, 2006, citing public comments by Russell Travers, a Deputy Director at the NCTC. Note that NCTC data come from a variety of open and closed sources both U.S. and foreign, public sector and private sector/academia, including efforts at rigorous tracking of incidents by U.S. Embassy personnel stationed overseas. However, it has always been difficult to pin down details of attacks in villages in rural areas such as those of Algeria or Egypt, for example, where the press and local government reporting of incidents may be incomplete and sketchy.

is consistent with the trends identified by the State Department in its recent report. In some instances, the emergence of additional trends is also suggested. For example, a 2006 report by the Netherlands Central Intelligence and Security Services cites trends of:

- increasing home grown terrorism;
- decentralization and implantation of international jihad;
- radicalization and emergence of local networks and;
- incitement of jihad through the internet—to include self- radicalization, possibly of lone operating terrorists.[19]

A multi-authored 2005 study by the RAND Corporation finds:

- increased focus on soft civilian-focused targets;
- ongoing emphasis on economic attacks; [20]
- continued reliance on suicide attacks;
- a desire to attack with WMD but little ability to execute attacks;
- more homegrown attacks and;
- the possibility of future attacks from the far right, anarchists, and radical environmentalists.[21]

Trends noted by others include

- decreases in the average age of terrorist recruits;
- greater organizational/operational roles for women and non-Muslims;
- potentially more terrorist acts rooted in a "backlash" against the impact of globalization;
- more near-simultaneous coordinated attacks with follow-up attacks on first responders;
- potentially wider use by criminals of terrorist-type tactics;
- more terrorists acts that remain unclaimed by those committing them; and

[19] *Violent Jihad in the Netherlands: Current Trends in the Islamist Terrorist Threat*, [http://english.nctb.nl/Images/Violent%20jihad%20in%20the%20Netherlands%202006_ tcm127-112471.pdf].

[20] When discussing attacks aimed to cause economic damage, analysts often cite as examples attacks on oil related targets such as planned attacks on Saudi oil installations in February and March 2006, the October 2002 attack on the French supertanker, Limberg, in the Straits of Hormuz off the Yemeni coast, and a likelihood of future attacks on oil installations in the Persian Gulf and possibly in Nigeria. Also notable and well documented are attacks aimed at damaging tourism (e.g. Bali, Luxor) and those disrupting transportation infrastructure (Madrid, London, and plots foiled in July 2006 reportedly aimed at the Holland tunnel in New York).

[21] *Trends in Terrorism, Threats to the United States and the Future of the Terrorism Risk Insurance Act*, by Peter Chalk et al, RAND, Center for Terrorism and Risk Management Policy, 2005.

- an overall rise in the number of terrorist attacks, potentially encompassing acts rooted in a variety of causes and committed by a growing diversity of groups and individuals.[22]

Some of the core "terrorism-enabling" factors that these sources view as contributing to and facilitating many of the trends highlighted by the Department of State and others include:

- Weak legal and law enforcement systems in some countries that enable terrorist and criminal networks to operate with relative ease;
- Expanded, instant, and often relatively anonymous or secure communications and networking channels offered to terrorists by the Internet;[23] and
- The potential for "spillover" of battlefield skills, technology and ordnance from Iraq.

Issues for Congress

Consistency/Compatibility and Significance of Data

One important issue raised by the Department of State report is whether data released by the NCTC concomitantly with the 2006 terror report can be used to support categorical assessments of trends in terrorist activity, since both the methodology for compiling such data and the resources devoted to the data have significantly changed over time.[24] Others might argue that in a long-term struggle against terror it may not be critical whether terrorist incidents are up or down within a particular time-frame.

---

[22] See the 2005 Princeton Colloquium on Public and International Affairs, "Rethinking the War on Terrorism," June 19, 2005. [http://uc.princeton.edu/main/index.php?option =com_content&task=view&id=21&Itemid=11].

[23] See "Jihad 2.0" by Nadya Labi, *Atlantic Monthly*, July/Aug. 2006, v.297, No.6, p. 102–108. Note that intelligence sources that at any one/given time there are some 4,500 active terrorist-affiliated websites in use. See also *Terror on the Internet. The New Arena the New Challenges*, by Gabriel Weimann, United States Institute for Peace, (Washington, D.C.) 2006, 309 p.

[24] The NCTC uses a definition of terrorism for its 2005 data collection that is significantly broader and includes acts of terror which formerly might have been excluded because they were not considered truly international or that may have previously been excluded because the victims might have not have been defined as non-combatants. See NCTC: *Report on Incidents of Terrorism, 2005, and NCTC: Country Reports on Terrorism 2005, Statistical Annex*. The revised/broader definition of terrorism used by the NCTC is "premeditated, politically motivated violence perpetrated against noncombatant targets." In past years, the report did not attempt to fully tally terrorist attacks that killed only the citizens of the country in which the attack took place. This was partly due to difficulties with the resources available to obtain accurate information on attacks that occurred in rural areas of some countries or where the United States did not see itself directly affected by the violence. However some observers argue that this resulted in not providing a sufficiently full picture of the terrorist situation, especially when a major attack might have had important political consequences, such as affecting peace talks or other developments.

In conjunction with the release of the 2006 State Department report, Rep. Henry A. Waxman, ranking minority member of the House Government Reform Committee, released a 4-page critique titled "The Bush Administration's Data on Global Terrorism in 2005," which expressed concerns about the meaning of the upsurge in incidents and the role of Iraq in the upswing.

In the view of these observers, what might be more critical is the need to recognize that terror remains an evolving widespread, ongoing, deadly, and sustained threat that must be addressed on many fronts, and even if the data should indicate downturns in terrorist incidents, policymakers need to beware a false sense of complacency or victory.

A Weakened al Qaeda?

A controversial and politically volatile issue raised by the Department of State report is to what extent al Qaeda has been weakened operationally in the wake of capture and killing of a substantial number of its leaders and operatives.[25] The common perception, correct or not, is that al Qaeda's command and control capabilities have been weakened to the point that the network is unwilling or unable to conduct operations, thereby prompting an evolution in al Qaeda's role to one of ideological inspiration and guidance. An alternate perspective is that a resilient and adaptive al Qaeda is planning the next mega-attack(s) and not wanting to get involved on the operational level in smaller scale attacks until execution of its next major operation.[26] Under such a mindset, involvement in operations before the next mega-attack is simply not a goal—topping the destruction and economic damage of 9/11 is. Moreover, the terrorists may calculate that

[25] Note that in many ways this is evidence of success in implementing the priorities set by the September 2002, *National Security Strategy of the United States*, which states: "Our priority will be first to disrupt and destroy terrorist organizations of global reach and attack their leadership; command, control, and communications; material support; and finances." [http://www.whitehouse.gov/nsc/nss3.html].

Contrast the new March 2006 *National Security Strategy of the United States*, which emphasizes that terrorism remains a global threat because of transnational inspiration, diffusion of tactics, and localized cells that require short-term and long-term responses: "Terrorist networks today are more dispersed and less centralized. They are more reliant on smaller cells inspired by a common ideology and less directed by a central command structure. . . From the beginning, the War on Terror has been both a battle of arms and a battle of ideas—a fight against the terrorists and against their murderous ideology. In the short run, the fight involves using military force and other instruments of national power to kill or capture the terrorists, deny them safe haven or control of any nation; prevent them from gaining access to WMD; and cut off their sources of support. In the long run, winning the war on terror means winning the battle of ideas, for it is ideas that can turn the disenchanted into murderers willing to kill innocent victims." [http://www.whitehouse.gov/nsc/nss/2006/sectionIII.html].

[26] See for example: "Al-Qaeda Still in Business" by Peter Bergen, *Washington Post*, July 2, 2006, p.B1. Historical data appear to indicate that al Qaeda has an established pattern of lying low between large-scale attacks as reflected by seemingly inactive periods between terror incidents in the 1990's. According to terrorism analyst Alexis Debat: "Al Qaeda's leadership has never made empty threats, which suggests that, while on the run, it is still connected to its "'foot soldiers." From Bin Laden's call on attacking the West in 2002 . . . to Ayman al Zawahiri's condemnation of Pervez Musharraf in 2003, which led to two unsuccessful assassination attempts on the Pakistani president, it seems that every warning formulated in these tapes was followed by action. There is also some evidence that the leaders of Al Qaeda remain in close touch with their "operational commanders." The interrogation of one of them, Abu Faraj al Libbi, shortly after his arrest in March 2005, established that he was in regular, if indirect, touch with Ayman al Zawahiri. Moreover, Pakistani intelligence sources tell ABC News that one of the suicide bombers in the July 7, 2005 terrorist attacks in London, personally spent three days with Ayman al Zawahiri in Pakistan's tribal areas in January 2005. See [ABCNews.com], January 2006 Terrorism column under the title "Al Qaeda Social Club." See also: Comments of Peter Bergen that "al Qaeda is not feeling the heat of the war on terror," CNN 360 Degree Report: "Ticking Time Bomb" by Anderson Cooper, July 6, 2006.

operational involvement prior to the next mega-attack could compromise both the mega-attack and the organization as well, a risk they may not want to take.[27] An exception however, would appear to be ongoing operational engagement in Afghanistan, Pakistan, and Iraq.

The Rise in Influence of Radical Islamist Political Parties

One trend that some observers view as not sufficiently emphasized in the State Department report is the overall growth in numbers and political influence of radical Islamist fundamentalist political parties throughout the world, some of which reportedly serve—or might serve—as fronts for terrorist activity. Even if not actively serving as fronts for terrorist activity, some are concerned that the actions and agendas of such groups could facilitate creation of a political climate in their home countries which views terrorism as a politically acceptable tactic and which might make their home countries appear as an attractive location for active terrorist groups to establish a secure base. Examples of such groups cited by scholars and the media include the Justice and Prosperity Party and the Mujaheddin Council (MMI) in Indonesia, the Party Islam in Malaysia, and more recently the Islamic Courts Union which, as of the writing of this report, controlled much of southern Somalia.[28] Groups in Pakistan are notable as well, especially the Muttahida Majlis-e-Amal (MMA or United Action Forum) and another long-standing Islamist party, the Jamiat Ulema-i-Islam faction led by Maulana Fazlur Rehman (JUI-F).[29]

---

[27] For example, if one gives credence to reporting in the *One Percent Doctrine, op. cit* (footnote #5), the al Qaeda leadership was both quite informed about plans in 2003 to release hydrogen cyanide gas in the New York subway system and quite capable of calling it off, arguably because some future mega-attack—designed to top that of 9/11—was in the pipeline.

[28] This is not to say that the State Department report does not address such groups individually. At issue here is the collective synergy and impact generated by the activities of such groups and any trends indicative of the growth or decline of such synergy. See for example: "Radical Islamic Strain Clouds the Tolerance Displayed by Indonesia," by Timothy Mapes and Andrew Higgins, *Asian Wall Street Journal*, Feb 25, 2005, p. A1. See also: "Indonesian Islamic Party Reaps Rewards of Goodwill" by Ellen Nakashima, *Washington Post*, Jan. 14, 2005, p. A13. See also: "Spread of Islamic Law in Indonesia Takes Toll on Women" by Jane Perlez, *New York Times*, June 27, 2006, p. A6; and "Out of the Woodwork: Islamist Militants in Aceh" by Zachary Abuza, research paper published Jan. 13, 2004. Note that the phenomenon of radical Islamist fundamentalist political parties, or like minded democratically elected representatives, is by no means limited to Indonesia and Malaysia.

For background on the Islamic Courts Union and U.S. concerns see "U.S. Puzzled by Changing Political Landscape in Somalia" by Michelle Kelemen, *National Public Radio*, Morning Edition, July 13, 2006. See also: "Q&A: Somali Islamist Advance," *BBC News* (international version) June 28, 2006 (17:01GMT).

[29] See CRS Report RL33498, *Pakistan-U.S. Relations* and CRS Report RL32615, *Pakistan's Domestic Political Developments*, both by Alan Kronstadt.

The Muttahida Majlis-e-Amal (MMA or United Action Forum) is a loose coalition of six Islamist parties formed for the 2002 elections. Its largest constituent is the Jamaat-i-Islami (JI), founded by Maulana Maududi in 1941 and considered to be Pakistan's best-organized religious party. JI chief Qazi Hussein Ahmed serves as MMA president. Another long-standing Islamist party is the Jamiat Ulema-i-Islam faction led by Maulana Fazlur Rehman (JUI-F). The JUI is associated with religious schools that gave rise to the Afghan Taliban movement. In addition to promoting a central role for

Additional examples of the success of terror linked political groups include (1) the Hizballah political party in Lebanon with 14 elected representatives in the National Assembly as well as two ministers in the Government; and (2) the popularly elected Hamas-led legislature of the Palestinian Authority, which won by a landslide in January 2006, giving the party control of the governing Palestinian National Authority. Any rise in the power and influence of terror-linked or terror-supportive political parties—especially should their representatives be elected through democratic processes—presents major policy dilemmas for the United States, since it pits U.S. support for democracy directly against America's commitment to aggressively combat terrorism.

Adequacy of International Anti-terror Cooperation

Another potential issue related to the State Department report involves the adequacy of international anti-terrorism cooperation, an avowed core component of U.S. anti-terror strategy. Whereas the State Department's *Country Reports on Global Terrorism Report* provides substantive in-depth data and analysis on levels of antiterrorism cooperation with individual countries on an individual basis, as well as cooperative efforts underway using international or regional organizations, some argue that it does not collectively link such levels of cooperation—or lack thereof—to any overall trend or trends. In the aggregate, are levels of foreign nation support or "buy-in" for U.S. counter-terror policy and programs increasing or decreasing? Critics suggest any effort to plot trends in international cooperation would be quite speculative and prone to stress quantitative factors, such as the number of countries meeting certain cooperative levels, rather than the relative importance of each country's cooperation to United States strategic goals and objectives.

What Are the Trends Related to Schools Teaching Radical Jihadism?

Schools for youth in countries where there is teaching of radical Jihadism and affiliated intolerance and hatred may serve as a breeding ground for terrorist ideology and pro-terrorist sentiment. Madrasas, religious schools

religion in Pakistani affairs, Islamists have been opposed to Westernization in both its capitalist and socialist forms. The leadership of the MMA's two main constituents—the Jamaat-i-Islami's (JI) Qazi Hussein Ahmed and the Jamiat-Ulema-Islami (JUI)-Fazlur's Maulana Fazlur Rehman—are notable for their sometimes virulent anti-American rhetoric; they have at times called for "jihad" against what they view as the existential threat to Pakistani sovereignty that alliance with Washington entails.

The May 2004 elevation of Jamiat-Ulema-Islami chief Maulana Fazlur Rehman to the position of Leader of the Opposition in Parliament spurred commentary that the "mullahmilitary alliance" had become a "Musharraf-Maulana alliance," further marginalizing Pakistan's more secular opposition parties. JUI leader Maulana Fazlur Rehman reportedly said he considers Americans to be "criminals" and the Taliban "innocent" See; "MMA Opposes Pak-US Military Drive," *News* (Karachi), June 24, 2003. See also: "Battle Ground: Despite U.S. Efforts, Pakistan Remains Key Terror Hub. . ." by Jay Solomon et al, Wall Street Journal, July 22, 2005, p.A1.

often backed by Saudi money, are often perceived to encourage militancy and are a particular concern in Pakistan, especially in areas along the Afghanistan border.[30] Therefore, it would seem important to have a better understanding of trends concerning these schools and their curricula.

Terror Groups Evolving into Criminal Groups

The overlap of terrorist activity with international crime presented by the Department of State's report suggests yet another challenge for consideration: To what degree, if at all, will terrorist organizations increasingly morph into criminal networks motivated by profit rather than ideology. It might be, at some later point in time, some terrorist groups would shy away from terrorism which is generally not considered good for criminal business activity. This is in line with thinking that engaging in criminal activity—especially the lucrative illicit drug trade—can become self-perpetuating as such criminal activity often becomes institutionalized making it difficult for groups to disengage themselves.[31] A classic example involves the so-called Revolutionary Armed Forces of Colombia (FARC) which initially provided hired protection to coca leaf growers and processors and subsequently moved into coca cultivation and processing. Notwithstanding, a more likely scenario appears to be that micro-terror actors will remain terror focused, but will increasingly turn to crime to finance terror.

Resource Allocation Between Larger and Smaller Attacks

Both the Department of State's trend analysis and that of non-government specialists paint a picture of Jihadist-inspired terror groups consumed by the desire to inflict major physical and economic damage with little ideological or moral constraints on mass casualty attacks. Some in these groups appear to be actively seeking the material, technology, and skills to carry out such attacks and, indeed, may already possess them. On the other hand, the number of day-to-day "low-tech" terror attacks using more traditional bombs and bullets appears to be dramatically rising in frequency and cannot be downplayed.

This situation might pose a challenge in allocating resources. Should antiterrorism efforts and resources worldwide concentrate on preventing or mitigating the growing phenomenon of day-to-day relatively low impact and low casualty terrorist attacks, or should they concentrate on preventing

[30] See "Pakistani Religious Schools Face Scrutiny," by Riaz Khan, AP dispatch of July 19, 2005 (07:13 GMT).

[31] See "Narco-Terrorism: International Drug Trafficking and Terrorism—a Dangerous Mix," testimony before the Senate Committee on the Judiciary, May 20, 2003. For a legal framework for countering such terror/crime activity see "The Legal Basis for Counterterrorism Activities In the United States," by Raphael Perl, in *Hi-Impact Terrorism: Proceedings of a Russian American Workshop*, National Research Council, National Academies Press (Washington, DC 2002), p. 5–15.

or mitigating possible catastrophic damage mass-casualty attacks on a scale heretofore not experienced, but which may not be imminent? Are there measures which could negatively impact on both types of terrorist interest and activity?

Responding to Unclaimed/Anonymous Terrorism

Another potential issue is how to respond to the growing number of terrorist attacks that are unattributed, or claimed in a manner in which the true identity of their perpetrators is masked. Such a trend might suggest that increasingly the goal of terrorist attacks is to inflict as much damage on the enemy as possible without linking attacks to specific goals, such as the release of prisoners, and with little importance given to gaining publicity for the specific group inflicting the damage. Terrorists may believe that recruitment and popular support for terrorism will increase after each successful attack, and that it is relatively immaterial for the perpetrating group to publically identify itself. Moreover, not revealing—or masking—the real identity of the perpetrating group makes it more difficult for law enforcement or retaliatory operations to effectively target them.

In some instances it may not even be possible to determine if a particular event is an act of terror. For example, is a particular train wreck, an explosion at a chemical plant, a forest fire, an increase in computer viruses, or an outbreak of B.S.E. or West Nile virus, the result of negligence, an act of terror or an act of God?

Although there may not yet be sufficient data to confirm such a trend towards anonymous terror attacks, some homed in on the phenomenon of "stealth terrorism" as early as June of 1991 when it was discussed at a joint American Academy of Science/Russian Academy of Science workshop on high-impact terrorism.[32] More recently, research conducted by the *National Journal*, which was largely based on State Department data, found that in 2001 about 20% of the attacks in the government's database were not claimed by any terrorist organization; in 2002, it was 40%; in 2003, it was slightly more than half; and in 2004, more than 70% of attacks carried no claim of responsibility.[33] If validated, such a trend would have a direct impact on anti-terror policies, since current doctrines of deterrence of, and

[32] See "Terrorism Future: Tactics, Strategy, and Stealth," by Peter Probst in *Hi-Impact Terrorism: Proceedings of a Russian American Workshop*, National Research Council, National Academies Press (Washington, D.C. 2002), p. 260–267.

[33] See "Foreign Policy—Terrorism Tally Not that Useless," by Corine Hegland, *National Journal*, May 14, 2005. Note however, that in some cases there may be conflicting claims of "credit" and it is not always possible to definitively sort them out. When a group is cited by the NCTC as the culprit rather than a competing terrorist group, this does not necessarily reflect the best consensus of the intelligence community as NCTC statistical reporting is not designed to confirm the accuracy of perpetrator claims and public allegations against groups.

retaliation for, terrorist acts are predicated on: (1) identifying acts of terrorism and (2) identifying those who commit them.

Some Implications for U.S. Policy

Looking at NCTC data in the aggregate, one might reasonably conclude that terrorists are becoming less constrained and more indiscriminate in their targeting, thereby inflicting casualties on a broader range of potential targets and victims. Moreover, the State Department's *Country Reports on Terrorism 2005* argues that the threat from small terrorist groups or lone terrorists is rising in frequency, as is the potential for these micro-actors to inflict deadly harm and costly economic damage. This finding appears consistent with other research and analyses. If the trend continues the immediate future is likely to bring "a larger number of smaller attacks, less meticulously planned, and local rather than transnational in scope." On the other hand, "an increasing number of such attacks could fail through lack of skill or equipment. . . ."[34]

Of growing concern is what many see as a trend by terrorists to launch near-simultaneous multiple attacks aimed at causing economic damage—such as attacks on transportation, tourism, and oil related targets and infrastructures. For example, in February 2006, Saudi security forces thwarted a suicide attack at an oil processing facility in the eastern part of that nation. An al Qaeda affiliated website subsequently claimed responsibility. A wave of arrests in the Saudi Arabia in late March 2006 reportedly thwarted a second refinery attack.[35]

If terrorist acts are becoming more the product of localized micro—actors, it raises the question of whether United States anti-terror strategy and tactics should reflect a more international law-enforcement oriented approach. Such an approach was envisioned in the February 2003 *National Strategy for Combating Terrorism*.[36] For example, the inclusion of the Drug Enforcement

[34] *Country Reports on Terrorism 2005*, p.13. Note however, that an attack(s) which is "unsuccessful" in terms of destruction and death may still have a devastating effect on the economy and emotional/social patterns of a nation, especially in terms of behavior and attitudes shaped by public perceptions of security.

[35] See "Saudis Thwart Oil Refinery Attack: al Qaeda claims responsibility on Web site," *CNN* World, February 24, 2006, and "Wave of Arrests in Saudi Arabia Thwarts Second Refinery Attack" by Stephen Ulph, in Terrorism Focus, Vol. 3 Issue 13 (April 4, 2006) published by the Jamestown Foundation.

[36] To the extent that terrorists interact with the criminal underworld for logistical support services—or to the extent that they bypass criminal groups and engage in other illegal activities themselves, their exposure and vulnerability to law enforcement activity increases as well. Much is being done to assist domestic law enforcement and security forces and institutions in foreign nations, especially training of investigators and prosecutors, through programs administered by the Department of Justice. In Mexico, for example, DEA has an extensive training program in place for both law enforcement personnel and prosecutorial staff. For background and analysis of the National Strategy for Combating Terrorism see CRS Report RL32522, U.S. *Anti-Terror Strategy the 9/11 Commission Report* by Raphael Perl. For the National Strategy see [http://www.whitehouse.gov/news/releases/

Administration's Office of National Security Intelligence as a member of the Intelligence Community will put in place new structures to share information on the ties between international terrorism and international drug trafficking. Increased sharing and cooperation between the law enforcement and the intelligence communities could well lead to disrupting some of the ties between terrorist and criminal groups, potentially "defunding" some terrorist activities.

Overall, policymakers may consider expanding programs that support foreign law enforcement training and educational exchanges, joint/multilateral training exercises, the creation of bi-lateral or multilateral law enforcement task forces, staff exchanges of detailees among foreign and domestic law enforcement agencies, and expansion of so-called "rule of law" programs. Some observers call for more vigorous, focused, and better funded public diplomacy initiatives to counter terrorist efforts to generate popular support and gain recruits.[37]

Collection and analysis of data which may reveal trends over time might also be strengthened. Some might argue that it could serve United States and allied interests to see more data analyzed and exchanged on terrorist motivations, tactics, and organizations by a wide range of institutions in the public and private sector. Greater participation in this process by industry, governments, and academia might prove fruitful. However, compiling and sharing the data on a timely basis may present yet another daunting challenge.[38]

Most agree that the evidence shows that terrorists are seeking to kill as many people as possible and concentrating on hitting economic targets such as support infrastructure and tourism—rather than seeking to achieve immediate political objectives such as gaining the release of prisoners. If correct, this might argue for hardening targets, improving the technology and placement of detection equipment, and generally beefing-up the nation's ability to respond to large scale disasters—whether caused by acts of God or acts of terror.[39]

2005/10/20051006-3.html] An NCTC coordinated interagency National Implementation Plan (NIP) for the National Strategy for Combating Terrorism is reportedly in final stages of review and approval.

[37] Of potential importance here is the need for enhanced data to facilitate understanding of the factors terrorists exploit to generate support and gain recruits. On the issue of public diplomacy and anti-terrorism generally, see CRS Report RL32607, *U.S. Public Diplomacy: Background and 9/11 Commission Recommendations*, by Susan B. Epstein.

[38] International/regional organizations, such as the United Nations, NATO, and/or INTERPOL, though not without downsides, might serve as useful clearing houses for such data.

[39] See generally, Homeland Security Secretary Michael Chertoff's "Remarks to the Commonwealth Club of California," July 28, 2005, especially those comments that discuss the importance of detection technology and the role of risk analysis. [http://www.dhs.gov/dhspublic/display?content=4700].

For Additional Reading

CRS Report RS21937. *9/11 Terrorism: Global Economic Costs,* by Dick K. Nanto.

CRS Report RL32759. *Al Qaeda: Statements and Evolving Ideology,* by Christopher M. Blanchard.

CRS Report RL33038. *Al Qaeda: Profile and Threat Assessment,* by Kenneth Katzman.

CRS Report RL30252. *Intelligence and Law Enforcement: Countering Transnational Threats to the U.S.,* by Richard A. Best, Jr.

CRS Report RS22211. *Islamist Extremism in Europe,* by Kristin Archick et al.

CRS Report RL32816. *The National Counterterrorism Center: Implementation Challenges and Issues for Congress,* by Todd M. Masse.

CRS Report RS22373. *Navy Role in Global War on Terrorism (GWOT)—Background and Issues for Congress,* by Ronald O'Rourke.

CRS Report RL31672. *Terrorism in Southeast Asia,* by Bruce Vaughn et al.

CRS Report 97-960. *Terrorism, the Media, and the Government: Perspectives. Trends, and Options for Policymakers,* by Raphael Perl. (Archived: available from the author.)

CRS Report RL32758. *U.S. Military Operations in the Global War on Terrorism: Afghanistan, Africa, the Philippines,* and Colombia, by Andrew Feickert.

B. COUNTRY REPORTS ON TERRORISM

COUNTRY REPORTS ON TERRORISM

Released by the Office of the Coordinator for Counterterrorism

April 30, 2007

Commentary

As mentioned in the first entry in this volume, each year, the U.S. Department of State (DOS) provides to the U.S. Congress a strategic assessment of terrorism trends, the nature of the terrorist threat, and information on anti-terror cooperation by other nations. The second document presented in this volume is the report released on April 30, 2007. It is a very comprehensive report replete with useful information for anyone who studies terrorism, or is responsible for formulating policies for preventing and defeating it. Due to the unclassified nature of the report, it lacks detail in several areas and is incomplete in others. Still, it serves a very important purpose in informing readers of the DOS's assessment of the terrorist threat to U.S. National Security and suggests actions that should be taken to thwart it.

The report addresses developments in countries that suffered acts of terrorism, are state sponsors of terrorism, and those determined by the Secretary of State to be integral to the Global War on Terror. The report covers terrorist groups responsible for the death, kidnapping, or injury of Americans and their parent organizations, groups financed by state sponsors of terrorism, terrorist organizations on the Foreign Terrorist Organization (FTO) list, other terrorist groups as determined by the Secretary of State to be relevant, terrorist sanctuaries, and terrorist attempts to acquire weapons of mass destruction. The report includes statistical information provided by the National Counterterrorism Center (NCTC) on the number of individuals killed, injured, or kidnapped by terrorist groups.

The report begins with a strategic assessment of terrorism trends and ongoing issues focused on 2006 to provide a framework for the detailed discussions in subsequent chapters. The chapter reports that five years after the September 11, 2001 attacks, progress to defeat transnational terrorists is mixed and the struggle continues, notwithstanding the absence of follow-on attacks in the United States. There have been tangible security improvements in securing borders and transportation, enhancing document security, disrupting terrorist financing, restricting terrorists' movement, dismantling terrorist organizations and disrupting terrorist leadership. These efforts have contributed to reduced terrorist activity and the elimination of some terrorist leaders.

The chapter also relates successes in organizing regional responses to terrorists who operate in under-governed or misgoverned territory. The successes resulted from both intra-governmental and intergovernmental cooperation and collaboration. Significantly, the DOS has developed strategic and deliberate operational planning capabilities that allow it to integrate all the tools of statecraft on an international basis, not only to deny terrorists their bases of support, but sanctuaries as well. Along these lines, the U.S. DOS is helping the ministries of partner nations apply their resources more effectively and efficiently to defeat terrorists.

These successes notwithstanding, the Global War Against Terrorists is far from won. Many states continue to sponsor terrorists, covertly and overtly. Iran, Syria, North Korea, Sudan, and Cuba view terrorism as a legitimate asymmetric means of countering conventional western power. Additionally, both Afghanistan and Iraq continue to be threatened by terrorists who attack U.S. and coalition forces, as well as civilians of all nationalities. Genuinely or not, many terrorist organizations continue to use the Israeli-Palestinian conflict as grounds for legitimizing their actions throughout the Middle East. Israeli policy in the Palestinian Territories has not reduced the terrorist threat. The inconvenient and unfortunate truth is that decades of use of terrorism in the Middle East, especially in and around the West Bank, Gaza, Lebanon, Syria, and Iran, have spawned generations of terrorists. The report wisely suggests that complete disarmament of terrorists groups may be the only answer to long-term peace in the region.

The report presents key al-Qaeda trends, such as the move toward fewer but more incendiary attacks like the bombing of the Askariya mosque in Samarra, Iraq on February 22, 2006. Al-Qaeda's strategy seems to be to apply limited resources to what it views as high-value targets to provoke widespread sectarian violence and change the character of the war in Iraq. That, in turn, is designed to trigger broader regional conflict which will destabilize governments friendly toward the West and set the stage for establishment of the caliphate. The fact that al-Qaeda's goal is not embraced by the vast majority of the region's population has not reduced the radical zeal of al-Qaeda and its affiliate movements, but ever-decreasing popular support has made it significantly more difficult for al-Qaeda to accomplish its objectives.

In addition to the insights discussed above, the report provides additional information on al-Qaeda that is very useful for understanding how the organization is evolving. Of particular interest is al-Qaeda's increased emphasis on winning the strategic communications war through the use of misinformation and anti-Western propaganda. Al-Qaeda's relegation to the cyber-battlefield largely resulted from the international community's success in disrupting and defeating it. The report does not go so far as to state that al-Qaeda can no longer mount a large-scale, horrific attack, but does suggest that to do so will require much greater effort than in the past and a degree of secrecy that al-Qaeda may not be able to achieve easily.

In a very disturbing way, the report refers to "the terrorist conveyor belt;" that is, the radicalization of immigrant populations, youth and alienated minorities. Terrorists and extremists have significantly increased their efforts to manipulate the grievances of such groups and then exploit them to subvert legitimate authority and create unrest. A pattern similar to that emerging within American and other prison populations is taking form. Terrorist leaders convert alienated or aggrieved populations to extremist viewpoints and turn them progressively into sympathizers, supporters, and ultimately, members of terrorist networks. The report correctly states that such populations should not be viewed as threats but as targets of enemy subversion to be protected and supported.

Perhaps the most tenuous position the report takes is to characterize al-Qaeda not merely as a transnational terrorist organization, but as a global insurgency, calling for a new paradigm. The report offers as evidence the fact that al-Qaeda openly describes itself as a transnational guerrilla movement and applies classic insurgent strategies at the global level; that it applies a full suite of tools including terrorism, subversion, propaganda, and open warfare, and seeks weapons of mass destruction in order to inflict the maximum possible damage on the West. The report states that al-Qaeda has formed a linked network of regional, national, and local actors who share some of its objectives, but also pursue their own local agendas, and that it works through regional and cross-border safe havens that facilitate its actions while hampering government responses.

These DOS claims are insufficient to show a global insurgency, however. Of course, it would serve al-Qaeda's interests if it could convince potential recruits and supporters that it is a global movement that will succeed in establishing the caliphate, but merely declaring itself to be a global insurgency does not make it one. Additionally, while many threat assessments refer to al-Qaeda and Affiliated Movements (AQAM), there is scant evidence that such a consolidated movement actually exists. On the contrary, probably the most significant flaw in the West's strategy for waging the Global War Against Terrorists is suggested by the name given to the effort—that it is a singular war against a monolithic enemy. The effort is described more accurately as war against terrorists waged on a global scale. Displaying some internal inconsistency, the report seems to recognize this and states that in order to win the Global War Against Terrorists, the United States must disaggregate the threat and counter each threat individually.

The report quite appropriately points out that in order to win the Global War Against Terrorists, three strategic components of the terrorist threat must be neutralized: leaders, safe havens, and underlying conditions. As mentioned previously, many key leaders have been eliminated through death or capture. Many others have been neutralized by being kept on the run. To be sure, there are almost always lieutenants prepared to step in and continue the effort, but in most cases they do not command the support their predecessors did. As a result, the organization progressively weakens with each successive change of leadership.

The report uses the terms ungoverned or under-governed spaces to refer to safe havens. That usage ignores two important points that are essential to effective strategy formulation. First, any area of the earth inhabited by humans is governed, in one way or another. The point is that some governing bodies knowingly and willingly afford safe haven to terrorists, some unknowingly and unwillingly provide safe haven, and some knowingly, but unwillingly provide safe haven. Knowing the difference is crucial to strategy formulation because each case requires a different approach. Additionally, whether the international community recognizes the legitimacy of the governing body also will help determine the appropriate strategy.

The report correctly states that employing its partial listing of counterinsurgency methods would be helpful in defeating terrorists; i.e., protecting and securing the population, politically and physically marginalizing the insurgents, and winning the support and cooperation of at-risk populations. However, one must be mindful that many terrorists today are different from their classical predecessors. Many do not seek political objectives beyond those needed for self-enrichment. Many are motivated by greed, not a political cause, and do not necessarily want to topple governments. Still, the report also is quite correct in its assessment that all instruments of national power including diplomatic, military, economic, and intelligence must be integrated into a whole-of-government approach to defeating terrorists.

Having established the strategic context for understanding detailed country- and region-specific analysis, the report proceeds to a comprehensive terrorism analysis of over 100 countries and regions. It then proceeds to an assessment of the five countries the United States considers sponsors of terrorism followed by a sobering discussion of the potential use of weapons of mass destruction (WMD) by terrorists.

The report accurately portrays the nexus of WMD and terrorism as one of the gravest potential risks to the national security of the United States and, indeed, to the world. The death, destruction, and economic loss that a nuclear or biological weapon could bring almost defies imagination. This chapter warrants a careful read. It discusses the key elements of the

United States' National Strategy for Combating WMD Terrorism; various types of materials terrorists may use in a WMD attack; resources of a state that could be directed or diverted to facilitate WMD terrorism; emerging WMD terrorism threats presented by non-state facilitators; and transformational U.S. partnerships to combat this growing global risk. This risk is real, severe, and imminent. Therefore, the U.S. Government places the highest priority on reducing it, through national and international efforts.

The report continues with a discussion of terrorist safe havens, specific terrorist organizations, other groups of concern, and closes anticlimactically with a discussion of legislative requirements and key terms. In summary, this rather lengthy report is an excellent primer on the threat of terrorism as viewed by the U.S. DOS. It is a valuable source for anyone interested in learning the contemporary nature of the terrorist threat to national security and what steps the U.S. Government intends to take to defeat it.

DOCUMENT NO. 2

COUNTRY REPORTS ON TERRORISM—2007

U.S. State Department
Office of the Coordinator for Counterterrorism

April 30, 2007

Chapter 1
Strategic Assessment

Introduction

This chapter highlights terrorism trends and ongoing issues, focusing on calendar year 2006 that will provide a framework for detailed discussion in later chapters. Since this issue of the *Country Reports on Terrorism* falls 5 years after the attacks of September 11, 2001, the chapter commences with a review of progress against the terrorist threat to date.

Five Years On, Progress is Mixed

Significant Achievements

Five years after 9/11, the international community's conflict with transnational terrorists continues. Cooperative international efforts have produced genuine security improvements—particularly in securing borders and transportation, enhancing document security, disrupting terrorist financing, and restricting the movement of terrorists. The international community has also achieved significant success in dismantling terrorist organizations and disrupting their leadership. This has contributed to reduced terrorist operational capabilities and the detention or death of numerous key terrorist leaders.

Working with allies and partners across the world, through coordination and information sharing, we have created a less permissive operating environment for terrorists, keeping leaders on the move or in hiding, and degrading their ability to plan and mount attacks. Canada, Australia, the United Kingdom, Saudi Arabia, Turkey, Pakistan, Afghanistan, and many other partners played major roles in this success, recognizing that international terrorism represents a threat to the whole international community.

Through the Regional Strategic Initiative, the State Department is working with ambassadors and interagency representatives in key terrorist theaters of operation to assess the threat and devise collaborative strategies, action plans, and policy recommendations. We have made progress in organizing regional responses to terrorists who operate in ungoverned spaces or across national borders. This initiative has produced better intra-governmental coordination among United States government agencies, greater cooperation with and between regional partners, and improved strategic planning and prioritization, allowing us to use all tools of statecraft to establish long-term measures to marginalize terrorists. (See *Chapter 5—Terrorist Safe Havens (7120 Report)* for further information on the Regional Strategic Initiative.)

Continuing Challenges

Despite this undeniable progress, major challenges remain. Several states continue to sponsor terrorism. Iran remains the most significant state sponsor of terrorism and continues to threaten its neighbors and destabilize Iraq by providing weapons, training, advice, and funding to select Iraqi Shia militants. Syria, both directly and in coordination with Hizballah, has attempted to undermine the elected Government of Lebanon and roll back progress toward democratization in the Middle East. Syria also supports some Iraqi Baathists and militants and has continued to allow foreign fighters and terrorists to transit through its borders into Iraq.

International intervention in Iraq has brought measurable benefits. It has removed an abusive totalitarian regime with a history of sponsoring and supporting regional terrorism and has allowed a new democratic political process to emerge. It also, however, has been used by terrorists as a rallying cry for radicalization and extremist activity that has contributed to instability in neighboring countries.

Afghanistan remains threatened by Taliban insurgents and religious extremists, some of whom are linked to al-Qaida (AQ) and to sponsors outside the country. In Afghanistan public support for the government remains high, national institutions are getting stronger and the majority of Afghans believe they are better off than under the Taliban. But to defeat the resurgent threat, the international community must deliver promised assistance and work with Afghans to build counterinsurgency capabilities, ensure legitimate and effective governance, and counter the surge in narcotics cultivation.

The Israeli/Palestinian conflict remains a source of terrorist motivation. The holding of free elections in the Palestinian Territories was a welcome sign of democratization, but HAMAS' subsequent refusal to disavow terrorism or accept Israel's internationally-accepted right to exist undermined the election's impact. Terrorist activity emanating from the Palestinian Territories remains a key destabilizing factor and a cause for concern.

The summer war in Lebanon between Israel and Hizballah was a prime example of how Hizballah's continued efforts to manipulate persisting grievances along the Israeli/Lebanese border can quickly escalate into open warfare. The conflict did force the international community again to demand Hizballah's complete disarmament, in UN Security Council Resolution (UNSCR) 1701, and generated a renewed international commitment to support a peaceful, stable, multi-sectarian democracy in Lebanon. Even so, Hizballah, a designated foreign terrorist organization, in combination with state sponsors of terrorism Iran and Syria, continues to undermine the elected Government of Lebanon and remains a serious security threat in the Middle East.

AQ and its affiliates have adapted to our success in disrupting their operational capability by focusing more attention and resources on their propaganda and misinformation efforts. They exploit and interpret the actions of numerous local, pseudo-independent actors, using them to mobilize supporters and sympathizers, intimidate opponents and influence international opinion. Terrorists consider information operations to be a principal part of their effort. The international community has yet to muster a coordinated and effectively resourced counter to extremist propaganda.

Overall, AQ and its loose confederation of affiliated movements remain the most immediate national security threat to the United States and a significant security challenge to the international community.

Key Al-Qaida Trends

Single terrorist events, like the Askariya mosque bombing in Samarra, Iraq on February 22, 2006, which provoked widespread sectarian violence and changed the character of the war in Iraq, can become triggers for broader conflict or templates for copycat attacks. Because terrorism is fundamentally political, the political significance of major events is vital in determining meaningful responses. Thus, the trends presented in this section are interpretive—they provide qualitative insight to complement the statistical detail covered in later chapters.

Transition from "Expeditionary" to "Guerrilla" Terrorism

Early AQ terrorist attacks were largely expeditionary. The organization selected and trained terrorists in one country, then clandestinely inserted a team into the target country to attack a pre-planned objective. The 1998 U.S.

embassy bombings in Nairobi and Dar es-Salaam, the 2000 attack on the USS *Cole*, and the 9/11 attacks were examples of this. Improved international border security, transportation security and document control have made this type of attack more difficult. Clandestine insertion across borders is harder, reconnaissance is more risky, and international movement of funds and equipment is more likely to be detected.

Thus we have seen a trend toward guerrilla terrorism, where the organization seeks to grow the team close to its target, using target country nationals. Through intermediaries, web-based propaganda, and subversion of immigrant expatriate populations, terrorists inspire local cells to carry out attacks which they then exploit for propaganda purposes. This circumvents the need to insert a team across borders or clandestinely transfer funds and materiel. The 2004 Madrid bombing, the London attacks of July 2005, and the thwarted August 2006 attempt to attack passenger jets operating from British airports include elements of this approach.

Both expeditionary and guerrilla approaches co-exist, alongside true "home-grown" terrorism involving local cells acting spontaneously rather than being than consciously inspired by trans-national terrorists. Rather than adopting a single *modus operandi*, AQ and its affiliated movements continue to be highly adaptive, quickly evolving new methods in response to countermeasures.

Terrorist Propaganda Warfare

As identified in the 2005 *Country Reports*, the international community's success in disrupting terrorist leadership and operational capacity led AQ to focus greater efforts on misinformation and anti-Western propaganda. This trend accelerated this year, with AQ cynically exploiting the grievances of local groups and attempting to portray itself as the vanguard of a global movement. AQ still retains some operational capability and the intent to mount large-scale spectacular attacks, including on the United States and other high-profile Western targets. Overall, however, AQ's current approach focuses on propaganda warfare—using a combination of terrorist attacks, insurgency, media broadcasts, Internet-based propaganda, and subversion to undermine confidence and unity in Western populations and generate the false perception of a powerful worldwide movement.

The Terrorist "Conveyor Belt"

Radicalization of immigrant populations, youth and alienated minorities in Europe, the Middle East, and Africa continued. It became increasingly clear, however, that such radicalization does not occur by accident, or because such populations are innately prone to extremism. Rather, there was increasing evidence of terrorists and extremists manipulating the grievances of alienated youth or immigrant populations and then cynically exploiting those grievances to subvert legitimate authority and create unrest.

Terrorists seek to manipulate grievances represent a "conveyor belt" through which terrorists seek to convert alienated or aggrieved populations, convert them to extremist viewpoints, and turn them, by stages, into sympathizers, supporters, and ultimately, members of terrorist networks. In some regions, this includes efforts by AQ and other terrorists to exploit insurgency and communal conflict as radicalization and recruitment tools, especially using the Internet to convey their message. Countering such efforts demands that we treat immigrant and youth populations not as a source of threat to be defended against, but as a target of enemy subversion to be protected and supported. It also requires community leaders to take responsibility for the actions of members within their communities and act to counteract extremist subversion.

A New Kind of Enemy

Al-Qaida as a Global Insurgency

The surface events mentioned above highlight a deeper trend: the transformation of international terrorism from the traditional forms that Congress intended to address when it established the annual *Country Reports* series into a broader, multifarious approach to transnational non-state warfare that now resembles a form of global insurgency. We have entered a new era of conflict that may demand new paradigms and different responses from those of previous eras.

AQ and its core leadership group represent a global action network that seeks to aggregate and exploit the effects of widely dispersed, semi-independent actors. It openly describes itself as a transnational guerrilla movement and applies classic insurgent strategies at the global level. AQ applies terrorism, but also subversion, propaganda, and open warfare, and it seeks weapons of mass destruction in order to inflict the maximum possible damage on its opponents. It links and exploits a wider, more nebulous community of regional, national, and local actors who share some of its objectives, but also pursue their own local agendas. Finally, it works through regional and cross-border safe havens that facilitate its actions while hampering government responses.

Disaggregating the Threat

To the extent that AQ succeeds in aggregating this broader constellation of extremist actors, it can begin to pursue more frequent and geographically extensive terror attacks. Therefore, we must act to disaggregate the threat, through international cooperation, counterpropaganda, counter subversion, counterinsurgency, and traditional counterterrorism.

Disaggregation breaks the links in the chain that exploit ordinary people's grievances and manipulates them into becoming terrorists. It seeks to provide those who are already radicalized with a way out and to create pathways for alienated groups to redress their legitimate grievances without joining the terrorist network. Disaggregation denies AQ its primary objective of achieving leadership over extremist movements worldwide and unifying them into a single movement. It does not remove the threat but helps reduce it to less dangerous local components, which can be dealt with by individual governments and communities working together.

Trusted Networks

Such cooperation requires the creation of trusted networks to displace and marginalize extremist networks. While killing and capturing key terrorist actors is fundamental in combating terrorism, it can have detrimental effects. These actions do not eliminate the threat and, if mishandled, can be actively counterproductive. Instead, we must seek to build trusted networks of governments, private citizens and organizations, multilateral institutions, and business organizations that work collaboratively to defeat the threat from violent extremism.

Such networks, over time, help wean at-risk populations away from subversive manipulation by terrorists and create mechanisms to address people's needs and grievances, thus marginalizing terrorists. Youth organizations, educational networks, business partnerships, women's empowerment, and local development initiatives can all play a role, with government as a supportive partner.

Leaders, Safe Havens, Underlying Conditions

To make such active measures effective, the three strategic components of the terrorist threat that must be neutralized are leaders, safe havens, and underlying conditions. Leaders provide a motivating, mobilizing, and organizing function and act as symbolic figureheads. Safe havens, which are often in ungoverned or under-governed spaces, provide a secure environment for training, planning, financial and operational support; and a base for mounting attacks. They may be physical or virtual in nature. In addition, underlying conditions provide the fuel, in the form of grievances and conflicts that power the processes of radicalization.

Treating this new era of conflict as a form of global insurgency implies that counterinsurgency methods are fundamental in combating the new form of transnational terrorism. These methods include firstly, a focus on protecting and securing the population; and secondly, politically and physically marginalizing the insurgents, winning the support and cooperation of at-risk populations by targeted political and development measures, and conducting precise intelligence-led special operations to eliminate critical enemy elements with minimal collateral damage.

Integrating All Elements of National Power

All elements of national power including diplomatic, military, economic, and intelligence, must be integrated and applied in a coordinated whole-of-government fashion. The intellectual and psychological dimensions of the threat are at least as important as its physical dimension, so countermeasures must be adequately coordinated and resourced. Thus, the military component of national power plays only a supporting role in this effort; the primary focus is on non-military influence.

Because the enemy is a non-state actor who thrives among disaffected populations, private sector efforts are at least as important as government activity. Citizen diplomacy, cultural activity, person-to-person contact, economic cooperation and development, and the application of media and academic resources are key components of our response to the threat. Motivating, mobilizing, and supporting such privately led activities are key leadership tasks in the new environment.

Commitment—the Key to Success

Experience since 9/11 has shown that the key success factor in confronting violent extremism is the commitment by governments to work with each other, with the international community, with private sector organizations, and with their citizens and immigrant populations.

Where governments cooperate, build trusted networks, seek active informed support from their people, provide responsive, effective and legitimate governance, and engage closely with the international community, the threat from terrorism has been significantly reduced.

Where governments have lacked commitment in working with their neighbors and engaging the support of their people, terrorism and the instability and conflict that terrorists exploit remain key sources of threat.

Summary

This chapter sets the scene for the detailed analysis that follows. In reviewing events since 9/11, it is clear that progress has been mixed. Significant achievements in border security, information sharing, transportation security, financial controls, and the killing or capture of numerous terrorist leaders have reduced the threat. But the threat still remains, and state sponsorship, the terrorist response to intervention in Iraq, improved terrorist propaganda capabilities, the pursuit of nuclear weapons by state sponsors of terrorism, and terrorist exploitation of grievances represent ongoing challenges.

Recent trends include the emergence of "guerrilla" terrorism in parallel with traditional "expeditionary" approaches, improved AQ propaganda warfare capacity, and emerging evidence of terrorist "conveyor belt" that seeks to deliberately manipulate and exploit grievances in at-risk populations.

A deeper trend is the shift in the nature of terrorism, from traditional international terrorism of the late 20th century into a new form of transnational non-state warfare that resembles a form of global insurgency. This represents a new era of warfare, and countering this threat demands the application of counterinsurgency techniques that focus on protecting, securing, and winning the support of at-risk populations, in addition to targeting violent extremist networks and individual terrorists.

Trusted networks of private and government organizations and individuals, and the application of integrated civil-military measures across all elements of national power are keys to this approach. Terrorist leaders, safe havens, and the underlying conditions that terrorists exploit are the principal strategic targets that we must address. The key success factor that has emerged so far is commitment by governments to work with the international community, their own populations, and at-risk immigrant or youth populations, to counter the threat collaboratively.

Within this framework, subsequent sections of this report will now present detailed analyses of each region and country.

Chapter 2
Country Reports: Africa Overview

"We also resolve, as all civilized nations have, to join the global effort to fight terrorism anywhere in the world recognizing that it is today the most single challenge to world peace and collective freedom . . ."

Ellen Johnson Sirleaf,
President, Republic of Liberia
Remarks, UN General Assembly, 61st Session
New York City, September 19, 2006

A small number of al-Qaida (AQ) operatives in East Africa, particularly Somalia, continued to pose the most serious threat to American and allied interests in the region. Although elements were severely disrupted at year's end, AQ continued to operate in Somalia and elsewhere in East Africa. Somalia remains a concern, as the country's unsecured borders and continued political instability provide opportunities for terrorist transit and/or organization. AQ remains likely to keep making common cause with Somali extremists in an attempt to disrupt international peacemaking efforts in Somalia.

There were few significant international terrorist incidents in Africa, but civil conflict and ethnic violence continued in a number of countries. AQ-affiliated terrorist groups were present and operated in Northwest Africa. These groups conducted small scale attacks on host governments and U.S. interests, raised funds, recruited, and conducted other support activities across the Trans-Sahara. The Salafist Group for Preaching and Combat (GSPC) merged with al-Qaida in September and changed its name to Al-Qaida in the Islamic Maghreb (AQIM). AQIM/GSPC continued to operate in the Sahel region, crossing difficult-to-patrol borders between Mali, Mauritania, Niger, Algeria, and Chad to recruit extremists within the region for training and terrorist operations in the Trans-Sahara and, possibly, for operations outside the region. Its new alliance with al-Qaida potentially has given it access to more resources and training.

Hizballah continued to engage in fundraising activities in Africa, particularly in West Africa, but did not engage in any terrorist attacks within the region. Many African governments improved their cooperation and strengthened their efforts in the War on Terror. Both the African Union (AU) and African regional organizations continued initiatives to improve counterterrorism cooperation and information sharing.

Trans-Sahara Counterterrorism Partnership (TSCTP)

The Trans-Sahara Counterterrorism Partnership is a multi-faceted, multi-year strategy aimed at defeating terrorist organizations by strengthening regional counterterrorism capabilities, enhancing and institutionalizing cooperation among the region's security forces, promoting democratic governance, discrediting terrorist ideology, and reinforcing bilateral military ties with the United States. The overall goals are to enhance the indigenous capacities of governments in the pan-Sahel (Mauritania, Mali, Chad, and Niger, as well as Nigeria and Senegal) to confront the challenge posed by terrorist organizations in the region and to facilitate cooperation between those countries and our Maghreb partners (Morocco, Algeria, and Tunisia) in combating terrorism.

The need for TSCTP stemmed from the potential for expansion of operations by Islamic terrorist organizations in the Sahel. TSCTP was developed as a follow-on to the very successful Pan-Sahel Initiative, which focused solely on the states of the Sahel. Ongoing concern that Islamist terrorists continue to seek to create safe havens and support networks in the remote expanses of the Sahel, as well as the public affiliation of some terrorist groups with AQ, led to its formal approval by the U.S. Government in early 2005.

TSCTP is a five-year program of counterterrorism, democratic governance, and military assistance and includes a public diplomacy component. Its main elements include:

- Counterterrorism (CT) programs to create a new regional focus for trans-Saharan cooperation, including use of established regional organizations like the African Union and its new Center for the Study and Research on Terrorism in Algiers. These programs include training to improve border and aviation security and overall CT readiness;
- Continued specialized Counterterrorism Assistance Training and Terrorist Interdiction Program (TIP) activities in the trans-Sahara region and possible regional expansion of those programs;
- Public diplomacy programs that expand outreach efforts in the Sahel and Maghreb regions, Nigeria, and Senegal and seek to develop regional programming embracing this vast and diverse region. Emphasis is on preserving the traditional tolerance and moderation displayed in most African Muslim communities and countering the development of extremism, particularly in youth and rural populations;
- Democratic governance programs that strive, in particular, to provide adequate levels of U.S. Government support for democratic and economic development in the Sahel, strengthening those states' ability to withstand internal threats; and
- Military programs intended to expand military-to-military cooperation, to ensure adequate resources are available to train, advise, and assist regional forces, and to establish institutions promoting better regional cooperation, communication, and intelligence sharing.

The African Union

The African Union (AU) has several counterterrorism legal instruments, including a Convention on Prevention and Combating of Terrorism (1999), a 2002 Protocol to the Convention, and a 2004 Plan of Action. The Addis Ababa-based AU Commission provided guidance to its 53 member states on ratification and implementation of continental and international counterterrorism commitments, and coordinated assistance to cover member states' counterterrorism gaps. The AU maintained that Africa's colonial legacy made it difficult to accept a definition of terrorism that excluded an exception for "freedom fighters." Still, the AU is on record strongly condemning acts of terrorism, such as those that occurred in Sharm El Sheik, Egypt, and London, England. Although AU Commission's political will to act as an effective counterterrorism partner was strong, capacity remained relatively weak. The AU sought to create a counterterrorism unit at its headquarters to promote member state counterterrorism efforts more effectively. The AU welcomes technical and financial assistance from international partners/donors to bolster both AU headquarters and African Centre for the Study and Research on Terrorism (ACSRT) activities approved by member states.

Botswana

Botswana established its National Counterterrorism Committee to address issues pertaining to terrorism and weapons of mass destruction and regularly participated in Antiterrorism Assistance (ATA) Programs offered at the International Law Enforcement Academy in Gaborone. The Botswana Defense Forces designated a squadron as its counterterrorist unit and several of its officers had counterterrorism training. The Bank of Botswana listed suspected terrorist assets and informed all banking institutions in the country by circulating an updated list of suspicious accounts. Although Botswana had no Financial Intelligence Unit, the Directorate on Corruption and Economic Crimes had a dedicated unit investigating suspicious transactions. As a member of the Southern Africa Development Community's (SADC) Organization on Politics, Defense, and Security, Botswana was responsible for the organization's counterterrorism efforts. SADC capabilities and its efforts in fighting terrorism were limited, however.

Burundi

The Government of Burundi attempted to improve its domestic efforts in the fight against international terrorism. With assistance from the United States, Burundi endeavored to pass new legislation on terrorist financing and other statutes that would specifically outlaw terrorist acts. Although members of the security sector were responsive to requests to assist the

United States, their training and meager resources severely limited their ability to prevent international terrorist acts. Burundi's porous border, coupled with daily incoming flights from East Africa, could allow terrorists easy entry into the country. Through its participation in the Tripartite Plus One group, Burundi joined with Rwanda, Uganda, and the Democratic Republic of Congo to identify and prevent regional insurgent forces from operating in its territory.

Comoros

International terrorism concerns in Comoros focused on Comorian national Fazul Abdullah Mohammed (a.k.a. Harun Fazul), who is suspected of involvement in the 1998 bombings of U.S. embassies in Nairobi and Dar es Salaam. His whereabouts were unknown, but he was believed to have maintained contacts in Comoros. The Comorian government's security forces had limited resources and training in counterterrorism and maritime security, so the country remained vulnerable to terrorist transit or safe haven. Comorian police and security forces continued to participate in U.S. antiterrorism assistance programs and cooperated with the Rewards for Justice Program.

President Sambi, a devout Muslim democratically elected in May, reconfirmed Comoros' rejection of terrorism and, with Comoros' religious leaders, publicly rejected Islamist extremism. President Sambi has sought close partnership with the United States to develop Comoros and to create opportunities for the country's youth. In September, President Sambi and agreed to establish a joint committee to improve bilateral relations, including cooperation on counterterrorism.

Djibouti

Djibouti hosted the only U.S. military base in Sub-Saharan Africa for U.S. and Coalition Forces and remained a staunch supporter of U.S. counterterrorism efforts. Djibouti was one of the most forward-leaning Arab League members supporting ongoing efforts against terrorism. President Ismail Omar Guelleh and many top leaders in Djibouti repeatedly expressed their country's full and unqualified support for the War on Terror. Djibouti was one of the very first Arab League nations to do so following September 11, 2001, even in the face of adversity and criticism from its neighbors.

U.S. security personnel continued to work closely with Djiboutian counterparts to monitor intelligence and follow up on prospective terrorism-related leads. Although the government's capabilities were limited, Djiboutian counterparts were very proactive, and were highly receptive and responsive to U.S. requests for cooperation. The Djiboutian National Security Services took extraordinary measures with its limited resources to ensure the safety and security of American citizens, the U.S. embassy, and the U.S. military base at Camp Lemonier.

Ethiopia

Although a developing nation with constrained resources in a tough neighborhood, Ethiopia demonstrated political will and intent to tackle the problem of terrorism. Ethiopia's counterterrorist capabilities were limited, but increasing. The government agreed to a number of new initiatives and cooperated in efforts to collect and share intelligence on terrorist groups.

In response to increasing threats against its security in December, the Government of Ethiopia conducted a counteroffensive in support of the internationally recognized Transitional Federal Government (TFG) of Somalia against the extremist dominated Council of Islamic Courts (CIC). Mid-year, the CIC gained control of Mogadishu and in a series of offensives in the second half of the year, extended its control over most of southern Somalia. The CIC made claims to large areas of Ethiopia and Kenya inhabited by ethnic Somalis. By the end of the year, Ethiopian and TFG advances routed the CIC out of Mogadishu, though there was concern that some CIC extremists would continue to reject peace overtures and could initiate an insurgency with AQ support.

The highest levels of the Ethiopian government recognized Ethiopia's vulnerability to financial crimes including terrorist financing and counterfeiting. The Penal Code adopted in early 2005 criminalized money laundering and a number of other financial crimes. The Central Bank (National Bank of Ethiopia) drafted specific anti-money laundering legislation, which included the establishment of a Financial Intelligence Unit.

Ethiopia's National Intelligence and Security Service (NISS), with broad authority for intelligence, border security, and criminal investigation, was responsible for overall counterterrorism management. Federal and local police counterterrorism capabilities were primarily focused on being able to respond to terrorist incidents. Draft counterterrorism legislation was before Parliament at year's end.

Ethiopia was an active participant in African Union (AU) counterterrorism efforts, was nominated as a focal point for the AU's Center for Study and Research on Terrorism, and participated in meetings of the Committee of Intelligence and Security Services of Africa.

Kenya

Kenya and the United States maintained generally good cooperation against terrorism throughout 2006, to the mutual benefit of both countries. Kenya was a capable and willing partner and took steps to interdict and apprehend terror suspects. Its cooperation, however, was uneven and constrained by domestic political pressures and considerations. Key among these were Kenyan Muslim and ethnic-Somali communities unsympathetic to cooperation with the United States, an inadequate legal and regulatory framework, and concerns about possible retribution from Somali Islamic extremists.

Kenya proved itself a solid and proactive partner during the Somali crisis that began in December, when Islamic extremists fleeing the Ethiopian advance threatened Kenya's national security. Kenya's borders remained porous and vulnerable to movement of potential terrorists as well as small arms and other contraband. In response to the crisis in Somalia, Kenya deployed its forces along its border with Somalia and at sea to apprehend fleeing CIC extremist fighters and prevent them from establishing safe haven in Kenya. Beginning in late 2006, the Kenyan government banned all flights to and from Somalia except for humanitarian aid flights and flights to the TFG's center of Baidoa. The order remained in effect, despite objections from growers of miraa, or qat, who were deprived of their main market (Somalia) by the ban.

Important Kenyan officials spoke out publicly about the dangers of terrorism and key elements of the Kenyan security apparatus took concrete steps to increase counterterrorism efforts, including the formation of an interagency Coastal Security Steering Committee. At the same time, however, political and bureaucratic resistance remained to the formation of an interagency Kenyan Joint Terrorism Task Force (JTTF).

Kenya still lacked counterterrorism legislation. In April 2003, Kenya published a draft "Suppression of Terrorism Bill," only to withdraw it after harsh criticism from human rights groups and Kenyan Muslim communities. The Kenyan government wrote another draft of the bill in May, according to the UN Office on Drugs and Crime, but did not officially publish the document or submit it to Parliament. In the absence of such legislation, it is difficult to detain terror suspects and to prosecute them effectively. Nonetheless, ATA-trained police investigators and counterterrorism prosecutors were credited with the re-arrest and successful prosecution of Kikambala bombing suspect Omar Said Omar after his acquittal on the main terrorism charge.[1] Omar was subsequently found guilty on April 4 and sentenced for illegal possession of a firearm, ammunition, and explosives.

The government made some progress on combating money laundering and terrorist financing. In November, the government published the text of the Proceeds of Crime and Money Laundering Bill for public comment and it is expected to be submitted to Parliament in March 2007. The Central

[1] Fifteen people were killed in the 2002 bombing of the Paradise Hotel in Kikambala, Kenya.

Bank of Kenya issued guidelines effective January 1, 2007, under Section 33K of the Central Bank of Kenya Act, to strengthen controls over foreign exchange bureaus to regulate their use of third party checks and telegraphic transfers, transactions that may have previously been used for money laundering or terrorist finance. Kenya took a major step to combat money laundering through the closure of Charterhouse Bank.

Senior Kenyan officials made clear their desire to achieve a Safe Skies agreement, but much work remained to be done to bring Kenya up to international standards. U.S. Federal Aviation Administration and Transportation Security Administration training efforts in recent years improved aviation security, but consistent planning and enforcement of security procedures remained a challenge in 2006, particularly at Wilson Airport in Nairobi. Security improved, however, at Kenya's main air entry point, Nairobi's Jomo Kenyatta International Airport.

Liberia

Despite limited resources, untrained personnel, and a weak judicial system, all products of 14 years of civil war, the Government of Liberia demonstrated a willingness to cooperate with the United States and the international community to combat terrorism. Through rule of law and security sector reform assistance programs, the United States supported a number of initiatives that addressed Liberia's vulnerabilities, which included porous borders, rampant identification document fraud, lax immigration controls, wide-scale corruption, and underpaid law enforcement, security, and customs personnel. The Liberian government was eager to engage the United States on counterterrorism, international crime issues, and security sector reform.

There have never been any acts of transnational terrorism in Liberia. Of concern, however, were reports that hundreds of Middle Eastern businessmen purchased legitimately issued but fraudulently obtained Liberian diplomatic passports from Ministry of Foreign Affairs (MFA) officials. These documents would permit free movement between the Middle East and West Africa. The government took steps to stop this Charles Taylor-era practice by requiring that diplomatic passports be issued only by the MFA in Monrovia.

The government's failure to surrender fugitives for extradition was a source of frustration in bilateral relations. In January, a circuit court erroneously held that the bilateral extradition treaty between the United States and Liberia expired in 1944. The Government of Liberia appealed that decision, and it is pending in the Supreme Court.

Since 2003, there has been a resurgence in the number of visits by foreign Islamic proselytizing groups, overwhelmingly Sunni organizations from

Pakistan, Egypt, and South Africa. Liberian security services reported that none of these groups publicly espoused militant or anti-U.S. messages. Liberia's indigenous, war-weary, and predominantly Sunni Islamic community, which represented roughly 20 percent of the country's population, has demonstrated no interest in militant strains of Islam to date. That said, outstanding land disputes negatively affecting large numbers of Muslim land owners in Nimba and other counties could fan ethnic and religious tensions with the predominantly Christian central government.

As in other West African states, reports of possible Hizballah connections within the Lebanese community in Liberia indicated that Lebanese businessmen provided financial support and engaged in fundraising activities for Hizballah. There were no other terrorist groups known to be operating within Liberia.

Madagascar

International terrorism was a concern in Madagascar because of the island nation's inadequately monitored 3,000 mile coastline. Limited equipment, personnel, and training for border control increased the risks of penetration. The Ministry of Defense and the U.S. Embassy co-hosted an International Maritime Security Conference in July with military and civilian participants from ten countries in the Indian Ocean and along the east coast of Africa. Malagasy police, military, intelligence, and security forces have not had much training in counterterrorism and maritime surveillance, but despite limited resources, government officials were willing to cooperate with the United States; the international maritime conference and the Rewards for Justice Program were two examples of cooperative ventures. At the main port in Tamatave, which handled 80 percent of maritime traffic and more than 90 percent of container traffic, access control and overall security improved substantially. The U.S. Coast Guard Port Security Liaison removed Tamatave Port from its Port Security Advisory for Madagascar, with an acknowledgement that the Port met minimum standards under the International Ship and Port Facility (ISPS) Code.

Mali

Inadequate resources continued to hamper the Malian government's ability to control its long and porous borders, thus limiting the effectiveness of military patrols and border control measures. Mali cooperated with U.S. efforts, and remained one of the largest recipients in the sub-region of military training and assistance through the Trans-Sahara Counterterrorism Partnership and other U.S. assistance programs. Northern Mali served as a potential safe haven for terrorists, traffickers, and smugglers due to the region's remoteness, harsh desert climate, and size. The AQIM/GSPC maintained a regular, small-scale presence, moving essentially without hindrance in the northern part of Malian territory, although it did not maintain any permanent facilities and was constantly on the move. In September and October, a group of Malian Tuareg rebels, known as the Alliance for Democracy and Change (ADC), engaged in two firefights with the AQIM/GSPC in northern Mali. The Malian government did not announce an official position on the violence between the ADC and AQIM/GSPC, nor did it attempt to confront AQIM/GSPC elements in the North or prevent their use of Malian territory. There were no confrontations between the Malian military and the AQIM/GSPC in 2006.

Mauritania

Mauritanian leaders continued to cooperate with the United States in the War on Terror. The transitional government took several positive steps toward creating an inclusive political environment that allowed moderate Islamic groups to participate in the political process. While the government continued not to recognize Islamic political parties, it did allow these groups to submit legislative and municipal candidates on independent lists.

On April 26, three suspected terrorists escaped from the central prison and apparently fled the country. Between May and August, the government arrested approximately ten individuals it claimed had links to terrorist groups. This brought the number of suspected terrorists in custody to approximately 20. The government did not try any of the suspected terrorists it held. Mauritanian officials dismantled a AQIM/GSPC network in May and June. The government did not tolerate the presence of AQIM/GSPC members on its territory, and several AQIM/GSPC members who attempted to infiltrate the country were arrested. In contrast with the previous year, there were no terrorist attacks on Mauritanian soil. However, fighting between the AQIM/GSPC and Tuareg rebels in Northern Mali occasionally threatened the border region. The Mauritanian Group for Preaching and Jihad (GMPJ) was not active during the year because most of its members were arrested in May 2005. Although eight of its members were released this year, the group's leaders remained in Mauritanian custody.

Nigeria

Although Nigeria wanted to be viewed as taking a leading counterterrorism role in West Africa, its security agencies remained reactive. Nigerian intelligence and security services worked hard, however, to improve intelligence sharing on counterterrorism issues, and the Nigerian military worked to establish units with counterterrorism capability. Nigerian security services were cooperative when asked to investigate potential terrorist threats to U.S. interests.

Nigeria took the lead in the Economic Community of West African States (ECOWAS) and the AU in sponsoring joint intelligence and security conferences on counterterrorism. The New Partnership for African Development (NEPAD), an organization founded by African heads of state, condemned terrorism and called for African nations to take concrete measures to combat it. Nigeria initiated legislative and regulatory steps to shore up its anti-money laundering regime to fight terrorism.

While Nigeria's current criminal law did not contain specific counterterrorism provisions, the penal code proscribed acts of violence that included terrorism. In August, the Nigerian cabinet approved a draft counterterrorism bill and sent it to the National Assembly for consideration. Under the new legislation, anyone convicted of a terrorist offense could be sentenced to as much as 35 years in prison. The National Assembly had not acted on the bill by year's end.

There was no special examining magistrate with specific powers in the counterterrorism area. In Nigeria, suspects by law must be charged within 48 hours, but in practice were held as long as deemed necessary. Most criminals were photographed and fingerprinted by security elements, but DNA samples were not taken due to resource constraints and a lack of scientific infrastructure.

While the Nigerian government did not support international terrorism or terrorists, there were some individuals and private groups in Nigeria with ties to probable terrorist elements in Sudan, Iran, Pakistan, and Libya. Members of terrorist groups, including al-Qaida and the AQIM/GSPC, have operated and recruited in Nigeria.

Rwanda

The Rwandan government made efforts to combat terrorism financing and continued to increase its border control measures to identify potential terrorists. Rwanda had an intergovernmental counterterrorism committee and a counterterrorism reaction team in the police intelligence unit. Central Bank and Ministry of Finance officials continued to provide outstanding cooperation on terrorist financing issues. While the Government of Rwanda had not yet fully developed its laws and regulations in accordance with international conventions and protocols concerning terrorism, it had the authority under local law to identify, freeze, and seize terrorist-related financial assets. Rwanda participated in regional initiatives on international counterterrorism cooperation, including active participation in the East African Stand-by Brigade. In September, it hosted the Third Regional Counter-Terrorism Conference for Chiefs of Security and Intelligence Services in Kigali, and it assumed the chairmanship of the organization. In October, Police Commissioner General Andrew Rwigamba was appointed the World Regional Chair for sub-Saharan Africa for the International Association of Chiefs of Police (IACP).

The Democratic Forces for the Liberation of Rwanda (FDLR)[2], an armed rebel force that included former soldiers and supporters of the previous government that orchestrated the 1994 genocide, continued to operate in the Democratic Republic of the Congo. Rwanda pressed for international action to pursue the FDLR. A unit of this organization was responsible for the kidnapping and murder of nine persons, including two American tourists, in Bwindi Park in 1999. The Rwandan government assisted U.S. law enforcement officials in an attempt to prosecute three individuals, suspected in the 1999 attack, who were transferred to the United States in 2003.

Senegal

The Government of Senegal cooperated with the United States in identifying terrorist groups operating in Senegal. More work remained to be done, however, to develop first responder services, to facilitate the quick sharing of information between agencies, and to control porous borders where police and security services are undermanned and ill-equipped to prevent illicit cross-border trafficking. The Government of Senegal affirmed its commitment to United States government-assisted efforts to augment its border security.

Senegal continued to enhance its ability to combat terrorism, prosecute terror suspects, and respond to emergencies. Despite advances, however, Senegal lacked specific counterterrorism legislation and current laws made it difficult to prosecute terror suspects. As participants in the Trans-Saharan Counterterrorism Partnership, more than 180 Senegalese government officials took part in ATA programs. Senegalese military officials attended a counterterrorism seminar in Algiers and attended the Chiefs of Defense and Directors of Military Intelligence conferences. The Defense International Institute of Legal Studies, the U.S. Treasury's Office of Technical Assistance, and the United Nations Office on Drugs and Crime (UNODC) gave separate seminars on the legal aspects of fighting terrorism.

During the year, President Wade met again with Imam Mamour Fall, a Senegalese deported from Italy in 2003 for praising Usama bin Laden, to counsel "moderation." President Wade also criticized members of the Senegalese press for exaggerating the level of public support for extremism.

[2] The Democratic Forces for the Liberation of Rwanda was known as the Army for the Liberation of Rwanda (ALIR) until 2001.

Sierra Leone

Sierra Leone's armed forces focused on border control because potential unrest in neighboring countries remained a threat. The government did not detect any radical Islamic activities. There were no identified terrorist groups or organizations in Sierra Leone, however, there were allegations that members of the Lebanese business community in Sierra Leone, many of whom are diamond traders, were sympathetic to and made financial contributions to Hizballah. The Bank of Sierra Leone established a Financial Investigations Unit, but it lacked the capacity to effectively monitor financial transactions. Financial constraints, corruption, and insufficient capacity continued to hinder Sierra Leone's counterterrorism and law enforcement capabilities.

Somalia

Somalia's weak central government, protracted state of violent instability, long unguarded coastline, porous borders, and proximity to the Arabian Peninsula made it a potential location for international terrorists seeking a transit or launching point for conducting operations in Somalia or elsewhere. The rise of the Council of Islamic Courts (CIC) and their expansion of control into southern and central Somalia created a more permissive operating environment and safe haven for foreign terrorists. In June, the CIC gained control of Mogadishu and were initially welcomed as bringing a modicum of peace and stability to the city. Over the course of the following months, the broader CIC organization was hijacked by al Shabaab (The Youth), a small, extremist group affiliated with AQ that consists of radicalized young men, between 20 and 30 years of age. Many of its senior leaders are believed to have trained and fought with AQ in Afghanistan. The CIC began to pursue an increasingly hostile strategy of military expansion and aggression designed to provoke a broader regional conflict. Al Shabaab militia participated in CIC military offensives and served as something akin to a "special forces" unit for the CIC. Although not formally a part of the CIC structure, members of al Shabaab held senior positions within the CIC, particularly in the security, finance, and education departments. The group was reputed to be extremely violent and brutal, and its members are suspected of murdering an Italian nun in Mogadishu in September, targeted assassinations of dozens of Somali nationals inside Somalia, including the murder of peace activist Abdulqadir Yahya Ali in July 2005 and the murder of foreign aid workers in the self-declared Republic of Somaliland in late 2003 to early 2004. In late June, the CIC elected Hassan Dahir Aweys chairman of the CIC Shura Council. Aweys is designated as a terrorist by the United States and the United Nations because of his links to AQ, the Taliban, or Usama bin Laden.

Among the foreign AQ operatives believed to have enjoyed protection by the CIC and al Shabaab leadership are individuals wanted for the 1998 embassy bombings in Kenya and Tanzania and a 2002 hotel bombing in Kenya, including Fazul Abdallah Mohammed (aka Harun Fazul), Abu Talha al-Sudani, and Saleh Ali Saleh Nabhan. At the end of the year, the Transitional Federal Government (TFG), backed by Ethiopia, succeeded in ending CIC control of Mogadishu and southern and central Somalia. Regional efforts to bring about national reconciliation and establish peace and stability in Somalia are ongoing. Although the capability of the TFG and other Somali local and regional authorities to carry out counterterrorism activities was limited, some have taken actions.

South Africa

South Africa continued to publicly support global efforts to combat terrorism and shared financial, law enforcement, and limited intelligence information with the United States. President Mbeki reiterated his support for such cooperation during his December meeting with President Bush. On several occasions President Mbeki voiced his opinion that "no circumstances whatsoever can ever justify resorting to terrorism." Members of Parliament from other parties, including Muslim legislators, have echoed Mbeki's sentiments.

The Government of South Africa supported multilateral counterterrorism efforts and bolstered its enforcement agencies. Resource constraints, however, limited the extent to which South Africa could fund its security forces for counterterrorist initiatives. The South African government is sensitive to distinctions between "terrorist organizations" and "liberation movements," since the ruling African National Congress was long branded a terrorist group during the struggle against apartheid.

Fraudulently obtained documents remained a significant problem for South African authorities. Although South African documents often include good security measures, but efforts to limit potential terrorists' access to passports and South African identity documents were limited by low capacity in the Department of Home Affairs, which handled identity documentation.

It was unclear to what extent terrorist groups were present in South Africa. Many analysts believed that AQ and other extremist groups have a presence within South Africa's generally moderate Muslim community. The South African government does not provide any type of material assistance to any group designated as a Foreign Terrorist Organization by the United States.

Sudan

See Chapter 3, *State Sponsors of Terrorism*.

Tanzania

Tanzania took significant steps to establish a National Counterterrorism Center. The purpose of this Center was to build Tanzania's capacity to prevent and respond to terrorist attacks. Working closely with the United States, Tanzania continued to disrupt terrorist networks to prevent acts of terrorism. Tanzanian law enforcement cooperated with the United States to exchange evidence and testimony on cases related to the 1998 bombing of the U.S. Embassy in Dar Es Salaam. Tanzania continued its participation in several multi-year programs to strengthen its law enforcement and military capacity, improve aviation and border security, and combat money laundering and terrorist financing. The Ministry of Finance and the Bank of Tanzania showed ongoing willingness to combat terrorist financing. Tanzania cooperated with the United States and complied with its obligations under UN Security Council resolutions. In November, the Tanzanian Parliament passed the Anti-Money Laundering (AML) Bill, ending a legislative process that began in 2002 with support from the United States. The AML Bill will lay the legal groundwork for Tanzania to create a Financial Intelligence Unit (FIU) and bolster Tanzania's ability to combat financial crime, including counterterrorist financing. With the Millennium Challenge Account Threshold Program, the United States will support Tanzania as it establishes a fully functional FIU. Tanzanian law enforcement and security forces attempted to identify and monitor terrorist activities and deny use of Tanzanian territory as a safe haven for terrorists. The government was aware that terrorists could use its territory for transit purposes and did not provide any kind of material assistance to terrorists or terrorist groups.

Uganda

The Ugandans have proved willing to locate, capture, and hold terror suspects. The Government of Uganda was actively involved in regional counterterrorism efforts, conferences, and workshops, and had a strong regional voice in opposing international terrorism and supporting U.S. counterterrorism initiatives. Although Uganda actively worked to root out possible terrorist threats, it was hampered by shortages in fuel, equipment, funding, and personnel.

Since 1987, the Lord's Resistance Army (LRA), which is on the U.S. Terrorist Exclusion List, has waged an insurgency in northern Uganda using camps in southern Sudan as bases for attacks on government forces and civilians. The LRA's tactics include murder, looting, burning houses, torture, mutilation, and abduction of children for the purposes of forced conscription, labor, and sexual servitude. The Government of Uganda deployed 45,000 troops in northern Uganda to protect civilians and combat the LRA. Uganda and Sudan also expanded an agreement that permitted the Ugandan military to attack LRA units operating in southern Sudan.

The Government of Uganda and the LRA began peace negotiations in July. The process yielded a Cessation of Hostilities Agreement (CHA) on August 26 that was poorly monitored and repeatedly violated. The CHA was renewed with strengthened monitoring provisions on November 1. The Government of Uganda remained committed to the ongoing peace process.

Zimbabwe

Despite the Government of Zimbabwe's self-imposed isolation on most diplomatic issues, local intelligence and criminal investigative agencies were responsive to U.S. needs in the War on Terror. Government agencies routinely provided assistance by conducting investigative inquiries, traces, and border checks of individuals thought to be threats to U.S. government facilities or personnel. In May, the Reserve Bank of Zimbabwe (RBZ) released new guidelines on anti-money laundering and combating the financing of terrorism for financial institutions and non-financial businesses and professionals. In August, Zimbabwe assumed the Presidency for the Eastern and Southern Africa Anti-Money Laundering Group (ESAAMLG) for the 2006/2007 administrative year and, in this capacity, hosted the group's Council of Ministers of Finance meeting in August. In August, Zimbabwe and the Republic of South Africa signed a memorandum of understanding for the exchange of information in combating money laundering and the financing of terrorism.

Country Reports: East Asia and Pacific Overview

"Our cause is a just cause. Terrorism respects no value system; terrorism does not respect the tenets of the great religions of the world; terrorism is based on evil, intolerance, and bigotry. And no free societies, such as Australia and the United States, can ever buckle under to bigotry and intolerance."

John Howard, Prime Minister of Australia
Remarks at the White House
Washington, DC, May 16, 2006

The Jemaah Islamiya regional terrorist network remained a serious threat to Western and regional interests, particularly in Indonesia and the Southern Philippines, although its capabilities were degraded due in large part to regional counterterrorism successes in 2005-2006. As 2007 began, DNA analysis conducted by the FBI confirmed the death of Abu Sayyaf Group's (ASG) nominal leader, Khaddafy Janjalani, at the hands of the Armed Forces of the Philippines (AFP). Early in 2007, Philippine forces also eliminated ASG spokesperson, Abu Solaiman. In August, the AFP killed a significant ASG sub commander, Ismin Sahiron. These deaths represented a major blow to JI, but did not eliminate the overall threat to U.S. interests in the Philippines. JI bombers Dulmatin and Patek remained on the run, probably on Jolo Island. Other terrorists remained at large in Southeast Asia, such as key JI operative Noordin Mat Top, in Indonesia.

Geography makes effective border control problematic for archipelagic states like Indonesia and the Philippines. Monitoring remote locations among the thousands of islands in the Sulawesi Sea and Sulu Archipelago that span the boundaries between Indonesia, Malaysia, and the Philippines is extremely difficult, which makes this tri-border area well suited to terrorist activities, including movement of personnel, equipment, and funds. Therefore, regional capacity building has emerged as a priority goal, in addition to bilateral cooperation and national capacity building. Institutes like the U.S.-Thailand International Law Enforcement Academy (ILEA) in Bangkok and the Southeast Asia Regional Center for Counterterrorism (SEARCCT) in Malaysia continued to expand their activities to provide effective counterterrorism training to law enforcement officers throughout the region. Likewise, the Australian-Indonesian Jakarta Center for Law Enforcement Cooperation (JCLEC) is a promising additional regional center for capacity building. Multilateral fora, including the United Nations Security Council's Counterterrorism Committee (UNCTC), the G8's Roma-Lyon Group and Counterterrorism Action Group (CTAG), the Asia-Pacific Economic Cooperation (APEC) forum, the Association of Southeast Asian Nations (ASEAN), which adopted a new ASEAN Convention on Counterterrorism pending ratification, and the ASEAN Regional Forum (ARF), continued their important roles as key organizations for regional counterterrorism cooperation.

Australia worked to strengthen the Asia-Pacific region's counterterrorism capacity through a range of initiatives, both bilaterally and in regional fora such as APEC, the ASEAN ARF, and the Pacific Island Forum (PIF). Australia increased its four-year counterterrorism assistance to the region by about $70 million to boost the capacity to combat terrorism, bringing the total amount committed to offshore counterterrorism activities since 2004 to $350 million. In March, Australian police arrested three suspected terrorists in Melbourne as part of an ongoing counterterrorism operation, disrupting a significant threat to the city.

China supported several operational and logistical aspects of the War on Terror. China participates in the United States Megaports Initiative designed to improve the security of U.S.-bound cargo. Container Security initiative programs are operating in the ports of Shanghai and Shenzhen. China increased its efforts to build its domestic counterterrorism capabilities with a focus on improving security for the 2008 Beijing Olympics. Beijing continued to express concern that terrorists operate on Chinese territory and has asserted that some members of the Uighur minority in Xingjiang Province pose a threat to China's domestic stability.

Japan strengthened its own security by contributing to counterterrorism capacity-building among Asian countries and by participating in a second trilateral counterterrorism dialogue with the United States and Australia in October. Japan is using Official Development Assistance (ODA) grants to expand counterterrorism capacity building in Southeast Asia. This $60 million dollar annual program, initiated in FY-2006, includes projects aimed at increasing maritime and port security. The Republic of Korea is shifting its attention to possible acts of terror beyond the Korean Peninsula. Reflecting this shift, the Ministry of Foreign Affairs and Trade (MOFAT) appointed its first Director for International Counterterrorism Cooperation in February.

Thailand's military staged a coup in September. An interim government has been attempting to address the ongoing violence connected to a separatist movement in the ethnic Malay, Muslim south. Although the roots of the problem are ethnic and not religious, there is concern that southern unrest has the potential to attract international terrorist groups such as JI and al-Qaida that may attempt to capitalize on the increasingly violent situation for their own purposes.

Australia

In addition to its substantial ongoing efforts to combat domestic and international terrorism, Australia launched new initiatives working with its regional neighbors to assist in building their resolve and capacity to confront terrorism. The Australian Federal Police (AFP) Joint Counterterrorism Teams' (JCTT) multi-agency effort to address domestic and international terrorism concerns in Australia's six largest cities became fully operational this year. In March, Australian police arrested three suspected terrorists in Melbourne as part of an ongoing counterterrorism operation, disrupting a significant threat to the community. In August, an Australian court sentenced Faheem Khalid Lodhi to 20 years in prison for plotting to bomb Australia's national electricity grid. Regional cooperation between Australian and Southeast Asian government agencies continued to disrupt terrorist operations. Active cooperation with immigration agencies in the region strengthened border controls and impeded terrorists' ability to travel, recruit, train, and operate.

In December, Australia enacted new anti-money laundering and counterterrorism financing (AML/CTF) legislation that would make the Australian Transaction Reports Analysis Centre (AUSTRAC), which monitors financial transactions, the national AML/CTF regulator with supervisory, monitoring, and enforcement functions over a diverse range of industry sectors. Australia strengthened its intelligence capabilities by funding additional staff and technical capabilities, and established identity security strike teams to investigate and prosecute people and syndicates involved in manufacturing false identities.

As part of measures Australia undertook in response to the 2005 *Wheeler Report on Aviation Security and Policing at Australian Airports*, airport police commanders began their new role overseeing crime and security-related matters at eleven counterterrorism first response airports in the country. Australia announced in its budget that it would enhance closed circuit television monitoring and analysis capability at its international airports. This will expand the deployment of explosives trace-detection equipment for the examination of domestic air cargo at each of Australia's major airports and will improve the quality of security training for cargo handlers. Australia committed to enhancing its capability to identify, inspect, and respond to high-risk export air cargo through the deployment of additional explosives detector-dog teams; the provision of additional mobile X-ray vans; and the trial of communications technology to achieve real-time air cargo reporting. The Australian government provided additional funding to enhance its ability to detect, deter, and respond to illegal activity near its borders, including illegal fishing and trafficking in persons, through increased surveillance and patrolling.

Australia used its position as Chair of the Wassenaar Arrangement on Export Controls for Conventional Arms and Dual-Use Goods and Technologies (WA) to increase awareness of the Man-Portable Air Defense Systems (MANPADS) threat and the need for more effective export controls, and to solicit greater cooperation, particularly from states that produce, export, or stockpile MANPADS. Australia also led outreach missions to non-Wassenaar states China, India, Belarus, Kazakhstan, and Singapore. In June, Australia hosted an international seminar in Geneva to promote the need for practical action to counter the global MANPADS threat. In the same month, Australia, the United States, and the Philippines hosted a workshop in Manila on the methodology of conducting airport MANPADS vulnerability assessments. In August, Australia advocated for increased efforts to counter the proliferation of MANPADS at the UN Conference on Disarmament. In October, Australia co-chaired with Thailand an ASEAN Regional Forum workshop on stockpile security of MANPADS and small arms and light weapons to help regional countries strengthen their domestic inventory controls.

The Australian ambassador for counterterrorism chaired the International Counterterrorism Coordination Group, Australia's interagency counterterrorism working group. Australia increased its four-year regional counterterrorism assistance package by about $70 million to boost the capacity of neighbor countries to combat terrorism, bringing the total amount committed to offshore counterterrorism activities since 2004 to $350 million. Building on successful regional cooperation among law enforcement, intelligence, and border control authorities, the package included new measures and a new emphasis on expanding regional cooperation. Cooperation will focus on countering the threat of terrorists acquiring or using weapons of mass destruction, building regional capability for responding to terrorist attacks, and commencing activities to promote tolerance and counteract terrorist propaganda. Key programs included funding for enhancing law enforcement counterterrorism capacity and liaison networks, expanding intelligence cooperation capabilities, improving border control capability and coordination in Southeast Asia, further developing the APEC Regional Movement Alert System, enhancing Indonesia's border alert system at major ports, building regional awareness of the terrorist WMD threat and strengthening regional controls on chemical, biological, radiological, and nuclear materials, and improving regional emergency response capacity and coordination. In July, Australia became an initial partner nation in the U.S. Global Initiative to Combat Nuclear Terrorism and, in October, it participated in a second Trilateral Counterterrorism Dialogue with the United States and Japan.

Australia continued to provide legal drafting assistance to regional states, including the South Pacific islands, seeking to adopt international conventions and protocols against terrorism and to bring their domestic laws into conformity with these conventions. In February, Australia opened the upgraded Transnational Crime Centre in Jakarta which was first established as a joint initiative between Australia and Indonesia in the aftermath of the 2002 Bali bombings. The center housed Indonesia's first national intelligence database, linking 30 locations throughout the country. The joint Australian-Indonesian Jakarta Centre for Law Enforcement Cooperation (JCLEC) located in Semarang, Indonesia has offered more than 50 courses and trained more than 1,200 officers to date. The AFP committed additional agents to Jakarta and Manila to work closely with those governments and the FBI to apprehend JI fugitives.

The AFP received funding to expand its investigative and specialist training, currently delivered to regional law enforcement partners through facilities like JCLEC. Funding was also targeted toward conducting offshore exercises and training with regional partners, increasing the number of counterterrorism advisers working in the AFP's international liaison officer network, introducing to high priority locations a custom-built Case Management and Information System developed for use in overseas jurisdictions, and enhancing specialist forensic and technical training for law enforcement agencies in the region. The Australian government substantially increased the AFP's International Deployment Group by over 400 personnel and created an Operational Response Group ready to respond on short notice to emerging law and order issues and to conduct stabilization operations.

Australia contributed an additional 500 troops to Afghanistan as part of a Dutch-led provincial reconstruction team. By year's end, there were 1,000 Australian troops in Iraq and 800 in Afghanistan. Australia designated a total of 19 terrorist organizations under its domestic criminal code.

The Government of Australia and its Muslim advisory body, the Muslim Community Reference Group, continued efforts begun in 2005 to develop and implement a National Action Plan to promote social cohesion, harmony, and security. The plan committed almost $30 million for a range of activities to address extremism and intolerance in the Australian community. Activities will include integration enhancement and crisis management training for Muslim communities, and education and employment programs that work to bring law enforcement agencies and Muslim communities together to resolve issues of conflict and discrimination.

Burma

Bilateral relations between Burma and the United States remained strained. The Burmese regime's willingness to cooperate and coordinate on counterterrorist activities within the country and throughout the region remains limited. However, Burma has cooperated with the United States on both transnational terrorist threats and law enforcement efforts to stem narcotrafficking and money laundering. Burmese Special Branch police created a new counterterrorism unit headquartered in Rangoon.

The Burmese judicial system lacked independence and transparency and suffered from corruption. The government defined almost all anti-regime activities "acts of terrorism" and made little distinction between peaceful political dissent and violent attacks by insurgents or criminals. Suspected perpetrators of any acts that opposed the regime were subject to lengthy detention without trial or due process. The government was quick to characterize dissident groups as aligned with terrorist organizations and used this as justification to scrutinize and disrupt their activities. The regime regularly labeled exile leaders and political activists as "terrorists." No reliable evidence existed that any terrorists, terrorist organizations, or affiliations, were using Burma as a safe haven.

No known anti-American terrorist groups were operating in Burma. However, some observers posited possible links between known terrorist organizations and two local insurgent groups: the Rohingya Solidarity Organization, and the Arakan Rohingya National Organization. There were few signs that either group remained active inside of Burma, although the Burmese regime's severe repression of the Rohingya Muslim population inside Burma could foster sympathy with extremist methods and objectives.

Indigenous violence in Burma generally was targeted against the ruling regime. Various insurgent groups in ethnic minority areas near borders with China, India, Bangladesh, Laos, and Thailand conducted small-scale actions against the Burmese authorities. The Government of Burma attributed several recent bombings in the capital and elsewhere to anti-regime elements, but did not publicly file charges against specific individuals.

On January 3, two small-scale bombings occurred in Bago. No deaths or injuries were reported. Police conducted an initial investigation and blamed ethnic Karen groups for attempting to disrupt the National Convention and Burmese Independence Day, which is January 4. On April 20, five small improvised explosive devices went off in downtown Rangoon; police reported minimal damage and no injuries. On September 21, Embassy contacts in the Burmese Special Branch Police reported that a small bomb exploded inside a women's bathroom at the Teachers Training College in Rangoon, but that no one was injured and the explosion caused very little damage. The Burmese police politely refused the Embassy's request to view either the scene or any remaining fragments. As in most such incidents, the Government of Burma claimed the incident was a subversive act, "committed by a group of insurgent destructive elements who wanted to disturb and destroy stability of the state." Authorities did not make public any evidence of a genuine investigation or identify the specific perpetrator(s).

Cambodia

Cambodia's ability to investigate potential terrorist activities was limited by a lack of training and resources. An absence of comprehensive domestic legislation to combat terrorism also hindered the government's ability to arrest and prosecute terrorists. Cambodia's political leadership, however, demonstrated a strong commitment to take aggressive legal action against terrorists.

There were no indications that specific terrorist groups operated in Cambodia, but porous borders and endemic corruption could make the country vulnerable to a terrorist presence. The Cambodian government believed that the Cambodian Freedom Fighters (CFF), which carried out an armed attack in November 2000 that killed eight people, are still capable of carrying out attacks in Cambodia. The leader of this group was arrested in California in 2005. The Cambodian government was working with the FBI to bring the leader of the CFF to trial in the United States.

Various officials were identified to take positions in Cambodia's National Counterterrorism Committee (NCTC), a policy level decision-making body established by the government in 2005 and chaired by the prime minister. The Australian military conducted a conference with the NCTC in August and expressed its intention to follow-up with a tabletop exercise with the Center.

In addition to providing assistance for the NCTC, the Australian government was helping Cambodia draft a new counterterrorism law. The draft law was being reviewed by the relevant legislative committee and the national legislature was expected to adopt it. The Australian and U.K. governments jointly sponsored a National Seminar on Counterterrorism in

April to help train the Cambodian military and police. The Malaysian government cooperated with the Cambodian government on Malaysia-specific cases.

In December, following the visit of the Sri Lankan prime minister, the Cambodian government announced that a Sri Lankan military intelligence official would work with police and defense officials on intelligence matters. His announcement followed Prime Minister Hun Sen's assurance to his Sri Lankan counterpart that the Tamil Tiger rebels would not receive arms smuggled from Cambodia, although the government acknowledged it was likely this has occurred in the past. Cambodia has destroyed 200,000 small arms over the last several years with EU assistance, and, with U.S. assistance, has destroyed its stockpile of MANPADS.

With U.S. assistance, the Government of Cambodia installed computerized border control systems at Phnom Penh and Siem Riep airports and at the land border crossing of Poipet and Koh Kong. The Cambodian government also cooperated fully with U.S. requests to monitor terrorists and terrorist entities listed as supporters of terrorist financing.

China

As Beijing prepares to host the 2008 Olympics, China increasingly reached out to the United States and other nations on counterterrorism cooperation. No acts of terrorism were committed in China this year, but Chinese citizens were victims of terrorist acts in Afghanistan, Iraq, Lebanon, and Pakistan.

China participated in the United States Megaports Initiative designed to improve security for United States-bound cargo. The U.S. Department of Energy and its Chinese counterparts made progress toward implementation of the November 2005 agreement allowing the installation of equipment at China's ports to detect hidden shipments of nuclear and other radioactive materials. China became an initial partner nation in the U.S. Global Initiative to Combat Nuclear Terrorism, attending the first meeting of the Global Initiative in Rabat, Morocco in October. China also continued its participation in the Container Security Initiative.

Chinese officials signed statements with counterterrorism counterparts in the Association of Southeast Asian Nations (ASEAN) Regional Forum (ARF), Asia Pacific Economic Cooperation (APEC), and the Shanghai Cooperation Organization (SCO). In April, China co-hosted the Fourth ARF Meeting on Counterterrorism and Transnational Crime in Beijing. China is a founding member of the SCO and has made counterterrorism one of the group's main objectives. In June, China hosted an SCO summit in Shanghai that included India, Iran, Pakistan, and Mongolia as observers. At the summit, the member states agreed to hold joint counterterrorism military exercises in Russia in 2007, with troops from all six SCO member states participating. In August, China and Kazakhstan held their first-ever joint counterterrorism exercises in Kazakhstan. In August, China signed agreements with Pakistan on border control, terrorism, and crime and, in December, held joint counterterrorism exercises in Pakistan.

China ratified the UN International Convention for the Suppression of the Financing of Terrorism in February and worked to expand its international cooperation on terrorist finance through mutual legal assistance agreements with foreign jurisdictions. In October, China passed a new Anti-Money Laundering Law, which took effect January 1, 2007, broadening the scope of existing anti-money laundering regulations to hold a greater range of financial institutions liable and to expand the powers of the People's Bank of China (PBOC). With the PBOC as the lead agency for all anti-money laundering activities in China, the Ministry of Public Security (MPS) is responsible for criminal investigations, and the State Administration of Foreign Exchange (SAFE) is the primary agency for countering illicit foreign exchange transactions.

Institutional obstacles and rivalries between domestic financial and law enforcement authorities hampered Chinese anti-money laundering work and other financial law enforcement aimed at countering terrorists. Still, China's Financial Intelligence Unit (FIU), established in 2004 to track suspicious transactions, worked closely with the Financial Crimes Enforcement Network (FINCEN) in the United States to develop its capabilities. China began requiring banks and financial institutions to establish anti-money laundering systems, record customer identities, and report suspicious transactions. In January, China launched a national credit information system to more efficiently monitor transactions, information collection, and dissemination. Nonetheless, anti-money laundering efforts were hampered by the prevalence of counterfeit identity documents and cash transactions conducted by underground banks, which, in some regions, reportedly accounted for over one-third of lending activities.

China refused to recognize the Egmont Group, an umbrella body coordinating the activities of over 100 FIUs worldwide, because the Group includes an FIU from Taiwan. Joining the Financial Action Task Force (FATF) remained an important priority for China. In 2004, China joined the Eurasia FATF-style regional group, and, in 2005, China was granted FATF observer status. In November 2006, an FATF Mutual Evaluation Team comprehensively reviewed China's anti-money laundering and counterterrorism finance regime. The results of the review and China's bid to join FATF will be discussed at the June 2007 FATF Plenary Meeting.

Human rights organizations have accused China of using counterterrorism as a pretext to continue efforts to suppress Uighurs, a predominantly

Muslim ethnic group that comprises the majority of the population of the Xinjiang Uighur Autonomous Region. In August, Chinese police officials announced that since 1990 they have seized 41 tons of explosives from separatists in Xinjiang, including grenades and materials to make bombs. Also in August, China convicted a Canadian citizen of Uighur ethnicity of involvement in East Turkistan terrorist activities. In November, China gave Canada assurances that he would not be executed for his alleged crimes; he remains in prison.

In May, the United States released five ethnic Uighur Chinese national detainees found not to be Enemy Combatants from Guantanamo (GTMO) to Albania. The Chinese government denounced the move as a violation of international law and demanded the return of the men to China. Some of the remaining Uighur detainees at GTMO were designated for transfer or release and others will have their status reviewed annually.

Formally established in 2004, the FBI Legal Attaché Office in Beijing bolstered U.S.-China cooperation on counterterrorism investigations. China provided substantive intelligence in some counterterrorism cases, but more work remained to be done in terms of its overall responsiveness to U.S. requests. In July, the first meeting between a standing Chinese Minister of Public Security and the Director of the FBI was held in Washington, D.C., where FBI Director Robert Mueller hosted Minister Zhou Yongkang, principally to discuss terrorism matters.

Following Secretary of Homeland Security Michael Chertoff's visit to Beijing in April, the United States and China signed a Memorandum of Understanding (MOU) to allow United States Federal Air Marshals (FAMS) to fly to China and Chinese air marshals to fly into the United States. In addition, the MOU provided for training and information exchanges. The first FAMS mission was completed in August, and the Chinese air marshals completed training at the FAMS Training Facility in September.

In February, the United States Coast Guard Liaison Office was established in Beijing as a focal point for United States-China exchanges to enhance the safety and security of ports around the world in compliance with the Maritime Transportation Safety Act. Activities included a visit by the U.S. Coast Guard Commandant, three expert-level delegations to conduct training and exchanges, two port visits in China by U.S. Coast Guard cutters, and one international exercise.

Although not publicly attributing any particular incident to terrorism, Chinese authorities asserted that terrorists, primarily based in Xinjiang, continued to operate clandestinely on Chinese territory. The Chinese government attempted to restrict foreign support for perceived terrorism and increased the number of deployed security personnel in response to perceived terrorist activities in Xinjiang. The United States has sanctioned

Chinese entities for missile and chemical weapons proliferation activities, including transfers to Iran, North Korea, and Libya.

Hong Kong

Hong Kong's role as a major transit point for cargo, finances, and people makes it an important counterterrorism partner, and the Hong Kong Special Administrative Region Government (HKSARG) continued to cooperate with the United States on counterterrorism efforts.

The high level of cooperation and the successful implementation of the Container Security Initiative (CSI) by Hong Kong Customs officials received continued praise from visiting U.S. government delegations, which described it as a model for CSI implementation. The U.S. government continued to work with one of Hong Kong's port terminal operators to develop and refine integrated container security architecture.

Hong Kong law enforcement agencies provided full support and cooperation to their overseas counterparts in tracing financial transactions suspected of being linked to terrorist activities. Hong Kong actively participated in various anti-money laundering and counterterrorist financing initiatives, including the Financial Action Task Force (FATF) and the Asia/Pacific Group on Money Laundering. Hong Kong's Joint Financial Intelligence Unit (JFIU), operated by Hong Kong Police and the Customs and Excises Department, is a member of the Egmont Group.

The UN International Convention for the Suppression of Financing Terrorism became applicable to Hong Kong when ratified by the People's Republic of China on April 19. The Hong Kong regional government published the list of individuals and entities designated as terrorists or terrorist associates under UNSCR 1267 and the financial regulators circulated the lists to financial institutions, advising them to check the lists and report any suspicious transactions to law enforcement agencies.

The Hong Kong Monetary Authority recently coordinated the establishment of an Industry Working Group on Anti-Money Laundering that included representatives from some 20 authorized institutions. The group established three sub-groups to address terrorist financing, transaction monitoring systems, and private banking issues.

Macau

The Macau Special Administrative Region Government (MSARG) passed both anti-money laundering and counterterrorism finance legislation. Still, Macau's lack of judicial and law enforcement experience in combating financial crimes, combined with its expanding casino industry and history as a base for organized crime, provided a potential site for money laundering and terrorist financing activities.

On March 23, the Macau government passed new counterterrorism legislation aimed at strengthening counterterrorist financing measures. The law made it illegal to conceal or handle finances on behalf of terrorist organizations. Individuals were liable even if they were not members of designated terrorist organizations themselves. The legislation also allowed, in certain cases, prosecution of persons who committed terrorist acts outside of Macau and mandated stiffer penalties. On the same day, the government also passed a money laundering bill that strengthened its oversight of financial institutions. The new law imposed requirements for the mandatory identification and registration of financial institution shareholders, customer identification, and external audits that includes reviews of compliance with anti-money laundering statutes.

The Macau government has the authority to freeze terrorist assets, although a judicial order is required. Macau financial authorities directed the institutions they supervise to conduct searches for terrorist assets using the UN 1267 Sanctions Committee consolidated list and the list of Specially Designated Global Terrorists designated by the United States pursuant to E.O. 13224. Bank examiners reviewed customer profiles, large cash transaction records, and suspicious bank reports. They also interviewed frontline staff, senior management and money laundering compliance officers.

The Government of Macau continued to exchange information with the Hong Kong Special Administrative Region and counterparts in mainland China. Additionally, Macau continued to cooperate internationally in counterterrorism efforts, through INTERPOL and other security-focused organizations within the Asia Pacific Region.

Indonesia

Since late 2004, the Indonesian government increased counterterrorism efforts and counterterrorism cooperation with both the United States and the international community. The Indonesian National Police (INP) had several successes in breaking-up terrorist cells and arresting terrorists with links to Jemaah Islamiya (JI). INP investigations into the October 2005 suicide attacks on Bali led to numerous successes for Indonesia's counterterrorism investigators. Links among violent Islamic radicals and extremist organizations, including JI and its associates, remained a serious security threat to both Western and domestic targets in Indonesia, although no major anti-Western terrorist incident occurred. Physical security at major hotels and tourist venues in Jakarta and Bali was upgraded significantly. At year's end, the main target of Indonesian CT units remained Malaysian JI operative and recruiter Noordin Mohammed Top, suspected in nearly every major terrorist attack in Indonesia since 2002.

The security situation in the previously strife-torn Maluku region improved, absent major incidents of interfaith violence. In central Sulawesi, where terrorist attacks in 2005 claimed several lives, a special taskforce led by the INP's top CT investigators identified and arrested several JI-linked terrorists responsible for the October 2005 Poso schoolgirl beheadings and other previously unresolved cases. The three main suspects arrested in April were brought to trial in Jakarta. In September, several days of street violence in Indonesia's eastern provinces followed the executions in Palu of three Christian men for their role in inciting deadly attacks against Muslims in 2000. However, the perpetrators behind the October shooting death of a Christian priest in Palu remained at large. Also at large were more than two dozen terrorist suspects in central Sulawesi who continued to evade INP investigators. The INP feared aggressive police operations would provoke the militants, and, in November, the INP unsuccessfully sought cooperation from the suspects' families to encourage the suspects to surrender.

The Indonesian attorney general's office continued to seek convictions in more than two dozen terrorism cases tried this year. Among those convicted were terrorist recruiter and trainer Subur Sugiyarto, terrorist financier Abdullah Sunata, and trained bomb maker Mohammad Cholily. In July, Indonesia's attorney general staffed the long awaited Terrorism and Transnational Crime Task Force, designed to oversee counterterrorism trials nationwide through a cadre of special terrorism prosecutors. Task Force members immediately began to take on over a dozen counterterrorism cases, including the three central Sulawesi cases.

Indonesia's policy of routinely granting sentence remissions to nearly all prisoners continued to benefit convicted terrorists, resulting in several early releases. JI figure Emir Abu Bakar Ba'asyir, sentenced in 2005 to 30 months in prison for his involvement in a "sinister conspiracy" to carry out the 2002 Bali attacks, was released in June after several routine sentence reductions. In December, the Indonesian Supreme Court overturned Ba'sayir's conviction based on a judicial review in which Ba'sayir's defense presented new evidence. Also released were several lesser known JI-linked figures and Rusman "Gun-gun" Gunawan, the younger brother of Indonesian-born Riduan bin Isomuddin, also known as Hambali, who was an operational leader in JI and served as the middleman between JI and al-Qaida from 2000 until his capture in 2003.[1] Hambali, a high value detainee, was transferred to Guantanamo Bay in September.

The Indonesian government continued its efforts to develop an effective anti-money laundering regime, but investigations and prosecutions in these cases continued to fall short. Indonesian police froze terrorist financial assets uncovered during investigations, but the government's implementation of the sanctions regime established pursuant to UNSCR 1267

[1] Hambali helped plan the first Bali bombings in 2002 that killed more than 200 persons and facilitated al-Qaida financing for the Jakarta Marriott Hotel bombing the following year.

was hampered by poor interagency coordination and by human and technical capacity deficits in both government and financial institutions. The USAID is promoting capacity building through its Financial Crimes Prevention Project, a multi-year program to provide technical advisors and support to Indonesia's effort to develop an effective and credible regime against money laundering and terrorism finance.

Indonesian counterterrorism efforts remained hindered by weak laws and enforcement, serious internal coordination problems, and systemic corruption that further limited already strained government resources. Lawmakers and other senior elected officials continued their slow pace toward needed legal reforms. A widely discussed plan to establish an official counterterrorism coordinating agency appeared to have been shelved after awaiting final presidential approval. Prospective members of the independent police commission designed to help guide police reform were identified this year, but they still need a formal presidential appointment before assuming their responsibilities. The government has not yet submitted a revision of the 2003 Counterterrorism Law to the House of Representatives. Indonesian authorities recognized that more effective prosecution of terrorism cases would require a revision of the law to include updated standards for introducing evidence in terror cases and comprehensive articles on conspiracy.

Japan

Domestically, Japan continued to bolster its defenses against terrorism. In March, the Cabinet approved emergency contingency plans for 47 prefectures to better protect the public from terrorist attacks. In May, Japan revised the Immigration Control and Refugee Recognition Act to enable immigration officials to collect and electronically store fingerprint and facial imagery from foreigners. The Ministry of Justice Immigration Bureau continued testing began in 2004 on a biometric fingerprint and facial recognition system at Narita and Kansai airports with the aim of identifying people trying to enter Japan on fake passports. In June, the government developed legislation designed to combat money laundering and terrorist financing and plans to submit the bill to the Diet. In a bid to clamp down on money laundering, the Ministry of Finance announced in August that Japanese financial institutions would be required to confirm the identity of customers sending 100,000 yen or more overseas. The Financial Services Agency announced a similar change for domestic remittances. On December 1, the Diet passed the Infectious Disease Law to prohibit possession and production of 12 pathogens, including Anthrax and the Ebola Virus to help prevent bioterrorism.

Japan used Official Development Assistance (ODA) grants to expand counterterrorism capacity in Southeast Asia. The Ministry of Foreign Affairs (MOFA) Economic Cooperation Bureau initiated the grant for

Cooperation on Counterterrorism and Security Enhancement. This nearly US$ 60.86 million annual program included projects aimed at bolstering piracy prevention, increasing maritime and port security, and preventing weapons proliferation.

Japan made valuable contributions to building counterterrorism capacity among Asian countries. In January, Japan hosted a two-day ministerial conference on international transport security to promote cooperation on ground transportation security; representatives from 14 countries attended. In June, Foreign Minister Aso signed a counterterrorism capacity building plan with Uzbekistan, Tajikistan, Kyrgyzstan, and Kazakhstan offering equipment and support for border control. In June, Japan hosted the ASEAN-Japan Counterterrorism Dialogue.

In July, the Japanese government held a seminar on the prevention and crisis management of bioterrorism to strengthen mechanisms to combat CBRN (chemical, biological, radiological, nuclear) terrorism in the Asia Pacific. In attendance were officials from 14 countries and representatives from the World Health Organization, the Institute of Defense and Strategic Studies, and the Southeast Asia Regional Centre for Counterterrorism (SEARCCT). Japan was an active partner in the Proliferation Security Initiative, participating in exercises, attending all meetings for intelligence experts and operational experts, and leading regional outreach efforts. In October, Japan became an initial partner nation in the U.S. Global Initiative to Combat Nuclear Terrorism, and attended its first Global Initiative meeting in Rabat, Morocco. Also in October, Japan hosted a counterterrorism trilateral meeting with the United States and Australia; the following month, these three countries participated in a trilateral strategic dialogue to better synchronize regional activities. Participants from 19 countries discussed measures to tighten nuclear and radiological security at the November International Atomic Energy Agence (IAEA)-Government of Japan Seminar on Strengthening Nuclear Security in Asia.

Japan continued to reach beyond the region in its fight against terrorism. In December, the Abe Cabinet approved the extension of Japan Air Self-Defense Force (JSDF) airlift operations until July 2007, enabling Japan to continue its support for Iraq. In October, the Diet extended for one year the Antiterrorism Special Measures Law that allows for JSDF support of Operation Enduring Freedom (OEF). The Japan Maritime Self-Defense Force (JMSDF) provided approximately 124 million gallons of fuel to U.S. and allied naval vessels engaged in OEF.

Bilaterally, Japan was a responsive partner in the fight against terrorism. In February, Japanese air marshals trained at the United States Federal Air Marshal Training Facility. Japan remained an advocate and active participant in the International Port Security Program (IPSP). Widely considered a regional leader in maritime security collaboration, the Government of Japan hosted a number of bilateral and multilateral maritime security events. Japan continued its participation in the Port State Control Officer exchange program with the U.S. Coast Guard, which worked to exchange best practices in implementing international ship security requirements.

The National Police Agency (NPA) and the Public Security Intelligence Agency (PSIA) continued to monitor the activities of Aum Shinrikyo, renamed Aleph. In January, the Public Security Examination Commission extended PSIA's legal authority to monitor Aleph for an additional three years. The Tokyo District Court, in August, upheld the death sentence for Aum Shinrikyo member Masami Tsuchiya, who was charged with making the sarin nerve gas used in the deadly 1995 attack on the Tokyo subway system. In September, the Supreme Court upheld the death sentence for Aum Shinrikyo founder Chizuo Matsumoto; he is not eligible to file future appeals. In February, the Tokyo High Court upheld the death sentence for Tomomitsu Niimi, convicted in 2002 for murdering 26 individuals in seven Aum Shinrikyo-related cases, including the 1995 sarin attack.

The Tokyo District Court sentenced Fusako Shigenobu, a former Japanese Red Army (JRA) member, to 20 years in prison in February. Members of the JRA were responsible for seizing the French Embassy in The Hague in 1974 and the U.S. Embassy in Kuala Lumpur in 1975. Prosecutors argued for a life sentence for Shigenobu, claiming she was the alleged mastermind of the "Hague Incident," but the court ruled that even though she conspired to take over the French Embassy, she was not physically present during the Embassy seizure. As of mid-December, former JRA member Jun Nishikawa remained on trial for his suspected role in a 1977 Japan Airlines hijacking.

Korea, North

See Chapter 3, *State Sponsors of Terrorism.*

Korea, South

The Republic of Korea (ROK) demonstrated excellent law enforcement and intelligence capabilities, and provided terrorism-related training to law enforcement officials from various developing countries. Traditionally focused on potential terrorism from the Democratic People's Republic of Korea (DPRK, or North Korea), the Korean government broadened its attention to possible acts of terror from beyond the Korean Peninsula. Reflecting this shift, the Ministry of Foreign Affairs and Trade (MOFAT), appointed the first Director for International Counterterrorism Cooperation in February. Seoul supported U.S. goals in Afghanistan and maintained the third-largest foreign troop contingent in Iraq, where it has committed $260 million in assistance since 2004. The Korean government remained a valued international partner in the fight against terror financing and money laundering.

In December, the Republic of Korea agreed to participate in the Secure Freight Initiative, which will provide screening for radiation of all cargo bound for the United States. On aviation security, the government participated in the International Civil Aviation Organization (ICAO)'s Universal Safety Oversight Audit Program and contributed over 500,000 US$ to ICAO activities. In November, the Republic of Korea joined other APEC member nations in endorsing U.S. security initiatives on aviation security, bioterrorism and food defense, and the protection of commercial and financial sectors from abuse by proliferators of weapons of mass destruction. It also took a number of bilateral antiterrorism measures in the region. In November, the governments of Korea and the Philippines launched a joint study on the development of a national computer emergency response team to combat cyber crime. In December, Korea and Indonesia agreed to continue cooperation against transnational crime, including terrorism and security in the Malaka and Singapore Straits. The Korean government also held bilateral counterterrorism consultations with Australia, Singapore, India, Vietnam, Russia, and China.

Korean immigration and law enforcement agencies have an excellent record of tracking suspicious individuals entering their territory and reacting quickly to thwart potential terrorist acts. The government conducted a Man Portable Air Defense System (MANPADS) vulnerability assessment of Incheon International Airport in September, and began examining various countermeasures, including a three-level alert system, increased local patrols, and enhanced public education.

Seoul continued its active participation in regional training and capacity building programs. The Korean government hosted representatives from the Middle East, Latin America, and elsewhere in Asia for training in crime prevention, criminal justice, counterterrorism, forensic science, anti-piracy and terrorism management, prevention of money laundering, and narcotics law enforcement.

Laos

Although the Government of Laos had positive intentions regarding counterterrorism, weak enforcement procedures, inefficient security organizations, and a fundamental misunderstanding of how its law applies to the UNSC counterterrorism conventions, all served to hamper the implementation of multilateral agreements. Border security was negligible. Since 2002, Laos consistently denounced international terrorism and expressed a willingness to cooperate with the international community on counterterrorism. Its actions, however, have mostly been disappointing, due to both a lack of resources and an attitude among Lao officials that Laos could not become a target of international terrorism. In spite of the presence of a domestic insurgency that has employed terrorist tactics, such as ambushing civilian buses and bombing civilian targets, Lao officials at many levels saw terrorism as an issue of only marginal relevance to Laos; they believed that Laos, as a small and neutral country, would not be targeted by international terrorists.

The Bank of Laos vetted government and commercial bank holdings for possible terrorist assets, as identified by U.S.-provided lists of terrorist organizations and individuals, and has issued freeze orders for assets of organizations and individuals named on these lists. However, the Bank has yet to require the freezing of assets of individuals and entities included on the UN 1267 Sanctions Committee consolidated list.

In accordance with its obligations under UNSCR 1373, the Bank of Lao issued freeze orders for assets of organizations and individuals named in lists provided by the United States. Lao authorities issued orders limiting the amount of cash that could be withdrawn from local banks or carried into or out of the country and strengthened reporting requirements of state and privately owned commercial banks. Banking regulation remained extremely weak, however, and the banking system was vulnerable to money laundering and other illegal transactions.

Laos does not have a separate counterterrorism law, but the Lao judicial system was prepared to prosecute acts of terrorism as serious crimes under the Lao criminal code, and recent amendments to the criminal code sought to strengthen counterterrorism sanctions. Still, a November UN-sponsored workshop on counterterrorism illustrated a myriad of shortcomings and vagaries in the theoretical application of the Lao criminal code to deal with terrorism-related crimes, and successful prosecution under these laws is speculative.

Laos' border security was weak; border officials could not effectively control access to the country even at its most sophisticated border checkpoints. Border crossing along the Mekong River into the surrounding countries of Burma, Thailand, and Cambodia could be accomplished easily and without detection. In more remote sections of the country, along borders with Vietnam and China, it is likely that unmonitored border crossings by locals occurred on a daily basis. Since 9/11, Lao authorities have strengthened airport security, but security procedures at both airport and land immigration points remained lax compared with most other countries in the region. In addition, official Lao identity documents, including passports and ID cards, were easy to purchase from corrupt officials. Laos has a small insurgency numbering perhaps 1,000 to 2,000 persons, including women and children, based in very remote areas of north/central Laos.

Malaysia

The Government of Malaysia took significant steps to improve its legal framework to deal with terrorists and their enablers. New provisions were added to Malaysia's Penal Code and Criminal Procedures Code that include clearer definitions of terrorism and related crimes and penalties including the death penalty or life in prison for terrorist-related crimes. In the Spring, police arrested 12 members of Darul Islam in Sabah, including citizens of Malaysia, Indonesia and the Philippines. The group was believed to have supported JI terrorists operating in Indonesia and the Philippines, and they were reportedly caught with illegal firearms and bomb making directions at the time of their arrest. Media reports also indicated that police made multiple interdictions of explosives and bomb making material transiting Malaysia via Eastern Sabah.

The police in Malaysia took the lead in counterterrorist investigations and operations. Malaysian police forces fall under the authority of the Ministry of Internal Security which is headed by Prime Minister Abdullah Badawi. To date, suspected terrorists have not been brought to trial but are held in detention under the country's Internal Security Act (ISA) where they undergo a program of rehabilitation. While in theory, ISA detentions can last indefinitely, sentences are for two years and must be renewed by a determination that the detainee remains a threat to national security. In October, the government unexpectedly released 17 individuals from ISA detention stating that they had been rehabilitated. Because they had been released before completing their sentences, these individuals were placed in probationary status and must periodically report to the authorities. Five of the released detainees had been members of the Kumpulan Mujahedin Malaysia (KMM), while the other eleven were believed to have had ties to Jemaah Islamiya (JI).

Counterterrorism finance-related amendments to the Anti-Money Laundering Act, the Subordinate Courts Act and the Courts of Judicature Act came into effect on January 1, 2007. Malaysia and the United States also signed a Mutual Legal Assistance Treaty.

The Malaysian government engaged with its neighbors on issues related to counterterrorism and transnational crime. It continued to operate and hoped to expand the Southeast Asian Regional Center for Counterterrorism (SEARCCT), an international center for training. Malaysian mediators continued to work in the southern Philippines to help end the dispute between the Philippine government and the separatist Moro Islamic Liberation Front (MILF). With the "Eyes in Sky" program, Malaysian military forces were working with Singapore and Indonesia to provide enhanced security to the Straits of Malacca, the world's busiest shipping lane. In December, the Malaysian Defense Minister/ Deputy Prime Minister and his Indonesian counterpart announced an initiative to enhance bilateral police cooperation along the land border on Borneo.

Mongolia

There were no known terrorist groups operating in Mongolia and no known bases of support. However, Mongolian government officials cited more than 6,000 kilometers of porous borders, easy entry for foreign travelers, and poverty as conditions that terrorists could exploit and moved to increase awareness of terrorism and to consider new laws. On July 8, a law to combat money laundering and terrorist financing offenses was approved by the Mongolian Parliament. The Mongolian police, Ministry of Justice, and the General Intelligence Agency's counterterrorism branch all cooperated with the U.S. to willingly provide requested support. As a result of resource and technical limitations, however, law enforcement capacities, including those related to counterterrorism, remained modest. Mongolia deployed a seventh rotation of 100 Mongolian soldiers to Iraq in October in support of Operation Iraqi Freedom, as well as a sixth rotation of 21 Mongolian soldiers to Afghanistan to train the Afghan National Army.

New Zealand

In June, the New Zealand Parliament passed the Terrorism Suppression Amendment Act 2005, which expanded criminalization of terrorist financing to include the intentional financing of non-designated organizations that engage in terrorism. New Zealand designated 68 terrorist organizations in 2006, bringing its total number of designated terrorist organizations to 488. Under the Financial Transactions Reporting Act of 1996, banks are required to report suspicious activities to the Financial Intelligence Unit (FIU) housed in the National Police Department. The FIU had received about 4,200 Suspicious Transaction Reports and referred 616 of these to various law enforcement agencies and units for investigation. The FIU received approximately 53 Suspicious Property Reports; none were found to have connections to terrorist entities or associated individuals.

New Zealand remained active in Operation Enduring Freedom in Afghanistan, where it has commanded the Provincial Reconstruction Team (PRT) in Bamiyan Province since September 2003. New Zealand also participated actively in the Proliferation Security Initiative (PSI) and took part in a U.S.-sponsored PSI tabletop exercise in October. On March 27, New Zealand and the U.S. signed a Memorandum of Understanding (MOU) through which New Zealand joined the United States and Australia in the Regional Movement Alert List (RMAL) passport alert system, an APEC forum initiative. In the Fall, an officer from the New Zealand police was seconded to the Joint Inter-Agency Task Force (JIATF-West) in the Pacific Command Center in Hawaii. New Zealand offered assistance to Pacific Islands Forum member countries to help them submit reports pursuant to UN Security Council Resolutions 1267, 1373, and 1540. Nine Pacific Island countries responded positively to this offer.

Philippines

The Philippines, one of the earliest supporters of the War on Terror, continued its bilateral and multilateral counterterrorism efforts. In August, the Armed Forces of the Philippines (AFP) launched "Operation Ultimatum", a concerted effort to capture or kill the top Jemaah Islamiya (JI) and Abu Sayyaf Group (ASG) operatives on Jolo Island in the South. The operation has been highly successful to date as a number of ASG and JI members have been captured or killed since its inception. Philippine forces recently eliminated both Khadaffy Janjalani, the nominal leader of the Abu Sayyaf Group, and ASG spokesperson, Abu Solaiman. Operation Ultimatum is one feature of a U.S.- assisted strategy to strengthen the rule of law in the Sulu archipelago. Joint U.S.-Philippines military exercises know as "Balikatan" supported the Philippine government's campaign to separate terrorists from the general population and diminish support for their cause. The Antiterrorism Task Force arrested, captured, or killed 88 suspected terrorists, and seized over 900 kilograms of explosive materials. Philippine authorities also made some progress in tracking, blocking, and seizing terrorists' assets.

Despite some successes, major evidentiary and procedural obstacles in the Philippines continued to hinder the building of effective terrorism cases. A large and growing case backlog and the absence of consistent trials against terrorists were impediments to the prosecution of suspected terrorists. Despite plans dating back to 2001, the Philippine Department of Foreign Affairs (DFA) had yet to introduce a digitized, machine-readable passport. While the Philippines cooperated with U.S. requests for prosecutions for persons who had tampered or altered travel documents, the prosecutions carried low-level penalties for those convicted of such fraud. In addition, there was a reluctance to investigate or charge vendors or users of false documents. Under current Philippine law, the suspect must present the fraudulent document to a Philippine government authority in order for a crime to have been committed. At year's end, a counterterrorism bill approved in April by the House of Representatives remained in the Senate.

The Philippines experienced 93 bombings, ranging from improvised explosive devices and grenades to landmines, including:

- In February, the bombing of a karaoke bar located near a Philippine military base in Jolo left one dead and 22 injured.
- In March, a bomb exploded at the Sulu Consumers Cooperative in Jolo killing nine people and injuring 20.
- In June, a roadside bombing in Shariff Aguak killed three people and injured eight.
- In August, two bombs exploded almost simultaneously in Kidapawan City injuring three people.

- In September, a bomb exploded at a public market in General Santos City killing two people and injuring six.
- In October, a bomb exploded near the headquarters of the Sulu Philippine National Police in Jolo injuring two persons.
- In a separate October attack, three bombs exploded in Tacurong, Sultan Kudurat; Makilala, North Cotabato; and Cotabato City killing eight people and injuring over 30.

The Anti-Money Laundering Council (AMLC) was empowered by the Philippines Anti-Money Laundering Act of 2001 (AMLA), as amended in 2003, to investigate and prosecute money laundering. The AMLC is the lead agency responsible for implementing the asset freeze measures called for by the UN Security Council 1267 Sanctions Committee. Under current law, however, the AMLC cannot take direct action against suspected terrorists or those supporting terrorism, but must apply for a court order to inquire into bank accounts and direct the freezing of assets and transactions. The AMLC sometimes needed several months to issue the relevant resolution to the Court of Appeals after receiving information about a newly-listed terrorist entity and circulating it to the financial institutions. The AMLC has 91 cases pending in various stages with the courts, including 34 for money laundering, 24 for civil forfeiture, and the rest pertaining to freeze orders and bank inquiries. The slow judicial process hindered efforts by the AMLC to see these cases through to conclusion; a trial can take up to seven years to complete.

In April, a bilateral U.S.-Philippines Security Engagement Board (SEB) was inaugurated to address non-traditional security issues, including counterterrorism and maritime security. The SEB set the stage for the "Kapid Bisig" (Shoulder-to-Shoulder) counterterrorism framework that focused on civil affairs, capability upgrades, and support for AFP operations. The United States assisted the Philippines in establishing an interagency intelligence fusion center in Zamboanga City to support both maritime interdictions against transnational criminal/terrorist organizations, and the "coast watch" system in Mindanao, established with Australian assistance.

Singapore

Singapore continued its bilateral and multilateral intelligence and law enforcement cooperation to investigate terrorist groups, focusing on Jemaah Islamiya (JI). In February, Indonesia extradited Mas Selamat bin Kastari to Singapore. Mas Selamat, reportedly the Singaporean leader of a local JI network, fled Singapore in 2001 following the arrest of other JI members by the Internal Security Department (ISD).

Singapore detained five members of the regional terrorist group JI, including Mas Selamat, under the Internal Security Act (ISA). As of November,

34 people with links to terrorist groups were in detention. Detainees included members of JI who had plotted to carry out attacks in Singapore in the past and members of the Moro Islamic Liberation Front (MILF). Under detention orders, the detainees were required to undergo a program of religious counseling with a group of volunteer religious counselors. Singapore enlisted the support of religious teachers and scholars to study JI's ideology, develop teachings to counter the group's spread within Singapore's Muslim community, and provide counseling to detainees.

In April, the Government of Singapore and the U.S. Department of Energy commenced joint operation of a Second Line of Defense (SLD) Megaports pilot project at Singapore's Pasir Panjang Terminal. Radiation detectors monitored export containers and a limited number of inter-terminal transshipped cargo containers. In July, Singapore announced a voluntary plan to enhance supply chain security. The plan included security guidelines and goals for companies to adhere to, in order to improve the security of their operations.

Since August, all new Singaporean passports were biometrically enabled. Singapore shared lost and stolen passport information with the U.S. and was working with its Association of Southeast Asian Nations (ASEAN) partners to develop similar data-sharing. Singaporean officials took strong measures to enhance maritime security in nearby waters, especially the Strait of Malacca, including countering terrorist threats, piracy, and other criminal attacks. In April, Singapore, Malaysia, and Indonesia signed the Malacca Strait Patrols (MSP) agreement linking naval and air patrols over the Strait of Malacca by the three littoral states. In November, Singapore hosted the inaugural meeting of the 14-member governing council of the Regional Cooperation Agreement on Combating Piracy and Armed Robbery Against Ships in Asia (ReCAAP). Singapore provided significant funding for the organization's Information Sharing Centre, based in Singapore. Singapore actively participated in counterterrorism efforts through various international fora, including the ASEAN Regional Forum, and continued to take part in the Proliferation Security Initiative (PSI), including the October Leading Edge PSI interdiction training exercise.

Taiwan

Taiwan is not a member of the United Nations and, therefore, is not subject to UNSC Resolutions and cannot join UN conventions and protocols related to terrorist financing. Nonetheless, Taiwan sought to implement, to the maximum extent possible, all UN resolutions relating to combating terrorism and terrorist finance issues. Taiwan continued to provide rapid and thorough responses on terrorism financing issues to the American Institute in Taiwan (AIT). Taiwan's Executive Yuan submitted an "Anti-terrorist Action Law" to the Legislative Yuan. This bill would empower the Financial

Supervisory Commission to seize assets of entities involved in terrorist activities, and employ a package of trade, travel, and financial sanctions against North Korea in response to UNSCR 1718. These items are under review.

The cabinet-level Counterterrorism Office conducted several large-scale training exercises. While its primary mission was counterterrorism, its focus broadened to include crisis management, disaster preparedness, and island-wide civilian military mobilization.

In September, the Container Security Initiative began operations at Taiwan's port of Kaohsiung and subsequently was expanded to Keelong harbor. Inspections in Kaohsiung have already yielded seizures of counterfeit currency and illegal drugs. In May, AIT and the Taipei Economic and Cultural Representative Office signed a Memorandum of Agreement to implement the U.S. Department of Energy's Megaports program in Kaohsiung to help prevent trafficking in radioactive materials. Taiwan's Ministry of Economic Affairs announced a more comprehensive requirement for official approval of commodities exported from or transshipped through Taiwan ports to Iran and North Korea. The Ministry of Foreign Affairs tightened regulations for issuing visas to nationals of North Korea and Iran.

Thailand

On December 31, a series of eight bomb attacks took place at six separate locations in Bangkok. The bombs killed three Thai citizens and injured dozens, including six foreign tourists. The locations targeted in the attacks were not specifically identified with foreign interests or tourists. The perpetrators of the attacks were not identified. Thailand's biggest domestic security challenge remained the ongoing separatist movement in the far southern provinces of Narathiwat, Yala, Pattani, and Songkhla. This region, bordering Malaysia, has experienced episodic, separatist-related violence for decades among the predominantly ethnic Malay-Muslim population. Since January 2004, violence increased dramatically and continued on a near daily basis. Suspected separatist militants carried out shootings, beheadings, and several coordinated bombings using improvised explosive devices, including an August 31 attack on 22 bank branch offices in Yala province.

In an effort to address local grievances, the interim government[2] made a series of conciliatory gestures towards southern ethnic-Malay Muslims, including a pledge to seek talks with separatist leaders. Additionally, on

[2] On September 19, a bloodless coup d'etat removed the elected civilian government of Prime Minister Thaksin Shinawatra from power, triggering congressionally mandated Section 508 sanctions that limited selected military training and exchange programs. Most counterterrorism programs were not subject to the sanctions, however.

November 1, the government reconstituted the Southern Border Provinces Administrative Center (SBPAC) and the Civilian, Military, and Police Command, two entities credited with effectively coordinating Thai government efforts in the region prior to their disbandment in 2002. The militants have not responded positively to these conciliatory gestures, and the violence continued.

The Government of Thailand maintained that the situation was a domestic issue. Elements of the government expressed concern, however, that militants involved in the violence may have received funding or training from outside Thailand. In November, interim Prime Minister Surayud said that militants were financing their activities in part through restaurants owned by Thai nationals living in Malaysia. Malaysian officials vehemently denied this allegation. Relations between Thailand and Malaysia remained strained as violence continued in Thai territory near their common border, but improved following visits to Kuala Lumpur by Surayud and other senior officials. The ongoing unrest received international attention and the concern of international Islamic organizations, including the Organization of the Islamic Conference, which expressed support for the reconciliation efforts made by the interim government.

Police forensics and ballistics work often failed to produce evidence that led to arrests following separatist attacks, and government prosecutors struggled to develop cases that could stand up in court. On November 18, three southern Thai Islamic teachers were convicted of criminal conspiracy charges related to their membership in the outlawed separatist group Pattani United Liberation Organization (PULO) and were sentenced to ten years in prison. This was one of the few successful prosecutions of southern militants by the government since the dramatic escalation in violence that began in 2004. In August, the Thai Attorney General held the first ever conference of Thai police and prosecutors working in the South, in part to improve cooperation between police and prosecutors. The newly reinstated SBPAC will also, for the first time, incorporate a special Ministry of Justice component offering legal aid to local citizens as well as serving to enhance police and prosecutor work in the South.

Thai security forces cooperated with the U.S. and other countries to deny safe haven for terrorists within their territory. In the past, Thailand has served as a transit point for regional terrorists, as evidenced by the 2003 capture in Central Thailand of Nurjaman Riduan bin Isomuddin (a.k.a. Hambali), JI's operations chief and the architect behind the 2002 Bali bombing. Thai and U.S. officials were concerned that transnational terror groups could establish links with southern Thailand-based separatist groups. However, there were no indications that transnational terrorist groups were directly involved in the violence, and there was no evidence of direct operational links between southern Thai separatist groups and regional terror networks.

There were several militant domestic separatist groups implicated in the ongoing violence besides PULO, including the Pattani Islamic Mujahideen Movement (GMIP) and the Barisan Revolusi Nasional Coordinate (BRN-C). Some Thai officials have publicly labeled the operational arm of the BRN-C as the Ruanda Kumpulan Kecil (RKK), which they blame for a significant number of attacks in the South. Some of these separatist groups may share elements of ideology and general rejection of Western influence held by international Islamic terrorists, but by all indications they remained primarily focused on seeking autonomy for the far southern provinces and historical grievances against the Thai state.

There was no evidence that foreign governments provided financial, military, or diplomatic support for militant separatist operations in the South of Thailand. However, Thai separatist groups such as PULO reportedly operated openly in Syria and a number of self-declared separatist leaders received asylum in Europe or were believed to be hiding in Malaysia. Officials in the Thai government expressed concern that money from Middle Eastern charities that supported religious or educational objectives could be diverted to support separatist activities, but there was no evidence of a direct link. Thai officials expressed concern that Thai students studying in madrassas in Pakistan and the Middle East might be exposed to extremist indoctrination. In November, Royal Thai Army Commander General Sonthi Boonyaratglin met with Thai students in Karachi, in part to address these concerns.

Since 2004, the militants appear to have limited their attacks to the geographic far South and have not specifically targeted U.S. persons or interests. On September 16, a U.S. citizen tourist was killed in Songkhla province by one of five coordinated bombs and on November 19, the local Ford and Chevrolet showrooms were among six car dealerships in Yala City targeted by bombers. No group claimed responsibility for these attacks.

Thai police and security officials participated in U.S. government training programs. The U.S. and Thai militaries conducted a number of joint exercises and training programs that supported counterterrorism. Bangkok's International Law Enforcement Academy (ILEA) began a series of training modules for Thai security officials and police that included post-blast and crime scene investigation courses. Under the auspices of the Container Security Initiative and the Megaport Initiative, Thailand engaged in a range of port security programs.

The Thai Anti-Money Laundering Office (AMLO) acted as the center for interdicting terrorist finance. UN 1267 resolutions were quickly implemented by Thai banks under instructions from AMLO. Thailand has engaged with the G-8 Counterterrorism Action Group on increasing penalties for document fraud, which is an ongoing problem in Thailand.

The Government of Thailand participated actively in international counterterrorism efforts through ASEAN and other fora, but areas of concern remained. Thailand was party to only six of the 13 international conventions and protocols relating to terrorism. Thailand has not endorsed the Proliferation Security Initiative (PSI), which negatively affects regional counter-proliferation cooperation given Thailand's regional leadership role and strategic location.

Country Reports: Europe and Eurasia Overview

"We must always keep in mind that terrorism, as an age-old method of coercion, has no deeper links to any culture or religion. Hence, we should be cautious not to associate any faith with terrorism."

Mr. Abdullah Gul, Deputy Prime Minister and Minister of Foreign Affairs, Republic of Turkey
Remarks, UN General Assembly, 61st Session
New York City, September 22, 2006

While no major terrorist attacks took place in Europe in 2006, foiled plots and concerns over increasing radicalization among immigrant youth served as stimulus for increased cooperation and efforts to strengthen counterterrorism capabilities. Italy and Germany worked closely with neighboring countries and held a successful and incident-free Winter Olympics and World Cup, respectively. European nations continued to work in close partnership with the United States on the global counterterrorism campaign and continued to enhance both their individual and collective abilities to deal with a terrorist threat characterized by both external and, increasingly, internal components. The contributions of European countries in sharing intelligence, arresting members of terrorist cells, and interdicting terrorist financing and logistics were vital elements in the War on Terror.

At the June 2004 U.S.—EU Summit, the sides agreed on a Declaration on Combating Terrorism that renewed the transatlantic commitment to develop measures to maximize capacities to detect, investigate and prosecute terrorists, prevent terrorist attacks, prevent access by terrorists to financial and other economic resources, enhance information sharing and cooperation among law enforcement agencies, and improve the effectiveness of border information systems. These commitments were reconfirmed at the 2006 Summit and work continued on implementation. In 2006, the ratification/implementation of the Extradition and Mutual Legal Assistance Treaties between the U.S. and EU Member States was ongoing. (In the United States, the treaties were submitted to the Senate Foreign Relations Committee.) In October, the U.S. and EU reached an interim agreement on the transferring of passenger name record data, which was necessitated by the nullification of the earlier agreement by a European court. On November 6, the U.S. and the EU signed an agreement to facilitate U.S. participation in Eurojust, the EU's prosecutorial liaison organization. Also in November, the U.S. and EU launched a formal dialogue to develop common data protection standards to facilitate efforts to share terrorist information.

European nations are active participants in a variety of multilateral organizations that contribute to counterterrorist efforts, including the G8, NATO, the Financial Action Task Force (FATF), the Organization for Security and Cooperation in Europe (OSCE), the International Maritime Organization (IMO), and the International Civil Aviation Organization (ICAO). The United States and its partners work through these organizations to establish and implement best practices, build the counterterrorism capabilities of "weak but willing" states, and help fight the War on Terror globally. OSCE members committed themselves to becoming parties to the 13 UN terrorism conventions and protocols, to work together to modernize travel documents and shipping container security, to prevent and suppress the financing of terrorist organizations, and to implement UNSC Resolution 1540 to counter WMD (related materials and the means of delivery) proliferation. *(See Chapter 5 for further information on the G8, NATO, FATF, and OSCE.)*

Terrorist activity and the presence of terrorist support networks in Europe remained a source of concern. Efforts to combat the threat in Europe were sometimes slowed by legal protections that made it difficult to take firm judicial action against suspected terrorists, asylum laws that afforded loopholes, inadequate legislation, or standards of evidence that limited the use of classified information in holding terrorist suspects. Terrorists are also able to take advantage of the ease of travel among Schengen countries.[1] Some European states have at times not been able to prosecute successfully or hold some of the suspected terrorists brought before their courts. The EU as a whole remained reluctant to take steps to block the assets of charities associated with HAMAS and Hizballah.

European governments were increasingly concerned about radicalization among their indigenous populations and sought greater understanding of the process of "radicalization" and how to prevent it. Several governments increased outreach to Muslim communities living within their countries and made attempts to gain support from within those communities to counter the appeal of extremist ideology.

---

[1] In June 1985, seven European Union countries signed a treaty in Schengen, Luxembourg, to end internal border checkpoints and controls. At present, there are 15 Schengen countries, all in Europe. The Schengen countries are: Austria, Belgium, Denmark, Finland, France, Germany, Iceland, Italy, Greece Luxembourg, Netherlands, Norway, Portugal, Spain, and Sweden.

The announcement by al-Qaida in the Islamic Maghreb (AQIM), formerly the Salafist Group for Preaching and Combat (GSPC), that it was merging with al-Qaida sparked concerns throughout Europe, in particular in France, after the AQIM/GSPC made more threats against what it termed "crusading" westerners, particularly American and French citizens.

In March, the Basque Fatherland and Liberty (ETA) terrorist group declared a "permanent cease-fire," leading to hopes that its long campaign would at last come to an end. On December 30, however, following street violence by ETA supporters and the organization's theft of 350 handguns from an armory in France, ETA set off a huge car bomb at the Madrid International Airport that killed two Ecuadorian immigrants.

In July, terrorists planted suitcase bombs that failed to detonate on two German trains.

In August, in cooperation with the U.S. and Pakistan, British authorities disrupted a terrorist plot to blow up aircraft traveling between the United Kingdom and the United States. Some 15 persons suspected of being involved in the U.K.-based plot were arrested.

Political progress in Northern Ireland continued, resulting in a marked decrease in terrorist incidents. The Independent Monitoring Commission (IMC), which monitors progress by paramilitary groups in ending violent activities, reported in October that evidence showed the leadership of the Provisional Irish Republican Army (IRA) was committed to following a peaceful path.

Cooperation among European law enforcement agencies was important to counterterrorism successes. France and Spain continued to cooperate effectively against ETA. Belgian courts convicted individuals connected to the 2003 Madrid bombings and several countries, including France, Spain and Italy, broke up terrorist networks facilitating travel by foreign fighters to Iraq.

U.S.- European bioterrorism cooperation expanded. The topic was addressed at high-level U.S.- EU counterterrorism talks and at the U.S.- Russia Counterterrorism Working Group. Switzerland and the U.S. co-sponsored the successful "Black Ice" bioterrorism coordination exercise in Montreux, hosting senior officials from numerous multilateral organizations. During its 2006 G8 presidency, Russia worked closely with the U.S. to launch the Global Initiative to Combat Nuclear Terrorism.

Several significant terrorist leaders were killed in Russia. In July, Russia's most wanted terrorist, Chechen separatist Shamil Basayev, was killed. In November, Russian security forces killed Abu Hafs al-Urdani, the al-Qaida-linked, Jordanian-born commander of foreign fighters in Chechnya. Central and Eastern European states made strides in countering terrorism in 2006. Many states across the Balkans, Baltics, and Caucasus sent troops to Iraq, Afghanistan, and Kosovo.

Albania

Albania contributed troops to both Afghanistan and Iraq, froze bank accounts related to money laundering and terrorism financing, and worked with the U.S. and other countries to combat terrorism. Albania made progress in identifying vulnerabilities at land and sea borders, but the government and police forces faced substantial challenges to fully enforce border security and combat organized crime and corruption.

In May, Albania granted political asylum to five Guantanamo Bay detainees, after the U.S. determined they were no longer considered enemy combatants. In November, Albania admitted an additional three former detainees who were designated for release. Albania has publicly committed to maintaining its presence in Iraq as long as required, and has a contingent of around 120 soldiers operating in the country. In Afghanistan, Albania deployed 26 troops to ISAF, including four members of a joint medical unit.

Although no new groups' assets were frozen this year under the Terrorism Financing Freeze (TFF) law enacted in 2004, the Albanian government found an additional seven holdings by already identified groups that were subsequently frozen. While the Albanian State Intelligence Service (SHISH) is the foremost counterterrorism unit within the Albanian government, much of their success went unnoticed due to the clandestine nature of their work. We note that the effectiveness of the government's counterterrorist financing efforts was hampered by inadequate financial resources, poor communications, a lack of data processing infrastructure, and the lack of experienced personnel due to frequent turnover.

Andorra

The Government of Andorra worked to build law enforcement capacity, enhance border security, and combat money laundering and terrorist financing. In September, the Minister's Council approved the ratification of the Council of Europe's Convention on Terrorism prevention signed by the Andorrans in Warsaw on May 16, 2005, and the Convention is pending approval by the Andorran Parliament. The Andorran government contributed to UNESCO's solidarity and international cooperation programs by sending financial support to Afghanistan, and provided financial support to OSCE to implement a rocket buster destruction project in Tajikistan.

Armenia

With substantial U.S. assistance, Armenia continued to strengthen its capacity to counter the country's few perceived terrorist threats. Armenia's geographic location, porous borders, and loose visa regime presents opportunities for traffickers of illicit materials, persons, and finances.

Armenia's reliance on ties with neighboring Iran have dampened Armenian criticism of Iranian extremism and led to closer trade relations between the two countries. Diplomatic and trade relations with Iran are seen as a geographic and strategic necessity for the landlocked country, in light of closed borders with Turkey and Azerbaijan, and the perceived risk of instability in Georgia. President Kocharian spoke out in November against the possibility of international sanctions against Iran.

The Financial Monitoring Center (FMC), a U.S.—supported financial intelligence unit within the Central Bank, is still developing as a regulatory body. Established in 2005, the FMC began to make investigative strides this year. The FMC received 23 suspicious transaction reports in 2006. After analyzing the reports, the FMC developed five suspicious transaction cases; three of the cases were subsequently referred to the Prosecutor General's office for further investigation. To date, the FMC has received no reports of transactions involving watch-list designees. The heavy flow of remittances, however, may hinder efforts to detect fund transfers in support of terrorism. The FMC has applied for Egmont Group membership.

Armenia introduced additional security features into the production of passports, continued to install passport readers at border posts, and continued efforts to increase the security of its vital documents, such as birth certificates. On November 1, the government implemented mandatory fingerprinting for travelers departing Zvartnots Airport, Armenia's only international airport. The National Security Service (NSS) and police shared information with the U.S. Embassy when they discovered fraudulent U.S. visas or other such documents.

In May, the UN Analytical Support and Sanctions Monitoring Team for al-Qaida and the Taliban visited Armenia to monitor the implementation of sanctions under UNSCR 1267 and successor resolutions. The team met with the Central Bank, the Ministry of Defense, the National Security Service and the Police, as well as the Ministry of Foreign Affairs. According to the MFA, the team said it was satisfied with Armenia's level of preparedness. Armenia supported U.S. efforts in Iraq with troops on the ground and provided overflight authorization in support of Operation Enduring Freedom.

In September, Armenia participated in a CIS-wide exercise called "Atom-Antiterror 2006." The Armenian Special Forces together with the Russian Federal Security Service, ran counterterrorism and hostage release drills at the Armenian Nuclear Power Plant.

Austria

In May, during its EU Presidency, Austria welcomed Attorney General Alberto Gonzales and Department of Homeland Security Deputy Secretary Michael Jackson to a conference of Justice and Interior Ministers from the

EU and Russia. The participants signed a declaration to increase cooperation against terrorism, organized crime, corruption, and illegal migration. In June, President Bush attended the U.S.-EU Summit in Vienna and discussed developing biometric standards and preventing WMD proliferation, terrorist financing, and radicalization and recruitment.

Austria promoted intercultural dialogues as a preventive strategy against radicalization and the isolation of ethnic and religious groups. In April, it hosted the second European Conference of Imams and convened a "Dialogue between Cultures and Religions" for high-ranking government and religious leaders from around the world in May. Austria has a comprehensive legal framework to combat money laundering and terrorism financing. It achieved a good level of compliance with FATF's nine Special Recommendations. Also in April, Austria hosted a joint EU-Gulf countries seminar in Brussels to strengthen international cooperation among financial intelligence units, non-profit organizations, and formal and informal banking systems. Austria allocated 12 million euros for counterterrorism measures and amended its export control legislation to further restrict transfers of chemicals, software, and weapons. In June, Austria hosted a U.S.-EU workshop on terrorist financing for 120 representatives from EU member state governments, and the private financial sector. The meeting focused on identifying best practices for ensuring private sector compliance with financial sanctions.

Austria maintained three instructors at the International Police Training Center in Jordan to train Iraqi police and four Austrian liaison officers served in the International Security Assistance Force (ISAF) headquarters in Kabul.

Azerbaijan

Azerbaijan's counterterrorism cooperation with the United States included granting blanket overflight clearance, engaging in information sharing and law-enforcement cooperation, and approving numerous landings and refueling operations at its civilian airport in support of OEF. Azerbaijan has supported peacekeeping operations in Iraq since August 2003 with an infantry company of approximately 150 soldiers stationed at the Haditha dam. A platoon of Azerbaijani soldiers has been working with the Turkish peacekeeping contingent in Afghanistan since November 2002, and President Aliyev announced plans to double this number to between 40 and 44 soldiers.

Azerbaijan stepped up its efforts and had some success in reducing the presence and hampering the activities of international mujahedin with ties to terrorist organizations seeking to move people, money, and material throughout the Caucasus. Azerbaijan took steps to combat terrorist financing and identify possible terrorist-related funding by distributing lists of suspected terrorist groups and individuals to local banks. In December, the inter-ministerial experts group responsible for drafting anti-money laundering and counterterrorist finance legislation, provided its most recent draft to the U.S. Department of Justice and the Council of Europe (COE) for comment. The draft law included the establishment of a Financial Intelligence Unit (FIU) and would expand the predicate crimes for money laundering beyond narcotics trafficking.

In April, the Azerbaijani Serious Crimes court sentenced six men in a group called Al-Muvahhidun Jamaat to prison terms ranging from ten to fifteen years. The group was convicted of purchasing illegal weapons, armed robbery, illegal border crossing, fabricating documents and resisting arrest. According to the Azerbaijani Ministry of National Security, the members of the group planned to travel to Afghanistan, Pakistan, Iran and Turkey for military training. The group was accused of planning bomb attacks on the U.S., Israeli and Russian embassies, the State Oil Company of the Azerbaijan Republic (SOCAR) building, and the National Bank of Azerbaijan; and "seeking the physical elimination of the leaders of Azerbaijan's government and security forces." (Members of the group were first arrested on July 13, 2005.)

Also in April, in a trial involving a group called al-Qaida Caucasus (separate from a group of the same name sentenced in 2005), 16 group members were sentenced to terms of up to life in prison. The group was convicted of the illegal purchase and bearing of firearms and for the July 2005 assassination of an officer of the Azerbaijani Ministry of Internal Affairs. The group consisted of citizens of Azerbaijan, Turkey, Russia and Yemen. Most of them were activists of various radical religious organizations that had undergone training at a camp in Georgia's Pankisi Gorge.

Azerbaijan extradited to Russia a terrorism suspect accused of a bombing in Dagestan in 2002. The suspect was originally arrested in Azerbaijan and, in April, was sentenced by an Azerbaijani court to seven years in prison. He was subsequently extradited to Russia.

Belgium

The Belgian government continued efforts to improve its ability to combat and control terrorist financing, including disrupting the possibility for untraced money flows through phone shops and other alternate remittance systems, value added tax refund carousels, laundered proceeds through narcotics trafficking or prostitution, and the diamond trade. Separately, the Belgian government enacted new legislation that broadened the definition of "bank account" to include insurance, stocks or other securities, and other financial instruments, for the purpose of investigating financial crimes, including the financing of terrorism. The burden of proof on judges to freeze terrorist assets was relatively high. To constitute a criminal offense, authorities had to demonstrate that support was given "with the knowledge that it would contribute to the commission of a crime by the terrorist group."

Belgium contributed 340 troops to the International Security Assistance Force (ISAF) in Afghanistan. The government also provided support for Afghan reconstruction. Belgium plans to expand its technical assistance efforts in Iraq and has begun implementing debt forgiveness within the framework of Paris Club agreements. It expanded its participation in the Jordan International Police Training Center in Amman, increasing the number of Belgian police officers at the facility from two to four. Other programs included training for Iraqi diplomats and magistrates in Belgium and training for Iraqi servicemen in Abu Dhabi, in cooperation with Germany.

Belgium is not a significant safe haven for terrorist groups, although the PKK operated television production facilities in the country. Belgian authorities were concerned about potential terror activities involving groups from Algeria and North Africa, and investigated groups such as the Moroccan Islamic Combatant Group (GICM), the Revolutionary People's Liberation Front (DHKP-C), and a far right group with links to neo-Nazi groups.

In February, a Belgian court convicted members of the GICM for belonging to a terrorist group linked to attacks in Madrid and Casablanca and providing logistical and financial support to the GICM. Under the antiterrorism law, prosecutors focused on the material support the suspects provided to terrorists, including lodging and false documents. Three of the 13 defendants were sentenced to terms of six to seven years. Six received three to five year sentences under the 2003 antiterrorism law, which criminalized membership in a terrorist group and broadened the definition of terrorist acts. In September, a Belgian appeals court upheld the convictions of five GICM members and imposed sentences ranging from 40 months to eight years.

In another case, also prosecuted pursuant to the 2003 antiterrorism law, members of the DHKP-C were convicted for membership in a terror organization and for providing material support to a terrorist group. In November, the Belgian court of appeals upheld those convictions. In September, Belgian authorities arrested 17 members of a loosely-organized far right group with links to neo-Nazi groups that was allegedly planning attacks to disrupt Belgian democratic institutions.

Bosnia and Herzegovina

Bosnia and Herzegovina's law enforcement organizations cooperated with the United States on international counterterrorism. Bosnia remained a weak state, however, with multiple semi-autonomous centers of power, vulnerable to exploitation as a terrorist safe haven or as a potential staging ground for terrorist operations in Europe. Nevertheless, there were notable signs of increased local operational capability to combat terrorism and terrorism finance.

Bosnian authorities continued to strengthen existing counterterrorism mechanisms and develop new ones. The Inter-Ministerial Counterterrorism Task Force (IMCTF), formed in December 2004, and currently responsible for coordinating all State-level institutions with counterterrorism responsibilities, directed two successful terrorism-related deportations in 2006. On February 8, the State Investigative and Protection Agency (SIPA), the State Border Police (SBP), the Foreigners Affairs Service (FAS), and the State Prosecutor worked together to remove convicted terrorist Said Atmani from the country. Atmani, a Moroccan national who fought in Bosnia during the war, served three years in jail for a bombing in France in the mid-1990s, before returning to Bosnia in 2005. On August 30, these agencies deported Tunisian national Bedrudin Ferchicij (a.k.a. Abu Malik), a mujahedin fighter who had remained illegally in Bosnia after the war. Despite these successes, the Task Force's operational effectiveness was generally hampered by insufficient coordination, such as infrequent communication and a lack of clear divisions of labor among the agencies.

In January, the Government of Bosnia and Herzegovina formed the Citizenship Review Commission (CRC). The Commission reviewed the status of foreign Mujahadin fighters and others who obtained Bosnian citizenship during and after the 1992-95 war, and withdrew citizenship from those who had obtained it improperly. In October the Council of Ministers adopted the Commission's interim progress report. According to the report, the CRC has completed preliminary reviews of approximately 600 cases (about half the total number pending), adjudicated 150 decisions, and stripped about 50 individuals of their citizenship. Among those stripped were three men listed under UNSC 1267 Committee for links with the Taliban, UBL and/or al-Qaida. The Foreigner Affairs Service had responsibility for determining the appropriate legal status of people stripped of citizenship and of initiating deportations when mandated under the Law on Movement and Stay of Aliens and Asylum. Although created in August 2005, vacant leadership positions stalled FAS institutional development until summer 2006. The process of drafting a revised Law on Movement and Stay of Aliens that would define and strengthen the FAS, which also began in 2005, remained unfinished.

The Bosnian State Court heard opening arguments in its first state-level terrorism trial in July. The trial remained underway with three individuals that were arrested in October 2005 and charged with terrorism, and two others charged with illegal possession of explosives. During the arrests, authorities confiscated weapons, explosives, a crudely fashioned suicide belt, and a video depicting masked men supposedly preparing to attack unspecified European targets. Lead defendants Mirsad Bektasevic (a Swedish citizen) and Abdulkadir Cesur were linked to terrorist networks elsewhere in Europe, and Cesur was also a named defendant in a terrorism trial concurrently underway in Denmark.

The Bosnian organization Aktivna Islamska Omladina (Active Islamic Youth, or AIO) spread extremist and anti-American rhetoric through its weekly print and on-line publication *SAFF Magazine*. AIO was founded in Zenica in 1995 by individuals with ties to the so-called "El Mujahid Brigade," a wartime unit comprised mainly of foreign extremists. There were indications that AIO conducted youth outreach in Bosnia during the year and maintained a presence in Western Europe.

In December, the Ministry of Defense pledged to donate 50,000 AK-47 rifles and necessary ammunition to security forces in Afghanistan in support of OEF. Bosnia and Herzegovina deployed a 36-member Explosive Ordinance Disposal (EOD) unit in Iraq in support of Operation Iraqi Freedom. The unit began its fourth rotation in Iraq in November.

Bulgaria

Bulgaria participated in both Operation Iraqi Freedom and the International Security Assistance Force (ISAF) in Afghanistan. Bulgaria's OIF contribution included a year-long deployment of a 154-person security company to Camp Ashraf in March, peace support operations training for 27 Iraqi officers at the National Military University in Veliko Turnovo in August as part of the NATO Training Mission in Iraq, and deployment of four officers to the NATO Training Mission in Iraq in October. In Afghanistan, Bulgaria maintained approximately 150 military personnel throughout the year, including soldiers assigned to HQ SEEBRIG; a separate mechanized infantry platoon assigned to the Kabul Multinational Brigade; a military police and counterintelligence platoon in Kabul; three military medical teams in Kabul and Herat; and Air Force personnel operating Kabul International Airport from October through December.

The Financial Intelligence Agency (FIA) continued efforts against terrorist financing and cooperated with the U.S. government on identifying terrorist assets. The FIA distributed lists of individuals and organizations linked to terrorism to all Bulgarian banks, the Ministry of Interior, Customs, and the Border Police. Parliament further strengthened the FIA's investigative powers by passing amendments enabling the FIA to obtain bank information without a court order.

Croatia

The Croatian government increased its contribution to the International Stabilization and Assistance Force (ISAF) in Afghanistan from 50 to 147 soldiers who served in military police, medical support and training roles. In addition, Croatia maintained a small civilian and police team deployment to the German-led Provincial Reconstruction Team in Feyzabad. On December 8, the Croatian Parliament approved a further increase to 200 troops in 2007, and to 300 troops in 2008.

Croatia's long land and sea borders presented a monitoring and enforcement challenge and guided continued efforts to improve its border integrity, its export control regime, and to prevent the proliferation of weapons of mass destruction. In November, Croatian police arrested in two men who were carrying explosives in Zadar, Croatia. The case was initially investigated as a terrorist plot to target and detonate the explosives on a ferry in the Adriatic Sea. Subsequent information pointed to the more likely scenario of an organized crime operation.

Cyprus

Despite limited resources, Cyprus took a clear stand against international terrorism and supported U.S. counterterrorism efforts. The government continued to allow blanket overflight and landing rights to U.S. military aircraft supporting operations in Iraq and Afghanistan. However, the government raised concerns about the allegations in a Council of Europe report identifying Cyprus as a "staging post" for U.S. rendition flights. Cyprus was generally supportive of international efforts to block and freeze terrorist assets, implemented Financial Action Task Force (FATF) recommendations, and conformed to EU directives on counterterrorism. In 2005, the Director of the Cyprus Central Intelligence Service (KYP) drafted and submitted to parliament legislation to restructure, modernize, and strengthen Cyprus's intelligence-gathering capabilities.

Third-country nationals comprised approximately ten percent of the Republic of Cyprus population, and the asylum community was growing. The government had concerns that this population was a potential source of recruits for terrorist groups looking to extend their reach into Europe. Moreover, the UN-patrolled "Green Line" dividing north and south is relatively porous. Immigration controls were uneven, and it was relatively easy for asylum seekers to cross from the Turkish Cypriot-administered area. Such conditions posed a potential vulnerability and access point for terrorist groups seeking entry into an EU member state (the EU's "acquis communitaire" currently is suspended in the north of Cyprus).

Cyprus's eastern Mediterranean location and the large volume of container traffic moving through its ports made the island potentially convenient for terrorist organizations seeking transshipment points for WMD and other items of concern. While Cypriot agencies responsible for nonproliferation assessed there was only a small risk that illicit materials might move through transit cargo, the United States continued to work for increased maritime cooperation.

In addition to EXBS activities, there was increased collaboration between the U.S. Embassy and the U.S. Defense Threat Reduction Agency (DTRA) in providing antiterrorism programming to Cyprus through the Department of Defense's International Counterproliferation Program (ICP). In October, the ICP provided an "Executive Seminar" on terrorist applications of weapons of mass destruction for 40 senior Republic of Cyprus officials.

The Kongra Gel/Kurdistan Workers' Party (KGK/PKK) maintained an active presence throughout Cyprus and reportedly used the island as both a fundraising and transit point. Experts estimated the Kurdish community in the government-controlled area to number 1,500. Among Kurdish-origin Turkish settlers in the north, the KGK/PKK reportedly enjoyed significant support. Cyprus maintained that it was fulfilling all responsibilities with respect to the EU designation of the KGK/PKK as a terrorist organization. Authorities in both the area under government control and in the area administered by Turkish Cypriots believed there was little risk the KGK/PKK would conduct operations on Cyprus and were reluctant to take any action that they perceived could make the island a potential target for PKK action. In addition, Turkish authorities believed that the large Turkish troop presence in the north acted as a significant deterrent to open KGK/PKK activity.

Czech Republic

The Government of the Czech Republic provided military assistance in Iraq and Afghanistan, cooperated in routine investigations, and worked with the U.S. to protect the Prague headquarters of Radio Free Europe/Radio Liberty. The Czech Republic contributed 101 troops to Coalition efforts in Iraq, 148 troops to the International Security Assistance Force (ISAF) in Afghanistan, and 120 Special Forces troops under Operation Enduring Freedom.

In December 2005, pursuant to a U.S. arrest warrant and INTERPOL Red Notice, Czech authorities arrested Oussama Kassir, a Lebanese-born Swedish national, in transit from Stockholm to Lebanon. Kassir was wanted in the United States on allegations that he conspired to provide material support to terrorists in the planned establishment of a terrorist training camp in Bly, Oregon. In June, a hearing was held to consider the extradition.

Kassir remained in Czech custody pending continued consideration of the U.S. extradition request.

Denmark

Denmark implemented several new measures as part of two anti-terror packages adopted by Parliament. These new measures criminalized the recruitment of persons to terrorism, and the training of others to assist in committing terrorist acts, including financing terrorism.

These new counterterrorism packages also enhanced the Danish government's ability to investigate and prevent terrorism and other serious crimes. Under the new acts, police may jam or disrupt communications to prevent criminal acts relating to terrorism or the security of Denmark. Information sharing between the Danish Security Intelligence Service (PET) and other agencies was made easier; and phone and internet providers must retain certain data for one year. In addition, the new legislation expanded the scope of certain warrants, allowing the police to conduct repeated searches under one warrant and to obtain intercept warrants covering an individual, rather than a particular phone number or single means of communication.

In January, the Danish government established the Center for Terrorism Analysis under the PET, which was composed of 15 analysts from five agencies. The government also transferred 150 employees from the national police to the PET to strengthen investigative capabilities within the intelligence service for terrorism and other serious crimes. In addition, the government proposed legislation that would prohibit private persons from purchasing fertilizer with ammonium nitrate levels of more than 28 percent, which could be used for improvised explosive devices.

Danish police and prosecutors cooperated closely on terror-related cases. Acting under the new counterterror measures and under provisions of its 2002 counterterrorism law, which explicitly criminalized both terrorism and providing financial and other support to terrorist groups, Danish authorities made several arrests on terrorism-related charges. In September, Danish officers arrested nine individuals suspected of planning a terrorist attack in Denmark in a suburb of Odense, Denmark's third-largest city. Five of the individuals remained in custody.

Danish authorities proceeded with several court trials on terrorism charges. In August, Danish prosecutors indicted four individuals, all born in Denmark, for attempting to conduct terrorist acts in cooperation with two men arrested in Bosnia in 2005. The four were charged under the terrorism statute; the trial began in December.

The trial continued against three members of the Danish branch of the Al-Aqsa Foundation (a Palestinian charity with suspected links to HAMAS) charged with supporting terrorism. They were indicted in 2003 for funneling money collected in Denmark, ostensibly for humanitarian purposes, to terrorist-related groups abroad. Danish authorities seized approximately $89,406 in funds from the organization. The case is Denmark's first prosecution under its financing of terrorism legislation.

The trial of Said Mansour, a Danish citizen originally from Morocco, began in December. Mansour was arrested in September 2005, by Danish police, for making and distributing CDs and videos throughout Europe that showed beheadings and killings and called for a violent jihad against the Western world. He was charged under the counterterrorism statute for attempting to recruit terrorists and facilitate terrorism, the first such case in Denmark. Mansour previously served a 90-day sentence from December 2004 on weapons possession charges.

Patrick MacManus, the spokesman of the Danish Non-Governmental Organization, "Opror" (Revolt) was indicted in October for violating Danish counterterrorism legislation by transferring approximately $17,000 to the Revolutionary Armed Forces of Colombia (FARC) and the Popular Front for the Liberation of Palestine (PFLP). In 2005, MacManus informed local media that the group's actions were a means to challenge Denmark's counterterrorism laws.

Denmark deployed more than 450 military personnel in southern Iraq to assist with security and reconstruction efforts, and contributed more than 350 military personnel to the International Security Assistance Force in Afghanistan. Denmark served as chair of the UN Security Council's Counterterrorism Committee.

Estonia

Estonia contributed 132 soldiers to participate in the U.K.-led provincial reconstruction team in Helmand, Afghanistan. The Estonian contribution consisted of an explosive ordnance disposal team, a national support element, a military observation team, a human intelligence team, a platform maintenance team in Kabul, and infantry. Estonia also sent 38 soldiers to participate in international peace support operations in Iraq. In addition, two staff officers served in the NATO-led training mission along with one police trainer in the Iraq training mission in Jordan.

In April, Estonian law enforcement, security police, and defense forces took part in Shamrock Key 2006, a regional counterterrorism exercise held in Lithuania, Latvia, and Estonia. The U.S., Norway, and Poland also participated as NATO partners. The exercise's objective was to improve cooperation and coordination between the various NATO allies' counterterrorism units, including synchronization of communications systems, coordination of logistical support, and cooperation on combat tactics.

On August 17, the Government of Estonia's antiterrorism council approved its antiterrorism policy's basic principles and action plan. The council consisted of representatives from the Ministries of Defense, Justice, Foreign Affairs, Economic Affairs and Communication, Internal Affairs (which included Security Police and Central Criminal Police), and the State Chancery's National Security Coordination Office. The Ministry of Internal Affairs headed the council.

Finland

Finland held the EU Presidency from July-December and made counterterrorism a top priority. The government led ongoing efforts within the EU to remove institutional barriers to counterterrorism cooperation and championed EU cooperation with the U.S. and international community. In November, Interior Minister Rajamaki visited Washington for discussions with Justice and Homeland Security officials, and FBI officials participated in Finnish-sponsored EU seminars.

Approximately 100 Finnish troops were deployed in Afghanistan in support of ongoing NATO operations, and a number of Finnish civilian crisis management experts were working in Afghanistan as well. Finland aims to provide ten million euros in development and humanitarian assistance to Afghanistan on an annual basis.

On October 1, 2005, new regulations entered into force requiring ships to submit security-related information prior to entry into port. Finland signed a Mutual Legal Assistance Treaty (MLAT) with the United States; the treaty is awaiting ratification by the Finnish Parliament.

In cases when another government presented a legal request for action or when an individual or organization was suspected of having committed an offense within Finland's borders, Finland implemented regulations that allowed it to freeze assets without EU or UN approval. Finland amended its criminal code to make it possible to sentence leaders of terrorist groups to 15 years in jail, although the group would have to have actually committed an act of terrorism in Finland before investigation or prosecution could begin. If the charge included murder, the maximum sentence would be life imprisonment.

France

France pursued aggressive counterterrorism measures, including dismantling terror networks on its territory, notably those assisting in the recruitment or financing of terrorists to Iraq. In total, French authorities arrested 317 people in connection with terrorism: 140 for links to Islamic terrorism, 150 for attacks in Corsica, and 27 with ties to Basque Fatherland and Liberty (ETA). Since 2002, French police have arrested 1,422 persons on terrorism related charges.

In September, the Salafist Group for Preaching and Combat (GSPC) announced its merger with al-Qaida, changed its name to al-Qaida in the Islamic Maghreb (AQIM), and declared France its number one target. Several high profile events—including the local publication of the Danish Mohammed cartoon pictorials, heated debate on the interdiction of the veil in French public institutions, and the presence of French troops in Afghanistan and Lebanon—were cited by various French authorities as factors manipulated by Islamic extremists to incite violence.

In May, 29 people were detained in France for suspected association with Iraq-related terror networks. In September, officials noted that at least nine terrorists, whose journey to Iraq began in France were killed, two were incarcerated, and another twelve-to-fifteen were likely still engaged in combat against Coalition Forces. Increasing Islamic radicalization in the prison system also continued to worry French officials.

On January 23, the French government adopted new counterterrorism legislation that considerably strengthened police powers in criminal law and codified some current practices. Preliminary detention for terrorism suspects was extended from a maximum of four to up to six days. Current legislation allowed the state to thereafter place suspects in pre-trial detention for up to four years when the evidence is strong or when they present an imminent threat. The law gave the government additional powers for the freezing of assets, video and telephone surveillance, allowed increased monitoring of public transport records, and granted broader powers of official access to connection data held by internet cafes and to various personal data records. Sentences for convicted terrorists were increased from 20 to 30 years for leading or organizing an attack, and from ten to twenty years for assisting a terrorist organization or operation. The new law also reinforced existing legislation that allowed for the revocation of French nationality and eventual expulsion if the terrorist became a citizen through naturalization within the preceding 15 years.

The French government published its White Paper on terrorism on March 7. The paper, a publicly available document, sets out the government's overall policy efforts to combat terrorism. It included attack scenarios, threat analyses, and technical as well as political responses to terrorism.

France continued its active engagement with the United Nation's Security Council (UNSC) Counterterrorism Committee (CTC), the G8's Counterterrorism Action Group (CTAG), the UN's 1267 Sanctions Committee (for the Taliban and al-Qaida), and the European Council's Anti-Terrorism Strategy action plan. In response to increasing calls, especially in some European and NAM delegations, that the process of listing and delisting of terrorist groups and entities under UNSCR 1267 lacked transparency, the United States and France co-sponsored UNSCR 1730, which made improvements in the process. The resolution was adopted in December. France is a founding member of the joint U.S./Russia Global Initiative to Combat Nuclear Terrorism that was inaugurated in October. France is a member and contributor to both the Proliferation and Container Security Initiatives. The U.S. and France maintained regular bilateral counterterrorism consultations.

On the military front, French Special Forces participated in coalition operations in Afghanistan as part of OEF. France was also a key participant in Coalition Task Force (CTF) 150, a multinational naval force that patrols the Red Sea and Gulf of Yemen to interdict the movement of suspected terrorists between Afghanistan, the Arabian Peninsula and the Horn of Africa. It has twice commanded the Task Force. France's overall contributions in Afghanistan increased.

French police cooperated closely with Spanish authorities in the Basque region. Several arms caches were discovered in France, and a number of arrests of Basque Fatherland and Liberty (ETA) suspects were made throughout the year. Several ETA members were extradited to Spain. One attack, allegedly claimed by Ipparetarek (a defunct French Basque nationalist group) or an Ipparetarek sympathizer, occurred in France on June 11 against the Hotel Ostap. There were no injuries and only minimal damage.

France continued to develop competencies and capabilities of TRACFIN, the Ministry of Finance's terrorism financing coordination and investigation unit. Within the European Union, France played an active role in the Clearinghouse, the EU process for designation of terrorist organizations. France did not designate HAMAS-affiliated charities, such as the French based Comite de Bienfaisance et Secours aux Palestiniens (Committee for the Well-Being and Assistance to Palestinians), arguing that it had no proven links to terrorism. France also opposed EU designation of Lebanese Hizballah as a terrorist organization, although it supported Hizballah's eventual disarmament, maintaining that disarmament would result in Hizballah's gradual integration into Lebanese politics.

Attacks on the French island of Corsica were up approximately 38 percent in 2006, totaling over 225. A majority of these attacks were claimed by the National Front for the Liberation of Corsica-Combatants Union, or by the National Front for the Liberation of Corsica of October 22. Three terrorists were killed during the year by accident while attempting to carry out attacks. The government had a widespread police presence in the region and arrested dozens of people throughout the year in connection with various attacks. The groups tended to target secondary residences, and avoided serious damage or casualties. Separatist groups appeared to have largely given up their political battle for independence but continued to wage an intimidation campaign aimed at foreigners or mainland French citizens interested in permanent residence or secondary homes on the small island.

Key judicial proceedings on Islamic terrorism related crimes included:

— On June 13, 25 Islamic militants tied to a Chechen extremist network that allegedly planned to bomb a commercial center in Paris and the Eiffel Tower were sentenced. Several members of the group, including Menad Benchellali and Merouane Benhamed, received the maximum sentence of ten years.[2]

— Five of six former Guantanamo detainees expelled to France in 2004 and 2005 were no longer in detention (they were initially detained for many months after their arrival in France). One, Brahim Yadel, remained in custody for violating the terms of his conditional release. All six former detainees faced further charges in France for terrorist conspiracy. In September the trial was halted when a judge ordered further investigations into the role of alleged visits of French intelligence authorities to Guantanamo.

— On October 26, Karim Mehdi, a Moroccan national, was sentenced to nine years for terrorism related activities. Mehdi is alleged to have ties with September 11 terrorists (Ramzi bin al Shaibah and Ziad Jarrah) and is suspected of planning an attack on the island of Reunion in 2003. Mehdi will be deported following his sentence and not allowed in France for a minimum of six years.

— On March 29, Rachid Ramda, who was extradited to France from the U.K. in December 2005 after ten years in detention, was sentenced to ten years for his role in the 1995 Paris subway and train attacks.

— On November 12, France's chief counterterrorism judge, Jean-Louis Bruguiere, sent to the Paris Court of Assises the cases of three suspects allegedly connected to the 2002 Djerba, Tunisia attacks. Khalid Sheikh Mohammed (KSM), Christian Ganczarski, and Walid Nawar are suspected of assisting convicted terrorist Belgacem Nawar in the Djerba AQ attacks whose victims included two French citizens. Khalid Sheikh Mohammed remained in U.S. custody at Guantanamo.

— In late November, three individuals were detained in France after being expelled from Syria; they were suspected of attempting to transit through Syria to join insurgents fighting against Coalition Forces in Iraq. Another nine individuals were deported from Egypt in mid-December under similar charges. All were released after a brief period of detention.

[2] The French government continued its policy of expelling non-French citizens engaged in terrorist activities or speech that promoted hate or incited violence. Among those ordered expelled from France were at least 20 imams from Algeria, Bangladesh, Morocco, and Pakistan.

— On July 19, Adel Tebourski, a Tunisian and French dual-national citizen, who was arrested in 2001 and sentenced in 2005 for his contribution to the September 9, 2001 assassination of Afghan War Chief Ahmad Shah Massood, was stripped of his French nationality by decree and expelled to Tunisia on August 7.

— Karim Bourti, a French AQIM/GSPC supporter, was also stripped of his citizenship in May.

— Since May 2005, the Government of France revoked the security clearances of 72 individuals working in private companies at Charles de Gaulle international airport. The majority of those were announced in early November. A few of those concerned brought legal action against the government and were subsequently reinstated. The government claimed that the individuals, while not terrorists, posed a security risk to the airport because background checks showed they had sympathies with Islamic extremists.

Georgia

Georgia is improving border security operations and made efforts to close its borders to those who wished to smuggle money, weapons, and supplies, but was hindered by corruption at border checkpoints, a general lack of resources, and obstructionism by Georgian separatists. Russia's July closure of its single legal border crossing with Georgia at Verkkhniy Lars (ostensibly a temporary closure for repairs) further hampered Georgia's control over its borders. All commerce and transit from Russia into Georgia had to thus pass illegally through the separatist regions of Abkhazia and South Ossetia, where Georgian authorities have no way to monitor or control the movement of goods and people as a result of the refusal of Russia and the separatists to permit joint monitoring of Georgia's borders between these separatist regions and Russia. Georgian internal troops carried out anti-terrorist operations in the Pankisi Gorge. The identification and safe removal of hidden weapons caches in Pankisi enabled Georgian security forces to better improve security in the area.[3]

The Georgian Ministry of Internal Affairs and the Prosecutor General's Office worked closely with U.S. law enforcement on counterterrorism. On January 12, a Georgian court sentenced Vladimir Arutunyan, who was convicted of throwing a grenade at President George Bush in 2005, to life in prison.

---

[3] Russia continued to charge Georgia with allowing Islamic fundamentalists that support Shechen insurgents to use Georgia, specifically the Parkisi Gorge region, as a staging area and transit point for fighters and materiel.

Germany

Germany participated in military operations overseas, provided leadership in multilateral settings, and fought terrorism within its borders. While no terrorist attacks took place in Germany, terrorists planted suitcase bombs that failed to detonate on two German trains, and German authorities uncovered a plot to smuggle a bomb aboard an Israeli jetliner. These incidents received extensive press coverage and were pointed to by German officials as reasons for Germany to take additional counterterrorism actions.

Germany was a leading contributor of troops to the International Security Assistance Force (ISAF) in Afghanistan with nearly 3000 troops deployed. The German Navy also participated in Operation Enduring Freedom off the Horn of Africa with roughly 330 military personnel involved. On October 25, a German Ministry of Defense White Paper outlined that, in the future, the international fight against terrorism would be a central task for the German military. Germany has resisted sending forces to Iraq, but provided equipment and training for the Iraqi military and training for the Iraqi police in the United Arab Emirates.

Eight EU member states joined the "Pruem" agreement, a German initiative from May 2005, to deepen law enforcement cooperation. The agreement enables faster sharing of car registration, DNA, and fingerprint data. Germany was active in the Global Initiative to Combat Nuclear Terrorism, in the Egmont Group of Financial Intelligence Units, and in seeking additional EU listings of terrorists.

The German government implemented legislation to strengthen its ability to fight terrorism. Federal reforms, enacted in July, granted the Federal Office of Criminal Investigation broader powers for terrorism investigations and for preventive arrest of would-be terrorists. On December 1, the German Bundestag approved two bills: one created a unified terrorism database, combining information from federal and state agencies as well as from law enforcement and security agencies; the second bill broadened and simplified the ability of German security agencies to obtain travel, financial, and telephone data.

The June 9–July 9 Soccer World Cup brought millions of fans from around the world to 64 matches in 12 German cities. Germany sought vigorous cooperation with law enforcement officials from neighboring and participating countries to prevent terrorist incidents. Several U.S. agencies developed new bilateral cooperative arrangements with German counterparts.

During the year, German law enforcement authorities arrested and investigated numerous individuals suspected of involvement in terrorism. At the end of the year, German authorities were investigating nearly 200 cases of terrorism-related crimes nationwide. Prominent new actions and arrests included:

- The November 17 raids and detention of six individuals who tried to bribe another person to smuggle a bomb aboard an Israeli aircraft during the summer. German authorities indicated the plot had been at an early stage; they released all individuals later in the day except for one wanted on another charge.
- The October 10 arrest of an Iraqi for posting AQ and other terrorist messages on the Internet.
- The August 19 and 25 arrests of a Lebanese and a Syrian, respectively, connected with the July 31 planting of two suitcase bombs aboard German regional trains in Dortmund and Koblenz. German prosecutors ordered the release of the Syrian on September 14 due to lack of evidence. German authorities worked closely with their Lebanese counterparts, who arrested another individual implicated in the plot.
- The July 6 arrest of a German citizen of Moroccan heritage charged with recruiting extremist fighters for battle in Iraq as well as for fundraising and providing logistical support for AQ.
- The June 12 arrest of an Iraqi charged with providing financial and logistical support for Ansar al-Islam.
- Additional arrests resulted in German prosecutors charging several with leadership of and fundraising for the Kurdistan Workers' Party (PKK) and the Revolutionary People's Liberation Party/Front (DHKP-C).

German courts began trials or reached verdicts in some notable counterterrorism cases. As in previous years, German laws and traditional procedures, as well as the courts' long-standing and expansive view of civil liberties, sometimes limited the success of cases prosecutors brought to trial:

- On November 16, ruling on an appeal, the Federal High Court convicted Moroccan citizen and 9/11 Hamburg cell member Mounir el Motassadeq of both membership in a terrorist organization and of 246 counts of accessory to murder (the 246 figure represented the number of passengers aboard the hijacked airliners of 9/11).[4]

[4] German courts convicted Motassadeq in 2003 of membership in a terrorist organization and accessory to 3,000 murders, but the Federal High Court subsequently ordered a retrial in 2004 due to the perceived lack of access to potentially exculpatory testimony from such individuals as Khaled Sheik Mohammed, whom the court presumed to be in U.S. custody. In August 2005, a Hamburg court convicted Motassadeq on the charge of membership in a terrorist organization and sentenced him to seven years in jail. As is possible in Germany, both the prosecution and the defense appealed. On February 6, the court released Motassadeq from custody pending the outcome of the appeal. Police re-arrested Motassadeq on November 17, the day after the Federal High Court's guilty verdict.

- On July 14, German prosecutors closed their investigation of Syrian-German dual national Mamoun Darkazanli, wanted in Spain on terrorism charges.
- On June 20, a Stuttgart court began the trial of three Iraqi alleged members of Ansar al-Islam: Ata Abdoulaziz Rashid, Rafik Mohamad Yousef, and Mazen al-Hussein. German prosecutors have charged the three, who have been in detention since December 2004, with a plot to assassinate former Iraqi Prime Minister Allawi during his visit to Berlin that month. Prosecutors also charged them with financial crimes and membership in, financing, and recruiting for a foreign terrorist organization.
- On May 9, a Düsseldorf court began the trial of one Iraqi (Ibrahim Mohamed Khalil) and two Palestinian defendants (brothers Yasser Abu Shaweesh and Ismail Abu Shaweesh) accused of membership in and/or support of Ansar al-Islam, insurance fraud, and attempted procurement of enriched uranium for a "dirty bomb." The three have been in German custody since their arrests in January and May 2005.
- On January 12, a Bavarian court convicted Iraqi citizen Lokman Amin Mohammed of membership in Ansar al-Islam and Ansar al-Sunna, providing them financial and logistical support, and smuggling terrorists into Iraq; he was sentenced to seven years in jail.

The German Interior Ministry used its authority under the Law on Associations to ban organizations that it believed were connected to terrorism. Germany banned a number of such organizations in recent years, including the DHKP-C, Dev Sol, Hizb-ut Tahrir, the PKK, and organizations connected with HAMAS. On January 25, a German court rejected an appeal of the ban against Hizb-ut Tahrir.

Germany participated in several U.S. programs to combat terrorism, including the Container Security Initiative in the ports of Hamburg and Bremerhaven. The Transportation Security Administration's presence in Frankfurt, together with U.S. and German air marshals, formed key parts of bilateral efforts to provide air transport security for the six German airports with flights to the United States.

Greece

With improved counterterrorism infrastructure in place following the 2004 summer Olympic Games in Athens, Greece continued to fight domestic and international terrorism. Greece sustained its participation in the International Security Assistance Force (ISAF) in Afghanistan by providing a unit from the Greek Corps of Engineers (511 troops) and a NATO medical unit in Kabul (209 troops). From October 2005 through April, Greece had the lead for security at Kabul International Airport. On October 12, Greece signed the

Council of Europe Convention on Laundering, Search, Seizure, and Confiscation of the Proceeds from Crime and on the Financing of Terrorism.

In July, convicted 17 November (17N) terrorist Nikos Papanastasiou, was released from prison for health reasons. Papanastasiou was sentenced to eight years imprisonment in 2003, for setting up and participating in the 17N terrorist group. Papanastasiou is the third convicted 17N terrorist to be granted an early release from prison on health grounds, being preceded by Konstantinos Telios and Pavlos Serifis in 2005. On April 12, an appellate criminal court unanimously acquitted Constantinos Avramidis, a self-confessed member of anarchist organizations who was arrested and indicted as a member of 17N in 2003, for lack of evidence.

Despite these early releases, on October 10, a Greek court denied 17N prisoner Savvas Xiros' pleas for release on medical grounds for the second time. Xiros' first plea was denied in October 2005. Xiros' botched bombing attempt in 2002 led to his arrest and the subsequent arrest and trial of several members of the November 17 organization.

In 2003, Greek courts handed down multiple life sentences to key 17N members who were responsible for hundreds of crimes and the murders of 13 Greeks and five U.S. government employees over a course of almost 30 years. A group appeals trial for 15 17N convicts and two previously acquitted individuals opened in December 2005. The appeals trials essentially represented a new trial for the convicts, since the Greek judicial system allows new facts and evidence to be introduced in the appeals phase.

The appeals trial lasted far longer than the original trial, in part due to the defense team's tactics and the court's decisions allowing defendants great leeway to make statements and interrupt witnesses. The defense attorney's strategy had been to dismiss defendant confessions rendered in the first trial as void due to alleged illegal interrogation methods. Investigation of 17N continued despite the arrest, trial, and conviction of what has been identified as "the main body" of the 17N terrorist group.

The Revolutionary Struggle (RS), an anti-Greek establishment radical leftist group, claimed responsibility for a May bomb explosion near the residence of former Minister of Public Order Giorgos Voulgarakis. The remotely detonated bomb was placed next to a school along the minister's usual route to work and exploded just minutes before he was due to pass. The explosion wrecked several cars but did not cause any injuries. Police have made no arrests in the case. Police officials have not closed their investigation into the 2004 killing of a Greek Special Guard at his post outside the residence of the British Defense Attaché, which they regarded as a domestic terrorist incident.

Self-styled anarchists attacked "imperialist-capitalist targets" with tools such as firebombs and Molotov cocktails. Since these attacks usually occurred in the middle of the night, few persons were seriously injured and there were no deaths. Several U.S. businesses were targeted. Police officials pursued a more pro-active approach to deterring violent attacks by anarchists and arrested perpetrators.

Hungary

Hungary deployed a provincial reconstruction team to Afghanistan and continued to fully implement domestic legislation to ensure compliance with EU norms regarding financial transactions and money laundering. Cooperation with U.S. and regional officials on export and border controls remained outstanding as Hungary continued its preparations to join the Schengen zone. Hungarian officials aggressively developed and pursued leads in cooperation with U.S. officials to prevent the transshipment of hazardous materials. Efforts to improve its technical ability to trace and control dangerous materials continued, consistent with EU membership obligations.

Iceland

Although Iceland does not have its own military, the government undertook efforts to review its national security policy following the withdrawal of U.S. military forces from Iceland. The Icelandic government made strong efforts to ensure that Iceland was not a haven for terrorist groups. In June, Iceland passed the "Act to Counter Money Laundering and the Financing of Terrorist Acts," which brought Icelandic law fully into compliance with FATF's recommendations regarding terrorist financing. In support of efforts to prevent trafficking in weapons of mass destruction, Iceland was a member of the Proliferation Security Initiative and participated in the U.S. Coast Guard's International Port Security Program. Through its participation in the Schengen Agreement, the Icelandic government consulted closely with other Schengen states on border control and security matters.

In September, the National Police Commissioner's Office confirmed it was investigating a case involving a resident who showed an interest in researching explosives and bomb making. No charges were brought in the case, but this was the first public confirmation that Iceland's police conduct preemptive investigations of possible terrorist activity.

On September 26, the government announced efforts to strengthen its security and counterterrorism capabilities, including: a legal review of intelligence and information sharing with foreign governments, the planned establishment of a national security unit within the National Police Commissioner's Office, and purchases of a new fixed-wing aircraft, helicopters, and a patrol vessel for the Icelandic Coast Guard (ICG).

On October 12, Iceland's Prime Minister and Foreign Minister and the U.S. Secretary of State signed a Joint Understanding on Defense and Security Issues, detailing new initiatives in training, exercises, and intelligence. The government conducted several joint counterterrorism training activities with the United States.

Iceland supported NATO counterterrorism operations in Afghanistan through the deployment of a mobile observation team to the provincial reconstruction team in Ghor Province and through its role as lead NATO nation at Kabul International Airport. Iceland also deployed personnel to the Sri Lanka Monitoring Mission, which reported violations of the cease-fire between the Sri Lankan government and the Liberation Tigers of Tamil Eelam (LTTE).

Ireland

The Irish government permitted the transit of U.S. military personnel and material through Irish airspace and airports for deployment to Iraq. The government also took steps to strengthen bilateral dialogue on terrorism issues, including establishing a security liaison office at the Irish Embassy in Washington and the visit of an Irish Justice Department delegation to meet with U.S. Government agencies to discuss terrorism. Ireland focused largely on implementing recent terrorism-related domestic legislation and on negotiations to bring republican groups into a political power-sharing arrangement in Northern Ireland.

The Irish media focused on concerns about the possible radicalization of small numbers of people within Ireland's 40,000-strong Muslim community. One imam told the press that recruits were targeting some Muslim youth to participate in terrorist activity, although most Muslim leaders strongly denied this claim.

The Irish government continued to work with the British government to bring republican groups into the Northern Ireland political process, the objective of the 1998 Good Friday Agreement. In October, representatives of Sinn Fein, formerly the political wing of the Provisional IRA (PIRA), and the Democratic Unionist Party announced their support for the Ireland/ U.K.-brokered "St. Andrews Agreement." The Agreement envisions a power-sharing arrangement between the two sides and a Sinn Fein endorsement of joint policing. The negotiation process leading to the Agreement followed steps by the IRA in 2005 to decommission its weapons and to announce an end to armed struggle.

In October, the Independent Monitoring Commission (IMC), a four-person body established by the Irish and British governments in 2004, published its twelfth report which concluded that the IRA "is firmly set on a political strategy, eschewing terrorism and other forms of crime." The IMC reported no acts of crime or violence that could be regarded as sanctioned by the PIRA. In April, however, former Sinn Fein leader Denis Donaldson was murdered in Ireland, roughly four months after his public admission that he had acted as an informant for the British government. While no suspects were apprehended in his murder, there is widespread suspicion that his murder was an act of republican retribution for his work as a double-agent.

Italy

Italy aggressively fought terrorism and dismantled terrorist-related cells within its borders, while it maintained high-level professional cooperation with its international partners. The Italian security services maintained a high-state of readiness at the 2006 Winter Olympic Games in Turin in February and during national elections in April, and closely collaborated with U.S. and other international partners to ensure that both events remained free of terrorist-related incidents. There was no discernible change in either the pace or scope on counterterrorism cooperation with the political change in government from the center-right to the center-left.

Italy contributed to Coalition peacekeeping activities in Iraq, Afghanistan, and Lebanon. Italy was an important partner in the Proliferation Security Initiative and the Container Security Initiative. In October, Italy became an initial partner nation of the Global Initiative to Combat Nuclear Terrorism, developed by the United States and Russia.

Italy's judiciary continued to be engaged in counterterrorism efforts, with several noteworthy cases during the reporting period. In September, a Milan court sentenced five members of an Ansar al-Islam cell to sentences ranging from five to ten years. The ruling overturned a January 2005 decision by another court that released two of the individuals and reduced the sentences of the other three, based on a judgment that their activities to recruit fighters for the insurgency in Iraq did not necessarily constitute terrorist activity.

In October, Italy's Court of Cassation (Italy's highest appellate court) overturned acquittals by two lower appellate courts for three individuals: Mohamed Daki, Maher Abdelaziz Bouyahia, and Ali Ben Sassi Toumi, suspected of supporting international terrorism. The higher court maintained there was sufficient evidence for a retrial of their alleged involvement in recruiting fighters for Iraq and facilitating the movement of suspected terrorists. In November, a court in Milan sentenced Rabei Osman Sayed Ahmed, an Egyptian national, to ten years in prison on charges of subversive association aimed at international terrorism for having recruited suicide bombers in Italy for Iraq. Rabei Osman will be extradited to Spain to stand trial on charges of being a key plotter in the 2004 Madrid bombings.

In July, the new Parliament, dominated by the center-left, approved a universal pardon in an effort to relieve prison overcrowding. The pardon allowed anyone serving a prison sentence (except for certain specified offenses) to be released from prison three years early. The pardon excluded those convicted of terrorism, but some individuals convicted of lesser crimes, but potentially having some terror connections, were pardoned. It is unknown how the pardon will affect other individuals with known or suspected ties to terrorism.

In May, the U.S. Ambassador and the Italian Justice Minister signed a new treaty on extradition and mutual legal assistance. The treaty, when ratified by the U.S. Senate, will allow for joint investigative teams, easier asset freezing and forfeiture, and faster sharing of bank account and other financial information.

The Italian security services engaged in raids, temporary detentions, prosecutions, and expulsions of known or suspected extremists to combat Islamic extremists. The Italian government benefited from reinforced counterterrorism legislation enacted in 2005, which made it easier to hold suspects; mandated arrest for crimes involving terrorism; and facilitated the deportation of persons who may be involved in terrorist activities. More than 25 individuals were arrested nationwide as a result of counterterrorism investigations, and approximately 20 suspected terrorists or facilitators were deported. The European Court of Human Rights is reviewing the Italian government's policy of expulsions and deportations without judicial review, which could impact the government's ability to uphold a key part of its counterterrorism policy.

Italian officials carefully monitored and dismantled groups with suspected links to the Balkans and Islamic terrorist groups. In a variety of operations, Italian officials maintained that some members of Balkan-based groups in Italy traveled throughout the country and elsewhere in Europe, possibly engaging in recruitment, support, and facilitation of terrorist activities. These individuals faced charges of membership to a terrorist organization and involvement in illegal immigration, both of which are considered a crime under the Italian Penal Code.

In February, two of the main plotters in terrorist cells that were planning attacks in Italy, including against Saint Petronio's Basilica in Bologna, were arrested in Algeria and Morocco with Italian support. The investigation and subsequent debriefing of the suspects identified seven other individuals residing in Italy linked to the plot; the seven were subsequently ordered deported. In April, as a result of a joint operation, Italian and French police detained 13 suspected Islamic militants linked to the Salafist Group for Preaching and Combat (AQIM/GSPC). Eight of the suspects were apprehended in Naples on suspicion of using or making forged documents.

In July, Italian police authorities arrested four Algerians suspected of belonging to the AQIM/GSPC and of fabricating false documentation. In October, Italian police services, in collaboration with the Federal Swiss Police, arrested six Algerians that belonged to the AQIM/GSPC and were suspected of promoting, financing, and supporting terrorist acts against the Algerian government. Individuals in the group reportedly were linked to at least two terrorist attacks in Algiers conducted in 2005. The investigation also revealed that the group managed more than $1.7 million through some 50 bank and postal accounts.

With respect to financial aspects of fighting terrorism, Italy aggressively identifies and blocks financial resources to suspected terrorist individuals and groups. Italy is second in the EU only to the United Kingdom in the number of individual terrorists and terrorist organizations the country has submitted to the United Nations UN 1267 Sanctions Committee for designation.

Domestic anarchist-inspired terrorist groups presented a diminished threat as a result of Italian authorities' continued efforts to dismantle their organizations. Nevertheless, anarchist groups sent letter bombs to Italian officials and placed package bombs near military installations and media outlets. In some cases, these devices caused minor injuries. Communist-inspired revolutionary groups occasionally placed improvised explosive devices outside military installations and in one case, a defense industrial firm.

In December, Italian authorities rearrested Fabio Matteini on charges of belonging to a terrorist and subversive organization and of participating in an armed organization. Matteini, who was released from prison in 1997 after serving time for similar charges, is connected to the new Red Brigades, which killed labor advisers Marco Biagi (in 2002) and Massimo D'Antona (in 1999). Biagi and D'Antona served as advisers to the center-right and center-left governments, respectively. Matteini previously was a member of the Combatant Communist Nuclei. In December, a Court of Appeals in Bologna confirmed the life sentences of four other individuals involved in Biagi's killing.

Latvia

Latvia's Financial Intelligence Unit continued to maintain a terrorist financing (OFAC) database that it shared with local banks. Although Latvia had previously passed legislation to improve government oversight, in May 2005, the Department of the Treasury designated two Latvian banks as institutions of "primary money laundering concern" under Section 311 of the Patriot Act, prohibiting them from having any dealings with U.S. financial institutions. Since then, the Latvian government and regulatory agencies have worked very closely with the United States to enhance their legislative and regulatory framework. In July, Treasury cleared one bank but continued sanctions against the second.

In April, Latvian law enforcement, security police, and defense forces took part in Shamrock Key 2006, a regional counterterrorism exercise held in Lithuania, Latvia, and Estonia. The United States, Norway, and Poland also participated as NATO partners. The exercise's objective was to improve cooperation and coordination between the various NATO Allies' counterterrorism units, including synchronization of communications systems, coordination of logistical support, and cooperation on combat tactics. In November, the NATO summit in Riga brought Heads of State and Government from 26 countries to Latvia. The summit provided an impetus for significant improvements in coordination among the various Latvian security-related agencies. Annual exercises are planned to ensure continuation of this high level of coordination. Latvia actively sought vigorous cooperation with law enforcement officials from neighboring and participating countries to prevent terrorist incidents. In securing the summit, Latvia also undertook significant cooperation with U.S. agencies and the U.S. military. Latvia used the Summit to strengthen its border control and inspection system, including data sharing with EU and other partners.

Latvia contributed 35 soldiers to support the International Security Assistance Force (ISAF) in Afghanistan; in October the team's mandate was renewed for one year and is now scheduled to expire the same day that the UNSCR mission mandate expires (October 13, 2007). In Iraq, Latvia has 120 soldiers under Polish command. Parliament renewed the authority for the Iraq deployment in December for an additional year.

Lithuania

In May, President Adamkus introduced a Lithuanian-Belarusian intergovernmental agreement to combat organized crime and trafficking in narcotics and psychotropic substances, terrorism, and other crimes (Decree No. 616), which is pending ratification. In June, the Parliament passed an amendment that allows for and formalizes the process by which the military can be used for counterterrorism purposes. In October, based on EU guidelines, the Lithuanian government approved a terrorist watch list of persons, groups, and organizations related to terror acts or suspected of terrorism. For EU citizens on the list, it limited their rights to own and use funds held by them in financial institutions (Decision No. 1027).

Lithuania has approximately 60 troops in Iraq, including infantry troops serving in Multinational Division South East (MND-SE) near Basra and trainers in the NATO Training Mission-Iraq (NTM-I). Lithuania also led a provincial reconstruction team in Afghanistan's remote Ghor Province.

This element consists of approximately 130 Lithuanian troops and civilians responsible for maintaining a stable environment throughout the province to enable reconstruction efforts.

Macedonia

Macedonia's active implementation of the Law on Export Control of Dual Use Goods and Technologies, through the establishment of an electronic system to review and issue export licenses for dual use technologies, demonstrated its commitment to preventing the sale of potentially dangerous technologies to terrorist and criminal regimes. Macedonia also passed legislation on nuclear security and terrorism, chemical weapons, and bilateral law enforcement, security, and extradition agreements.

Macedonia continued to support troop rotations to Afghanistan and Iraq. The government removed five of seven caveats on its troops deployed to both countries so Macedonian soldiers can better support ISAF and other allied military operations. The United States trained several hundred police and military personnel in counter and antiterrorism techniques, technologies, and methods.

Malta

Although the Government of Malta has expressed political will, counterterrorism efforts in Malta remained in a nascent stage and are in need of development, enlargement, training, and financial assistance. Deputy Prime Minister Tonio Borg acknowledged this during his September visit to the United States.

In February, Malta's Prevention of Money Laundering Regulations was extended to include "financing of terrorism," which criminalized terrorist financing and imposed additional obligations, namely customer due diligence, record keeping, reporting, and training procedures. Like other EU countries, Malta has not yet adopted the Directive but was already in substantial compliance with the enumerated requirements. The Government of Malta made significant strides to reform and regulate the banking laws, most significantly, ending its offshore investment regime. The Ministry of Finance's Financial Intelligence and Analysis Unit continued to expand and upgrade its capabilities.

The Maltese government was concerned about the proliferation and trafficking of weapons of mass destruction (WMD) in and through its territory. A particular vulnerability is Malta's Freeport which transshipped approximately 1.2 million containers per year. Most of the containers through Freeport were heading to, or coming from, nations along the North African littoral. Through the Export Control and Border Security assistance program, the United States has for several years provided training and advanced equipment that have increased Maltese authorities' capability to monitor what passes through its ports. The Maltese have seized many shipments of stolen and counterfeit goods as a direct outcome of the U.S. assistance. Malta and the United States agreed in October on the text for a bilateral Proliferation Security Initiative Ship Boarding Agreement. After Malta and the United States sign the agreement, which is set to occur in March 2007, the Maltese Parliament must approve legislation for it to enter into force.

Technology, funding, and training of Maltese agencies contributed to improved port security and the ability to inspect goods transiting the Freeport and Malta International Airport. With Malta's geographic location between northern Africa and the European mainland, Malta could become increasingly attractive to terrorist organizations seeking entry into Europe.

Moldova

Moldova deployed four separate contingents of servicemen (a total of 76 servicemen) to Iraq, where they specialized in demining, liaison, and convoy security. The Moldovan government continued to manage a counterterrorism strategy based on its 2003–2008 National Action Plan on Combating Terrorism. The SECI/GUAM National Virtual Center, aimed at combating terrorism, organized crime, and narcotics trafficking, was created on January 27. On November 13, a Counterterrorism Center within the Information and Security Service (SIS) was created and staffed by 18 employees.

The separatist-controlled Transnistria region of Moldova remained a potential area for terrorist recruitment. Moldovan law enforcement worked hard to track the whereabouts and activities of a sizeable Arab student population, as many often move in and out of Transnistria, an area where the Moldovan police and security services do not have the authority to operate. Many of these students remained in Moldova illegally, as the government lacked the resources to deport them when their visas expired. Corruption was endemic, and it was easy to obtain false travel documents. The U.S. embassy does not maintain liaison relationships or contacts with Transnistrian law enforcement and/or security service personnel. To date, Embassy has not obtained any information about known terrorist organizations or terrorists operating from or within this region.

Montenegro

Montenegro became independent on June 3, after a May 21 public referendum. The Government of Montenegro, before and after independence from the State Union of Serbia and Montenegro, has taken a serious and considered approach to combating international terrorism, including terrorism finance. Although Montenegro made considerable progress in its efforts to combat corruption and organized crime, weak border control and high levels of organized crime make Montenegro a potential harbor for organized crime and extremist groups that seek to operate in Montenegro and the Balkan region. Montenegro sits along several major smuggling routes between Southern and Western Europe.

Montenegro does not tolerate the activity of terrorist groups on its territory. The Administration for the Prevention of Money Laundering, which was established with and continues to receive assistance and training from the United States, works closely and shares information with regional and international Financial Intelligence Units (FIUs). The Montenegrin FIU also conducted local investigations of terrorism finance and initiated investigations potentially leading to future criminal prosecution in three cases this past year. Montenegro joined INTERPOL in September.

On September 9, the day before parliamentary elections, Montenegrin police raided arms caches in a suburb of Podgorica, the nation's capital, initially arresting 14 persons, including three foreign nationals, on suspicion that the group planned to carry out armed attacks on election day. The Government described the group as comprising of ethnic Albanian extremists. On December 7, 18 persons, including four fugitives and, non-exclusively, five foreign nationals, were criminally charged with planning terrorist acts, financing of terrorism, and other acts constituting organized crime. Subsequently, one foreign national fugitive was arrested in Austria upon an Interpol warrant filed by Montenegro. The State Prosecutor, in the indictment, stated that additional planning for the terrorist acts took place in Skoder, Albania. Some opposition political parties criticized the arrests, claiming the raid was aimed at suppressing legitimate political dissent. At year's end, all of the defendants were still awaiting trial. Since September 9, there were numerous unconfirmed reports of similar ethnic-Albanian extremist groups operating within Montenegro.

Netherlands, The

The Dutch continued to respond to the global terrorist threat with leadership and energy in the areas of border and shipping security, terrorist financing, and Coalition efforts in Afghanistan. The Netherlands deployed over 1900 troops to Afghanistan as part of NATO's International Security Assistance Force (ISAF) mission and in support of Operation Enduring Freedom (OEF). The Dutch led a Provincial Reconstruction Team (PRT) in Uruzgan province, and in November assumed a six-month rotational command in Kandahar of NATO's efforts in southern Afghanistan. For 2004-2006, the Dutch pledged 75 million euros toward the Afghanistan Reconstruction Trust Fund to support the transition from humanitarian to reconstruction assistance. From December 2005 to May 2006, the Government of the Netherlands commanded OEF's Combined Task Force 150, committing a fast frigate, a submarine, and a support ship to the mission. Dutch troops ended their deployment in Iraq as part of SFIR in March 2005 following two extensions. The Netherlands deployed 14 trainers and security guards in support of the NATO Training Mission in Iraq and pledged 21 million euros for Iraqi reconstruction.

In its October quarterly terrorism threat analysis, the Dutch National Counterterrorism Coordinator (NCTb) maintained the "substantial threat" level, citing significant threats against other European countries, and Western countries in general. The NCTb also highlighted concern about continuing radicalization among young Muslims, particularly through the Internet. The report cited the increasing presence of susceptible teenagers, particularly those of Dutch-Turkish descent, in local Jihad networks as evidence of continuing radicalization, noting that frustration about the position of Muslims in the Netherlands and fury about events in conflict areas appeared to nourish the feeling of "having to do something." The NCTb also highlighted the role of the Internet as a platform for radical Islamic propaganda.

In February, the Dutch government launched a national counterterrorism public information campaign, "The Netherlands against Terrorism." The campaign was designed to make the public aware of government counterterrorism actions and what individuals could do to minimize the risks of an attack. In March a special notification center for radical statements and hate mail became operational via the new cyber crime website. The Dutch hosted the first ever U.S.-Netherlands Cyber-Crime Conference in October. The conference, attended by Attorney General Gonzales and Dutch Justice Minister Hirsch Ballin, included discussions on bilateral counterterrorism investigations and combating internet radicalization.

The Dutch prosecuted two major terrorism cases. In March, the Rotterdam court ruled the Hofstad group a terrorist organization that aimed to incite hatred, violence, and intimidation. Nine of 14 defendants, including Mohammad Bouyeri, the convicted murderer of film director Theo Van Gogh, were found guilty of membership in a criminal organization "with terrorist intent." Two of the nine, Jason Walters (a dual U.S.—Dutch national) and Ismael Akhnikh, were also convicted for attempted murder and violating the Weapons and Ammunition Act for throwing a hand grenade at The Hague police officers in November 2004. They were sentenced to 15 and 13 years, respectively. Noureddin el Fatmi, also charged in the Piranha case (see below), was sentenced to five years. Bouyeri, considered the group's leader, did not receive an additional sentence in the Hofstad case because he already was serving a life term for Van Gogh's murder. This was the first case to be tried under the 2004 Terrorist Crimes Act, which made membership in a terrorist group and conspiracy to commit terrorist attacks criminal offenses.

The second major prosecution concluded in December, when Samir Azzouz and four additional defendants in the "Piranha" trial were found guilty of planning terrorist attacks on politicians and the national intelligence office. Samir Azzouz, the alleged leader of the group, was sentenced to eight years in prison.

In November, the National Crime Squad arrested five men and one woman on suspicion of terrorist recruitment, participating in a terrorist organization, and obtaining false travel documents.

Dutch officials remained committed to active cooperation with the United States in freezing the assets of known terrorist organizations. In March, the Netherlands Finance Ministry hosted an international conference on terrorist financing issues. In April, the Hofstad group and nine convicted members of the group were put on the Dutch Terrorist Sanctions List, freezing all their assets; in June the government decided, on humanitarian grounds, to ease financial sanctions on some members of the group who already served their sentences. The Netherlands sought EU designations of the Hofstad group and Hizballah as terrorist groups.

The Netherlands adopted three new counterterrorism laws that were expected to facilitate the investigation and prosecution of terrorism suspects. The Protected Witness Act permitted the use of intelligence information in criminal proceedings by establishing procedures to allow the examining judge to assess the reliability of intelligence information without exposing the identities of intelligence officers or sharing confidential intelligence information with the public. The provisions went into effect November 1. The "special investigative methods" bill expanded the use of special investigative techniques in terror investigations by lowering the threshold for the use of surveillance, infiltration, undercover purchases, and wiretapping. This allows the police to initiate investigations at a much earlier stage in terrorist planning. The final law forbade the operation in the Netherlands of terrorist organizations on the UN or EU designations lists. (Previously, only the bank accounts of such groups were frozen.) The law also provided for action, including the confiscation and liquidation of the group's Dutch assets, to be taken against foreign organizations, including those not appearing on the UN or EU terror lists, conducting activities or pursuing objectives in the Netherlands deemed contrary to public order. These new laws complemented the 2004 Terrorist Crimes Law and were expected to facilitate the successful investigation and prosecution of terrorist suspects.

The National Police Service's Special Intervention Unit became operational in June. It integrated various special police and defense units engaged in counterterrorism activities.

The government's sectoral terror alert system, which became operational in June 2005, now includes nine economic sectors: Schiphol Airport, the Rotterdam Port, and the petrochemical industry, drinking water, railway, natural gas, electricity, nuclear, municipal and regional transport, and financial sectors. This early-warning system was designed to trigger a clear and rapid response to terrorist threats by both the public and private sectors. It links sector-specific measures to be taken to the latest threat information from the National Counterterrorism Coordinator. There are four alert levels: basic, low, moderate, and high-threat. A total of 14 sectors are anticipated.

On October 11, the Justice Minister approved the extradition to the United States of Wasem Al Delaema, an Iraqi-born Dutch citizen. Al Delaema was charged with conspiring to attack U.S. troops in Iraq in 2003, and was the first person to be charged in U.S. courts for terrorist activities in Iraq. The Supreme Court's September ruling that Al Delaema was eligible for extradition was the first time a Dutch court approved the extradition of a Dutch citizen on terrorism-related charges. Al Delaema filed for an injunction against the Minister's extradition order; his appeal was rejected on December 19, paving the way for his extradition. In September, the Dutch Supreme Court blocked the extradition of alleged female PKK leader Nuriye Kesbir to Turkey, citing concerns over Turkey's human rights practices and insufficient guarantees against torture.

Norway

Norway took steps to improve its counterterrorism capabilities but more work remains to be done. The government's efforts to address serious shortages in equipment, training, and capabilities were complicated by the widespread belief among the general public that no one would attack Norway. In October, the Ministry of Interior conducted a large-scale exercise in Oslo designed to test emergency response capabilities to a London and Madrid-type terrorist attack on transit infrastructure.

In October 2005, Norway passed an antiterrorism law that gave the police greater leeway to investigate and prosecute terror suspects. The September 2006 arrest of four individuals suspected of shooting an Oslo synagogue and planning attacks on the U.S. and Israeli embassies was the first test of this law. Some of the new investigative tools were used in the case. However, the prosecution of the case highlighted concerns that the law's definition of a conspiracy to commit a terror act was restrictive and could limit its usefulness. Reported miscommunication among various police offices and mishandling of information and suspects illustrated the need for improvement.

Alleged Ansar al-Islam leader Mullah Krekar, an Iraqi Kurd listed in December 2006 under UNSCR 1267, continued to reside in Norway but was unable to travel abroad, as his travel documents were confiscated and he remained under a government expulsion order. In the fall of 2005 the Oslo City Court rejected Krekar's suit against the government's expulsion decision. His subsequent appeal was rejected one year later. Despite the failure of his appeal, Krekar remained in Norway because the government was unable to receive sufficient human rights assurances from Iraq to proceed with deportation.

Poland

Poland supplied about 100 troops to the International Security Assistance Force (ISAF) in Afghanistan while leading the Multinational Division Center South (MND-CS) in Iraq with 900 troops. Domestically, Poland hosted the global Proliferation Security Initiative (PSI) policy meeting in June, conducted a PSI maritime interdiction exercise in September, and cooperated with the United States in various counterterrorism training opportunities. There were no reported terrorist groups or incidents in Poland, but a growing population of Chechen migrants vulnerable to radicalization was a cause for concern.

Through the bilateral Joint Counterterrorism Working Group (JCTWG), Poland cooperated with various U.S. government agencies on synchronizing counterterrorism policy and training counterterrorism specialists. The United States trained 16 Polish Air Marshals, eight Polish officials in cargo inspection procedures, and about 100 Polish officials in topics ranging from bioterrorism to the psychology of terrorism.

Poland continued to closely monitor incoming Chechen migrants for signs of radicalization. According to the Office for the Repatriation of Foreigners, about 4,500 Chechens entered Poland in 2006. Most of them continued on to other EU destinations in search of work, however, approximately 5,500 Chechens were residing in Poland, of whom approximately 100 were known to be extremists.

Portugal

Portugal supported international efforts to combat terrorist networks and actively pursued indications of extremist group activity in Portugal. Portuguese government agencies took steps to minimize exploitation of its financial sector and to maintain the integrity of its passports and other documents.

On November 14, Portugal's Judicial Police (PJ) simultaneously executed 48 search warrants on small currency exchange operations. The effort, in cooperation with the Bank of Portugal, was intended to investigate money laundering operations with links to Lusophone Africa and South Asia that could be exploited by extremist organizations. The investigation into the "mixed Hawala" system netted equipment, documents, and over 300,000 Euros, but no arrests. Portugal announced it would restructure the Judicial Police to create four major operational commands regarding terrorism, corruption, drug trafficking, and technological investigation.

In August, Portugal began issuing biometric passports with greater protections than previous iterations. In addition to the additional security features, the new Portuguese passport law passed July 16 centralized the production of all passports to counter the fraudulent acquisition of Portuguese documents by criminal and extremist organizations. Portugal maintained its active participation in both the Proliferation Security Initiative and the Container Security Initiative.

Romania

Approximately 1,500 Romanian troops served in Iraq and Afghanistan as part of coalition and NATO efforts to combat terrorism and to deny terrorists operational and political opportunities. President Basescu reaffirmed his commitment to keep Romanian troops in Iraq and Afghanistan for as long as they are needed. Romania made available its airspace, ground infrastructure, and naval facilities to support U.S. and NATO forces. The Romanian frigate *Regina Maria* deployed from September to November with NATO counterterrorism forces in the Mediterranean Sea as part of Operation Active Endeavor.

The Romanian government strengthened its national policies as part of a strategic approach to combat terrorism. Romania included proactive language on counterterrorism in its National Security Strategy, in its National Antiterrorism Strategy, and in guidelines for preventing and combating terrorist financing activities. Romania continued to promote the Bucharest-based South East Europe Cooperation Initiative (SECI), a regional center that provides law enforcement training and intelligence sharing to prevent trans-border criminal activities, including terrorist-related activities, for the 12 member countries in South Eastern and Central Europe.

In April, Romania hosted the first meeting of counterterrorism chiefs within the framework of the Regional Conference of Interior Ministers under the Brdo Process (a regional initiative involving Interior Ministries from Central and Southern European states). In October 2005, the Government of Romania first released a list of over 250 individuals and legal entities suspected of committing or financing terrorist acts. The 21 official agencies that form Romania's National System to Prevent and Combat Terrorism routinely update this list based on information from the UN Security Council. The list was compiled by the Ministry of Public Finance, which was responsible for monitoring and blocking the movement of terrorist funds.

In October, the Romanian Parliament ratified the UN International Convention for the Suppression of Acts of Nuclear Terrorism; in November, it ratified two Council of Europe Conventions related to counterterrorism: the Convention on the Prevention of Terrorism and the Convention on Money Laundering, and the Search, Seizure, and Confiscation of Criminal Proceeds.

In June, a Romanian citizen, Ioan Les, was detained by Romanian intelligence agents near the town of Buzias in Western Romania, for allegedly planning an act of terrorism. According to Romanian authorities, the suspect was arrested in transit to Timisoara, where he planned to use a remote control device to blow up a car in the city center. The suspect told investigators that his motive was to force Romania to withdraw its troops from Iraq. Investigators linked the suspect to a Bosnia-based terrorist network. The Romanian Intelligence Service (SRI) placed Les under surveillance for several months after he allegedly made several threats via the internet to various entities, including CNN and Al-Jazeera television stations. Les was charged under a 29-day preventive arrest warrant.

Omar Hayssam, a businessman with strong connections both to the Arab world and the now-in-opposition Social Democratic Party (PSD) was arrested on terrorism-related charges in 2005 for his involvement in the abduction of three Romanian journalists and another businessman in Iraq. Although prohibited from leaving the country, Hayssam fled Romania for Syria on June 30, following his conditional April release on medical grounds. As a result of the ensuing public scandal, the General Prosecutor, the Police Information Service chief, and both Internal and External Intelligence chiefs resigned.

On November 13, four Romanian-Muslim citizens were arrested in Iasi under suspicion of supporting Middle Eastern terrorist groups. On November 14, an Iraqi citizen Shaker A. Shaker was arrested in Bacau under suspicion of terrorist-related activities. Romanian Intelligence Services had evidence that Shaker possessed a false passport, and that his real name was in fact Mahmoud Chaker, a former Iraqi Embassy diplomat, who had been deported previously from Romania in 2003 along with 40 other Iraqi citizens for planning terrorist attacks against Israeli interests in Bucharest.

Russia

The Russian government continued to view counterterrorism as a top priority and considered cooperation with the United States in this area as one of the pillars of the bilateral relationship. Much of the terrorist activity in Russia was homegrown and linked to both the Chechen separatist movement and in some ways, to separate, but overlapping, North Caucasus-wide extremism.

However, there was evidence of a foreign terrorist presence in the North Caucasus with financial and ideological ties to international terrorism. There were no high-profile terrorist incidents involving large numbers of civilian casualties, as had been the case in the four previous years.

Russian security forces carried out operations that led to the deaths of two significant terrorist leaders. In July, Russia's most wanted terrorist, Chechen separatist Shamil Basayev, was killed in the North Caucasus. Russian officials claim he was targeted by security forces but there were reports he was killed accidentally by his own explosives. In November, Abu Hafs al-Urdani, the AQ-linked, Jordanian-born commander of foreign separatist forces in Chechnya, was killed by security forces. In June Russian security forces killed Chechen separatist leader Abdul Khalim Sadulayev, whom the Russian government considered a terrorist, and who was nominal head of the Chechen separatist "government" to which Basayev belonged.

The most significant terrorist incident for Russia took place outside the borders of the Russian Federation. In June, five employees of the Russian Embassy in Baghdad were abducted and murdered, reportedly by members of the Mujahideen Shura Council, an umbrella group incorporating al-Qaida in Iraq. This was followed by a Presidential decree that ordered Russian security forces to "eliminate" those responsible and authorized the deployment of Russian security forces abroad to prevent "international terrorist activity."

The Russian government continued to take steps to improve coordination of counterterrorism activities and expand law enforcement responsibilities domestically. In February, President Putin signed a decree creating the National Counterterrorism Committee (NCC), to be headed by the Federal Security Service (FSB). The NCC was an effort to rationalize the decision-making process following the 2004 Beslan school siege, and was designed to establish a single chain of command and centralize the decision-making process at the national level, subordinating the Regional Counterterrorism Committees headed by governors. In March, the Russian legislature approved the law "On Counteracting Terrorism," which further defined the role of the NCC. The legislation expanded the concept of terrorism under Russian law, going beyond physical involvement in planning or carrying out terrorist attacks. Under the law, terrorism also included promotion of "terrorist ideas" and distributing materials or information to encourage terrorist activity or inciting individuals to commit a terrorist act.

The government provided further transparency about its counterterrorist efforts in July by releasing, for the first time, a list of 17 organizations it designated as terrorist entities. All entries to the list must be approved by the Supreme Court, and must meet the following criteria:

— Activities aimed at changing Russia's constitutional system through violence, including terrorism;

— Links to illegal armed groups and other extremist organizations operating in the North Caucasus; and

— Association with, or links to, groups regarded as terrorists by the international community.

The list includes the following organizations: AQ; Supreme Military Majlisul Shura of the Caucasus Mujahedin United Forces; Ichkeria and Dagestan People's Congress; Asbat al-Ansar; Holy War (Al Jihad or Egyptian Islamic Jihad); Islamic Group (Al-Gamaa al Islamia); Moslem Brothers (Al-Ikhvan al-Muslimun); Party of Islamic Liberation (Hiz'but-Tahrir al-Islami); Lashkar-I-Taiba; Islamic Group (Jamaat-i-Islami); Taliban Movement; Islamic Party of Turkestan (former Islamic movement of Uzbekistan); Social Reform Society (Jamiyat Ikhya al-Islakh al-Ijtimai); Islamic Heritage Renaissance Society (Jamiyat Ikhya at-Turaz al-Islami); Two Holies' House (Al Kharamein); Islamic Jihad—Mujahidin Jammat; and Jund ash-Sham.

There were three known organizations operating within the Russian Federation that the United States designated terrorist entities in February 2003, under Executive Order 13224. They have not been designated as Foreign Terrorist Organizations under 8 USC Section 1189. These include:

— The Special Purpose Islamic Regiment (SPIR). The SPIR was one of three Chechen-affiliated terrorist groups that furnished personnel to carry out the seizure of the Dubrovka Theater in Moscow in October 2003. It is not clear if the SPIR was still active, nor is it clear who commanded the organization.

— Riyadus-Salikhin Reconnaissance and Sabotage Battalion of Chechen Martyrs. The group had been led by Basayev. It used terrorism as part of an effort to secure an independent Muslim state in the North Caucasus. The group has not mounted a terrorist attack since the Beslan school attack in September 2004. The group's strength is probably no more than 50 fighters at any given time.

— Islamic International Peacekeeping Brigade (IIPB). The IIPB is a terrorist group affiliated with the Chechen separatist movement demanding a single Islamic state in the North Caucasus. Arab mujahedin still operating in Chechnya fell under the command of Abu Hafs al-Urdani, until his death in November. According to the pro-separatist website Kavkaz Center, Saudi national "Mukhanned" (full name not known) is the group's new commander. The IIPB has engaged in terrorist and guerrilla operations against Russian forces, pro-Russian Chechen forces, and Chechen non-combatants. At its peak, the group had up to 400 fighters, including as many as 100 Arabs and other foreign fighters, but almost certainly has suffered significant attrition. It operates primarily in Russia in adjacent areas of the North

Caucasus, particularly in the mountainous south of Chechnya, with major logistical activities in Georgia, Azerbaijan, and Turkey. The IIPB and its Arab leaders appear to be a primary conduit for Islamic funding of the Chechen guerrillas, in part through links to AQ-related financiers on the Arabian Peninsula. The IIPB was also listed under UNSCR 1267 for its associations with AQ, and the Terrorist Exclusion List.

Noteworthy court cases involving terrorist suspects included:

— In May, Nurpashi Kulayev was found guilty of all charges for his role in the 2004 Beslan school siege and was sentenced to life in prison. He was charged with murder and terrorism. Kulayev was the sole known survivor among the Beslan hostage takers. Kulayev claimed he did not kill anyone during the siege.

— In November, the highest court in the Russian Republic of Dagestan found Magomed Salikhov innocent of the 1999 apartment bombing that killed 64 people. Russian authorities cited that attack and a series of other bombings to justify sending troops back into Chechnya in 1999. The court had previously found Salikhov not guilty but that decision was overturned by the Federal Supreme Court, which ordered him retried.

— In December, Spanish police arrested suspected Chechen terrorist Murat Gasayev in Mislata, Valencia. Russian authorities were preparing an extradition request. Under Spanish law, Gasayev would first have to be found guilty in a Spanish court.

The United States and Russia continued to cooperate on a broad range of counterterrorism issues, including efforts to destroy, safeguard, and prevent the proliferation of WMD. The U.S.- Russian Counterterrorism Working Group (CTWG) met for its fifteenth session September 13–14 in Washington, fostering cooperative, operational links between numerous U.S. and Russian agencies. Law enforcement, intelligence, and policy cooperation have increased as a result of the work of the CTWG. At the St. Petersburg G8 Summit in July, the United States and Russia jointly announced the Global Initiative to Combat Nuclear Terrorism, and Russia and the United States invited other nations to join. The Initiative demonstrates Russia's effort to take a leadership role in establishing a partnership amongst nations to accelerate efforts to combat nuclear terrorism. Partner nations are committed to steps to combat nuclear terrorism in a variety of ways, to include safeguarding radioactive and nuclear materials, preventing nuclear smuggling, and sharing information. The first meeting of the Initiative took place in Morocco in October.

Russia was an active member of the Financial Action Task Force on Money Laundering and Terrorist Financing (FATF). Russia fulfilled its pledge to create a Eurasian FATF-style regional body (FSRB) in 2004, known as the Eurasia Group on Money Laundering (EAG), and as the group's leading force remained its chair. The EAG, whose members also include Belarus, China, Kazakhstan, Kyrgyzstan, and Tajikistan, made significant progress toward building Financial Intelligence Units (FIUs) and established the necessary legislative and regulatory frameworks in member states to help those states improve their compliance with international standards.

Russia used its position in international fora to build cooperative mechanisms and programs to counter terrorism. For example, Russia led efforts to make counterterrorism cooperation a key element in the Shanghai Cooperation Organization (SCO) and the Collective Security Treaty Organization (CSTO). Russia has also promoted counterterrorism within the framework of the Organization for Security and Cooperation in Europe, the G8, and the United Nations.

Serbia

Serbia was eager to cooperate with the United States on a wide range of issues including border security, information sharing, antiterrorism financing, and export control. Internally, the Serbian government consistently demonstrated a strong commitment to counterterror operations. Serbia and the United States signed an agreement on countering proliferation of weapons of mass destruction; the agreement was provisionally in force upon signature and awaited ratification by the Serbian parliament. While still largely complacent about the prospect of an attack in Serbia by international terrorists, Belgrade officials were significantly concerned about the potential for an increase of Middle Eastern terrorist transit through Serbia.

Kosovo

Kosovo's counterterrorism efforts were hampered by porous boundary lines easily crossed by individuals trafficking in people or goods. The Kosovo border police service is new and lacks basic equipment: Underpaid border and customs officials were often easily corrupted. While NATO has roving teams patrolling the green border right up to the border and administrative boundary lines, terrorists could exploit numerous passable roads leading into Kosovo.

The United Nations Interim Administration Mission in Kosovo (UNMIK) continued to administer Kosovo pursuant to UN Security Council Resolution 1244, and to monitor suspected terrorist activity with the Provisional Institutions of Self-Government (PISG). The Provisional Institutions and UNMIK monitored NGOs suspected of funding Islamic extremist and Albanian extremist movements. Officials believed only several of the more than 400 NGOs operating in Kosovo were involved in suspicious activities, and sought to prevent extremists from using NGOs to gain a foothold in Kosovo. Consequently, municipalities authorized NGO use of public facilities for religious gatherings only if the relevant religious community consented. The Kosovo Islamic Community (KIC) reported that it evaluated about 20 applications of mostly foreign NGOs and rejected four due to reservations about their proposed programs and participants.

The UNMIK Police's Counterterrorism Task Force (CTTF) is primarily responsible for Kosovo's counterterrorism efforts, and reported that its objectives shifted in 2006 from reactive to preventive measures. It received information and analysis support from the UNMIK Central Intelligence Unit (CIU) and the UNMIK Police Intelligence Liaison Unit (ILU). In October, with UNMIK Police's support and guidance, the Kosovo Police Service established its own Counterterrorism Unit (CTU), with six officers.

While there were no new terrorism cases, UNMIK's Department of Justice (DOJ) reported that intimidation of witnesses during investigation and trial phases hampered ongoing terror prosecutions. According to UNMIK's DOJ, a weak domestic witness protection program and the absence of witness relocation agreements to places outside of Kosovo made it difficult to convince witnesses to come forward. Moreover, international officials still handled terrorism cases due to concerns that local officials could be susceptible to intimidation.

While Kosovo officials struggled to bring the perpetrators of terrorist acts to justice, domestic extremists, acting individually and in groups, continued to commit violence, sometimes directed towards local government institutions and UN facilities. Approximately 15 attacks by such groups or individuals occurred and included use of hand grenades, rocket propelled grenades, explosive devices, and shots fired. There were a few fatalities and injuries as a result of these attacks. In early December, groups of armed, masked men reportedly presenting themselves as members of the Albanian National Army (AKSH), intermittently stopped pedestrians and vehicles in western Kosovo to check their identification documents. On December 5, the masked men fired at Kosovo Police Service officers in the village of Gercine near Gjakove. AKSH's Tirana-based spokesman, Gafurr Adili, told Kosovo media that these groups were not affiliated with the AKSH.

Slovakia

Slovakia contributed a team of 57 deminers and construction engineers to the International Security Assistance Force (ISAF) in Afghanistan and 112 personnel to Operation Iraqi Freedom (OIF). In late 2006 Slovakia decided to withdraw the bulk of its forces from Iraq with effect from February 2007.

Slovenia

Slovenia participated in four training sessions for dual-use licensing as part of its ongoing cooperation with the United States under the Export

Control and Border Security Program, as well as several Proliferation Security Initiative exercises. Slovenia continued to provide police instructors in Amman, Jordan, to train Iraqi policemen, instructors as part of the NATO training mission in Iraq, and troops as part of the International Stabilization Forces in Afghanistan.

Spain

Spain cooperated closely with the United States and worked aggressively to investigate and prosecute acts of terrorism, to prevent future attacks, and to disrupt terrorist acts that possibly were directed against U.S. interests.

Spain has decades of experience with terrorism involving the Basque terrorist group Basque Fatherland and Liberty (ETA). Despite the "permanent ceasefire" declared by the group in March, on December 30 the group exploded a massive car-bomb at Madrid's Barajas International Airport, killing two individuals. The government of Spanish President Jose Luis Rodriguez Zapatero announced political negotiations with the group had ended. ETA supporters continued to carry out acts of street violence and vandalism in the Basque region and Navarra. The group was weakened by the continued arrests of senior members and logistical supporters by Spanish and French authorities.

Spain arrested 47 individuals with possible links to al-Qaida and related extremist organizations. The National Court Chief Prosecutor reported in July that Spain held a total of 145 Islamist extremist terrorist suspects that were either under prison sentence or awaiting trial. Detainees included individuals arrested in 2004 for the March 11 train bombings and others for conspiring to bomb Spain's High Court. Authorities continued to hold eleven Pakistani nationals arrested in Barcelona in 2004, for allegedly providing logistical support to al-Qaida, and the prosecutor asked for sentences ranging from 22 to 32 years in jail. In April, the U.K. extradited Tunisian citizen Hedi Ben Youseff Boudhiba to Spain, where he was awaiting trial for membership in a Spanish terrorist cell that provided false passports and other identification to the March 11, 2004 bombers.

Spain remained both a target for international terrorist groups and an important transit point and logistical base for terrorist organizations operating in Western Europe. Spain did not serve as a safe haven for terrorists or terrorist organizations, but the large population of immigrants from North Africa, the opportunities that exist for raising funds through illicit activities, and the ease of travel to other countries in Europe, made Spain a strategic location for international terrorist groups. Spanish authorities put great effort into investigating, disrupting, and prosecuting members of such groups.

Many of the 2004 Madrid train bombing suspects had direct or indirect relationships with members of the Moroccan Islamic Combat Group (GICM), and, in 2006, several GICM members were arrested. A splinter group, known as the Moroccan Salafiya Jihadiya, was also increasingly on the radar screen of Spanish law enforcement.

The Salafist Group for Preaching and Combat (GSPC), who later in the year changed its name to al-Qaida in the Islamic Maghreb, was known to use Spain as a logistical base and transit point. Several alleged AQIM/GSPC members were arrested this year and Joan Mesquida, Director of the Police and Civil Guard, announced in November that the Spanish and French Ministries of Interior had created a "Joint Investigation Team" to investigate the financial network of the group. This was the first joint team the two countries have created to fight Islamist terrorism.

Spanish police worked to thwart terrorist facilitation networks that sought both to funnel potential extremists from Spain to Iraq, primarily through Syria, as well as bring fighters seasoned in Iraq into Spain. In November, police arrested four individuals charged with cooperating with an Islamist terrorist organization, forging official documents to support terrorist activities, and aiding extremists who tried to enter Spain after having fought in Iraq. In a separate case pending before Spanish courts, the national prosecutor will seek a prison sentence of 124 years for six alleged Islamist extremists arrested in January 2003 in Barcelona and Girona. These individuals are known in Spain as "The Detergent Command," because of their possession of large quantities of detergents that police believed were to serve as ingredients for explosive devices. In June, police arrested eleven individuals on charges of recruiting terrorists for terrorist organizations operating in Iraq.

Also in June, the Supreme Court reduced the prison sentence of Imad Eddin Barakat Yarkas, aka Abu Dahdah, from 27 years to 12 years. Barakat Yarkas, a Syrian immigrant to Spain, was detained in November 2001 on charges of providing support to AQ and of helping Mohammed Atta organize the September 11 terrorist attacks. Yarkas and 17 co-defendants were convicted in September 2005 for their roles in supporting AQ, but three codefendants were later released on appeal. Among those convicted was al-Jazeera journalist Taysir Alony, who was sentenced to seven years in prison for transporting funds from Yarkas to terrorists in Afghanistan under his cover as a journalist. Spanish authorities released Alony in October for humanitarian reasons stemming from a serious heart problem, but he remained under surveillance.

Spanish authorities continued their investigation into the March 2004 Madrid train bombings that killed 191 people and wounded hundreds of others, and the trials of 29 suspected perpetrators of the attacks were scheduled to begin in February 2007. This year, police arrested an additional 31 individuals in connection with the attacks, bringing to 110 the total number of suspects detained as part of the investigation. In November, Italian authorities extradited Egyptian national Osman El Sayed, known as "the Egyptian," to Spain in response to an international arrest warrant for his alleged role in the Madrid bombings. Later that month, Osman was sentenced in Italy to ten years in jail for international terrorist crimes.

Key arrests by Spanish security forces of suspected international terrorists included:

— January: A joint Civil Guard-SNP operation culminated in the arrest of 19 people associated with Islamist terrorism in Catalonia, Madrid, and Guipuzcoa Province (15 of them were sent to jail). Among the group arrested in Catalonia were seven Moroccans and one Spaniard who were alleged members of the GICM, and allegedly were responsible for sending the suicide bomber who struck the Italian base of Nasiriyah in southern Iraq in November 2003, killing 20 Italian soldiers.

— May: the Civil Guard arrested Issa Ben Othman in Barcelona, an alleged member of the terrorist network dismantled in the January operation. He was accused him of recruiting and sending foreign combatants to Iraq.

— November: Two individuals accused of belonging to the GICM and of having links with the 2003 Casablanca terrorist attack were arrested by Spanish police in Melilla.

— December: Spanish National Police arrested ten Spanish nationals and one Moroccan national in the North African enclave of Ceuta on charges that the men were plotting to carry out a terrorist attack.[5]

Spain continued to make progress in its decades-old campaign to eliminate the Basque Fatherland and Liberty (ETA) terrorist group, but a new phase in the struggle began in March when ETA declared a "permanent ceasefire." The government of President Jose Luis Rodriguez Zapatero agreed to begin peace talks with ETA and its outlawed political wing Batasuna if the group put an end to all violence. ETA supporters continued to engage in street violence and vandalism, and in October alleged ETA supporters stole 350 handguns from an armory in the French town of Vauvert. As of mid-December, Spanish authorities had arrested 15 individuals for membership in or association with ETA. On December 30, ETA exploded a massive

[5] Among the detainees were two brothers of former Spanish national Guantanamo detainee Hamed Abderrahaman Ahmed (known in Spain as the *Spanish Taliban*), whose conviction on terrorism charges was overturned earlier this year by the Spanish Supreme Court. According to initial reports, the eleven men were accused of membership in the GICM or the related "Al Haraka Salafiya Jihadiya" organization. In announcing the arrests, Minister of Interior Alfredo Perez Rubalcaba said the group had not selected a specific target, but was in the initial stages of planning an attack.

car-bomb that destroyed much of the covered parking garage outside the new Terminal 4 of Madrid's Barajas International Airport and effectively broke its nine-month "permanent cease-fire." Two individuals killed in the blast became ETA's first fatalities in more than three years. The government suspended talks with ETA, and government officials subsequently said political negotiations with the group had ended. The bombing came on the heels of extensive vandalism by street gangs in various Basque cities.

Spain cooperated with French authorities in its ETA effort, with French police arresting 22 suspected members and extraditing seven of them to Spain to stand trial. Cooperation with Mexico resulted in the extradition to Spain of four additional ETA members. Spanish authorities charged 41 members of ETA's illegal political front group Batasuna, including senior Batasuna figure Arnaldo Otegi, with membership in a terrorist organization and of providing financial support to ETA. Before the fatal December 30 airport bombing, ETA had carried out 12 bombings, all of them before the March 22 cease-fire announcement, resulting in injuries and significant property damage, but no fatalities.

Spain made great strides in disrupting terrorist cells and frustrating would-be terrorist plots. Under Spanish law, however, the standards of evidence for conviction are high and this affects terrorism cases. For example, the Spanish National Court in September 2005 convicted Spanish national Hamed Abderrahman (known as the "Spanish Taliban", who was transferred to Spain from the U.S. naval base at Guantanamo in February 2004 at the request of Spanish authorities), and sentenced him to six years imprisonment for membership in a terrorist organization. The Supreme Court overturned that decision in July. In its decision, the Supreme Court excluded all evidence obtained during the more than two years that Abderrahman spent in Guantanamo, as well as communications intercepts by Spanish authorities that had also served as evidence against him. It threw out other evidence collected against Abderrahman prior to his capture in Afghanistan and determined that prosecutors had skewed Abderrahman's testimony to incriminate him. This finding had an immediate affect on the case of Lahcen lkassrien, a Moroccan national and former Guantanamo detainee transferred to Spanish custody in July 2005. Spain's National Court, in October, acquitted lkassrien after finding insufficient evidence that he was a member of either AQ or of the Abu Dahdah terror cell in Spain, or that he fought alongside the Taliban in Afghanistan. The Court excluded the prosecution's evidence that was obtained during his detention in Guantanamo and any information gleaned from intercepted phone calls in Spain.

The U.S.—Spain Counterterrorism Working Group (CTWG) met in Madrid in October, and was addressed by U.S. Attorney General Gonzales, Spanish Minister of Justice Lopez Aguilar, and Spanish Attorney General Conde Pumpido.

The group helped foster counterterrorism cooperation between numerous U.S. agencies and their Spanish law enforcement and judicial counterparts. The sides agreed to designate a point of contact on counterterrorism issues in the U.S. Department of Justice and in the Spanish Prosecutors' office to streamline future collaborative efforts.

Spain participated in the Container Security Initiative to scan containers bound to the United States from the port of Algeciras for hazardous and illicit materials. The Megaports initiative was inaugurated in Algeciras in June. Spain and the United States co-chaired the Financial Action Task Force (FATF) Terrorism Finance Working Group, and Spain participated in all meetings of the G8 Counterterrorism Action Group (CTAG).

Sweden

In his first policy statement in October, newly elected Prime Minister Fredrik Reinfeldt called for increased international cooperation against terrorism, to include preventive measures and greater coordination of operational activities and intelligence. Authorities considered the threat of terrorist attacks in Sweden low, but monitored a number of known extremists and extremist organizations within the country. Such groups, including AQ, Ansar-Al-Islam, FARC, Hizb Al-Tahrir, Hizballah, and Islamic Jihad, provided logistical and financial support to their respective organizations abroad.

While the Government of Sweden did not provide safe haven for terrorists or terrorist organizations, terrorist organizations exploited its considerable legal protections of personal freedoms and civil liberties to maintain a presence in the country. Sweden's immigration policy, based on political asylum, attracted individuals from troubled countries, including some that sponsor terrorism.

The government augmented law enforcement funding and passed new laws to fight terrorism. In July, a law entered into force that enabled the military to assist police in responding to terrorist incidents. The Swedish government provided an extra $10 million to strengthen the work on serious crime and to increase capabilities at the Prosecutors Office and the National Police Board.

The Stockholm District Court in June convicted three men: 22-year-old Nima Ganjin, 25-year-old Andreas Fahlen, and 19-year-old Albert Ramic; for attempting to commit a terrorist act, and conspiracy to commit a terrorist act, in connection with a December 2005 botched arson attack on a Stockholm polling center for expatriate Iraqis. Prison sentences for the three ranged from two to three years. In September an appeals court reduced the sentences of Ganjin and Fahlen to two years for Mr. Ganjin, and 15 months for Mr. Fahlen, and reversed the conviction of Mr. Ramic.

In April, authorities in Bosnia and Herzegovina confirmed the indictment of Swedish citizen Mirsad Bektasevic on charges, inter alia, of terrorism under Article 201, Paragraph 1, in conjunction with Article 29 of the Criminal Code of Bosnia and Herzegovina. Bektasevic's formal trial opened in July and was ongoing. He has remained in Bosnian custody since his arrest in Sarajevo in 2005.

Pursuant to a U.S. arrest warrant and INTERPOL Red Notice, in December 2005, Czech authorities arrested Oussama Kassir, a Lebanese-born Swedish national, while he was in transit from Stockholm to Lebanon. Kassir is wanted in the United States on allegations that he conspired to provide material support to terrorists in the planned establishment of a terrorist training camp in Bly, Oregon. In June, a hearing was held to consider the extradition. Kassir remained in Czech custody pending continued consideration of the U.S. extradition request.

Swedish law did not provide the government independent national authority to freeze assets, unless in connection with an ongoing criminal investigation. Noteworthy cases concerning asset freezing included:

— In September, Sweden unfroze the assets of Ahmed Yusuf, one of three Swedes designated on UN and EU lists in 2002; after he was delisted from UNSCR 1267 and the EU formally de-listed him.

— In November, authorities froze assets of a grain trading company "al-Aqsa" in Malmo (southern Sweden), and arrested its head Marwan el-Ali; they subsequently released him and unfroze the assets due to lack of evidence.

— Subsequent to his listing in December 2006 under UNSCR 1267 (as well as U.S. and EU designations), Sweden froze the financial assets of, and imposed travel restrictions on AQ-linked Mohamed Moumou, a Swedish citizen of Moroccan origin.

Sweden actively contributed to EU counterterrorism efforts. Through the European Common Foreign and Security Policy (EFSP), Sweden coordinated EU counterterrorism cooperation with Morocco and Algeria. Sweden participated in EUROPOL and EUROJUST, European law enforcement institutions that coordinated member states' counterterrorism cooperation and activities. Further, the government participated in the Nordic Council of Ministers Regional Forum for Nordic Governmental Cooperation. Sweden contributed $900,000 to the Terrorism Prevention Branch of the United Nations Office on Drugs and Crime. It additionally provided $150,000 to the UN Counterterrorism Implementation Taskforce. In Asia, Sweden continued to provide funding for the Jakarta Center for Law Enforcement Cooperation, with a contribution of $150,000.

Switzerland

In 2006, the Swiss became more conscious of the presence of terrorist groups on their own soil, with the Swiss Federal Police describing Switzerland as a "jihadi field of operations" in its 2005 terrorism report. Due in part to increased pressure in neighboring EU countries, several non-al-Qaida terrorist groups, including the Tamil Tigers (LTTE), Kurdish Workers Party (PKK), and Colombian FARC, appeared to have increased their presence in Switzerland. Existing Swiss law and practice limited the government's ability to designate these as terrorist entities, but Swiss officials have expressed willingness to pursue criminal investigations of such "violent extremist" groups. Swiss officials have provided information to U.S. officials when information had a specific U.S. angle; however, law and practice continued to limit the scope of intelligence sharing and joint investigations.

The Department of Foreign Affairs (DFA) noted that, in the past, Swiss officials were primarily concerned that outside radical networks might try to use the country as a logistical base to raise money or support operations elsewhere. Whereas most terrorism suspects arrested or questioned after September 11, 2001, were foreigners just transiting, most of the ten North African suspects arrested for alleged involvement in a plot against a U.S. or Israeli commercial aircraft at Geneva or Zurich airport were immigrants who had been granted Swiss residency. The accused were believed to be members of the Salafist Group for Preaching and Combat (AQIM/GSPC).

On May 12, the Swiss Federal Police arrested seven North African terrorists in Basel and Zurich, following a lengthy investigation in Switzerland, including close cooperation with the police and legal authorities in several European countries. This operation was followed in July with the arrest of another North African terrorist in July and other arrests abroad.

In a parallel investigation, federal police arrested another AQIM/GSPC member in October following an international warrant issued by Italian authorities. Afif Mejri, also known as Lofti, is believed to be a member of a Milan cell that had raised 1.62 million Euros (SFr 2.57 million) to finance at least two AQIM/GSPC attacks on January 3, 2005, and another on March 27, 2005, in towns southwest of Algiers. Two others, Yacine Ahmed Nacer and Ali El Heit have been jailed in Italy since May 2005 for weapons trafficking for terrorist groups. Three other suspects, identified as Rabah Bouras, Lamine Ahmed Nacer and Farid Aider are fugitives and are believed to have left Europe last year. They are being sought on the more serious charge of having criminal associations with terrorism.

The Government of Switzerland estimated there were 4,000 sympathizers of the PKK/Kongra-Gel in Switzerland and approximately 100 individuals in the Kongra-Gel's central coordinating cadre, although no training camps were found in Switzerland during the last four years. Swiss police still experienced problems when tracking them, because their leaders changed jobs about every six months. Most Kongra-Gel's activities in Switzerland consisted of media relations, training management staff, and fundraising. Swiss authorities also noted that the Turkish Communist Party/Marxist-Leninists (TKP/ML) and the successor organizations of Devrimci Sol, the Revolutionary Peoples' Liberation Party/Front (DHKP-C), and the Turkish Peoples' Liberation Party/Front (THKP-C) remained active in Switzerland.

The Sri Lankan Ambassador to the UN in Geneva met with Swiss authorities on June 6, and expressed concerns about the presence of members of the separatist movement Tamil Tigers, and pointed to the EU's inclusion of the Tamil rebels on its terrorist list in May. While Norway is an official mediator in the Sri Lankan conflict, Switzerland has offered its services several times in the past. Swiss officials asserted that since September 2005, Switzerland "has implemented a very selective visa policy" for Sri Lanka, especially regarding sympathizers of Tamil rebels.

Similarly, the Colombian Ambassador raised concerns with Swiss officials over the presence of the Colombian Marxist guerrilla movement FARC in Switzerland. The Swiss press reported not only the presence of the FARC member Marcos Calarca, but also noted that the group's website was based in Switzerland.

Investigations continued against individuals suspected of supporting the 2002 Jerba and 2003 Riyadh bombings, although only three suspects remained imprisoned.

On March 29, the Federal Council agreed that authorities must be able to better supervise new technologies and in particular those related to the Internet.

Counterterrorism activities were carried out by several police units: the Federal Criminal Police's Counterterrorism Unit focused on al-Qaida-related cases and employed 21 officials—eleven working on terrorism, nine working on terrorism financing, and a chief. Another 15 analysts worked in the Department for Analysis and Prevention (DAP) in the Federal Office for Police. There were also 70 policemen in the cantons working on counterterrorism activities.

The Federal Council extended its ban on AQ and kept frozen approximately $28 million in AQ and Taliban assets in 82 separate accounts. One recent Swiss investigation centered on Al-Taqwa Management, a financial firm based in Switzerland until it went into liquidation in December 2001. The United States accused the company of funding al-Qaida. Al-Taqwa was founded in 1988 and was run from Lugano, canton Ticino, by its Egyptian-born managing director, Youssef Nada, and his Syrian-born associate, Ali Himat. The company is on the Office of Foreign Assets Control (OFAC)'s list of organizations accused of helping to fund terrorism and is listed under UNSCR 1267. Soon after the list was published, Swiss police raided the firm's headquarters in Lugano. The company's bank accounts, as well as those belonging to its board members, were subsequently frozen. Swiss authorities acknowledged that their investigations showed that the Al-Taqwa directors' ties to leadership could go back as far as the late 1990s.

In September, Switzerland and the United States co-sponsored the successful "Black Ice" bioterrorism coordination exercise in Montreux, hosting senior officials from numerous multilateral organizations. The Swiss also sponsored several conferences on civil infrastructure protection and terrorism finance under the auspices of NATO's Partnership for Peace.

Turkey

Domestic and transnational terrorist groups have targeted Turkish nationals and foreigners, including, on occasion, U.S. Government personnel, for more than 40 years. International and domestic terrorist groups that operated in Turkey included Kurdish separatist, Marxist-Leninist, radical Islamist, and pro-Chechen groups.

Most prominent among terrorist groups in Turkey is the Kurdistan Workers' Party (PKK), subject to regular name changes, currently operating as Kongra-Gel (KGK/PKK). Composed primarily of Kurds with a historically separatist agenda, the KGK/PKK operated from headquarters in part of northern Iraq and directed forces to target mainly Turkish security forces, government offices, and villagers who opposed the KGK/PKK. The Kurdistan Freedom Falcons (TAK), a group affiliated with the KGK, assumed responsibility for attacks on resort areas in southern and western Turkey, an attack on the office of a political party, and the bombing of a minibus carrying schoolchildren.

KGK/PKK attacks against Turkey increased significantly and claimed as many as 600 lives in 2006. In October, the KGK/PKK declared a unilateral cease-fire that slowed the intensity and pace of its attacks but attacks continued in response to Turkish security forces significant counterinsurgency and counterterrorism operations, especially in the southeast.

Other prominent terrorist groups included the Revolutionary People's Liberation Party/Front (DHKP/C), a militant Marxist-Leninist party with anti-U.S. and anti-NATO views that seeks the violent overthrow of the Turkish state; and Turkish Hizballah (not affiliated with Lebanese Hizballah), an organization of Sunni Kurds with a violent history, which appeared to be providing social services and promoting Sharia in parts of the southeast.

At year's end, a criminal trial was underway for the 72 defendants allegedly involved in the four November 2003 Istanbul bombings. The trial concluded on February 16, 2007, with 48 of the 72 receiving jail sentences.

Seven of those were sentenced to life in prison; 26 were acquitted. The lead defendants admitted to contacts with AQ and warned of further attacks. Most of the other defendants denied responsibility for, or knowledge of, the bombings. Four of the suspects, including the brother of one of the four suicide bombers, were released pending trial in May after spending more than two and half years in prison.

As of late November, Turkish prosecutors were seeking life imprisonment for Luay Sakka, a Syrian national linked to AQ and the Zarqawi network. Sakka was connected to the funding of the November 2003 Istanbul bombings and the deaths of U.S. and Coalition Forces in Iraq, and was allegedly plotting a terrorist attack on Israeli cruise ships in Turkish ports when he was apprehended in August 2005.

In addition to sharing intelligence information on various groups operating in Turkey, the Turkish National Police (TNP) and the National Intelligence Organization (MIT) conducted an aggressive counterterrorist campaign and detained numerous suspected terrorists in scores of raids, disrupting these groups before terrorist acts could be carried out. For example, in December, TNP counterterrorism units simultaneously raided ten addresses in Istanbul that were suspected of housing leftist militants. Twenty suspects were arrested. Turkish law defined terrorism as attacks against Turkish citizens and the Turkish state, and government left the definition unchanged when Parliament enacted a package of amendments to its antiterrorism law.

Turkey has consistently supported Coalition efforts in Afghanistan. After commanding ISAF II in 2002 and ISAF VII in 2005, in August, Turkey began a two-year joint rotational command of the International Security Assistance Force (ISAF) in Afghanistan for the Capital Regional Command along with France and Italy. Turkey also opened its first Provincial Reconstruction Team (PRT) in November in Wardak Province and pledged $100 million in humanitarian assistance for the reconstruction and operation of schools and hospitals.

Turkey has provided significant logistical support to Coalition operations in Afghanistan and Iraq, authorizing the use of Incirlik Air Base as an air-refueling hub for OEF and OIF and as a cargo hub to transport non-lethal cargo to U.S. troops in Afghanistan and Iraq. Almost 60 percent of air cargo for U.S. troops in Iraq transits Incirlik. Establishment of this hub allows six C-17 aircraft to transport the amount of goods it took nine to ten aircraft to move from Germany, and saves the United States almost $160 million per year.

One-third of the fuel (has been as high as two-thirds) destined for the Iraqi people and more than 25 percent of fuel for Coalition Forces transits from Turkey into Iraq via the Habur Gate border crossing. Turkey was active in reconstruction efforts, including providing electricity to Iraq. Turkish citizens continued to be killed, providing logistical support to Coalition Forces or performing reconstruction in Iraq. Turkey contributed headquarters personnel to the NATO Training Mission in Iraq (NTM-I), helped train Iraqi diplomats and political parties, and completed military leadership training in Turkey for 90 Iraqi officers as a further contribution to the NATO NTM-I.

The Financial Action Task Force (FATF) conducted a peer review of Turkey's regime against the financing of terrorism and money laundering in September and planned to publicize the report in early 2007. Pursuant to its obligations under UNSCR 1267 and subsequent resolutions, Turkish officials continued to pass UN and U.S.-designated names of terrorists to all law enforcement and intelligence agencies, as well as to financial institutions. Only UN-designated names, however, were subjected to asset freezes enforced through a Council of Ministers decree. This legal mechanism for enforcing the sanctions under UNSCR 1267 was challenged in Turkish courts by UN-designated terrorist financier Yasin al-Qadi. A lower-court ruled in July that the Council of Ministers lacked the authority to freeze assets, but in February 2007, an appeals court overturned the lower court ruling and confirmed the Council of Ministers' authority to freeze. In the meantime, al-Qadi's assets remain frozen. Separately, in October, Parliament enacted legislation to reorganize MASAK, Turkey's anti-money laundering agency, which doubled as Turkey's Financial Intelligence Unit. This law explicitly criminalized terrorism finance and provided legal protections for filers of suspicious transaction reports.

Ukraine

Ukraine did not suffer from domestic terrorism incidents, although law enforcement authorities sometimes labeled ordinary criminal activity as terrorist acts. Still, the Ukrainian government instituted legislative and regulatory changes to improve its ability to investigate and prosecute acts of terrorism. In September, the Ukrainian Parliament amended the Criminal and Criminal Proceedings Codes of Ukraine to conform to commitments resulting from Ukraine's ratification of the Council of Europe Convention on Prevention of Terrorism. The amendments to the codes introduced punishments for inducing people to participate in an act of terror, public calls to commit an act of terror, formation of a terrorist group/organization, and facilitating an act of terror through provision of financing, material, or arms. The Ukrainian State Financial Monitoring Agency signed bilateral agreements with Croatia, Canada, and China, which stipulated cooperation in the prevention of money laundering and prevention of terrorist financing. Ukrainian banks and other financial institutions were required to screen all transactions against a consolidated list of terrorists approved by the Cabinet of Ministers.

United Kingdom

There were no successful terrorist attacks in the United Kingdom in 2006. In August, British, Pakistani, and American officials worked together to disrupt a terror plot involving British citizens intent on detonating aircraft traveling between the United Kingdom and the United States. The British government arrested over 20 individuals suspected of being involved in that plot, many of whom were subsequently charged with criminal acts and intent to carry out acts of terrorism. Their cases remained before the courts. Some of those arrested had spent time in or had ties to Pakistan. The British and American governments instituted new restrictions to trans-atlantic airline travel in response to the revealed airline plot. The United States and United Kingdom enjoyed a wide-range of bilateral information sharing on threat assessments and terror networks, and government responses to both. Cooperation in derailing the transatlantic terror plot in August was evidence of the ability of the two governments to work together, in real-time, to avert loss of life from terrorism.

The British government acknowledged the existence of some 200 known terror networks in the United Kingdom. In November, Dame Eliza Manningham-Buller, head of the domestic security service (known as MI5), made a stark announcement that there were some "1,600" individuals, "200 networks," and an estimated "30 terror plots" in the United Kingdom. The British government viewed radicalization of young people in the U.K. and elsewhere, regardless of whether those radicalized in the U.K. had ties to AQ or are "homegrown," as a growing threat to international and British security.

The government enacted new counterterrorism legislation that made the "glorification of terrorism" illegal, and expanded the government's ability to detain terror suspects before charging them. The government has a mechanism for deporting foreign terror suspects to their home countries once those countries agreed to provide assurances that the suspects' human rights will not be violated upon their return. The courts tried and convicted several prominent terror suspects involved in terror plots prior to 2006. The British government also increased its efforts at outreach to Muslim communities within the U.K. It sought to support advocates of moderate interpretations of Islam and to gain support from within British Muslim communities to counter the appeal of extremist ideology and radicalization.

The United States and the U.K. worked closely within the UN and the FATF to deny terrorists and their supporters access to the international financial system. The United Kingdom had strong legal provisions for freezing assets related to terrorist financing, including the Terrorism (United Nations Measures) Order 2001, the al-Qaida and Taliban (United Nations Measures) Order 2001, and the Antiterrorism Crime and Security Act 2001. In October, the British government took measures to further strengthen its terrorist financing legislation when Chancellor Gordon Brown announced that Her Majesty's Treasury, on the advice of law enforcement agencies, had agreed to use "closed source evidence" (classified materials) in asset freezing cases where there were strong operational reasons to impose a freeze but insufficient unclassified information available. He also announced that the government would seek to amend its existing domestic legislation to give "the Treasury the power to stop funds reaching anyone in the U.K. suspected of planning terror or engaging with terror."

Northern Ireland

Political progress in Northern Ireland, including prospects for the establishment of a devolved government and continuing cease-fires by paramilitary organizations, have created a marked decrease in terrorist incidents in Northern Ireland. In October, the Independent Monitoring Commission (IMC), which was established in 2004 by the British and Irish governments to monitor progress made by paramilitary groups in ending their violent activities, reported that evidence showed the Provisional Irish Republican Army had committed itself to following a peaceful path.

Loyalist paramilitary groups, however, were thought to be responsible for two killings in Northern Ireland from September 2005 to August 2006. The IMC was unable to place blame in three other killings, including the April murder of Sinn Fein member Denis Donaldson, who admitted publicly in December 2005 to having been a British spy.

Loyalist paramilitary Michael Stone disrupted a session of the Northern Ireland Assembly on November 24 as he tried to enter the parliament building with a viable bomb, a knife, and an imitation pistol. Afterwards, Stone, who was sentenced to over 600 years in prison for killing three mourners at a 1988 Sinn Fein funeral but released in 2000 under the terms of the 1998 Good Friday Agreement, had his license for liberty under that agreement revoked. He will now serve out the remainder of his term and faces additional charges stemming from the November 24 incident including attempted murder for targeting the leader of Sinn Fein (Gerry Adams).

Country Reports: Middle East and North Africa Overview

"In Saudi Arabia, we strongly believe that international cooperation is crucial for fighting terrorism. It also goes without saying that the will and resolve to fight terrorism must begin at home; the national will then must be extended to a universal collective resolve, for no country can afford to stay on the sidelines."

Prince Saud Al-Faisal
Foreign Minister of Saudi Arabia

Address to Britain's Royal United Services Institute
London; January 16, 2006

Iraq remained at the center of the War on Terror battling al-Qaida and affiliated terrorist organizations, insurgent groups fighting against Coalition Forces (CF), militias and death squads increasingly engaged in sectarian violence, and criminal organizations taking advantage of Iraq's deteriorating security situation. Terrorist organizations and insurgent groups continued to attack Coalition Forces primarily utilizing improvised explosive devices (IEDs) and vehicle-borne improvised explosive devices (VBIEDs). The U.S. Government continued with focused efforts to mitigate the threat posed by foreign fighters in Iraq, coordinating both with the interagency and with our embassy officials overseas. State sponsors of terrorism, Iran and Syria, continued to play destabilizing roles in the region. (See Chapter 3, *State Sponsors of Terrorism.*)

Israel faced a new situation when HAMAS, a designated Foreign Terrorist Organization, assumed control of the Palestinian Authority's (PA) Palestinian Legislative Council (PLC). After HAMAS' election win in January, the Israeli government declared it would not meet with PA representatives, and that it would hold HAMAS responsible for all terrorist attacks and rocket launches emanating from PA territory.

In the past year, major terrorist attacks occurred in Algeria, Iraq, Saudi Arabia, Israel, Lebanon, and Egypt. In Lebanon, in addition to the war precipitated by Hizballah against Israel in July, political violence continued throughout the year. Most notable was the assassination of Industry Minister Pierre Gemayel by a team of gunmen in the streets of a northern suburb of Beirut on November 21. This act, the latest in a series of assassinations and attempted assassinations over the last two years, seemed designed to inflame tensions and intimidate forces opposing Syrian interference in Lebanon. Algiers experienced its first terrorist attacks since 2004, including one that targeted westerners. Past attacks targeted Algerian government interests. On April 24 in Egypt, three suicide bombers detonated their explosive charges in rapid succession at three popular tourist locations in the Sinai resort town of Dahab. The bombers killed at least 24 people, including six foreigners. At least 87 were injured, among them four Americans and 25 other foreigners. In Saudi Arabia, one failed attack attempted to target a critical petroleum installation.

Almost all governments in the region cooperated with the United States in counterterrorist activities and undertook efforts to strengthen their capabilities to fight the War on Terror. These efforts included active participation in USG-sponsored antiterrorism assistance (ATA) programs and bolstering banking and legal regimes to combat terrorist financing. Many countries continued to provide some form of assistance to Coalition efforts to bring peace and stability to Iraq and Afghanistan.

The United States rescinded Libya's designation as a state sponsor of terrorism on June 30. Full diplomatic relations were resumed and Libya continued to cooperate closely with the United States and the international community on counterterrorism efforts.

Some countries made impressive strides. In Saudi Arabia, the government announced in December that it had captured 136 suspected terrorists over a three month period. In Morocco and Jordan, authorities disrupted a number of terrorist cells, some with connections to AQ and the Salafist Group for Preaching and Combat (GSPC), now known as al-Qaida of the Islamic Maghreb (AQIM). The Government of Jordan moved forward with prosecuting several terrorism-related cases, including the sentencing of seven individuals connected to the 2005 Amman hotel bombings. The Kuwaiti government sentenced several individuals who intended to travel to Iraq to join the insurgency. In Algeria, as part of the government's National Reconciliation Project, over 350 terrorists turned themselves over to authorities. The Moroccan government continued to implement internal reforms that aimed to address the socioeconomic conditions extremists exploit for recruitment.

The Summer War

On July 12, Hizballah terrorists entered Israel from southern Lebanon, abducted two Israeli soldiers and killed eight others. During the next 34 days, Hizballah fired over 4,000 Katyusha rockets and other missiles into northern Israel, forcing the residents of Haifa, Nahariya, Tiberias, and other northern communities into bunkers. Hizballah also launched weaponized drones toward Israel and struck an Israeli naval vessel with an anti-ship missile. Israel responded by sending the Israeli Air Force (IAF) to attack rocket launchers and Hizballah infrastructure throughout southern Lebanon and in select areas north of the Litani River. The IAF also bombed Hizballah offices in southern Beirut, and roads, bridges, and power plants throughout Lebanon. Israeli Defense Force (IDF) artillery struck Hizballah targets in southern Lebanon and paved the way for an incursion of more than a division of mechanized and infantry forces into southern Lebanon, aimed at pushing Hizballah forces north of the Litani River and laying the groundwork for a cessation of hostilities. During this period, Israel imposed an air and sea blockade on Lebanon to prevent the resupply of Hizballah by Syria and Iran. At least 110 Israeli soldiers and 43 Israeli civilians died in the conflict. The conflict also resulted in more than 1,000 Lebanese civilian deaths, and four UN observers died following an Israeli air attack.

The war ended with a UN-sponsored cessation of hostilities on August 14. Despite the cessation of hostilities and the deployment of Lebanese Armed Forces (LAF) and additional United Nations Interim Forces in Lebanon (UNIFIL) troops in the south, Lebanese militias, particularly designated

Foreign Terrorist Organization Hizballah, retained significant influence over parts of the country. UN Security Council (UNSC) resolutions 1559 and 1701 required the government to take effective control of all Lebanese territory and disarm militia groups operating in Lebanese territory. Due to several factors, including internal political differences, resource shortages, and the unstable political situation following the conflict, the government was not able to disarm fully various extralegal armed groups or Hizballah. The conflict did not resolve Hizballah's claim of its right to conduct hostile operations against Israel along the Blue Line on the premise of legitimate self-defense of Lebanese territory and sovereignty. Hizballah has contended, with the support of many Lebanese, that the Shebaa Farms area of the Israeli-occupied Golan Heights is Lebanese territory.

The Israeli government and IDF report they dealt a serious blow to Hizballah, degrading its medium to long-range missile capability, destroying its infrastructure in southern Lebanon, and killing up to 700 of its fighters. By the end of the year, however, Israeli security experts suggested that Hizballah had recovered much of its manpower and equipment losses through recruitment and resupply from Syria and Iran. Hizballah nonetheless was keeping a low profile on the Israel-Palestinian border, and the provocations that preceded the July outbreak of hostilities have not resumed.

Algeria

For the majority of 2006, the security situation in Algeria remained relatively unchanged, marked by stability in the major urban areas and low-level terrorist activities in the countryside. The last quarter of the year, however, witnessed four attacks in the province of Algiers, including one that targeted Westerners. These were the first attacks inside the province since 2004. Until these recent attacks, terrorism in Algeria was generally not aimed at foreign entities. Instead, the country's major terrorist group, the Salafist Group for Preaching and Combat (GSPC), preferred to target Algerian government interests.

Two events helped fuel terrorism concerns in Algeria: the GSPC's September merger with al-Qaida and the conclusion of the amnesty period for Algeria's National Reconciliation project. Following al-Qaida's September 11 announcement of the GSPC's status as an AQ affiliate in North Africa, the group changed its name to al-Qaida in the Islamic Maghreb (AQIM), and subsequently made more threats against what it termed "crusading" westerners, particularly American and French citizens. On October 19, an improvised explosive device (IED) exploded outside a military barracks in an Algiers suburb, wounding six; and on October 30 two bombs killed two persons approximately 20 kilometers from downtown Algiers. On December 10, a shuttle bus carrying expatriate workers of an American oil services company was ambushed in an Algiers suburb thought to be secure because of its proximity to residences of senior government officials and a major western hotel. This attack, done with a road-side IED, killed two foreigners and wounded several others, including an American worker. The terrorists escaped. The December 10 attack against a relatively soft American target generated greater global media attention than nearly all of AQIM/GSPC past attacks against Algerian government targets. Given the success of this attack in terms of media attention, the AQIM/GSPC likely will attempt further attacks.

Even before its affiliation with AQ, the GSPC was an organization whose regional ties were expanding. AQIM/GSPC support cells have been discovered and dismantled in Spain, Italy, Morocco, and Mali; it maintains training camps in the Pan-Sahel. The AQIM/GSPC's regional scope, however, is thought to be the result of successful Algerian security service and military operations against it on Algerian soil that compelled it to operate outside Algerian territory. The Algerian services killed approximately 260 terrorists and arrested an additional 450 in 2006, compared to the combined killed and arrested figure of about 400 for 2005.

The counterterrorism successes of the Algerian services, combined with the public's continued rejection of terrorists, led the AQIM/GSPC to seek new methods to finance attacks. Algerian media reported the use of extortion in concert with 16 instances of fake roadblocks and 55 kidnappings inside Algeria. The kidnappings, sometimes in coordination with fake roadblocks, often targeted wealthy Algerians. Not all these methods were attributed solely to the AQIM/GSPC as there was also a growing crime problem in Algeria. AQIM/GSPC terrorists such as Mokhtar Belmokhtar have also taken an active role in regional smuggling to finance terrorism.

The final stages of implementation of the national reconciliation, a major policy initiative of Algerian President Abdelaziz Bouteflika, took place in 2006, and sought to bring closure to the near civil war between Algeria's secular government and Islamic terrorists in the 1990s. A cornerstone of this initiative was the six-month amnesty program from March to September 2006 for repentant imprisoned or active terrorists who had not committed bombings, massacres, or rapes. As of September, over 2,300 convicted terrorists were released and more than 350 terrorists surrendered to authorities in order to benefit from the amnesty; statistics on the recidivism of these individuals were not available. Despite a September deadline for amnesty, the government has quietly extended the amnesty grace period indefinitely. In addition, some members of the banned political party Islamic Salvation Front returned to the country from self-imposed exile as part of the amnesty.

The National Reconciliation policy was an effort to resolve divisions that had resulted during more than a decade of civil strife. The amnesty, however, paradoxically appeared to harden the resolve of the remaining terrorists. Indeed, there were reports of terrorists killing cohorts who surrendered to the authorities. During the March through September amnesty period, 199 security officials and civilians were killed, compared to 107 during the rest of the year. Perhaps as a show of defiance and renewed determination, the AQIM/GSPC was responsible for the death of 78 security officials and civilians in October and November, immediately after the amnesty period ended. The AQIM/GSPC, thanks in part to high unemployment among Algerian youth, was partially successful in replenishing its numbers after the arrests, surrenders, and deaths of over 1,000 terrorists. Those remaining appear to be more hard-line and resistant to the government's amnesty offer.

Despite the upsurge of AQIM/GSPC activity toward the end of the year, overall, the government has greatly improved security from the situation of the late 1990s. The Algerian security services and military remained capable of handling the prolonged effort against internal terrorist threats and continued to be a reliable ally in the War on Terror.

Bahrain

In 2006, the Government of Bahrain enacted important legislation to combat terrorism and its financing. In August, Bahrain enacted its first law (Law 58 of 2006) specifically criminalizing terrorism. The law, officially titled "Protecting Society from Terrorist Acts," enumerated the types of crimes considered to be terrorism and established punishments, ranging up to and including the death penalty. The law criminalized conspiracy to carry out an act of terror, although it did not specify a precise penalty of imprisonment or fine.

In August, the King signed amendments to an anti-money laundering law (Law 4 of 2001) that specifically addressed terror financing. These amendments criminalized the undeclared transfer of money across international borders for the purpose of money laundering or in support of terrorism. Anyone convicted under the law of collecting or contributing funds, or otherwise providing financial support to a group or people who practiced terrorist acts, was subject to imprisonment and/or fine. Law 54 also codified a legal basis for a disclosure system for cash couriers although the government must still enact supporting regulations.

The new law included a definition of terrorism based upon the Organization of the Islamic Conference definition. The law excludes from the definition of terrorism acts of struggle against invasion or foreign aggression, colonization, or foreign supremacy in the interest of freedom and the nation's liberty, according to the principles of international law. There are various legal interpretations about the possible application of this clause, and its impact is not yet known.

Bahrain actively monitored terrorist suspects. Domestic legal constraints, particularly prior to the promulgation of the new counterterrorism and CFT laws, at times have hamstrung its ability to detain and prosecute suspects. The legal case of four Bahrainis arrested in mid-2004 on suspicion of plotting terrorist attacks was resolved conclusively on November 20 when Bahrain's Higher Criminal Court ruled that the four accused were not guilty of any remaining charges. This step followed a June 26 ruling by the Constitutional Court that conspiracy charges filed against the suspects were unconstitutional.

In September, security services arrested eight Bahrainis on suspicion of planning possible terrorist activities. During the interrogations, several of the suspects admitted they intended to travel to Afghanistan to fight allied forces. The prosecutor general subsequently decided he did not have enough evidence to charge them under the counterterrorism law and released them on bond in late September.

Bahrain continued to host the Middle East and North Africa Financial Action Task Force (MENA FATF) secretariat. At the Bahraini government's request, the International Monetary Fund and World Bank conducted a financial sector assessment program (FSAP). The FSAP made recommendations to improve the anti-money laundering/combating the financing of terror environment in Bahrain, among other items. The Bahraini delegation briefed MENA FATF members on the FSAP during the November plenary in Abu Dhabi.

Egypt

Egypt was a victim of domestic terrorism in 2006. On April 24, three suicide bombers detonated explosive charges in rapid succession at three popular tourist locations in the southern Sinai resort town of Dahab. The bombers killed at least 24 people, including six foreigners. At least 87 were injured, among them four Americans and 25 other foreigners. As with the 2005 triple bombing in Sharm el-Sheikh, the attacks seemed to target the Egyptian tourism industry, not Americans or foreigners specifically.

On April 26, two suicide bombers attacked a vehicle belonging to the Multinational Force and Observers (MFO) in northern Sinai and the Egyptian police, but the bombers were the only casualties. In the first attack, a suicide bomber wearing a belt bomb threw himself on the hood of an unarmored MFO vehicle, shattering the windshield. In the second attack, several kilometers away, another man with a belt bomb rode a bicycle to an Egyptian police vehicle and blew himself up. The police vehicle was responding to the first attack on the MFO vehicle.

Following these attacks, Egyptian police conducted major security sweeps of the Sinai. According to police, al-Tawhid wa al-Jihad ("Unity and Holy War"), an indigenous group comprised mostly of radicalized Bedouin extremists was responsible for the Sinai bombings. Although the group espouses a pro al-Qaida, Salafist ideology, there were no indications the group was specifically targeting Americans. Egyptian authorities believed they have arrested or killed most of its leadership and operational planners, but members are very likely still at large in the Sinai.

Although al-Tawhid wa al-Jihad was the only terrorist group to successfully commit attacks in Egypt this year, the Egyptian government broke up two other alleged terrorist groups before the groups could conduct operations. One group was reportedly planning attacks; the other was reportedly planning to send foreign fighters to Iraq. There was no further evidence of operational domestic or foreign terrorist groups in the country.

The Egyptian government's well-known opposition to Islamist terrorism and its effective intelligence and security services have made it less likely that terror groups will seek safe haven there. However, Egypt's rugged northern Sinai region remained a haven for smuggling arms and explosives into Gaza and a transit point for Gazan Palestinians trying to infiltrate Israel. In addition, Palestinian HAMAS officials have allegedly carried millions of U.S. dollars in cash across the Gaza-Egypt border. Criminal networks that smuggle weapons and other contraband through the Sinai into Israel and the Gaza Strip may be associated with or used by terrorist groups in the region. The apparent radicalization of some Sinai Bedouin might be linked in part to these smuggling networks, to heavy-handed Egyptian efforts to dismantle them, and to the Bedouin's long-standing distrust of the central government.

In the past three years, Egypt has tightened its terror finance regulations. Egypt maintained its strengthened security measures for airports, seaports, and the Suez Canal.

The Egyptian judicial system does not allow plea bargaining, and terrorists have historically been prosecuted to the full extent of the law. Terrorism defendants may be tried in military tribunals or emergency courts. Under the framework of the Mutual Legal Assistance Treaty, the Egyptian regime provided evidence for counterterrorism cases in the United States.

Many of the Egyptian President's far-reaching counterterrorism authorities are derived from a decades-old Emergency Law that was renewed by Parliament in 2006 for two years. President Mubarak called for new counterterrorism legislation to replace the Emergency Law. Such legislation is reportedly being drafted by a governmental interagency committee, although pursuit of the legislation will likely follow passage and public approval of constitutional amendments which maintain wide latitude for government action against terrorist suspects.

Iran

See Chapter 3, State *Sponsors of Terrorism*.

Iraq

Iraq remained at the center of the War on Terror with the Iraqi Government and the Coalition battling al-Qaida in Iraq (AQI) and affiliated terrorist organizations, insurgent groups fighting against Coalition Forces (CF), militias and death squads increasingly engaged in sectarian violence, and criminal organizations taking advantage of Iraq's deteriorating security situation. Terrorist organizations and insurgent groups continued to attack CF primarily using Improvised Explosive Devices (IEDs) and Vehicle-Borne Improvised Explosive Devices (VBIEDs). The Iraqi government universally condemned terrorist groups and supported CF against AQI and its affiliates.

The June 7 death of AQI's leader, Abu Musab al-Zarqawi, damaged the group's leadership but did not diminish attacks against Coalition Forces and Iraqis nor did it halt overall increasing attack trends by the group. AQI's new leader is Abu Ayyub al-Masri, also known as Abu Hamza al-Muhajir. January press reports indicated that AQI teamed with several smaller Sunni Islamist groups devoted to continuing the insurgency calling themselves the Mujahideen Shura Council. By the end of the year, this group had renamed itself the Islamic State of Iraq. AQ and affiliated groups continued attacks on Iraq's infrastructure and claimed responsibility for kidnappings and attacks against Coalition Forces.

The Government of Iraq sponsored reconciliation programs to reduce the sources of violence. The government organized conferences involving tribal and religious leaders, politicians, and civil society organizations to counter support for terrorist organizations and to promote dialogue between Iraq's ethnic and religious groups in an effort to decrease violence. Tribal leaders in Ramadi, a volatile city in Anbar province, banded together late in the year and pledged to fight against AQ instead of the coalition. While the tribal leaders' full effectiveness remained uncertain, this represented an important step.

Iraq's sectarian divide increased dramatically following the February 22 bombing of the al-Askariyah Mosque, one of the holiest sites to Shia Muslims, located in Salah ad Din province. While violence against both CF and Iraqis had increased prior to the bombing, this event exacerbated sectarian tensions and led to increased violence in Iraq's ethnically-mixed areas, especially Baghdad. Sectarian attacks, including car bombs, suicide vests, sniper fire, targeted assassinations, and death squad murders, occurred on a close-to-daily basis with Iraqi civilians suffering the majority of causalities. Iraq's sectarian violence furthered the terrorists' goals by creating instability and weakening the government.

Neighboring countries, specifically Iran, continued to interfere in Iraq's internal affairs by allowing, condoning, or in some cases, actively smuggling weapons, people, materials, and money to terrorist, insurgent, and militia groups inside Iraq. Iranian agents and sympathizers utilized an 800-mile long, porous border with limited security to transport goods, which increasingly included Iranian-made weapons such as IEDs or their components, which proved effective in attacks against Coalition Forces.

In recent statements, Iraqi government leaders, including the Prime Minister, the President and the Foreign Minister, have called on neighboring countries to stop interfering in Iraq's internal affairs and to stop supporting elements actively fighting against Iraq's elected government. Syria's Foreign Minister traveled to Baghdad and agreed to cooperate more closely on border security in an effort to reduce the number of foreign fighters entering Iraq. Senior Iraqi officials, including Iraqi President Talabani, traveled to Iran throughout the year encouraging the Iranian government to support Iraq's political process and to stop material support of terrorist groups and militias.

To demonstrate that the Iraqi government does not wish to allow Iraq to become a safe haven for terrorist organizations, Prime Minister al-Maliki appointed the Minister of State for National Security, Shirwan al-Waeli, as the Iraq coordinator for issues involving the Kurdistan Workers Party (Kongra-Gel/PKK), a designated Foreign Terrorist Organization. Tension between Turkey and the Iraqi government increased as Turkish leaders expressed increasing frustration at what they viewed as Iraq's inaction against the PKK.

Although Iraq is a proven ally in the War on Terror, Iraq's developing security and armed forces will require further training and resources before they can effectively address the terrorist groups already operating within their borders. Iraq's intelligence services continued to improve in both competency and confidence, but they also will require additional support before they will be able to adequately identify and respond to internal and external terrorist threats. The international community's support for investment and reconstruction are critical components needed to ensure that the Government of Iraq's plans to reduce violence, improve services, and increase economic opportunities are successful.

Israel, the West Bank, and Gaza

Israel faced a new situation when HAMAS, a designated Foreign Terrorist Organization, assumed control of the Palestinian Authority's (PA) Palestinian Legislative Council (PLC). After HAMAS' electoral victory in January, the Israeli government declared it would not meet with PA representatives, initiated a diplomatic campaign to secure international isolation of the HAMAS-led PA government, and withheld the disbursement of hundreds of millions of dollars of value-added tax and customs revenues collected by Israel on behalf of the PA. Following the formation of a new

HAMAS-led government in March, the Israeli government declared it would hold HAMAS responsible for all terrorist attacks and rocket launches emanating from PA territory. IDF officials were instructed to suspend all contact with Palestinian security forces in the Gaza Strip. Israeli security experts increasingly expressed concern that terrorist know-how and capabilities would be transferred from the Gaza Strip to the West Bank.

Throughout the year, Israel grappled with the problem of Qassam rocket launches from the Gaza Strip. On numerous occasions, rockets struck Israeli communities in the western Negev desert, including Sderot, or landed near or in the city of Ashkelon. Evidence suggested that Palestinian terrorists were able, on occasion, to improve the range of the Qassams. On at least three occasions, longer-range Katyusha rockets were launched from the Gaza Strip. To address the problem of rocket launches from populated areas, the IDF modified its rules of engagement to permit its forces to fire on targets a few hundred meters from Palestinian homes and police positions. During an IDF incursion into the northern Gaza Strip in November (Operation Autumn Cloud), an errant IDF artillery strike destroyed an apartment complex, and killed 18 Palestinian civilians and wounded over 50. A HAMAS spokesman called on all Palestinian factions to renew attacks, including suicide bombings, inside Israeli territory. Beginning in late November, however, HAMAS was the primary group observing a cessation of rocket fire from Gaza into green-line Israel. Although other groups have disregarded the cease-fire, HAMAS has upheld it, according to Israeli security experts.

Israel also grappled with a growing concern that terrorists, weapons, and funds were being smuggled between Egypt and the Gaza Strip through the Rafah crossing—manned by the PA Border Crossing Authority, international observers, and Egyptian border guards—and a series of tunnels under the 12 km Philadelphi Corridor (PC) separating Gaza from Egypt. Israeli security experts voiced concern that Palestinian militants were exiting the Gaza Strip via Rafah, and then infiltrating Israel across the Egypt-Israel border. After HAMAS staged a June 25 attack on IDF soldiers near Kerem Shalom that resulted in two deaths and the abduction of Corporal Gilad Shalit, Israel took steps that severely limited the operation of the Rafah crossing. The IDF also carried out operations to locate tunnels under the PC, destroying at least 17 during the year.

Early in 2006, Israeli security officials said Israel was not targeting HAMAS because it forbade its members to participate in Qassam rocket launches. The Israelis maintained, however, that HAMAS activists were providing assistance to militants from other terrorist groups launching Qassams. HAMAS called Palestinian Islamic Jihad's (PIJ) April 17 suicide bombing attack in Tel Aviv a legitimate act of resistance. PIJ launched Qassam rockets into Israel, carried out the January 19 and April 17 suicide bombings at the old central bus station in Tel Aviv (which killed ten Israeli civilians and an American citizen, and injured 98 Israeli civilians), participated in a foiled February attack against the Erez crossing between Israel and the Gaza Strip, and attempted to carry out a number of other suicide bombings. Israeli security sources said PIJ made significant efforts to carry out terror attacks in Israel prior to the March 28 Knesset elections. The IDF believed PIJ was behind the launch of a Katyusha rocket from the Gaza Strip into Israel during Knesset elections.

Israeli security officials also maintained that various Fatah-affiliated groups carried out Qassam launches, particularly the Fatah-linked al-Aqsa Martyrs Brigade (AAMB) and the Abu Rish Brigades. Using stolen bulldozers, AAMB demolished part of the border wall between Gaza and Egypt on January 4, allowing hundreds of Palestinians to surge through the wall and enter Egypt. AAMB also claimed that it participated in two failed attempts in February to attack the Erez crossing between Israel and the Gaza Strip. AAMB claimed, on the Hizballah-operated Al-Manar TV station in Lebanon that it was responsible for the March 30 suicide car bombing at the entrance to a West Bank settlement that killed four Israeli civilians. On April 17, AAMB issued a statement threatening to target Zionists outside Palestine until Israel released its prisoners.

Lebanese Hizballah continued to provide support to select Palestinian groups to augment their capacity to conduct attacks against Israel. Hizballah also continued to call for the destruction of Israel, and directly launched a number of attacks from Lebanon, including a May 28 attack against Israel and the July 12 attack (see "The Summer War", earlier in this chapter).

Israeli security services maintained that Palestinian terrorists attempted numerous times to perpetrate attacks in Israel, but were thwarted. Palestinians in the Gaza Strip attempted to infiltrate Israel by breaching the security fence around the Gaza Strip, and PIJ members were stopped en route to suicide bombings in Israeli territory. Israeli security officials claim they thwarted numerous attempts by Popular Resistance Committees (PRC) operatives and other Palestinian militants to detonate explosives at the Karni crossing between Israel and the Gaza Strip.

According to claims by HAMAS, AAMB, PIJ, PFLP, and the PRC, a number of terrorist attacks and Qassam launches were carried out by two or more organizations acting together. AAMB, PRC and PIJ claimed to have cooperated in a foiled February 9 attempt to attack the Erez crossing between Israel and the Gaza Strip. In February, the IDF and ISA shut down a Fatah-Tanzim infrastructure in Bethlehem that was receiving instructions and professional and financial assistance from PRC terrorists in the Gaza Strip.

Israeli security sources expressed concern that AQ and other external Sunni extremists were attempting to infiltrate the West Bank and Gaza Strip.

On March 21, an Israeli military court in the West Bank charged two Palestinians with conspiracy to cause death, active membership in AQ, illegal assembly, and other charges. According to the charges, the two men created an al-Qaida cell in the West Bank city of Nablus, were recruiting to form other AQ cells in the West Bank, were preparing to carry out large-scale terrorist attacks in Israel, and were receiving funds and instructions from al-Qaida in Jordan. One of the two men had also been a member of HAMAS and AAMB.

In response to continuing threat information, Israeli security forces launched frequent arrest and detention raids throughout the West Bank and the Gaza Strip, conducted targeted killings of suspected Palestinian terrorists, imposed strict and widespread closures and curfews in Palestinian areas, conducted aerial attacks on buildings affiliated with designated Foreign Terrorist Organizations in the Gaza Strip, and continued the construction of an extensive security fence in the West Bank. Israeli security forces arrested and held without trial or charges HAMAS and other Palestinian lawmakers and PA ministers from the West Bank. In the wake of the June 25 kidnapping by HAMAS of an IDF corporal posted outside the Gaza Strip, IDF troops arrested 64 HAMAS ministers and members of parliament. On August 5, the IDF arrested the speaker of the PA parliament.

On March 14, the IDF carried out an operation to seize Palestinian terrorists held in a prison in the West Bank city of Jericho within minutes after international monitors left the prison. The IDF took into custody five PFLP members, including four held responsible for the 2001 murder of an Israeli government minister, a prisoner responsible for the foiled "Karine A" weapons smuggling attempt, and over 100 other prisoners (most of whom were soon released). Israel's Attorney General said the prisoners believed responsible for the Israeli minister's murder would stand trial.

In December 2005, the IDF declared a 16 square kilometer zone in the northern Gaza Strip off-limits, warning the PA and general public that anyone in the zone could be targeted. The area remained off-limits in 2006. The IDF carried out ground and naval artillery and aerial strikes against wanted terror suspects and terrorists attempting to launch Qassam rockets into Israel, access roads to Qassam rocket launch sites, terrorist training camps, and weapons manufacturing and storage facilities. The IDF also conducted air strikes against the offices and official establishments of the PA in the Gaza Strip, including the office of PA Prime Minister Haniyeh, the PA ministries of interior, foreign affairs, and finance; and the offices of HAMAS' security force located in the Jabalya refugee camp.

Israeli security forces carried out several operations to shut down terrorist finance networks and seize terrorist funds. In the port city of Ashdod, Israeli Customs authorities seized containers of goods worth millions of dollars that they claimed were to be sold as part of a money laundering and transfer operation aimed at providing funds to HAMAS and PIJ. Another container from China destined for the Gaza Strip was confiscated because it allegedly contained combat support equipment. On numerous occasions, Israeli security forces raided the West Bank offices of HAMAS' "Dawaa" organization, charging that the offices were providing financial support to families of suicide bombers and imprisoned terrorists under the guise of charity. Israeli security forces also raided foreign exchange bureaus in the West Bank, confiscating millions of counterfeit shekels that Israeli security sources suspected originated in Iran, were transferred by HAMAS, PIJ, and Hizballah offices in Syria and Lebanon, and were earmarked for terrorist acts.

Israeli security experts cited occasions when HAMAS-affiliated PA officials smuggled millions of dollars into the Gaza Strip from Egypt. In June, PA Foreign Minister Zahar carried 20 million Euros in his suitcases into the Gaza Strip from Egypt. On October 22, the PA Interior Minister carried $2 million into the Gaza Strip in his suitcases. On November 28, the PA Foreign Minister crossed into Gaza through Rafah with $20 million. In an effort to stop another such effort, Israel closed the Rafah crossing on December 14, to prevent PA Prime Minister Haniyeh from entering the Gaza Strip from Egypt carrying $35 million. Haniyeh was eventually allowed to enter Gaza after he agreed to deposit the money in an Egyptian bank.

Jordan

The Government of Jordan retained its keen interest in combating Takfiri[1]-inspired extremism, and has actively supported forums for tolerance and religious education during the last year. Polls indicate, however, that only one-half of Jordanians considered AQ a terrorist organization, but many Jordanians viewed U.S. operations in Iraq as terrorist operations. King Abdullah continued to be an outspoken critic of terrorism and Islamic extremism—condemning as a "criminal cowardly attack" the September 4 shooting of a British tourist in downtown Amman. The King also continued to promote a tolerant and moderate brand of Islam. The Jordanian government publicly condemned terrorist acts throughout the world, practiced strict security measures, and passed new anti-terror legislation. Jordanian security forces disrupted several terrorist plots during the year, while Jordan's State Security Court (SSC), which has purview over terrorism-related cases, maintained a heavy caseload.

In March, Jordanian and Arab intellectuals participated in a conference titled "Terrorism: The Phenomenon and Mechanisms to Combat It." Hosted by

[1] Takfiri is a an Arabic word applied to Muslims who assert that other self-professed Muslims are not true followers of Islam. Some takfiri groups are willing to kill other Muslims whom they regard as insufficiently Muslim.

Public Security Director Lieutenant General Mohammad Eitan and Interpol Secretary General Ronald Nobel, the conference highlighted the threats from terrorism and the need to understand and fight its origins. In April, Prince Ghazi bin Mohammad inaugurated the 17th annual Fiqh Academy Conference—a three-day conference on Islamic doctrine. Prince Ghazi delivered a speech on behalf of King Abdullah calling on Muslims "to work honestly and seriously to eradicate terrorism and expose misguided Takfiri thought." Also in April, the King signed the Amman Declaration, which calls for more dialogue, cooperation, and understanding between Western and Muslim civilizations and stressing that ties must be built on mutual respect rather than conflict and rivalry. King Abdullah told reporters during a subsequent TV interview, "[w]e believe fighting terrorism does not take place through employing direct security measures alone, but through a comprehensive strategy to strengthen the culture of dialogue and renounce the culture of violence."

The General Intelligence Directorate and Public Security Directorate actively defended Jordan throughout the year. In February, Jordan's security forces disrupted an al-Qaida-linked cell plotting to attack Queen Alia International Airport. In June, the State Security Court indicted seven Iraqi, Libyan, and Saudi suspects involved in the airport plot for conspiracy to carry out terrorist attacks. In mid-April, the Government of Jordan announced it had discovered a cache of weapons, including rockets, C-4 explosives, and small arms, in northern Jordan. The government said that several militants associated with the cache were arrested while planning attacks in Jordan with instructions from HAMAS leaders in Syria. In early November, the State Security Court indicted three of the HAMAS-affiliated defendants for plotting attacks in Jordan. Jordanian security forces quickly apprehended Nabil Ahmed Issa al-Jaaourah, a Jordanian citizen, after he shot and killed a British tourist and injured five tourists from the Netherlands, Australia, and New Zealand, and a Jordanian tourist police officer, while shouting "God is great" at Amman's Roman Amphitheater in early September.

Jordan's lower house of Parliament ratified a bill on the prevention and punishment of terrorism in late August; the bill became law in early November following a royal decree. Highlights of the bill include: authority for the government to freeze the assets of persons suspected of terrorist conspiracy, place them under surveillance, and prevent them from leaving Jordan; a provision that would limit investigative detention to 30 days; and a definition of terrorism. The approved bill defined terrorism as "every intentional action committed by any means that leads to killing anyone or causing him physical harm or inflicting damages to public or private property . . . if the intention of that action was to disturb public order and endanger public safety and security or impede the implementation of the law or the constitution."

The Government of Jordan moved forward on several high-profile al-Qaida-related terrorism cases:

- In February, the State Security Court sentenced nine men to hang for the 2004 plot to carry out a chemical/vehicle-borne explosive attack against the U.S. embassy and Government of Jordan targets.
- On March 11, Jordanian authorities executed Libyan national Yasser Saad bin Suway for the October 2002 assassination of USAID officer Lawrence Foley.
- In September, the State Security Court sentenced seven terrorist plotters to hang, including would-be suicide bomber Sajidah al-Rishawi, for the November 2005 Amman Hotel Bombings. The King must review and approve the death warrant before the execution can take place.
- In September, the Court sentenced Omar Jamil Nazzal al-Khalayleh, a cousin of the late terrorist Abu Musab al-Zarqawi, to six months in prison for planning to recruit fighters in Syria to fight against U.S. and Iraqi forces in Iraq.
- On December 7, Ali Muhammad Hasan al-Sahli was sentenced to death, and Abd-al-Rahman Ismai'l and Samih al-Nubani to two years in prison, for their roles in the August 2005 rocket attack against U.S. naval vessels (USS Ashland and USS Kearsarge) visiting the port of Aqaba.

Several non-al-Qaida-related cases were also concluded:

- In the first quarter of 2006, the State Security Court sentenced Abdullah al-Mrayat and seven men from the Horani cell to prison for recruiting fighters for operations against U.S. and Iraqi government forces in Iraq;
- In March and September, the State Security Court sentenced four members of the Qteishat cell and six members of the Khattab Brigade for plotting attacks against hotels, liquor stores, tourist sites, and security officers.
- In October, the Court found eight Mansurah cell militants guilty of plotting to kill American and Iraqi trainers at the Jordan International Police Training Center; and in November, the court sentenced five men from the Khaled Mohammad cell to prison for planning attacks against Israel.
- In December, the Court sentenced three men to prison for attempting to join Iraqi insurgents.

Border security remained a top concern. The Jordanian government enforced security measures at each of its ports of entry, including thorough manual and electromagnetic searches of vehicles and persons attempting to enter

Jordan through the Karama-Trebil border crossing in the West Bank. The Jordanian and Iraqi Interior Ministers met in Amman in mid-December to discuss the formation of joint committees aimed at countering terrorism and enhancing control along the 180 km Jordanian—Iraqi border.

Kuwait

Kuwaiti officials condemned terrorism in regional and international fora, drafted stronger money laundering and terrorist finance legislation, and implemented a government-funded moderation campaign to combat extremism. Despite these efforts, the risk of a terrorist attack in Kuwait remained high because of the Government of Kuwait's continued reluctance to confront domestic extremists and Kuwaiti supporters of terrorism active in Iraq and Afghanistan, and regional tensions, particularly sectarian violence in Iraq.

The Government of Kuwait continued to pursue prosecutions of 36 members of the "Peninsula Lions" terrorist cell involved in the January 2005 confrontations with police, 22 Kuwaiti citizens accused of "jihad in Iraq," 12 Kuwaitis involved in the 2002 Failaka Island shooting, and eight Guantanamo detainees released to Kuwaiti custody. In November, the Appeals Court upheld most of the verdicts in the "Peninsula Lions" case, including four death sentences, four prison sentences of ten years or more, two seven-year sentences, and six sentences of four years or less. The Court commuted two death sentences to life imprisonment and reduced seven other prison sentences; it also increased four sentences from seven to ten years imprisonment.

In the "Jihadists in Iraq" case, 15 defendants were sentenced to three years, three received small fines, and four were acquitted by the Appeals Court in June. The government is still pursuing cases against 12 of the defendants. In January, the Appeals Court increased the sentences of six of the 12 defendants in the Failaka Island shooting case, and imposed heavier fines, longer probation periods, and travel restrictions. Of the eight Guantanamo detainees released to Kuwait, two remained in Kuwaiti custody awaiting trial. The other six were tried. Five were found not guilty and released; the government is appealing the verdicts. One was initially found guilty, but in an appeal, Kuwait's highest court overturned the decision and issued a not guilty verdict.

Kuwait still lacked strong legal provisions to deal effectively with those engaged in conspiracy to commit terrorist acts. Kuwaiti officials stated that insufficient and incomplete evidence prevented the conviction of, or more robust sentences for, many suspected terrorists.

In August, Kuwaiti police apprehended Hamid Nawaf al-Harbi, a suspect in the "Peninsula Lions" case who was sentenced in absentia to seven years in prison. Mohsen al-Fadhli, a known Kuwaiti terrorist believed to be in the country, remains at large. In December, the U.S. Treasury Department designated Kuwaiti extremist cleric Hamid al-Ali and terrorist facilitators Mubarak Bathali and Jabir Jalahmah as terrorist supporters. Kuwait continued to pursue upgrades to its border security, and worked closely with Iraq and other countries to secure the Iraqi border area. Kuwait also significantly increased security at oil installations after AQ threatened to attack oil facilities in the Gulf.

The Kuwaiti government continued to strengthen its legal regime for combating money laundering and terrorist financing, but problems persisted, particularly with enforcement. Although money laundering was a criminal offense, terrorist financing was not specifically prohibited. Currency smuggling into Kuwait was illegal, but cash reporting requirements were not uniformly enforced and there were no currency reporting requirements for individuals leaving the country. Members of the Kuwait National Committee for Anti-Money Laundering and Combating Terrorist Financing represented a wide range of government ministries and domestic financial institutions, but vague delineations of the roles and responsibilities continued to hinder their overall effectiveness. Kuwait was also an active member of the Middle East and North Africa Financial Action Task Force and had a Financial Intelligence Unit in accordance with current international standards, although it was not well-organized nor an independent body.

The Ministry of Social Affairs and Labor took steps to increase the monitoring and regulation of the domestic fundraising activities of Kuwait-based Islamic charities, but the Kuwaiti government was less effective in monitoring the operations of Kuwaiti charities abroad. The government needed to accelerate its efforts to pass counterterrorism legislation, strengthen charity oversight, empower its FIU, monitor cash couriers, and fully conform to international standards and conventions on terrorist financing.

Toward the end of the year, Kuwait's Ministry of Awqaf and Islamic Affairs opened its World Moderation Center, a special agency responsible for implementing an initiative launched in 2005 to combat extremism and spread moderation among Muslims through education, training, international dialogue, and research.

Lebanon

Political violence continued throughout the year. Most notable was the assassination of Industry Minister Pierre Gemayel by a team of gunmen in the streets of a northern suburb of Beirut on November 21. This act, the latest in a series of assassinations and attempted assassinations over the last two years, seemed designed to inflame tensions and intimidate forces opposing Syrian interference in Lebanon. An assassination attempt on

Internal Security Forces (ISF) Colonel Samir Shehade took place on September 5. Colonel Shehade was injured by the explosion of a roadside bomb which went off as his car passed by the village of Rmaileh, near the southern port city of Sidon. Lebanese officials suspected that the attempt on his life was in retaliation for his role in the investigation into former Prime Minister Rafiq Hariri's murder.

Between October and November, several attacks targeted ISF barracks in different areas in Beirut. On October 8 and November 1, Energa grenade-type shells were fired at al-Helou ISF barracks, causing damage to the ISF dormitory. On October 10, the Barbar el-Khazzen ISF barracks were also the target of an Energa shell that caused no casualties. The Tareek el-Jedideh ISF barracks were targeted on November 5. In what may have been a related incident, on October 15, two Energa shells exploded in downtown Beirut, injuring five and causing damage to the Credit Libanais Bank building.

Since October 2004, there have been at least 18 bombings and assassination attempts that resulted in more than 32 deaths, including that of former Prime Minister Rafiq Hariri on February 14, 2005. Other attacks have targeted Lebanese journalists and politicians critical of Syrian interference in Lebanon, including Telecom Minister Marwan Hamadeh, MP Gebran Tueni, journalist May Chidiac, Deputy Prime Minister and Defense Minister Elias Murr, and journalist Samir Kassir. Each of these attacks remained unsolved. The UN International Independent Investigation Commission (UNIIIC) has been investigating the Hariri assassination and other possibly related crimes, pursuant to UNSC Resolution 1644. The Lebanese government also continued to investigate the acts of political violence.

The government of Prime Minister Fouad Siniora has taken some gradual steps to prevent terrorist activities. In accordance with UNSC Resolution 1701, the Lebanese Armed Forces (LAF) strengthened its border presence and increased patrols in the south, with assistance from UNIFIL. The LAF deployed 15,000 troops in the south, establishing itself in this region for the first time in 30 years. Also, the ISF created a special unit to combat terrorism, and established branches of this unit to preempt terrorist activity in northern and central Lebanon.

Even with these steps, there are many concerns about Lebanon's ability to combat terrorism. Hizballah still remains the most prominent terrorist group in Lebanon. It has strong influence among Lebanon's Shia community, which comprises about one-third of Lebanon's population. The Lebanese government still recognizes Hizballah as a legitimate "resistance group" and political party. Hizballah maintains offices in Beirut and elsewhere in the country, has official liaison officers to the security services, is represented by elected deputies in parliament, and until recently had one minister in the cabinet.

The unstable political situation in Lebanon also contributed to enabling suspected foreign terrorist organizations, such as AQ and Fatah-Islam, to infiltrate Lebanon and set up operational cells within the Palestinian refugee camps. Some of these groups, such as AQ affiliate Asbat al-Ansar, have been able to find safe haven within the camps to support their actions.

Although Syria withdrew its military forces from Lebanon in April 2005, it still maintained a covert intelligence presence. The Lebanese government accused Syria of continuing to support and facilitate arms smuggling to Hizballah and Palestinian terrorist groups. Even with the post-conflict LAF troop deployments, the Government of Lebanon did not exercise full control over areas in the Hizballah-dominated south, the southern suburbs of Beirut, parts of the Biqa Valley, and inside the Palestinian-controlled refugee camps or Palestinian paramilitary bases. This lack of control provided opportunity for terrorist groups to operate relatively freely in some of these locations. During the national dialogue held in March that aimed to generate consensus among the country's major parliamentary groups, Lebanese leaders agreed to disarm the Palestinian factions located outside the 12 Palestinian refugee camps by September. The intended disarming of the Palestinian factions was derailed by the Summer War and the subsequent unsettled internal political situation.

At the end of 2006, the Lebanese government had not fully complied with UNSC Resolution 1559, which calls for respect for the sovereignty and political independence of Lebanon, the end of foreign interference in Lebanon, and the disarming and disbanding of all Lebanese and non-Lebanese militias. While Lebanon was committed to fulfilling UNSC Resolution 1559, its political leaders maintained that implementation of Hizballah's disarmament should be accomplished through a national dialogue rather than force. Lebanon's 12 Palestinian refugee camps, safe havens for several armed Palestinian factions and numbers of Sunni extremists, remained no-go zones for the LAF.

Lebanese authorities maintained that the amnesty for Lebanese individuals involved in acts of violence during the civil war prevented the government from prosecuting terrorist cases of concern to the United States. These cases included individuals involved in the 1985 hijacking of TWA Flight 847, during which a U.S. Navy diver was murdered, and the abduction, torture, and murder of U.S. hostages in Lebanon from 1984 to 1991. U.S. courts brought indictments against Lebanese Hizballah operatives responsible for a number of those crimes. Despite evidence to the contrary, some Lebanese government officials have insisted that Imad Mughniyah,[2] wanted in connection with the TWA 847 hijacking and other terrorist acts,

[2] Late in 2006, Mughniya was indicted by the Argentine government in connection with the AMIA bombing in 1994.

and placed on the FBI's list of most-wanted terrorists in 2001, was no longer in Lebanon. Mohammad Ali Hamadi, who spent 18 years in a German prison for his role in the TWA hijacking, was released in December 2005 and was believed to be in Lebanon. The United States continued its efforts to bring him to trial before a U.S. court and formally requested his extradition.

With regard to terrorism finance, Lebanese officials played an active leadership role in the Middle East and North Africa Financial Action Task Force (MENA/FATF). The Central Bank of Lebanon's Special Investigation Commission (SIC), an independent legal entity with judicial status that is empowered to investigate suspicious financial transactions, investigated 123 cases involving allegations of money laundering and terrorist financing activities. On two occasions, the SIC was unable to designate or freeze the assets of two groups affiliated with Hizballah, on the ground that the groups were affiliated with a political party participating in the Lebanese government, and thus, a decision to freeze their assets would have been a political, rather than a legal, decision.

Libya

On May 15 the United States announced its intention to restore full diplomatic relations with Libya and to rescind Libya's designation as a state sponsor of terrorism. The United States formally rescinded Libya's designation as a state sponsor of terrorism on June 30. Libya continued to cooperate closely with the United States and the international community on counterterrorism efforts.

Since pledging to renounce terrorism in 2003, Libya has endeavored to show its commitment to the War on Terror. Libya cooperated with the United States to combat the Libyan Islamic Fighting Group (LIFG), an AQ affiliate dedicated to the overthrow of the Qadhafi regime. Libya also worked with the United States to curtail terrorist activities of al-Qaida in the Islamic Maghreb (AQIM), an Algeria-based al-Qaida associate formerly known as the Salafist Group for Preaching and Combat (GSPC).

A number of U.S. court cases seeking compensation from Libya for its past support for terrorism remained unresolved.

Morocco

The Moroccan government continued with internal reforms that aimed to address the socio-economic conditions extremists exploit for recruitment. The National Initiative for Human Development (INDH), launched by King Mohammed VI in 2005, is designed to combat poverty, generate employment, and improve infrastructure. INDH projects have focused on rural areas. Morocco's Ministry of Religious Endowments and Islamic Affairs (MOIA) continued reforms begun in 2004 to counter extremist ideology and promote religious tolerance and moderation. Thirty Imams were dismissed in an effort to eliminate extremist ideology in the mosques, and the Ministry supervised revisions to the country's religious curriculum, broke with precedent by appointing 50 women to serve as Islamic spiritual guides in mosques across the country, and installed a closed circuit television network that broadcast moderate religious lectures and sermons to 2,000 mosques daily.

Moroccan efforts to combat terrorism were overhauled and upgraded following coordinated suicide bombings in Casablanca in May 2003 that left 45 persons dead. In the investigation that followed, approximately 3,000 persons suspected of connections to the network were detained, some of whom remain imprisoned. The Moroccan government continued to aggressively investigate and detain terrorist suspects. Minister of Interior Chakib Ben Moussa announced in late November that 300 terrorist suspects had been detained during the year.

Several terrorist cells were identified and disrupted. In March, members of the "Ben Hadi Cell," allegedly tied to (AQIM/GSPC) were arrested. In July, 56 alleged members of the "Mehdi Support Group," led by Hassan al-Khatab, an extremist first jailed after the 2003 Casablanca bombings, were arrested. In November, 13 alleged members of another group were arrested. All three terror cells had identified targets, procured explosives, and initiated planning for attacks against both domestic and foreign interests in Morocco.

Morocco continued with steps to counter terrorism finance and to strengthen controls against money laundering. At the end of 2006, the Parliament was in the final stages of preparing new anti-money laundering legislation that will provide a comprehensive legal basis for the monitoring, investigation, and prosecution of illegal financial activities.

Oman

Oman remained proactive in developing counterterrorism programs and strategies to ensure that it does not become a terrorist safe haven. Oman has worked extensively with neighboring countries to delineate border regions to help prevent the ability of terrorists to move freely throughout the Arabian Peninsula. These efforts resulted in a December agreement between Oman and Saudi Arabia to establish a formal Port of Entry along Oman's western border to better control border transit operations between the two countries.

Although Oman does not have a significant money laundering problem, its government launched the "Oman Program for Anti-Money Laundering" (OPFAM) in August. The purpose of this initiative was to promote greater cohesion among Omani policy-makers, regulators, law enforcement agencies, and financial institutions. Through OPFAM the Omani government hopes to promote information exchanges among relevant actors, standardize indicators to report suspicious transactions, and develop common guidelines to address anti-money laundering challenges.

The Omani government has expressed concern about the increasing number of illegal immigrants attempting to enter Oman. Oman's long coastline and porous borders offered significant challenges as they remained vulnerable to illegal transit by immigrant workers, smugglers, terrorists, and individuals involved in the traffic and sale of illegal drugs. No known terrorists were apprehended during immigration enforcement operations, but Omani officials were aware of the possibility of such individuals using human smuggling organizations to enter Oman. To date, illegal immigrants used Oman primarily as a transit point to other destinations in the Arabian Peninsula, particularly the United Arab Emirates. The majority of illegal immigrants apprehended were Pakistani, Afghani, and, to a much lesser extent, Iranian nationals who were smuggled across the Gulf of Oman.

The Omani government has been aggressive in obtaining training and equipment through the U.S. military to support efforts to control its land and maritime borders. This included the purchase of night vision equipment, an upgraded communication system used by the Royal Omani Police (ROP) and Coast Guard units, open-water patrol boats for the Coast Guard with advance radar systems, and ground surveillance radar systems to assist in border interdiction efforts. The Royal Omani Police, Sultan's Special Force, and the Royal Omani Police Coast Guard participated in U.S. Antiterrorism Assistance Programs.

Qatar

The Qatari government's 2004 *Combating Terrorism Law* defined terrorism and terrorist acts, provided measures against terrorist financing or fund-raising activities, gave the government the authority to take action against terrorist activities, and listed specific punishments, including the death penalty, for terrorist crimes.

The Qatar Authority for Charitable Works monitored all domestic and international charitable activities and approved international fund transfers by charities. The Authority had primary responsibility for monitoring overseas charitable, development, and humanitarian projects; and reported annually to Qatari government ministries on their status.

Cooperation with U.S. authorities on counterterrorism finance was strong. Qatar's Financial Information Unit resided in the Qatar Central Bank. Local banks worked with the Central Bank and the FIU on counterterrorism finance and anti-money laundering issues, and bank officials attended U.S.-sponsored conferences.

There has not been a terrorist attack in Qatar since the March 19, 2005, suicide car bomb attack at an amateur theater playhouse, which killed a British citizen. Cooperation with U.S. authorities improved during the course of the investigation of this unresolved case.

Saudi Arabia

The Government of Saudi Arabia continued to experience a mix of successes and setbacks in its efforts to combat terrorism. Government security forces conducted successful operations against terrorist cells, capturing or killing large numbers of wanted terrorist suspects, as well as members of their support networks. The government has made some progress in other aspects of its counterterrorism effort, such as financing and education, but it still has significant ground to cover to address these issues.

Saudi efforts suffered setbacks with prison breaks and an attack that led to the discovery of extensive support networks in the Kingdom. Prison escapes occurred in March at the al-Kharj prison and in July from al-Malaz jail in Riyadh. On February 24, a Saudi-based AQ cell conducted a suicide attack utilizing vehicle-borne improvised explosive devices on Saudi Aramco's Abqaiq oil stabilization and processing facility near Dammam, which resulted in the death of two security guards and several of the bombers.

Saudi security forces achieved several successes, both in response to these attacks and independently of them. Saudi security forces killed or captured all of the members of the Abqaiq cell and all but three of the Maraz prison escapees. On August 21, five wanted terrorists surrendered in response to government assurances in the media that they would receive mitigated sentences. In December, the government announced the capture during the previous three months of 136 suspected terrorists who were involved in terrorist support networks in the Kingdom.

The Saudi government initiated several programs to support its counterterrorism efforts and bolster its campaign against extremists. King Abdullah created a special security court, the Court of the Divergent, to prosecute terrorist suspects. Interior Minister Prince Nayif gave public assurances that the Court would not be a military tribunal, but would conform to existing judicial practices and law. Additionally, the government began planning a border security system, including fences and sensors, to prevent infiltration of terrorists or terrorist funding into the kingdom. In December, the Gulf Cooperation Council (GCC) summit reiterated its calls to criminalize terrorism, and called for a comprehensive effort against terrorism to include intellectual, social, and educational efforts.

The Saudi government moved to monitor and enforce its anti-money laundering and terrorist finance laws, regulations, and guidelines. However, it still had not established a High Commission for Charities. As in many countries in the Middle East, there was still an over-reliance on suspicious transaction reporting to generate money laundering investigations. Saudi Arabia's unwillingness to publicly disseminate statistics regarding money laundering prosecutions impeded the evaluation and design of enhancements to the judicial aspects of its anti-money laundering system. The Saudi government did not subject Saudi international charities to the same government oversight as domestic charities. In August, the UN 1267 Sanctions Committee designated the International Islamic Relief Organization's (IIRO) branches in Indonesia and the Philippines, and the Kingdom's Eastern Province Branch Director, Abdulhamid Al-Mujil.

In late 2005, the government enacted stricter regulations on the cross-border movement of money and precious metals. Money and gold in excess of $16,000 must be declared upon entry and exit from the country. While the regulations were effective immediately, Customs has not issued new cash declaration forms, and therefore has not yet been able to enforce the current regulation.

In the cultural arena, official visits by a number of U.S. officials, including Ambassador-at-Large for International Religious Freedom John Hanford, highlighted the government's efforts to remove references in textbooks that called for violence against non-Muslims and Muslims of different sects. The government also initiated the National Campaign to Counter Terrorism, which included publications, lectures, and workshops intended to educate school-age girls and boys about the evils of terrorism. To promote tolerance, the government began revising curricula and teaching methods, screening and reevaluating existing teachers, improving selection of future teachers, and better monitoring of teachers.

The government continued to require religious leaders to attend courses designed to eradicate extremist ideology in the mosques and monitor mosque sermons to promote tolerance and eliminate extremism. Several religious leaders were fired or subjected to punitive actions for failure to abide by government instructions to avoid provocative speeches against non-Muslims and non-Sunni Muslims. In previous years in some mosques, a second preacher would appear after the main preacher during the Friday prayer and speak provocatively against Jews, Americans, or non-orthodox Muslims. This practice is less prevalent now, due in large part to the government's efforts to combat extremism in the mosques.

The Saudi government remained engaged in its efforts to root out terrorists and their support networks in the Kingdom, but continued to face difficulties in combating the appeal of AQ ideology. Despite significant efforts and successes in the counterterrorism realm, Saudi security forces continued to discover new terrorist networks in the Kingdom. The Saudi government will need to further address the social and religious underpinnings that sustain the Saudi form of Islamic extremism.

Syria

See Chapter 3, *State Sponsors of Terrorism.*

Tunisia[3]

Tunisian law enforcement organizations carefully monitored the activities of Tunisian extremists, both in Tunisia and abroad during 2006. Tunisia's active monitoring and law enforcement activities challenged the ability of terrorists to organize internally. However, Tunisian extremists were arrested for or implicated in terrorist activities abroad, including in Algeria, Turkey, Egypt, Italy, and Iraq. Domestically, the Government of Tunisia worked to improve security procedures at borders and at Tunisian airports.

The Tunisian government actively works to prevent the formation of terrorist groups inside Tunisia, including prohibiting the formation of religious-based political parties and groups that it believed would pose a terrorist threat. Overall, the government is responsive to U.S. requests for information and assistance in counterterrorism investigations.

United Arab Emirates (UAE)

The Government of the United Arab Emirates (UAE) repeatedly condemned terrorist acts in Iraq, Egypt, and elsewhere in the region throughout the year. In order to prevent extremist preaching in UAE mosques, the General Authority of Islamic Affairs and Endowments provided prescribed guidelines for all Friday sermons, and required all 1,500 mosques that delivered sermons to record them each Friday to ensure that imams adhered to the guidelines. The UAE undertook several border security measures to deter terrorists from reaching UAE soil.

The UAE was generally cooperative in counterterrorism and law enforcement efforts, although cooperation on law enforcement matters was hampered by the lack of a mutual legal assistance treaty (MLAT) between the UAE and the United States. In February, the UAE passed a cyber-crimes law criminalizing the use of the internet for terrorist groups to "promote their ideologies and finance their activities." In June, the UAE established a National Security Council charged with formulating and implementing a national strategic plan.

The Container Security Initiative (CSI), which became operational at the ports of Port Rashid and Jebel Ali in the Emirate of Dubai in 2005, had five U.S. Customs officers co-located with the Dubai Customs Intelligence Unit at Port Rashid. On average, CSI reviewed approximately 250 bills of lading

[3] Due to an inadvertent omission, the report was updated on May 1, 2007 to include an entry on Tunisia.

each week, resulting in 15-20 non-intrusive inspections of U.S.-bound containers; examinations were conducted jointly with Dubai Customs officers. In addition, Dubai Customs made requests for most, if not all, containers that originated in Iran to be designated for inspection.

The U.S./UAE Joint Terrorist Finance Coordinating Committee met three times during the year, directly resulting in affirmative changes to the UAE's anti-money laundering laws. The UAE Central Bank provided training programs to financial institutions on money laundering and terrorist financing. The Central Bank initiated memoranda of understanding with regional financial intelligence units, and performed anti-money laundering training both locally and regionally. The Central Bank investigated financial transactions and froze accounts in response to internal investigations. Nine prosecutions for money laundering were in process at year's end. The Central Bank has registered 201 hawala dealers to date.

Yemen

The Republic of Yemen took action against al-Qaida and local extremists, arresting several individuals suspected of having AQ ties, and prosecuting the perpetrators of previous terrorist acts. Yemen also experienced several setbacks to its counterterrorism efforts with the February 3 escape of 23 suspected AQ supporters and the September 15 terrorist attacks on two oil facilities.

On September 15, two coordinated attacks on oil facilities in eastern Yemen resulted in the deaths of all four attackers and one Yemeni security official. A group calling itself al-Qaida in Yemen claimed responsibility. One day after the attack, security forces arrested four individuals on suspicion of links to the attack and for planning attacks in Sanaa on Yemeni government and Canadian Nexen oil company facilities. The investigations into the oil facility and Sanaa attacks continued but no charges were filed.

On February 3, 23 suspected AQ supporters escaped from a maximum security prison in Sanaa. Among the escapees were individuals convicted of participating in the 2000 USS Cole and 2002 M/V Limburg attacks, including the alleged organizer of the Cole attack, Jamal Badawi. On October 1, the U.S.-trained Central Security Force/ Counterterrorism Unit killed two of the most dangerous escapees, Foaz al-Rabi'i and Mohammed al-Dhailami. Rabi'i was sentenced to death, in absentia, in 2004 for his role in the M/V Limburg attack. Rabi'i and Dhailami were alleged to have organized the September oil facility attacks. In total, eight escapees surrendered and security forces killed three.

Yemeni security forces continued to arrest and try suspected members of AQ and other terrorist groups throughout the year. On May 3, a security court convicted Mohammed Hamdi al-Ahdal, alleged to be AQ's number two in Yemen, of financing terrorist groups associated with AQ. Al-Ahdal was sentenced to 37 months in prison, much of which was credited as time served while awaiting trial.

On July 8, the Special Penal Court (SPC) acquitted 19 individuals charged with conspiring to attack U.S. and Yemeni interests. The defendants admitted to traveling to Iraq to "conduct jihad," but the judge ruled that jihad was not illegal under Yemeni law. Also in July, the SPC acquitted 23 other individuals on conspiracy charges relating to traveling to Iraq to attack U.S. forces and found 21 of the defendants guilty on fraudulent document charges. Both cases are currently under appeal. In March, the Sanaa Appellate Court upheld the acquittal of four Iraqis charged with plotting to attack the U.S. and British Embassies in 2003.

In August, the Sanaa Appellate Court returned the case of two individuals accused of plotting to assassinate the U.S. Ambassador in 2004 to a lower court, claiming the judge did not follow correct sentencing procedures. Hizam al-Mass and Khalid al-Halilah were sentenced on March 5 to five years in prison.

Yemen used its Islamic Dialogue Committee, headed by a leading judge, to continue its dialogue with detainees arrested for connections to terrorist groups and extremist elements. The government released detainees it considered rehabilitated after they pledged to uphold the Yemeni constitution and laws, the rights of non-Muslims, and the inviolability of foreign interests. No comprehensive program existed to monitor recidivism rates. An undisclosed number of released detainees from previous years reportedly have traveled to Iraq to participate in attacks against Coalition Forces.

The government's capacity for stemming terrorism financing remained limited. In 2004, the UN 1267 Sanctions Committee designated prominent Yemeni Sheikh Abd al-Majid al-Zindani for his association with AQ. The Yemeni government took no action to bar his travel or freeze his assets in compliance with its UN obligations. Throughout the year, President Saleh voiced public support for Zindani and his Al-Iman University.

Country Reports: South and Central Asia Overview

"We must look beyond Afghanistan to the sources of terrorism. We must destroy terrorist sanctuaries beyond Afghanistan, dismantle the elaborate networks in the region that recruit, indoctrinate, train, finance, arm, and deploy terrorists. We must ensure that political currents and entities in the region are not allowed to use extremism as an instrument of policy."

Hamid Karzai
President of the Islamic Republic of Afghanistan

Statement, 61st UN General Assembly
New York, September 20, 2006

Terrorism remained a problem in the region, directly and indirectly threatening American interests and lives. To varying degrees, U.S. cooperation with regional partners on counterterrorism issues continued to increase, but much is left to be accomplished.

Despite considerable progress in Afghanistan, the Taliban-led insurgency remained strong and resilient, particularly in the Pashtun south and east. Although the insurgency absorbed heavy combat losses, its ability to recruit foot soldiers from its core base of rural Pashtuns remains undiminished.

Pakistan executed effective counterterrorism cooperation and captured or killed many terrorists. In August, close cooperation between Pakistani, British, and American law enforcement agencies exposed the London-Heathrow bomb plot, leading to the arrest in Pakistan of Rashid Rauf and other conspirators believed to be connected to the case. However, the United States remained concerned that the Federally Administered Tribal Areas (FATA) of Pakistan are a safe haven for al-Qaida, the Taliban, and other militants.

Terrorists staged numerous attacks in India, including a series of commuter train bomb attacks in Mumbai which killed over 200 people and injured more than 700. Despite challenges associated with its law enforcement and judicial systems, India achieved major successes this year, including numerous arrests and the confiscation of explosives and firearms. Neighboring Bangladesh continued to arrest extremists, but the deteriorating political situation in Bangladesh may increase the opportunity for terrorists to find refuge or transit.

In Nepal and Sri Lanka, terrorism carried out by the Maoists and the Liberation Tigers of Tamil Eelam (LTTE) posed a severe challenge to those governments. On an encouraging note, in November, the Maoists signed a peace agreement with the Government of Nepal that provided, under certain disarmament conditions, that the Maoists could be admitted into an interim government. In Sri Lanka, the LTTE continued attacks including targeted assassinations against political and military opponents.

A sustained commitment to counterterrorism by Central Asian states resulted in relatively few terrorist attacks. Yet terrorism and the underlying conditions and porous borders it exploits still pose a significant threat to the region. In May, terrorists attacked border posts in Tajikistan and Kyrgyzstan but were subsequently killed and captured by joint operations in the Ferghana Valley. With U.S. support, Central Asian states have undertaken to improve the capabilities of their border forces and build new border posts to impede terrorist movements and interdict drug smuggling, some of which financed terrorism in the region. The sheer length of the border and local corruption remained obstacles in Central Asia's efforts to control its borders. More widely, popular grievances over governance and poor economic growth enhance conditions terrorists and other extremists could exploit to recruit and operate in the region.

Central Asia's most notorious terrorists are the Islamic Movement of Uzbekistan (IMU) and a splinter group, the Islamic Jihad Union (IJU). However, radical extremist groups such as Hizbut-Tahrir (HT) may also present a danger to the region. HT, an extremist political movement advocating the establishment of a borderless, theocratic Islamic state throughout the entire Muslim world, has followers in Kyrgyzstan, Kazakhstan, Tajikistan, Uzbekistan, Germany, the United Kingdom, Turkey, and the Middle East. The United States has no evidence that HT has committed any acts of international terrorism, but the group's radical anti-American and anti-Semitic ideology is sympathetic to acts of violence against the United States and its allies. HT has publicly called on Muslims to travel to Iraq and Afghanistan to fight Coalition Forces.

Afghanistan

Afghanistan continued its progress toward building a stable and democratic government, despite a strong Taliban offensive and an increase in suicide bombings and attacks on soft targets throughout the country. Programs designed to combat the Taliban and other lawlessness were the principal focus of the Afghan government and international community.

At year's end, the Program for Strengthening Peace and Reconciliation (PTS), which worked to reconcile Taliban and Hizb-i-Islami Gulbuddin (HIG) members, had eleven regional offices, and over 2,500 former Taliban fighters and other insurgents had left the battlefield and joined the program. Plans were underway to strengthen and expand PTS, provided sufficient funding was available. The Disarmament, Demobilization, and Reintegration (DDR) program processed more than 63,000 former combatants in 2005, and 380 in 2006, as the program successfully wound down in June. The Disbandment of Illegal Armed Groups (DIAG) began work in June 2005 vetting parliamentary candidates to ensure they had no ties to illegal armed groups (IAGs). The DIAG disqualified a number of candidates, using the program more as an effort to push compliance rather than to punish individuals for past and present actions. The program's second phase began in early 2006, and undertook a province-by-province effort to identify and remove government officials with links to IAGS and disband the most notorious IAGs. Progress has been slow because of a lack of government enforcement of mandatory compliance and the unwillingness of many to disarm given the security situation.

Coalition Forces, in particular the U.S.-led Combined Joint Task Force-76, conducted a series of sub-campaigns during 2006. These actions utilized effective counterinsurgency means and methods, including the simultaneous use of kinetic (air and ground forces) and non-kinetic means to counter terrorism, extremism, and anti-government forces. This regional strategy, focusing on the south and east, destroyed many anti-government forces and attempted to restore the flow of reconstruction and development. Coalition Forces killed over 2,000 anti-government forces and provided hundreds of millions of dollars in reconstruction and development aid.

Increasingly, the rapidly professionalizing Afghan National Army (ANA), with more than 31,000 personnel trained and equipped, and to a lesser extent the Afghan National Police (ANP), with 61,500 trained and equipped, have taken the lead in counterterrorism operations and cooperated closely with the U.S. Afghan security forces have arrested presumed terrorists, disrupted several IED cells, and prevented many bombings, particularly in Kabul.

Despite this progress, the Taliban-led insurgency remained a capable and resilient threat to stability, particularly in the Pashtun south and east. Although the insurgency absorbed heavy combat losses, its funding and ability to recruit foot soldiers from its core base of rural Pashtuns remained undiminished. This was due in part to aggressive Taliban propaganda. Taliban information operations have grown increasingly sophisticated. Seemingly reliable streams of Taliban financing from various sources, including collusion with narcotraffickers responsible for 92 percent of the world's opium supply, as well as safe haven in the FATA across the border in Pakistan, have allowed the insurgency to strengthen its military and technical capabilities.

Afghanistan saw an increasing number of violent incidents during 2006. More than 1,400 civilians were killed in terrorist attacks during the year. The use of IEDs and suicide bombings in Afghanistan increased fourfold. Militants launched approximately 130 suicide attacks this year. Insurgents targeted provincial governors, NGOs, women's affairs officials, and ministry buildings and officials during the year. Insurgents increased their use of IEDs and suicide attacks against Coalition Forces, NATO/ISAF, Afghan National Security Forces, and Government of Afghanistan targets, while maintaining a steady level of direct and indirect fire attacks against these same forces.

Overall attacks against non-combatants (government officials, civilians, religious figures, teachers, and students) appeared to increase, and international NGOs, UN workers, and recipients of NGO assistance were attacked on approximately 57 occasions. Thirty-one NGO staff members were killed compared to 33 in 2005 and 23 in 2004. Insurgents targeted Provisional

Reconstruction Teams and construction crews in a possible effort to hamper reconstruction and drive the international assistance community out of Afghanistan.

Bangladesh

Bangladesh continued to arrest, prosecute, and convict top leaders and activists of Jamaatul Mujahedin Bangladesh (JMB), the banned Islamic extremist group responsible for a wave of bombings and suicide attacks in late 2005. In response to the attacks, the government's Rapid Action Battalion, a paramilitary organization, emerged as Bangladesh's lead counterterrorism unit responsible for the arrests of significant numbers of JMB leaders and activists. Although JMB remnants have threatened violence if the death sentences of JMB leaders under appeal are carried out, there was no JMB-linked violence in 2006. In September, authorities arrested four members of another banned terrorist organization, Harakat ul-Jihad-I-Islami/Bangladesh (HUJI-B), two of whom confessed involvement with the 2004 grenade attack that severely injured the British High Commissioner, the 2005 assassination of opposition Awami League elder statesman Shah Kibria, and three attacks on two other Awami League leaders.

The Government of Bangladesh stated that it intended to close permanently the local office of the radical Kuwait-based Revival of Islamic Heritage Society, but has yet to do so. The Central Bank of Bangladesh fined Islami Bank for violating anti-money laundering laws in connection with possible financing of JMB activities. Islami Bank has a number of board members who are associated with the Jamaat Islami Party, a member of the ruling coalition.

India continued to allege that the United Liberation Front of Assam (ULFA) and other anti-India insurgency groups operated from Bangladesh with the concurrence of senior Bangladeshi government officials. The Government of Bangladesh strongly denied these allegations. Nonetheless, the arrest in India of two Pakistanis linked to the Mumbai train bombings who allegedly entered India from Bangladesh underscored how porous the Indo-Bangladeshi border is. The absence of counterterrorism cooperation between India and Bangladesh fueled mutual allegations that each country facilitated terrorism inside the borders of the other.

U.S. and Bangladeshi law enforcement agencies cooperated well on several cases related to domestic and international terrorism. With U.S. technical assistance, Bangladesh drafted an improved anti-money laundering law, and put into operation basic elements of a Financial Intelligence Unit. Bangladesh also continued cooperation with the United States to strengthen control of its borders and land, sea, and air ports of entry.

India

As in previous years, terrorists staged hundreds of attacks on people and property in India. The most prominent terrorist groups were violent extremists operating in Jammu and Kashmir; Maoists operating in the "Naxalite belt" in eastern, southern and central India; and ethno-linguistic nationalists in India's northeastern states. The federal and state governments tried various strategies to address some of these grievances within the context of Indian democracy, but the government was firm: groups must cease violence before negotiations can begin, and the government will not entertain territorial concessions.

India alleged, based on numerous arrests and several major attacks, that UN designated Foreign Terrorist Organizations (FTOs) began a campaign in the Indian heartland to gain support from India's minority Muslim population for terrorist attacks. The Indian government blamed two prominent Pakistani-based FTOs, Lashkar-e-Taiba (LT) and Jaish-e-Mohammad (JEM), for several attacks in major Indian cities.

On July 11, terrorists set off seven blasts on packed commuter trains in Mumbai, killing at least 209 people and injuring more than 700. On March 7, terrorists set off three blasts in the holy city of Varanassi, killing 21 and injuring 62 people. On September 9, terrorists set off a series of blasts outside a mosque in the western Indian city of Malegon that killed 38 people and wounded more than 50. Police claimed the Malegon attack was conducted by Islamic extremists hoping to incite further anger between the Hindu and Muslim communities.

On October 27, Karnataka state police in Mysore arrested two suspected terrorists who allegedly belonged to the terrorist group Al-Badr. Police believed the suspects were inserted as an advance team to establish a base in southern India from which they would facilitate terrorist attacks on economic and government targets, especially in nearby Bangalore, a high-tech hub.

In addition, terrorist groups continued their attacks in Jammu and Kashmir against Indian and Kashmiri politicians, civilians in public areas, and security forces. Hundreds of non-combatants were killed, most of whom were Kashmiri Muslims. Indian experts asserted that the July 11 attack that killed eight tourists and injured 43 in Srinagar was designed to inhibit growth in the tourism industry and to hamper increasing Kashmiri enthusiasm for normalization of ties with New Delhi and between Indian and Pakistani controlled Kashmir. Unfortunately, Kashmir continued to be a dangerous area as an American citizen was injured in a grenade attack in Srinagar in June. Indian officials said that terrorist infiltration into Jammu and Kashmir increased in 2006, although they also pointed to an overall decline in violence and infiltration since 2000.

Naxalite (a Maoist agrarian peasant movement) terrorism, which covered a broad region of eastern, central, and southern India, grew in sophistication and lethality. Naxalites launched several high-level attacks, raising the insurgency's profile, and expanded the rural territory under their control. On July 17, at least 25 people were killed, 80 injured, and approximately 250 people were missing following an attack by some 800 armed Naxalites in the Dantewada district of Chhattisgarh.

The United Liberation Front of Assam (ULFA), an ethnic separatist group, conducted multiple terrorist attacks against civilians and security forces in the Northeastern Indian state of Assam resulting in numerous deaths and injuries. In one of the more violent series of attacks attributed to ULFA, on November 5 several bombs exploded in a crowded market and at an oil refinery in Assam's capital city Guwahati, killing 12 people and injuring a few dozen.

In Manipur, a Northeast Indian state affected by over 20 insurgent groups, two American citizens were seriously injured on August 16 in a grenade attack on a Hindu temple in the capital, Imphal. Four people died, including two children, and 34 were injured. An ethnic Meitei separatist group, Kanglei Yawol Kanna Lup (KYKL), was suspected to have been the perpetrator.

Indian security agencies and the police in Tamil Nadu remained active to prevent infiltration into the state by members of the Liberation Tigers of Tamil Eelam (LTTE) who were engaged in violent conflict with the army in neighboring Sri Lanka.

U.S. Government and military cooperation with India on counterterrorism continued to expand. In October, a company of U.S. Marines traveled to India for a counterterrorism exercise with the Indian army. In September, the Indian Army sent a company to Hawaii to train with U.S. Army Pacific forces. In August, the Indian Army sent two experts to observe a military exercise in Hawaii.

The U.S.-India Counterterrorism Joint Working Group (CTJWG) has met eight times since its creation in 2000. India also participated in CTJWGs with 15 other countries, and in multilateral CTJWGs with the EU and BIMSTEC (an organization promoting economic cooperation among Bangladesh, India, Myanmar, Sri Lanka, Thailand, Bhutan, and Nepal).

The Indian government supported ongoing U.S. investigations in cases involving American citizens that were victims of terrorism. On April 26, in part due to U.S. evidence, a special court in Kolkata convicted seven men for the January 2002 attack on the American Center in Kolkata that left five Indian police officers dead and over 20 injured.

India's counterterrorism efforts were hampered by its outdated and overburdened law enforcement and legal systems. The Indian court system was slow, laborious, and prone to corruption; terrorism trials can take years to complete. An independent Indian think tank determined that the thousands of civilians killed by terrorism in Jammu and Kashmir from 1988 to 2002 received justice in only 13 convictions through December 2002; most of the convictions were for illegal border crossing or possession of weapons or explosives. Many of India's local police forces were poorly staffed, trained, and equipped to combat terrorism effectively. Despite these challenges, India scored major successes this year, including numerous arrests and the seizure of explosives and firearms during operations against Lashkar-e-Taiba and other terrorist groups.

Kazakhstan

Kazakhstan continued to aggressively combat terrorism and extremism locally and strengthened its cooperation and timeliness in sharing information with the United States. There was little movement, however, on counterterrorism legislation. The draft law on money laundering that the government has worked on since 2005 remained stalled in Parliament.

In January, authorities arrested a number of individuals from two extremist cells in Almaty on terrorism charges. Eight of those arrested remain in prison with trials ongoing. In November, authorities arrested eleven people from a terrorist group in Stepnogorsk and confiscated arms, explosives, and extremist printed materials. According to press reports, members of the terrorist group were planning hostage sieges, lethal attacks on state employees, and several explosions. In December, three Kazakhstani nationals were returned to Kazakhstan from the Guantanamo Bay detention facility.

Kazakhstan continued to face a growing problem with the Islamic extremist group Hizb'ut Tahrir (HT). HT remained outlawed as an "extremist" organization through the Law on Extremism and continued to be the only group so designated under this law.

In November, the Government of Kazakhstan added the East Turkistan Liberation Organization and Aum Shinrikyo to the national list of banned terrorist organizations, accusing these groups of using terrorist means in an attempt to achieve an independent state in Central Asia and in China, respectively. The list of banned groups also included al-Qaida, the East Turkistan Islamic Party, the Kurdish People's Congress, Asbat al-Ansar, the Muslim Brotherhood, the Taliban, the Boz Gurd, Jamaat of Central Asian Mujahadins, Lashkar-e-Tayyiba, the Social Reform Society, the Islamic Movement of Uzbekistan, and its splinter group, the Islamic Jihad Union.

In July, Kazakhstan became an initial partner nation in the Global Initiative to Combat Nuclear Terrorism. Kazakhstan was one of the first countries to endorse and participate in the Global Initiative after its inception.

Kazakhstan, along with China, Kyrgyzstan, Russia, Tajikistan, and Uzbekistan, is a member of the Shanghai Cooperation Organization, which established a Regional Antiterrorism Center in Tashkent. Kazakhstan is also a member of the CIS Collective Security Treaty Organization and the Eurasia Group, a regional anti-money laundering organization modeled on the Financial Action Task Force, which has as its objective the integration of Kazakhstan, Belarus, China, Kyrgyzstan, Tajikistan, Russia, and Uzbekistan into the global system of anti-money laundering and combating the financing of terrorism.

Kyrgyzstan

The Republic of Kyrgyzstan took new political, legislative, and law enforcement steps to disrupt terrorism. Since 2001, Kyrgyzstan has hosted the Operation Enduring Freedom Coalition airbase at Manas International Airport near Bishkek. In October, Kyrgyzstan adopted an antiterrorism law that authorized an antiterrorism center to coordinate state agencies and facilitate international cooperation. In November, President Bakiyev signed a comprehensive law on "Counteracting Terrorist Financing and Legalization (Money Laundering) of Proceeds from Crime." The law authorized the establishment of a Financial Intelligence Unit (FIU), and obligates financial institutions to report any suspicious activity and bank transactions that exceed the threshold amount of $25,000.

Kyrgyzstan's military and internal forces worked to improve their counterterrorism capabilities and to expand cooperation with regional partners. Kyrgyzstan is a member of the Shanghai Cooperation Organization (SCO) and the Central Asian Cooperation Organization (CACO), which established lists of banned terrorist groups in an effort to streamline cooperation.

On May 12, an attack on Tajik and Kyrgyz border posts in the southern Batken region left six Kyrgyz servicemen and civilians dead. Kyrgyz authorities blamed the attack on Islamic militants crossing from Tajikistan. In response to a request from the Kyrgyz government following the attack, the United States provided $280,000 in radio and communication equipment to the Kyrgyz Border Guards in December to help improve their operational effectiveness in the mountainous border regions. In addition, the United States is funding $5 million in infrastructure improvements for the Kyrgyz Border service in the southern regions.

During the summer, Kyrgyz security services conducted operations in southern Kyrgyzstan against alleged terrorists from banned groups such as Hizb ut-Tahrir and the Islamic Movement of Uzbekistan (IMU). A July 14 raid killed five suspected IMU militants near Jalalabad. In September, a raid on the home of the alleged leader of the Islamic Movement of Turkestan, Rasul Akhunov, resulted in his death; authorities later claimed that Akhunov died of a heart attack.

Hizbut-Tahrir (HT) has been banned in Kyrgyzstan since 2003. Local specialists estimate that there are more than 5,000 HT members in Kyrgyzstan, located primarily among Kyrgyzstan's ethnic Uzbek population in the south but with growing support in the north as well. Kyrgyz authorities continued to report seizures of HT leaflets and small arms.

Nepal

Through April 2006, Nepal's primary counterterrorism focus remained the Maoist insurgency but the focus shifted dramatically after Nepal's political parties, the Maoists, and civil society led a popular uprising against the King. King Gyanendra was compelled to restore parliament and cede his authoritarian powers to a government run by an alliance of the seven main political parties. The Maoists declared a unilateral cease-fire on April 27. The government followed suit on May 3, formally lifting its designation of the Maoists as a terrorist organization. Months of negotiations resulted in a comprehensive peace agreement on November 21 that formally ended the insurgency. The agreement also provided that the Maoists would be admitted into an interim government once Maoist combatants were in camps and relinquished their weapons under UN monitoring.

From January to November, Maoist rebels were responsible for the deaths of 165 security personnel and 46 civilians. During the same time period, the government killed 182 suspected Maoist militants. Nepal's National Human Rights Commission (NHRC) reported that murders by Maoists lessened after the cease-fire in April, but still totaled 28 from May until November. Security force killings of Maoist insurgents were also significantly lower after the cease-fire, totaling nine during the same period.

Despite the cease-fire, Maoist rebels continued to conduct abductions, extortion, and violence. In the Kathmandu Valley, Maoists took advantage of their dramatically increased presence and the government's reluctance to upset the peace process to expand their use of extortion and efforts to undermine trade unions and student groups affiliated with the political parties. They also continued forced recruitment of schoolchildren, with thousands targeted after the signing of the initial November 8 peace accord. On September 20, and again on December 19, the Maoists declared nationwide transportation strikes. Both events were accompanied by the stoning of vehicles, and each lasted only for the declared period, demonstrating Maoist command and control.

This year also saw the beginning of a disturbing new trend with the activation of the separatist Maoist-splinter terrorist group called the Janatantrik Terai Mukti Morcha (JTMM), which aimed to bring about the secession of the southern Terai plains from the rest of Nepal. This group was responsible for the assassination of a Nepali Member of Parliament in September.

"Imperialist" United States and "expansionist" India were the targets of considerable Maoist venom, especially in the period leading up to the April uprising. A trip by Maoist Supremo Prachanda to New Delhi on November 18, however, seemed to mark the culmination of a shift in the Maoist view of Nepal's large neighbor to the south. At the end of the year, the United States was the only country to maintain its designation of the Maoist insurgency as a terrorist organization. Several countries, including India, were waiting for the Maoist entry into government to authorize open contacts at all levels.

The United States provided substantial antiterrorism assistance and training to Nepal's security forces, including courses on crisis management and critical incident management.

Pakistan

The Government of Pakistan is a frontline partner in the War on Terror. Nevertheless, Pakistan remains a major source of Islamic extremism and a safe haven for some top terrorist leaders. Credible reports estimated that as many as 900 Pakistanis lost their lives in more than 650 terror attacks in 2006, with another 1,500 people seriously injured. Pakistan has experienced attacks from international terror networks such as AQ and its supporters, as well as violence stemming from Sunni-Shia sectarian strife and militant sub-nationalists. Attacks occurred with greatest frequency in the regions bordering Afghanistan: Balochistan, the North West Frontier Province (NWFP), and the adjacent Federally Administered Tribal Areas (FATA).

Al Qaida's continued calls for the overthrow of President Musharraf remained a threat to Pakistan, despite the government's efforts to eliminate AQ elements. Pakistan continued to pursue AQ and its allies aggressively through nationwide police action and military operations in the FATA. Despite having approximately 80,000 troops in the FATA, including Army and Frontier Corps (FC) units, the Government of Pakistan has been unable to exert control over the area.

Pakistan Army and FC units have targeted and raided AQ and other militant safe havens in the FATA. In November, a suicide bomber killed 43 Army recruits and injured more than 40 others at a Pakistani military training facility in Dargai, NWFP, in retaliation for raids on AQ installations.

Operations throughout the year against both AQ and Taliban command and control capabilities helped disrupt support for the anti-Coalition insurgency in Afghanistan and anti-militant activity in Pakistan. In the early part of the year, recognizing that military operations alone would not restore security and stability to the FATA, President Musharraf directed governmental agencies to devise a comprehensive strategy to accelerate economic and social development, strengthen political administration and enhance security in the region. By year's end, the FATA Sustainable Development Plan was undergoing a final review before being presented to the Pakistani public and international community.

Pakistani security services cooperated with the United States and other nations to attack terrorism both within Pakistan and abroad. Hundreds of suspected AQ operatives have been killed or captured by Pakistani authorities since September 2001. Close cooperation between Pakistani, British and American law enforcement agencies exposed the August London-Heathrow bomb plot, leading to the arrest in Pakistan of Rashid Rauf and other alleged conspirators connected to the case. Pakistani authorities arrested two suspects in the March bombing of the U.S. Consulate in Karachi, which killed American diplomat David Foy and two others and injured more than 50 bystanders.

Pakistan's leaders took steps to prevent support to the Kashmiri militancy and denounced acts of terrorism in India, including bombings in Varanasi in March and Mumbai in July. Meeting in September on the margins of the Non-Aligned Movement Summit in Havana, President Musharraf and Indian Prime Minister Manmohan Singh agreed to establish an Anti-Terrorism Mechanism to coordinate bilateral exchange of information on terrorist threats.

Armed conflict between the national government and militant Baloch nationalists escalated, culminating in the August 26 death of Nawab Akbar Khan Bugti[1] during a raid by security forces on his mountain hideout. The "Balochistan Liberation Army" (BLA) claimed responsibility for dozens of terror attacks on government offices and economic infrastructure in the province, as well as in neighboring Sindh and Punjab. The government declared the BLA a terrorist organization in April. In addition to violence related to the militant Baloch nationalists, a series of bomb attacks in the provincial capital of Quetta followed police actions against suspected Taliban fighters in the last quarter of the year.

Sectarian violence, a scourge in Pakistan for more than two decades, claimed hundreds of lives, although the total number of sectarian terror attacks continued to decline for the second year in a row. A suicide bomber killed over two dozen and injured approximately 50 people participating in a February 9 Shia religious procession in Hangu, NWFP. On April 11, at least 57 people were killed in a bombing of a gathering of Sunni (Barelvi) religious leaders in Nishtar Park, Karachi. Although media reports blamed intra-Sunni Muslim sectarian rivalry, the results of the government's investigation have not been made public.

[1] Nawab Akbar Khan Bugti was rebel leader of the Balochistan nationalist movement and played a major role in Pakistani politics for decades.

President Musharraf remained a forceful advocate for his vision of "enlightened moderation," calling on Pakistanis to reject extremism and terrorist violence. The government's crackdown on banned organizations, hate material, and incitement by religious leaders continued unevenly. Madrassa registration, foreign student enrollment in madrassas, and financial disclosure requirements remained a source of friction between government and religious leaders.

Although Pakistan continued to work with the UNSCR 1267 Committee to freeze the assets of individuals and groups identified as terrorist entities linked to AQ and the Taliban, several UN-sanctioned entities continued to operate. An anti-money laundering bill introduced into the National Assembly in September 2005 remained under consideration in 2006. Adoption of anti-money laundering legislation consistent with international standards would significantly broaden Pakistan's ability to cooperate internationally on counterterrorism finance issues. Pakistani customs officials continued to enhance controls to interdict bulk cash couriers at key ports of entry to prevent unregulated cross-border cash flows, which are a potential source of terrorism funding.

Pakistan's courts, including the Anti-Terrorism Court (ATC), presided over several high-profile terror-related cases. Prosecuting terrorism cases presented considerable challenges for the government, which obtained convictions in some cases but suffered reversals in others. On May 22, the Rawalpindi ATC sentenced four men to death and ordered life imprisonment for three others for their part in a July 2004 plan to assassinate Prime Minister Shaukat Aziz. On May 30, a Multan ATC judge sentenced Lashkar-e-Jhangvi activist Qari Omar Hayat to death on 16 counts of murder for a 1999 attack on a Shia prayer gathering. On November 23, the Sindh High Court reversed the convictions of nine Harkat-ul Mujahideen members for killing three during the May 2004 bombing of the honorary Macedonian Consulate in Karachi.

The United States and Pakistan engaged in a broad range of counterterrorism cooperative efforts including border security and criminal investigations, as well as several long-term training projects. A Joint Working Group (JWG) on Counterterrorism and Law Enforcement, established in 2002, convened in Washington, DC in April to assess ongoing efforts and discuss enhanced cooperation.

Sri Lanka

The 2002 cease-fire between the Sri Lankan government and the Liberation Tigers of Tamil Eelam (LTTE), a designated Foreign Terrorist Organization, continued to erode amidst numerous violations and escalating military engagement between the LTTE and government security forces. The Sri Lankan Army remained deployed across the country to fight the insurgency. The paramilitary Special Task Force (STF) police were deployed both in the east and in strategic locations in the west.

The LTTE conducted a campaign of targeted assassinations against political and military opponents. This included the April assassination attempt of Sri Lanka Army Commander General Sarath Fonseka and the assassination of the Army Third-in-Command; the August 12 assassination of the Government of Sri Lanka's Secretariat for the Coordination of the Peace Process, Deputy Director Keteshwaran Loganathan; and the December 1 suicide bomber's attempt on the life of Defense Secretary Gothabaya Rajapaksa, the President's brother. The Karuna faction, a dissident faction of the LTTE, conducted its own assassination campaign against the LTTE and pro-LTTE civilians in the east.

Following the assassination of Foreign Minister Kadirgamar in August 2005, the government enacted emergency regulations giving arrest power to members of the armed forces, who were required to turn suspects over to the police within 24 hours. Individuals arrested under the emergency regulations may be detained for up to one year. Under these regulations, 148 persons were arrested; most have already been released. A revised Prevention of Terrorism Act (PTA), enacted in December, strengthened these powers.

The LTTE financed itself with contributions from the Tamil Diaspora in North America, Europe, and Australia, and by imposing local "taxes" on businesses operating in the areas of Sri Lanka under its control. Using this money, LTTE weapons were purchased on the international black market or captured from the Sri Lankan Army. Many LTTE innovations, such as explosive belts, vests, and bras, using female suicide bombers, and waterborne suicide attacks against ships, have been copied by other terrorist groups.

In general, the LTTE did not target U.S. citizens or assets, limiting attacks to Sri Lankan security forces, political figures, civilians, and businesses. However, two suicide bomb attacks on VIP motorcades in Colombo occurred within half a mile of the U.S. embassy on roads frequently traveled by Embassy employees.

Sri Lankan cooperation with the FBI has resulted in arrests of persons charged with material support to terrorist groups. The Sri Lankan government cooperated with U.S. efforts to track terrorist financing, although no assets were identified. The United States also provided training for relevant Sri Lankan government agencies and the banking sector. The government cooperated with the United States to implement both the Container Security Initiative and the Megaports program at the port of Colombo.

Tajikistan

Sharing a 1,400-kilometer border with Afghanistan, Tajikistan offered its limited resources to assist the United States with Operation Enduring

Freedom almost unconditionally. Following the deployment of U.S. troops to Afghanistan, Tajikistan allowed its territory and air space to be used for counterterrorist actions. The Tajik government's main impediment to counterterrorism performance remained its lack of resources. The fact that Tajikistan remained the poorest of all the former Soviet republics, and the ninth poorest country in the world in per capita GDP, puts these funding issues into context.

Tajikistan is not known to harbor terrorist groups, but extremists have transited Tajikistan to and from Afghanistan and Pakistan through the porous 1,400 kilometer Tajik-Afghan border. The United States spent over $5.8 million in 2006 to train and equip the Tajik Border Guards, improve border fortifications, and related capacity-building assistance. These measures will help stem the flow of potential terrorists attempting to cross the border and allow Tajikistan to better monitor its own borders.

Tajikistan prohibited extremist-oriented activities and closely monitored terrorist groups like the Islamic Movement of Uzbekistan (IMU) and extremist groups like Hizbut-Tahrir (HT). The Government of Tajikistan believed HT was active in the Ferghana Valley. The Tajik legal system convicted 32 alleged HT members (19 men and 13 women) in 2006. Analysts believed that the IMU also operated in Tajikistan. Recent press reports indicated that Tajik authorities arrested 30 suspect IMU members in Tajikistan; figures were not available regarding how many of them have been convicted. Tajik authorities arrested five additional alleged IMU members in Isfara. During a search of their house, police claimed that they found 80 kilograms of ammoniac nitrate and four kilograms of aluminum powder.

In May, a small group of armed bandits attacked Tajik and Kyrgyz border posts. The fighters seized several weapons, including 17 Kalashnikov assault rifles, a PK light machine-gun, and 3,000 rounds of ammunition. The date of the attack coincided with the one-year anniversary of the Andijan uprising in Uzbekistan leading authorities to suspect that the IMU was responsible for these attacks. Kyrgyz security services killed four militants during the attack and arrested one other. Tajik authorities later convicted seven IMU members for their participation in the attacks.

Tajikistan participated in the counterterrorist activities of the Shanghai Cooperation Organization (SCO), the Commonwealth Security Treaty Organization (CSTO), and the CIS Counterterrorist Center.

Turkmenistan

While the Government of Turkmenistan strictly controlled access into and passage through Turkmenistan at official border crossings and along main roads, clandestine passage could not be eliminated because of the extended border through mountainous and desert terrain, as well as the small size and uneven quality of Turkmenistan's border guard, customs service, and law enforcement agencies. Turkmenistan government officials exert stringent security control over the country. The Government of Turkmenistan strictly controlled religious expression, and radical or extremist forms of Islam were not tolerated. The military-style counterterrorism unit with hostage rescue and explosives threat management capability, inaugurated in 2005, and the Department for the Prevention of Terrorism and Organized Crime in the Ministry of Internal Affairs, were used largely to investigate and harass real or perceived opposition to the regime, relatives of those implicated in the 2002 coup attempt, religious groups, and non-governmental organizations. The Government of Turkmenistan supported humanitarian assistance related to the War on Terror and Operation Enduring Freedom in Afghanistan. The government entered the names of individuals and organizations on terrorist financing lists into its banking system.

Uzbekistan

There remained a clear potential for Islamic extremism and acts of international terrorism in Uzbekistan. Supporters of terrorist groups such as al-Qaida, the Islamic Movement of Uzbekistan (IMU), the Islamic Jihad Union (IJU), and the East Turkistan Islamic Movement (ETIM), were active in the region. Members of these groups expressed anti-U.S. sentiments and have attacked U.S. interests in the past, including a 2004 suicide bombing at the U.S. embassy in Tashkent, which was clamed by the Islamic Jihad Group (IJU), now the IJU. U.S. Government personnel and facilities continued to operate at a heightened state of alert.

The Government of Uzbekistan did not provide safe haven for terrorists or terrorist organizations. However, the country's poor economic climate and repressive government policies created conditions in which large portions of the population were increasingly susceptible to extremist ideologies. Uzbekistan's porous borders, particularly in the Ferghana Valley, allowed for people and illicit goods to move in and out of the country with relative freedom. The government responded to these threats with even more repressive actions against regime opponents and those it deemed to be religious extremists. However, it failed to address the conditions terrorists might exploit to gain popular support and recruits for their cause.

Although Uzbekistan was among the first states to support U.S. efforts in the War on Terror, the Government of Uzbekistan ended virtually all counterterrorism cooperation with the United States in mid-2005. In November 2005, the United States fully vacated, at Uzbekistan's request, the Karshi-Khanabad airbase. Authorization for U.S. aircraft to overfly Uzbekistani territory ended in January 2006, although an agreement was signed in November allowing Department of Defense-contracted civilian aircraft to overfly Uzbekistan on a fee-per-flight basis.

Tashkent hosted the Shanghai Cooperation Organization's (SCO) Regional Antiterrorism Center Secretariat (RATS), which claimed to have begun to focus on operational activities such as developing a coordinated list of terrorist groups and facilitating joint counterterrorism exercises among SCO member states. In the past, the government participated in UNODC and OSCE programs aimed at ensuring that it enacted appropriate terrorism legislation. However, Uzbekistani participation in these programs has virtually ended, and the government has made little progress in this regard.

Country Reports: Western Hemisphere Overview

"It is true that, somewhere in some community, we will find the apostles of terror—people who use the symbols of culture or faith to justify crimes of violence. They hate open, diverse, and democratic societies like ours because they want the exact opposite, a society that is closed, homogeneous, and dogmatic. But they and their vision will be rejected—rejected by men and women of generosity and goodwill in all communities, and rejected most strongly by those men and women in the very community they claim to represent . . ."

Stephen Harper, Prime Minister of Canada
Address to the World Urban Forum
Vancouver, Canada; June 19, 2006

Terrorism in the Western Hemisphere was primarily perpetrated by Foreign Terrorist Organizations based in Colombia and by the remnants of radical leftist Andean groups. With the exception of the United States and Canada, where some prosecutions of suspected terrorists were underway, there were no known operational cells of Islamic terrorists in the hemisphere, although pockets of ideological supporters and facilitators in South America and the Caribbean lent financial, logistical, and moral support to terrorist groups in the Middle East.

The Secretary of State certified Venezuela as "not fully cooperating" with U.S. antiterrorism efforts. The designation, included in Section 40A of the Arms Export Control Act, was based on a review of Venezuela's overall efforts to fight terrorism. The certification became active October 1 and will remain in effect until the end of the fiscal year, when it may be renewed by a determination by the Secretary of State. Cuba remained a State Sponsor of Terrorism.

On October 25, the Argentine special prosecutors who investigated the July 18, 1994, terrorist bombing of the Argentine-Israeli Mutual Association (AMIA) building that killed 85 and injured over 200 people, issued an 801-page indictment charging eight Iranian government officials and one member of Hizballah with the attack. On November 9, Judge Canicoba-Corral ratified the indictments and maintained charges against former Iranian Ambassador Soleimanpour. The judge issued arrest warrants, and on November 15, the Argentine government transmitted a request to INTERPOL for new Red Notices[1] for the nine suspects. The year ended with action in INTERPOL pending.

The threat of a major terrorist attack remained low for most countries in the hemisphere. Overall, governments took modest steps to improve their counterterrorism (CT) capabilities and tighten border security, but corruption, weak government institutions, ineffective or lack of interagency cooperation, weak or non-existent legislation, and reluctance to allocate sufficient resources limited progress. Some countries, like Panama, Mexico, and El Salvador, made serious prevention and preparedness efforts. Others lacked urgency and resolve to address deficiencies in their counterterrorism posture. Caribbean and Central American nations, recognizing their attractiveness and vulnerability to attack or transit by terrorists, took steps to improve their border controls and to secure key infrastructure, especially air and maritime ports. Most countries began to look seriously at possible connections between transnational criminals and terrorist organizations.

The United States enjoyed solid cooperation on terror-related matters from most hemispheric partners, especially at the operational level. The United States maintained excellent intelligence, law enforcement, and legal assistance relations with most countries. The hemisphere boasts the OAS' Inter-American Committee against Terrorism, the only permanent regional multilateral organization focused exclusively on counterterrorism.

Mexico and Canada were key partners in the War on Terror and for U.S. homeland security. Cooperation with them was broad and deep, involving all levels of government and virtually all agencies, in several initiatives. Mexico represented primarily a terrorist transit threat, and the Mexican government worked with the United States to enhance aviation, border, maritime, and transportation security, to secure critical infrastructure, and to combat terrorism financing. In the first case of its kind in Canada, law enforcement officials in June arrested 18 individuals, all Canadian citizens or residents, who were allegedly planning terror attacks on Canadian soil. The group was arrested with bomb building materials and was attempting to buy an additional three tons of ammonium nitrate and detonators.

The United States remained fully committed to assisting the government and people of Colombia in their efforts to defeat Colombian-based Foreign Terrorist Organizations. President Alvaro Uribe continued vigorous law

[1] An Interpol Red Notice is not an international arrest warrant. The persons concerned are wanted by national jurisdictions. Interpol's role is to assist the national police forces in identifying or locating those persons with a view to their arrest and extradition. Interpol red notices allow the warrant to be circulated worldwide with the request that the wanted person be arrested with a view to extradition.

enforcement, intelligence, military, and economic measures against the Revolutionary Armed Forces of Colombia (FARC), the National Liberation Army (ELN), and remaining elements of the former United Self-Defense Forces of Colombia (AUC). The Colombian government also increased its efforts with neighboring countries to thwart terrorist expansion, investigate terrorist activities inside and outside Colombia, seize assets, and bring terrorists to justice.

Colombia's neighbors had varied reactions to the threat from Colombian based terrorists. While none condemned the terrorists or outlawed membership in such groups in their countries, for the most part, they responded positively to Colombian requests to arrest specific fugitives. Brazil and Peru improved cross-border cooperation with Colombia (often based on local, rather than national, arrangements), but their security forces remained under formal or informal orders to avoid military confrontations with encroaching foreign terrorists. Forces in those countries pursued renascent domestic terrorist groups aggressively. It remained unclear to what extent the Government of Venezuela provided material support to Colombian terrorists. However, weapons and ammunition—some from official Venezuelan stocks and facilities—have turned up in the hands of Colombian terrorist organizations. The Venezuelan government did not systematically police the 1,400-mile Venezuelan-Colombian border to prevent the movement of groups of armed men or interdict arms flows to narcoterrorists.

Argentina hosted a meeting of the 3+1 Security Group (Argentina, Brazil, Paraguay, and the United States) in December. Delegates highlighted the importance of early warnings among States and the immediate exchange of information in order to prevent and combat illegal activities, and to deny refuge to those who finance, plan or commit acts of terrorism. In November, Brazil inaugurated a new Regional Intelligence Center, in Foz do Iguacu, dedicated to coordinating intelligence activities of the police forces of Argentina, Brazil, and Paraguay, and invited Argentina and Paraguay to send official representatives to the center.

OAS Inter-American Committee against Terrorism (CICTE)

CICTE delivered more than $5 million in counterterrorism capacity-building assistance in the region. CICTE provided training to nearly 500 port and airport security officials from 29 member states to help meet the requirements of the International Maritime Organization's International Ship and Port Facility Security (ISPS) code, and the International Civil Aviation Organization's (ICAO) new air security standards. CICTE advised 15 member state governments on how to meet the requirements of UNSC Resolution 1373, the 13 international conventions and protocols relating to terrorism, and the Inter-American Convention against Terrorism (IACAT), which complements and expands on international conventions and protocols. CICTE also organized its sixth annual regular session in Bogotá, Colombia.

Tri-Border Area (Argentina, Brazil, and Paraguay)

The governments of the Tri-Border Area (TBA) have long been concerned with arms and drugs smuggling, document fraud, money laundering, and the manufacture and movement of contraband goods through this region. In the early 1990s, they established a mechanism to address these illicit activities. In 2002, at their invitation, the United States joined Argentina, Brazil, and Paraguay in what became the "3+1 Group on Tri-Border Area Security" to improve the capabilities of the three TBA states to address cross-border crime and thwart money laundering and potential terrorist fundraising activities. The United States remained concerned that Hizballah and HAMAS were raising funds in the TBA by participating in illicit activities and soliciting donations from extremists within the sizable Muslim communities in the region and elsewhere in the territories of Argentina, Brazil, and Paraguay, although there was no corroborated information that these or other Islamic extremist groups had an operational presence in the area.

Argentina

Argentina cooperated well with the United States at the operational level, and began to address legal and institutional weaknesses that have hindered its counterterrorism efforts. The Argentine government amended its money laundering legislation to strengthen and reorganize its Financial Intelligence Unit (FIU), and created a new national Coordination Unit in the Ministry of Justice and Human Rights to oversee and manage the government's money laundering and terrorism finance efforts. The Attorney General's Office and the Central Bank both established special investigative units to handle money laundering and terrorism finance cases. In order to comply with a Financial Action Task Force (FATF) mandate, on December 20, President Kirchner approved a draft antiterrorism and counterterrorism finance law and sent it to Congress for review. If passed, the draft law would criminalize both terrorist acts and the financing of terrorism, and would provide the legal foundation for the FIU, Central Bank, and other law enforcement bodies to investigate and prosecute such crimes. The Argentine government and Central Bank have committed to freeze assets of terrorist groups identified by the United Nations if detected in Argentine financial institutions. Implementation will determine whether Argentine law enforcement institutions, including the Central Bank and FIU, aggressively apply the newly strengthened legal and administrative measures available to them.

Since President Bush's visit during the November 2005 Summit of the Americas, there were no reported incidents similar to the 20 small-scale bombings, attempted bombings, or acts of arson noted in *Country Reports on Terrorism 2005*. American businesses received e-mail threats and bomb threats, and were at times the focus of protests and demonstrations, but actual reporting and confirmation of these types of incidents declined.

Hizballah and Iran remained the chief suspects for the July 18,1994 terrorist bombing of the Argentine-Israeli Mutual Association (AMIA) that killed 85 and injured over 200 people. On October 25, AMIA special prosecutors issued an 801-page indictment charging eight Iranian government officials and one member of Hizballah with the attack.[2] On November 9, Judge Canicoba-Corral ratified the indictments and maintained charges against former Iranian Ambassador Soleimanpour. The judge issued arrest warrants and on November 15, the Argentine government transmitted a request to INTERPOL for new Red Notices for the nine suspects. The year ended with action in INTERPOL pending.

Bolivia

Bolivia's counterterrorism efforts were hindered by inadequate resources, corruption, and a weak legal framework. The Bolivian government's ineffective anti-money laundering regime failed to comply with international norms.

In April, the Bolivian government released Francisco "Pacho" Cortez, a member of the National Liberation Army (ELN), who was arrested in Bolivia after the statute of limitations on his case expired. Bolivian authorities arrested Aida Ochoa, a suspected member of the Tupac Amaru Revolutionary Movement (MRTA), in October 2005, but then released her in early 2006. After a four month delay, the Government of Bolivia issued an arrest warrant, as requested by the Peruvians, for Ochoa, who by that time was a fugitive. In a separate case in late May, Bolivia's Vice-Minister of the Interior directly intervened to arrange the release of Paraguayan Free Fatherland Party (PPL) member Angel Acosta, after he was arrested on an Interpol warrant for his involvement in the kidnapping and murder of Cecilia Cubas, claiming the warrant was invalid.

Peruvian terrorist organizations appear to be extending their influence to Bolivia. The Bolivian district attorney prosecuting a gang leader allegedly responsible for the murders of three foreign tourists in Bolivia said the gang had received training from Sendero Luminoso (Shining Path),

[2] The completion of the Special Prosecutors' investigation is the latest and, perhaps, the most important and promising development in the saga of a mismanaged and overly politicized 12-year investigation into the AMIA bombing. The attack destroyed the seven-story structure, killed 85 people and injured more than 300 Argentine citizens. In many ways, it was Argentina's September 11, and remains one of four major attacks by international terrorist groups in this hemisphere—the others being the Israeli Embassy bombing in Buenos Aires in 1992, the World Trade Center bombing in 1993, and the 9/11 attacks.

a designated Foreign Terrorist Organization from Peru. Additionally, a December press article highlighted a Peruvian intelligence report claiming that the Tupac Amaru Revolutionary Movement (MRTA) was rebuilding its capabilities in Bolivia and was receiving aid from supporters in La Paz and Cochabamba.

Brazil

The Government of Brazil vigorously condemned international terrorism, but did not provide the necessary political and material support to strengthen domestic counterterrorism institutions. A government commission proposed a new national interagency counterterrorism structure, but the government did not present legislation to implement it.

Brazil chose not to establish a terrorist-designation regime that would make support for and membership in terrorist organizations a crime. Moreover, the Government of Brazil considers Hizballah a legitimate political party. Brazilian law prohibits the extradition of native-born Brazilian citizens and imposes tight constraints on the extradition of naturalized citizens and foreigners, which complicates foreign governments' efforts to bring terrorist fugitives to justice. In August 2005, the Brazilian Federal Police arrested Revolutionary Armed Forces of Colombia (FARC) "spokesman" Francisco Antonio Cadena Collazos under an international warrant. In August 2006, the Government of Brazil granted him political asylum and denied Colombia's extradition request.

Brazil continued to improve aspects of its counterterrorism capabilities, such as more effectively using its financial intelligence unit (COAF) to monitor and prevent possible funding for terrorist groups. With assistance and training from the United States, COAF upgraded its database and data collection mechanisms. The government also invested in border and law enforcement infrastructure with a view toward gradually controlling the flow of legal and illegal goods through the Tri-Border Area. The United States continued to work with Brazil in several bilateral, multilateral, and international fora, including CICTE and the 3+1 group.

Canada

The United States and Canada collaborated extensively on a broad array of initiatives, exercises, and joint operations that spanned virtually all agencies and every level of government. Canada added the Liberation Tigers of Tamil Eelam (LTTE) to its list of terrorist organizations, preemptively arrested 18 Canadian citizens in June for suspected terrorist activity, and sought to amend the country's terrorist financing act to strengthen its information sharing and reporting provisions.

In the first case of its kind in Canada, law enforcement officials in June arrested 18 individuals, all Canadian citizens or residents, who were planning terror attacks on Canadian soil. Individual members of the Toronto-based group (the Toronto 18) were under investigation since August 2005. Two group members had been previously arrested by Canadian authorities on charges of bringing weapons from the United States to Canada and were already in custody. Two other individuals traveled from the United States to Canada in March 2005 to meet with the group's leader, and were subsequently arrested in the United States where they were awaiting trial. The group was arrested with bomb building materials and was attempting to buy an additional three tons of ammonium nitrate and detonators. The group's targets reportedly included the Parliament Building and Peace Tower in Ottawa, and the CN Tower and Stock Exchange in Toronto. Reactions by Canadians were measured but sober, and sparked a national discussion on multiculturalism, immigration, and the necessary balance between protective security and respecting civil liberties.

The Toronto 18 were charged under Canada's Antiterrorism Act, which was enacted in December 2001 to provide law enforcement with new tools for the War on Terror. In October, the Supreme Court of Canada struck down one piece of the Act that required the specification of motive in proving terrorist offenses. Two other provisions that allow for preventive arrest and permit judges to compel testimony, are subject to mandatory Parliamentary review and renewal and were under consideration at year's end.

U.S.-Canadian counterterrorism cooperation rested on a number of established forums, including the terrorism sub-group of the Cross Border Crime Forum, the Shared Border Accord Coordinating Committee, and the Bilateral Consultative Group. In September, the latter brought together counterterrorism officials from over a dozen agencies on both sides of the border to coordinate policy on bioterrorism, information sharing, and joint counterterrorism training.

In Afghanistan, Canada stood firm in fighting the resurgent Taliban in Kandahar province, where it led Regional Command South and provided a battalion-sized battle group and a Provincial Reconstruction Team for stabilization and development efforts.

Canada also helped key countries address terrorism and terrorism financing with new training programs. For example, Canada provided 18 trainers to the Iraqi police training program in Amman and had four senior advisors attached to the U.S. Security Coordinator for the West Bank and Gaza. In other supportive efforts, its Counterterrorism Capacity Building Program became a fully operational mechanism for providing Canadian expertise to other countries in border security, transportation security, and antiterrorism legislation drafting.

The United States and Canada continued to work on mechanisms to accommodate Canadian concerns about information sharing in the wake of the Arar affair, in which a Canadian-Syrian citizen and terror suspect was removed from New York to Syria in 2002. A Canadian government commission said in September that there was no evidence of Arar's involvement in terrorism or any Canadian government participation in the U.S. decision to detain and remove Arar. This has made certain aspects of information sharing more challenging, although it was noteworthy that the commission also recommended that "the Royal Canadian Mounted Police (RCMP) should maintain its policy of sharing information obtained in the course of national security with other agencies and police departments, both domestic and foreign. . .in accordance with clearly established policies." The commission also recognized that it did not have access to all the information on Arar available to the United States.

The Canadian government introduced legislation before Parliament to amend the Proceeds of Crime and Terrorist Financing Act to make Canada's anti-money laundering and anti-terrorist financing regime consistent with new Financial Action Task Force (FATF) standards. It would allow Canada to enter into Memorandums of Understanding (MOUs) with international and third country law enforcement organizations to strengthen information sharing and to create penalties to improve compliance with the act.

In May, the Canadian government announced $56 million in additional funding over the next two years for the Financial Transactions And Reports Analysis Centre of Canada (FINTRAC), the RCMP, and the Department of Justice, to increase their capability to combat terrorist financing and money laundering. Additionally, Toronto was selected as the permanent headquarters of the Egmont Group, a worldwide organization of financial intelligence units including FINTRAC. For the first time ever, Canada assumed the presidency of FATF, the international body that develops and promotes policies to combat terrorist financing and money laundering.

In April, the government announced that it was listing the Liberation Tigers of Eelam (LTTE) as a terrorist group, pursuant to the Criminal Code, making it illegal for any person to provide support, facilitate, or participate in the activities of the listed group, including providing financial support. The move brought the total number of listed entities in Canada to 40. The large Tamil community in Toronto has traditionally been a key source of funding for the LTTE. The RCMP assisted the FBI in an investigation that led to the arrest on August 19 of seven Canadians, three in New York and four in Canada, involved in trying to buy weapons for the LTTE.

Chile

Chilean law enforcement actively cooperated in international terrorism investigations and cooperated with the United States to monitor and combat terrorist financing. Law enforcement officials monitored possible extremist links between Chile's Iquique Free Trade Zone and the Tri-Border Area; trade links between these two areas are increasing. Chile's National Intelligence Agency remained an analytical body, relying on law enforcement and investigative agencies for collection and operations.

Chile hosted an Interpol working group meeting on terrorism in Central and South America in October to discuss the activities of individuals related to radical fundamentalist movements in the region. The meeting was attended by members of both the law enforcement agencies and the intelligence communities from Chile, the United States, Peru, Bolivia, Colombia, and Argentina.

Thirty-eight members of Chile's law enforcement agencies participated in money-tracing and document-tracking techniques training, and several investigators and lawyers took part in a cyber-crime seminar. The United States worked closely with Chilean counterparts to combat money laundering and terrorist financing. Senior analysts from Chile's armed forces, academia, and non-governmental organizations participated in a counterterrorism seminar with an OAS counterterrorism expert. The seminar highlighted the role of illegal financing, corruption, and drug trafficking in enabling terrorists to carry out attacks.

Grupo de Operaciones Especializados (GOPE), a 300-person unit of the Carabinero police force, served as the nation's primary counterterrorist reaction force. The force is well-trained and participates each year in Exercise Fuerzas Comando, a SOCOM-sponsored special operations seminar designed to refine the tactics, techniques, and procedures used by Special Operations counterterrorism forces.

Colombia

The Government of Colombia, facing a domestic terrorist threat, continued vigorous law enforcement, intelligence, military, and economic measures against three designated Foreign Terrorist Organizations: the Revolutionary Armed Forces of Colombia (FARC), the National Liberation Army (ELN), and remaining elements of the former United Self-Defense Forces of Colombia (AUC). Colombia increased its efforts with neighboring countries to thwart terrorist expansion, investigate terrorist activities inside and outside Colombia, seize assets, and bring terrorists to justice. The U.S.-Colombia extradition relationship remained the most successful in the world. The Colombian government cooperated fully with U.S. efforts to recover three U.S. citizens kidnapped by the FARC in February 2003, and remained open to third-party proposals for a hostage-prisoner exchange, but at year's end talks had not progressed.

Colombian based terrorist groups were weakened as a result of aggressive actions by the military and police, but these groups continued to murder, kidnap, and terrorize Colombians from all walks of life. The Uribe administration maintained its focus on defeating and demobilizing Colombia's terrorist groups through its "democratic security" policy. In the course of an increased tempo of offensive military, intelligence, and police operations, combined with efforts to demobilize combatants, the security services captured or killed numerous terrorists and mid-level commanders, debriefed terrorist group deserters for detailed information on their terrorist cells, and reduced the amount of territory where terrorists can freely operate. The government increased offensive operations against the FARC and ELN along the Venezuelan and Ecuadorian borders, and restarted anti-drug fumigation operations along the Ecuadorian border. Overall, aerial spraying in 2006 covered 425,000 acres of illegal drug crops (coca and opium poppies).

Colombia continued its close cooperation with the United States to block terrorists' assets, and financial institutions continued to close narcotrafficking and terrorism-related accounts on government order. In December, the Colombian Congress passed a law that, upon final presidential approval, will make terrorist financing an autonomous crime. Where financial institutions previously cooperated with authorities in specific cases of terrorist finance, the new law will require them to screen all new clients, and to file suspicious transaction reports (STRs) with the country's financial intelligence unit when they suspect terrorist finance activities.

Colombia emerged as a regional leader for improving counterterrorism capabilities and for strengthening political will to combat terrorism in the region, and intends to expand its leadership role in counterterrorism training in the region. Building on U.S. Antiterrorism Assistance (ATA), Colombia provided training to regional neighbors on anti-kidnapping, VIP protection, and cyber-investigation, and took over the Chair of the Organization of American States' Inter-American Committee against Terrorism (CICTE). The government continued to seek enhanced regional CT cooperation to target terrorist safe havens in vulnerable border areas.

The threat of extradition to the United States is a strong weapon against the FARC, the ELN, and ex-AUC leaders. In 2006, Colombia extradited 102 criminals to the United States, the vast majority of whom were Colombian nationals. Trials for extradited FARC leader Ricardo Palmera "Simon Trinidad" and financier Omaira Rojas Cabrera "Sonia" on terrorism and drug related charges were scheduled when the year ended. The Uribe administration suspended two more extraditions of alleged AUC members, bringing the total to five, who were cooperating with the peace process, but the United States continued to seek their extraditions. However, the Colombian government denied a request from two other AUC leaders to suspend their extradition based on their demobilization; the extraditions are proceeding.

The FARC continued tactical-level terrorist and narcotrafficking activities, despite the ongoing military campaign against it, and launched several bombings against military targets in urban areas, including Bogotá. The FARC also targeted numerous rural outposts, infrastructure targets, and political adversaries in dozens of attacks, and continued kidnappings across Colombia. A sample of the FARC's daily criminal activity included:

— In February, the FARC killed eight town councilmen in Rivera, Huila;

— In April, Liliana Gaviria, sister of former-President Cesar Gaviria, was killed by the FARC;

— In October, the FARC launched car bomb attacks in Bogotá, Villavicencio, and Fusagasuga,

— In November, the FARC attacked rural National Police post in Tierradientro, killing 17 police officers;

— In December, the FARC ambushed the military in Ocana, North Santander, killing 17 soldiers; and

— In December, the FARC killed 15 soldiers near La Julia (Meta).

Three Irish Republican Army (IRA) members who were awaiting final sentencing for training the FARC on IRA bomb tactics fled Colombian parole and resurfaced in Ireland in August 2005. They were detained and questioned by the Irish national police and released without charge. The Colombian government requested their extradition. Ireland does not have an extradition treaty with Colombia; the case remained under review and the three fugitives at large.

The Government of Colombia and the ELN conducted several rounds of peace talks, but no agreements were reached. The ELN remained in the field, but with limited resources, a dwindling membership, and reduced offensive capability. The ELN and FARC clashed over territory in northeastern Colombia regularly, which further weakened the ELN.

AUC blocs continued to demobilize under the Justice and Peace Law, which offers judicial benefits and reduced prison sentences for qualifying demobilizing terrorists. The law requires all participants to confess fully their crimes as members of a terrorist group and to return all illicit profits. More than 32,000 AUC members have demobilized, and the government is attempting to reintegrate them into society through a newly created high commissioner for reintegration. At year's end, the Colombian Prosecutor's office began taking sworn confessions from ex-members of the AUC as part of the Justice and Peace process. Some AUC renegades continued to engage in criminal activities after demobilization, but the AUC as a formal organization largely ceased to function.

Cuba

See Chapter 3, *State Sponsors of Terrorism.*

Ecuador

Ecuador's greatest counterterrorism and security challenge was the presence of Colombian Foreign Terrorist Organizations, frequently linked with narcotics trafficking organizations, along its northern border. Members of the Revolutionary Armed Forces of Colombia (FARC) and the National Liberation Army (ELN) were widely present on the Colombian side of the border and regularly entered Ecuadorian territory (generally as unarmed civilians) for rest and resupply. Training camps for these groups were discovered on the Ecuadorian side of the border.

In response, the Government of Ecuador continued troop shifts to the northern border region, and publicly affirmed the need to maintain effective presence and control of the border. This position was taken in the Ministry of Defense White Paper and in the Foreign Ministry's forward-looking foreign policy White Paper, referred to as PLANEX 2006–2020.

Greater troop presence and more frequent patrolling led to the discovery and dismantling of over 30 clandestine FARC camps in northern Ecuador. The Ecuadorian National Police continued efforts to strengthen border crossing security and worked with the military to deepen national security cooperation to combat illegal armed groups. Ecuador strengthened its dialogue with Colombia on sensitive cross-border issues and initiated bilateral development planning. Ecuador worked closely with the United States and other donors to promote lawful economic activity and development in the north. In May, the Ecuadorian Congress ratified the Inter-American Convention Against Terrorism.

Ecuadorian police suspected several small Ecuadorian groups of domestic subversion and involvement in terrorism. Of greatest concern was the estimated 200-member Popular Combatants Group (GCP), a faction of the Marxist-Leninist Communist Party of Ecuador. Its members are mainly students and are trained in the use of firearms and low-yield pamphlet bombs, which they deployed in major cities without casualties. Also of concern were the Political Military Organization (OPM) and Alfarista Liberation Army (ELA), which were reputed to have ties with and support from Colombian narcoterrorists.

El Salvador

El Salvador, the only Western Hemisphere country with troops serving alongside U.S. forces in Iraq, continued its support for the Coalition by dispatching an eighth contingent of troops to Iraq in December, and President Tony Saca publicly expressed his intention to deploy a ninth unit.

In September, the Legislative Assembly passed new counterterrorism legislation, which President Saca quickly signed into law. The law featured new sentencing requirements for certain terrorist-related crimes, but fell short of international recommendations on terrorist finance. Rather than distinguishing terrorism from regular crime by defining it as politically-motivated violence, the new legislation lists some 27 types of acts as terrorism,[3] punishable by a maximum sentence of 86 1/2 years in prison in the case of aggravating circumstances and, in a controversial provision, the law provides for 25–30 years in prison for armed occupation of public buildings (a tactic favored by some militant groups affiliated with the opposition FMLN party). The FMLN legislators, many of whom are former guerrilla insurgents, voted unanimously against the legislation, charging that its measures would restrain their right of free association. A group of different organizations is planning constitutional challenges and threatened to take the case to the Inter-American Court of Human Rights if necessary.

The Civilian National Police (PNC) is a professional force that is well-regarded by Salvadorans and international observers. The PNC coordinated its work with the Immigration Service, the Office of the Attorney General (FGR), and the National Intelligence Service (OIE). The new CA-4 agreement, implemented among El Salvador, Guatemala, Honduras, and Nicaragua, allowed for the inspection-free movement of citizens among these countries, and reduced overall inspection at land crossings. While important for improving overall integration and trade among the four member nations, the system has raised concerns that it could facilitate easier international movement of terrorists.

Guatemala

Guatemala continued to strengthen its anti-money laundering and terrorism finance regime since its 2004 removal from the Financial Action Task Force list of Non-Cooperative Countries. The Financial Intelligence Unit is an active partner of U.S. and multilateral efforts to track terrorism finance and reduce financial sector vulnerabilities. With U.S. assistance, Guatemala formed an interagency money laundering task force with representation from the Financial Intelligence Unit, the Guatemalan tax authority, and the Public Ministry (prosecutors office). There was no credible evidence of terrorism financing in Guatemala, and the Guatemalan government, along with private financial sector actors, actively cooperated in looking for such funds.

[3] The 27 acts include: murder or grave injury of public officials, diplomats, or other international figures; kidnapping; terrorist attacks against aircraft or maritime vessels; crimes against port and maritime security; participation in terrorist finance (though lacking internationally-accepted language on cash couriers and wire transfers); tampering with chemicals and medicines; inciting acts of terror; publicly defending or supporting acts of terror; membership in terrorist organizations; use of WMD; and acts of cyber-terrorism.

An organized crime bill passed by the Guatemalan Congress on July 19 provided the Guatemalan government with the tools to investigate criminal activities including those related to terrorism, but is not yet operational. The Guatemalan military's deployment of a western border task force at the beginning of the year continued the government's initial efforts to secure control of its borders with Mexico that began with the deployment of a northern border task force in September 2005.

Severe resource constraints of both technology and manpower, corruption, and an ineffective criminal justice system hindered efforts against transnational crime threats such as drug trafficking and alien smuggling, especially through remote areas of the country. Guatemala's northern and western borders with Mexico lacked effective coverage by police or military personnel, and controls at its southern and eastern borders with El Salvador have been relaxed as part of the Central American integration process. Nevertheless, Guatemalan civil aviation and port authorities provided strong cooperation to U.S. requests for assistance in investigating potential terrorism leads. Deployment of the military-led border task forces provided a new governmental presence in the previously lawless northwest and western border regions. The Guatemalan government worked to enhance overall maritime and aviation security and counterterrorism capabilities to remain in compliance with rising international standards.

Mexico

Mexico demonstrated a strong commitment to work with the United States to preempt terrorist activity and entry through our shared border. There were no known international terrorists residing or operating in Mexico, and no terrorist incidents have occurred on or originated from its territory. Mexico represented primarily a terrorist transit threat, and our bilateral efforts focused squarely on minimizing that threat.

Counterterrorism cooperation steadily increased through the end of the Fox administration. President Calderon entered office on December 1, committed to prioritizing national security. U.S. law enforcement agencies enjoyed particularly strong relationships with the Center for National Security Investigations (CISEN), the Attorney General's Office (PGR), and the National Migration Institute (INM). Mexico worked with the United States to enhance aviation, border, maritime, and transportation security, secure critical infrastructure, and combat terrorism financing.

The Mexican government further professionalized federal law enforcement institutions, restructured and strengthened the institutions directly responsible for fighting organized crime, and developed tools under the framework of the Security and Prosperity Partnership (SPP) to better address national security threats.

The March 2005 launch of the SPP, which consists of ten security-related goals within its Security Pillar, institutionalized mechanisms for information exchange across agencies and levels of our respective governments. While a solid foundation has been built, we are working towards further cooperation and information sharing.

Mexico continued to make steady progress on border security projects focused on counterterrorism and alien smuggling. Mexico acknowledged and responded thoughtfully to U.S. reports concerning terrorist transit and the smuggling of aliens who may raise terrorism concerns. Cooperation between the United States and Mexico was especially positive in alien smuggling initiatives along Mexico's northern and southern borders. Initiatives included exchanges of information on and screening of individuals suspected of cooperation with terrorist organizations as well as smugglers whose activities presented terrorist concerns. This cooperation led to the deployment of the Operation Against Smugglers Initiative on Safety and Security (OASSIS) system, which allowed Mexican and U.S. law enforcement officials to share real-time information regarding ongoing alien smuggling investigations in a systemized fashion. OASISS enhanced the ability to prosecute alien smugglers and human traffickers on both sides of the border and to avoid situations where smugglers responsible for life-threatening behavior (even deaths) on one side of the border could evade justice by escaping to the other side. The U.S. Government would like to see more cooperative efforts to identify smuggling organizations operating along Mexico's southern border that may raise terrorism concerns.

An ongoing issue of strategic concern was the continued exploitation of smuggling channels traversing the U.S.-Mexico border and the lack of enforcement along the southern Mexican border with Guatemala and Belize. The southern border, in particular, could be vulnerable to the movement of terrorists. In the wake of increasing narcotics-related border violence, bilateral cooperation on border security issues has increased.

The Mexican government coordinated with the United States on information sharing of air passenger data. The United States was also planning to support Mexico's plans to develop a national center for migratory alerts, which would coordinate information drawn from various other agencies to alert officials of possible suspect entries into Mexico.

Mexico and the United States began negotiations on programs designed to deter terrorists from using Mexico's seaports to ship illicit materials, detect nuclear or radioactive materials if shipped via sea cargo, and interdict harmful material before it could be used against the United States or U.S. allies. The cooperative effort will include installation of specialized equipment to screen cargo containers for nuclear or other radioactive materials.

Despite excellent U.S.-Mexico cooperation, money laundering remained a significant problem. The United States and the new Mexican government are discussing the dedication of greater resources to combating it. The underlying legal framework remained inadequate, and the establishment of a specific Mexican penal charge against money laundering connected to terrorism is needed. Both chambers of the Mexican legislature have passed legislation outlawing terrorist financing and associated money laundering; the two bills must still be consolidated in conference. The Mexican government notably deployed a task force to the Mexico City airport that included elements from the Agencia Federal de Investigacion (Federal Investigative Agency), Mexican Customs, and prosecuting attorneys from the PGR's anti-money laundering criminal prosecution section.

The Mexican Armed Forces continued to expand its counterterrorism capabilities. The Secretariat of the Navy improved maritime air surveillance by returning to service two of three E-2C Hawkeye command and control aircraft and acquiring more MI-17 helicopters. This capability related directly to efforts to secure key national strategic facilities, including those related to oil production in the Bay of Campeche. It remains difficult to accurately assess Mexican Army counterterrorism capabilities because the U.S. and Mexican Armed Forces had limited interoperability in counterterrorism.

The U.S.-Mexico Border Security and Public Safety Working Group, formed in March, has become another important tool for bilateral cooperation, establishing protocols between both governments to respond cooperatively at a local level to critical incidents and emergencies along the border. It remains in the pilot stage. The United States was able to further develop its border security relationship with the Government of Mexico through training programs, which focused on using non-intrusive inspection equipment, detecting weapons of mass destruction, and identifying fraudulent documents.

Nicaragua

The most pressing counterterrorism issue for the United States concerning Nicaragua was the stalled destruction of Nicaragua's stocks of man-portable air defense systems (MANPADS). While the Nicaraguan executive branch under outgoing President Enrique Bolanos, as well as the armed forces, recognized the danger of these weapons falling into the hands of terrorists and cooperated with the United States, the opposition-controlled legislature refused to allow the MANPADS destruction program to move forward. The Nicaraguan legislature also failed to act on a comprehensive counterterrorism law that would create a national counterterrorism operations unit and address deficiencies in existing criminal and money laundering statutes. The latter, coupled with both the lack of a Financial

Intelligence Unit, and a Prosecutor General who refused to prosecute money laundering cases brought to him by the existing cash-starved Commission on Financial Analysis, amounted to an ineffective anti-money laundering and terror financing regime. Nicaragua's court system was politicized and mired in corruption that reached right up to the Nicaraguan Supreme Court. Nicaragua's immigration system suffered from corrupt practices and could be exploited by terrorist groups.

Panama

The Panama Canal remains Panama's most important economic asset. Any act of terrorism that could close off the Canal would severely impact the economies of Panama, the United States, and other countries that rely heavily on the Canal for commerce. The government undertook a review of the structure of its Public Forces and conducted exercises to ensure its ability to protect the Canal and residents of Panama against a possible terrorist act.

Panama's highly developed commercial transport sector and shared border with Colombia makes it a transshipment point for arms, drugs, and smuggling of illegal aliens. Panama's Public Forces (PPF) closely monitored FARC activities in the Darien Province on the Colombian border. In January, the FARC kidnapped two Spanish citizens near the town of Jaque in the Darien. The group held and later released the two individuals. This incident indicated that the FARC continued to have a presence and activity in the Darien[4]. Panama created a dedicated border patrol force for both the Colombian and Costa Rican borders. The Border Protection Force was a separate service with its own command and headquarters under direction of the Panamanian National Police (PNP).

Panama provided enhanced force protection for U.S. military vessels, including submarines, during "high value transits" (HVT) of the Canal; U.S. officials praised Panama's level of support and security. The Ministry of Government and Justice (MOGJ) used classroom training, table-top exercises, and field visits to improve coordination among the PPF agencies. Panama was also the sponsor and host of the annual PANAMAX exercise, a multinational civil and military forces training exercise tailored to the defense of the Panama Canal. The exercise replicated real world threats to the Canal in order to develop appropriate responses and guarantee safe passage through the waterway. Fifteen nations, including the United States, participated.

The Ministry of Government and Justice, the U.S. Department of Homeland Security and the Department of Justice worked together on joint

[4] Panama's remote border region with Colombia, the Darien Province, served in the past as a rest and regrouping point for the FARC.

counterterrorist initiatives, including the malafide traveler interdiction operation at Tocumen Airport, Operation Firewall. Panama worked closely with DHS to finalize the Declaration of Principles for Panama's Container Security Initiative.

On October 30–31, Panama hosted a multilateral conference for Inter-American Committee Against Terrorism (CICTE) members from the United States, Panama, Colombia, and Brazil to discuss strategies and preventative measures to protect critical infrastructure from potential terrorist activities. The conference included expert presentations on topics such as telecommunications, cyber security, and international port security. The October meetings were held in preparation for the upcoming CICTE General Assembly scheduled to take place in late February 2007.

Panama is an international offshore banking center. While the government has taken extensive measures to combat money laundering, the banking system and the Canal Free Zone continue to serve as vehicles for illicit finance. Panama's Foreign Ministry, Council for Public Security and National Defense, Financial Analysis Unit, and the Superintendent of Banks were fully cooperative in reviewing terrorism finance lists. The Panamanian legislature passed legislation that toughened laws on money laundering.

Paraguay

Although Paraguay was generally cooperative in counterterrorism and law enforcement efforts, its judicial system remained severely hampered by a lack of strong anti-money laundering and counterterrorism legislation. Such legislation is essential for Paraguay to meet its counterterrorism obligations under UN Security Council Resolutions and, equally important, acquire the tools it needs to effectively obstruct and prosecute money laundering and terrorist financing occurring in the Tri-Border Area, particularly Ciudad del Este.

Paraguay did not exercise effective immigration or customs controls at its borders. Efforts to address illicit activity occurring in the Tri-Border Area were uneven due to a lack of resources and, more principally, corruption within customs, the police, and the judicial sector. In October, a Legal Reform Commission introduced to Congress a Penal Code Reform bill that included provisions to update Paraguay's money laundering law. The Legal Reform Commission was also working on a Procedural Code Reform bill that would include provisions on money laundering and terrorism. Separately, Congress must pass another bill that would give Paraguay's Financial Intelligence Unit (FIU), the Secretariat for the Prevention of Money Laundering (SEPRELAD), the autonomy it would need to function effectively. Without this law, in June 2007 SEPRELAD could be suspended from the Egmont Group, the international group that facilitates information exchange among the Financial Intelligence Units of its 100 members. Despite expanded cooperation with other government entities and significant assistance from the United States over recent years, SEPRELAD has yet to demonstrate the ability to monitor and detect money laundering. Absent effective money laundering and terrorist financing legislation, it remained difficult for Paraguay to prosecute terrorist financiers or seize their assets.

Without effective counterterrorism legislation, Paraguay has successfully prosecuted suspected terrorist financiers under tax evasion or other statutes. The tax evasion case against Kassem Hijazi, a suspected Hizballah money launderer connected to 113 businesses and 46 individuals, remains ongoing. This case was set to go to trial pending Hijazi's latest appeal to the Supreme Court. Suspected terrorist fundraiser Hatim Ahmad Barakat was convicted of document fraud and was sentenced to six years in jail in June. Paraguayan authorities continued to seek the arrest of fugitive Hassan Ali Barakat (Ahmad Barakat's cousin), for conspiracy, piracy, and contempt of court.

Twelve of the 15 individuals charged with the 2004-5 kidnapping and murder of Cecilia Cubas, daughter of former President Raul Cubas, were convicted in November. Their sentences ranged from 10 to 35 years. Several of the defendants were tied to the leftist Free Fatherland Party (PPL) which, in turn, has allegedly received support from the Revolutionary Armed Forces of Colombia (FARC) and other foreign governments. The PPL supports armed struggle as a means to overthrow the Paraguayan elected government. Several co-conspirators remained at large. Six escaped to Argentina, one of whom subsequently fled to Bolivia after the others were captured, and were awaiting the possibility of extradition. Two escaped to Bolivia and extradition was pending.[5] An additional nine individuals remained at large and were under investigation.

The United States assisted Paraguay with training for judges, prosecutors, and police in investigating, preventing and prosecuting individuals involved in money laundering, bulk cash smuggling, and terrorism, including terrorism financing. Paraguay qualified for participation in the Millennium Challenge Account (MCA) Threshold Program and received a $35 million dollar grant to develop and strengthen institutions. Paraguay is a member of the Financial Action Task Force of South America Against Money Laundering (GAFISUD), which has been critical of Paraguay for its failure to adopt strong money laundering legislation. A delegation from the UN Security Council's Counterterrorism Committee visited Paraguay

[5] The two that escaped to Bolivia initially received refugee status in Bolivia but the Supreme Court overturned that decision in August. They remained at large.

in June urging it to move expeditiously to adopt counterterrorism legislation that would meet its international obligations.

Peru

Peru's top counterterrorism concern was preventing the reemergence of the militant Maoist Sendero Luminoso (SL or Shining Path), a designated Foreign Terrorist Organization that convulsed the country in the 1980s and1990s at a cost of more than 69,000 lives. SL members continued to engage in narcotrafficking and killed eight civilians and five counternarcotics police officers. SL members also intimidated voters during the election year, but it suffered significant setbacks in 2006 when SL founder and leader Abimael Guzman was sentenced to life in prison, SL's number two military leader Hector Aponte Sinarahua "Clay" was killed, and a boat capsized in the Ene River drowning some 40 members.

Although previous Peruvian administrations nearly eliminated SL in the 1990s, the organization, now entwined with narcotics trafficking, reemerged and remained a threat. Now estimated to include hundreds of armed combatants, Sendero Luminoso conducted 92 terrorist acts in remote areas. While the new SL is shorter on revolutionary zeal than its predecessor, reports suggested it was attempting to rebuild support in the university system, where it exercised considerable influence in the 1980s. Meanwhile, the drug trade provided SL with a greater source of funding to conduct operations, to improve relations with local communities in remote areas, and to gain recruits. Lack of government presence in these areas and deterioration in Peruvian security capabilities complicated efforts to counter or disrupt SL activity.

Since SL remnants operated in coca growing regions and relied on narcotrafficking income, the Peruvian National Police (PNP) in these regions and U.S.-Peruvian counternarcotics operations were on alert for possible attacks based on SL threats. SL presence and activity near Aucayacu in Huanuco limited voluntary eradication and alternative development projects, as SL members reportedly owned and operated coca fields in this area.

SL killed five Peruvian Police officers and two employees of the government-regulated licit coca company (ENACO) in an ambush attack on December 16 in the Apurimac and Ene River Valley (VRAE) of Ayacucho. The ENACO staff, protected by the PNP officers, was tasked to confiscate illegal coca and cocaine precursor chemicals. The Armed Forces reported three soldiers wounded by SL. Two sustained injuries in May and July when their base came under SL fire, and the other soldier was wounded when his convoy was ambushed by SL guerillas.

In rural areas of the Huallaga Valley and the Apurimac and Ene River Valley, SL called for the boycott of April presidential elections and stepped up its recruitment before the elections. Five murders were linked to SL either as voter intimidation during the presidential elections or as revenge for the police operation resulting in the death of SL military leader Hector Aponte Sinarahua "Clay". In March, three people were tortured and mutilated for allegedly providing information to the PNP that led to the police operation against Clay. Their bodies were found with anti-election/pro-revolution notes attached. In March, three residents of Leoncio Prado, Huanuco were murdered; one body was found with a note stating that other informants would also be murdered. SL declared that the killings would continue until Clay's death was avenged. In August, SL murdered a fifth civilian from Tocache, San Martin for working as an informant in Clay's case. SL's propaganda and intimidation activities peaked around the first round of the presidential elections and were less pronounced for the subsequent runoff and regional/municipal elections.

From January through June, then-President Toledo undertook a counterterrorism campaign (the Huallaga Police Front) in response to the deadly attacks on police in 2005. This strategy remained in effect. Alan Garcia's government announced a new counterterrorism strategy in November. Under Garcia's strategy, 2,000 troops and 19 antiterrorism bases in the Apurimac and Ene River Valley operated under a central command. The plan also called for new health, education, and infrastructure investment in these isolated communities where the state lacked presence. The government also sought to improve interagency cooperation and strengthen prosecutors. Police units specializing in counterterrorism and counternarcotics conducted joint operations with the Peruvian Army. President Garcia proposed a law in November that called for the death penalty for those convicted of acts of terrorism, but Congress has yet to take action.

President Garcia and former President Toledo repeatedly reauthorized a 60-day state of emergency in parts of Peru's five departments where SL operates, suspended some civil liberties and gave the armed forces authority to maintain public order.

The Tupac Amaru Revolutionary Movement (MRTA) has not conducted a significant terrorist attack since the December 1996 hostage taking at the Japanese Ambassador's residence in Lima. However, there were indications that ex-MRTA members were trying to reconstitute an organizational structure. These MRTA activists were infiltrating far left civil society organizations. For example, the MRTA participated in a conference with left-wing fringe parties in Chile in an attempt to rejuvenate their organization. Police also found MRTA propaganda distributed during the election season.

Authorities arrested 155 suspected SL members and nine Tupac Amaru Revolutionary Movement (MRTA) members. On February 19, the PNP killed Clay, military leader and number two in the Huallaga branch of the SL. The PNP also arrested Mansueto Ausencio "Mansho" and Juan Chujutalli "Pablito", two top political-military operatives in November. Reportedly the result of a boat accident, almost 40 SL members, a third of the force in the region, drowned in the Ene River.

Government records indicated that 145 former SL members were released from jail in November after completing their sentences. Some of these members rejoined political movements but there was no evidence that they have engaged in violent acts.

The Government of Peru aggressively prosecuted terrorist suspects, led by special counterterrorism prosecutors. A special terrorism court was in the process of retrying the remaining SL and MRTA members whose convictions were overturned by Peru's Constitutional Tribunal in 2003. Following a trial that lasted over a year, Abimael Guzman was convicted and sentenced to life in prison on October 13 for acts of terrorism and for founding and leading SL. Elena Iparraguirre, his partner and co-conspirator, was also sentenced to life in prison. Oscar Ramirez Durand 'Feliciano', former leader of SL was sentenced to 24 years prison in June for acts of terrorism. Guzman and his accomplices will continue to face other judicial processes.

The Revolutionary Armed Forces of Colombia (FARC) used remote areas along the Colombian/Peruvian border for rest and to make arms purchases. According to the Peruvian police, the FARC has forced indigenous groups in remote jungle areas to cultivate coca crops. The outgoing Loreto Regional President made headlines in November when he claimed the FARC operated in the region and had begun to recruit locals to fight in Colombia. Peru, Colombia, and Brazil are party to a 2004 border security agreement to cooperate against terrorism and arms trafficking.

Suriname

Suriname's lead agency for counterterrorism, the Central Information and Security Agency (CIVD); and the Ministry of Justice and Police (MOJP) have a police Anti-Terrorist Team (ATE) and a 28 person "capture team" for use in the interior. Suriname has not yet signed the UN Convention for the Suppression of the Financing of Terrorism and does not have laws or regulations that would enable the authorities to freeze and seize funds and assets related to terrorist financing, but does have legislation to allow authorities to freeze assets of those suspected of money laundering.

Suriname began issuing CARICOM-compliant machine-readable passports in 2004, yet there are still numerous valid old passports in circulation, which can easily be tampered with in order to assume a false identity to travel across borders. An unknown number of blank old-style passports remained unaccounted for. The United States provided watch lists of known terrorists to Suriname police, but if any terrorists were present, the likelihood of apprehending them is low because of the lack of border and immigration control by police and officials, and because Suriname has no system for registering and monitoring visitors. According to police sources, the FARC conducted arms-for-drugs operations with criminal organizations in Suriname.

Trinidad and Tobago

In October, Trinidad and Tobago signed a U.S.-CARICOM Memorandum of Intent for the creation of an Advance Passenger Information System (APIS) in preparation for the 2007 Cricket World Cup, and the Parliament passed implementing legislation for the system. The Opposition United National Congress Party failed in its attempt to challenge the constitutionality of the 2005 Antiterrorism Act, and Imam Yasin Abu Bakr became the first person to be prosecuted under the Act. Law enforcement officials participated in U.S. Antiterrorism Assistance programs, and in December, the Trinidad and Tobago government hosted a seminar on "Tourism and Recreational Security", sponsored by the OAS' Inter-American Committee against Terrorism (CICTE).

Venezuela

In reviewing Venezuela's overall level of cooperation in U.S. efforts to fight terrorism, the Secretary of State certified Venezuela as "not fully cooperating" with U.S. antiterrorism efforts. In light of Venezuela's actions, the United States imposed an arms ban effective August 17. The Secretary's designation became a matter of law October 1, and will remain in effect until the end of the fiscal year, when it may be renewed by a determination by the Secretary of State.[6]

President Hugo Chavez persisted in public criticism of U.S. counterterrorism efforts, deepened Venezuelan relationships with Iran and Cuba, and was unwilling to prevent Venezuelan territory from being used as a safe haven by the FARC and ELN, effectively flouting UN Security Council Resolutions 1373 and 1540, which form part of the legal basis of international counterterrorism efforts.

Chavez' ideological sympathy for the Revolutionary Armed Forces of Colombia (FARC) and the National Liberation Army (ELN) limited Venezuelan cooperation with Colombia in combating terrorism. FARC and ELN units often crossed into Venezuelan territory to rest and regroup with relative impunity. Splinter groups of the FARC and another designated

[6] Venezuela is the only nation certified as "not fully cooperating" that is not a state sponsor of terrorism. Sanctions ended all commercial arms sales and retransfers to Venezuela.

Foreign Terrorist Organization, the United Self- Defense Forces of Colombia (AUC), operated in various parts of Venezuela and were involved in narcotrafficking.

It remained unclear to what extent the Venezuelan government provided material support to Colombian terrorists. However, limited amounts of weapons and ammunition—some from official Venezuelan stocks and facilities—have turned up in the hands of Colombian terrorist organizations. The Venezuelan government did not systematically police the 1,400-mile Venezuelan-Colombian border to prevent the movement of groups of armed terrorists or to interdict arms or the flow of narcotics.

An individual claiming to be a member of an Islamic extremist group in Venezuela placed two pipe bombs outside the American Embassy in Caracas on October 23. Venezuelan police safely disposed of the two pipe bombs and immediately made one arrest. The investigation by Venezuelan authorities resulted in the additional arrest of the alleged ideological leader of the group. At year's end, both suspects remained in jail and prosecutors were pressing terrorism charges against them.

Responding to a complaint filed by two deported ETA terrorists in the Interamerican Human Rights Commission in June, Venezuelan officials negotiated and signed an "amicable settlement" to facilitate the naturalization of Basques who came to Venezuela as political refugees in the 1980s as a result of a bilateral agreement between the governments of Spain and Venezuela. After media reports revealed that ETA terrorists would obtain substantial benefits from the settlement, Venezuela repudiated the terms of the agreement in December.

Venezuelan citizenship, identity, and travel documents remained easy to obtain, making Venezuela a potentially attractive way-station for terrorists. International authorities remained suspicious of the integrity of Venezuelan documents and their issuance process.

Chapter 3
State Sponsors of Terrorism Overview

State sponsors of terrorism provide critical support to non-state terrorist groups. Without state sponsors, terrorist groups would have much more difficulty obtaining the funds, weapons, materials, and secure areas they require to plan and conduct operations. Most worrisome is that some of these countries also have the capability to manufacture weapons of mass destruction (WMD) and other destabilizing technologies that could get into the hands of terrorists. The United States will continue to insist that these countries end the support they give to terrorist groups.

As a result of the historic decisions taken by Libya's leadership in 2003 to renounce terrorism and to abandon its WMD programs, the United States rescinded Libya's designation as a state sponsors of terrorism on June 30. Since pledging to renounce terrorism in 2003, Libya has cooperated closely with the United States and the international community on counterterrorism efforts.

Sudan continued to take significant steps to cooperate in the War on Terror. Cuba, Iran, and Syria, however, have not renounced terrorism or made efforts to act against Foreign Terrorist Organizations. Iran and Syria routinely provided safe haven, substantial resources, and guidance to terrorist organizations.

Venezuela was certified by the Secretary of State as "not fully cooperating" with U.S. counterterrorism efforts. The designation, included in Section 40A of the Arms Export Control Act, was based on a review of Venezuela's overall efforts to fight terrorism. Effective October 1, the decision imposed sanctions on all commercial arms sales and transfers. It remains in effect until September 30, 2007, when it may be renewed by a determination by the Secretary. (Venezuela is the only nation certified as "not fully cooperating" that is not a state sponsor of terrorism.)

State Sponsor: Implications

Designating countries that repeatedly provide support for acts of international terrorism as state sponsors of terrorism imposes four main sets of U.S. Government sanctions:

1. A ban on arms-related exports and sales.
2. Controls over exports of dual-use items, requiring 30-day Congressional notification for goods or services that could significantly enhance the terrorist-list country's military capability or ability to support terrorism.

3. Prohibitions on economic assistance.
4. Imposition of miscellaneous financial and other restrictions, including:
   - Requiring the United States to oppose loans by the World Bank and other international financial institutions;
   - Lifting diplomatic immunity to allow families of terrorist victims to file civil lawsuits in U.S. courts;
   - Denying companies and individuals tax credits for income earned in terrorist-listed countries;
   - Denial of duty-free treatment of goods exported to the United States;
   - Authority to prohibit any U.S. citizen from engaging in a financial transaction with a terrorist-list government without a Treasury Department license; and
   - Prohibition of Defense Department contracts above $100,000 with companies controlled by terrorist-list states.

Cuba

Cuba continued to publicly oppose the U.S.-led Coalition prosecuting the War on Terror. To U.S. knowledge, Cuba did not attempt to track, block, or seize terrorist assets, although the authority to do so is contained in Cuba's Law 93 against Acts of Terrorism, as well as Instruction 19 of the Superintendent of the Cuban Central Bank. No new counterterrorism laws were enacted, nor were any executive orders or regulations issued in this regard. To date, the Cuban government had not undertaken any counterterrorism efforts in international and regional fora or taken action against any designated Foreign Terrorist Organizations. The Government of Cuba provided safe haven to members of ETA, FARC, and the ELN, and maintained close relationships with other state sponsors of terrorism such as Iran. The Cuba-Iran Joint Commission met in Havana in January.

The Cuban government continued to permit U.S. fugitives to live legally in Cuba and is unlikely to satisfy U.S. extradition requests for terrorists harbored in the country. The United States periodically requested that the government return wanted fugitives,[1] and Cuba continued to be non-responsive. The Cuban regime publicly demanded the return to Cuba of five of its agents convicted of espionage in the United States. The five were variously accused of being foreign intelligence agents and infiltrating U.S. military facilities, but the Cuban government continued

[1] U.S. fugitives range from convicted murderers, two of whom killed police officers, to numerous hijackers. Most of those fugitives entered Cuba in the 1970s. In previous years, the Government of Cuba responded to requests to extradite U.S. fugitives by stating that approval would be contingent upon the U.S. returning wanted Cuban criminals.

to refer to these individuals as heroes in the fight against terrorism. One was accused of conspiracy to murder for his role in the Cuban Air Force's shooting down of two small civilian planes. Cuba has stated, however, that it will no longer provide safe haven to new U.S. fugitives who may enter Cuba.[2]

Although Cuba did not extradite suspected terrorists during the year, the government demanded that the United States surrender Luis Posada Carriles, whom it accused of plotting to kill Castro and bombing a Cubana Airlines plane in 1976, which resulted in more than 70 deaths. Posada Carriles remained in U.S. custody. Cuba also asked the United States to return three Cuban-Americans implicated in the same cases.

Iran

Iran remained the most active state sponsor of terrorism. Its Islamic Revolutionary Guard Corps (IRGC) and Ministry of Intelligence and Security (MOIS) were directly involved in the planning and support of terrorist acts and continued to exhort a variety of groups, especially Palestinian groups with leadership cadres in Syria and Lebanese Hizballah, to use terrorism in pursuit of their goals.

Iran maintained a high-profile role in encouraging anti-Israeli terrorist activity, rhetorically, operationally, and financially. Supreme Leader Khamenei and President Ahmadi-Nejad praised Palestinian terrorist operations, and Iran provided Lebanese Hizballah and Palestinian terrorist groups—notably HAMAS, Palestinian Islamic Jihad, the al-Aqsa Martyrs Brigades, and the Popular Front for the Liberation of Palestine-General Command—with extensive funding, training, and weapons.

Iran continued to play a destabilizing role in Iraq, which appeared to be inconsistent with its stated objectives regarding stability in Iraq. Iran provided guidance and training to select Iraqi Shia political groups, and weapons and training to Shia militant groups to enable anti-Coalition attacks. Iranian government forces have been responsible for at least some of the increasing lethality of anti-Coalition attacks by providing Shia militants with the capability to build IEDs with explosively formed projectiles similar to those developed by Iran and Lebanese Hizballah. The Iranian Revolutionary Guard was linked to armor-piercing explosives that resulted

[2] During September, a U.S. fugitive sequestered his son, stole a plane at a local airport in the Florida Keys, and landed illegally in Varadero, east of Havana. American Interests Section efforts resulted in a visit to the male individual and his son in Varadero. After several meetings between the aforementioned USINT Offices and Cuban government officials, the son was returned in October to his mother in Mexico, who had legal custody. Simultaneously, the father was returned to the United States via charter flight to Miami, where he is being prosecuted. The stolen private plane was later returned to the United States. This was the first instance in which the Cuban government permitted the return of a fugitive from U.S. justice.

in the deaths of Coalition Forces. The Revolutionary Guard, along with Lebanese Hizballah, implemented training programs for Iraqi militants in the construction and use of sophisticated IED technology. These individuals then passed on this training to additional militants in Iraq.

Iran remained unwilling to bring to justice senior AQ members it detained in 2003, and it has refused to publicly identify these senior members in its custody. Iran has repeatedly resisted numerous calls to transfer custody of its AQ detainees to their countries of origin or third countries for interrogation or trial. Iran also continued to fail to control the activities of some al-Qaida members who fled to Iran following the fall of the Taliban regime in Afghanistan.

North Korea

The Democratic People's Republic of Korea (DPRK) was not known to have sponsored any terrorist acts since the bombing of a Korean Airlines flight in 1987. The DPRK continued to harbor four Japanese Red Army members who participated in a jet hijacking in 1970. The Japanese government continued to seek a full accounting of the fate of the 12 Japanese nationals believed to have been abducted by DPRK state entities; five such abductees have been repatriated to Japan since 2002. In the February 13, 2007 *Initial Actions* Agreement, the United States agreed to "begin the process of removing the designation of the DPRK as a state-sponsor of terrorism."

Sudan

The Sudanese government was a strong partner in the War on Terror and aggressively pursued terrorist operations directly involving threats to U.S. interests and personnel in Sudan. In recent months, Usama Bin Laden and other senior al-Qaida leaders have called for the expansion of AQ's presence in Sudan in response to possible deployment of UN peacekeepers in Darfur. This has led to speculation that some individuals with varying degrees of association with AQ have taken steps to establish an operational network in Darfur, but there were no indications that AQ affiliated extremists were active there.

With the exception of HAMAS, the Sudanese government did not openly support the presence of extremist elements in Sudan. The Sudanese government took steps to limit the activities of these organizations. For example, Sudanese officials welcomed HAMAS members as representatives of the Palestinian Authority (PA), but limited their activities to fundraising. The Sudanese government also worked to disrupt foreign fighters from using Sudan as a logistics base and transit point for Jihadists going to Iraq. There was some evidence to suggest that individuals who were active participants in the Iraqi insurgency have returned to Sudan and were in a position to use their expertise to conduct attacks within Sudan or to pass on their knowledge.

The Lords Resistance Army (LRA) continued to be a threat to Uganda, the Democratic Republic of the Congo (DRC), and Southern Sudan. The Government of Southern Sudan worked to mediate peace between the LRA and the Government of Uganda and sought to curb LRA raids, but achieved little tangible progress. Although LRA attacks declined significantly, renewed violence remains a threat. Formal negotiations commenced in Juba in July 2006. The LRA continued to stall the talks, however, most recently with demands for a change of venue and a halt to all Ugandan People's Defense Forces activity in southern Sudan. Both parties signed a Cessation of Hostilities agreement in August 2006 identifying areas where the LRA could assemble for the negotiations without fear of being attacked by the Ugandan People's Defense Forces.

Syria

The Syrian government continued to provide political and material support to Hizballah and political support to Palestinian terrorist groups. Palestinian Islamic Jihad (PIJ), HAMAS, the Popular Front for the Liberation of Palestine (PLFP), and the Popular Front for the Liberation of Palestine-General Command (PFLP-GC), among others, base their external leadership in Damascus. The Syrian government insisted that the Damascus-based groups undertake only political and informational activities, but Palestinian groups with leaders in Syria have claimed responsibility for anti-Israeli terrorist acts.

Syria's public support for the Palestinian groups varied, depending on its national interests and international pressure. In April, visiting PA Foreign Minister Zahar (HAMAS) met with Damascus-based Palestinian leaders and attended a rally at the Palestinian Yarmouk refugee camp alongside HAMAS Political Bureau Chief Khalid Mish'al and representatives of other terrorist groups and Hizballah. In July, Mish'al held a highly publicized press conference under tight security at a Damascus hotel, expressing gratitude for Syria's unconditional support to the Palestinian cause.

The Government of Syria has not been implicated directly in an act of terrorism since 1986, although preliminary findings of a UN investigation into the February 2005 assassination of former Lebanese Prime Minister Rafik Hariri indicated a strong likelihood of official Syrian involvement. That investigation remains in process.

On September 12, four Syrian nationals with alleged Islamist ties used grenades, guns, and a small truck bomb to launch an attack against the U.S. embassy in Damascus. All four of the assailants were killed as was a Syrian security officer who responded to the attack. In the incident's aftermath, the Syrian government enhanced security for the embassy and American personnel in Syria, although it declined to provide the embassy with the findings of its internal investigation into the attack. Damascus repeatedly assured the United States that it will take every possible measure to protect U.S. citizens and facilities in Syria, but at the same time has not taken the measures considered necessary by the United States.

In 2004-2005, Syria upgraded physical security conditions on the border and began to give closer scrutiny to military-age Arab males entering Syria. (Visas are still not required for citizens of Arab countries.) It also highlighted the repatriation of more than 1,200 foreign extremists and the arrest of more than 4,000 Syrians trying to go to Iraq to fight. In November, Syria's foreign minister announced the resumption of diplomatic relations with Iraq after a 25-year rupture, and, a month later, the Syrian and Iraqi Ministers of Interior signed a five-year memorandum of understanding to boost, among other things, joint efforts to control the borders and combat terrorism.

As in recent years, Damascus highlighted in Syrian government-controlled press, information about clashes on Syrian territory with terrorist groups, particularly with the Jund a-Sham group. Separately, in November, security agents on the Syrian side of the border with Lebanon engaged in a gun battle with a Syrian Islamic militant from the Tawhid and Jihad group. The militant, who was trying to use fake documents to cross into Lebanon, subsequently blew himself up with a hand grenade.

Chapter 4
The Global Challenge of WMD Terrorism

Introduction

The nexus of weapons of mass destruction (WMD) and terrorism poses one of the gravest potential risks to the national security of the United States and its global partners. A successful major WMD terrorist attack could result in hundreds of thousands of casualties and produce far-reaching economic and political consequences that would affect all members of the international community. This chapter outlines:

- The key elements of the United States' National Strategy for Combating WMD Terrorism;
- The various types of materials terrorists may use in a WMD attack;
- The potential that resources of a state could be directed or diverted to facilitate WMD terrorism;
- The emerging WMD terrorism threat presented by non-state facilitators; and
- Transformational U.S. partnerships to combat this growing global risk.

The U.S. Government places the highest priority on working with a broad range of international partners, international organizations and national governments, as well as local governments and private sector organizations, to develop effective partnerships to meet the global challenge of WMD terrorism.

Diplomatic Strategic Priorities for Combating WMD Terrorism

U.S. diplomatic priorities for combating WMD terrorism build on the comprehensive approach set forth in the U.S. National Strategy for Combating WMD Terrorism. Specifically, our strategic approach hinges on the six objectives outlined in the National Strategy. We work across all objectives simultaneously to maximize our ability to eliminate the threat.

- **Determine terrorists' intentions, capabilities, and plans to develop or acquire WMD.** We need to understand and assess the credibility of threat reporting and provide technical assessments of terrorists' WMD capabilities.
- **Deny terrorists access to the materials, expertise, and other enabling capabilities required to develop WMD.** We seek to deny our enemies access to WMD-related materials (with a particular focus on weapons-usable fissile materials), methods of transport, sources of funds, and

other capabilities that facilitate the execution of a WMD attack. In addition to building upon existing initiatives to secure materials, we are developing innovative approaches that blend classic counterproliferation, nonproliferation, and counterterrorism efforts.

- **Deter terrorists from employing WMD.** A new deterrence calculus combines the need to deter terrorists, facilitators, and supporters from contemplating a WMD attack and, failing that, to dissuade them from actually conducting an attack. Traditional threats may not work because terrorists generally show a wanton disregard for the lives of innocents and, in some cases, for their own lives. We require a range of deterrence strategies that are tailored to the various WMD threats and the individual actors who facilitate or enable those threats. We will employ diplomatic strategies that seek to address extremism and diffuse volatile conditions to discourage populations from considering WMD an appropriate tool to address perceived injustices.
- **Detect and disrupt terrorists' attempted movement of WMD-related materials, weapons, and personnel.** We will seek to expand our global capability for detecting illicit materials, weapons, and personnel transiting abroad or heading for the United States or U.S. interests overseas. We will use our global partnerships, international agreements, and ongoing border security and interdiction efforts. We also will continue to work with countries to enact and enforce strict penalties for WMD trafficking and other suspect WMD-related activities.
- **Prevent and respond to a WMD-related terrorist attack.** Once the possibility of a WMD attack against the United States has been detected, we will seek to contain, interdict, and eliminate the threat. We will continue to develop requisite capabilities to eliminate the possibility of a WMD operation and to prevent a possible follow-on attack. We will prepare ourselves for possible WMD incidents by developing capabilities to manage the range of consequences that may result from such an attack against the United States or our interests around the world.
- **Define the nature and source of a terrorist-employed WMD device.** Should a WMD terrorist attack occur, the rapid identification of the source and perpetrator of an attack would enable our response efforts and may be critical in disrupting follow-on attacks. We will maintain and improve our capability to determine responsibility for the intended or actual use of WMD via accurate attribution—the rapid fusion of technical forensic data with intelligence and law enforcement information.

As we move forward in the implementation of our diplomatic strategic priorities for combating WMD terrorism, we will take special care to work closely with the full range of foreign partners to prioritize and to tailor our capacity-building approaches to the regional and local conditions we face across the world.

The Material Threats

There are four generally accepted categories of weapons of mass destruction that terrorists may seek to acquire and use in a WMD terrorist attack: nuclear, radiological, biological, and chemical.

Nuclear

Some terrorist organizations, such as AQ, have openly stated their desire to acquire and use nuclear weapons. The diffusion of scientific and technical information regarding the assembly of nuclear weapons, some of which is now available on the Internet, has increased the risk that a terrorist organization in possession of sufficient fissile material could develop its own nuclear weapon. The complete production of a nuclear weapon strongly depends on the terrorist group's access to fissile material and scientific expertise. Terrorists may, however, seek to link up with a variety of facilitators to develop their own nuclear capability. These facilitators include black market proliferators or transnational criminal networks that may seek to profit from the sale of nuclear material, a weaponized device, or technical knowledge gathered from nuclear experts involved in a national nuclear program.

Radiological

Some terrorists seek to acquire radiological materials for use in a radiological dispersal device (RDD) or "dirty bomb." Most radiological materials lack sufficient strength to present a public health risk, but public panic and the economic disruption caused by a radiological dispersal device would be significant. Radiological materials are used widely across the medical industry including medical isotopes and sources used in some X-ray machines; and in the oil industry they are used in well-logging devices and other measuring instruments. Its widespread use makes radiological material significantly easier to procure than fissile nuclear material.

Biological

Biological weapons, another deadly threat, consist of pathogens that are deliberately dispersed through food, air, water, or living organisms. If properly produced and released, biological weapons can kill on a massive scale, even spreading across oceans to distant continents and population centers.

Like other WMD, developing a biological weapons capability represents scientific and operational challenges. The quality of a biological weapon greatly determines its ability to harm people. It requires scientific expertise to assemble a biological weapon or develop and disperse a suitable pathogen such as the one used in the 2001 anthrax attacks in the United States. Some terrorist organizations, however, remain interested in developing a bioweapons capability.

Among present-day terrorist organizations, AQ is believed to have made the greatest effort to acquire and develop biological weapons. U.S. forces discovered a partially built biological weapon laboratory near Kandahar after expelling the Taliban from Afghanistan. Although it was not conclusive that AQ succeeded in obtaining a biological weapon, the discovery demonstrated a concerted effort to acquire a biological weapons capability.

Chemical

Chemical weapons represent another highly dangerous potential tool in the hands of terrorists. Effectively dispersed and in sufficient dosages, chemical weapons could injure tens of thousands. Not since the 1995 sarin attack conducted by Aum Shinrikyo in the Tokyo subway system has an attack been conducted with a sophisticated chemical device. Since then, only materials with legitimate dual uses, such as pesticides, poisons, and industrial chemicals, have been used. The growth and sophistication of the worldwide chemical industry, including the development of complex synthetic and dual-use materials, may make the task of preventing and protecting against this threat more difficult. Preventing chemical terrorism is particularly challenging as terrorists can, with relative ease, use commercial industrial toxins, pesticides, and other commonly available chemical agents as low-cost alternatives to conventional attacks—though likely with limited effects rather than mass casualties.

Dual-Use Materials, Equipment, Research and Technology of Concern

Reducing the risk of terrorist acquisition of, access to, and use of dual-use materials, equipment, research, and technology of concern also remains a critical challenge. Terrorists have shown an interest in developing improvised devices leveraging such capabilities, and the diffusion of information on the Internet regarding dual-use research of concern has compounded this challenge. Recent attacks in Iraq involving improvised devices containing chlorine, a dual-use chemical used in water treatment facilities, offer a notable example. Effective partnerships with private sector organizations—industry, academia, and the scientific research community—as well as with local governments will play an important role in mitigating the risk of dual-use capabilities falling into the wrong hands.

State Sponsorship of Terrorism: A Key Concern

A state that directs WMD resources to terrorists, or one from which enabling resources are clandestinely diverted, may pose a potentially grave WMD terrorism threat. Although terrorist organizations will continue to seek a WMD capability independent of state programs, the sophisticated WMD knowledge and resources of a state could enable a terrorist capability. State sponsors of terrorism and all nations that fail to live up to their international counterterrorism and nonproliferation obligations deserve greater scrutiny as potential facilitators of WMD terrorism.

Non-State Facilitators: An Emerging Threat

State sponsors of terrorism represent just one facet of the overall risk of WMD terrorism. Non-state facilitators have emerged as a growing WMD proliferation threat in recent years. In 2003, the United States and its international partners succeeded in interdicting a shipment of WMD-related material destined for Libya's then active nuclear weapons program. As facts emerged regarding this shipment and its origin, the U.S. Government gained insight into an emerging WMD terrorism risk. Pakistani nuclear scientist A.Q. Khan had developed a transnational nuclear proliferation network reaching from Southeast Asia to Europe, and was making available sensitive technology and WMD-related materials to nations willing to pay.

The dismantling of the A.Q. Khan network revealed an uncomfortable truth about globalization. The very trends driving globalization—improved communications and transportation links—can enable development of extended proliferation networks that may facilitate the terrorist acquisition of WMD. Globalization requires that partner nations work together closely to prevent, detect, and disrupt linkages that may develop between terrorists and facilitators such as A.Q. Khan.

Transformational Partnerships to Combat WMD Terrorism

Since September 11, 2001, the international community has taken significant strides in responding to the threat of WMD terrorism. States are working together bilaterally and multilaterally to address these threats and protect their populations. The United States has taken concrete measures to build a layered defense against the WMD terrorism threat. In 2003, the U.S. Government announced the first National Strategy to Combat Weapons of Mass Destruction. Through a variety of multinational initiatives such as the Global Partnership against the Spread of Weapons of Mass Destruction, the Global Threat Reduction Initiative, and the Proliferation Security Initiative, and most recently, through the Global Initiative to Combat Nuclear Terrorism, the United States has taken a leadership role in reducing the threat of WMD in the hands of non-state actors and terrorists.

The Proliferation Security Initiative

Announced by President Bush in 2003, the Proliferation Security Initiative (PSI) deserves special mention as a particularly well received and effective international initiative. The PSI is a global effort that aims to stop the trafficking of WMD, their delivery systems, and related materials to and from states and non-state actors of proliferation concern worldwide. States that wish to join the PSI are asked to endorse a Statement of Interdiction Principles that identifies specific measures participants intend to undertake for the interdiction of WMD and related materials. PSI participants also conduct exercises to improve their operational capabilities to conduct interdictions, and meet periodically to develop new operational concepts and share information. PSI has led to a number of important interdictions over the last two years and is an important tool in the overall U.S. strategy to combat WMD terrorism.

The Global Initiative to Combat Nuclear Terrorism

Presidents Bush and Putin announced the Global Initiative to Combat Nuclear Terrorism on July 15, 2006 to expand and accelerate the development of partnership capacity against one of the most serious threats to international security. Although PSI has marshaled resources to support interdiction, the Global Initiative focuses on strengthening the other defensive layers necessary to prevent, protect against, and respond comprehensively to the nuclear terrorist threat.

Australia, Canada, China, France, Germany, Italy, Japan, Kazakhstan, Morocco, Russia, the United Kingdom, and the United States agreed to and endorsed a Statement of Principles and Terms of Reference for the Initiative in a meeting in Rabat, Morocco on October 30-31. The International Atomic Energy Agency (IAEA) attended as an observer. By agreeing to the Statement of Principles, partner nations committed themselves to:

- Develop, if necessary, and improve accounting, control, and physical protection systems for nuclear and other radioactive materials and substances;
- Enhance security of civilian nuclear facilities;
- Improve the ability to detect nuclear and other radioactive materials and substances in order to prevent illicit trafficking in such materials and substances, to include cooperation in the research and development of national detection capabilities that would be interoperable;
- Improve capabilities of participants to search for, confiscate, and establish safe control over unlawfully held nuclear or other radioactive materials and substances or devices using them;
- Prevent the provision of safe haven to terrorists and financial or economic resources to terrorists seeking to acquire or use nuclear and other radioactive materials and substances;

- Ensure adequate respective national legal and regulatory frameworks sufficient to provide for the implementation of appropriate criminal and, if applicable, civil liability for terrorists and those who facilitate acts of nuclear terrorism;
- Improve capabilities of participants for response, mitigation, and investigation, in cases of terrorist attacks involving the use of nuclear and other radioactive materials and substances, including the development of technical means to identify nuclear and other radioactive materials and substances that are, or may be, involved in the incident; and
- Promote information sharing pertaining to the suppression of acts of nuclear terrorism and their facilitation, taking appropriate measures consistent with their national law and international obligations to protect the confidentiality of any information which they exchange in confidence.

Additional U.S. Efforts Supporting a Global Layered Defense

The United States has also worked with partner nations through the United Nations and the IAEA to reduce the threat of WMD in the hands of terrorists. In the past few years, the UN Security Council has passed two important resolutions related to the prevention of terrorism and the proliferation of WMD. In 2001, the Security Council adopted Resolution 1373, which requires all UN member states to refrain from providing any support, active or passive, to terrorists, and to work together to limit terrorist movement and safe haven. In 2004, the Security Council adopted Resolution 1540, which requires all UN member states to refrain from providing support to non-state actors that attempt to develop or acquire WMD and their means of delivery. The United States remains committed to full implementation of both UN Security Council Resolutions 1373 and 1540 and stands ready to support our partners in this area.

In 2005, the UN General Assembly adopted the Convention on the Suppression of Acts of Nuclear Terrorism (Nuclear Terrorism Convention). The United States was one of the first signatories. There are now over 100 signatories to this Convention, and the United States is taking steps to prepare for ratification. The adoption of the Nuclear Terrorism Convention, and the recent adoption of the Amendment to the Convention on the Physical Protection of Nuclear Material and the Protocol to the Convention for the Suppression of Unlawful Acts against the Safety of Maritime Navigation, both U.S. initiatives, underscore the importance that many countries are now placing on cooperating to reduce the risk of WMD terrorism.

Conclusion

The potential threat of terrorists acquiring and using WMD poses one of the greatest security challenges facing the United States and our international partners today. During the past year, the U.S. Government has built on a range of activities and launched new efforts to prevent, protect against, and respond to the threat or use of WMD. Together with partner nations and international organizations, the United States will continue to take the initiative to reduce the global risk of WMD terrorism.

Chapter 5
Terrorist Safe Havens (7120 Report)

Update of Information Originally Reported Under Section 7120(b) of the Intelligence Reform and Terrorist Prevention Act

Section 2656f(b) requires that this report include "an update of the information contained in the report required to be transmitted to Congress under Section 7120(b) of the 9/11 Commission Implementation Act." Section 7120(b) includes certain reporting requirements relating to terrorist "sanctuaries" in addition to other reporting requirements. [We have integrated the terrorist sanctuary reporting required under Section 7120(b) in the present chapter. Because the term "sanctuary" is commonly associated with places of worship, we have, for greater clarity and for consistency with the terminology used elsewhere in *Country Reports on Terrorism*, referred instead here to terrorist "safe havens." We interpret terrorist "safe haven" to have the same meaning as terrorist "sanctuary" for purposes of Section 7120(b).

The 7120 report includes:

1. Terrorist Safe Havens: Strategies, Tactics, Tools for Disrupting or Eliminating Safe Havens
2. Support for Pakistan
3. Collaboration with Saudi Arabia
4. Struggle of Ideas in the Islamic World
5. Outreach through the Broadcast Media
6. Visas for Participants in United States Programs
7. Basic Education in Muslim Countries
8. Economic Reform

5.1. Terrorist Safe Havens

Terrorist safe havens are defined in this report as ungoverned, under-governed, or ill-governed areas of a country and non-physical areas where terrorists that constitute a threat to U.S. national security interests are able to organize, plan, raise funds, communicate, recruit, train, and operate in relative security because of inadequate governance capacity, political will, or both. Physical safe havens provide security for terrorist leaders, allowing them to plan acts of terrorism around the world. Global communications and financial systems, especially those created by electronic infrastructure such as the internet, global media, and unregulated economic activity, further allow terrorists to carry out activities, particularly the dissemination of propaganda and misinformation, without the need for a physical safe haven. These "virtual" havens are highly mobile, difficult to track, and difficult to control, and are not based in any particular state. This part of the report, however, will not address virtual safe havens, focusing instead on physical safe havens.

Africa

Somalia

A small number of al-Qaida operatives found safe haven in East Africa, particularly Somalia, where they continued to pose a serious threat to American and allied interests in the region. Although these elements were severely disrupted at year's end as a result of Ethiopian and Somali Transitional Federal Government military actions, AQ continued to operate in Somalia and elsewhere in East Africa. Somalia remains a concern given the country's long unguarded coastline, porous borders, continued political instability, and proximity to the Arabian Peninsula all of which provide opportunities for terrorist transit and/or safe haven. AQ remains likely to make common cause with Somali extremists.

The Trans-Sahara

The Algeria based Salafist Group for Preaching and Combat (AQIM/GSPC) officially merged with al-Qaida in September, and subsequently changed its name to al-Qaida in the Islamic Maghreb (AQIM). The AQIM/GSPC continues to operate in the Trans-Sahara region, crossing difficult-to-patrol borders between Mali, Mauritania, Niger, Algeria, and Chad to recruit extremists within the region for training and terrorist operations in the Trans-Sahara, and possibly for operations outside the region. Its new alliance with Al-Qaida potentially has given it access to more resources and training.

Northern Mali served as a potential safe haven for terrorists, traffickers, and smugglers because the region's remoteness and harsh desert climate discouraged effective assertion of central government control. The al-Qaida-aligned AQIM/GSPC maintained a small-scale presence using sparsely populated areas in northern Mali as a safe haven, although the group does not maintain permanent facilities and is constantly on the move. Since a brief exchange of gunfire in April 2004, during which four Malian armed forces personnel were wounded, there have been no confrontations between the Malian military and the AQIM/GSPC. In September and October, a group of Malian Tuareg rebels, known as the Alliance for Democracy and Change (ADC), engaged in two fire-fights with the AQIM/GSPC in northern Mali. The Malian government has announced no official position on the violence between the ADC and AQIM/GSPC, nor did it attempt to confront AQIM/GSPC elements in the North or prevent their use of Malian territory in 2006.

The Government of Mauritaniaaggressively pursued AQIM/GSPC members on its territory, and several AQIM/GSPC members who attempted to infiltrate the country were arrested. In contrast with 2005, there were no terrorist attacks on Mauritanian soil. However, fighting between the AQIM/GSPC and Tuareg rebels in Northern Mali occasionally threatened the border region.

East Asia and Pacific

The Sulu/Sulawesi Seas Littoral.

Southeast Asia includes a safe haven area composed of the Sulawesi Sea and Sulu Archipelago, which sit astride the maritime boundary between Indonesia, Malaysia, and the Philippines. The geography of the thousands of islands in the region makes them very difficult for authorities to monitor. The range of non-terrorist activities, both licit and illicit, that are occurring in this maritime area pose another challenge to identifying and countering the terrorist threat. Although Indonesia, Malaysia, and the Philippines have improved their efforts to control their shared maritime boundaries, the area remained difficult to control. Surveillance is partial at best, and traditional smuggling and piracy groups provided an effective cover for terrorist activities in the area, such as movement of personnel, equipment, and funds. This area represents a safe haven for the AQ-linked Jemaah Islamiya (JI) organization and the Philippine Abu Sayyaf Group (ASG).

In 2006, Malaysian authorities arrested several members of a JI support cell in Sabah, Malaysia, who were facilitating JI activities across the tri-border area. In December, the Malaysian Defense Minister/Deputy Prime Minister and his Indonesian counterpart announced an initiative to enhance bilateral police cooperation along the land border on Borneo.

- **The Southern Philippines**. The Abu Sayyaf Group (ASG), responsible for multiple bombings and kidnappings throughout the southern Philippines in recent years, remained active, although weakened. Several key operatives, including ASG leader Khadaffy Janjalani and his lieutenant Abu Solaiman, were killed during a counterterrorism offensive by the Armed Forces of the Philippines. JI and ASG operatives continued to enjoy safe haven in the Southern Philippines, but sustained, effective counterterrorist field operations by Philippine military forces on key islands of the Sulu archipelago have had a marked impact on the terrorists' freedom of action. Development programs, civil-military affairs projects such as infrastructure construction, medical and dental clinics, and other measures have undermined public sympathy for terrorist groups and boosted popular support for the government.

- **Indonesia**. Although Indonesia has made significant progress in weakening the JI terrorist organization, JI continues to operate in Indonesia, a geographically widespread archipelago country with porous borders and CT resource constraints. Key JI operational planner Noordin Mat Top remains on the run, although aggressively pursued by Indonesian CT authorities.

Near East Asia

Iraq

Iraq is not currently a terrorist safe haven, but terrorists, including Sunni groups like al-Qaida in Iraq (AQI), Ansar al-Islam (AI), and Ansar al-Sunna (AS), as well as Shia extremists and other groups, view Iraq as a potential safe haven and are attempting to make it a reality.

The June 7 death of AQI leader, Abu Musab al-Zarqawi, damaged the group's leadership but did not diminish attacks against Coalition Forces, Iraqi civilians and infrastructure nor did it halt overall increasing attack trends by the group and other affiliated groups. Senior Iraqi officials, including Iraqi President Talabani, traveled to Iran throughout the year encouraging the Iranian government to support Iraq's political process and to stop material support of terrorist groups and militias. Although efforts by the Iraqi government, the United States, Coalition partners, and the international community are helping to thwart the terrorists' ambitions, the battle is not over. Prospects for increasing stability in Iraq over the next year will depend on: the extent to which the Iraqi government and political leaders can establish effective national institutions that transcend sectarian or ethnic interests and, within this context, the willingness of the security forces to pursue extremist elements of all kinds; the extent to which extremists, most notably AQI, can be defeated in their attempt to foment inter-sectarian struggle between Shia and Sunnis; and the extent to which Iraq's neighbors, especially Iran and Syria, can be persuaded to stop the flow of militants and munitions across their borders.

- **Northern Iraq**. The Kongra-Gel/PKK maintains an active presence in northern Iraq, from which it coordinates attacks in the predominantly ethnic Kurdish areas of southeastern Turkey and provides logistical support to forces that launch attacks into Turkey, primarily against Turkish security forces, local Turkish officials, and villagers who oppose the organization. In an effort to demonstrate further that the Iraqi government would not allow Iraq to become a safe haven for terrorist organizations, Prime Minister Nuri al-Maliki appointed the Minister of State for National Security, Shirwan al-Waeli, as the Iraq coordinator for PKK issues.

Lebanon

In accordance with UNSC Resolution 1701, the Lebanese Armed Forces (LAF) strengthened its border presence and deployed 15,000 troops to patrols in the south, establishing itself in this region for the first time in 30 years. The LAF was assisted by UNIFIL, authorized to deploy up to 15,000 international peacekeepers south of the Litani River. Also, the Internal Security Force created a special unit to combat terrorism and established branches of this unit to preempt terrorist activity in northern and central Lebanon. Despite these steps, Lebanon remains a safe haven for terrorist activities. Hizballah remains the most prominent and powerful terrorist group in Lebanon, with a strong influence among Lebanon's large Shia community. Hizballah maintains offices in Beirut and elsewhere in the country, has official liaison officers to the security services, is represented by elected deputies in parliament, and has two ministers in the cabinet (although they have suspended their participation in the government). Hizballah is still recognized by the Lebanese government as a legitimate "resistance group" and political party.

The unstable political situation in Lebanon also contributed to enabling foreign Sunni extremists with links to AQ to infiltrate Lebanon and to set up cells, including within the Palestinian refugee camps. Palestinian extremist groups also have exploited the absence of Lebanese government authority within the 12 refugee camps, which have become terrorist safe havens and LAF no-go zones. We believe that some of these groups, such as AQ-associated Asbat al-Ansar, and Fatah al-Islam, have used the safe haven within the camps to train for terrorist attacks in Lebanon proper.

See Chapter 3, State Sponsors of Terrorism, for discussions on **Iran** and **Syria**, which provide safe haven to Hizballah and Palestinian terrorist groups, and are used as safe havens by al-Qaida-linked operatives and groups.

Yemen. AQ's operational structure in Yemen has been weakened and dispersed, but concerns remain about the organization's attempts to reconstitute operational cells there. Yemen continues to increase its maritime security capabilities, but land border security along the extensive frontier with Saudi Arabia remains a problem, despite increased Yemeni-Saudi cooperation on bilateral security issues.

Southwest Asia

Afghan-Pakistan Border

Historically, Islamabad and Kabul have not exerted comprehensive control over the mountainous and sparsely populated Afghan-Pakistan border—the famed "Durand Line." Fiercely independent Pashtun and Baluch tribes straddle the border, which is routinely crossed by militants and extremists.

Pakistan

The Federally Administered Tribal Areas (FATA) of Pakistan have become a safe haven for AQ terrorists and Afghan insurgents since the fall of the Taliban in December 2001. Islamist Deobandi groups and many local tribesmen in the FATA continue to resist the government's efforts to improve governance and administrative control at the expense of longstanding local autonomy. Despite Pakistan's efforts to eliminate threats and establish effective governance in the FATA, these tribal areas continued to be terrorist safe havens and sources of instability for Pakistan and its neighbors. The government maintains approximately 80,000 troops, including Army and Frontier Corps (FC) units, along the Afghanistan border. The U.S. plans to help modernize and increase the capacity of the Frontier Corps so they can become a more effective force. The Pakistani government expects to close four Afghan refugee camps-in which terrorists and violent extremists often hide - this year. Pakistan Army and FC units have targeted and raided AQ and other militant safe havens in the FATA. The failure of the tribal leaders in the FATA to fulfill their promises to the government under the terms of the North Waziristan agreement signed in September, failed to stem insurgent infiltration into Afghanistan.

In order to increase the central government's writ in the FATA, the Government of Pakistan is implementing a comprehensive approach with three prongs: political, security, and developmental. For the political prong, Pakistan seeks to bolster effective governance by empowering local officials. For the security prong, Pakistan's objective is to increase the capacity and efficacy of local security forces. For the developmental prong, the Government of Pakistan has designed a comprehensive sustainable development plan for the region. The plan concentrates on four sectors (basic human services, natural resources, communication/ infrastructure, and economic development) and, if fully implemented, would cost $2 billion. The plan was developed with the extensive grassroots participation of all stakeholders and will provide essential economic and livelihood opportunities while upgrading and expanding social services to a population at risk for recruitment by extremist and terrorist organizations.

- **Afghanistan**. The Afghan government, in concert with ISAF/NATO forces and the international community, continues efforts to build security on the Afghan side of the border. The border areas remain contested, however, with ongoing insurgent and terrorist attacks, to include al-Qaida activity. Taliban terrorist attacks, alongside with those of associated extremist movements such as Hizb-e-Islami Gulbuddin (HIG) and the Haqqani network, continued throughout Afghanistan. Taliban-sponsored insurgency, terrorism, and related narcotics cultivation remained particularly prevalent in the South and East of the country.

Western Hemisphere

Colombia Border Region

This region includes the borders between Colombia on one side, and Venezuela, Ecuador, Peru, Panama, and Brazil on the other. Rough terrain, dense forest cover, low population densities, and lack of government authority and presence in this area create an area of safe haven for insurgent and terrorist groups, including especially the Revolutionary Armed Forces of Colombia (FARC). Brazil, Ecuador, Peru, and Panama have adopted an tacit policy mix of containment and non-confrontation with Colombian narcoterrorist groups, with, however, some confrontations occurring. Much of this depends on local decisions and relations. The FARC uses remote areas in Colombia's border regions to rest and regroup, procure supplies, and stage and train for terrorist attacks. In addition, the FARC and another designated terrorist organization, the National Liberation Army (ELN) regard Venezuelan territory near the border as a safe haven and often use the area for cross-border incursions. Splinter groups of the FARC and breakaway members of another designated terrorist organization, the United Self-Defense Forces of Colombia (AUC), operate in various parts of Venezuela and are involved in drug trafficking.

The Tri-Border Area (Argentina, Brazil, and Paraguay)

The United States remains concerned that Hizballah and HAMAS are using the Tri-Border area as a safe haven in which to raise funds by participating in illicit activities and soliciting donations from extremists within the sizable Muslim communities in the region and elsewhere in Argentina, Brazil, and Paraguay. Although there was no corroborated information that these or other Islamic extremist groups used the region for military-type training, or planning of terrorist operations, suspected supporters of Islamic terrorist groups, including Hizballah, take advantage of loosely regulated territory and proximity to Muslim communities in Ciudad del Este, Paraguay, and Foz do Iguacu, Brazil, to engage in illegal activity and illicit fundraising. The governments of the TBA have long been concerned with arms and drugs smuggling, document fraud, money laundering, and the manufacture and movement of contraband goods through this region. In the early 1990s, the governments established a mechanism to address these illicit activities.

Strategies, Tactics, Tools for Disrupting or Eliminating Safe Havens

Corruption, poverty, a lack of civic institutions and social services, politically repressive governments, inadequate or unjust law enforcement and legal systems are conditions terrorists exploit for recruitment, operational planning or physical safe haven. Efforts to build partner capacity and encourage states to cooperate more effectively at the local and regional level are key to denying terrorists safe haven. U.S. Ambassadors, as the President's personal representatives abroad, have a unique responsibility to bring all elements of national power to bear against the terrorist enemy. They lead interagency Country Teams that develop strategies to help host nations understand the threat and to strengthen their political will and capacity to counter it.

Defeating the terrorist enemy requires a comprehensive effort executed locally, nationally, regionally and globally. Working with partner nations, we must eliminate terrorist leadership, but incarcerating or killing terrorists will not achieve an end to terrorism. We must simultaneously eliminate terrorist safe havens, tailoring regional strategies to disaggregate terrorist networks, breaking terrorist financial, travel, communications and intelligence links. Finally, and most challenging, we must address the underlying conditions that terrorists exploit. These include geo-political issues, lack of economic opportunity and political participation, ethnic conflict, ungoverned space, or political injustice.

Regional Strategic Initiative

Building on this understanding, we have worked to develop the Regional Strategic Initiative (RSI), an effort to develop flexible regional networks of interconnected Country Teams. The State Department's Office of the Coordinator for Counterterrorism (S/CT) is working with ambassadors and interagency representatives in key terrorist theaters of operation to assess the threat and devise collaborative strategies, action plans, and policy recommendations.

The RSI is a key tool in promoting cooperation between our partners in the War on Terror—for example with Malaysia, Indonesia and the Philippines as they confront terrorist transit across the Sulawesi Sea; or among Mauritania, Algeria, Morocco, Niger, Chad, and Mali, to counter a GSPC/AQIM enemy recruiting and hiding in the desert that sits astride national borders. Terrorists are highly adaptable; defeating them requires both centralized coordination and field authority. Resources and responses must be applied in a rapid, flexible, and focused manner. The RSI helps achieve this coordinated approach.

As of December 2006, RSI strategy groups were in place for Southeast Asia, Iraq and its neighbors, the Eastern Mediterranean, the Western Mediterranean, and the Horn of Africa. These groups are chaired by Ambassadors, with interagency representatives participating. RSI programs focus on developing a common understanding of the strategic situation in a region. Using this shared perspective, networked Country Teams then identify opportunities for collaboration and pool resources not only to eliminate terrorism safe havens, but also to address the conditions that terrorists exploit for recruitment.

Terrorists operate without regard to national boundaries. To effectively counter terrorists, we are working to strengthen our regional and transnational partnerships and increasingly operate in a regional context. Denying safe haven plays a major role in undermining terrorists' capacity to operate effectively and forms a key element of U.S. counterterrorism strategy as well as the cornerstone of UN Security Council Resolution 1373, adopted in September 2001. UNSCR 1373 specifically targets terrorists' ability to move across international borders and find safe haven, to solicit and move funds, and to acquire weapons. It also calls on UN member states to enact laws criminalizing terrorist activity and support to enact such laws.

Countering Terrorism on the Economic Front

Since the terrorist attacks of September 11, 2001, the United States has acted to block funding of terrorists and their supporters and to promote international cooperation against them. On September 23, 2001, the President signed E.O. 13224, giving the United States a powerful tool to impede terrorist funding. This executive order provides a means to disrupt the financial support network for terrorists and terrorist organizations by authorizing the U.S. government to designate and block assets of foreign individuals and entities that commit, or pose a significant risk of committing, acts of terrorism. In addition, because of the pervasiveness and expansiveness of the financial base of foreign terrorists, the order authorizes the U.S. government to block the assets of individuals and entities that provide support, offer assistance to, or otherwise associate with designated terrorists and terrorist organizations. The order also covers their subsidiaries, front organizations, agents, and associates.

The Secretary of State, in consultation with the Attorney General and the Secretary of the Treasury, continues to designate Foreign Terrorist Organizations (FTOs) pursuant to Section 219 of the Immigration and Nationality Act, as amended. These designations play a critical role in the U.S. fight against terrorism and are an effective means of curtailing support for terrorist activities and pressuring groups to get out of the terrorism business. Among the consequences of such a designation, it is unlawful for U.S. citizens or any persons subject to the jurisdiction of the U.S. to provide funds or material support to a designated FTO. U.S. financial institutions are also required to freeze the funds of designated FTOs.

Executive Order and Foreign Terrorist Organization designations support U.S. efforts to curb the financing of terrorism and encourage other nations to do the same. They internationally stigmatize and isolate designated terrorist entities and individuals. They also deter donations or contributions to, and economic transactions with, named entities and individuals. In addition, they heighten public awareness and knowledge of terrorist organizations and signal to other governments U.S. concerns about named entities and individuals.

International cooperation remains fundamental to our common endeavors for the simple reason that most of the funds used to support terrorism are located outside the jurisdiction of the United States. International cooperation is essential to initiatives in fields ranging from intelligence and law enforcement coordination to targeted financial sanctions to norms and standards of financial regulation.

United Nations Security Council Resolution 1267 and successor resolutions require member states to impose financial and other sanctions on listed groups and individuals associated with Usama bin Ladin, the Taliban, or al-Qaida. In 2006, UNSCR 1735 was adopted, clarifying procedures for both listing and delisting terrorist groups and entities under 1267 in an effort to increase transparency. UNSCR 1735, also encourages member states and the 1267 Committee to update the Taliban section of the 1267 consolidated sanctions list, both by submitting additional names for inclusion on the Consolidate List of individuals and entities associated with the Taliban, especially those responsible for the recent upsurge of Taliban violence in Afghanistan, as well as considering petitions to remove listed members and/or associates no longer associated with the Taliban. In December 2006, the United States and France co-sponsored UNSCR 1730 in response to a call for improving procedures for delisting individuals and entities from the 1267 Committee's Consolidated List.

In 2006, the United States and other UN members designated a number of individuals and entities:

- On February 8, the United States designated five individuals and four entities for their role in financing the Libya Islamic Fight Group (LIFG), an AQ affiliate known for engaging in terrorist activity in Libyan and cooperating with AQ worldwide. Abd Al-Rahman Al-Faqih, Ghuma Abd'rabbah, Abdulbaqi Mohammed Khaled, Tahir Nasuf, and Mohammed Benhammedi were designated pursuant to E.O.13224 as were the four entities Sara Properties Ltd., Meadowbrook Investments Ltd., Sanabel Relief Agency Ltd., and Ozlam Properties, Ltd. On February 7, the UN 1267 Sanctions Committee added these individuals and entities and entities to its list of individuals and entities associated with Usama bin Ladin, the Taliban, or al-Qaida.
- On March 23, the United States designated Al-Manar, a satellite owned or controlled by the Iran-funded Hizballah terrorist network. Also designated were Al-Nour Radio and the Lebanese Media group, the parent company to both Al-Manar and Al-Nour.

- On April 13, the United States designated four top leaders of the al-Qaida-linked Southeast Asian terrorist organization Jemaah Islamiya (JI) pursuant to E.O. 13224: Abdullah Anshori, Abu Bakar Ba'asyir, Gun Gun Rusman Gunawan, and Taufik Rifki.
- On July 20, the United States designated Abu Sufian Al Salambai Muhammed Ahmed Abd Al-Razziq for high level ties to and support for the al-Qaida network pursuant to E.O.13224.
- On August 4, the United States designated the Indonesian and Philippine branches of the Saudi-based International Islamic Relief Organization (IIRO) for facilitating fundraising for al-Qaida and affiliated terrorist groups pursuant to E.O. 13224. The Executive Director of the Eastern Province Branch of IIRO in Saudi Arabia, Abd Al Hamid Sulaiman Al-Mujil, was also designated for using his position to bankroll the al-Qaida network in Southeast Asia. On August 4, the UN 1267 Sanctions Committee added Abd Al Hamid Sulaiman Al-Mujil and the Philippine branch of the IIRO to its list of individuals and entities associated with Usama bin Ladin, the Taliban, or al-Qaida.
- On August 30, the Islamic Resistance Support Organization (IRSO), a key Hizballah fund-raising organization, was designated under E.O.13224.
- On September 7, the United States designated two financial companies and one individual that provided financial support to the Iran funded Hizballah terrorist network. Bayt al-Mal and the Yousser Company as well as Husayn al-Shami, the head of Bayt al-Mal and a senior Hizballah leader, were designated under E.O.13224.
- On December 6, the United States designated nine individuals and two entities located in the triple frontier of Argentina, Brazil and Paraguay that provided financial and logistical support to Hizballah. Muhammad Yusuf Abdallah, Hamzi Ahmad Barakat, Hatim Ahmad Barakat, Muhammad Fayez Barakat, Muhammad Tarabain Chamas, Saleh Mahmud Fayad, Sobhi Mahmud Fayad, Ali Muhammad Kazan, and Farouk Omairi, and two businesses, Casa Hamze and Galeria Page; were designated under E.O. 13224.
- On December 7, the United States designated five individuals under E.O.13224 for providing financial support to al-Qaida and other terrorist organizations as well as facilitating terrorist activity. Mullah Krekar, Hamed Al Ali, Jaber Al Jalamah, Mubarak Al Btahali, and Mohamed Moumou were designated. On December 7, the UN 1267 Sanctions Committee approved the request that Mohamed Moumou and Mullah Krekar be added to its list of individuals and entities associated with Usama bin Ladin, the Taliban, or al-Qaida.

- December 12, Mohammed Al-Ghabra, a British citizen who provided material and logistical support to al-Qaida and other terrorist organizations, was added to the UN 1267 Sanctions Committee list. On December 19, the United States designated Mohammed Al-Ghabra under E.O. 13224.
- As of December 31, 2006, the United States has designated a total of 469 individuals and entities as terrorists, their financiers, or facilitators, since 2001. The global community has frozen more than $153 million in terrorist-related assets.

Bringing Terrorists to Justice

The Rewards for Justice(RFJ) Program continues to be one of America's most valuable assets in the War on Terror. Through RFJ, the Secretary of State may offer rewards for information that prevents or successfully resolves an act of international terrorism against the United States. Rewards of up to $25 million have been authorized for information leading to the capture of Usama bin Laden and other key al-Qaida leaders. Since its inception in 1984, RFJ has paid more than $62 million to over 40 people who provided credible information. In 2006, rewards totaling $1.1 million were approved for the successful resolution of terrorist cases in Afghanistan and the Philippines. In January, the Department of State paid a reward of $500,000 to an individual who assisted U.S. authorities in resolving a terrorist case involving al-Qaida operative Habis Abdulla al-Saoub.

In January and May, two public rewards ceremonies were jointly sponsored by the U.S. Embassy in Manila and the Government of the Philippines. In January, the Department paid a reward of $100,000 to an individual who helped the Government of the Philippines bring to justice Abu Sayyaf Group member Toting Craft Hanno. In May, the Department paid rewards of $250,000 each to two persons who supported Filipino authorities in their efforts to bring Rajah Solaiman Movement leader Ahmad Santos to justice.

New initiatives included adding five new reward offers at $1 million each for key al-Qaida leaders. In June, Abu Ayyub al-Masri was added to the RFJ program upon the death of Abu Musab al-Zarqawi, the former leader of al-Qaida in Iraq. In addition, the Secretary approved a reward of up to $1 million for the American-born al-Qaida terrorist Adam Gadahn. In October, the Bureau of Diplomatic Security and the FBI conducted a joint press conference announcing the RFJ reward offer and the indictment of Gadahn on charges of treason.

Bilateral and Multilateral Efforts to Identify and Address Terrorist Safe Havens

Throughout the year, the United States worked closely with multilateral partners in numerous counterterrorist financing efforts, including the Counterterrorism Committee of the United Nations, the Egmont Group of Financial Intelligence Units, the Financial Action Task Force (FATF), the G8's Counterterrorism Assistance Group (CTAG), and international financial institutions. In addition, the United States continued its regular dialogue on terrorism finance with the European Union. Since its launch in September 2004, the dialogue has served as the framework for ongoing exchanges to promote information sharing and cooperation on FATF and on technical assistance issues.

European nations are active participants in a variety of multilateral organizations that contributed to counterterrorist efforts, including the G8, NATO, the Financial Action Task Force (FATF), the Organization for Security and Cooperation in Europe (OSCE), the International Maritime Organization (IMO), and the International Civil Aviation Organization (ICAO). The United States and its partners worked through these organizations to establish and implement best practices, build the counterterrorism capabilities of "weak but willing" states, and institutionalize the War on Terror globally. The World Bank and International Monetary Fund also have pledged to provide countries with training to increase their capacity to combat money laundering and terrorist financing.

The United Nations

The United Nations continued to devote energy to the fight against terrorism. The Security Council adopted four resolutions related to terrorism:

- Resolution 1673, adopted in April, reauthorized and improved the mandate of the 1540 committee, which deals with nonproliferation and preventing terrorist access to WMD.
- Resolution 1686, adopted in June, extended the mandate of the International Independent Investigation Commission and supported its intention to extend further technical assistance to the Lebanese authorities regarding their investigations in terrorist attacks in Lebanon since October 1, 2004.
- Resolution 1699, adopted in August, endorsed and encouraged increased cooperation between the UN and INTERPOL to help facilitate the implementation of sanctions, including counterterrorism sanctions.
- Resolution 1735, adopted in December, strengthened the current sanctions regime against the Taliban, Usama bin Laden, and al-Qaida.

The Counter-Terrorism Committee (CTC) was established by Security Council Resolution 1373 after September 11, 2001, with the goal of enhancing the ability of UN member states to combat terrorism. The Counter-Terrorism Committee's Executive Directorate (CTED), established by Resolution 1535 in 2004, became fully operational in December 2005. CTED's mandate is to enhance the Committee's ability to monitor the implementation of Resolution 1373 and to continue its capacity-building work by facilitating technical assistance to member states and promoting closer cooperation and coordination with international, regional, and subregional organizations. It also conducts visits in member states to assess the implementation of Resolution 1373. CTED visited ten states in 2006, and the CTC has approved another 17 visits for the future. Resolution 1624 (2005), concerning incitement to terrorism and denial of safe havens, also directs the CTC, among other things, to include implementation of Resolution 1624 (2005) in its dialogue with states. CTED is doing so in its visits to member states.

The 1267 Sanctions Committee, also established by the Security Council, maintains a list of individuals and entities associated with al-Qaida, the Taliban, and/or Usama bin Ladin who are subject to international sanctions—assets freeze, travel ban, and arms embargo—that member states are obligated to implement. The Committee entered into an agreement to exchange information with Interpol with the goal of better enforcing the sanctions.

In 2006, the UN General Assembly took several important steps to counterterrorism. The General Assembly negotiated and adopted three terrorism-related resolutions, 61/40, 61/86, and 61/161, and continued work on the negotiation of a Comprehensive Convention on International Terrorism. The General Assembly concluded the International Convention for the Suppression of Acts of Nuclear Terrorism in 2005, and, by July 2006, 106 states had signed this important new instrument. In September 2006, the United Nations General Assembly adopted the United Nations Global Counter-Terrorism Strategy.

Then-UN Secretary General, Kofi Annan continued to use his office to focus the international community on terrorism. He took steps to institutionalize the Counterterrorism Implementation Task Force, which brings together 23 United Nations system entities that address different aspects of terrorism. He also established a focal point within the Secretariat to help coordinate a civil society campaign to counterterrorism and suggested the creation of an informal group of UN technical assistance providers, donors and recipients to exchange information and coordinate efforts.

UN Secretariat staff of the Terrorism Prevention Branch in Vienna, Austria, continued to help countries build the legal framework necessary to become party to and implement the international counterterrorism conventions and protocols.

UN Specialized Agencies are also involved in the work of fighting terrorism. For example, the International Civil Aviation Organization adopted passport security standards, and the International Maritime Organization engaged in security-related activities designed to make it harder for terrorists to operate in the commercial shipping arena. In February, a new protocol to the 1988 Convention for the Suppression of Unlawful Acts against the Safety of Maritime Navigation and a new protocol to the 1988 Protocol for the Suppression of Unlawful Acts against Fixed Platforms on the Continental Shelf opened for signature. The International Atomic Energy Agency (IAEA) launched a nuclear security action plan to combat the threat of terrorism involving nuclear and other radioactive materials. The IAEA also promoted more rigorous standards for securing radioactive sources and released the first international export control framework for radioactive sources. In February, under a global security initiative, an IAEA-supported operation safely conditioned, packaged, and shipped radioactive neutron sources from three African countries to the United States for ultimate disposition. In April, the IAEA supported the removal of potentially weapon-usable highly enriched uranium from a civilian research reactor in Uzbekistan. In July, two potentially dangerous radioactive devices were successfully secured in the Republic of Georgia. In December, the IAEA supported the return to Russia of over 200 kg of highly enriched uranium from a research reactor in Germany.

G8 Counterterrorism Actions

The Group of Eight (G8), the United States, Canada, France, Germany, Italy, Japan, Russia, and the United Kingdom, has been instrumental in developing cutting-edge counterterrorism standards and practices. These included enhanced travel document security standards, as well as strengthened controls over exports and stockpile security to mitigate the threat to airports from illicit acquisition of shoulder-fired anti-aircraft missiles (man portable air defense systems, or MANPADS).

G8 counterterrorism initiatives often have an impact well beyond the borders of G8 member states since the group actively seeks to promulgate the standards and practices it develops to international standard-setting organizations. In 2006, the G8 completed the Secure and Facilitated International Travel Initiative (SAFTI) and produced two counterterrorism-related documents for the St. Petersburg Summit.

Since 2004, G8 leaders have expressed their commitment to defending against bioterrorism. Through the work of the Bioterrorism Experts Group (BTEX), G8 efforts to counter bioterrorism include strengthening national and international biosurveillance capabilities, increasing protection of the global food supply, and improving bioterrorism response and mitigation capabilities.

Securing Critical Energy Infrastructure

At the July 2006 St. Petersburg Summit, President Bush and the other leaders of the G8 announced a plan of action to secure global critical energy infrastructures, including:

- Defining and ranking vulnerabilities of critical energy infrastructure sites;
- Assessing emerging and potential risks of terrorists attacks; and
- Developing best practices for effective security across all energy sectors.

Counterterrorism Action Group (CTAG)

At the June 2003 Evian Summit, G8 leaders adopted a plan to build political will and capacity to combat terrorism globally, and established the Counterterrorism Action Group (CTAG) to implement this plan. CTAG supports the UN Counter-Terrorism Committee's efforts to monitor and promote implementation of UNSCR 1373 by developing an active forum for donors to coordinate counterterrorism cooperation with, and assistance to, third countries. CTAG promotes counterterrorism by prioritizing needs, and targeting and coordinating assistance to expand counterterrorism capacity in recipient countries. CTAG also encourages all countries to meet their obligations under UNSCR 1373 and, for states party to them, the 13 international counterterrorism conventions and protocols.

Under the leadership of the rotating G8 presidency, CTAG meets three times per year with the active participation of G8 member states, the European Commission, the UN Counterterrorism Committee, and other countries and organizations. Coordination meetings hosted by the local embassy of the G8 presidency were also held among CTAG members' diplomatic missions in recipient countries.

In 2006, CTAG coordinated diplomatic, donor cooperation, and donor assistance efforts, including:

- Cooperated with the UN Counterterrorism Committee Executive Directorate (CTED) during country visits by contributing significantly to the preparation of the visits, meeting with CTED during those visits, and monitoring the implementation by visited countries of the CTC's recommendations;
- Facilitated universal adherence to the 13 international counterterrorism conventions and protocols by encouraging more than a dozen countries to approve unratified instruments;
- Focused counterterrorism donor assistance on needs in the Asia-Pacific Economic Cooperation (APEC) region, especially port and maritime security gaps, in concert with APEC's Counterterrorism Task Force;

- Coordinated donor assistance to help countries in the Asia and South America assess and improve airport security; and
- Promoted and assisting implementation of travel security and facilitation standards and practices being developed by the G8 under its Secure and Facilitated International Travel Initiative (SAFTI).

Financial Action Task Force (FATF)

Under the Department of Treasury's leadership, the United States played a strong role in developing new initiatives within FATF to meet evolving anti-money laundering and counterterrorism finance threats. The United States became a co-chair, with Italy, of the newly created International Cooperation Review Group to examine AML/CTF systemic threats and participated in major FATF studies (e.g., Trade-Based Money Laundering) and FATF mutual evaluations.

European Union (EU)

The United States and the European Union's Judicial Cooperation Unit (Eurojust) agreed to improve cooperation and information exchange among investigators and prosecutors, posting a U.S. Liaison Prosecutor at Eurojust. We continue to make progress toward ratification and entry into force of the U.S.-EU Extradition and Mutual Legal Assistance Agreements between the United States and EU member states. Expert level discussions have begun on mutual recognition of the EU Authorized Economic Operator provisions and the U.S. Customs -Trade Partnership Against Terrorism. We have begun a pilot project to the Container Security Initiative for feeder ports, to increase security of goods transiting our ports, and continue to work jointly to refine our risk assessments. A pilot in Southampton under the U.S. Secure Freight Initiative should improve detection and response capabilities for high-risk container traffic.

In October, the United States and the EU concluded an interim agreement on the processing of passenger name record data. We are studying the comparability of our airport assessment programs and will continue to refine international airport security measures, as in our successful joint effort to establish a common standard for liquids in carry-on baggage.

The United States and the EU continued to improve procedures for information sharing and for proactively implementing FATF Special Recommendations, including enforcing cash declaration regulations for travelers and getting private sector financial institutions to improve implementation of asset freeze measures. We continue to exchange information and best practices in expert-level discussions. In 2006, conferences on terrorism finance and money laundering issues were held with sanctions implementers, analysts, and prosecutors and investigators. We are working on a public outreach statement on fairness and transparency in the implementation of sanctions regimes.

Organization for Security and Cooperation in Europe (OSCE)

The United States worked with the OSCE to establish and implement best counterterrorism practices and help build the capacity of OSCE members. OSCE members committed themselves to becoming parties to the 13 UN terrorism conventions and protocols, to work together to modernize travel documents and shipping container security, to prevent and suppress the financing of terrorist organizations, and to implement UNSC Resolution 1540 to counter WMD (related materials and the means of delivery) proliferation. The OSCE also held two regional workshops on ICAO's minimum security standards for handling and issuance of passports, sponsored visits by ICAO and other experts to provide technical advice to requesting countries on new travel document security features, and increased OSCE countries' cooperation with Interpol in reporting lost or stolen passports. The OSCE, in conjunction with the UNODC, held its second experts workshop in 2006 on promoting legal cooperation in criminal matters as related to terrorism, which covered such issues as extradition and mutual legal assistance. The OSCE also held a conference on countering the use of the Internet for terrorist purposes.

North Atlantic Treaty Organization (NATO)

The North Atlantic Treaty Organization (NATO) plays a key role in combating terrorism at the regional level in Europe. First and foremost, NATO is contributing to the War on Terror by leading security and stability operations in Afghanistan and continuing Operation Active Endeavor (OAE), a naval operation that aims to combat terrorism by monitoring maritime traffic in the Mediterranean. The Alliance is also engaged in a far-reaching transformation of its forces and capabilities to better deter and defend against 21st Century threats, including terrorism, and is working closely with partner countries and organizations to ensure interoperability of forces and broad cooperation.

Trans-Sahara Counterterrorism Partnership (TSCTP)

The Trans-Sahara Counterterrorism Partnership (TSCTP) is a multi-faceted, multi-year strategy aimed at defeating terrorist organizations by strengthening regional counterterrorism capabilities, enhancing and institutionalizing cooperation among the region's security forces, promoting democratic governance, discrediting terrorist ideology, and reinforcing bilateral military ties with the United States. The overall goals are to enhance the indigenous capacities of governments in the pan-Sahel (Mauritania, Mali, Chad, and Niger, as well as Nigeria and Senegal) to confront the challenge posed by terrorist organizations in the region, and to facilitate cooperation between those countries and our Maghreb partners (Morocco, Algeria, and Tunisia) in combating terrorism. See Chapter 2, *Country Reports, Africa,* for further information on the TSCTP.

The African Union

The African Union (AU) has several counterterrorism legal instruments, including a Convention on Prevention and Combating of Terrorism (1999), a 2002 *Protocol to the Convention, and a 2004 Plan of Action*. See Chapter 2, *Country Reports, Africa,* for further information on the AU.

Association of Southeast Asian Nations (ASEAN) and the ASEAN Regional Forum (ARF)

The United States works closely with the ten-member Association of Southeast Asian Nations (ASEAN), comprising Brunei, Burma, Cambodia, Indonesia, Laos, Malaysia, Philippines, Singapore, Thailand, and Vietnam to enhance counterterrorism cooperation. In July 2006, Secretary of State Rice and her ASEAN counterparts signed the "Framework Document for the Plan of Action to Implement the ASEAN-U.S. Enhanced Partnership." The Plan of Action identifies a range of measures to strengthen cooperation on maritime security, law enforcement, border security, information sharing, suppressing illicit money transfers and terrorist financial flows, curbing the abuse of NGOs and charities, as well as on other transnational crime issues. The United States actively participates in counterterrorism-related activities of the 26-member ASEAN Regional Forum (ARF), including the annual meetings on counterterrorism and transnational crime. The United States has continued efforts to increase maritime security cooperation by co-chairing with Singapore an ARF confidence-building measure in 2005 focused on preventing and countering terrorist attacks and other unlawful acts. This event built on earlier efforts to strengthen agreement on the key elements of maritime security among participants. Subsequent events, hosted by India and Japan respectively, have focused on expanding cooperation in capacity building for maritime security. In July of 2005, ARF Foreign Ministers adopted the "Statement on Information Sharing and Intelligence Exchange and Document Integrity and Security in Enhancing Cooperation to Combat Terrorism and other Transnational Crimes" in which ministers committed to improve cooperation among participants in these areas.

Asia Pacific Economic Cooperation (APEC)

The 21 member economies of APEC (Australia, Brunei, Canada, Chile, China, Hong Kong, Indonesia, Japan, Republic of Korea, Malaysia, Mexico, New Zealand, Papua New Guinea, Peru, Philippines, Russia, Singapore,

Chinese Taipei, Thailand, the United States, and Vietnam) are committed to creating a safe environment for the movement of goods, services, and people throughout the region. The APEC Counterterrorism Task Force (CTTF) was established in 2003 to coordinate implementation of Leaders' and Ministers' statements on counterterrorism and non-proliferation. The United States works within APEC to dismantle transnational terrorist groups and to eliminate the severe and growing danger posed by proliferation of weapons of mass destruction and their means of delivery.

In 2006, with Australian and Chilean co-sponsorship, the United States introduced the first bioterrorism/biodefense initiative in APEC to protect the food supply from deliberate contamination. The United States co-hosted an experts-level workshop in Bangkok in November to share experiences and develop best practices. APEC is also committed to bolstering regional maritime and port security, and to strengthening international non-proliferation regimes. In 2005, APEC members adopted the Framework for Secure Trade and provided capacity building to seven economies to assist with implementation of the International Ship and Port Facility Security code. APEC export control systems were strengthened through capacity building initiatives, such as the 2005 Export Control Conference for APEC Economies. APEC also ensured the safe handling of radioactive sources through an agreement to implement the International Atomic Energy Agency (IAEA) Code of Conduct and Import/Export Guidelines for Radioactive Sources by the end of 2006. Airport Security was further enhanced through APEC members' agreement to undertake Man Portable Air Defense Systems (MANPADS) Vulnerability Assessments at international airports based on ICAO or similar international guidelines. APEC enhanced travel security through improvements in travel document security standards and the launch of a pilot project to share lost and stolen passport data between Australia, New Zealand, and the United States. APEC also continues to combat terrorist financing in APEC economies through efforts to strengthen financial intelligence units.

OAS Inter-American Committee against Terrorism (CICTE)

CICTE delivered more than $5 million in counterterrorism capacity-building assistance in the region. CICTE provided training to nearly 500 port and airport security officials from 29 member states to help meet the requirements of the International Maritime Organization's International Ship and Port Facility Security (ISPS) code, and the International Civil Aviation Organization's (ICAO) new air security standards. CICTE advised 15 member state governments on how to meet the requirements of UNSCR 1373, the 13 international conventions and protocols relating to terrorism, and the Inter-American Convention against Terrorism (IACAT), which complements and expands on international conventions and protocols. CICTE also organized its sixth annual regular session in Bogota, Colombia.

Three Plus One Group on Tri-Border Area Security (3+1)

Argentina hosted a meeting of the 3+1 Group (Argentina, Brazil, Paraguay, and the United States) in December. Delegates highlighted the importance of early warnings among States and the immediate exchange of information to prevent and combat illegal activities, and to deny refuge to those who finance, plan, or commit acts of terrorism. In November, Brazil inaugurated a new Regional Intelligence Center, in Foz do Iguacu, dedicated to coordinating intelligence activities of the police forces of Argentina, Brazil, and Paraguay, and invited Argentina and Paraguay to send official representatives to help staff the center.

Long-Term Goals and Programs/Actions Designed to Reduce Conditions that Allow Terrorist Safe Havens to Form

The Middle East Partnership Initiative

As President Bush noted, when an "entire region sees the promise of freedom in its midst, the terrorist ideology will become more and more irrelevant, until that day when it is viewed with contempt or ignored altogether." Conversely, systems characterized by an absence of political choice, transparent governance, economic opportunities, and personal freedoms can become incubators for extremism, hate, and violence.

To this end, in 2006, the State Department's Middle East Partnership Initiative (MEPI) continued to provide tangible support to reformers in the region so democracy could spread, education could thrive, economies could grow, and women could be empowered. Working in 16 countries and the Palestinian territories, MEPI invested in programs ranging from campaign schools to civic education to an Arab businesswomen's network. Despite a difficult political environment in the region throughout the year, reformers continued to provide reasons to believe that positive change is possible for the people of the Middle East. Examples of MEPI's work with reformers include the following:

Political

- MEPI-supported local and regional election monitors in Yemen reported a process with an absence of the violence of previous electoral contests in the country and with an opposition candidate garnering over 20 percent of the vote against the incumbent leader, a rarity in the region. Technical support also was provided to all parties contesting provincial and municipal elections on the same day;
- MEPI-supported domestic monitors in Bahrain observed the most competitive elections in the kingdom's history with a turnout of more than 70 percent and without the opposition boycotts that undermined the last round of elections.;

- Provided technical assistance to women candidates and voter awareness campaigns in Kuwait's first parliamentary elections through universal suffrage as Kuwait joined Oman, Bahrain, Qatar, and the UAE in enfranchising women in electoral processes;
- Continued to provide technical assistance to parties and candidates across the region in anticipation of new rounds of municipal and parliamentary elections in 2007;
- Strengthened the role of civil society in the democratic process by facilitating dialogue among activists, NGOs, and their respective governments within the framework of the G8's Broader Middle East and North Africa Initiative and by awarding direct grants to numerous civil society organizations across the region to advance the Freedom Agenda; and
- Trained journalists in free and independent media techniques to support greater transparency and accountability in their countries.

Economic

- Provided technical and other assistance in support of successfully completed free trade agreements with Bahrain and Oman;
- Expanded trade capacity of Arab countries with training and technical assistance; a number of Gulf countries are drafting new labor laws and updating new customs codes and agricultural import/export standards;
- Provided entrepreneurial training for more than 300 participants, almost half of them women, from 16 Middle Eastern and North African countries, with 35 alumni going on to start or expand businesses. At least 500 new jobs have been created following their participation in MEPI programs;
- Extended credit and services to small- and medium-sized businesses through peer consultation and training for regional banks and financial organizations;
- Established self-sustaining Junior Achievement chapters in 12 countries throughout the Middle East, with more than 10,000 students participating. Created public-private partnerships that assisted in the sustainability of Junior Achievement chapters; and
- Expanded commercial and legal reform efforts in the Gulf by working to update legal curricula at law schools in Qatar and Oman, update commercial codes to meet international standards in Bahrain and Oman, and provide continuing education programs for the judiciary.

Education

- Provided English language study to more than 4,500 underserved youth from 13 countries in the Middle East through a micro-scholarship program, bringing the total number of students reached with MEPI support to more than 12,000;
- Empowered young, highly motivated Arab men and women with leadership, problem-solving, and entrepreneurial skills through intensive five-week institutes. More than 200 students have participated, and most have started their own civic projects back home;
- Supported a regional civic-education network that promotes youth civic awareness and involvement. Examples of resulting youth-led projects included starting after-school classes for poor students and improving health services at local hospitals. The program is being widely accepted and adopted; for example, education officials committed to adopting Project Citizen in all schools in Marrakesh, Morocco; and
- Promoted critical thinking and independent reading with an initiative to provide more than 80 titles of high-quality American children's books to more than 3,000 schools in three Middle Eastern countries.

Women's Empowerment

- Strengthened the technology, business and advocacy skills of women across six Gulf nations;
- Established the first U.S.-Middle East Partnership for Breast Cancer Awareness and Research, which activated women across the region in private-public partnerships, civic engagement, and networking;
- Established business network hubs in six countries, focusing on training, professional development, and information sharing on laws, business opportunities, skills, and the global economy; and
- Focused on women's rights, particularly family law, in three Gulf states and Morocco.

Antiterrorism Assistance Program (ATA). The Antiterrorism Assistance Program (ATA) provides partner countries with the training, equipment, and technology needed to increase their capabilities to find and arrest terrorists, and to build the kind of cooperation and interactivity between law enforcement officers that has a lasting impact.

At the operational level, ATA alumni have led the investigation of a number of recent terrorist attacks. In Indonesia, a special unit trained and equipped by DS/ATA tracked SE Asia's most wanted terrorist, Dr. Azahari. The suspect refused to give himself up and was killed along with another accomplice.

Azahari and his accomplice were responsible for the Bali bombing in 2002, the J.W. Marriott attack in 2003, and the bombing of the Australian Embassy in 2004. The ATA program has also been crucial in helping local initiatives take root. In Tanzania, ATA assistance mapped out the foundation for the establishment of a counterterrorism center and the implementation of an innovative mechanism to regularly communicate with Kenyan counterparts. In Colombia, ATA financed a training facility in Sibate, which has become an international training hub for officials across the Hemisphere.

ATA sponsored 289 courses and technical consultations and trained approximately 4,816 participants from 77 countries in 2006. In its two-decade long existence, ATA has trained more than 57,116 students from 151 countries, providing programs tailored to the needs of each partner nation and to local conditions. Such training included crisis management and response, cyber terrorism, dignitary protection, bomb detection, airport security, border control, kidnap intervention and hostage negotiation and rescue, response to incidents involving weapons of mass destruction, countering terrorist finance, and interdiction of terrorist organizations. All courses emphasized law enforcement under the rule of law and respect for human rights.

Terrorist Interdiction Program (TIP). The Terrorist Interdiction Program (TIP) assisted priority countries at risk of terrorist activity to enhance their border security capabilities. TIP provided participating countries with a computerized watch listing system to identify suspect travelers at air, land, or sea ports of entry. TIP further promotes expanded cooperation and close liaison with host governments in the areas of rule of law, anticorruption, and law enforcement. Since 2001, the State Department has provided TIP assistance to more than 20 countries, assistance that was instrumental in impeding terrorist travel. Hundreds of individuals traveling on stolen passports in Pakistan, as well as wanted criminals, narcotics smugglers, and human traffickers have been identified and intercepted worldwide. The Terrorist Interdiction Program complements other counterterrorism-related U.S. Government efforts to enhance aviation, border, cyber, maritime, and transportation security.

Counterterrorist Finance Training. In response to the development of new international standards against the growing threat of illicit cash couriers and bulk cash smuggling, the State Department worked with its interagency partners to develop a training course on interdicting bulk cash smuggling. This course provided operational training to foreign customs officers, investigators, and other officials on the detection, interdiction, analysis, investigation, and seizure of illicit cross-border cash used to facilitate terrorism and criminal activities. The training, conducted in three Middle Eastern countries, emphasized the need to investigate the source, destination, and organization behind cash smuggling, and stressed FATF requirements on reporting of outbound/inbound currency and working with Financial Intelligence Units. Based on the vulnerabilities uncovered during this training, one country moved aggressively to implement new laws and regulations. Due to high demand, the State Department is planning to increase the number of courses offered and to provide this training to countries in other geographical regions.

Increasing Economic Development. Development is central to the President's National Security Strategy. Expanding the circle of prosperity is critical to our national security. Poverty, weak institutions, and corruption can turn nations of great potential into recruiting grounds for terrorists. Well-conceived targeted aid is a potential leveraging instrument that can help countries implement sound economic policies, helping to improve the conditions that terrorists exploit.

The Millennium Challenge Account, established by Congress in 2004 based on President Bush's concept, represents a new model for achieving transformational development by providing assistance to those countries that rule justly, invest in their people and encourage economic freedom. The prospect of an MCA Compact provides a powerful incentive for the poorest countries to reform. Good governance and sound policies, not foreign aid, are the keys to economic development. U.S. private sector flows to the developing world, including trade and investment ($450.2 billion in 2004), dwarf our foreign aid ($19.7 billion). Unutilized capital in developing countries, owing to weak policies and poor property rights, is estimated to be as high as $9 trillion.

Debt relief for the poorest is another element of our development strategy. Our long-standing support for the Heavily Indebted Poor Countries (HIPC) initiative, as well as for the Multilateral Debt Relief Initiative (MDRI) introduced in 2006, promotes debt sustainability, reduces the likelihood of debt distress and enables the poorest countries to devote additional resources to reducing poverty and promoting economic growth. Our aggressive multilateral and bilateral trade agenda to open agricultural and non-agricultural markets and liberalize financial services, transportation, telecommunications, and government procurement all support development.

The U.S. Agency for International Development (USAID), carries out foreign assistance programs that support key U.S. foreign policy interests and have a positive public diplomacy impact for many people in the developing world. USAID's humanitarian aid programs and its activities in the areas of economic growth, agriculture, trade, health, democracy, and conflict prevention help reduce the risk of countries becoming breeding grounds for terrorism. In Afghanistan, USAID is helping to build a safe, stable society that meets the needs of its people and eliminates an environment in which terrorist groups have flourished. USAID has been on the front lines of support to tsunami-affected countries, garnering goodwill toward the United States among people in the hardest-hit areas. Our rapid humanitarian assistance and generous reconstruction pledge in response to the devastating South Asian earthquake helped Pakistan in its hour of need, tangibly changing hearts and minds about the U.S. role in this predominately Muslim country.

5.2. Support for Pakistan

The 9/11 Commission recommended that the United States "make the difficult long-term commitment to the future of Pakistan" and "support Pakistan's government in its struggle against extremists with a comprehensive effort that extends from military aid to support for better education, so long as Pakistan's leaders remain willing to make difficult choices of their own."

Composition and Levels of Assistance, Including Security and Other Assistance

The USG commitment to a long-term relationship with Pakistan is highlighted by President Bush's pledge to Pakistani President Musharraf to seek from Congress $3 billion in Economic Support Funds (ESF) and Foreign Military Financing (FMF) for Pakistan during the five-year period from FY-2005 through FY-2009. In addition to Economic Support Funds and Foreign Military Financing, the United States Government is also providing other forms of assistance to Pakistan, including funding for Child Survival and Health (CSH), Development Assistance (DA), International Military Education and Training (IMET), International Narcotics and Law Enforcement (INCLE), Anti-Terrorism Assistance (NADR-ATA), Export Control and Border Security (NADR-EXBS), Small Arms and Light Weapons (NADR-SALW), Terrorism Interdiction Programs (NADR-TIP), Food for Peace (P.L. 480 Title I & II), and Emergency Refugee and Migration Assistance (ERMA). The chart below offers a comparison of levels:

Assistance to Pakistan

($ in millions)

Account	FY-2005 (Includes Supplemental.)	FY-2006	FY-2006 Supplemental	FY-2007 Request	FY-2008 Request
CSH	21.000	22.757	5.300	21.700	39.800
DA	29.000	26.990	10.500	29.000	18.000
ESF	297.600	296.595	40.500	350.000	382.900
FMF	298.800	297.000	-	300.000	300.000

Account	FY-2005 (Includes Supplemental.)	FY-2006	FY-2006 Supplemental	FY-2007 Request	FY-2008 Request
IMET	1.885	2.037	-	2.075	2.000
INCLE	32.150	34.97	-	25.500	32.000
NADR-ATA	6.051	6.885	-	8.590	8.000
NADR-CTF	-	-	-	0.100	0.400
NADR-EXBS	1.000	0.700	-	0.600	0.500
NADR-SALW					0.500
NADR-TIP	0.900	1.000	-	1.000	0.900
P.L. 480 Title I & II	-	17.675	-	TBD	TBD
ERMA	-	0	-	-	-
IDFA	-	-	70.000	-	-
TOTAL	688.386	706.609	126.300	738.565	785.000

Approximately $706.6 million in U.S. assistance was provided to Pakistan from monies appropriated for Fiscal Year 2006. In addition, the Administration received a supplemental Fiscal Year 2006 appropriation from Congress for $126.3 million for Pakistan to meet relief needs from the devastating October 8, 2005, earthquake. The Administration requested $738.565 million in assistance for Pakistan for Fiscal Year 2007 and is requesting $785 million for Fiscal Year 2008.

The mix of U.S. assistance for Pakistan reflects the diverse ways that the U.S. Government is cooperating with Pakistan in pursuit of critical U.S. policy goals. These include prosecuting the War on Terror; countering nuclear proliferation; building a stable and democratic Afghanistan; ensuring peace and stability in South Asia through the continuation of the India-Pakistan reconciliation process; supporting Pakistan's efforts to become a modern, prosperous, democratic state; and assisting it in recovering from the October 8, 2005, earthquake.

U.S. Foreign Military Financing (FMF) funding for Pakistan is designed to enhance Pakistan's capabilities in the War on Terror; help it to better control its borders; meet its legitimate defense needs; and make Pakistan more secure so that it can more readily take the steps necessary to build a durable peace with all its neighbors-thus fostering security and stability throughout the South Asia region. FMF is being used by Pakistan to purchase helicopters, aircraft, weapons systems, munitions, and other equipment, which, *inter alia*, has enabled Pakistan's armed forces to operate effectively against foreign terrorists and militants in the rugged border areas along the Pakistan-Afghanistan border. The Pakistani military is continuing major military operations along that border, which to date have resulted in the capture or death of several hundred foreign terrorists and militants, at the expense of the lives of several hundred Pakistani servicemen.

International Military Education and Training (IMET) assistance for Pakistan complements Foreign Military Financing by providing training to Pakistani officers with the aim of promoting military-to-military cooperation, increased professionalism, and enhanced military interoperability between Pakistan and the United States. IMET also assists Pakistan in developing expertise and systems to more effectively manage its defense establishment; builds technical skills for better operation and maintenance of U.S.-origin equipment; and promotes military subordination to democratic civilian rule and respect for human rights. For Fiscal Year 2008, the Administration's International Military Education and Training request is $2.0 million, a slight decrease over the $2.075 million requested for Fiscal Year 2007.

Measures to Ensure that Assistance Has the Greatest Long-Term Positive Impact on the Welfare of Pakistani People and Their Ability to Cooperate Against Terror

Economic Support Funds, Development Assistance, and Child Survival and Health assistance is being used to improve the lives of ordinary Pakistanis; lay the groundwork for the country's sustained economic growth; and strengthen social, political, and economic institutions, thus alleviating the conditions that breed extremism while demonstrating that the U.S. interest in Pakistan extends beyond the War on Terror to concern for the Pakistani people as a whole. Economic Support Funds reduced Pakistan's bilateral debt to the United States by $1 billion in Fiscal Year 2003 and a further $460 million in Fiscal Year 2004. This debt reduction, together with prior comprehensive donor debt rescheduling, enabled Pakistan to reduce its total sovereign debt from 89 percent of gross domestic product in 2000 to 64 percent of gross domestic product in 2004, laying the groundwork for the implementation of economic reforms designed to stabilize its macroeconomic environment, boost economic growth, and reduce poverty.

During Fiscal Year 2007, $200 million in Economic Support Funds are being provided to the Government of Pakistan as budget support to enable the country to carry out further economic and social reforms, expand its poverty alleviation programs, and reform and expand access to public education and health care. Pakistan's use of this money is guided by the Shared Objectives agreed to with the U.S. Government.

A total of approximately $61 million in Fiscal Year 2007 Economic Support Funds and Development Assistance funds ($69 million in Fiscal Year 06) were requested to implement education reform programs in Pakistan and support the Government of Pakistan's education sector reform initiative. Pakistan's literacy rate greatly hampers its ability to develop and expand its economic base. Literacy averages 49 percent nationwide, and in Pakistan's remote tribal areas can be as low as 0.5% for women. The dearth of good public schools results in thousands of youth attending private madrassas, schools teaching only religious subjects, some of which also inculcate a radical, jihadist ideology. To tackle these problems, U.S. Government-funded education programs in Pakistan are aimed at improving the quality of education in Pakistani primary and secondary schools, especially in Baluchistan and Sindh provinces; improving early childhood education; training teachers; increasing parental and community involvement in schools, ensuring that teachers have adequate classroom materials; and promoting the development of a new generation of Pakistani leaders by providing scholarships for disadvantaged students to obtain a higher education. Adult and youth literacy education programs are targeting out-of-school youth and illiterate adult populations, with a focus on women and girls. In addition, student exchanges play a large part in our education efforts, with Pakistan's Fulbright program being the largest in the world.

Democratization is a key focus of U.S. Government assistance toward Pakistan. One of the fundamental tools for combating terrorism over the long-term is democracy. The programs include several mutually reinforcing components: legislative training to increase the effectiveness, transparency, and accountability of Pakistan's provincial and national parliaments; political party strengthening focused on identifying and training young reformers—tomorrow's political leadership; support for increased women's political participation; civil society development designed to increase the capacity of indigenous nongovernmental organizations to serve as policy watchdogs and promote human rights; and independent media training for journalists.

Pakistan trails its South Asian neighbors in almost all key health areas: maternal and infant mortality; safe, affordable family planning; and control of infectious diseases. Fiscal Year 2007 Child Survival and Health funds will be used to increase availability of maternal and child health services, especially in rural areas; to improve healthcare at the provincial and district level through better resource management; to help maintain Pakistan's low human immunodeficiency virus prevalence rate by increasing awareness; to control other infectious diseases; and to improve water and sanitation.

Throughout 2007, Economic Support Funds, Development Assistance, and Child Survival and Health will support reconstruction efforts to rebuild, furnish, and supply health and education sector infrastructure and human resource capacities; to re-establish the livelihoods of earthquake victims; to relocate displaced victims; and to train skilled and unskilled individuals in vocational training, agriculture and livestock development, asset formation, enterprise development, micro-credit, and market restoration.

The Administration is requesting $382.9 million in Economic Support Funds and $39.8 million in Child Survival and Health for Pakistan for Fiscal Year 2008, a combined increase of $51 million from its Fiscal Year 2007 request. This increase is designed to complement Musharraf's Federally Administered Tribal Areas Sustainable Development Plan to improve governance, provide security, and encourage economic development of the border area between Afghanistan and Pakistan. These funds will also help meet earthquake reconstruction needs, with a focus on rebuilding education, economic, social and health care infrastructure, including human capital, in the earthquake zone. The Administration is requesting for Fiscal Year 2008 $18 million in Development Assistance and $39.8 million in Child Survival and Health funds, a decline from the $29 requested for Development Assistance and an increase from the $21.7 requested for Child Survival and Health in Fiscal Year 2007.

International Narcotics and Law Enforcement funds for Pakistan continue to strengthen border security and enable law enforcement access to remote areas along the Pak-Afghan border—thus enhancing the country's capability to interdict traffickers in narcotics, arms, persons, and contraband, as well as terrorists. International Narcotics and Law Enforcement funds are used to reform, strengthen, and improve cooperation among Pakistan's law enforcement agencies, all of which play an important role in the War on Terror. International Narcotics and Law Enforcement funds support a counternarcotics Air Wing based in Quetta, Baluchistan, operated by Pakistan's Interior Ministry, which includes fixed-wing surveillance aircraft and Huey II helicopters. International Narcotics and Law Enforcement funds are used to procure vehicles and communications, surveillance, and related equipment for border control and counter-narcotics activities. Border security roads that facilitate law enforcement access to inaccessible parts of Pakistan's Federally Administered Tribal Areas are also funded by International Narcotics and Law Enforcement, as are an Automated Fingerprint Identification System and National Criminal Database, and training and equipment to expand law enforcement investigative skills and forensic capacities. In tackling poppy cultivation, International Narcotics and Law Enforcement funds also support crop control, alternative livelihood, and demand reduction programs.

Nonproliferation, Anti-terrorism, Demining, and Related Programs/Export Control and Related Border Security assistance strengthens Pakistan's export control system and thus prevents weapons of mass destruction and related technology transfers that raise proliferation concerns. Nonproliferation, Anti-terrorism, Demining, and Related Programs/Export Control and Related Border Security funds are used for nonproliferation export control training addressing legal/regulatory reform, export licensing systems, and customs enforcement; for general inspection and weapons of mass destruction detection training for border control personnel; and for procuring specialized radiation/chemical-detection equipment. The Administration's $500,000 Fiscal Year 2008 request in Nonproliferation, Anti-terrorism, Demining, and Related Programs/Export Control and Related Border Security assistance represents a slight decrease from the $600,000 requested for Fiscal Year 2007.

Nonproliferation, Anti-terrorism, Demining, and Related Programs/Anti-terrorism Assistance funding for Pakistan enhances the capabilities of elite national police units responsible for counterterrorism investigations and tactical operations. Nonproliferation, Anti-terrorism, Demining, and Related Programs/Anti-terrorism Assistance trained the Special Investigation Group and crisis response teams that were integral in making arrests after the December 2003 assassination attempts on President Musharraf and the May 2004 car bombs near the U.S Consulate in Karachi. The Administration's Fiscal Year 2008 request of $8 million for Nonproliferation, Anti-terrorism, Demining, and Related Programs/Anti-terrorism Assistance represents a decrease from the $8.59 million requested in Fiscal Year 2007.

Nonproliferation, Anti-terrorism, Demining, and Related Programs/Terrorism Interdiction Programs funding for Pakistan is being used to support the Personal Identification Secure Comparison Evaluation System automated border control system, including to sustain ongoing program operations and to expand coverage to additional Pakistani ports-of-entry. The Administration is requesting $900,000 in Nonproliferation, Anti-terrorism, Demining, and Related Programs/Terrorism Interdiction Programs funds for Pakistan for Fiscal Year 2008, a slight decrease from the $1 million requested for Fiscal Year 2007.

The Administration is requesting $400,000 in Nonproliferation, Anti-terrorism, Demining, and Related Programs/Counter-Terrorism Finance funds for Fiscal Year 2008, an increase from the $100,000 requested in Fiscal Year 2007, to support assignment of a resident legal advisor to U.S. Embassy Islamabad. The legal advisor will assist the Pakistani government in establishing the counter-terrorist finance infrastructure needed to prevent money flows to terrorist groups.

Measures to Alleviate Difficulties, Misunderstandings, and Complications in U.S.-Pakistani Relations

The United States and Pakistan engage in extensive consultations to ensure that U.S. foreign assistance has the greatest long-term benefit for Pakistanis and also enhances the country's ability to cooperate in the global War on Terror. This is exemplified by the annual consultations that result in mutually-agreed Shared Objectives for the Government of Pakistan's use of $200 million in Economic Support Funds in direct budget support. The United States also participates in the annual Pakistan Development Forum, which brings together the Government of Pakistan and bilateral and multilateral donors to discuss Pakistan's development priorities and assistance needs. The United States holds regular consultations with major donors, including the European Union, Japan, and World Bank, to ensure that assistance to Pakistan is effectively coordinated and that its impact is maximized.

U.S. public diplomacy programs in Pakistan play a critical role in improving mutual understanding; garnering Pakistani support for United States policies; supporting Pakistani reforms; and laying the foundation for a stable, productive, long-term U.S.-Pakistan relationship. U.S. public diplomacy efforts include: people-to-people exchanges to bring Pakistani students, journalists, academics, politicians, and other opinion leaders to the U.S. for academic programs and study tours; placement of articles and opinion pieces in the Pakistani media and interaction with Pakistani journalists to explain U.S. policies; and public speeches and appearances by the U.S. Ambassador to Pakistan, other U.S. mission staff, and American exchange visitors.

5.3. Collaboration with Saudi Arabia

Steps to Institutionalize and Make More Transparent Government-to-Government Relations

The U.S.-Saudi Strategic Dialogue, inaugurated in November 2005 by Secretary Rice and Foreign Minister Saud al-Faisal and reporting to President Bush and King Abdullah, continues to be the highest level institutionalized forum for coordinating U.S. and Saudi interests. The Strategic Dialogue consists of six working groups focusing on human development, economy, energy, consular affairs, military cooperation, and counterterrorism. These Strategic Dialogue working groups meet periodically to address issues ranging from reform to human rights to visas to child custody cases to security cooperation. Ministerial-level meetings, dealing with bilateral issues of strategic importance, are held as part of the Strategic Dialogue.

Intelligence and Security Cooperation in the Fight against Islamic Terrorism

The United States and Saudi Arabia have an ongoing and robust dialogue on a full range of counterterrorism issues, including regular high-level discussions and close working-level collaboration. Saudi cooperation in this area is significant, and U.S. law enforcement and intelligence agencies have benefited and continue to benefit greatly from Saudi information and intelligence on individuals and organizations. U.S. law enforcement agencies have provided counterterrorism training to Saudi security services in both Saudi Arabia and in the United States. We hope to continue to build upon past cooperation and training through additional CT initiatives.

In 2006, Saudi Arabia improved its capabilities to disrupt terrorist organizations and operations and attempted to preempt the resurgence of al-Qaida and any potential attacks. Since May 2003, the Saudi government has killed or captured al-Qaida's operational Saudi-based senior leadership, as well as almost all of the network's key operatives and many of the Kingdom's most wanted individuals. Saudi security forces killed or captured within four months all of the members of the al-Qaida cell that conducted the February 2006 attack on Aramco's Abqaiq facility. On August 21, five wanted terrorists surrendered in response to government assurances in the media that they would receive mitigated sentences. The Saudi government continues to arrest individuals associated with terrorism, including nascent operational cells and members of facilitation networks for terrorist groups in Iraq and South Asia, including al-Qaida.

In November 2006, the Saudi government announced that security forces had captured 136 known or suspected terrorists or those who supported terrorist networks during the previous three months, continuing a trend in which hundreds of terrorist suspects have been killed or captured since 2003. However, the United States continues to urge Saudi Arabia to take action against additional key terrorist financiers and facilitators in the Kingdom. The U.S. and Saudi Arabian cooperation on designations in the UN 1267 Committee has also been good. The Saudi Arabian Monetary Authority circulates to all financial institutions under its supervision the names of suspected terrorists and terrorist organizations on the UNSCR 1267 Sanctions Committee's consolidated list.

Saudi Contribution to Stability in the Middle East and Islamic World, Including the Middle East Peace Process, by Eliminating Support for Extremist Groups

Saudi Arabia was one of the first countries to condemn the September 11 attacks and provided key logistical support to U.S. forces in Afghanistan. Saudi Arabia has been an important partner in the War on Terror, particularly since the onset of the al-Qaida-sponsored terror campaign inside the Kingdom in 2003. Saudi Arabia also has strengthened its border controls and security and, in particular, its border with Iraq. These efforts have hampered the flow of terrorists and weapons across the border.

The United States and Saudi Arabia have worked closely to combat extremist groups and tendencies in Saudi Arabia. The government continued its wide-ranging re-education and training program that requires all government-sponsored religious leaders to attend courses designed to eliminate extremist ideology from mosques. Those who fail to abide by government directives have been fired or reassigned. Several religious leaders were fired or subjected to punitive action for failure to abide by government instructions to avoid provocative speeches against non-Muslims and non-Sunni Muslims. In previous years in some mosques, a second preacher would appear after the main preacher during the Friday prayer and speak provocatively against Americans, Jews, or non-orthodox Muslims. This practice is less prevalent now, due in large part to the government's efforts to combat extremism in the mosques.

In the cultural arena, official visits by a number of U.S. officials, including Ambassador-at-Large for International Religious Freedom John Hanford, highlighted the government's efforts to remove references in textbooks that promote hatred towards non-Muslims and Muslims of different sects. Senior Saudi officials have acknowledged the need to combat extremism by addressing comprehensive education reform. In November 2006, the King Abdul Aziz Center for National Dialogue held the Sixth National Dialogue Forum in Al-Jawf called "Education: Reality and Promises." The Dialogue produced a "road map" for educational reform, including revision of textbooks, curricula, and teaching methods to promote tolerance. The government also initiated the National Campaign to Counter Terrorism, which includes publications, lectures, and workshops intended to educate school-age girls and boys about the evils of terrorism. Additionally, The Ministry of Education recently issued a new regulation that allows only Ministry-approved summer camps to operate.

Political and Economic Reform in Saudi Arabia and Throughout the Islamic World

Since 2005, Saudi Arabia has taken incremental steps toward political reform through holding municipal city council elections and allowing women to both vote in and compete for seats in chamber of commerce elections and the Saudi Engineer's Council. The United States welcomed the municipal elections as an opportunity to increase citizen participation in government and to increase government accountability. However, in the future the United States hopes to see the inclusion of women in the municipal elections, further expansion of citizen participation in politics, and the development of independent political and civil society institutions.

In 2006, there was also greater involvement in government activities by the Majlis Al-Shura (the Consultative Council) and the 178 municipal councils. Despite increased public and media discourse about human rights, the overall human rights environment remained poor.

The United States sponsors a variety of initiatives focused on increasing freedom and opportunity for Saudi citizens, including the Middle East

Partnership Initiative (MEPI), support to the Middle East Democracy Assistance Dialogue and the Broader Middle East and North Africa (BMENA) Civil Society Dialogue, and a broad variety of public diplomacy educational, exchange, and outreach programs of the State Department's Bureaus of Educational and Cultural Affairs and International Information Programs. With MEPI support, Junior Achievement International—a program to educate youth on the benefits of free enterprise, business, and economics—will focus on opening a new chapter in Saudi Arabia this summer. MEPI also is supporting the creation of a women's business hub in the kingdom to expand the participation and variety of economic opportunities for women.

Higher oil prices bolstered the Saudi economy in 2006, resulting in a budget surplus of roughly $71 billion. In addition to reducing the national debt, Saudi Arabia is re-investing much of the surplus revenue in ambitious social development and massive infrastructure projects. The government also has supported investments to diversify the economy away from petroleum and the petrochemical industry. Saudi Arabia's accession to the World Trade Organization in December 2005 strengthened the Kingdom's ability to attract foreign investment.

Ways to Promote Greater Tolerance and Respect for Cultural and Religious Diversity in Saudi Arabia and Throughout the Islamic World

In November 2006, the Secretary of State designated Saudi Arabia a "Country of Particular Concern" pursuant to the International Religious Freedom Act. This is an important element of our bilateral dialogue with the Saudi government. The United States is working to promote religious and cultural diversity in Saudi Arabia and counter the spread of extremist ideology through high-level engagement and through exchange programs aimed at reaching key population groups. We also support efforts to promote moderation and tolerance, such as King Abdullah's National Dialogue initiative.

On April 25, 2005, following the visit of then-Crown Prince Abdullah to Crawford, Texas, the United States and Saudi Arabia issued a joint declaration noting that "future relations must rest on a foundation of broad cooperation. We must work to expand dialogue, understanding, and interactions between our citizens." The declaration noted that such cooperation would include programs designed to:

- Increase the number of young Saudi students traveling and studying in the U.S.;
- Increase military exchange programs so that more Saudi officers visit the U.S. for military training and education; and
- Increase the number of Americans traveling to work and study in Saudi Arabia.

In 2005, Saudi Arabia initiated a scholarship program to increase the number of young Saudi men and women pursuing undergraduate and graduate studies in the United States. By 2006, more than 15,000 Saudis were studying in the United States on government scholarships.

Ways to Assist Saudi Arabia in Reversing the Impact of Financial, Moral, Intellectual, or Other Support to Extremist Groups in Saudi Arabia and Other Countries, and to Prevent this Support from Continuing in the Future

The United States and Saudi Arabia work closely together to combat terrorism in Saudi Arabia and abroad. This includes collaboration on countering terrorist financing. The United States and Saudi Arabia have established a Joint Task Force on Terrorism Finance (JTFTF) that has strived to improve cooperation on combating terrorist financing. However, the Saudis still have not established a High Commission for Charities to oversee all charities in Saudi Arabia. Although the Saudis have increased oversight and monitoring of domestic charities, the government does not subject the foreign activities of Saudi-based international charities to the same level of scrutiny. Additionally, although the Saudis announced plans to establish the Commission for Relief and Charitable Works Abroad to oversee the activities of Saudi charities overseas, this body is not yet functioning.

The United States and Saudi Arabia have worked together to jointly designate entities to the UN 1267 Committee, and the Saudis have submitted over 20 names. To combat terrorist financing, Saudi Arabia has instituted new anti-money laundering and counterterrorism finance laws and regulations, including removing charity boxes from mosques, restricting the amount of cash that can be carried into or out of the Kingdom, and establishing a Financial Investigations Unit (FIU) in the Ministry of Interior to investigate money-laundering cases. However, the Customs authorities have not yet implemented the new regulations governing the movement of cash across Saudi Arabia's border.

5.4. The Struggle of Ideas in the Islamic World

Public diplomacy is essential to a successful foreign policy and to America's national security. The United States recognizes that the global and generational challenge of countering terrorism is, at its heart, a contest of ideas and values, and that America is more secure when people around the world share the same hopes and freedoms.

Goals for Winning the Struggle of Ideas

The State Department's public diplomacy work is guided by three strategic imperatives. First and foremost, it continues to offer a positive vision of hope and opportunity rooted in the enduring U.S. commitment to freedom.

It promotes the fundamental and universal rights of free speech and assembly, the freedom to worship, the rule of law, and rights for women and minorities. It strives to isolate and marginalize violent extremists and undermine their efforts to exploit religion to rationalize their acts of terror. Finally, it fosters a sense of common interests and common values between Americans and people around the world.

Tools to Accomplish Such Goals

The United States advances these strategic objectives by vigorously engaging foreign publics to explain and advocate American policies. Reaching foreign audiences with core policy messages on democracy, tolerance, and the universal values of liberty, justice, and respect are at the center of U.S. efforts to counter extremist rhetoric and disinformation coming from hostile groups.

The United States is promoting increased exchanges, which exemplify the transformative power of American global engagement. The significance of people-to-people exchanges has never been more clear or compelling. The 9/11 Commission Report recognizes the essential contribution exchanges make to national security. The National Intelligence Reform Act of 2004 reaffirms the importance of America's commitment to exchanges.

The United States is expanding educational opportunities as the path to hope and opportunity. English language programs not only provide crucial skills but also open a window to information about the United States, its people, and its values. Americans must also better educate themselves about the world; the President's National Strategic Languages Initiative will encourage more American students to study critical languages such as Chinese and Arabic.

Responding to and quickly debunking misinformation, conspiracy theories, and urban legends is crucial for success in the war of ideas. The State Department maintains a public "Identifying Misinformation" website, in English and Arabic, devoted to countering false stories that appear in extremist and other web sources. The site focuses on disinformation likely to end up in the mainstream media. Embassies have used information from this site to counter disinformation in extremist print publications in Pakistan and other countries. One article, "A Trio of Disinformers," was the subject of a 1,100-word front-page article in an issue of the influential pan-Arab newspaper al-Sharq al-Awsat. "Identifying Misinformation" is featured on the usinfo.state.gov website, and is listed first of 17.6 million sites in a Google search for the term "misinformation." At least 49 websites have direct links to it.

The Internet, radio, television, and video products remain powerful tools for bringing America's foreign policy message to worldwide audiences.

The State Department produces a wide array of print and electronic materials describing for foreign audiences, in their own languages, the need to counter those who have committed or wish to commit terrorist acts, as well as the achievements made in that struggle.

The State Department's premier web page to explain U.S. counterterrorism policy is "Response to Terrorism," created more than seven years ago and featured on usinfo.state.gov. The site is listed third out of 241 million sites in a Google search for the terms "terrorism U.S." At least 133 websites link directly to it.

In addition to featuring articles, texts, and transcripts from key policymakers, this site provides valuable links to the Electronic Journals series, the National Strategy for Combating Terrorism, the designated Foreign Terrorist Organization list, and the State Department's Country Reports on Terrorism. "Response to Terrorism" is located on the Internet at: http://usinfo.state.gov/is/international_security/terrorism.html.

Support for and understanding of the United States go hand-in-hand with strengthening and empowering the voices most credible to speak out in favor of tolerance and rule of law to counter the violent extremists' message of hate and terror. One of public diplomacy's greatest assets is the American people. Empowerment of individuals and groups—from all walks of life—is a key aspect of the Department's public diplomacy efforts.

As we actively prosecute the struggle of ideas, we need to recognize that this will require a long-term effort spanning years and generations. For that reason, we are placing increased emphasis on programs directed at younger audiences, including undergraduate and, in select cases, high school students.

The U.S. Government's assistance programs, administered through USAID, the Middle East Partnership Initiative, the Millennium Challenge Corporation, and other U.S. entities, advance U.S. interests in this area directly through programs to increase access to education, improve health care and empower people to build better lives. Civic engagement is an important component. Assistance programs to strengthen and professionalize independent media and civic society contribute to opening the "marketplace of ideas," as well as support development and reform across the board.

Through the $66 million in FY 2006 supplemental funds for civil society development, broadcasting, and exchange efforts related to Iran, we have dramatically increased our ability to speak directly to the Iranian people and Diaspora. This supports efforts to clarify U.S. policy objectives to the Iranian people and to increase pressure on the Iranian regime to suspend its funding of extremist activities abroad.

Benchmarks for Measuring Success and Linking Resources to Accomplishments

In 2004, State established the Public Diplomacy Evaluation Office (PDEO). Its mandate is to evaluate all major public diplomacy and exchange programs individually as well as provide an overall strategic framework for public diplomacy assessment.

The PDEO has researched other government public diplomacy evaluation and measurement tools and it is considered one of the most advanced in terms of measuring outcomes of public diplomacy. Organizations as diverse as the Peace Corps, Department of Defense, the British Council, the World Bank, and non-profits in Italy, Japan, and the Netherlands have all consulted with the PDEO on how to measure public diplomacy activities.

The measures used by the PDEO are based upon recognized social and behavioral science methodologies and include measuring changes in audience attitudes (knowledge, skills, perceptions, and understanding), behavior, and condition. Examples include:

- Improved or increased understanding of the United States, its policies and values;
- Initiated or implemented "positive" change within an individual's organization—positive referring to changes that support U.S. ideals and values;
- Institutional partnerships and linkages and on-going collaboration; and
- Changes in editorial content in major media.

Participation in International Institutions for the Promotion of Democracy and Economic Diversification

The United States is a leading participant in many international organizations, such as the United Nations and NATO, that are important to the struggle of ideas and the War on Terror. We also play a leading role in other initiatives, such as the Forum for the Future and the Community of Democracies, which stimulate cooperation with other nations to advance the agenda of freedom. For the first time since its creation in 2000, the Community of Democracies, in response to U.S. recommendations, created regional dialogues which brought together governmental and non-governmental organization representatives from each region, including the Middle East, to discuss the particular challenges and solutions unique to their area. We will continue to seek opportunities to build on the momentum coming out of the April ministerial, particularly in support of the Forum for the Future and the Broader Middle East and North Africa (BMENA) processes.

U.S. Assistance Sufficient to Convince Allies and People in the Islamic World that the United States Is Committed to Winning This Struggle

U.S. assistance programs are intended to improve economic conditions and opportunities in developing countries around the world, thereby serving the U.S. national interest in a more prosperous and secure international community. Our assistance can have the additional impact of demonstrating our commitment to help poorer countries or countries in special need, as we saw after the tsunami of 2004, and the Pakistan earthquake of 2005. There is, however, no set amount of money or time that we could identify as being sufficient to win the struggle of ideas.

5.5. Outreach through Broadcast Media

This section is provided by the Broadcasting Board of Governors (BBG).

Broadcasting Board of Governors Initiatives: Outreach to Foreign Muslim Audiences

The Broadcasting Board of Governors (BBG) continues to build its capacity to broadcast to Muslim populations in the Middle East and other parts of the world. In the past four years, the establishment of the Middle East Broadcasting Networks (MBN) illustrates the urgency and gravity of the broadcast priorities associated with the nation's War on Terror. Radio Sawa and Alhurra television's 24/7 Arabic broadcasts reach audiences in 22 countries in the Middle East as well as throughout Europe.

In 2006, the BBG made further progress in implementing its broadcast strategy across the broad geographical and cultural landscape of the Middle East and beyond. A dramatic increase in the Persian language television programming of the Voice of America has been a singular accomplishment, providing four hours of original television news and information each day to the people of Iran. A 12-hour stream of programming is expected to be on line by April 2007. At the same time, Radio Free Europe/Radio Liberty strengthened its 24/7 Persian broadcasts via Radio Farda by adding 30 minutes of additional daily news programming, as well as creating a more substantive, interactive website that enhances our ability to communicate directly with the Iranian people.

Through the combined skills of broadcasters at MBN, VOA, RFE/RL, and Radio Free Asia, the BBG is securing a public diplomacy strategy that mirrors U.S. national security priorities and focuses on nations that may suffer from, or contribute to, the scourge of terrorism. The implementation of this strategy focuses on building BBG's reach and impact within the Islamic world; facilitating citizen discourse; engaging the world in conversation about America; enhancing program delivery; helping audiences understand the principles of democratic societies; and employing modern communication techniques. The rigorous use of research, more frequent program review and oversight, and more compelling broadcast formats that will resonate in competitive, but critical, international markets remain crucial to this strategy. But underlying these techniques, the journalistic product and integrity remain the same. BBG broadcasters provide accurate, objective, and comprehensive news and information.

As BBG resources have shifted from areas of the world where the local media are increasingly free and robust to the Middle East and Southwest Asia, the BBG has created a new broadcast entity, MBN, and refocused the broadcasts of others. RFE/RL is now a major broadcaster to Iran, Iraq and Afghanistan. RFE/RL reaches audiences in the Muslim countries of Uzbekistan, Kazakhstan, Turkmenistan, Kyrgyzstan, Tajikistan, and Azerbaijan as well as the majority Muslim populations of Tatarstan, Bashkortostan, and the North Caucasus. VOA has similarly reduced its broadcasts to Europe, increasing its focus on Iran, Afghanistan, Indonesia, Pakistan, and other critical nations.

During the past year, BBG's broadcasters harnessed their broad journalistic resources to fully report on issues such as the Israeli-Hezbollah conflict in Lebanon, to provide a program perspective that is often lacking in media outlets abroad. BBG correspondents in the Unites States and around the world contribute to coverage available in 58 languages. Live, simultaneous interpretation of Presidential speeches, such as the State of the Union, and of Congressional hearings enables Muslim audiences to hear the President's message, as well as the Democratic response.

Arabic Broadcasting

To effectively communicate with the predominantly young audiences in the Middle East, the BBG created a new concept in international broadcasting—Radio Sawa—a 24/7 network of stations specifically designed to reach the large segment of the Arabic-speaking population under the age of 35. Radio Sawa went on the air in March 2002, quickly attracting and sustaining a loyal audience throughout the Middle East, as new transmission sites were added throughout the region. In 2007, Radio Sawa continues to broadcast accurate, authoritative, comprehensive, and timely news about the Middle East, the U.nited States, and the world. In addition to 325 newscasts per week, Radio Sawa offers discussion and informational programs such as the popular "Sawa Chat" interactive feature and the "Free Zone," a weekly review and discussion of democracy and freedom as they relate specifically to the Middle East. Feature programs encourage discussion of key social and political issues in a manner very different from indigenous Arab media.

Radio Sawa broadcasts on FM in Morocco (Rabat, Casablanca, Tangier, Meknes, Marrakesh, Agadir and Fes), Jordan (Amman and Ajlun), the Palestinian Territories (Ramallah and Jenin), Kuwait (Kuwait City), Bahrain (Manama), Qatar (Doha), U.A.E. (Abu Dhabi and Dubai), Iraq (Baghdad, Nasiriya, Basra, Mosul, Kirkuk, Sulimaniya and Erbil), Lebanon (Beirut, North Lebanon, South Lebanon and Bekaa Valley), and Djibouti. Radio Sawa broadcasts on medium wave to Egypt, Yemen, Saudi Arabia, and Sudan. However, Radio Sawa recently received permission from Sudan to expand its reach in that country and broadcast Radio Sawa on FM transmitters throughout Sudan. By broadcasting on FM, Radio Sawa increases the number of listeners who can receive objective news and information about Sudan, the Middle East, and the world.

Building on the success of Radio Sawa, the BBG launched Alhurra Television on February 14, 2004, covering 22 countries in the Middle East via the same satellites used by major indigenous Arabic channels. In the three years Alhurra has been broadcasting 24/7, the channel has provided in-depth coverage of historic events, such as elections throughout the Middle East including Iraq, the Palestinian Territories, Egypt, U.A.E., Kuwait, Bahrain, and Israel. Alhurra has been a consistent leader reporting on and analyzing new democratic trends in the Middle East. Through objective and accurate reporting, Alhurra has been an example of a free press to the region and has become a trusted source of news for its estimated 20 million weekly viewers. In 2006, Alhurra expanded its live and breaking news coverage to provide viewers with the latest news and information as it is happening.

Alhurra also gives its audience insights into life in America and the American system of government. During the U.S. electoral campaign in 2004 and the midterm elections in 2006, Alhurra provided daily in-depth coverage of the candidates and the issues that impacted the U.S. elections. Broad coverage of the U.S. elections provided an opportunity to showcase the political institutions of the United States. Alhurra also dramatically increased its live news coverage of events and speeches by President Bush, Secretary of State Rice, and members of Congress. Additionally, Alhurra has reporters that cover the White House, Congress, State Department and the Pentagon. Alhurra's current affairs programs also highlight the U.S. Inside Washington takes viewers behind the scenes of the political process in Washington with guests such as Supreme Court Justice Antonin Scalia, former Secretary of State Alexander Haig, and Representatives Howard Berman, Ileana Ros-Lehtinen, Tom Lantos, and Peter Hoekstra. The network also produced a documentary series on American culture and values, and Americans, which proved to be a popular program with audiences and the Arabic press.

Alhurra is also producing programs to provide a forum for discussion on sensitive issues such as human rights and the rights of women. Current affairs programs like Alhurra's Equality continue to be unique in the region's media, due to the limitations imposed by the countries that finance regional television networks. Hosted by Saudi journalist Nadine Al-Bdair, the program discusses the rights of women and tackles subjects such as young girls being forced into marriage, the right of women to drive and the rights of women in Islam. There has been incredible feedback on this program and others, some praising the courageousness of this program and others condemning Alhurra for discussing these topics. In 2006, Alhurra also launched Eye on Democracy focusing on democratic efforts throughout the Middle East and human rights abuses in the region.

Throughout its three-year history, Alhurra has provided a forum for discussion of important topics by a wide variety of experts including the all-important voices of moderation. Alhurra's talk shows, roundtables, and documentaries have routinely tackled vital topics that are taboo on many other stations in the region, including the struggle for human rights, the position of women in Arab society, religious freedom, freedom of the press, and freedom of expression.

Radio Sawa and Alhurra Television continue to grow in popularity and credibility and now reach a total unduplicated audience of 35 million adults 15 and older according to international research firms such as ACNielsen and Ipsos. The surveys show that, despite high levels of anti-American sentiment throughout the region, both Alhurra and Radio Sawa are regarded as credible sources of news and information by their audiences.

Iraq

Alhurra Iraq, a special television stream containing more concentrated news and information to and about Iraq, began broadcasting in April 2004. Through satellite and terrestrial broadcasting in Iraq, Alhurra has gained a foothold in one of the most competitive TV marketplaces in the world. Alhurra's goal is to help its viewers make educated and informed decisions about political, social, and economic events affecting their lives. To this end, during the historic elections in Iraq, Alhurra produced and broadcast the first televised electoral debate in Iraq's history, featuring six candidates representing the major political parties. This historic debate brought about a candid discussion among the candidates and provided a forum for the viewers to be able to compare and contrast each of the parties' candidates.

RFE/RL's **Radio Free Iraq** continues to provide the Iraqi people with breaking news and in-depth coverage of developments in Iraq and the Middle East. RFI appeals to a wide spectrum of listeners in Iraq, covering the most significant political issues in the country through its extensive network of stringers reporting through its Baghdad bureau. During 2006, the editors in Prague continued to develop thematic programming focused on democracy-building, and an enhanced website has shown strong growth topping more than 170,000 page views in December. A December 2005 survey showed listening rates for RFI at a weekly level of 21.6 percent.

Radio Free Iraq provided extensive coverage of President Bush's trip to the Middle East in November 2006, and aired a special broadcast on President Bush's talks in Jordan with Iraqi Prime Minister Nuri Kamal al-Maliki. The program included reports from RFI correspondents in Amman on the President's joint press conference with al-Maliki, with lengthy excerpts of statements by the two leaders, analysis and reactions within Iraq.

Throughout December, RFI devoted substantial airtime to the report of the Iraq Study Group. Coverage focused on the report's content, analysis by experts, and local and international reactions to its findings. RFI presented the positions of Iraqi national and regional leaders, and statements by leaders in the United States, Britain, Israel, Jordan, Syria, and Egypt. RFI correspondents interviewed political analysts, commentators and advisers to politicians in Baghdad, Damascus, Tel Aviv, Washington, Arbil, and Kut, airing a range of views and responses.

Weekly programs such as "Human Rights in Iraq" provided a forum for extensive coverage of the trial of Saddam Hussein, in addition to the daily coverage of the trial when it was in session. On November 5, RFI broke into regular programming to bring a live report with the verdict, followed by a special half-hour program of live reactions from five Iraqi cities—Baghdad, Tikrit, Mosul, Amara, and Basra—and statements from President Bush and Iraqi government officials. The same format was used the day of the execution.

Arabic In Europe

In August 2006, Alhurra Europe was launched to bring together the best programs of Alhurra and Alhurra-Iraq to the Arabic-speaking population in Europe. Alhurra Europe can be seen on the Hotbird satellite system that reaches all of Europe.

Kurdish

Broadcasting four hours of daily radio programming, VOA's Kurdish Service remains highly popular. According to a 2006 survey conducted by InterMedia Research, VOA's Kurdish Service scored a 31 percent audience share among the Kurds of Iraq. The survey stated: "In fact, no radio station ranks higher in terms of reliability," and added: "VOA occupies a unique position among Iraqi Kurds as it is the only major international broadcaster offering programs in the Kurdish language." VOA Kurdish focuses on the Iraqi scene through a network of stringers, with special programs and call-in shows devoted to combating extremism inside the country and the surrounding region. Special coverage highlighted the debate among Kurds on the role of Islam in the regional and national constitutions of Iraq. In interviews with VOA Kurdish, moderate Kurdish-speaking clerics tried to calm the passions raised by the Pope's comments on Islam. The Iranian regime's nuclear ambitions and its support for extremist groups in Iraq and in the Middle East received particular coverage in the form of interviews and panel discussions.

Iran

Broadcasting to Iran remains a key BBG priority. Pursuant to increased funding, VOA Persian television to Iran essentially doubled its broadcast hours over 2005 levels by June 2006, and expanded fourfold by October 2006. This programming has been met in Iran with open arms.

VOA's current television lineup includes: NewsTalk, a discussion program with a panel of experts who examine the day's headlines; News and Views, VOA Persian's flagship program featuring live news coverage of the latest headlines from Iran and the world; Roundtable, a call-in and discussion program on politics and current affairs; and Late Edition, a daily nightly wrap-up of the day's news, which is targeted to a younger audience. Programming on human rights, democratic governance, freedom of speech, the rights of women and ethnic minorities, the issue of nuclear energy vs. nuclear weapon development, and news and analysis are constant features of our programming.

This year, Persian television featured an impressive array of prominent guests including Under Secretary of State Nicholas Burns; Principal Deputy Assistant Secretary for Near Eastern Affairs James Jeffrey; Nobel Peace Prize laureate Shirin Ebadi; journalist Akbar Gandji, recently released from jail; Holocaust survivor Elie Wiesel; and many U.S. senators and representatives. VOA TV has also covered Senate and House hearings on Iran. In the near future, the Service will launch a series on 28 years after the Islamic Revolution in Iran and the impact it has had on that country and the region.

Other program examples include: an interview with Ted Koppel about his documentary, "Iran—the Most Dangerous Nation," which explored the generation gap in Iran between aging clerics and the 70 percent of the population below the age of 30; an interview with former CIA Director James Woolsey at the American Foreign Policy Council conference, "Understanding the Iranian Threat"; coverage of testimony by General John Abizaid, Senior Advisor to the Secretary of State and Coordinator for Iraq David Satterfield, and CIA Director Michael Hayden before the Senate Armed Services Committee; live broadcast, with simultaneous translation into Persian, of President Bush's January 11 address to the nation about increasing the number of troops in Iraq; commentaries from Iraqi government officials welcoming President Bush's new strategy for their country; U.N. Secretary-General Ban Ki-Moon's statement that the UN backs any genuine efforts to improve security for Iraqis and to stabilize the country; and commentaries from Capitol Hill on the President's new Iraq strategy.

VOA devotes significant effort to hard-hitting topics on the role of religion in society, including Iranian regime's use or abuse of Islam to solidify its control of power, as well as to justify the oppression of women and limit free speech, free association and freedom of religion. These stories generate massive email response and other feedback from Iran, as well as from Persian-speaking populations in Kuwait, the UAE, Qatar, Saudi Arabia, Iraq, Turkey, Syria, and Lebanon.

In 2006, **Radio Farda**, a joint service of RFE/RL and VOA, continued to broadcast to Iran 24 hours a day, with a goal of providing Iran's predominantly young population news and information. As Radio Farda has matured, and as funding has supported the addition of larger blocks of news and information, it has done so in its tradition as a "surrogate" broadcaster, presenting news about the country to which it broadcasts. Current broadcasts include over eight hours of news and information programming daily, with popular Persian and western music drawing in the younger audience. Radio Farda finds direct sources of information from within Iran in spite of the challenging environment for journalism.

Radio Farda reaches significant audiences in Iran, in spite of Iran's consistent jamming. Listening remained stable at 13.5 percent—the highest weekly reach rate of any international broadcaster, and more than double that of BBC's Persian service. Among its key target group, youth aged 18-29, Farda's weekly reach was 28.7 percent. Utilizing new resources provided by the U.S. Congress, Radio Farda has augmented its website to expand breadth of content—more stories to read, more images to view, and more opportunities to comment on news and information. December 2006 was the first full month of operations for the revamped Farda site, which showed a million-page increase in usage over the previous month.

The Internet will become increasingly important in the lives of Iranians seeking objective news and information about Iran and the world. Radio Farda's new site also brings a new level of interactivity to Radio Farda. This includes the "Most Popular and Most Emailed Stories" and "Farda Club"—for moderated discussions and blogs, providing immediate feedback from users to Radio Farda and other users.During the first 30 minutes that the site was live, about 500 visitors viewed a story on a protest at the Amir Kabir University.

Farda also provided thorough news coverage and analysis of the December 15, 2006, Assembly of Experts and municipal elections held throughout Iran, widely considered a setback for conservative forces aligned with

President Mahmoud Ahmadinejad. In addition to pre-election analysis and hour-by-hour coverage of the voting from correspondents in all provinces on Election Day, Radio Farda broadcast comments from both Iranian party leaders and international experts on Iran.

Radio Farda provides Iranians with both breaking news and updates on social and political movements and unrest in their country, including such issues as the strikes by Iranian workers. Farda aired comments from student leaders, who proclaimed their solidarity with striking workers, as well as an exclusive eyewitness account from an Iranian trade union official of the surprise arrest of union leader Mansour Osanlou in Tehran. Radio Farda has provided ongoing coverage of ethnic unrest among the Azeri and Kurdish population of Iran.

In its human rights reporting, Radio Farda covered government attacks against women, including the Tehran police dispersing a gathering to mark International Women's Day by beating the assembled women. On December 11, 2006, within minutes of receiving word that students at Tehran's Amir Kabir University were heckling President Ahmadinejad during a speech he was giving, Radio Farda reported the news to its listeners around the country.

Pakistan

Since VOA introduced a new, youth-oriented, 12/7 radio station called ***Radio Aap ki Dunyaa*** *(Your World)* in 2004, the station has continued to attract a growing number of listeners with its contemporary format that includes news, information, roundtable discussions, call-in shows, interviews, features, and music. Research indicates that *Radio Aap ki Dunyaa's* audience has doubled since its debut. The programs target Pakistani listeners between the ages of 15 and 39—which account for some 60 million of Pakistan's 150 million residents—as well as millions more potential listeners in India, the Gulf, and the Diaspora. To increase *Radio Aap ki Dunyaa's* reach, VOA introduced a bilingual web page that offers live audio streaming of news and entertainment programming.

Stories of interest to VOA's Muslim audience are a central part of the Urdu Service's programming on radio, the Web, and television. The Service provided detailed coverage of the 2006 U.S. mid-term elections, with a particular focus on the perspectives of American Muslims, both Republican and Democratic. VOA followed the campaign and successful election of Congressman Keith Ellison (D-MN), the first Muslim member of Congress. The Urdu Service also covered the observations by American Muslims of Raman, the month of fasting, with daily television features, including special packages on iftar (breaking of the fast) at the White House, and on the participation of Karen Hughes, Under Secretary of State for Public

Diplomacy, in Washington-area celebrations of Eid, the last day of Ramadan and the most important holy day in Islam. A five-part interfaith discussion underscored freedom of religion in the United States.

VOA's Urdu Service entered the television market in November 2005 with a 30-minute program, "Beyond the Headlines," a news magazine featuring current affairs, discussions of issues behind the news, and feature stories illustrating shared values between Pakistanis and Americans. The show airs every weekday during prime time on GEO, Pakistan's most widely watched satellite TV channel. The program includes in-depth reports from VOA's Islamabad bureau on Pakistani politics and cultural issues; hard-hitting interviews with newsmakers, policy experts, diplomats and journalists; and stories examining the similarities between life in Pakistan and the United States, including Pakistani-American life and its contribution to both cultures. "Beyond the Headlines" newsmaker interviews have generated widespread coverage in the Pakistani press. According to GEO-TV's market research, "Beyond the Headlines" is the most widely watched program in Pakistan during the 7:30 to 8:00 p.m. local time slot.

Afghanistan

Since 9/11, the BBG increased radio broadcasting to Afghanistan pursuant to the Radio Free Afghanistan Act. Together RFE/RL and VOA provide a 24-hour daily radio service in the Dari and Pashto languages that has a vast audience reach in Afghanistan. In addition, VOA provides a one hour daily program of branded TV news and cultural features to state-owned Kabul TV.

An InterMedia survey in September 2006 found **RFE/RL's Radio Free Afghanistan** to have the highest weekly reach of any communications medium in Afghanistan, including domestic radio and TV, at 58.0 percent. Afghanistan is the only country in the RFE/RL broadcast region where a U.S. government-funded broadcaster is the dominant media.

With its wide audience and high level of public trust, Radio Free Afghanistan is a key media outlet in Afghanistan for both U.S. and Afghan officials. For example, during the last year, Radio Free Afghanistan covered President Bush's March 1 visit to Afghanistan, the surprise first stop his tour of South Asia. Radio Free Afghanistan provided a simultaneous translation of his joint press conference with President Karzai after their meeting at the presidential palace in Kabul. On June 28, U.S. Secretary of State Rice's exclusive interview to Radio Free Afghanistan during her visit to Kabul assured the Afghan people that "the American people are committed to Afghanistan's future . . ."

The Service provides reports from Washington, Prague, and Kabul, exclusive interviews and roundtables, and ongoing coverage of the efforts by Coalition Forces to subdue the insurgency. During June, Radio Free

Afghanistan reporters in the Kandahar and Helmand provinces went out with Afghan and Coalition Forces in southern Afghanistan to report on the launch of the second phase of Operation Mountain Thrust, the largest counterinsurgency operation in the country since the Taliban regime was toppled in 2001.

An example of Radio Free Afghanistan's thought-provoking programming was its comprehensive coverage of the apostasy case of Abdul Rahman, from his arrest in mid-March for his conversion to Christianity, to his release March 28 and request for asylum in Italy. Correspondents in Kabul interviewed Ministry of Justice and Afghan Supreme Court officials about the charges and the specific laws on apostasy. Radio Free Afghanistan aired statements from Afghan judicial officials, reactions from ordinary Afghans, and from leaders around the world including President Bush and Pope Benedict XVI. Radio Free Afghanistan's weekly live call-in show March 30 was dedicated to the Rahman case, inviting listeners to exchange views on religious tolerance.

Human rights programming provides interviews with senior U.S. officials, and features Afghan citizens struggling with everyday issues, such as an interview with 14-year-old Zohra Amiri, a student who was criticized for attending a music academy for women sponsored by the United Nations and the European Union because of prohibitions under Islamic law for women to play music. On October 12, Radio Free Afghanistan for the first time broadcast a call-in show conducted in three languages: Dari, Pashto, and English, featuring Mark Laity, the senior spokesman for NATO/ISAF in Afghanistan, as a guest in the Kabul bureau.

VOA shares the 24 hour radio broadcast clock with RFE/RL, providing up to the minute news and information to large Afghan audiences. In addition, VOA has also launched new television and radio programming to engage broad Afghan audiences and to focus on the Pashto-speaking people in the Afghanistan-Pakistan border region. In September, VOA launched "TV Ashna", a Saturday through Thursday 60-minute TV news program (30 minutes each in Dari and Pashto) broadcast directly to viewers nationwide via satellite and its affiliate Radio and TV Afghanistan (RTA). This coverage now complements VOA's 12 hours of extensive radio programming to the country. TV and Radio Ashna feature regular segments on American Muslims and Civil Rights, Islam in America, and Islam and Democracy through the segment's interviews and daily live call-in programs.

Ashna provided extensive coverage of the first Muslim Member of Congress being sworn into office, using the Koran that belonged to Thomas Jefferson. Highlights of Ashna's information programming in 2006 included:

- An exclusive interview with General Richard Myers, former General Chief of Staff, in which he said NATO and Coalition Forces will respond to any attack across the border of Pakistan only when they are under attack;

- An interview with General David Richards, Commander of ISAF forces in Afghanistan in Kabul, who said that NATO and Afghan forces are preparing themselves for anticipated Spring attacks by the Taliban, and described efforts by NATO and the PRT (Provincial Reconstruction Team) to help the Afghan people rebuild their country;
- A profile of Zinedine Zidane, the world champion soccer star for the French national team, and his return to Algeria for the first time in 20 years to be honored by President Bouteflika; and
- Interviews with both the Imam and Chairman of the Mustafa Center in Virginia, and the president of the Afghan Academy in Virginia, regarding the freedom of practicing Islam in America.

The Pakistan/Afghanistan Border Region

In August, VOA introduced **Radio Deewa** (Light), a new broadcast stream aimed at the 40 million Pashto-speaking people living in the Afghanistan-Pakistan border region. This three hour daily program offers local, regional, and international news as well as features on Islam in America, including interviews with prominent Muslim leaders. VOA Pashto Deewa Radio features a daily segment called "Islam in America," and recently had live reports from Eid Celebrations by Muslims in America. Additionally, Deewa Radio focuses on the Islamic world through its daily call-in shows.

Deewa has interviewed dozens of Muslims of South Asian origin residing in America and has aired profiles of Islamic Centers and Mosques in its programming (i.e., the Islamic Center in Washington DC, the Mustafa Masjid in Virginia, and the Mustafa Mosque in New York). During the month of Ramadan, Deewa aired daily interviews with Muslims in America, from Washington, D.C., New York, the Carolinas and Texas. These interviews tackle the topic of freedom of religion in America, the observance of fasting, and attendance at area mosques for late night prayers and ceremonies.

Last month Radio Deewa had four call-in shows during Eid celebrations in America and its reporters reported live from area mosques on Eid Prayers. The Service also regularly interviews American Pashtuns, both men and women of every walk of life, to talk about their experiences of practicing their religion and culture in the United States. A call-in show on "Islamic Mysticism" featured a prominent mystic scholar, Tahir Bukhari, from the Northwest Frontier Province of Pakistan responding to questions posed by more than a dozen callers from Pakistan, Afghanistan and the Diaspora.

The Service regularly interviews the Pakistani Foreign Ministry spokesperson, Afghan officials, and Pakistani federal and state cabinet ministers and religious and tribal leaders on political and social issues.

Turkey. In recognition of media listening habits in Turkey, VOA's Turkish Service is moving to devote more of its existing resources to TV and the Internet. In 2006, VOA Turkish expanded its TV affiliation in Turkey by launching two weekly live broadcasts on TGRT News TV network, a 24-hour nationwide news network with a weekly audience share of over 30 percent of Turkey's estimated 25 million regular viewers. A 15-minute wrap of the latest developments in news and current affairs, VOA-TGRT Live is broadcast at 9:00 p.m. local time in Turkey on Tuesdays and Fridays. In addition, VOA Turkish Service produces a weekly 30-minute news and magazine program that is aired on TGRT News network 9:30 p.m. local time on Sundays. Managers of TGRT News TV are pleased with this cooperation and have indicated that they would like to increase the VOA-TGRT Live broadcasts to five days per week.

VOA Turkish radio broadcasts include two news shows (Mon-Fri) on NTV-FM, Turkey's largest FM news network. Discussions are underway with another Turkish network, TGRT-FM, to carry the 30-minute evening radio show. VOA has also been working to attract more users to the VOA Turkish website. The average number of monthly visitors to the VOA Turkish site has tripled this year to almost 65,000/month. VOA Turkish is also one of the first VOA languages to offer text versions of top news stories for use on web-enabled handheld devices such as cell phones and PDAs (Personal Digital Assistants). This service was launched in June 2006.

VOA Turkish Service summarized the U.S. State Department's 2006 Annual Report on International Religious Freedom and reported on the reactions from Turkish officials and experts. In an exclusive interview to VOA in July 2006, Turkish Foreign Minister Abdullah Gul responded to questions about issues of religious tolerance in Turkey and shared his views on the so-called "clash of civilizations." The Service aired original radio and TV reports on how U.S. Muslims celebrated the month of Ramadan and other Muslim holidays last year. In a series of reports and interviews during Pope Benedict's highly sensationalized visit to Turkey in November 2006, Turkish Service focused on issues related to "the current lack of dialogue between Christianity and Islam." Those interviewed included Andrew Duff, member of British Parliament and Joost Lagendijk, Dutch member of the European Parliament and co-chairman of the EU-Turkey Joint Parliamentary Committee.

Indonesia

VOA expanded its reach to Indonesia's more than 200 million Muslims in 2006 by launching six news and information programs for Indonesia's top three TV networks. VOA also peppered the TV market with a dozen or more special series on subjects ranging from illegal arms sales by Indonesians to the diverse faces of Islam in America and how Americans celebrate the fasting month of Ramadan. VOA is now seen on five national TV networks and 16 regional TV stations. In late 2006, VOA conducted a five-week promotional campaign on Indonesian TV. The one-minute "VOA World News Quiz" spots aired several times a day on the top four national stations and attracted over 450,000 text and email quiz entries. Additionally, more than 200 radio stations now carry one or more of VOA's program offerings, including the youth-oriented "VOA Direct Connection" and "VOA Headline News." This year also saw greater VOA outreach to Indonesian youth. Three times a day the popular youth station, Prambors, airs "VOA Minute", a rapid-fire segment of breaking news and information of interest to youth. As a result of this growth in TV and radio, 7.9 million Indonesians now tune in to VOA regularly, making VOA the number one international broadcaster in Indonesia.

With more and more Indonesians jumping into digital communications, VOA has begun providing a range of information services including a dynamic webpage, a weekly electronic newsletter and daily email news bulletins direct to cell phones.

Finally, VOA's presence on the ground inside Indonesia solidified and grew in 2006, with its Jakarta news bureau becoming a valuable resource for coordinating VOA's local TV and radio news coverage and for developing new programs, especially for television.

Uzbekistan and Central Asia

VOA Uzbek reaches Muslim audiences in Uzbekistan, the most populous Muslim country in Central Asia, with a total population of 27 million. VOA broadcasts are carried on short wave, medium wave from Tajikistan, and two FM frequencies in Osh and Jalalabad, Kyrgyzstan. Both reach a key area of Uzbekistan, the Ferghana Valley, a hotbed of Islamic fundamentalism. VOA's daily 30-minute broadcasts feature high profile interviews with various U.S. and international sources discussing critical issues, such as the War on Terror and the future of U.S. relations with Uzbekistan. Interviews with Members of the U.S. Congress and key policymakers, bring U.S. policy and debate alive for listeners. Pegged to the State Department's annual report on religious freedom, VOA Uzbek aired two series on Islam in Central Asia and women's rights. When Uzbek-speaking Muslims living in the United States observed their religious holidays, VOA Uzbek covered their stories as examples of tolerance in the American way of life. On television, VOA continues to produce a weekly 30-minute feature magazine called *Exploring America*, which is being placed on a TV satellite network reaching Uzbek-speakers in Afghanistan and the rest of Central Asia, and on two local stations in the Uzbek-speaking area of Osh, home to Uzbek and Kyrgyz Muslims.

RFE/RL's programming to Uzbekistan, Turkmenistan, Tajikistan, Kyrgyzstan and Kazakhstan continued despite various forms of harassment and even repression against its correspondents and editors. In Turkmenistan, an RFE/RL correspondent died while in prison. The recent death of President Saparmurat Niyazov of Turkmenistan may provide an opportunity for RFE/RL to register its in-country correspondents, and eventually open its first bureau in the country if there is a political realignment in Turkmenistan. In Uzbekistan, RFE/RL's bureau remains closed by Uzbek government order. The service continues to provide news coverage and democracy promotion under harsh conditions reminiscent of the Soviet era. In Kyrgyzstan, RFE/RL has been able to work with Kyrgyz National Television (KTR) to produce and air local television news programming.

Azerbaijan

According to a March 2006 InterMedia national survey in Azerbaijan, VOA Azerbaijani had emerged as the leading international broadcaster in Azerbaijan with an audience share of 34 percent. In addition to TV and radio offerings, VOA Azerbaijani maintains two web sites, one in Farsi to reach the large Azeri-speaking minority in Iran (estimated at 15 million). Azerbaijani Foreign Minister Elmar Mammadyarov was interviewed exclusively for TV by the VOA Azerbaijani Service in September 2006. Among other issues, he commented on "tensions between Muslims and followers of other faiths throughout the world." In November 2006, when an article published in an Azerbaijani newspaper was seen as denigrating Islam, leading Muslim clerics in neighboring Iran issued a religious order calling for the killing of its author. VOA's Azerbaijani Service interviewed several religious experts as well as men and women on the street both in Azerbaijan and Iran to get their reactions. This issue, and the U.S. State Department's Annual Report on Religious Freedom, were discussed in two separate live radio call-in shows produced by VOA's Azerbaijani Service.

RFE/RL's Azerbaijan service drew a 7.6 percent audience on radio only in 2006 maintaining its status as the lead international radio broadcaster in the country. RFE/RL lived through the same setbacks in local delivery of programming as VOA during the past year. Programming remains a mix of newscasts and democracy programming on political issues and civil society such as: human rights, media rights, minorities, judicial rights, religion and elections. Social issues of health care, pensions, public welfare, unemployment and drugs are increasingly a component of the programming. The service, working in concert with RFE/RL's Armenian Service, provided comprehensive coverage of intensified negotiations over a settlement to the longstanding dispute over Nagorno-Karabakh including on-the-scene coverage of summits in Rambouillet, France in February, and Brussels, Belgium in November.

Africa

VOA reaches a large percentage of the almost 250 million Muslims in Sub-Saharan Africa. One in every five Muslims in the world lives in Africa, and one-third of Sub-Saharan Africa's population is Muslim. VOA Hausa reaches 51 percent of the Hausa-speaking Muslim population in Nigeria (about 20 million), and about 65 percent of the Muslim population in Niger.

VOA's broadcasts serve an important role in easing tensions and presenting the facts about local, international, and U.S.-based news stories. For example, when Danish cartoons depicting Muhammed generated protests throughout the Muslim world, including many countries in Africa, VOA was able to provide needed perspective to the story. The Africa Division covered this major story from every angle, while giving special attention to the African reaction. In Nigeria, the northern city of Maiduguri was the scene of rioting. Muslims attacked Christians and burned churches and shops owned by Christians. The services contacted Muslim, Christian and civic leaders as well as politicians, journalists and ordinary people in Africa, in the United States and in other parts of the world to ensure that listeners could evaluate the situation fairly.

Northern Nigeria

A VOA Africa Division program targeting Hausa speaking Muslims in northern Nigeria, "Political Crossfire" (Tsaka Mai Wuya), has been praised by ordinary listeners and many Muslim political leaders. In this lively program with listener participation, politicians representing different points of view discuss the hottest political issues of the day. In a ceremony in late June of 2006, many citizens, leading media outlets, leaders of several political parties, and the Nigerian Vice-President participated in a ceremony where a national Nigerian NGO with 2.5 million members, Friends of Nigeria, presented an award to "Political Crossfire," the first award of its kind. The leader of Friends of Nigeria called VOA Hausa "a watchdog of democracy in Nigeria."

Amharic

On December 28, 2006, the Horn of Africa Service added an additional half-hour morning radio news program in Amharic to cover the crisis in the predominantly Muslim country of Somalia. The program, whose centerpiece is an integrated newscast with correspondent reports and actualities, is broadcast on shortwave in the target area Monday through Friday. The program is heard in the region at 6:00 a.m. local time, with a repeat at 7:00 a.m. local time. The new program supplements the regular evening programs in Amharic, Afan Oromo and Tigrigna, which also give extensive coverage to Somalia-related news. VOA Amharic attracts an audience of 18 percent of the adult population of Ethiopia on a weekly basis.

New VOA Somali Broadcast. VOA is scheduled to begin a new half-hour, seven day a week Somali broadcast on Monday, February 12. The new program will be heard at 7:00 PM local time and again at 8:00 PM on shortwave, medium wave, and on FM through local affiliates. The program will follow fast changing news developments in Somalia and the sub-region; it will also include interviews with Horn newsmakers, U.S. policymakers and experts, interviews with the Somali Diaspora, analysis and cultural features and music. The re-launched VOA Somali-language programming to the Horn of Africa will aim to reach millions of Somali speakers in predominantly Muslim Somalia, Djibouti and in the greater Horn of Africa and will target listeners, ages 17 to 35.

Bangladesh

Bangladesh, with a population of over 140 million, has one of the largest Muslim populations in the world. VOA Bangla TV & Radio produced features regarding Muslim youth, Islamic Centers, Eid festivals and Ramadan. Interviews were aired with Nobel Peace Prize Winner Dr. Muhammad Yunus, Assistant Secretary of State for South Asia Richard Boucher, Congressman Joseph Crowley (D) from New York, U.S. Ambassador in Bangladesh Patricia Butenis, Bangladesh Foreign Minister Morshed Khan, Home Minister Lutfuzzaman Babar, and Bangladesh Ambassador in Washington Shamsher M. Choudhury.

India

With Muslims numbering over 145 million, India has the second largest Muslim population, after Indonesia. VOA Hindi TV and radio programming reaches them. Whether it is a discussion about the Iraq war, the situation in Afghanistan, the nuclear ambitions of Iran, the recent India-Pakistan peace initiatives, the situation in Kashmir, or the Bombay Blats of 7/11, the Hindi Service covers issues of interest to the Muslim world. In 2006, VOA Hindi offered exclusive TV interviews with U.S. UnderSecretary of State R. Nicholas Burns, Assistant Secretary of State for South and Central Asian Affairs Richard Boucher, dozens of U.S. senators and representatives, and Muslim leaders, scholars, and experts regarding India's relations with Iran, Pakistan, and the United States.

Bosnia and Herzegovina

VOA broadcasts to Bosnia and Herzegovina include programming targeted to the 49 percent of the population that are Bosnian Muslims. Bosnian Service has a 15-minute daily live radio show; a half hour daily live television show (news and current affairs); a 4-minute daily satellite television feed; and a variety of short programs aired by the best rated Bosnian television station, BHT1. Programs are also aired by 15 television and 15 radio affiliate stations throughout Bosnia, and are available via satellite.

The Service has been at the forefront of promoting reconciliation between the three ethnic groups in Bosnia, still widely divided, even twelve years after the signing of the Dayton Agreement, which ended the war. VOA's news and current affairs programs are tailored to address concerns of the Muslim population in Bosnia, providing exclusive interviews with religious leaders in Bosnia. Interviews such as those with the Grand Mufti of Bosnia Mustafa Ceric; Catholic Cardinal Vinko Puljic; Orthodox Metropolitan Nikolai Dabrobosanski; and Bosnian Jewish Community leader Jacob Finci, were aimed toward promoting inter-religious dialogue, and healing the wounds of war.

The Service continues to address the problem of terrorism, beginning with the allegations of a serious threat posed by foreign Islamic militants in Bosnia after the Bosnian war was over. Interviews with Ilan Berman of the American Foreign Policy Council; Juan Zarate, Deputy Assistant to the President and Deputy National Security Advisor for Combating Terrorism; Bosnian Americans Bajram ef. Mulic and Senad Agic; and Lorenzo Vidino with the Investigative Project have focused on the problem of terrorism in Europe. Recently Grand Mufti Ceric gave an exclusive interview to VOA Bosnian on his initiative for a new Islamic Declaration which would condemn Wahabism and its violent influence on Bosnian Muslim Community.

China

Radio Free Asia provides service to Muslim audiences through its Uigher language service launched in December 1998. It is the only international radio service providing impartial news and information to the Uighur Muslim population in Western China in the Uigher language. The Xinjiang Uigher Autonomous Region (XUAR) comprises roughly one-sixth of China's territory and an estimated 10 million Uigher speakers. Like Tibetans, the Turkic Uighers have faced extreme repression from the Chinese government since the People's Republic took control of their home territory. In recent years, Beijing has stepped up their control over Uighers, using the War on Terror to justify harsh crackdowns on religious practice and political and social dissent.

Consistent with RFA's mandate, the Uigher service acts as a substitute for indigenous media reporting on local events in the region. The service, broadcasting two hours daily seven days a week, breaks many stories that go unreported by China's state-run media or foreign news organizations including programs on Sino-Central Asia, Sino-Russia, Sino-America relationship, democratic development in Central Asia, Uigher history, culture, literature, language, arts, human rights, corruption in the communist leadership system, the environment, AIDS and other health issues, as well as Internet control in China.

RFA provides a forum for a variety of opinions and voices from within the XUAR. Programming includes: breaking news, analysis, in-depth reporting, interviews, commentary, a hotline call-in show, weekly news review, and feature stories. A listener call-in hotline airs five days per week, allowing callers a platform to discuss current events in the region.

RFA's Uigher service Web site, launched in September 2004, provides continuously updated news in all three writing systems used to convey the Uigher language—Arabic, Latin, and Cyrillic. RFA's site is the only non-Chinese Uigher news Web site and the only Unicode Uigher news Web site. The site streams the daily RFA broadcast in Uigher and offers ongoing coverage of events in the XUAR in text, image and video. The archived audio files can be retrieved on a special page or downloaded via podcast. RSS feeds are also available, making it possible for people to automatically update their news readers or Web pages with RFA news content.

RFA continues to be confronted with unrelenting jamming of broadcasts and blocking of its Web site. Research conducted between June 2005 and August 2006 shows that fear is the main tool used to prevent Uigher people from accessing RFA, whether on air or online. RFA's confronts Chinese censorship by broadcasting on multiple short-wave frequencies and by regularly e-mailing instructions on accessing the banned www.rfa.org through proxy Web servers. Despite Chinese censorship and the dangers involved, research indicates that Uigher listeners and Web users consider RFA a lifeline in a hostile media environment—a station offering unique content worth taking risks to access.

Transmission

Since September 11, 2001, the BBG has transformed its transmission capabilities, continuing its move from a shortwave environment to one that uses AM, FM, satellite, and Internet capabilities to reach its audience. By bolstering transmission capabilities to the Muslim world, BBG has improved opportunities to deliver news and information clearly, reliably, and effectively. New transmission capabilities have been added, and assets reallocated from regions of lesser geopolitical importance and from technologies of declining effectiveness.

The BBG has worked to ensure that we deliver programming to in the media that are most effective in reaching local populations. Recent transmission enhancements include: the delivery of Persian television broadcasts to Iran through two satellites; transmission of Alhurra Europe on a new satellite channel widely viewable throughout Europe; the launch of two additional Alhurra TV transmitters in Iraq (Mosul and Al Hillah) bringing to four the total number of BBG-funded TV transmitters in that country; the construction of a new medium wave antenna in Tajikistan that is increasing the strength of VOA's Aap ki Dunyaa radio programs to Pakistan. In addition, a number of new FM transmitters became operational in 2006. Subsequent to an agreement with Sudan, we hope to establish FM radio transmitting stations in Khartoum and up to 11 other locations in Sudan.

The BBG is currently supporting the construction of three high power medium wave radio transmitters that should come on the air in the next year: one for Pashtun programming in Afghanistan, one for Radio Farda programs to Iran, and one for Aap ki Dunyaa programs to Pakistan. VOA's launch of www.voamobile.com provides an innovative service that offers news content on a mobile phone or Internet-enabled handheld device in ten languages including English, Persian, Turkish, and Indonesian.

U.S. international broadcasting must meet and serve U.S. national security priorities, and must also meet the needs and technological capabilities of the audiences and regions to which we broadcast.

Presenting the U.S. Point of View through Indigenous Broadcast Media

At the Department of State, the Bureau of Public Affairs, Office of Broadcast Services uses television and video products as strategic tools for bringing America's foreign policy message to Middle East and worldwide audiences. A state-of-the-art digital broadcast television facility enables the Department to deliver messages instantly, using the same technology as professional broadcast television networks. Public Affairs facilitates live and taped interviews with the Secretary of State and other State Department principals to all the major Arab networks such as Middle East Broadcasting Corporation (MBC), Al Arabiya, Al Iraqiya, Abu Dhabi TV, Dubai Television, Arab Radio and Television Network (ART), Al Hurra, Kuwait TV, Egyptian TV (ETV), and Lebanese Broadcasting Corporation (LBC). This investment in people and technology was developed to give senior U.S. government officials an opportunity to engage and inform the widest audiences possible about our foreign policy and public diplomacy objectives.

Furthermore, to specifically enhance the capacity of the U.S. Embassy in Iraq, the Department of State recently opened atelevision studio inside the U.S. Embassy in Baghdad. This fully functioning studio allows top U.S. officials to conduct live interviews via satellite with national and international media on a range of topics related to the current situation and future of Iraq as well as America's role in the greater Middle East.

The Department of State Near East Asia Public Affairs and Public Diplomacy Directorate's Arab/Regional Media Outreach Program has achieved tremendous success in directly engaging Middle East media and broadcast services. Since its creation, it has recorded an ever-increasing number of interviews with Arab and regional media outlets—during 2006, 820 interviews with 1200 Arab and regional journalists/media outlets occurred, with a record 486 conducted primarily in Arabic. Networks aired many of the interviews repeatedly and the broadcasts were often picked up by other outlets or wire services.

This capacity was further enhanced by the creation of *Regional Public Diplomacy Hubs* in London, Brussels and Dubai, key media markets where the full-time job of spokesmen is to advocate U.S. policies on regional media, especially television.

A Rapid Response Unit (RRU) was created within the Bureau of Public Affairs to monitor and translate major world media in real-time, produce an early morning daily report on stories driving news around the world, and to craft language to explain the U.S. position on these issues. It is distributed daily worldwide, to U.S. cabinet and sub-cabinet officials, U.S. ambassadors, public affairs officers, regional combatant commanders, and others across the U.S. Government.

The Department of State directly engages foreign audiences on the Internet through the Digital Outreach Team. The Team directly engages in discussions of policy issues and related developments on websites, primarily in the Arabic language. Openly representing the Department, but using informal language, the Team seeks to ensure that the U.S. perspective is heard in cyberspace, providing a counterpoint to extremist ideological arguments and misinformation. Other interagency public diplomacy efforts targeted at countering extremist use of the internet are coordinated through the interagency Public Diplomacy Working Group, chaired by the Bureau of International Information Programs.

In the absence of a U.S. embassy, the Bureau of International Information Programs manages a Persian-language website directing policy and general information into Iran. The website supports active engagement via web chats, web casts and listservs to connect U.S. policymakers and subject-matter experts and Iranian citizens.

Another tool used to enhance communications not just within the Middle East, but with the entire world, is the use of "Echo Chamber" Messages. These messages have given U.S. ambassadors and other U.S. Government officials clear, common-sense guidance that enables them to better advocate U.S. policy on major news stories and policy issues. Additionally, these messages are provided to the Voice of America Policy Office for use in crafting editorials reflecting the views of the U.S. Government.

The Strategic Speakers Initiative (SSI)identifies, recruits, and programs prominent U.S. experts to engage foreign opinion leaders on key strategic themes such as democracy/rule of law, terrorism/security, energy/environment and trade/development. Such speakers can be deployed rapidly to focus IIP resources where the need is greatest to address the most crucial U.S. policy priorities. Strategic Speaker participants are often part of a bigger public diplomacy package that includes webchats, DVCs and other outreach. This program represents collaboration throughout the State Department.

Major Themes of Biased or False Media Coverage of the United States in foreign countries and the actions taken to address this type of media coverage.

The Department of State is taking a leading role to counter misinformation and falsehoods about the United States and its policies or intentions. For example, recent false themes about the United States in foreign media included that the United States has devised an "American Koran," and it is pressing Muslims to adopt it, and that depleted uranium, which the United States uses in its anti-tank ammunition, has caused a massive upsurge in cancers and birth defects. Actions the Department of State has taken to address these false allegations include:

- Launching a Department of State webpage entitled "Identifying Misinformation," appearing in English and Arabic, provides truthful information and analysis to the public to debunk these false allegations. (English-language website url: http://usinfo.state.gov/media/misinformation.html)
- Instructing Public Affairs Officers at our Embassies around the world to use this information on the website to counter false stories in the local media.
- Creating the position of Counter-Misinformation Officer in the Bureau of International Information Programs (IIP) to respond to Embassy requests regarding false stories about the United States.

Potential incentives for and costs associated with encouraging United States broadcasters to dub or subtitle into Arabic and other relevant languages their news and public affairs programs broadcast in the Muslim world in order to present those programs to a much broader Muslim audience than is currently reached.

The single greatest incentive for U.S. broadcasters to dub or subtitle their news and public affairs programs would be evidence that there is adequate demand for the programming among the targeted foreign publics. The Office of the Under Secretary for Public Diplomacy and Public Affairs is working with the Bureau of Public Affairs and other elements within the Department to explore avenues to demonstrate that a potentially profitable market exists for this programming. These offices will continue to do such work, and if data emerges that indicates that this translation makes sense from a business standpoint, will present the data to broadcasters in an effort to encourage this activity.

Any recommendations the President may have for additional funding and legislation necessary to achieve the objectives of the strategy?

The President's budget and legislative requests for FY-2008, and supplemental request for FY-2007, include a number of authorities that would aid the strategic objectives of U.S. international broadcasting. The pending supplemental contains a request for $10 million for the Middle East Broadcasting Networks. As part of the Administration's strategy to counter violent extremism, Alhurra television would launch a signature three-hour daily program to provide additional information about American policies, people, institutions, and perspectives to its audiences across 22 countries in the Middle East. The three-hour daily program capitalizes on Alhurra's unique perspective in a growing market of over 200 channels, and would provide a format and information mix unavailable in the region today. The programming would focus on the news of the day, discuss compelling social issues, broadcast investigative reporting and a spectrum of information not presented in the region's media.

The Administration's budget and legislative requests for FY-2008 would provide ongoing support for this new Alhurra programming effort, increase Alhurra's newscast capability to 24 hours a day (expanding from the current 16 hour capability), and allow Radio Sawa to grow as a news source in the region. The FY-2008 budget also continues VOA's program initiative Somalia, begun in 2007, and maintains program strength in Iran, Afghanistan, and Pakistan. Further, our pending legislative request to the Congress to permanently adopt the BBG's pilot program for personal services contracting (PSC) authority—up to a ceiling of 200 PSCs at any given time—would assure the agency the flexibility to quickly meet staffing needs to respond to broadcast requirements.

6. Visas for Participants in U.S. Programs

According to the State Department's Bureau of Consular Affairs, current visa processing guidelines are sufficient to meet any requirements for the issuance of appropriate visas to individuals from predominantly Muslim nations to participate in any new exchange program, as envisioned by the Intelligence Reform and Terrorism Protection Act of 2004.

The Bureau of Consular Affairs' policy is to expedite all student and exchange visitor applications, with the goal of giving every student and exchange visitor applicant the opportunity to meet their program start date in the United States. This policy is in place at every embassy and consulate worldwide. In countries with a significant waiting period for a visa appointment due to high demand, this policy reduces the wait time for students and exchange visitors from weeks to mere days. In all cases requiring a separate security clearance, the average processing time is now about 25 days.

Processing they can take longer, however, and applicants should allow additional time. Security clearances can be expedited when circumstances so warrant.

The most important factor in expediting visa applications is for the applicants, in conjunction with their program sponsors, to initiate their visa applications well in advance of their planned travel. Most problems in the visa process can be resolved given sufficient time. New exchange programs should be planned far enough in advance to allow the necessary time for visa processing. Candidates should be advised to obtain passports immediately; visit embassy websites for instructions on applying for U.S. visas; and ensure that they follow the instructions concerning required documents and procedures they must complete, as well as how to complete an EVAF and how to arrange an appointment as soon as all required documents are available to them.

The Bureau of Consular Affairs is prepared to work with the Bureau of Educational and Cultural Affairs, or any other government and/or private sector implementing agency to facilitate the timely issuance of visas to exchange visitors.

7. Basic Education in Muslim Countries

The Department of State, the U.S. Agency for International Development (USAID), and other United States agencies continue to support an increased focus on education in predominantly Muslim countries and those with significant Muslim populations. The ongoing U.S. approach stresses mobilizing public and private resources as partners to improve access, quality and the relevance of education, with a specific emphasis on developing civic-mindedness in young people. In many Muslim-majority countries, such as Afghanistan and Yemen, the challenge is to increase country capacity to provide universal access to primary education and literacy. Countries face increasing enrollments and low education quality in the classroom while struggling with limited budgets.

In the Middle East, USAID and the Department of State's Middle East Partnership Initiative (MEPI) are responding to these needs by promoting quality education through improved policy, teacher training, education finance/governance, and community participation. These U.S. efforts complement investments of partner countries and other donors. MEPI funding for projects in basic education totals $34.5 million (FY-2002-06).

In 2006, USAID/Asia Near East Bureau's total education assistance for the region was approximately $365 million, of which $336 million was targeted in predominantly Muslim countries—Afghanistan, Bangladesh, Egypt, Indonesia, Jordan, Lebanon, Morocco, Pakistan, Philippines (Mindanao),

West Bank/Gaza, and Yemen. Out of the $336 million total, approximately $237 million goes toward basic education programs.

In 2006, USAID/Africa Bureau's total education assistance for the region was approximately $185.4 million in DA Basic Education (includes the Africa Education Initiative, Fast Track Initiative and School Fees), of which $36.6 million benefits Muslim populations in Chad, Djibouti, Ethiopia, Kenya, Mali, Mauritania, Niger, Nigeria, Senegal, Somalia, Tanzania, and Uganda.

USAID/Europe and Eurasia (E&E) Bureau implements a regional program for primary and secondary education in the Muslim-majority countries of Tajikistan, Kyrgyzstan, and Turkmenistan. The program is approximately $3.5 million per year, of which $0.58 million was FY-2006 funding.

The U.S. Strategy to Meet Challenges in Education

To promote transformational diplomacy and development, the Department of State and USAID have articulated a common Foreign Assistance Framework. In the "Investing in People" objective of this framework, education is a major element with basic education as an important sub-element. This strategy is applied to programs worldwide, including Muslim countries.

Basic Education: USAID has an Agency-wide *Basic Education Strategy* that targets underserved populations and promotes free universal basic education. The goal is to help learners gain the general skills and knowledge needed to function effectively in life. Basic education programs focus on three areas:

- **Increasing Access:** Targeting groups that have been marginalized in the education system such as minority, rural, out-of-school youth, girls, and young adults, and those who have been impacted by conflict or disaster, thus helping ensure equitable access to education.
- **Improving Quality:** Improving the quality of education is pivotal for ensuring attendance and learning outcomes of basic education. Increasing attention is placed on curriculum reform and measuring learning outcomes.
- **Improving Relevance:** Education programs that develop human capacities and livelihood skills, and aim to link learning with skill development and employment opportunities, particularly in areas with high youth unemployment.

In designing and implementing basic education programs throughout the world, USAID works closely with host-country governments (national and local), non-governmental organizations, communities, and the private sector to maximize program impact and sustainability.

Working with the International Community

The U.S. Government continues to be an active member of several international bodies and activities to achieve universal basic education, including the International Working Group on Education, which originally proposed the "Education for All" (EFA) initiative begun in the late 1980s.

Coordination of the International Effort

USAID provides technical guidance to the EFA effort through the UNESCO-aligned International Institute for Educational Planning. The U.S. Director of Foreign Assistance represents the U.S. at the annual High Level Group meeting for "Education for All," and the USAID Office of Education participates in the annual EFA Working Group meeting. In 2004, USAID served as the G-8 co-chair of the global EFA Fast Track Initiative (FTI) focused on universal primary education; the Agency has participated in all FTI meetings since its inception in 2000.

In engaging the G-8 and Muslim country governments for Broader Middle East and North Africa (BMENA) initiatives, USAID collaborates closely with the State Department and key cooperating United States agencies, especially on literacy.At the Sea Island Summit, the G-8 launched the Broader Middle East and North Africa (BMENA) Literacy Initiative aimed at halving illiteracy rates in the region by 2015. This initiative launched a series of Literacy Working Group and Education Ministerial Dialogues in the BMENA region. Education Ministers from the BMENA region and the G-8 met in Jordan in May 2005 and in Egypt in May 2006, and confirmed their commitment to the process of cooperation under the umbrella of the Forum for the Future launched in Rabat in December 2004. Following the Egypt Ministerial, USAID took over as G-8 co-chair of the BMENA Literacy Task Force with Egypt as regional co-chair. USAID continues to collaborate closely with the State Department and the U.S. Department of Education on literacy reform. As part of the U.S. contribution to this international effort, USAID is supporting literacy assessments in the region and has developed the BMENA 'Literacy Hub' database of global best practices in promoting literacy. The 'Literacy Hub' will be transferred to the BMENA region by March 2008.

Leveraging Other Donors

Of all bilateral aid to the education sector in 2003-2004, the United States with France, Germany, Japan and the United Kingdom contributed 72 percent of the total, according to the *EFA Global Monitoring Report for 2007*." For basic education, over two-thirds were contributed by Canada, Japan, the Netherlands, the United Kingdom, and the United States." Both the United States and the United Kingdom have the greatest focus on basic education, with over 80 percent of their resources focused on that level.

USAID coordinates closely with multilateral (e.g. World Bank and the Asian Development Bank) and other bilateral donors in each country often extending the reach of USAID programs. In Indonesia, for example, the Australian bilateral aid agency, AusAID, used USAID pilot education program as the basis for its new basic education project, using USAID's methodology for supporting local government management of education and for promoting active learning in classrooms. Collaboration with AusAID, as well as other donors such as UNICEF, continues during implementation in the form of jointly-prepared training materials and activities in communities to avoid duplication as well as combined approaches in working with local and national officials. This coordinated approach has extended donor program coverage in Indonesia in the education sector.

In Tajikistan, USAID-developed training modules on interactive learning and teaching methods and teacher trainers support the Government of Tajikistan's implementation of the "Education for All" Fast Track Initiative, leveraging funds of approximately $1.6 million. The USAID basic education project also complements World Bank and Asia Development Bank (ADB) projects in the area of education finance, curriculum revision, teacher training, and strengthening capacity of teacher training institutes. In Kyrgyzstan, USAID-supported independent testing organization won a World Bank tender to implement student assessments; USAID-developed teacher standards are used in revision of the teacher incentive system; and the basic education project collaborates with the ADB project by providing training for textbook authors.

Leveraging Contributions from the Private Sector and Civil Society Organizations

The U.S. Government uses its official development assistance to leverage other resources for education by developing alliances or partnerships with the private sector and non-governmental organizations (NGOs), including civil society organizations. USAID's Global Development Alliances (GDAs), also known as public-private partnerships, are tailored to country-specific needs and the private sector partners' interests. Between the years 2000–2006, USAID received on average a greater than a three-to-one match for education alliances in the Asia Near East region. Below are several examples of ongoing and new country-specific partnerships in the region:

In Western and Central Mindanao, as well as the Autonomous Region of Muslim Mindanao in the Philippines, there are currently six GDA partnerships to increase educational opportunities for children by ensuring access to quality education; to improve the capacity of teachers, and raise math, science and English skills among elementary school beneficiaries; to increase employment opportunities and engage young leaders; and, to provide business and skills training for out-of-school youth; and, to provide opportunity for school drop-outs and out-of-school youths to rejoin formal schooling through an accreditation and equivalency mechanism. With approximately $12 million in USAID funding, an additional $42.7 million was leveraged (more than a one-to-three leverage) from private businesses, local NGOs, foundations, and national government agencies.

In Indonesia, public private partnerships are being used to expand the reach of USAID activities and to respond in natural disaster situations. A partnership with BP is helping improve education quality in Papua, one of the most under-served and isolated areas of Indonesia. An alliance with ConocoPhillips is helping restore education services in communities affected by the May 2006 earthquake that struck Yogyakarta and Central Java.

In Morocco and Jordan, a USAID information technology partnership with CISCO, UNIFEM, and the Governments of Morocco and Jordan has introduced CISCO Certified Network Associate and job-readiness training to eleven Moroccan institutions (900 students, 49 percent women) and to over 600 students (all women) in Jordan. In both countries, there is a focus on job skills and placement for women. In Morocco, 900 students, more than 50 percent of whom are women, have benefited (or are still benefiting) from the CISCO Certificate programs combined with job-preparedness training. Fifty percent of the first student cohort who completed the program found jobs within six months after graduation.

USAID's Office of Middle East Affairs recently finalized a new GDA that will engage and support emerging youth leaders in five Middle Eastern countries Egypt, Jordan, Lebanon, West Bank Gaza and Yemen. Partnering with the Ford Foundation, Save the Children International will create a youth development toolkit and link emerging young leaders to a network of youth development workers and institutions that assist young people build leadership capacity and exercise positive, moderate leadership behaviors within a community development context.

In cooperation with the Middle East Partnership Initiative (MEPI), Scholastic Inc., is providing millions of Arabic-language classroom libraries to thousands of schools in the Middle East and North Africa Scholastic's substantive contribution allows MEPI to leverage its $12 million investment in this critical-thinking and independent reading skills development program. In another example, MEPI's partnership with the CISCO Learning Institute, is developing on-line English language curricular materials to complement the efforts of the private sector-based World Economic Forum (WEF)—sponsored Jordan Education Initiative.

USG Coordination to Reduce Duplication and Waste

The Department of State and USAID work closely together implementing their Foreign Assistance Framework, which includes education. Through this framework and a joint Operational Plan process, State, and USAID coordinate to reduce duplication of effort and/or waste.

USAID collaborates actively with the Department of State/Middle East Partnership Initiative (MEPI) to promote education in Muslim countries within the Near East region, with a focus on civic education. The MEPI education pillar supports education systems that enable all people, especially girls, to acquire the knowledge and skills necessary to compete in today's economy, participate actively and effectively in the civic arena, and improve the quality of their lives and that of their families. MEPI and USAID coordinate to minimize any potential duplication of efforts and investments. A modest number of MEPI-funded education programs, notably the support for the Arab Civitas network, are implemented in conjunction with USAID. Other examples of collaboration include: support for a women's literacy in Morocco; development of e-learning modules for civics in Jordan; and, in Yemen, pending funds availability, the design and implementation of an Internet communication and collaborative learning network for 20 high schools. (This program will end March 31, 2007; there is no additional funding for it.) MEPI is also providing funding for an Arabic version of the Global Learning Portal, a project under the auspices of the Broader Middle East and North Africa (BMENA) initiative; the Portal will provide new means for professional collaboration and benefit educators and idea leaders across the Arab world.

Training and Exchange Programs

Bridging both basic and higher education, USAID, State Department Bureau of Education and Cultural Affairs (ECA) and MEPI coordinate in the area of providing training and exchanges for students from Muslim-majority countries to the United States. In addition to the educational value of these kinds of interventions, participants are exposed to American values, culture, and democratic institutions. Many of these programs directly benefit basic education. In Egypt, 100 scholarships will be awarded to enhance the Ministry's technical college instructor capacity through "Train-the-Trainer" teacher preparation programs, of which 25 will be financed by the current ECA community college scholarship program. In Pakistan, secondary school educators will attend a five-week program in the United States, focusing on mathematics, science, and classroom technology.

For younger students, there are some programs such as State Department's **English Microscholarship Access Program**, which provides English classes for deserving high school students from non-elite sectors in countries with significant Muslim populations. The program, funded by MEPI in the Middle East and North Africa region, delivers language instruction in a civic education context, and helps students compete for future job and educational opportunities. It also prepares them to be considered for a U.S.

exchange program. During FY-2006, U.S. embassies selected schools in 45 countries to enroll approximately 10,000 students in the program. In addition to teaching English, the program provides an American classroom experience using U.S. materials and emphasizes active learning.

The State Department's **Youth Exchange and Study Program (YES)** and **Future Leaders Exchange Program (FLEX)** bring high school students from Muslim countries to live with American host families and attend American public high schools for an academic year. The FLEX students also receive special training in civics and work as volunteers. Similarly, MEPI's **Student Leaders/Study of the United States Institutes** provide young people with intensive training in civic engagement and leadership skills in both U.S. and regionally-based settings.

The State Department's **"Leaders in Education Program"** is specifically designed to bring K-12 educators and administrators from all regions of the world, including Muslim countries, to the United States to visit schools, meet with teachers, administrators, and representatives of Parent Teacher Associations and other community organizations. The **Teaching Excellence and Achievement Program** (TEA) provides secondary school teachers from Eurasia, South Asia, and Southeast Asia with unique opportunities to enhance their teaching skills and increase their knowledge about the United States. The participants participate in a professional teacher development program in the United States. The six-week program also includes a three-week internship at a secondary school where participants actively engage with American teachers and students. Also, the TEA program provides follow-on grants to the international teachers to purchase essential materials for their schools, to offer follow-on training for other teachers, and to conduct other activities that will build on the exchange visits.

USAID's **Training Future Leaders** initiative highlights the importance of U.S.-trained scholars and their unique role in developing their nations upon returning home. USAID is carrying out an analytical study on prior USG investments. This research will inform future program design and provide a "best practices" framework for long-term training programs. Currently, field research is being done in Yemen, Egypt, Nepal, and Indonesia. This program complements ongoing efforts carried out by State/ECA and MEPI.

Funds Needed to Achieve Universal Basic Education

UNESCO estimates that $5.6 billion are needed per year to achieve "Education for All" by 2015. Globally UNESCO estimated that 103 million children were out of school in 2002/2003. For the countries in the Muslim world, this figure is estimated to be around 45 million. Estimating that it costs roughly $50 per year per child to complete basic education (6 years of schooling), it would cost $2.2 billion per year in Muslim countries as a whole to achieve universal basic education.

Efforts to Encourage Development and Implementation of a National Education Plan

In countries with predominantly Muslim populations, the effectiveness of basic education systems is at the crux of their development future and potential to moderate the influence of low growth, joblessness, lagging social services and despair. The United States encourages countries to develop and implement national education plans by offering assistance to support education reform developments and program funding once reforms have moved into the implementation phase. The United States has influenced national education plans and reform by way of pilot programs that model best practices in education. These positive experiences galvanize support for broader change and can impact the education system beyond the pilots programs' localities. Model programs also potentially have an impact outside of targeted interventions. In Indonesia, USAID helped the provincial government of Aceh with its new long-term education strategy, developed after decades of conflict and the 2004 tsunami. This strategic plan was recently endorsed by the Government of Indonesia's Ministry of National Education.

In December 2006, the USAID basic education project in Central Asia organized a regional conference on school governance which gathered over 60 representatives from ministries of education and finance, local authorities, schools, and national and international organizations from Kyrgyzstan, Tajikistan, Turkmenistan, and Uzbekistan. The participants reviewed policy guidelines on community participation in education decision making developed by the USAID project, discussed relevant national and international legal frameworks and recommended changes which will help the decision makers in the region to increase community involvement in school activities and provide input to education reform.

Closing the Digital Divide and Expanding Vocational/Business Skills

To "close the digital divide" and expand vocational/business skills, USAID, State, and other agencies implement public-private partnerships, information technology in the classroom, school-to-work and workforce training programs, improved quality of basic and secondary education programs, scholarships and exchanges. A few programs are highlighted below.

— USAID/ANE Bureau **Education and Employment Alliance** promotes private sector participation in Egypt, Morocco, Pakistan, India, Indonesia, and the Philippines to enhance skills and improve education and employment opportunities among over 1 million underserved youth. In addition to local partners (profit and non-profit), corporate partners include Chevron/Unocal, GE, Ink Media, Lucent, Microsoft, Nike, and Oracle.

— The State Department's **Global Connections and Exchange Program** seeks to promote mutual understanding and civic education in countries with significant Muslim populations by bringing together more than 1,000 schools from 16 countries for online collaborative projects that focus on professional development, media literacy, and civic education. Teachers also develop skills needed to participate in collaborative activities with U.S. schools, and teachers and students are offered opportunities to travel to their partner schools as a way to strengthen mutual understanding and solidify virtual relationships through face-to-face meetings.

— The USAID **Internet Access Training Program** (IATP), administered by the International Research and Exchanges Board (IREX) since 1995, provides free internet access and training in 11 countries throughout Central Asia, the Caucasus, and Western Eurasia. From major cities to small communities, IATP encourages information sharing, network building, and collaboration among U.S. Government exchange alumni and other targeted audiences. IATP staff train alumni and other targeted audiences in the effective use of the Internet and sponsor the development of local language web sites. The centers also conduct training in basic civics, entrepreneurship, and English.

— **USAID and the Intel Corporation** signed Memorandum of Understanding in December 2006 to broaden access and usage of information and communications technologies (ICT) in developing commu nities around the world. This alliance envisions collaboration and partnership in the following areas: enabling "last mile" internet connectivity and locally relevant applications; supporting ICT usage and deployment by small and medium-sized enterprises to enhance economic development opportunities; and increasing the use of ICTs to support education and health. Intel prior experience in the education sector includes software development and teacher training programs for K-12.

Countries Eligible for Assistance

USAID has education programs in Muslim-majority countries and countries with large Muslim populations, which potentially overlap those which might be targeted by the President under an International Youth Opportunity Fund [section 7114(b)]. Below is a list, though not exhaustive, of programs in the Asia Near East, Africa, Europe, and Eurasia regions.

The Asia Near East region contains several Muslim-majority countries with significant education needs. Basic education program highlights include:

In **Afghanistan**, because many children and youth lost years of formal schooling, students need to catch up to their appropriate grade level. USAID created an accelerated learning program, compressing two years of study into a single year through innovative teaching techniques. This program has trained around 10,500 teachers and enrolled nearly 170,000 students. More than half the students are girls. In addition, USAID has printed and distributed nationwide 48.5 million textbooks for grades 1-12. Since 2002, USAID in conjunction with the Ministry of Education has built or refurbished 622 schools, mostly in remote areas.

In Bangladesh, Sesame Street Bangladesh, known locally as Sisimpur, is USAID's most recognized activity in the country. The program began airing in April 2005 and is the first show of its kind in Bangladesh. The half-hour television programs provide access to literacy, numeracy, and critical thinking skills for almost half of the estimated nine million three to six-year-olds in Bangladesh. This prepares them for learning success and helps to combat traditionally low achievement and high drop out rates in the lower primary grades. Secondly, USAID supports the Early Learning for School Success Program (SUCCEED) operation of 1,800 preschools which prepare preschool-aged children for school by improving reading and mat skills and expanding access to primary schools. A further aim of the program is to increase children's confidence and to reduce high dropout rates by enriching early learning opportunities prior to formal education. The program has established 1,800 preschools across the country (600 are based in schools and 1,200 are based in homes) and trained over 1,800 preschool teachers in new interactive methodologies.

USAID/Egypt supports the Government of Egypt in sustaining improvements in learning outcomes in grades K-12. The program focuses on improving teaching and learning, increasing equitable access to education, and strengthening management and governance in seven governorates. Activities include in-service teacher training, school libraries, information technology, and some school construction in remote and densely populated areas. To date, USAID has also provided 5 million books to over 5,000 Egyptian primary schools. Over 39,000 students now have access to computer technology. USAID has built 70 new girls schools serving almost 40,000 students. USAID supported the development of the Egyptian Sesame Street, which helps over 85 percent of all children under age eight acquire early literacy and numeracy skills.

USAID works in **Indonesia**, the world's largest Muslim country. The USAID program there works with over 100 districts (25 percent of the nation), providing training and technical assistance to school officials, communities and local governments on education management and finance. This Presidential initiative also includes in-service teacher training, mentoring, and teacher resource centers to improve the quality of classroom instruction. Over 245,000 junior secondary students and out-of-school youth are learning employment-related life skills while working toward school completion or its equivalency. USAID is supporting the creation of an Indonesian *Sesame Street*, which will debut in 2007. Through direct assistance and dissemination of best practices, education programs are expected to reach 9,000 public and private schools, 2.5 million students, 90,000 educators and one million out-of-school youth by 2010.

In July 2003, the Government of **Jordan** launched a five-year, $380 million program, developed with USAID assistance, Education Reform for the Knowledge Economy (ERfKE) initiative. This initiative is one of the most ambitious education reform programs in the Arab region to date; its goal is to re-orient education policy, restructure education programs and practices, improve physical learning environments, and promote learning readiness through improved and more accessible early childhood education. USAID, in coordination with Jordan and eight other donor nations and multi-lateral organizations, will provide $80 million during this strategy period to support reform efforts through ERfKE. USAID's efforts under this initiative (1) assist the Government of Jordan's early child care initiative, creating 100 public kindergartens, field-test curriculum, and develop an accreditation system; (2) develop school-to-work programs and an IT curriculum stream for high school students; (3) connect 100 'Discovery' schools to broadband and test e-learning modules for all subject; (4) expand youth and life skills programs to secondary schools in new underserved areas in Jordan; and, (5) construct up to 28 new schools and rehabilitate another 100 schools to create the appropriate learning environment that supports the reform efforts and accommodates the recent influx of refugees from the region.

In **Pakistan**, USAID supports the Government of Pakistan's education reform strategy by: (1) strengthening education policy and planning; (2) improving the skills and performance of teachers and administrators; (3) increasing youth and adult literacy; (4) expanding public-private partnerships; and (5) providing school improvement grants and involving parents and communities in public schools. Over 9,000 parent-teacher associations received school improvement grants helping communities to build over 3,000 new classrooms, reconstruct over 1,000 more classrooms, build over 1,200 toilets, and repair another 1,000. In addition, in the Federally Administered Tribal Areas, USAID is constructing and furnishing 65 primary, middle, and high schools. USAID is building or restoring water and sanitation facilities at 190 girls' schools. Scholarships have been awarded to

57 women from this area to attend a one-year, pre-service teacher education program.

In the **Philippines (Mindanao)**, USAID education programs aim at improving education quality and access, and providing livelihood skills training for out-of-school youth. USAID and the U.S. Peace Corps jointly help improve instruction in English, science, and math by training over 21,000 elementary and secondary school teachers, as well as mobilizing over 300 Parent-Teacher Community Associations. Computer and internet education has also been introduced.

The Asia Near East regionalso contains countries with significant Muslim populations though not in the majority, such as India (second largest Muslim population in the world).

USAID/India's pilot program introduces the formal curriculum in eleven Islamic religious schools (madrassas), complementing the Indian Government's efforts to modernize madrassa education. The program reaches over 2,500 out-of-school youth and working children, particularly adolescent girls. A state government has decided to scale-up this model with its own resources, benefiting over 90,000 children in 1,200 madrassas by September 2008.

The sub-Saharan Africa region contains a number of important Muslim and Muslim majority countries, in which support to basic education activities and improved learning opportunities for in-school and out-of-school youth figure prominently. While USAID has been working with predominately Muslim countries and communities in the education sector in Africa from the 1960s, since the events of 9/11, the Bureau for Africa's Office of Sustainable Development (AFR/SD) has re-evaluated the role of education and taken a more strategic approach to address the concerns of a post-9/11 society. USAID partners with Muslim communities to ensure that children in these communities are receiving the best and broadest education possible and that USAID is working collaboratively to create an enabling socio-economic environment that will ultimately lead to greater global peace, security and understanding.

In support of President Bush's $100 million **East Africa Counter Terrorism Initiative (EACTI)**, AFR/SD initiated programs in East Africa in 2003 that provide basic education opportunities in marginalized Muslim communities. The targeted countries include Kenya, Uganda, Tanzania, and Ethiopia. Eritrea had been part of the original list, but eliminated during the USAID/Eritrea closeout. A summary of these programs include:

- **USAID/Ethiopia** implements various activities in Muslim-dominated areas particularly in Somali, Afar, and Oromia regions. The activities include: support to pre-service and in-service teacher training to improve the quality of primary education; provision of capacity building training for Parent Teacher Associations (PTAs) and community members to increase parent and community involvement in school management; building the capacity of education officers to improve the planning and management of the education system; and establishment and expansion of alternative basic education centers to provide non-formal primary education to children, especially girls, and adult literacy classes for illiterate Muslim men and women.

- **USAID/Kenya's** basic education program, Education for Marginalized Children in Kenya (EMACK), is concentrated in the North Eastern and Coast Provinces. Both Provinces have predominantly Muslim populations and the lowest education statistics in the country. This education portfolio began in 2004 with supplemental funding specifically targeted at Muslim communities. At the end of two years the project has had a tremendous impact on enrollment and retention. Over 100,000 children have been reached in the Coast Province. Approximately 250 Early Childhood Development Centers have been supported; over 2,000 teachers were trained in child-centered teaching methods. To date, the School Infrastructure Program has successfully built 107 classroom, three dining halls, eight dormitories, and supplied 2,000 desks along with 300 bunk-beds with mattresses.
- **USAID/Tanzania's** program focuses on strengthening primary performance in general and secondary math and sciences over the next five years. USAID will focus basic education activities for underserved children (especially girls in Muslim and pastoral areas). The United States' basic education initiative will provide training and materials to teachers and students, allowing thousands of Tanzanian students to receive textbooks written in Kiswahili and allowing girls to receive scholarships. United States resources will enable two programs to lay the groundwork over the next five years to: increase the number of girls receiving preschool, primary, and secondary education; improve primary and secondary skills in math and science; and provide specialized training for teachers in math, science, English, and the needs of children with disabilities.

USAID works with Muslim and pastoralist populations in geographic areas where there is little or no donor support. USAID/Tanzania will continue enhancing service delivery in Zanzibar, while adding two pilot districts (Lindi Urban and Mtwara Urban) on the southern Tanzanian mainland. Over 36,000 secondary, 64,000 primary, and 7,000 pre-primary school students will benefit from U.S. support targeting education delivery systems at local, district, and regional levels. In addition, an innovative radio instruction activity will focus on pre-primary and primary-level education. The radio instruction activity will establish 100 informal learning centers, as well as pilot radio instruction in 40 primary-school classrooms in Zanzibar. In addition, isolated communities in pastoralist areas will establish 70 Community Learning Centers providing equitable access to education for 14,000 children by FY-2008. Children will benefit from quality basic education in Kiswahili, English, math, social studies, science, and life skills.

- **USAID/Uganda** supports Madrassa Early Childhood Development (ECD), which targets poor communities and builds on existing informal early child education at selected community mosques. Through the Madrassa Resource Centre communities are supported to establish and manage their own pre-schools by using intense community participation in pre-primary education. The education activities follow a unique structure that was exclusively designed for Madrassa for use in the Ugandan context. The project seeks to provide access to high quality, culturally relevant and affordable early childhood education and development in order to increase the chances of children from underprivileged communities to access and succeed in later formal education. To date the project has achieved the following: 15 community schools have been mobilized and are participating in the program; 13 community schools are being supported under post graduation continuous support to ensure the long-term sustainability of the pre-schools; 1,207 children are currently enrolled in the new schools and other schools supported by the ECD activity; 282 Schools Management Committee members received training on how to manage their schools; 120 ECD teachers have been trained in ECD methodologies; and 1,810 parents have been mobilized to send their children to the community schools.

In support of the **Trans-Sahara Counter-Terrorism Partnership (TSCTP)**:

- **USAID/Mali's** basic education program focuses on supporting moderate Islamic schools (madrassas) and improving the quality of primary education for Mali's predominantly Muslim population. The program reinforces the Ministry of Education's management capacity; provides school-based and radio-based teacher training; develops interactive radio instruction for students; promotes adult literacy, and mobilizes communities to better manage and advocate for their local primary schools. In the three northern regions of the country, USAID provides scholarships for over 6,000 disadvantaged girls each year.
- **USAID/Senegal's** program aims at improving basic education in Koranic schools currently benefits approximately 4,800 vulnerable children living and studying in these schools. The pilot activity, funded with TSCTP ESF funds, was launched in late 2005. It supports improvements in the living, health, nutrition, and learning conditions of children in Koranic schools. It accomplishes this through the provision of hot meals; basic learning materials such as pens, books, and notebooks;

and first aid kits. The program also provides training to teachers in how to effectively teach languages, math, life skills, and health education. Vocational training is also offered in the areas of carpentry, sewing, masonry, and tannery. Over the past few months, the leaders of these schools have become increasingly receptive to incorporating secular education in their curriculum and in promoting better nutrition and hygiene among their students.

- AFRD/SD's efforts through the President's Africa Education Initiative (AEI) in **Niger, Chad, and Mauritania** complement the TSCTP's efforts to counter extremism and terrorism. In these countries, USAID has used the AEI's Ambassador Girls' Scholarship Program to improve access to quality education for girls and to engage parents and communities in the north of Mali and throughout Niger, Chad, and Mauritania.

While not part of EACTI or TSCTP, other countries have benefited from USAID's Bureau for Africa's efforts to reach out to Muslim populations, including Somalia, Sudan, and Djibouti in the Horn of Africa and Nigeria in the West.

- **USAID/East Africa** has been supporting education programs in **Somalia** since 1994. The current education program uses radio to deliver high-quality, interactive instructional programs to marginalized children. The radio programs are currently being broadcast throughout Somalia, including in Mogadishu. The instructional radio program will target out-of-school youth and Koranic schools in Muslim communities.
- **USAID/Sudan** efforts are focused on the Three Areas and southern Sudan and engaging in national development. USAID continues to implement programs to enhance inter-religious peace-building through improving education access. Formal and non-formal programs focus on primary and girls' education, teacher training and institutional development—targeting out-of-school youth, women girls, returnees, and other vulnerable groups. The U.S. Government is expediting the provision of primary education and adult literacy through radio-based instruction to provide a quality standard of learning both for students and teachers. Conflict resolution, recovery, and prevention are integrated to support the peace process.
- **USAID/Djibouti**. Since 2003, USAID has supported Djibouti's education reform program, to (a) increase access through school rehabilitation, renovating/building water and sanitation facilities, and the provision of textbooks, equipment and kits; (b) improve quality through teacher training, development of teachers' and school principals' guides, provision of English Language teaching and teacher training for secondary and university levels, and construction and

equipment of pedagogic resources centers, as well as improving supervision; and (c) improve community participation and increase girls' education through the provision of scholarships to 1,000 girls and non-formal education programs for out-of-school youth, especially girls. USAID collaborates with the U.S. Embassy and the Combined Joint Task Force/ Horn of Africa.

- **USAID/Nigeria** began support to the education sector in 1999. The first three-year program focused on increasing teachers' instructional skills in English literacy and numeracy; used interactive radio instruction; increased community/PTA involvement in schools' management; increased child-focused classroom instructional methods; and increased local and state government skills in school-based data collection and use (this aspect evolved into the current GON National EMIS model). Some 25 percent of participating schools were Islamiyyah, the balance were public. The current program integrates health and education activities, focusing on increasing teachers' instructional skills in English literacy and numeracy; uses interactive radio instruction; increases community/PTA involvement in schools' management; and deals with school health and nutrition issues.

In **Europe and Eurasia** the dissolution of the Soviet Union, followed by creation of new independent countries in place of the former Soviet republics, and the drastic deterioration of the economic situation during the 1990s, forced many of the new governments to drastically reduce the country's share of the Gross Domestic Product (GDP) allocated for the education sector. The economic downturn and the challenges of restructuring the economy and the education sector have been particularly severe in Tajikistan, which suffered from a five-year civil war (1992–97).

In 2003, to support the efforts of the Central Asian countries to reform the education sectors, USAID has implemented a regional education project in Tajikistan, Kyrgyzstan, Uzbekistan, and Turkmenistan. Although regional in implementation, the project allows for and takes into account the specific needs of each country and aims to utilize windows of opportunity as they arise. The **Basic Education Strengthening Program (PEAKS)** focuses on five major aspects of the education system: (1) in-service teacher training; (2) classroom-level learning materials and textbook development; (3) parent and community involvement in education decision making; (4) management and technical capacity at all levels of the education system; and (5) rehabilitation of school infrastructure. The program is implemented in close collaboration with the respective Ministries of Education, Ministry of Finance, teacher training institutes and other pedagogical and research institutions. USAID also facilitates donor-host country dialogue and to the extent possible collaborates with other donors to ensure complementary design and delivery of education activities.

USAID/E&E EDUCATION PROGRAM IMPACT IN FOUR MUSLIM MAJORITY CENTRAL ASIAN COUNTRIES (2002–2006)		
TYPE OF PROGRAM	**MAJOR PROGRAM COMPONENTS**	**REGIONAL IMPACT (approximate numbers)**
Increase Access to Education Opportunities	• School and classroom construction and rehabilitation	• Rehabilitated 113 schools (Kyrgyzstan, Tajikistan, Uzbekistan)
	• School finance	• Piloted new school finance mechanism based on per capita funding formula to improve efficiency. Results include more efficient student/teacher ratios in pilot areas. (Kyrgyzstan, Tajikistan, Uzbekistan)
Increase the Quality of Education	• Teacher training	• 8,142 primary and secondary school teachers trained in interactive, student-centered methods with mentoring and other follow-up support (Kyrgyzstan, Tajikistan, Uzbekistan, Turkmenistan)
	• Community and parental involvement	• 174 school community committees strengthened to support school quality improvements (Kyrgyzstan, Tajikistan, Uzbekistan,)
	• Model school program	• 300 "Model Schools" model best practices in the use of new teaching methods, management practices and community involvement. (Kyrgyzstan, Tajikistan, Uzbekistan, Turkmenistan)

Kyrgyzstan

After the Tulip Revolution, the country continues to hang in a tenuous balance. Strengthening the ability of the education sector to deliver quality education relevant to the needs of market-based democracy will facilitate the democratic transition and economic performance and competitiveness. USAID provides teacher training and resource development for 11 pilot schools, which in turn will serve as teacher training centers for 84 cluster schools. The professional Development Schools (PDS) have been recognized by the Government of Kyrgyzstan as the alternative teacher training providers, a significant accomplishment in a country with a highly centralized educational system that does not readily look to alternative service providers. The Government of Kyrgyzstan also pays a salary for a PDS coordinator.

From the inception of the project, 90,268 students benefited from this program and 12,062 teachers received training. In addition, USAID funds the Kyrgyz National Scholarship Test, which helps to fight corruption by enabling high school graduates to receive merit-based scholarships for higher education.

Tajikistan

Keeping momentum towards democratic reform in Tajikistan is critical, and a strong education system is an important tool to support that goal. While the basic education project initially focused on primary grades, deemed to be in the most urgent need of support, in 2005, additional resources allowed the project to expand the spectrum of interventions to cover grades 5-11 and introduce the Reading, Writing, and Critical Thinking Program. From the inception of the project, 53,105 students benefited from this program and 481 teachers received training.

In addition to the regionally implemented PEAKS project, USAID is also supporting a basic education project through the Aga Khan Foundation (AKF). This project works in remote, mountainous areas where teachers seldom have access to professional development activities. As a result of teacher training improvements, teachers report increased attendance, return to school of students who stopped attending, and new motivation to study among the students. From its inception, the USAID-AKF project has benefited 5,000 students and trained 1,057 teachers.

Uzbekistan

Although USAID was forced to halt project activities in 2006 due to the deteriorating political situation, the overall project achievements to date may be noted here. Since its inception, the basic education project has benefited 102,412 students and trained 676 teachers. The success of the project is also evidenced by the fact that many of the Uzbek trainers continue to support the regional project activities in Kyrgyzstan and Tajikistan.

Turkmenistan

Turkmenistan has taken the disturbing step of essentially eliminating upper secondary education by reducing the length of study to nine years instead of the standard ten years (under the Soviet system). In addition, the shift to the almost total reliance on the late President Niyazov's books (Rukhnama) as the primary curriculum which emphasizes loyalty to the president and his spiritual teachings, resulted in devastating deterioration of education quality and relevance and created a vast knowledge vacuum which will affect many generations to come. Young people under the age of 15 make up nearly 35 percent of the population in Turkmenistan—the second largest percentage of youth in the Europe and Eurasia region.

As a result of the President Niyazov's education reforms, upper secondary enrollments have fallen from 67 percent to 27 percent since 1991. This means that approximately one in four students between ages of 15 and 18 are enrolled in school.

Besides a small-scale UNICEF initiative in primary and secondary education, USAID has been the only other donor involved in education. Although the Government of Turkmenistan has not formally endorsed the program, it has allowed interested schools to work with the USAID-funded project. Assistance-to-date has focused on teacher training in interactive teaching and learning methods. Up to now, 57,335 students have benefited from the project and 533 teachers received training. In FY-2006, USAID did not fund the basic education project.

The change of leadership following the recent death of President Niyazov may create opportunities for broader engagement. President Berdimuhammedov announced that Turkmenistan will embark on reform to align the education system with international standards. If implemented, this may provide an opportunity for U.S. involvement in basic education reform.

8. Economic Reform

High unemployment and underemployment, often a result of slow economic growth, are among the most critical issues in predominantly Muslim countries. U.S. assistance programs attempt to address this issue with reforms to improve the investment climate. Such reforms could include business registration, dispute settlement, financial sector and agricultural reforms, combined with education, job training, and health programs.

The United States strategy of *Total Economic Engagement* pursues economic reform, rule of law, and global economic integration worldwide, including countries with predominantly Muslim populations. *Total Economic Engagement* includes:

- Regular bilateral discussions on these topics with host government officials, with both U.S. Embassy officials and officials from a wide range of U.S. agencies participating in these talks;
- Formal structured dialogues, high-level Economic Dialogues, and Trade and Investment Framework Agreement (TIFA) Councils;
- U.S. bilateral and multilateral assistance programs for economic reform, trade capacity building, and rule of law are managed chiefly through USAID, the Millennium Challenge Corporation, and the State Department's Middle East Partnership Initiative. Programs are often

complemented with technical assistance provided by specialized U.S. agencies and offices;

- Working through our membership in such international organizations as the International Monetary Fund (IMF), World Bank (WB), World Trade Organization (WTO), and OECD (MEAN-OECD Investment); we coordinate bilateral policies and assistance strategies with these organizations and other bilateral donors to advance reform goals; and
- Working with non-governmental organizations (NGOs), such as Transparency International, and U.S. and foreign business associations, such as American Chambers of Commerce and Business Councils, to advance reform issues of mutual concern.

Integrating Predominantly Muslim Countries into the Global Trading System

There are a number of USG-funded programs to promote predominantly Muslim countries' integration into the global trading system and promotion of regional trade and rule of law.

The following table lists USG funding for trade and capacity building programs. USAID/Asia and Near East Bureau currently funds 86 percent of these programs in these countries.

USG Funding for Trade and Capacity Building	
Country	**USG FY-2006 Funding**
Afghanistan	$59,337,037
Bangladesh	$879,412
Egypt	$29,678,973
Indonesia	$13,873,877
Iraq	$9,482,830
Jordan	$10,960,695
Lebanon	$50,000
Morocco	$10,867,389
Pakistan	$3,929,000
West Bank/Gaza	$0
Yemen	$448,824
TOTAL TCB Funding	**$139,508,037**

WTO Awareness and Accession

FY-2006 USAID programs with components dealing withWTO awareness and accessionare being implemented in Afghanistan ($11,000,000), Egypt ($7,500,000), Iraq ($5,029,501), and Yemen ($100,000):

- **USAID/Afghanistan's Strengthening Private Sector through Capacity Building** goal is to establish sound economic governance within the economic ministries and agencies of the Government of Afghanistan. Activities include customs operations and administration and other related reforms supporting progress toward WTO accession.
- **USAID/Egypt's Assistance for Customs and Trade Facilitation Project** targets all aspects of trade capacity building, including trade policy, trade facilitation, inspections, import and export procedures, trade agreements, and WTO awareness.
- **USAID/Iraq's Trade Policy and Market Access Support—Iraq**. Key objectives include assisting with the Government of Iraq's accession to the World Trade Organization, supporting trade policy reform, and training and capacity building on trade-related matters.
- **USAID/Yemen's Agricultural Support Project** supports both Yemen's capacity to increase its exports of traditional and non-traditional commodities, and Yemen's WTO accession.

USAID Global Export Promotion Programs

USAID global export promotion programsin FY-2006 included Afghanistan/ Pakistan ($493,000), Bangladesh ($630,000), Egypt (the $7,500,000 mentioned previously and $4,000,000), Jordan ($1,000,000), Morocco ($3,587,706 and $5,600,000), Pakistan ($2,500,000 and $240,000), and Yemen ($73,000):

- A U.S. Interagency Working Group supporting the Presidential Initiative for Reconstruction Opportunity Zones (ROZs) sponsored a study on the most feasible locations and products to be included in ROZs to be located in **Afghanistan and adjacent border areas of Pakistan**. Goods produced in the ROZs could enter the U.S. market duty free. The study was funded and implemented by USAID/ Afghanistan, USAID/Pakistan, and USAID/ANE.
- In **Bangladesh**, the Shrimp Quality Support Project focuses on improving the quality and quantity of shrimp exports by Bangladesh in socially and environmentally acceptable ways by transferring appropriate applied research to farmers.
- USAID/Egypt's Assistance for Customs and Trade Facilitation Project (mentioned previously).

- USAID/**Egypt's Information Communication Technology** works to establish the legal and regulatory framework necessary to strengthen e-commerce and information and communication technology; these investments are designed to support business development, trade, and investment.
- USAID/Jordan supports the **Business Development Center—Jordan**, which provides assistance to firms in Jordan to help them adapt to the integration of Jordan into the global economy, and enhances their ability to export to international markets.
- USAID's **Morocco Fast Track Trade** is designed to help Moroccan companies identify U.S. business partners and provide advice on marketing, packaging, and exporting to the United States. The Project prepares export-ready Moroccan small and medium enterprises to use the U.S.—Morocco Free Trade Agreement to their best advantage.
- USAID's **Morocco New Business Opportunities** supports the U.S.—Morocco Free Trade Agreement by providing technical assistance, training, and business contacts to Moroccan manufacturing enterprises to enable them to successfully export to the United States.
- The **Pakistan Initiative for Strategic Development and Competitiveness** provides technical assistance and training to increase the competitiveness of Pakistani small and medium sized enterprises. This USAID/Pakistan project works with a number of sectors, including gems, jewelry, dairy, marble, horticulture, and furniture, to improve their capacity to market and export their product. In addition, USAID's Embroidery Value Chain in Pakistan project is linking rural female embroiderers to agents, who in turn sell their product to urban and rural export markets.

Customs Reforms

Customs reformsare supported by USAID FY-06 programs in Afghanistan ($11,000,000), Egypt ($7,500,000, mentioned previously), Iraq ($1,453,334), and Jordan ($6,437,695):

- **Afghanistan's Customs Reform Program** is imbedded in USAID's Strengthening Private Sector through Capacity Building Project, which is designed to establish sound economic governance in economic ministries and agencies, including the Ministry of Finance and Customs Service. Customs generated some $150 million in Afghan fiscal year 2004-5, surpassing the IMF revenue generation goal.
- **Customs Reform for Trade Improvements—Iraq** is a USAID project to assist the government of Iraq to develop the necessary customs reforms to rebuild the economic infrastructure in Iraq. A modern customs

service is essential for revenue collection and international trade management.

- **Jordan's Customs Reform Program** is embedded in USAID's Achievement of Market Friendly Initiatives and Results (AMIR), which supports private sector development and trade capacity building.

USAID Africa Bureau Programs

Programs managed within the USAID Africa Bureau include Sub-Saharan integration into the global trading system, the driving forces of which are the African Growth and Opportunity Act (AGOA) and the Presidential Initiative—African Global Competitiveness Initiative (AGCI). The African Global Competitiveness Initiative promotes export competitiveness and growth of African enterprises to expand trade with the United States under the African Growth and Opportunity Act, other international trading partners, and within Africa. Program efforts are focused on helping countries build a sound enabling environment including policies, laws and regulations governing business and trade; improving infrastructure to facilitate trade; strengthening financial services to small and medium-sized enterprises and other businesses; and developing the energy sector to meet the needs of growing African economies.

USAID Europe and Eurasia Bureau Programs

Albania

USAID's objective in Albania is to strengthen its integration into the Euro-Atlantic community and promote its contribution to ethnic integration in the region. USAID/Albania's programs worked with the government to improve the business climate for private sector growth and investment and to improve private sector competitiveness to meet international export requirements. The Albanian Center for International Trade, founded in 2003, currently assists the Government of Albania to improve the quality of its trade policies. The Enterprise Development and Export Market Services Project, scheduled to run through September 2008, promotes the competitiveness of small and medium Albanian enterprises in domestic and foreign markets, and accelerates the entry of Albanian exports into global markets.

Azerbaijan

Azerbaijan's program emphasizes economic growth and reform, with a focus on developing the non-oil sectors of the economy. In 2006, USAID worked to develop a well-functioning private sector to increase job creation and regional economic development.

Bosnia and Herzegovina

The program in Bosnia and Herzegovina (BiH) supports progress towards full integration into the EU. USAID/BiH worked to integrate the energy sector into the regional European framework and supported the development and implementation of a coherent direct taxation system that is regionally competitive. USAID's competitiveness projects promote trade and investment in agribusiness, wood processing, and tourism by improving the competitiveness of the firms, industries, and training firms to meet EU standards.

Central Asia Region

The Trade Facilitation and Investment (TFI) Project has been operating in Kazakhstan and the Kyrgyz Republic since 2001 and in Tajikistan and Uzbekistan since 2002. The project seeks to improve the trade and investment environment for small and medium-sized enterprises through the reduction of investment constraints, trade facilitation, and accession to and active participation in the WTO (Kyrgyz Republic joined in 1998).

Building on USAID's TFI Project, the **U.S. Central Asia Trade Facilitation Initiative** works to foster greater regional trade through reduced transaction costs for businesses by harmonizing, strengthening, and streamlining customs functions.

The Business Environment Improvement Project (BEI) was launched for Kazakhstan, the Kyrgyz Republic and Tajikistan in October. This program supports the streamlining of legal and regulatory processes and facilitates multi-party engagement to improve the business, trade, and legal environment.

The Central Asia Infrastructure Integration Initiative, under the Regional Electricity Market Assistance Project (REMAP) helps to establish a transparent and competitive regional electricity market to increase regional electricity trade, stimulate economic growth, and provide market-based solutions for regional disputes related to hydro facilities and reservoirs.

Kazakhstan

USAID's Trade Facilitation and Investment (TFI) Project operates five offices in Kazakhstan and was directly involved in the drafting of Kazakhstan's Customs Code, bringing the country into greater compliance with WTO principles and agreements. TFI is also financing the training of front-line customs officers in the identification and seizure of pirated goods which will help Kazakhstan meet the standards of the Agreement on Trade Related Aspects of Intellectual Property Rights (TRIPS) and achieve removal from the Special 301 Watch List, both of which will help

Kazakhstan's accession process to the WTO. The Kazakhstan Small Business Development Project, funded in October 2006, aims to promote development of small business, resulting in an increase of sales domestically and regionally.

Kosovo

USAID's objective in Kosovo is to strengthen its integration into the Euro-Atlantic community and promote its contribution to ethnic integration in the region. USAID's goal is to help Kosovo make the transition from international administration to self-governance in an effective and peaceful manner. USAID provides training and expert counsel to ensure Kosovars quickly build capacity in the fiscal and economic policy sectors, private enterprise development, and energy management. One such program is the Cluster and Business Support Project, assisting businesses in the construction materials, livestock, and fruit and vegetables sectors by promoting productivity, trade and investment, identifying trade, marketing and import-substitution opportunities and providing training to meet European Union standards.

Kyrgyz Republic. USAID's Trade Facilitation and Investment Project provides support to the WTO Department within the Kyrgyz Ministry of Economic Development and Industry & Trade (MEDIT) to increase its technical capacity in the legal and regulatory process. The Kyrgyz Agri-Enterprise Development Program works closely with the USAID Ferghana Valley Agribusiness Initiative, and provides development assistance to private agricultural-input suppliers that share the Ferghana Valley with Uzbekistan and Tajikistan.

Tajikistan. USAID's Trade Facilitation and Investment Project works directly with the Tajik government to prepare it to meet its WTO commitments by revising and updating the Legislative Action Plan to bring trade-related legislation into conformity with the provisions of WTO Agreements. Patent, copyright, trademark, and geographic indication legislation are revised to reach conformity with the provisions of the Trade-Related Aspects of the Intellectual Property Rights (TRIPS) Agreement. USAID's programs support small and medium enterprise development, customs reform, and the creation of agricultural value chains. Fiscal reform projects focus on reducing regional disparities by increasing the effectiveness of local tax administration and increasing the capacity of local governments to develop and execute budgets.

Turkmenistan. USAID works to foster trade advisory services and implement International Financial Reporting Standards in Turkmenistan. In FY-06, USAID implemented its Agricultural Improvement Project to improve competitiveness and increase the rural incomes of farmers through the production of quality goods for domestic and international markets.

Uzbekistan. In FY-06 USAID assisted Uzbekistan in its WTO accession process supporting the drafting of new legislation and amending the existing legislation required, and worked to implement the reforms required for liberalizing Uzbekistan's trade regime and increasing its participation in the global economy.

Stability Pact for Southeastern Europe

The Stability Pact for Southeastern Europe (SP) has several relevant programs related to global trade that affect parts of the region with significant Muslim populations, including Albania, Bosnia and Herzegovina, and Kosovo. In December, under Stability Pact leadership, the countries of Southeastern Europe signed the amended and enlarged Central European Free Trade Agreement (CEFTA), which brings the region the benefits of freer trade, improve the climate for investment, and bolster stability by increasing economic cooperation. The SP's Trade Working Group has encouraged the negotiation, ratification and implementation of a network of bilateral free trade agreements among the members of the Stability Pact and supports negotiation of a single regional trade agreement aimed at harmonizing the bilateral trade agreements to encompass all SP members. The U.S. supports this process by providing technical assistance to lower non-tariff barriers within the region, consistent with WTO principles.

The SP has also helped develop a common energy market between the European Union and Southeastern Europe. On October 25, Albania, Bosnia-Herzegovina, and UNMIK/Kosovo (among other Southeastern European parties) signed the Energy Community Treaty in Athens. This treaty will establish a common regulatory framework for trade in electricity and gas and facilitate financing and investment by both official donors and private investors in the rehabilitation of existing infrastructure and construction of new infrastructure.

Under Stability Pact auspices, the OECD Investment Compact for Southeastern Europe aims to improve the region's investment conditions, by setting out commitments for policy reform, which countries need to implement in order to create a robust and sustainable market economy and to encourage increasing local and foreign direct investment. Albania and Bosnia and Herzegovina (among other Southeastern Europe nations) are signatories.

Possible Actions to Promote Intraregional Trade and Rule of Law in the Region

Supporting intraregional trade and rule of law is a key aspect of U.S. policy in the Middle East and around the world.

Intraregional Trade

- The President's vision of a Middle East Free Trade Area (MEFTA) by 2013, linking countries in the region with each other and the U.S, is the centerpiece of our effort to promote intraregional trade. Our strategy for attaining MEFTA includes:
  - Negotiating Free Trade Agreements (FTAs) with countries ready for that step. The U.S. has concluded FTAs with Israel, Jordan, Morocco, Bahrain, and Oman;
  - Working with additional countries through the TIFA process to advance readiness for FTA negotiations; and
  - Assisting reform-minded Middle East countries that are not yet in the WTO accession process.
- The Middle East Partnership Initiative (MEPI), MCC, and USAID Missions in the Middle East, provide support for the MEFTA initiative through a variety of programs in trade capacity building. MEPI and USAID Missions in the Middle East are supporting the WTO accession efforts of Iraq, Yemen, and Lebanon. U.S. assistance programs assist FTA partners Jordan, Morocco, Bahrain, and Oman to implement their FTAs with the United States.
- USAID/Jordan's Achievement of Market Friendly Initiatives and Results (AMIR), supports implementation of the FTA between the United States and Jordan. It offers support to Jordan as it liberalizes its economy and works to meet the requirements of regional and global trade opportunities. USAID/Morocco assists the government and private sector to successfully respond to the challenges and opportunities that the FTA with the United States will bring.

The Rule of Law

- **USAID/Egypt's Administration of Justice Support II project** promotes the rule of law by reforming and modernizing the commercial court system and improving the access to quality legal services. FY-2006 funding is $5,000,000.
- **USAID/Morocco's Commercial Court Judges Training in Trademark Opposition Process** promotes mandatory continuing education for judges and lawyers, including trademark opposition. This builds on the work of a previous USAID project on modernization of commercial laws and of the judiciary. The project will also cooperate with USAID funded training provided the U.S. Patent and Trademark Office regarding implementation of the system for both judges and customs officials.

The Millennium Challenge Corporation (MCC)

In addition, the Millennium Challenge Corporation (MCC) provides assistance for transformational development in countries that perform well on 16 independent, transparent policy indicators in the areas of ruling justly, investing in people, and economic freedom. Besides the financial support provided by MCC programs, MCC creates an incentive for candidate countries to adopt legal, policy, regulatory, and institutional reforms related to the MCC selection criteria. Such reforms will contribute to countries' efforts to reduce poverty and increase economic growth.

Summary of MCC Activities in Predominantly Muslim Countries:

Compact-Eligible Countries

Based on their good performance on the 16 policy indicators mentioned above, Compact-Eligible countries are invited to apply for substantial grants from MCC for programs that they design and implement through a "Compact."

Mali

Mali signed a five-year, $460.8 million Compact with MCC in November. Its Compact aims to reduce rural poverty and help achieve national food security through a sustainable increase in the economic performance of the agricultural sector. The Compact also intends to spur economic growth and reduce poverty by increasing the competitiveness of light industry and increasing the value-added of exports and tourism. The Compact's objectives will be met through investments aimed to increase farmers' incomes, enhance agricultural supply chains, reduce transport costs and create a platform for industrial production. The Compact focuses on key infrastructure investments that capitalize on two of Mali's major assets, the Bamako-Senou International Airport, gateway for regional and international trade, and the Niger River, a source of water for irrigated agriculture.

Burkina Faso

Burkina Faso submitted a Compact proposal to MCC in October. It aims to promote economic growth in the rural sector by fostering land tenure security; investing in irrigation and watershed management infrastructure for agricultural purposes; constructing national roads, feeder roads, and market infrastructure; and improving existing agro-industrial supply chains.

Jordan

In November,MCC's Board of Directors selected Jordan as eligible to apply for Compact funding. Jordan is currently preparing a proposal for submission to MCC.

Morocco

Morocco submitted its Compact proposal to MCC in August. The proposal focuses on relieving constraints to growth in the agriculture, fishing, artisan, and small enterprise finance sectors.

Threshold Programs are designed to assist countries that have demonstrated significant commitment to improving their performance on MCC selection criteria, but do not yet pass more than half the indicators in each of the three selection categories of ruling justly, investing in people, and encouraging economic freedom. A Threshold Program provides financial assistance to help improve a low score on at least one of MCC's policy indicators.

Albania

Reducing corruption is the primary focus of the $13.8 million Albanian program. Albania is receiving assistance from MCC to fund three programs designed to reform tax administration, public procurement and business administration. The program anticipates reducing the extensive red tape and below-board payments needed to start a business while increasing the national tax base.

Burkina Faso

The $12.9 million program is a pilot program that seeks to improve performance on girls' primary education completion rates. Specific interventions include the construction of 132 "girl-friendly" schools, teacher training, providing take-home dry rations to girls who maintain a 90 percent school attendance rate, and providing literacy training for mothers. Burkina Faso is now eligible for Compact assistance.

Indonesia

The $55 million program with Indonesia seeks to immunize at least 80 percent of children under the age of one for diphtheria, tetanus, and pertussis and 90 percent of all children for measles. The Threshold Program also has a component aimed at curbing public corruption by reforming the judiciary.

Jordan

The $25 million Jordanian program aims to strengthen democratic institutions by supporting Jordan's efforts to broaden public participation in the political and electoral process, increasing government transparency and accountability, and enhancing the efficiency and effectiveness of customs administration. The Threshold Program is a part of Jordan's reform efforts focused on improvements in public administration, civil liberties, infrastructure, and the economy. Jordan has now become eligible for Compact assistance.

Kyrgyz Republic

Selected as eligible for the Threshold Program in FY-2006 and reselected in FY-2007, the Kyrgyz Republic has requested MCC funding to improve performance on MCC indicators in the *Ruling Justly* category. The Kyrgyz Republic submitted a Threshold Country Plan to MCC, which is currently under review.

Yemen

In February 2007, the Republic of Yemen was reinstated into the Threshold Program. The MCC Board of Directors found that the Yemeni government worked aggressively and demonstrably to address the country's performance on the MCC selection criteria. Yemen may now apply for a Threshold Program agreement.

The Middle East Partnership Initiative (MEPI)

In 2006, the State Department's Middle East Partnership Initiative (MEPI) provided tangible support to reformers in the region so democracy could spread, education could thrive, economies could grow, and women could be empowered. Working in 16 countries and the Palestinian territories, MEPI invested in programs ranging from trade technical assistance to commercial code reform to a network for Arab businesswomen.

Examples of MEPI's work with reformers include the following:

- Provided technical and other assistance in support of successfully completed free trade agreements with the Bahrain and Oman.
- Expanded trade capacity of Arab countries with training and technical assistance; a number of Gulf countries are drafting new customs codes and updating agricultural import/export standards.
- Provided entrepreneurial training for more than 300 participants, almost half of them women, from 16 Middle Eastern and North African countries, with 35 alumni going on to start or expand businesses. At least 500 new jobs have been created following their participation in MEPI programs.
- Extended credit and services to small- and medium-sized businesses through peer consultation and training for regional banks and financial organizations.
- Established self-sustaining Junior Achievement chapters in 12 countries throughout the Middle East, with more than 10,000 students

participating. Created public-private partnerships that assisted in the sustainability of Junior Achievement chapters.

- Expanded commercial and legal reform efforts in the Gulf by working to update legal curricula at law schools in Qatar and Oman, update commercial codes to meet international standards in Bahrain and Oman, and provide continuing education programs for the judiciary.
- Established business network hubs in six countries, focusing on training, professional development, and information sharing on laws, business opportunities, skills, and the global economy.

Chapter 6
Terrorist Organizations

Foreign Terrorist Organization (FTO) aliases cited are consistent with and drawn from the Specially Designated Nationals list maintained by the Department of Treasury. The full list can be found at the following website: http://www.treasury.gov/offices/enforcement/ofac/sdn/sdnlist.txt

Abu Nidal Organization (ANO)

Abu Sayyaf Group (ASG)

Al-Aqsa Martyrs Brigade

Ansar al-Sunna (AS)

Armed Islamic Group (GIA)

Asbat al-Ansar

Aum Shinrikyo (Aum)

Basque Fatherland and Liberty (ETA)

Communist Party of Philippines/New People's Army (CPP/NPA)

Continuity Irish Republican Army (CIRA)

Gama'a al-Islamiyya (IG)

HAMAS

Harakat ul-Mujahedin (HUM)

Hizballah

Islamic Jihad Union (IJU)

Islamic Movement of Uzbekistan (IMU)

Jaish-e-Mohammed (JEM)

Jemaah Islamiya Organization (JI)

Al-Jihad (AJ)

Kahane Chai (Kach)

Kongra-Gel (KGK/PKK)

Lashkar e-Tayyiba (LT)

Lashkar i Jhangvi (LJ)

Liberation Tigers of Tamil Eelam (LTTE)

Libyan Islamic Fighting Group (LIFG)

Moroccan Islamic Combatant Group (GICM)

Mujahedin-e Khalq Organization (MEK)

National Liberation Army (ELN)

Palestine Liberation Front (PLF)

Palestinian Islamic Jihad (PIJ)

Popular Front for the Liberation of Palestine (PFLP)

Popular Front for the Liberation of Palestine-General Command (PFLP-GC)

Al-Qaida (AQ)

Al-Qaida in Iraq (AQI)

Al-Qaida in the Islamic Maghreb (AQIM) [Formerly Salafist Group for Call and Combat (GSPC)]

Real IRA (RIRA)

Revolutionary Armed Forces of Colombia (FARC)

Revolutionary Nuclei (RN)

Revolutionary Organization 17 November

Revolutionary People's Liberation Party/Front (DHKP/C)

Shining Path (SL)

United Self-Defense Forces of Colombia (AUC)

Abu Nidal Organization (ANO)

a.k.a. Arab Revolutionary Brigades; Arab Revolutionary Council; Black September; Fatah Revolutionary Council; Revolutionary Organization of Socialist Muslims.

Description

The ANO international terrorist organization was founded by Sabri al-Banna (a.k.a. Abu Nidal) after splitting from the Palestine Liberation Organization (PLO) in 1974. The group's previous known structure consisted of various functional committees, including political, military, and financial. In August 2002, Abu Nidal died in Baghdad; the new leadership of the organization remains unclear.

Activities

The ANO has carried out terrorist attacks in 20 countries, killing or injuring almost 900 persons; however, the group has not staged a major attack against Western targets since the late 1980s. Major attacks included the Rome and Vienna airports in 1985, the Neve Shalom synagogue in Istanbul, the hijacking of Pan Am Flight 73 in Karachi in 1986, and the City of Poros day-excursion ship attack in Greece in 1988. The ANO is suspected of assassinating PLO deputy chief Abu Iyad and PLO security Chief Abu Hul in

Tunis in 1991. The ANO was responsible for the December 1985 simultaneous Rome and Vienna airport attacks in which 12 people died, including five American citizens.

Strength

Current strength and operational status are unknown.

Location/Area of Operation

Although former and possibly current ANO associates may be in Iraq and Lebanon, the group is largely considered inactive.

External Aid

The ANO received considerable support, including safe haven, training, logistical assistance, and funding from Iraq, Libya, and Syria (until 1987). The ANO's current access to resources is unclear, but it is likely severely impacted by the decline in state support.

Abu Sayyaf Group (ASG)[1]

a.k.a. Al Harakat al Islamiyya

Description

The ASG is a violent Muslim terrorist group operating in the southern Philippines. Some ASG leaders allegedly fought in Afghanistan during the Soviet invasion and are students and proponents of radical Islamic teachings. The group split from the much larger Moro National Liberation Front in the early 1990s under the leadership of Abdurajak Abubakar Janjalani, who was killed in a clash with Philippine police in December 1998. His younger brother, Khadaffy Janjalani, replaced him as the nominal leader of the group. In September 2006, Janjalani was killed in a gun battle with the Armed Forces of the Philippines. Radullah Sahiron is assumed to be the new ASG leader.

Activities

The ASG engages in kidnappings for ransom, bombings, beheadings, assassinations, and extortion. The group's stated goal is to promote an independent Islamic state in western Mindanao and the Sulu Archipelago, areas in the southern Philippines heavily populated by Muslims, but the ASG primarily has used terror for financial profit. Recent bombings may herald a return to a more radical, politicized agenda, at least among certain factions. In August 2006, the Armed Forces of the Philippines began "Operation Ultimatum," a sustained campaign that has disrupted ASG

[1] Listed on the UN 1267 Committee List.

forces in safe havens on Jolo Island in the Sulu archipelago, and resulted in the killing of ASG leader Khadafy Janjalani in September 2006.

The group's first large-scale action was a raid on the town of Ipil in Mindanao in April 1995. In April 2000, an ASG faction kidnapped 21 persons, including ten Western tourists, from a resort in Malaysia. In May 2001, the ASG kidnapped three U.S. citizens and 17 Filipinos from a tourist resort in Palawan, Philippines. Several of the hostages, including U.S. citizen Guillermo Sobero, were murdered. A Philippine military hostage rescue operation in June 2002 freed U.S. hostage Gracia Burnham, but her husband Martin Burnham and Filipina Deborah Yap were killed. U.S. and Philippine authorities blame the ASG for exploding a bomb near a Philippine military base in Zamboanga in October 2002 that killed a U.S. serviceman. In February 2004, Khadaffy Janjalani's faction bombed SuperFerry 14 in Manila Bay, killing 132. In March 2004, Philippine authorities arrested an ASG cell whose bombing targets included the U.S. Embassy in Manila. The ASG also claimed responsibility for the 2005 Valentine's Day bombings in Manila, Davao City, and General Santos City, which killed eight and injured more than 150.

Strength

ASG is estimated to have 200 to 500 members.

Location/Area of Operation

The ASG was founded in Basilan Province and operates primarily in the provinces of the Sulu Archipelago, namely Basilan, Sulu, and Tawi-Tawi. The group also operates on the Zamboanga peninsula, and members occasionally travel to Manila. In mid-2003, the group started operating in Mindanao's city of Cotobato and on the provincial coast of Sultan Kudarat, Mindanao. The ASG was expelled from Mindanao proper by the Moro Islamic Liberation Front (MILF) in mid-2005. The group expanded its operational reach to Malaysia in 2000 with the abduction of foreigners from a tourist resort there.

External Aid

The ASG is funded through acts of ransom and extortion, and receives funding from both regional terrorist groups such as Jemaah Islamiya (JI), which is based mainly in Indonesia, and Middle Eastern Islamic extremists.

Al-Aqsa Martyrs Brigade (al-Aqsa)

a.k.a. al-Aqsa Martyrs Battalion; Fatah Tanzim

Description

The al-Aqsa Martyrs Brigades consists of localized cells of Palestinian militants loyal to the secular-nationalist Fatah movement. Al-Aqsa emerged at the outset of the 2000 Palestinian al-Aqsa Intifadah, splitting from the Fatah party to attack Israeli military targets and settlers with the aim of driving Israel from the West Bank and Gaza Strip and establishing a Palestinian state. Al-Aqsa has no central leadership; the cells operate with autonomy, although they remained ideologically loyal to Palestinian Authority (PA) President and Fatah party head Yassir Arafat until his death in 2004.

Activities

Al-Aqsa initially focused on small arms attacks against Israeli military personnel and settlers in the West Bank. In 2002, the group began to conduct suicide bombings against Israeli civilians. After a March 2002 bombing, the U.S. State Department designated Al-Aqsa a foreign terrorist organization. Al-Aqsa suspended most anti-Israel attacks as part of the broader unilateral Palestinian ceasefire agreement during 2004 but resumed them following HAMAS's electoral victory in January 2006. Al-Aqsa members have continued anti-Israeli as well as intra-Palestinian violence and contribute to the overall chaotic security environment inside the Palestinian territories. Al-Aqsa has not targeted U.S. interests as a policy, although its anti-Israeli attacks have killed some dual U.S.-Israel citizens.

Strength

Current strength is unknown.

Location/Area of Operation

Al-Aqsa operates mainly in the West Bank but has conducted attacks inside Israel and the Gaza Strip. The group has members in refugee camps in southern Lebanon and overseas, although it has not demonstrated transnational capability.

External Aid

Iran has exploited Al-Aqsa's lack of leadership and funds by providing aid and exerting influence over the organization.

Ansar al-Sunna (AS)[1]

a.k.a. Ansar al-Islam; Ansar Al-Sunna Army; Devotees of Islam; Followers of Islam in Kurdistan; Helpers of Islam; Jaish Ansar Al-Sunna; Jund Al-Islam; Kurdish Taliban; Kurdistan Supporters of Islam; Partisans of Islam; Soldiers of God; Soldiers of Islam; Supporters of Islam in Kurdistan.

[1] Listed on the UN 1267 Committee List.

Description

Ansar al-Sunna (AS) is a Salafi terrorist group whose goals include expelling the U.S.- led Coalition from Iraq and establishing an independent Islamic Iraqi state. This amorphous group has changed its name several times over the years and was last known as Ansar al-Islam. AS announced its creation in 2003 by posting a statement to the Internet calling all extremists in Iraq to unite under the new name. The bid to become a jihadist umbrella organization failed, but the name AS stuck. AS has ties to the al-Qaida central leadership and al-Qaida in Iraq (AQI); it has a competitive relationship with AQI, and did not join the AQI-dominated "Islamic State of Iraq." Some members of AS trained in al-Qaida camps in Afghanistan, and the group provided safe haven to al-Qaida fighters before Operation Iraqi Freedom (OIF). Since OIF, AS has become the second-most prominent group engaged in anti-Coalition attacks in Iraq behind AQI and has maintained a strong propaganda campaign.

Activities

AS continues to conduct attacks against a wide range of targets including Coalition Forces, the Iraqi government and security forces, and Kurdish and Shia figures. AS has claimed responsibility for many high profile attacks, including the simultaneous suicide bombings of the Patriotic Union of Kurdistan and Kurdistan Democratic Party offices in Irbil in February 2004, the bombing of the U.S. military dining facility in Mosul in December 2004, and numerous kidnappings, executions, and assassinations.

Strength

Precise numbers are unknown, but AS is the second largest Sunni jihadist group in Iraq, behind AQI.

Location/Area of Operation

Primarily central, western, and northern Iraq.

External Aid

AS receives assistance from a loose network of associates in Europe and the Middle East.

Armed Islamic Group (GIA)[1]

a.k.a. Al-Jama'ah al-Islamiyah al-Musallah; Groupement Islamique Arme.

[1] Listed on the UN 1267 Committee List.

Description

An Islamic extremist group, the GIA aims to overthrow the Algerian regime and replace it with a fundamentalist Islamic state. The GIA began its violent activity in 1992 after the military government suspended legislative elections in anticipation of an overwhelming victory by the Islamic Salvation Front, the largest Islamic opposition party.

Activities

The GIA has engaged in attacks against civilians and government workers. The GIA began conducting a terrorist campaign of civilian massacres in 1992, sometimes wiping out entire villages and killing tens of thousands of Algerians, thus alienating itself from the Algerian populace in the process. Since announcing its campaign against foreigners living in Algeria in 1992, the GIA killed more than 100 expatriate men and women, mostly Europeans, in the country. Many of the GIA's members have joined other Islamist groups or have been killed or captured by the Algerian government. The government's September 2005 reconciliation program led to an increase in the number of GIA terrorist suspects who surrendered to security forces. The GIA's most recent significant attacks occurred in August 2001.

Strength

Precise numbers are unknown, but probably fewer than 100.

Location/Area of Operation

Algeria, the Sahel, and Europe.

External Aid

The GIA has members in Europe that provide funding but mostly the group engages in criminal activity to finance activities and raise funds.

Asbat al-Ansar

a.k.a. League of the Followers; Partisans' League

Description

Asbat al-Ansar, the League of the Followers or Partisans' League, is a Lebanon-based Sunni extremist group composed primarily of Palestinians with links to Usama bin Ladin's al-Qaida organization and other Sunni extremist groups. Asbat is well positioned to play an important role should al-Qaidaattempt to expand further its terrorist operations to Lebanon. The group follows an extremist interpretation of Islam that justifies violence against civilian targets to achieve political ends. Some of the group's goals include overthrowing the Lebanese government and thwarting perceived anti-Islamic and pro-Western influences in the country.

Activities

Asbat al-Ansar maintains close ties with the al-Qaida network, and had a "front-line" command post relatively close to Israel's border in the Ain al-Hilwah (Palestinian) refugee camp. In early to mid-March, Lebanese authorities arrested several members of the group. Some were Palestinians, some were Lebanese. Members of this group were believed by some to have been responsible for a Katyusha rocket attack on the Galilee (Israel) in December 2005. On April 3, 2006, a video was posted to an Islamic website claiming that five members of Asbat al-Ansar were killed fighting in Iraq; the date of death was not provided. Asbat al-Ansar members have been involved in fighting Coalition Forces in Iraq since at least 2005 and several members of the group have been killed in anti-Coalition operations.

Since it first emerged in the early 1990s, Asbat al-Ansar has carried out multiple terrorist attacks in Lebanon; in the mid-1990s the group assassinated Lebanese religious leaders and bombed nightclubs, theaters, and liquor stores. It was involved in clashes in northern Lebanon in December 1999, and carried out a rocket-propelled grenade attack on the Russian Embassy in Beirut in January 2000. Asbat al-Ansar's leader, Ahmad Abd al-Karim al-Sa'di a.k.a. Abu Muhjin, remains at large despite being sentenced to death in absentia for the 1994 murder of a Muslim cleric. In September 2004, operatives with links to the group were believed to be involved in a planned terrorist operation targeting the Italian Embassy, the Ukrainian Consulate General, and Lebanese government offices. In October 2004, Mahir al-Sa'di, a member of Asbat al-Ansar, was sentenced in absentia to life imprisonment for plotting to assassinate then U.S. Ambassador to Lebanon David Satterfield in 2000. Al-Sa'di was working in cooperation with Abu Muhammad al-Masri, the head of al-Qaida at the 'Ayn al-Hilwah refugee camp, where fighting has occurred between Asbat al-Ansar and Fatah elements.

Strength

The group commands about 300 fighters in Lebanon.

Location/Area of Operation

The group's primary base of operations is the 'Ayn al-Hilwah Palestinian refugee camp near Sidon in southern Lebanon.

External Aid

Probably receives money through international Sunni extremist networks.

Aum Shinrikyo (Aum)

a.k.a. A.I.C. Comprehensive Research Institute; A.I.C. Sogo Kenkyusho; Aleph; Aum Supreme Truth

Description

Shoko Asahara established Aum in 1987, and the cult received legal status as a religious entity in 1989. At first, Aum aimed to take over Japan and then the world, but over time it began to emphasize the imminence of the end of the world. Asahara predicted 1996, and 1999 to 2003, as likely dates and said that the United States would initiate Armageddon by starting World War III with Japan. The Japanese government revoked its recognition of Aum as a religious organization following Aum's deadly sarin gas attack in Tokyo in March 1995. In 1997, however, a government panel decided not to invoke the Operations Control Law against the group that would have outlawed it. A 1999 law authorized the Japanese government to maintain police surveillance over the group because of concerns that Aum might launch future terrorist attacks. Under the leadership of Fumihiro Joyu, the chief of Aum's once thriving Moscow operation, Aum changed its name to Aleph in January 2000 and tried to distance itself from the violent and apocalyptic teachings of its founder. In late 2003, however, Joyu stepped down under pressure from members who wanted to return fully to the worship of Asahara. A growing divide between members supporting Joyu and those who remain loyal to Asahara is splitting the cult into factions. In 2006, Joyu officially split from Aleph over recognizing Shoko Asahara as the sole authority.

Activities

In March 1995, Aum members simultaneously released the chemical nerve agent sarin on several Tokyo subway trains, killing 12 persons and causing up to 6,000 to seek medical treatment. Subsequent investigations by the Japanese government revealed the group was responsible for other mysterious chemical incidents in Japan in 1994, including a sarin gas attack on a residential neighborhood in Matsumoto that killed seven and hospitalized approximately 500. The group's attempts to conduct attacks using biological agents were unsuccessful. Japanese police arrested Asahara in May 1995, and in February 2004 authorities sentenced him in to death for his role in the 1995 attacks. In September 2006, Asahara lost his final appeal against the death penalty.

Since 1997, the cult has recruited new members, engaged in commercial enterprises, and acquired property, although it scaled back these activities significantly in 2001 in response to a public outcry. In July 2001, Russian authorities arrested a group of Russian Aum followers who had planned to set off bombs near the Imperial Palace in Tokyo as part of an operation to free Asahara from jail and smuggle him to Russia.

Strength

Aum's current membership in Japan is estimated to be about 1,650 persons. At the time of the Tokyo subway attack, the group claimed to have as many as 40,000 members worldwide, including 9,000 in Japan and 30,000 members in Russia.

Location/Area of Operation

Aum's principal membership is located in Japan, while a residual branch comprising about 300 followers lives in Russia.

External Aid

None.

Basque Fatherland and Liberty (ETA)

a.k.a. Askatasuna; Batasuna; Ekin; Epanastatiki Pirines; Euskal Herritarrok; Euzkadi Ta Askatasuna; Herri Batasuna; Jarrai-Haika-Segi; K.A.S.; Popular Revolutionary Struggle; XAKI

Description

ETA was founded in 1959 with the aim of establishing an independent homeland based on Marxist principles encompassing the Spanish Basque provinces of Vizcaya, Guipuzcoa, and Alava, as well as the autonomous region of Navarra and the southwestern French territories of Labourd, Basse-Navarre, and Soule. Spain and the European Union both have listed ETA as a terrorist organization, and in 2002 the Spanish parliament banned the political party Batasuna, ETA's political wing, charging its members with providing material support to the terrorist group. In 2004, Spain and France formed a joint counterterrorism and judicial unit to combat ETA and Islamic terrorist groups. During 2005 and 2006, police in both countries together arrested around 100 individuals associated with ETA, dismantled several of the group's cells, and dealt a significant blow to its operational capability. Spanish and French prisons are estimated to hold a total of more than 500 ETA members. In March 2006, ETA announced that it would implement a "permanent" cease-fire. On December 30, ETA exploded a massive car-bomb that destroyed much of the covered parking garage outside the new Terminal 4 of Madrid's Barajas International Airport and effectively broke its nine-month "permanent cease-fire." Two individuals killed in the blast became ETA's first fatalities in more than three years. The Government of Spain suspended talks with ETA, and government officials subsequently said political negotiations with the group had ended.

Activities

ETA primarily conducts bombings and assassinations; targets are typically Spanish government officials, security and military forces, politicians, and judicial figures, but the group also has targeted journalists and tourist areas. The group is responsible for killing more than 800 and injuring thousands more since it began its lethal attacks in the late 1960s. Security service scrutiny and a public outcry after the Islamic extremist train bombings in Madrid in March 2004, have limited ETA's capability and willingness to inflict casualties. ETA conducted no fatal attacks in 2005, but did mount more than 30 low-level bombings, most preceded by a warning call, that caused minor injuries and property damage. In February 2005, ETA detonated a car bomb in Madrid at a convention center where Spanish King Juan Carlos and then Mexican President Vicente Fox were scheduled to appear, wounding more than 20 people. In June 2005, ETA launched grenades at the airport that serves the city of Zaragoza, shutting down the airport but causing no damage or injuries. ETA also detonated an explosive device at a stadium constructed as part of Madrid's bid to host the 2012 Olympic Games; there were no injuries in that attack. Just days before its March 2006 cease-fire announcement, ETA claimed responsibility for a spate of roadside blasts in northern Spain that caused no injuries. Its late 2006 attack at Madrid's airport is the group's first fatal attack since March 2003. ETA finances its activities primarily through bribery and extortion.

Strength

Not precisely known, but believed to number in the low hundreds.

Location/Area of Operation

Operates primarily in the Basque autonomous regions of northern Spain and southwestern France, but also has attacked Spanish and French interests elsewhere.

External Aid

Has received training at various times in the past in Libya, Lebanon, and Nicaragua. Some ETA members allegedly fled to Cuba and Mexico, while others reside in South America. ETA members have operated and been arrested in other European countries, including Belgium, the Netherlands, and Germany.

Communist Party of Philippines/New People's Army (CPP/NPA)

a.k.a. Communist Party of the Philippines; CPP; New People's Army; NPA

Description

The military wing of the Communist Party of the Philippines (CPP), the NPA is a Maoist group formed in March 1969 with the aim of overthrowing the government through protracted guerrilla warfare. Jose Maria Sison, the chairman of the CPP's Central Committee and the NPA's founder, reportedly directs CPP and NPA activity from the Netherlands, where he lives in self-imposed exile. Luis Jalandoni, a fellow Central Committee member and director of the CPP's overt political wing, the National Democratic Front (NDF), also lives in the Netherlands and has become a Dutch citizen. Although primarily a rural-based guerrilla group, the NPA has an active urban infrastructure to support its terrorist activities and at times uses city-based assassination squads.

Activities

The NPA primarily targets Philippine security forces, government officials, local infrastructure, and businesses that refuse to pay extortion, or "revolutionary taxes." The NPA extorts politicians running for office in NPA-influenced areas, charging them for "campaign permits." The group opposes any U.S. military presence in the Philippines and in the past has attacked U.S. military interests; it killed several U.S. service personnel before the U.S. base closures in 1992. The NPA claimed responsibility for the assassination of two congressmen, from Quezon in May 2001 and Cagayan in June 2001, among other killings. Periodic peace talks with the Philippine government stalled after these incidents. In December 2005, the NPA publicly expressed its intent to target U.S. personnel if they were discovered in NPA operating areas.

Strength

Estimated at less than 9,000, a number significantly lower than its peak strength of approximately 25,000 in the 1980s.

Location/Area of Operations

Operates in rural Luzon, Visayas, and parts of northern and eastern Mindanao. Has cells in Manila and other metropolitan centers.

External Aid

Unknown.

Continuity Irish Republican Army (CIRA)

a.k.a. Continuity Army Council; Continuity IRA; Republican Sinn Fein

Description

CIRA is a terrorist splinter group formed in 1994 as the clandestine armed wing of Republican Sinn Fein, which split from Sinn Fein in 1986. "Continuity" refers to the group's belief that it is carrying on the original Irish Republican Army's (IRA) goal of forcing the British out of Northern Ireland. CIRA's aliases, Continuity Army Council and Republican Sinn Fein, are included in its FTO designation. CIRA cooperates with the larger Real IRA (RIRA).

Activities

CIRA has been active in Belfast and the border areas of Northern Ireland, where it has carried out bombings, assassinations, kidnappings, hijackings, extortion, and robberies. On occasion, it has provided advance warning to police of its attacks. Targets have included the British military, Northern Ireland security forces, and Loyalist paramilitary groups. CIRA did not join the Provisional IRA in the September 2005 decommissioning and remains capable of effective, if sporadic, terrorist attacks. In late 2006 CIRA members issued a list of up to 20 individuals they were targeting for paramilitary attacks, several of whom were wounded in subsequent shootings.

Strength

Membership is small, with possibly fewer than 50 hard-core activists. Police counterterrorist operations have reduced the group's strength, but CIRA continues to recruit, train, and plan operations.

Location/Area of Operation

Northern Ireland and the Irish Republic. Does not have an established presence in Great Britain.

External Aid

Suspected of receiving funds and arms from sympathizers in the United States. May have acquired arms and materiel from the Balkans in cooperation with the Real IRA.

Gama'a al-Islamiyya (IG)

a.k.a. Al-Gama'at; Egyptian al-Gama'at al-Islamiyya; Islamic Gama'at (IG); Islamic Group

Description

The IG, Egypt's largest militant group, has been active since the late 1970s and is a loosely organized network, whose primary goal is to overthrow the Egyptian government and replace it with an Islamic state. It has an external wing with supporters in several countries. The group's issuance of a cease-fire in 1997 led to a split into two factions: one, led by Mustafa Hamza, supported the cease-fire; the other, led by Rifa'i Taha Musa, called for a return to armed operations. The IG issued another ceasefire in March 1999, but its spiritual leader, Shaykh Umar Abd al-Rahman, sentenced to life in prison in January 1996 for his involvement in the 1993 World Trade Center bombing and incarcerated in the United States, rescinded his support for the cease-fire in June 2000. IG has not conducted an attack inside Egypt since the 1997 Luxor attack, which killed 58 tourists, four Egyptians, and wounded dozens more. In February 1998, a senior member signed Usama bin Ladin's fatwa calling for attacks against the United States.

In early 2001, Taha Musa published a book in which he attempted to justify terrorist attacks that would cause mass casualties. Taha Musa disappeared several months thereafter, and there is no information as to his current whereabouts. In March 2002, members of the group's historic leadership in Egypt declared use of violence misguided and renounced its future use, prompting denunciations by much of the leadership abroad. The Egyptian government continues to release IG members from prison; approximately 900 were released in 2003, and most of the 700 persons released in 2004 at the end of the Muslim holy month of Ramadan were IG members. Ayman al-Zawahiri announced in August 2006 that IG had merged with al-Qaida, but the group quickly denied this claim.

Activities

IG conducted armed attacks against Egyptian security and other government officials, Coptic Christians, and Egyptian opponents of Islamic extremism before the 1997 cease-fire; after the cease-fire, the faction led by Taha Musa launched attacks on tourists in Egypt, most notably the 1997 Luxor attack. IG claimed responsibility for the June 1995 assassination attempt on Egyptian President Hosni Mubarak in Addis Ababa, Ethiopia.

Strength

Unknown. At its peak IG probably commanded several thousand hard-core members and a like number of sympathizers. The 1999 cease-fire, security crackdowns following the 1997 attack in Luxor, and post-September 11 security efforts, have probably resulted in a substantial decrease in the group's numbers.

Location/Area of Operation

IG Operates mainly in the Al-Minya, Asyut, Qina, and Sohaj Governorates of southern Egypt. It also appears to have support in Cairo, Alexandria, and other urban locations, particularly among unemployed graduates and students. The IG has an external presence, including in the United Kingdom, Afghanistan, Yemen, and in various locations in Europe.

External Aid

Unknown. Usama Bin Ladin and Afghan militant groups support the organization. IG also may obtain some funding through various Islamic non-governmental organizations.

The Islamic Resistance Movement (HAMAS)

a.k.a. Harakat al-Muqawama al-Islamiya; Izz al-Din al Qassam Battalions; Izz al-Din al Qassam Brigades; Students of Ayyash; Students of the Engineer; Yahya Ayyash Units

Description

HAMAS, which includes military and political wings, was formed at the onset of the first Palestinian uprising or Intifadah in late 1987, as an outgrowth of the Palestinian branch of the Muslim Brotherhood. The armed element, called the Izz al-Din al-Qassam Brigades, conducts anti-Israeli attacks, including suicide bombings against civilian targets inside Israel. Social-political elements engage in "Dawa" or ministry activities, which include running charities and schools, fund-raising and political activities. A Shura council based in Damascus, Syria, sets overall policy. Since winning Palestinian Authority (PA) elections in 2006, HAMAS has taken control of significant PA ministries, including the Ministry of Interior. HAMAS formed an expanded, overt militia called the Executive Force, subordinate to the Ministry.

Activities

Prior to 2005, HAMAS conducted numerous anti-Israeli attacks including suicide bombings, rocket attacks, IED attacks, and shootings. The group curtailed terrorist attacks in February 2005 after agreeing to a temporary period of calm brokered by the PA, and ceased most violence after winning control of the PA legislature and cabinet in 2006. After HAMAS staged a June 25 attack on IDF soldiers near Kerem Shalom that resulted in two deaths and the abduction of Corporal Gilad Shalit, Israel took steps that severely limited the operation of the Rafah crossing. HAMAS maintained and expanded its military capabilities during this time. HAMAS has not directly targeted U.S. interests, although the group makes little or no effort to avoid targets frequented by foreigners.

Strength

HAMAS probably has several hundred members in its armed wing, the al-Qassam Brigades, along with its reported 6,000-man Executive Force and tens of thousands of supporters and sympathizers.

Location/Area of Operation

HAMAS has an operational presence in every major city within the Palestinian territories and has focused its anti-Israeli attacks on targets in those territories and Israel. The group retains a cadre of leaders and facilitators that conduct diplomatic, fundraising, and arms smuggling activities in Lebanon, Syria, and other states.

External Aid

Receives some funding, weapons and training from Iran. Also receives donations from Palestinian expatriates around the world and private benefactors in Arab states. Some fundraising and propaganda activity takes place in Western Europe and North America.

Harakat ul-Mujahedin (HUM)[1]

a.k.a. Al-Faran; Al-Hadid; Al-Hadith; Harakat ul-Ansar; Harakat ul-Mujahideen; HUA; Jamiat ul-Ansar (JUA)

Description

HUM, an Islamic militant group based in Pakistan, is politically aligned with the radical political party Jamiat Ulema-i-Islam's Fazlur Rehman faction (JUI-F), and operates primarily in Kashmir. Reportedly under pressure from the Government of Pakistan, HUM's long time leader Fazlur Rehman Khalil stepped down and, in January 2005, was replaced by Dr. Badr Munir as the head of HUM. Khalil has been linked to Usama bin Ladin, and his signature was found on Bin Ladin's fatwa in February 1998 calling for attacks on U.S. and Western interests. HUM operated terrorist training camps in eastern Afghanistan until Coalition air strikes destroyed them in autumn 2001. Khalil was detained by Pakistani authorities in mid-2004 and subsequently released in late December.In 2003, HUM began using the name Jamiat ul-Ansar (JUA). Pakistan banned JUA in November 2003.

Activities

HUM has conducted a number of operations against Indian troops and civilian targets in Kashmir. It is linked to the Kashmiri militant group al-Faran that kidnapped five Western tourists in Kashmir in July 1995; one was killed in August, and the other four reportedly were killed in December of the same year. HUM was responsible for the hijacking of an Indian airliner in December 1999 that resulted in the release of Masood Azhar, an important leader in the former Harakat ul-Ansar who was imprisoned by India in 1994 and founded Jaish-e-Mohammed (JEM) after his release.

[1] Listed on the UN 1267 Committee List.

Ahmed Omar Sheik also was released in 1999, and was later convicted of the abduction and murder in 2002 of U.S. journalist Daniel Pearl.

Strength

HUM has several hundred armed supporters located in Azad Kashmir, Pakistan, and India's southern Kashmir and Doda regions and in the Kashmir valley. Supporters are mostly Pakistanis and Kashmiris, but also include Afghans and Arab veterans of the Afghan war. HUM uses light and heavy machine guns, assault rifles, mortars, explosives, and rockets. In 2000, HUM lost a significant share of its membership in defections to the JEM.

Location/Area of Operation

Based in Muzaffarabad, Rawalpindi, and several other towns in Pakistan, HUM conducts insurgent and terrorist operations primarily in Kashmir, but members have also been found operating in Afghanistan. HUM trains its militants in Afghanistan and Pakistan.

External Aid

Collects donations from wealthy and grassroots donors in Pakistan, Kashmir, Saudi Arabia, and other Gulf and Islamic states. HUM's financial collection methods also include soliciting donations in magazine ads and pamphlets. The sources and amount of HUM's military funding are unknown. Its overt fundraising in Pakistan has been constrained since the government clampdown there on extremist groups and the freezing of terrorist assets.

Hizballah

(Common alternate spellings: Hezbollah, Hizbullah, Hizb`allah)a.k.a. Party of God; Islamic Jihad

Description

Formed in 1982 in response to the Israeli invasion of Lebanon, this Lebanese-based radical Shia group takes its ideological inspiration from the Iranian revolution and the teachings of the late Ayatollah Khomeini. The group follows the religious guidance of Khomeini's successor, Iranian Supreme Leader Ali Khamenei. Hizballah is closely allied with Iran and often acts at its behest, but it also can and does act independently. Although Hizballah does not share the Syrian regime's secular orientation, the group has been a strong ally in helping Syria advance its political objectives in the region. The Majlis al-Shura, or Consultative Council, is the group's highest governing body and has been led by Secretary General Hasan Nasrallah since 1992.

Hizballah remains the most technically capable terrorist group in the world. It has strong influence in Lebanon's Shia community, which comprises about one-third of Lebanon's population. The Lebanese government still recognizes Hizballah as a legitimate "resistance group" and political party. Hizballah maintains offices in Beirut and elsewhere in the country, has official liaison officers to the security services, claims 14 elected officials in the 128-seat Lebanese National Assembly and was represented in the Cabinet for the first time, by the Minister of Water and Electricity Mohammed Fneish, until his resignation, along with other Shia ministers on November 11, 2006. Hizballah has largely withdrawn its military presence from southern Lebanon in accordance with UNSCR 1701, although likely maintains weapons caches in southern Lebanon and justifies its continued arms status by claiming to act in defense of Lebanon against acts of Israeli aggression, such as regular Israeli overflights of Lebanese airspace. Hizballah alleges that Israel has not withdrawn completely from Lebanese territory because, in Hizballah's view, the Shebaa Farms and other areas belong to Lebanon. Hizballah supports a variety of violent anti-Western groups, including Palestinian terrorist organizations. This support includes the covert provision of weapons, explosives, training, funding, and guidance, as well as overt political support.

Activities

In 2006, Hizballah launched a number of attacks on Israel, including the May 28 and July 12 attack, which resulted in the capture and kidnapping of two Israeli soldiers. (*See Chapter 2, Country Reports.*) Hizballah continued to call for the destruction of Israel and provided support to select Palestinian groups to augment their capacity to conduct attacks against Israel. Since at least 2004, Hizballah has provided training and logistics to select Iraqi Shia militants, including for the construction and use of shaped charge IEDs, which Hizballah developed against Israeli forces in southern Lebanon during the late 1990s and which can penetrate heavily armored vehicles. Hizballah is known to have been involved in numerous anti-U.S. and anti-Israeli terrorist attacks, and prior to September 11, 2001, was responsible for more American deaths than any other terrorist group; its terrorist attacks have included the suicide truck bombings of the U.S. Embassy and U.S. Marine barracks in Beirut in 1983 and the U.S. Embassy annex in Beirut in 1984. Four members of Hizballah, Imad Mughniyah, Hasan Izz-al-Din, Mohammed Hamadei, and Ali Atwa, are on the FBI's list of most wanted terrorists for the 1985 hijacking of TWA flight 847, during which a U.S. Navy diver was murdered. Elements of the group were responsible for the kidnapping, detention, and murder of Americans and other Westerners in Lebanon in the 1980s. Hizballah also has been implicated in the attacks on the Israeli Embassy in Argentina in 1992 and the Argentine-Israeli Mutual

Association (AMIA) in Buenos Aires in 1994.* The U.S. Government has indicted a member of Lebanese Hizballah for his participation in the June 1996 truck bomb attack of the U.S. Air Force dormitory at Khobar Towers in Saudi Arabia. In 2000, Hizballah operatives captured three Israeli soldiers in the Sheba'a Farms area and kidnapped an Israeli non-combatant.

Strength

Thousands of supporters, several thousand members, and a few hundred terrorist operatives.

Location/Area of Operation

Operates in the southern suburbs of Beirut, the Beka'a Valley, and southern Lebanon. Has established cells in Europe, Africa, South America, North America, and Asia.

External Aid

Receives training, weapons, and explosives, as well as political, diplomatic, and organizational aid, from Iran, and diplomatic, political, and logistical support from Syria. Hizballah also receives funding from religious donations, and profits from legal and illegal businesses.

Islamic Jihad Union (IJU)[1]

a.k.a. Al-Djihad al-Islami; Dzhamaat Modzhakhedov; Islamic Jihad Group of Uzbekistan;Jama'at al-Jihad; Jamiat al-Jihad al-Islami; Jamiyat; The Jamaat Mujahedin; The Kazakh Jama'at; The Libyan Society

Description

The IJU is an extremist organization which splintered from the Islamic Movement of Uzbekistan. They oppose secular rule in Uzbekistan and seek to replace it with a government based on Islamic law.

Activities

The IJU issued a statement in May 2004 fully supporting the armed attacks on Uzbek police and military personnel in Andijon, Uzbekistan, and called for the overthrow of the Uzbekistani regime. The group first conducted attacks in March-April 2004 targeting a popular bazaar and police at several roadway checkpoints. These attacks killed approximately 47 people,

* On October 25, 2006, the Argentine AMIA special prosecutors issued an indictment charging eight Iranian government officials and one member of Hizballah with the attack.

[1] Listed on the UN 1267 Committee List.

including 33 terrorists, some of whom were suicide bombers. The IJU's claim of responsibility, which was posted to multiple militant Islamic websites, denounced the leadership of Uzbekistan. These attacks marked the first use of suicide bombers in Central Asia. In July 2004, the group struck again with near-simultaneous suicide bombings of the U.S. and Israeli Embassies and the Uzbekistani Prosecutor General's office in Tashkent. The IJU again claimed responsibility via an Islamic website and stated that martyrdom operations by the group would continue. The statement also indicated that the attacks were done in support of IJU's Palestinian, Iraqi, and Afghan brothers in the global insurgency. The date of the July attack corresponded with the trial of individuals arrested for their alleged participation in the March-April attacks.

Strength

Unknown.

Location/Area of Operation

Militants are scattered throughout Central Asia and probably parts of South Asia.

External Aid

Unknown.

Islamic Movement of Uzbekistan (IMU)[1]

Description

The IMU is a group of Islamic militants from Uzbekistan and other Central Asian states. The IMU's goal is to overthrow Uzbekistani President Islam Karimov and establishing an Islamic state in Uzbekistan. The IMU is affiliated with al-Qaida and, under the leadership of Tohir Yoldashev, has embraced Usama bin Ladin's ideology.

Activities

Since Operation Enduring Freedom, the IMU has been predominantly occupied with attacks on U.S. and Coalition soldiers in Afghanistan. Although it is difficult to differentiate between IMU and Islamic Jihad Union members, Pakistani security forces continue to arrest probable IMU operatives in the Federally Administered Tribal Areas (FATA).

The IMU was active in terrorist operations in Central Asia. Tajikistan arrested several IMU members in 2005. In November 2004, the IMU was

[1] Listed on the UN 1267 Committee List.

blamed for an explosion in the southern Kyrgyz city of Osh that killed one police officer and one terrorist. In May 2003, Kyrgyz security forces disrupted an IMU cell that was seeking to bomb the U.S. Embassy and a nearby hotel in Bishkek, Kyrgyzstan. The IMU was also responsible for explosions in Bishkek in December 2002 and Osh in May 2003 that killed eight people. The IMU primarily targeted Uzbekistani interests before October 2001, and is believed to have been responsible for several explosions in Tashkent in February 1999. IMU militants took foreigners hostage in Kyrgyzstan for two consecutive years: in August 1999, IMU militants took four Japanese geologists and eight Kyrgyz soldiers hostage, and in August 2000, they took four U.S. mountain climbers hostage.

Strength

Approximately 500 members.

Location/Area of Operation

IMU militants are scattered throughout South Asia, Central Asia, and Iran. Their area of operation includes Afghanistan, Iran, Kyrgyzstan, Pakistan, Tajikistan, Kazakhstan, and Uzbekistan.

External Aid

The IMU receives support from a large Uzbek diaspora, Islamic extremist groups and patrons in the Middle East, Central Asia, and South Asia.

Jaish-e-Mohammed (JEM)[1]

a.k.a. Army of Mohammed; Jaish-i-Mohammed; Khudamul Islam; Khuddam-ul-Islam; Kuddam e Islami; Mohammed's Army; Tehrik ul-Furqaan

Description

Jaish-e-Mohammed is an Islamic extremist group based in Pakistan founded by Masood Azhar, a former senior leader of Harakat ul-Ansar, upon his release from prison in India in early 2000. The group's aim is to unite Kashmir with Pakistan, and it has openly declared war against the United States. It is politically aligned with the radical political party Jamiat Ulema-i-Islam's Fazlur Rehman faction (JUI-F). Pakistan outlawed JEM in 2002. By 2003, JEM had splintered into Khuddam ul-Islam (KUI),headed by Azhar, and Jamaat ul-Furqan (JUF), led by Abdul Jabbar, who was released from Pakistani custody in August 2004 after being detained for suspected involvement in the December 2003 assassination attempts

[1] Listed on the UN 1267 Committee List.

against President Pervez Musharraf. Pakistan banned KUI and JUF in November 2003.

Activities

Jaish-e-Mohammed continues to operate openly in parts of Pakistan despite President Musharraf's 2002 ban on its activities. The group is well-funded, and is said to have tens of thousands of followers who support attacks against Indian targets, the Pakistani government, and sectarian minorities. Since Masood Azhar's 2000 release from Indian custody in exchange for 155 hijacked Indian Airlines hostages, JEM has conducted many fatal terrorist attacks in the area. JEM continues to claim responsibility for several suicide car bombings in Kashmir, including a suicide attack on the Jammu and Kashmir legislative assembly building in Srinagar in October 2001 that killed more than 30. The Indian government has publicly implicated the JEM, along with Lashkar e-Tayyiba, for the December 2001 attack on the Indian Parliament that killed nine and injured 18. Pakistani authorities suspect that JEM members may have been involved in the 2002 anti-Christian attacks in Islamabad, Murree, and Taxila that killed two Americans. In December 2003, Pakistan implicated elements of JEM in the two assassination attempts against President Musharraf. In July 2004, Pakistani authorities arrested a JEM member wanted in connection with the 2002 abduction and murder of U.S. journalist Daniel Pearl. In 2006, JEM claimed responsibility for a number of attacks, including the killing of several Indian police officials in the Indian-administered Kashmir capital of Srinagar.

Strength

JEM has at least several hundred armed supporters, including a large cadre of former HUM members, located in Pakistan, in India's southern Kashmir and Doda regions, and in the Kashmir Valley. Supporters are mostly Pakistanis and Kashmiris, but also include Afghans and Arab veterans of the Afghan war. The group uses light and heavy machine guns, assault rifles, mortars, improvised explosive devices, and rocket-propelled grenades.

Location/Area of Operation

Pakistan and Kashmir. Until autumn 2001, JEM maintained training camps in Afghanistan.

External Aid

Most of JEM's cadre and material resources have been drawn from the Pakistani militant groups Harakat ul-Jihad-i-Islami (HUJI) and the Harakat ul-Mujahedin (HUM). In anticipation of asset seizures by the Pakistani government, JEM withdrew funds from bank accounts and invested in legal businesses, such as commodity trading, real estate, and production of consumer goods. In addition, JEM collects funds through donation requests in magazines and pamphlets, and al-Qaida is suspected of providing funding.

Jemaah Islamiya (JI)[1]

Description

The Southeast Asia-based Jemaah Islamiya (JI) is a terrorist group that seeks the establishment of an Islamic caliphate spanning Indonesia, Malaysia, southern Thailand, Singapore, Brunei, and the southern Philippines. More than 300 JI operatives, including operations chief Hambali, have been captured since 2002. Several are no longer incarcerated, however, including JI emir Abu Bakar Bashir who was released from prison in 2006 after serving a 25-month sentence for his involvement in the 2002 Bali bombings. The death of top JI bombmaker Azahari bin Husin in November 2005, and further arrests of several close associates of senior JI operative Noordin Mat Top in 2006 likely disrupted JI's anti-Western attacks that occurred annually from 2002-2005.

Activities

The group's most recent high-profile attack occurred in Bali on October 1, 2005 and left 26 persons dead. Other major JI attacks include the September 2004 bombing outside the Australian Embassy in Jakarta, the August 2003 bombing of the J. W. Marriott Hotel in Jakarta, and the October 2002 Bali bombing. The 2002 Bali attack, which killed more than 200, remains one of the deadliest terrorist attacks since 9/11. In December 2001, Singaporean authorities uncovered a JI plot to attack the U.S. and Israeli Embassies and British and Australian diplomatic buildings in Singapore. JI is also responsible for the coordinated bombings of numerous Christian churches in Indonesia in December 2000 and was involved in the bombings of several targets in Manila the same month.

Strength

Exact numbers currently are unknown. Estimates of total JI members vary from the hundreds to one thousand.

Location/Area of Operation

JI is based in Indonesia and believed to have cells in Indonesia, Malaysia, and the Philippines.

[1] Listed on the UN 1267 Committee List.

External Aid

Investigations indicate that JI is fully capable of its own fundraising, although it also receives financial, ideological, and logistical support from Middle Eastern contacts, and non-governmental organizations.

Al-Jihad (AJ)

Egyptian Islamic Jihad (EIJ); Egyptian al-Jihad; New Jihad; The Jihad Group

Description

This Egyptian Islamic extremist group merged with Usama Bin Ladin's al-Qaida organization in 2001. Usama Bin Ladin's deputy, Ayman al-Zawahiri, was the former head of AJ. Active since the 1970s, AJ's primary goal has been the overthrow of the Egyptian government and the establishment of an Islamic state. The group's targets, historically, have been high-level Egyptian government officials as well as U.S. and Israeli interests in Egypt and abroad. Regular Egyptian crackdowns on extremists have greatly reduced AJ capabilities in Egypt.

Activities

The original AJ was responsible for the 1981 assassination of Egyptian President Anwar Sadat. It claimed responsibility for the attempted assassinations in 1993 of Interior Minister Hassan al-Alfi and Prime Minister Atef Sedky. AJ has not conducted an attack inside Egypt since 1993 and has never successfully targeted foreign tourists there. The group was responsible for the Egyptian Embassy bombing in Islamabad in 1995 and a disrupted plot against the U.S. Embassy in Albania in 1998.

Strength

Believed to have several hundred hard-core members inside and outside of Egypt.

Location/Area of Operation

Most AJ members today are outside Egypt in countries such as Afghanistan, Pakistan, Lebanon, the United Kingdom, and Yemen. AJ activities have been centered outside Egypt for several years under the auspices of al-Qaida.

External Aid

Since 1998 AJ has received most of its funding from al-Qaida; these close ties culminated in the eventual merger of the groups in June 2001. Some funding may come from various Islamic non-governmental organizations, cover businesses, and criminal acts.

Kahane Chai (Kach)

a.k.a. American Friends of the United Yeshiva; American Friends of Yeshivat Rav Meir; Committee for the Safety of the Roads; Dikuy Bogdim; DOV; Forefront of the Idea; Friends of the Jewish Idea Yeshiva; Jewish Idea Yeshiva; Jewish Legion; Judea Police; Judean Congress; **Kach; Kahane; Kahane** Lives; **Kahane** Tzadak; **Kahane**.org; Kahanetzadak.com; Kfar Tapuah Fund; Koach; Meir's Youth; New **Kach** Movement; Newkach.org; No'ar Meir; Repression of Traitors; State of Judea; Sword of David; The Committee Against Racism and Discrimination (CARD); The Hatikva Jewish Identity Center; The International **Kahane** Movement; The Jewish Idea Yeshiva; The Judean Legion; The Judean Voice; The Gomemiyut Movement; The Rabbi Meir David **Kahane** Memorial Fund; The Voice of Judea; The Way of the Torah; The Yeshiva of the Jewish Idea; Yeshivat Harav Meir

Description

Kach's stated goal is to restore the biblical state of Israel. Kach was founded by radical Israeli-American rabbi Meir Kahane. Its offshoot Kahane Chai, (translation: "Kahane Lives") was founded by Meir Kahane's son Binyamin following his father's 1990 assassination in the United States. Both Kach and Kahane Chai were declared terrorist organizations in 1994 by the Israeli Cabinet under its 1948 Terrorism Law. This designation followed the groups' statements in support of Dr. Baruch Goldstein's attack in February 1994 on the Ibrahimi Mosque (Goldstein was affiliated with Kach) and their verbal attacks on the Israeli government. Palestinian gunmen killed Binyamin Kahane and his wife in a drive-by shooting in December 2000 in the West Bank.

Activities

Kach has harassed and threatened Arabs, Palestinians, and Israeli government officials, and has vowed revenge for the death of Binyamin Kahane and his wife. Kach is suspected of involvement in a number of low-level attacks since the start of the al-Aqsa intifada in 2000.

Strength

Unknown.

Location/Area of Operation

Israel and West Bank settlements, particularly Qiryat Arba' in Hebron.

External Aid

Receives support from sympathizers in the United States and Europe.

Kongra-Gel (KGK/PKK)

(Despite name changes, the group is still most commonly referred to as the PKK; for the purposes of this report we refer to the group as Kongra-Gel/ PKK or KGK/PKK.)

a.k.a. Kurdish Freedom Hawks (TAK); Kurdistan Workers' Party (PKK); Freedom and Democracy Congress of Kurdistan (KADEK); Halu Mesru Savunma Kuvveti (HSK); Kurdistan Freedom and Democracy Congress; Kurdistan People's Congress (KHK); Partiya Karkeran Kurdistan; People's Congress of Kurdistan; The People's Defense Force.

Description

The KGK/PKK was founded by Abdullah Ocalan in 1974 as a Marxist-Leninist separatist organization. The group, composed primarily of Turkish Kurds, launched a campaign of violence in 1984. The KGK/PKK aspired to establish an independent Kurdish state in southeastern Turkey, but in recent years has spoken more often about cultural or linguistic rights. In the early 1990s, the KGK/PKK moved beyond rural-based insurgent activities to include urban terrorism. In the 1990s south-eastern Anatolia was the scene of significant violence; some estimates place casualties at approximately 30,000 persons. Following his capture in 1999, Ocalan announced a "peace initiative," ordering members to refrain from violence and requesting dialogue with Ankara on Kurdish issues. Ocalan's death-sentence was commuted to life-imprisonment; he remains the symbolic leader of the group. The group foreswore violence until June 2004, when the group's hard-line militant wing took control and renounced the self-imposed cease-fire of the previous five years. Striking over the border from bases within Iraq the KGK/PKK engaged in terrorist attacks in eastern and western Turkey.

Activities

Primary targets have been Turkish government security forces, local Turkish officials, and villagers who oppose the organization in Turkey. The group conducted attacks on Turkish diplomatic and commercial facilities in West European cities in 1993 and again in spring 1995. In an attempt to damage Turkey's tourist industry, the KGK/PKK bombed tourist sites and hotels and kidnapped foreign tourists in the early-to-mid-1990s. Turkish authorities have confirmed or suspect that the group is responsible for dozens of bombings since 2004 in western Turkey, particularly in Istanbul and increasingly in resort areas on the western coast where foreign tourists, among others, have been killed. There have also been dozens of military clashes between Turkish security forces and KGK/PKK militants.

Strength

Approximately 4,000 to 5,000; 3,000 to 3,500 are currently located in northern Iraq.

Location/Area of Operation

Operates primarily in Turkey, Iraq, Europe, and the Middle East.

External Aid

Kongra-Gel/PKK has historically received safe haven and modest aid from Syria, Iraq, and Iran. Since 1999, Syria and Iran have cooperated with Turkey against the PKK, in a limited fashion. The KGK/PKK funds raise in Europe.

Lashkar e-Tayyiba (LT)[1]

a.k.a. Al Mansooreen; Al Mansoorian; Army of the Pure; Army of the Pure and Righteous; Army of the Righteous; Jamaat ud-Dawa and Al Monsooreen; Lashkar e-Toiba; Lashkar-i-Taiba; Paasban-e-Ahle-Hadis; Paasban-e-Kashmir; Paasban-i-Ahle-Hadith; Pasban-e-Ahle-Hadith; Pasban-e-Kashmir

Description

LT began as the militant wing of the Islamic extremist organization Markaz Dawa ul-Irshad (MDI), which was formed in the mid-1980s. MDI changed its name to Jamaat ul-Dawa (JUD) in 2001, probably in an effort to avoid Pakistan government restrictions. LT, which is not connected to any political party, is led by Hafiz Muhammad Saeed and is one of the three largest and best-trained groups fighting in Kashmir against India. The Pakistani government banned the group and froze its assets in January 2002. Elements of LT and Jaish-e-Muhammad combined with other groups to mount attacks as "The Save Kashmir Movement."

Activities

LT has conducted a number of operations against Indian troops and civilian targets in Jammu and Kashmir since 1993. LT claimed responsibility for numerous attacks in 2001, including an attack in January on Srinagar airport that killed five Indians; an attack on a police station in Srinagar that killed at least eight officers and wounded several others; and an attack in April against Indian border security forces that left at least four dead. The Indian government publicly implicated LT, along with JEM, for the December 2001 attack on the Indian Parliament building, although concrete evidence is lacking. LT is also suspected of involvement in May 2002 attack on an Indian Army base in Kaluchak that left 36 dead. India blamed LT for an October 2005 attack in New Delhi and a December 2005 Bangalore attack. Senior al-Qaida lieutenant Abu Zubaydah was captured at an LT safe house in Faisalabad in March 2002, which suggested that some members

[1] Listed on the UN 1267 Committee List.

were facilitating the movement of al-Qaida members in Pakistan. Government of India officials hold LT responsible for the July 11, 2006 train attack in Mumbai.

Strength

LT has several thousand members in Azad Kashmir, Pakistan, in the southern Jammu and Kashmir and Doda regions, and in the Kashmir Valley. Almost all LT members are Pakistanis from madrassas across Pakistan or Afghan veterans of the Afghan wars.The group uses assault rifles, light and heavy machine guns, mortars, explosives, and rocket-propelled grenades.

Location/Area of Operation

Based in Muridke (near Lahore) and Muzaffarabad.

External Aid

Collects donations from the Pakistani expatriate communities in the Middle East and United Kingdom, Islamic NGOs, and Pakistani and other Kashmiri business people. LT also maintains a website under the name Jamaat ud-Daawa through which it solicits funds and provides information on the group's activities. The precise amount of LT funding is unknown.

Lashkar i Jhangvi (LJ)[1]

a.k.a. Lashkar e Jhangvi; Lashkari-i-Jhangvi

Description

Lashkar i Jhangvi (LJ) is the militant offshoot of the Sunni Deobandi sectarian group Sipah-i-Sahaba Pakistan. LJ focuses primarily on anti-Shia attacks and was banned by Pakistani President Musharraf in August 2001 as part of an effort to rein in sectarian violence. Many of its members then sought refuge in Afghanistan with the Taliban, with whom they had existing ties. After the collapse of the Taliban, LJ members became active in aiding other terrorists with safe houses, false identities, and protection in Pakistani cities, including Karachi, Peshawar, and Rawalpindi. In January 2003, the United States added LJ to the list of designated Foreign Terrorist Organizations.

Activities

LJ specializes in armed attacks and bombings and has admitted responsibility for numerous killings of Shia religious and community leaders in Pakistan.

[1] Listed on the UN 1267 Committee List.

In January 1999, the group attempted to assassinate former Prime Minister Nawaz Sharif and his brother Shabaz Sharif, Chief Minister of Punjab Province. Pakistani authorities have publicly linked LJ members to the 2002 abduction and murder of U.S. journalist Daniel Pearl. Media reports linked LJ to attacks on Christian targets in Pakistan, including a March 2002 grenade assault on the Protestant International Church in Islamabad that killed two U.S. citizens, but no formal charges were filed against the group. Pakistani authorities believe LJ was responsible for the July 2003 bombing of a Shiite mosque in Quetta, Pakistan. Authorities also implicated LJ in several sectarian incidents in 2004, including the May and June bombings of two Shiite mosques in Karachi that killed more than 40 people. In May 2006, Pakistani police arrested two LJ militants suspected of involvement in the April bombing outside the U.S. Consulate in Karachi that killed one U.S. official; investigations are ongoing. In late 2006, Pakistani security agencies arrested eight suspects allegedly involved in the October blast at the Ayub Park in Rawalpindi and in planting anti-tank rockets at several locations in Islamabad. The Pakistani Interior Minister claimed these suspects have links to LJ and al-Qaida.

Strength

Probably fewer than 100.

Location/Area of Operation

LJ is active primarily in Punjab and Karachi. Some members travel between Pakistan and Afghanistan.

External Aid

Unknown.

Liberation Tigers of Tamil Eelam (LTTE)

a.k.a. Ellalan Force; The Tamil Tigers

Description

Founded in 1976, LTTEis the most powerful Tamil secessionist group in Sri Lanka. LTTE wants to establish an independent Tamil state in the island's north and east. It began its insurgency against the Sri Lankan government in 1983 and has relied on a guerrilla strategy that includes the use of terrorist tactics. LTTE nominally hasobserved a cease-fire agreement with the Sri Lankan government since 2002. The United States designated LTTE as a Foreign Terrorist Organization in October 1997.

Activities

LTTE has integrated a battlefield insurgent strategy with a terrorist program that targets key personnel in the countryside and senior Sri Lankan political and military leaders in Colombo and other urban centers. It also has conducted a sustained campaign targeting rival Tamil groups and figures, and assassinated the head of government of two countries: Prime Minister Rajiv Gandhi of India in 1991 and President Premadasa of Sri Lanka in 1993. LTTE is most notorious for the Black Tigers, its cadre of suicide bombers. Political assassinations and bombings were commonplace tactics prior to the cease-fire and have increased again since mid-2005. Fighting between LTTE and the Sri Lanka government escalated in 2006.

Strength

Exact strength is unknown, but LTTE is estimated to have 8,000 to 10,000 armed combatants in Sri Lanka, with a core of 3,000 to 6,000 trained fighters.LTTE also has a significant overseas support structure for fundraising, weapons procurement, and propaganda activities.

Location/Area of Operations

Headquartered in northern Sri Lanka, LTTE controls portions of the northern and eastern coastal areas of Sri Lanka, where it has set up a comprehensive administrative structure, but also has conducted operations throughout the island. LTTE leader Velupillai Prabhakaran has established an extensive network of checkpoints and informants to keep track of any outsiders who enter the group's area of control.

External Aid

LTTE's overt organizations support Tamil separatism by lobbying foreign governments and the United Nations. LTTE also uses its international contacts and the large Tamil Diaspora in North America, Europe, and Asia to procure weapons, communications, funding, and other needed supplies.

Libyan Islamic Fighting Group (LIFG)[1]

Description

The Libyan Islamic Fighting Group (LIFG) emerged in the early 1990s among Libyans who had fought Soviet forces in Afghanistan and the Qadhafi regime in Libya. The LIFG declared Libyan President Muammar Qadhafi un-Islamic and pledged to overthrow him. Some members maintain a strictly anti-Qadhafi focus and organize against Libyan government interests, but others, such as Abu al-Faraj al-Libi, who was arrested in

[1] Listed on the UN 1267 Committee List.

Pakistan in 2005, are aligned with Usama bin Ladin and believed to be part of al-Qaida's leadership structure or active in the international terrorist network. The United States designated the LIFG a Foreign Terrorist Organization in December 2004.

Activities

Libyans associated with the LIFG are part of the broader international terrorist movement. Spanish media in August 2005 linked Ziyad Hashem, an alleged member of the LIFG's media committee, as well as the imprisoned amir Abdullah al-Sadeq, with the Tunisian Islamist Serhane Ben Abdelmajid Fakhet, the suspected ringleader in the 2004 Madrid attacks. The LIFG is one of the groups believed to have planned the Casablanca suicide bombings in May 2003. The LIFG continues to target Libyan interests, and attempted to assassinate Qadhafi a total of four times; the last attempt was in 1998. The LIFG engaged Libyan security forces in armed clashes during the 1990s.

Strength

Probably has several hundred active members or supporters.

Location/Area of Operation

Since the late 1990s many members have fled to various Asian, Arabian Gulf, African, and European countries, particularly the United Kingdom. It is likely that LIFG maintains a clandestine presence in Libya.

External Aid

Unknown. The LIFG has used Islamic charitable organizations as cover for raising and transferring money and documents.

Moroccan Islamic Combatant Group (GICM)[1]

a.k.a. Groupe Islamique Combattant Marocain

Description

The Moroccan Islamic Combatant Group (GICM) is a clandestine transnational terrorist group currently centered in the Moroccan diaspora communities of Western Europe. Its goals include establishing an Islamic state in Morocco and supporting al-Qaida's war against the West by assisting in the assimilation of al-Qaida operatives into Moroccan and then European society. The group appears to have emerged in the 1990s and is comprised of Moroccan recruits who trained in armed camps in Afghanistan, including some who fought in the Soviet Afghan war. GICM members interact

[1] Listed on the UN 1267 Committee List.

with other North African extremists, particularly in Europe. In November 2002, the United States designated the GICM for asset freeze under EO 13224 following the group's submission to the UNSCR 1267 Sanctions Committee. The United States designated GICM as a Foreign Terrorist Organization on October 11, 2005.

Activities

The GICM carried out its first attack in Casablanca, Morocco on May 16, 2003, and GICM members were responsible for the Madrid attack. Moroccans associated with the GICM are part of the broader international terrorist movement; GICM members have been implicated in the recruitment network of individuals for Iraq, and at least one GICM member has carried out a suicide attack against Coalition Forces in Iraq.

Strength

Much of the GICM's leadership in Morocco and Europe have been killed, imprisoned, or are awaiting trial. Alleged leader Mohamed al-Guerbouzi has been convicted in absentia by the Moroccan government for his role in the Casablanca attacks but remains free in exile in the United Kingdom.

Location/Area of Operation

Morocco, Western Europe, Afghanistan, and Canada.

External Aid

The GICM is involved heavily in narcotics trafficking in North Africa and Europe to fund their operations. Moroccan security officials believe money from drug trafficking largely financed the 2003 Casablanca attacks. The Madrid attacks were financed mainly by the narcotics trafficking of Moroccan jihadist Jamal Ahmidan.

Mujahedin-e Khalq Organization (MEK)

a.k.a. MKO; Mujahedin-e Khalq; Muslim Iranian Students' Society; National Council of Resistance; National Council of Resistance (NCR); Organization of the People's Holy Warriors of Iran; The National Liberation Army of Iran (NLA); The People's Mujahedin Organization of Iran (PMOI); National Council of Resistance of Iran (NCRI); Sazeman-e Mujahedin-e Khalq-e Iran

Description

The MEK advocates the violent overthrow of the Iranian regime and was responsible for the assassination of several U.S. military personnel and civilians in the 1970's. MEK leadership and members across the world maintain the capacity and will to commit terrorist acts in Europe, the Middle East, the United State, Canada, and beyond.

The MEK emerged in the 1960s as one of the more violent political movements opposed to the Pahlavi dynasty and its close relationship with the United States. MEK ideology has gone through several iterations and blends elements of Marxism, Islam, and feminism. Following its participation in the 1979 Islamic Revolution, the group rapidly fell out of favor with the Iranian people. The new Iranian government under Supreme Leader Khomeini systematically arrested and targeted many MEK members, causing most MEK leadership to flee to Europe. In 1986, MEK leaders and operatives were evicted from France and provided a safe haven in Iraq by Saddam Hussein. The group has planned and executed terrorist operations against the Iranian regime for nearly three decades from its European and Iraqi bases of operations. Additionally, it has expanded its fundraising base, further developed its paramilitary skills, and aggressively worked to expand its European ranks. In addition to its terrorist credentials, the MEK has also displayed cult-like characteristics. Upon entry into the group, new members are indoctrinated in MEK ideology and revisionist Iranian history. Members are also required to undertake a vow of "eternal divorce" and participate in weekly "ideological cleansings." Additionally, children are reportedly separated from parents at a young age. MEK leader Maryam Rajavi has established a "cult of personality." She claims to emulate the Prophet Muhammad and is viewed by members as the "Iranian President in exile."

Activities

The group's worldwide campaign against the Iranian government uses propaganda and terrorism to achieve its objectives and has been supported by reprehensible regimes, including that of Saddam Hussein. During the 1970s, the MEK assassinated several U.S. military personnel and U.S. civilians working on defense projects in Tehran and supported the violent takeover in 1979 of the U.S. Embassy in Tehran. Despite U.S. efforts, MEK members have never been brought to justice for the group's role in these illegal acts.

In 1981, MEK leadership attempted to overthrow the newly installed Islamic regime; Iranian security forces subsequently initiated a crackdown on the group. The MEK instigated a bombing campaign, including an attack against the head office of the Islamic Republic Party and the Prime Minister's office, which killed some 70 high-ranking Iranian officials, including Chief Justice Ayatollah Mohammad Beheshti, President Mohammad-Ali Rajaei, and Prime Minister Mohammad-Javad Bahonar. These attacks resulted in a popular uprising against the MEK and an expanded Iranian government crackdown which forced MEK leaders to flee to France. For five years, the MEK continued to wage its terrorist campaign from its Paris headquarters. Expelled by France in 1986, MEK leaders turned to Saddam Hussein's regime for basing, financial support, and training. Near the end of the 1980-1988 Iran-Iraq War, Baghdad armed the MEK with heavy military equipment and deployed thousands of MEK fighters in suicidal, mass wave attacks against Iranian forces.

The MEK's relationship with the former Iraqi regime continued through the 1990s. In 1991, the group reportedly assisted in the Iraqi Republican Guard's bloody crackdown on Iraqi Shia and Kurds who rose up against Saddam Hussein's regime; press reports cite MEK leader Maryam Rajavi encouraging MEK members to "take the Kurds under your tanks." In April 1992, the MEK conducted near-simultaneous attacks on Iranian embassies and installations in 13 countries, demonstrating the group's ability to mount large-scale operations overseas. In April 1999, the MEK targeted key Iranian military officers and assassinated the deputy chief of the Iranian Armed Forces General Staff, Brigadier General Ali Sayyaad Shirazi.

In April 2000, the MEK attempted to assassinate the commander of the Nasr Headquarters, Tehran's interagency board responsible for coordinating policies on Iraq. The pace of anti-Iranian operations increased during "Operation Great Bahman" in February 2000, when the group launched a dozen attacks against Iran. One of those attacks included a mortar attack against a major Iranian leadership complex in Tehran that housed the offices of the Supreme Leader and the President. In 2000 and 2001, the MEK was involved in regular mortar attacks and hit-and-run raids against Iranian military and law enforcement personnel, as well as government buildings near the Iran-Iraq border. Also in 2001, the FBI arrested seven Iranians in the United States who funneled $400,000 to an MEK-affiliated organization in the UAE which used the funds to purchase weapons. Following an initial Coalition bombardment of the MEK's facilities in Iraq at the outset of Operation Iraqi Freedom, MEK leadership negotiated a cease-fire with Coalition Forces and voluntarily surrendered their heavy-arms to Coalition control. Since 2003, roughly 3,400 MEK members have been encamped at Ashraf in Iraq, under the supervision of Coalition Forces.

In 2003, French authorities arrested 160 MEK members at operational bases they believed the MEK was using to coordinate financing and planning for terrorist attacks. Upon the arrest of MEK leader Maryam Rajavi, MEK members took to Paris' streets and engaged in self-immolation. French authorities eventually released Rajavi. Although currently in hiding, Rajavi has made appearances via video-satellite to "motivate" MEK-sponsored conferences across the globe.

According to evidence which became available after the fall of Saddam Hussein, the MEK received millions of dollars in Oil-for-Food program subsidies from Saddam Hussein from 1999 through 2003, which supported planning and executing future terrorist attacks. In addition to discovering 13 lists of recipients of such vouchers on which the MEK appeared, evidence linking the MEK to the former Iraqi regime includes lists, as well as video footage of Saddam Hussein handing over suitcases of money to known MEK leaders, and video of MEK operatives receiving training from the Iraqi military.

Strength

Estimates place MEK's worldwide membership in the several thousands, with large pockets in Paris and other major European capitals. In Iraq, roughly 3,400 MEK members are gathered under Coalition supervision at Camp Ashraf, the MEK's main compound north of Baghdad, where they have been designated as "protected persons" under Article 27 of the Fourth Geneva Convention. This status does not affect the group's members outside of Camp Ashraf or the MEK's designation as a Foreign Terrorist Organization. As a condition of the 2003 cease-fire agreement, the MEK relinquished more than 2,000 tanks; armored personnel carriers; and heavy artillery. A significant number of MEK personnel have voluntarily left Ashraf, and an additional several hundred MEK defectors have been voluntarily repatriated to Iran. Many MEK leaders and operatives, however, remain at large, and the number of at-large MEK operatives who received weapons and bomb-making instruction from Saddam Hussein's regime remains a source of significant concern.

Location/Area of Operation

In the 1980s, the MEK's leaders were forced by Iranian security forces to flee to France. Following France's recognition of the Iranian regime in 1986, the group's leadership was forced out of France and took up residence in Iraq. The MEK maintains its main headquarters in Paris and has concentrations of members across Europe, in addition to the large concentration of MEK located at Camp Ashraf in Iraq. The MEK's global support structure remains in place with associates and supporters scattered throughout Europe and North America. Operations target Iranian regime elements across the globe, including in Europe and Iran. MEK's political arm, the NCRI, has a global support network with active lobbying and propaganda efforts in major Western capitals. NCRI also has a well-developed media communications strategy.

External Aid

Before Operation Iraqi Freedom began in 2003; the MEK received all of its military assistance and most of its financial support from Saddam Hussein. The fall of Saddam's regime has led MEK to increasingly rely on front organizations to solicit contributions from expatriate Iranian communities.

National Liberation Army (ELN)

a.k.a. Ejercito de Liberacion Nacional

Description

The ELN is a Colombian Marxist insurgent group formed in 1965 by urban intellectuals inspired by Fidel Castro and Che Guevara. It is primarily rural-based, although it possesses several urban units. In December 2005, the ELN began preliminary talks with the Colombian government in Cuba, but had not yet agreed to begin a formal peace process.

Activities

ELN conducts kidnapping, hijacking, bombing, and extortion. It has minimal conventional military capability. The group conducts kidnappings for ransom, often targeting foreign employees of large corporations, especially in the petroleum industry. ELN derives some revenue from taxation of the illegal narcotics industry, and its involvement may be increasing. It assaults energy infrastructure and has inflicted major damage on pipelines and the electrical distribution network but has lost much of its capacity to carry out attacks in the past few years.

Strength

Approximately 3,000 armed combatants and an unknown number of active supporters.

Location/Area of Operation

Mostly in rural and mountainous areas of northern, northeastern, and southwestern Colombia, and Venezuelan border regions.

External Aid

Cuba provides some medical care and political consultation.

Palestine Liberation Front (PLF)

a.k.a. PLF-Abu Abbas Faction

Description

In the late 1970s the Palestine Liberation Front (PLF) splintered from the Popular Front for the Liberation of Palestine-General Command (PFLP-GC), and later split into pro-PLO, pro-Syrian, and pro-Libyan factions. The pro-PLO faction was led by Muhammad Zaydan (a.k.a. Abu Abbas) and was based in Baghdad prior to Operation Iraqi Freedom.

Activites

Abbas's group was responsible for the 1985 attack on the Italian cruise ship Achille Lauro and the murder of U.S. citizen Leon Klinghoffer. In 1993, the PLF officially renounced terrorism when it acknowledged the Oslo accords, although it was suspected of supporting terrorism against Israel by other Palestinian groups into the 1990s. In April 2004, Abu Abbas died of natural causes while in U.S. custody in Iraq. Current leadership and membership of the relatively small PLF appears to be based in Lebanon and the Palestinian territories.

Strength

Unknown.

Location/Area of Operation

Based in Iraq from 1990 until 2003, the group currently is based in Lebanon.

External Aid

Unknown.

Palestine Islamic Jihad (PIJ)

a.k.a. Islamic Jihad of Palestine; PIJ-Shaqaqi Faction; PIJ-Shallah Faction; Al-Quds Brigades

Description

Formed by militant Palestinians in the Gaza Strip during the 1970s, Palestine Islamic Jihad (PIJ) is committed to the creation of an Islamic state in all of historic Palestine and the destruction of Israel through attacks against Israeli military and civilian targets.

Activities

PIJ terrorists have conducted numerous attacks, including large-scale suicide bombings against Israeli civilian and military targets. In 2006, the group conducted two suicide bombings and launched numerous home-made rockets from the Gaza Strip into neighboring Israeli towns. PIJ continues to plan and direct attacks against Israelis both inside Israel and in the Palestinian territories. Although U.S. citizens have died in PIJ mounted attacks, the group has not directly targeted U.S. interests.

Strength

Unknown.

Location/Area of Operation

Primarily Israel, the West Bank, and the Gaza Strip. The group's central leadership resides in Syria. Other leadership elements reside in Lebanon and official representatives are scattered throughout the Middle East.

External Aid

Receives financial assistance primarily from Iran. Syria provides the group with safe haven.

Popular Front for the Liberation of Palestine (PFLP)

Description

Formerly a part of the PLO, the Marxist-Leninist PFLP was founded by George Habash when it broke away from the Arab Nationalist Movement in 1967. The PFLP does not view the Palestinian struggle as religious, seeing it instead as a broader revolution against Western imperialism. The group earned a reputation for spectacular international attacks in the 1960s and 1970s, including airline hijackings that killed at least 20 U.S. citizens.

Activites

The PFLP has stepped up its operational activity since the start of the current intifada, highlighted by at least two suicide bombings since 2003, multiple joint operations with other Palestinian terrorist groups, and the assassination of Israeli Tourism Minister Rehavam Ze'evi in 2001, to avenge Israel's killing of the PFLP Secretary General earlier that year. In March 2006, the PFLP's current Secretary General, Ahmed Sa'adat, who had been imprisoned by the Palestinian Authority for his involvement in the Ze'evi assassination, was seized from the Jericho prison compound by Israeli forces and is now awaiting trial.

Strength

Unknown.

Location/Area of Operation

Syria, Lebanon, Israel, the West Bank, and the Gaza Strip.

External Aid

Receives safe haven and some logistical assistance from Syria.

Popular Front for the Liberation of Palestine-General Command (PFLP-GC)

Description

The PFLP-GC split from the PFLP in 1968, claiming it wanted to focus more on fighting and less on politics. Originally, the group was violently opposed to the Arafat-led PLO. Ahmad Jibril, a former captain in the Syrian Army, whose son Jihad was killed by a car bomb in May 2002, has led the PFLP-GC since its founding. The PFLP-GC is closely tied to both Syria and Iran.

Activites

The PFLP-GC carried out dozens of attacks in Europe and the Middle East during the 1970s and 1980s. The organization was known for cross-border terrorist attacks into Israel using unusual means, such as hot-air balloons and motorized hang gliders. The group's primary focus now is on guerrilla operations in southern Lebanon, training members of other Palestinian terrorist groups, and weapons smuggling. The PFLP-GC maintains an armed presence in several refugee camps and military bases throughout Lebanon.

Strength

Several hundred.

Location/Area of Operation

Headquartered in Damascus with bases in Lebanon.

External Aid

Receives logistical and military support from Syria and financial support from Iran.

Al-Qaida[1]

a.k.a. International Front for Fighting Jews and Crusaders; Islamic Army; Islamic Army for the Liberation of Holy Sites; Islamic Salvation Foundation; The Base; The Group for the Preservation of the Holy Sites; The Islamic Army for the Liberation of the Holy Places; The World Islamic Front for Jihad Against Jews and Crusaders; Usama bin Ladin Network; Usama bin Ladin Organization; Qaidat al-Jihad

Description

Al-Qaida was established by Usama bin Ladin in 1988 with Arabs who fought in Afghanistan against the Soviet Union. The group helped finance,

[1] Listed on the UN 1267 Committee List.

recruit, transport, and train Sunni Islamic extremists for the Afghan resistance. Al-Qaida's goal is uniting Muslims to fight the United States and its allies, overthrowing regimes it deems "non-Islamic," and expelling Westerners and non-Muslims from Muslim countries. Its ultimate goal is the establishment of a pan-Islamic caliphate throughout the world. Al-Qaida leaders issued a statement in February 1998 under the banner of "The World Islamic Front for Jihad Against the Jews and Crusaders" saying it was the duty of all Muslims to kill U.S. citizens, civilian and military, and their allies everywhere. Al-Qaida merged with al-Jihad (Egyptian Islamic Jihad) in June 2001, renaming itself "Qaidat al-Jihad."

Activities

Even as al-Qaida's top leaders continue to plot and direct terror attacks worldwide, terrorists affiliated with al-Qaida but not necessarily controlled by bin Ladin have increasingly carried out high-profile attacks. Over the past four years, al-Qaida, its affiliates, and those inspired by the group were also involved in anti-U.S. and anti-Coalition attacks in Africa, Europe, the Middle East, Afghanistan, Pakistan, and Iraq, including suicide bombings and vehicle-borne improvised explosive devices.

In 2006, al-Qaida and affiliated organizations continued major efforts to attack the West and its interests. For example, in mid-August, U.K. and U.S. authorities foiled a plot to blow up as many as ten aircraft. Al-Qaida may have been complicit in the plot but the group has made no public statement claiming its involvement. Additionally, al-Qaida in the Arabian Peninsula claimed responsibility for the February 24, 2006, attack on the Abqaiq petroleum processing facility, the largest such facility in the world, in Saudi Arabia. The Salafist Group for Preaching and Combat (GSPC) officially merged with al-Qaida in September 2006, subsequently changed its name to al-Qaida in the Islamic Maghreb (AQIM), and attacked a U.S. contractor bus in December 2006 in greater Algiers, marking its first attack against a U.S. entity.

Bin Ladin's deputy Ayman al-Zawahiri claimed responsibility on behalf of al-Qaida for multiple attacks in 2005 against the London public transportation system. The extent of senior leadership involvement in planning the July 2005 attacks is unclear, however, some suspects in the attacks included homegrown United Kingdom-based extremists who were inspired by al-Qaida.

In 2003 and 2004, Saudi-based al-Qaida operatives and associated extremists launched more than a dozen attacks, killing at least 90 people, including 14 Americans in Saudi Arabia. Al-Qaida may have been connected to the suicide bombers and planners of the November 2003 attacks in Istanbul that targeted two synagogues, the British Consulate, and the HSBC Bank, and resulted in the deaths of more than 60 people. Pakistani President Musharraf blames al-Qaida for two attempts on his life in December 2003.

In October 2002, al-Qaida directed a suicide attack on the French tanker MV Limburg off the coast of Yemen that killed one and injured four. The group also carried out the November 2002 suicide bombing of a hotel in Mombasa, Kenya, which killed 15. Al-Qaida probably provided financing for the October 2002 Bali bombings by Jemaah Islamiya that killed more than 200.

On September 11, 2001, 19 al-Qaida members hijacked and crashed four U.S. commercial jets—two into the World Trade Center in New York City, one into the Pentagon near Washington, DC, and a fourth into a field in Shanksville, Pennsylvania—leaving nearly 3,000 individuals dead or missing. In October 2000, al-Qaida conducted a suicide attack on the USS Cole in the port of Aden, Yemen, with an explosive-laden boat, killing 17 U.S. Navy sailors and injuring 39. Al-Qaida also carried out the August 1998 bombings of the U.S. Embassies in Nairobi and Dar es Salaam killing at least 301 individuals and injuring more than 5,000 others. Al-Qaida and its supporters claim to have shot down U.S. helicopters and killed U.S. servicemen in Somalia in 1993, and to have conducted three bombings that targeted U.S. troops in Aden in December 1992.

Strength

Al-Qaida's organizational strength is difficult to determine in the aftermath of extensive counterterrorist efforts since 9/11. The arrests and deaths of mid-level and senior al-Qaida operatives have disrupted some communication, financial, and facilitation nodes and disrupted some terrorist plots. Additionally, supporters and associates worldwide who are inspired by the group's ideology may be operating without direction from al-Qaida's central leadership; it is impossible to estimate their numbers. Al-Qaida also serves as a focal point of inspiration for a worldwide network that is comprised of many Sunni Islamic extremist groups, including some members of the Gama'at al-Islamiyya, the Islamic Movement of Uzbekistan, the Islamic Jihad Group, Lashkar i Jhangvi, Harakat ul-Mujahedin, Ansar al-Sunnah, the Taliban, Jemaah Islamiya, and the Libyan Islamic Fighting Group.

Location/Area of Operation

Al-Qaida's worldwide networks are augmented by ties to local Sunni extremists. The group was based in Afghanistan until Coalition Forces removed the Taliban from power in late 2001. While the largest concentration of senior al-Qaida members now reside in Pakistan, the network incorporates members of al-Qaida in Iraq and other associates throughout the Middle East, Southeast Asia, Africa, Europe, and Central Asia who continue working to carry out future attacks against U.S. and Western interests.

External Aid

Al-Qaida primarily depends on donations from like-minded supporters and individuals who believe that their money is supporting a humanitarian or other cause. Some funds are diverted from Islamic charitable organizations. Additionally, parts of the organization raise funds through criminal activities; for example, al-Qaida in Iraq raises funds through hostage-taking for ransom, and members in Europe have engaged in credit card fraud. U.S. and international efforts to block al-Qaida funding have hampered the group's ability to raise money.

Al-Qaida in Iraq (AQI)[1]

a.k.a. Al-Qaida Group of Jihad in Iraq; Al-Qaida Group of Jihad in the Land of the Two Rivers; Al-Qaida in Mesopotamia; Al-Qaida in the Land of the Two Rivers; Al-Qaida of Jihad in Iraq; Al-Qaida of Jihad Organization in the Land of The Two Rivers; Al-Qaida of the Jihad in the Land of the Two Rivers; Al-Tawhid; Jam'at al-Tawhid Wa'al-Jihad; Tanzeem Qaidat al Jihad/Bilad al Raafidaini; Tanzim Qaidat al-Jihad fi Bilad al-Rafidayn; The Monotheism and Jihad Group; The Organization Base of Jihad/Country of the Two Rivers; The Organization Base of Jihad/Mesopotamia; The Organization of al-Jihad's Base in Iraq; The Organization of al-Jihad's Base in the Land of the Two Rivers; The Organization of al-Jihad's Base of Operations in Iraq; The Organization of al-Jihad's Base of Operations in the Land of the Two Rivers; The Organization of Jihad's Base in the Country of the Two Rivers

Description

In an attempt to unify Sunni jihadists in Iraq, in January 2006, al-Qaida in Iraq (AQI) created the Mujahidin Shura Council (MSC), an umbrella organization meant to encompass the various Sunni jihadist groups in Iraq. AQI claimed its attacks under the MSC until mid-October, when Abu Mus'ab al-Zarqawi's successor, Abu Ayyub al-Masri, took the first step toward al-Qaida's goal of establishing a caliphate in the region by declaring the "Islamic State of Iraq" (ISI), under which AQI now claims its attacks.

On June 7, 2006, AQI leader Abu Mus'ab al-Zarqawi was killed in a U.S. airstrike. Following his death, the MSC announced Abu Hamza al-Muhajir, also known at Abu Ayyub al-Masri, as Zarqawi's successor. Abu Ayyub

[1] Listed on the UN 1267 Committee List.

promptly issued a statement pledging to continue what Zarqawi had started, and AQI has continued its strategy of targeting Coalition Forces and Shi'a civilians in an attempt to foment sectarian strife. Although Coalition and Iraqi security force operations also have cost AQI dozens of lieutenants and high-ranking network members, overall violence in Iraq is at a higher level than it was while Zarqawi was alive.

Activities

In August 2003, Zarqawi's group carried out a major terrorist attack in Iraq when it bombed the Jordanian Embassy in Baghdad, followed 12 days later by a suicide vehicle-borne improvised explosive device (VBIED) attack against the UN Headquarters in Baghdad that killed 23, including the Secretary-General's Special Representative for Iraq, Sergio Vieira de Mello. That same month the group conducted a VBIED attack against Shia worshippers outside the Imam Ali Mosque in al Najaf, killing 85, including the leader of the Supreme Council for the Islamic Revolution in Iraq (SCIRI). The group kept up its attack pace throughout 2003, striking numerous Iraqi, Coalition, and relief agency targets such as the Red Cross. Zarqawi's group conducted VBIED attacks against U.S. military personnel and Iraqi infrastructure throughout 2004, including suicide attacks inside the Green Zone perimeter in Baghdad. The group successfully penetrated the Green Zone in the October 2004 bombing of a popular café and market. It also claimed responsibility for the videotaped execution by beheading of Americans Nicholas Berg (May 8, 2004), Jack Armstrong (September 20, 2004), and Jack Hensley (September 21, 2004). AQI was likely involved in other hostage incidents as well. In 2005, AQI largely focused on conducting multiple high-profile, coordinated suicide attacks. AQI claimed numerous attacks primarily aimed against civilians, the Iraqi government, and security forces, such as the coordinated attacks against polling sites during the January elections and the coordinated VBIED attacks outside the Sheraton and Palestine hotels in Baghdad on October 24. The group also continued assassinations against Shia leaders and Shia militia—Jaysh al-Mahdi and Badr Corps.

AQI increased its external operations in 2005 by claiming credit for three attacks: suicide bomber attacks against hotels in Amman on November 9; a rocket attack against U.S. Navy ships in the port of Aqaba in August, which resulted in limited damage in Jordan and in Eilat, Israel; and the firing of several rockets into Israel from Lebanon in December. In August 2005, an AQI operative was arrested in Turkey while planning an operation targeting Israeli cruise ships. Prior to 2005, AQI planned and conducted limited attacks in Jordan, including the assassination of USAID official Laurence Foley in 2002. In October 2006, AQI declared the ISI would become a platform from which AQI would launch jihad throughout the world. Following the announcement, AQI members marched through cities they considered to be part of their new state as a show of force. AQI attack claims, which the group released under the auspices of the Mujahidin Shura Council and now the ISI, increased in 2006.

Strength

Precise numbers are unknown, but AQI is the largest terrorist group in Iraq.

Location/Area of Operation

AQI's operations are predominately Iraq-based, but the group maintains an extensive logistical network throughout the Middle East, North Africa, Iran, South Asia, and Europe.

External Aid

AQI probably receives funds from donors in the Middle East and Europe, local sympathizers in Iraq, a variety of businesses and criminal activities, and other international extremists throughout the world. In many cases, AQI's donors are probably motivated by support for terrorism rather than affiliation with any specific terrorist group.

Al-Qaida in the Islamic Maghreb (AQIM) [Formerly Salafist Group for Preaching and Combat (GSPC)]

a.k.a. Le Groupe Salafiste pour la Predication et le Combat; Salafist Group for Call and Combat

Description

The Salafist Group for Preaching and Combat (GSPC) officially merged with al-Qaida in September 2006, and subsequently changed its name to al-Qaida in the Islamic Maghreb (AQIM). GSPC members abandoned the Armed Islamic Group (GIA) over disagreements about leadership and tactics, but retained the mission of overthrowing the Algerian Government and installing an Islamic regime. AQIM/GSPC is the most effective and largest armed group inside Algeria. In contrast to the GIA, it has pledged to avoid civilian attacks inside Algeria.

Activities

AQIM/GSPC attacked a U.S. contractor bus in December 2006 in greater Algiers. In Zawahiri's September 11 speech announcing the GSPC's merger with al-Qaida, Zawahiri called on it to be "a bone in the throat of the American and French crusaders" and to sow fear "in the heart of the traitors and apostate sons of France." AQIM/GSPC continues to conduct operations aimed at government and military targets, primarily in rural areas, although civilians are sometimes killed. AQIM/GSPC executed simultaneous attacks on October 30 on two police stations just east of Algiers, killing three civilians, wounding 14 police officers, and causing substantial damage to both facilities. In 2005, the GSPC claimed responsibility for an attack on a remote Mauritanian military outpost, killing 15, while indicating a shift in its strategy toward a more global war beyond Algerian borders.

Police in France, Italy and Spain arrested several Algerians suspected of providing support to AQIM/GSPC, and French officials announced that the AQIM/GSPC had issued an Internet call-to-action against France, declaring France "public enemy number one." The Government of Algeria scored major counterterrorism successes against AQIM/GSPC in 2004, killing AQIM/GSPC leader Nabil Sahraoui and separately taking custody of Abderazak al-Para, who led a AQIM/GSPC faction that held 32 European tourists hostage in 2003.

Strength

Several hundred fighters with an unknown number of facilitators outside Algeria.

Location/Area of Operation

Algeria, the Sahel, Canada, and Western Europe.

External Aid

Algerian expatriates and AQIM/GSPC members abroad, many residing in Western Europe, provide financial and logistical support. AQIM/GSPC members also engage in criminal activity.

Real IRA (RIRA)

a.k.a. 32 County Sovereignty Committee; 32 County Sovereignty Movement; Irish Republican Prisoners Welfare Association; Real Irish Republican Army; Real Oglaigh Na Heireann

Description

Like the Continuity IRA, RIRA did not participate in the September 2005 weapons decommissioning. RIRA was formed in 1997 as the clandestine armed wing of the 32 County Sovereignty Movement, a "political pressure group" dedicated to removing British forces from Northern Ireland and unifying Ireland. RIRA also seeks to disrupt the Northern Ireland peace process. The 32 County Sovereignty Movement opposed Sinn Fein's adoption in September 1997 of the Mitchell principles of democracy and non-violence; it also opposed the amendment in December 1999 of Articles 2 and 3 of the Irish Constitution that laid claim to Northern Ireland. Despite internal rifts and calls by some jailed members, including the group's founder Michael "Mickey" McKevitt, for a cease-fire and disbandment, RIRA has pledged additional violence and continues to conduct attacks.

Activities

Many RIRA members are former Provisional Irish Republican Army members who left that organization after it renewed its cease-fire in 1997. These members brought a wealth of experience in terrorist tactics and bomb-making to RIRA. Targets have included civilians (most notoriously in the Omagh bombing in August 1998), British security forces, police in Northern Ireland, and local Protestant communities. RIRA's most recent fatal attack was in August 2002 at a London army base, killing a construction worker. The organization wants to improve its intelligence-gathering ability, engineering capacity, and access to weaponry; it also trains members in the use of guns and explosives. RIRA continues to attract new members, and its senior members are committed to launching attacks on security forces. Three suspected RIRA members that engaged in cigarette smuggling were arrested in Spain in 2006.

Strength

The number of activists may have fallen to less than 100. The organization may receive limited support from IRA hardliners and Republican sympathizers dissatisfied with the IRA's continuing cease-fire and with Sinn Fein's involvement in the peace process. Approximately 40 RIRA members are in Irish jails.

Location/Area of Operation

Northern Ireland, Great Britain, and the Irish Republic.

External Aid

Suspected of receiving funds from sympathizers in the United States and of attempting to buy weapons from U.S. gun dealers. RIRA also is reported to have purchased sophisticated weapons from the Balkans.

Revolutionary Armed Forces of Colombia (FARC)

a.k.a. Fuerzas Armadas Revolucionarias de Colombia

Description

The FARC is Latin America's oldest, largest, most capable, and best-equipped insurgency. It began in the early sixties as an outgrowth of the Liberal Party-based peasant self-defense leagues, but took on Marxist ideology, although it only nominally fights in support of Marxist goals today. The FARC is governed by a general secretariat led by long-time leader

Manuel Marulanda (a.k.a. "Tirofijo") and six others, including senior military commander Jorge Briceno (a.k.a. "Mono Jojoy"). The FARC is organized along military lines and includes some specialized urban fighting units. A Colombian military offensive targeting FARC fighters in their former safe haven in southern Colombia has experienced some success, with several FARC mid-level leaders killed or captured. France, Spain, and Switzerland formed an international commission in November 2005 to aid the Colombian government and the FARC with humanitarian exchange negotiations, which are currently stalled.

Activities

FARC has carried out bombings, murder, mortar attacks, kidnapping, extortion, and hijacking, as well as guerrilla and conventional military action against Colombian political, military, and economic targets. In February 2003, when a U.S. plane crashed in a FARC-held area, the FARC murdered a U.S. citizen and a Colombian; it continues to hold hostage the three other U.S. citizens that were on the plane. Foreign citizens often are targets of abductions that FARC carries out in pursuit of ransom and political leverage. The FARC has well-documented ties to the full range of narcotics strafficking activities, including taxation, cultivation, and distribution.

Strength

Approximately 15,000 combatants and several thousand more supporters, mostly in rural areas.

Location/Area of Operation

Primarily in Colombia with some activities such as extortion, kidnapping, weapons sourcing, logistics, and R&R in neighboring countries.

External Aid

Cuba and Venezuela provide some medical care, safe haven, and political consultation. The FARC often uses the Colombia/Venezuela and Colombia/Ecuador border areas for cross-border incursions and Venezuelan and Ecuadorian territory as a safe haven, although the degree of government acquiescence is not clear and seems to vary.

Revolutionary Nuclei (RN)

a.k.a. Revolutionary Cells

Description

Revolutionary Nuclei (RN) emerged from a broad range of anti-establishment and anti-U.S./NATO/EU leftist groups active in Greece between 1995 and 1998. The group is believed to be the successor to or offshoot of Greece's most prolific terrorist group, Revolutionary People's Struggle (ELA), which has not claimed an attack since January 1995. Indeed, RN appeared to fill the void left by ELA, particularly as lesser groups faded from the scene. RN's few communiqués show strong similarities in rhetoric, tone, and theme to ELA proclamations. RN has not claimed an attack since November 2000, nor has it announced its disbandment.

Activites

Since it began operations in January 1995, the group has claimed responsibility for some two dozen arson attacks and low-level bombings against a range of U.S., Greek, and other European targets in Greece. In its most infamous and lethal attack to date, the group claimed responsibility for a bomb it detonated at the Intercontinental Hotel in April 1999 that resulted in the death of a Greek woman and injury of a Greek man. RN's modus operandi includes warning calls of impending attacks, attacks targeting property instead of individuals, use of rudimentary timing devices, and strikes during the late evening to early morning hours. RN may have been responsible for two attacks in July 2003 against a U.S. insurance company and a local bank in Athens. RN's last confirmed attacks against U.S. interests in Greece came in November 2000, with two separate bombings against the Athens offices of Citigroup and the studio of a Greek-American sculptor. Greek targets have included judicial and other government office buildings, private vehicles, and the offices of Greek firms involved in NATO-related defense contracts in Greece. Similarly, the group has attacked European interests in Athens.

Strength

Group membership is believed to be small, probably drawing from the Greek militant leftist or anarchist milieu.

Location/Area of Operation

Primary area of operation is in the Athens, Greece metropolitan area.

External Aid

Unknown but believed to be self-sustaining.

Revolutionary Organization 17 November (17N)

a.k.a. Epanastatiki Organosi 17 Noemvri; 17 November

Description

17 November (17N) is a radical leftist group established in 1975 and named for the student uprising in Greece in November 1973 that protested the

ruling military junta. 17N is an anti-Greek establishment, anti-United States, anti-Turkey, and anti-NATO group that seeks the ouster of U.S. bases from Greece, the removal of Turkish military forces from Cyprus, and the severing of Greece's ties to NATO and the European Union (EU).

Activities

Initial attacks were assassinations of senior U.S. officials and Greek public figures. Five U.S. Embassy employees have been murdered since 17N began its terrorist activities in 1975. The group began using bombings in the 1980s. In 1990, 17N expanded its targets to include Turkish diplomats, EU facilities, and foreign firms investing in Greece, and added improvised rocket attacks to its methods. The group supported itself largely through bank robberies. A failed 17N bombing attempt in June 2002 at the port of Piraeus in Athens, coupled with robust detective work, led to the arrest of 19 members, the first 17N operatives ever arrested, including a key leader of the organization. In December 2003, a Greek court convicted 15 members, five of whom were given multiple life terms. Four other alleged members were acquitted for lack of evidence. In December 2005, against the backdrop of a sympathetic press, a group appeals trial opened for the 15 convicted members and two of the previously acquitted members. The appeals trial essentially represents a new trial for the convicts because new evidence and facts can be introduced under Greek law. Moreover, convicted 17N terrorist Nikos Papanastasiou was released from prison in July 2006 on medical grounds. Papanastasiou was the third convicted 17N terrorist to be granted early release from prison for health reasons, following Konstantinos Telios and Pavlos Serifis in 2005.

Strength

Unknown but presumed to be small.

Location/Area of Operation

Athens, Greece.

External Aid

Unknown.

Revolutionary People's Liberation Party/Front (DHKP/C)

a.k.a. Dev Sol; Dev Sol Armed Revolutionary Units; Dev Sol Silahli Devrimci Birlikleri; Dev Sol SDB; Devrimci Halk Kurtulus Partisi-Cephesi; Devrimci Sol; Revolutionary Left

Description

This group originally formed in 1978 as Devrimci Sol, or Dev Sol, a splinter faction of Dev Genc (Revolutionary Youth). It was renamed in 1994 after factional infighting. "Party" refers to the group's political activities, while "Front" is a reference to the group's militant operations. The group espouses a Marxist-Leninist ideology and is vehemently anti-U.S., anti-NATO, and anti-Turkish establishment. Its goals are the establishment of a socialist state and the abolition of F-type prisons, which contain one- to three-man prison cells. DHKP/C finances its activities chiefly through donations and extortion.

Activities

Since the late 1980s, the group has targeted primarily current and retired Turkish security and military officials. It began a new campaign against foreign interests in 1990, which included attacks against U.S. military and diplomatic personnel and facilities. To protest perceived U.S. imperialism during the Gulf War, Dev Sol assassinated two U.S. military contractors, wounded an Air Force officer, and bombed more than 20 U.S. and NATO military, commercial, and cultural facilities. In its first significant terrorist act as DHKP/C in 1996, the group assassinated a prominent Turkish businessman and two others. DHKP/C added suicide bombings to its repertoire in 2001, with successful attacks against Turkish police in January and September. Since the end of 2001, DHKP/C has typically used improvised explosive devices against official Turkish targets and soft U.S. targets of opportunity; attacks against U.S. targets beginning in 2003 probably came in response to Operation Iraqi Freedom. Operations and arrests against the group have weakened its capabilities.

Strength

Probably several dozen terrorist operatives inside Turkey, with a large support network throughout Europe.

Location/Area of Operation

Turkey, primarily Istanbul, Ankara, Izmir, and Adana. Raises funds in Europe.

External Aid

Widely believed to have training facilities or offices in Lebanon and Syria.

Shining Path (SL)

a.k.a. Sendero Luminoso; Ejercito Guerrillero Popular (People's Guerrilla Army); Ejercito Popular de Liberacion (People's Liberation Army); Partido

Comunista del Peru (Communist Party of Peru); Partido Comunista del Peru en el Sendero Luminoso de Jose Carlos Mariategui (Communist Party of Peru on the Shining Path of Jose Carlos Mariategui); Socorro Popular del Peru (People's Aid of Peru)

Description

Former university professor Abimael Guzman formed SL in Peru in the late 1960s, and his teachings created the foundation of SL's militant Maoist doctrine. In the 1980s, SL became one of the most ruthless terrorist groups in the Western Hemisphere. Approximately 35,000 persons have died since Shining Path took up arms in 1980. The Peruvian government made dramatic gains against SL during the 1990s, but recent SL attacks against Peruvian counternarcotics police and kidnappings of counternarcotics NGO workers underscore the continuing threat SL poses, as well as the group's increasing ties to narcotrafficking. SL's stated goal is to destroy existing Peruvian institutions and replace them with a communist peasant revolutionary regime. It also opposes any influence by foreign governments. In response to SL's bloody attacks in late 2005, Peruvian authorities have stepped up counterterrorism efforts against the group. More recently, SL members have attempted to influence the local populace through indoctrination versus violence.

Activities

SL has conducted indiscriminate bombing campaigns, ambushes, and selective assassinations. Its increased drug ties have raised operating revenue.

Strength

Unknown but estimated to be some 300 armed militants.

Location/Area of Operation

Peru, with most activity in rural areas, specifically the Huallaga Valley, the Ene River, and the Apurimac Valley of central Peru.

External Aid

None.

United Self-Defense Forces of Colombia (AUC)

a.k.a. Autodefensas Unidas de Colombia

Description

The AUC, commonly referred to as the paramilitaries, is an umbrella group formed in April 1997 to organize loosely affiliated illegal paramilitary groups that emerged to retaliate against leftist guerillas fighting the Colombian government and the landed establishment. The AUC increasingly discarded its counter-guerilla activities, electing instead to involve itself in the illegal drug trade. Recently, as the result of a large demobilization process, most of the AUC's centralized military structure has been dismantled, all the top paramilitary chiefs have stepped down, and the majority of the chiefs are being held in a maximum security facility. More than 31,000 paramilitary members demobilized bloc by bloc from 2003 to 2006. Colombia now faces criminal gangs formed by demobilized paramilitaries and other individuals, as well as a few paramilitary groups that refused to disarm. Unlike the AUC, the new criminal groups make little claim to fighting guerrillas and are more clearly criminal enterprises focused primarily on drug trafficking, other lucrative illicit activity, and controlling local politics. They are not part of the AUC.

Activities

Paramilitary operations vary from assassinating suspected insurgent supporters to engaging guerrilla combat units. As much as 70 percent of the paramilitary operational costs are financed with drug-related earnings, with the rest coming from "donations" from sponsors. These groups generally avoid actions against U.S. personnel or interests. Paramilitary operations are reduced as a result of the demobilization of all AUC groups, although some individuals appear to be violating the commitments they made when they demobilized. Colombia's homicide rate is at its lowest level in 18 years, in part because of the cease-fire agreement and demobilization. Other violence indicators such as kidnapping and terror attacks have also decreased significantly.

Strength

The Colombian government has stated that the AUC no longer exists. An estimated 3,000 former members have re-engaged in criminal activities.

Location/Areas of Operation

Paramilitary forces were strongest in northwest Colombia in Antioquia, Cordoba, Sucre, Atlantico, Magdelena, Cesar, La Guajira, and Bolivar Departments, with affiliate groups in the coffee region, Valle del Cauca, and Meta Department.

External Aid

None.

OTHER GROUPS OF CONCERN

The following groups of concern have not been designated as Foreign Terrorist Organizations under 8 USC Section 1189, although many have been designated under other U.S. Government counterterrorism authorities.

Contents

New Red Brigades/Communist Combatant Party (BR/PCC)

People Against Gangsterism and Drugs (PAGAD)

Rajah Solaiman Movement (RSM)

Red Hand Defenders (RHD)

Revolutionary Proletarian Initiative Nuclei (NIPR)

Revolutionary Struggle (RS)

Riyadus-Salikhin Reconnaissance and Sabotage Battalion of Chechen Martyrs (RSRSBCM)

Sipah-I-Sahaba/Pakistan (SSP)

Special Purpose Islamic Regiment (SPIR)

Al-Tawhid w'al Jihad (TWJ)

Tenrik Mifaz-E-Shariah Mohammadi (TNSM)

Tunisian Combatant Group (TCG)

Tupac Amaru Revolutionary Movement (MRTA)

Turkish Hizballah

Ulster Defense Association/Ulster Freedom Fighters (UDA/UFF)

Ulster Volunteer Force (UVF)

United Liberation Front of Assam (ULFA)

Al-Badhr Mujahedin (al-Badr)

Description

The al-Badhr Mujahedin split from Hizbul-Mujahedin (HM) in 1998. It traces its origins to 1971, when a group named al-Badr attacked Bengalis in East Pakistan. The group later operated as part of Gulbuddin Hekmatyar's Hizb-I Islami (HIG) in Afghanistan and, from 1990, as a unit of HM in Kashmir. The group was relatively inactive until 2000. Since then, it has increasingly claimed responsibility for attacks against Indian military targets. Since the late 1990s, al-Badhr leader Bakht Zamin repeatedly has expressed his support for Usama bin Ladin and the Taliban, and in 2002 declared jihad against U.S. forces in Afghanistan.

Activities

The organization has conducted a number of operations against Indian military targets in Jammu and Kashmir. Since late 2001, al-Badhr members have reportedly targeted Coalition Forces in Afghanistan.

Strength

Perhaps several hundred.

Location/Area of Operation

Jammu and Kashmir, Pakistan, and Afghanistan.

External Aid

Unknown.

Al-Ittihad al-Islami (AIAI)[1 2 3]

Description

AIAI, a Somali extremist group that was formed in the 1980s and reached its peak in the early 1990s, failed to obtain its objective of establishing a Salafist emirate in Somalia and steadily declined following the downfall of the Siad Barre regime in 1991 and Somalia's subsequent collapse into anarchy. AIAI was not internally cohesive, lacked central leadership, and suffered divisions between factions. AIAI was militarily defeated by Ethiopian forces in 1997. In recent years, the existence of a coherent entity operating as AIAI has become difficult to prove. After the downfall of the Somali Council of Islamic Courts in late 2006, AIAI has re-emerged. Former elements of AIAI continue to pursue a variety of agendas ranging from social services and education to insurgency activities in the Ogaden region of eastern Ethiopia. Some sheikhs formerly associated with AIAI espouse a fundamentalist version of Islam, with particular emphasis on a strict adherence to Sharia (Islamic law), a view often at odds with Somalis' emphasis on clan identity. A small group of former AIAI members embrace global jihad and support al-Qaida members in East Africa. 1267 al-Qaida/Taliban/Usama bin Laden Sanctions Committee has listed AIAI for its associations with al-Qaida.

Activities

Individuals formerly associated with AIAI may have been responsible for several kidnappings and murders of relief workers in Somalia and Somaliland since 2003 and in the late 1990s. Prior to its destruction in 1997, factions of AIAI also may have been responsible for a series of bomb attacks in public places in Addis Ababa in 1996 and 1997. Most AIAI factions in recent years have concentrated on broadening their religious base, renewed an emphasis on building businesses, and undertaken "hearts and minds"

1 Listed on the UN 1267 Committee List.
2 Listed on the Terrorist Exclusion List.
3 Designated under Exclusion Order 13224.

actions, such as sponsoring orphanages and schools and providing security that uses an Islamic legal structure in the areas where it is active.

Strength

The actual membership strength is unknown.

Location/Area of Operation

Primarily in Somalia, with a presence in the Ogaden region of Ethiopia, Kenya, and possibly Djibouti.

External Aid

Receives funds from Middle East financiers and Somali diaspora communities in Europe, North America, and the Arabian Peninsula.

Alex Boncayao Brigade (ABB)[2]

Description

The ABB, the breakaway urban hit squad of the Communist Party of the Philippines/New People's Army, was formed in the mid-1980s. The ABB was added to the Terrorist Exclusion List in December 2001.

Activities

Responsible for more than 100 murders, including the murder in 1989 of U.S. Army Col. James Rowe in the Philippines. In March 1997, the group announced it had formed an alliance with another armed group, the Revolutionary Proletarian Army (RPA). In March 2000, the group claimed credit for a rifle grenade attack against the Department of Energy building in Manila and strafed Shell Oil offices in the central Philippines to protest rising oil prices. The group has not been active/conducted attacks in recent years.

Strength

Unknown, but believed to number below 500.

Location/Area of Operation

The largest RPA/ABB groups are on the Philippine islands of Luzon, Negros, and the Visayas.

External Aid

Unknown.

[2] Listed on the Terrorist Exclusion List.

Anti-Imperialist Territorial Nuclei for the Construction of the Communist Combatant Party (NTA-PCC)

a.k.a. Anti-Imperialist Territorial Units

Description

The NTA-PCC is a clandestine leftist extremist group that first appeared in Italy's Friuli region in 1995. It adopted the class struggle ideology of the Red Brigades of the 1970s and 1980s, and a similar logo—an encircled five-point star—for its declarations. It seeks the formation of an "anti-imperialist fighting front" with other Italian leftist terrorist groups, including Revolutionary Proletarian Initiative Nuclei and the New Red Brigades. The group opposes what it perceives as U.S. and NATO imperialism, and condemns Italy's foreign and labor policies. In a leaflet dated January 2002, NTA-PCC identified experts in four Italian government sectors—federalism, privatizations, justice reform, and jobs and pensions—as potential targets.

Activities

To date, NTA-PCC has conducted attacks only against property. During the NATO intervention in Kosovo in 1999, NTA-PCC members threw gasoline bombs at the Venice and Rome headquarters of the then-ruling party, Democrats of the Left. NTA-PCC claimed responsibility for a bomb attack in September 2000 against the Central European Initiative office in Trieste and a bomb attack in August 2001 against the Venice Tribunal building. In January 2002, police thwarted an attempt by four NTA-PCC members to enter the Rivolto military air base. In 2003, NTA-PCC claimed responsibility for the arson attacks against three vehicles belonging to U.S. troops serving at the Ederle and Aviano bases in Italy. There has been no reported activity by the group since the arrest in January 2004 of NTA-PCC's founder and leader.

Strength

Accounts vary from one to approximately 20 members.

Location/Area of Operation

Primarily northeastern Italy and U.S. military installations in northern Italy.

External Aid

None evident.

Cambodian Freedom Fighters (CFF)

a.k.a. Cholana; Kangtoap Serei Cheat; Kampouchea

Description

The Cambodian Freedom Fighters (CFF) emerged in November 1998 in the wake of political violence that saw many influential Cambodian leaders flee and the Cambodian People's Party assume power. With an avowed aim of overthrowing the government, the U.S.-based group is led by a Cambodian-American, a former member of the opposition Sam Rainsy Party. The CFF's membership reportedly includes Cambodian-Americans based in Thailand and the United States, and former soldiers from the Khmer Rouge, Royal Cambodian Armed Forces, and various political factions.

Activities

Alleged CFF leader Chhun Yasith was arrested in June in the United States on charges of conspiracy to kill in a foreign country, conspiracy to damage or destroy property in a foreign country, and engaging in a military expedition against a nation with which the United States is at peace. If convicted, Yasith faces life imprisonment without parole for each of the charges. Meanwhile, a Cambodian court in October dropped charges against five alleged CFF members arrested in April 2004 in connection with a bombing at a ferry, which slightly injured three persons. In 2003, the Cambodian government arrested seven CFF members who were reportedly planning an unspecified terrorist attack in southwestern Cambodia. Cambodian courts in February and March 2002 prosecuted 38 CFF members suspected of staging an attack in Cambodia in 2000. The courts convicted 19 members, including one U.S. citizen, of "terrorism" and/or "membership in an armed group," and sentenced them to terms of five years to life imprisonment. A Cambodian court later judged that the three-year sentences of six other members were too light and decided in December 2005 to extend them to 6 to 10 years. The group had claimed responsibility for an attack in late November 2000 on several government installations that killed at least eight persons and wounded more than a dozen. In April 1999, five CFF members also were arrested for plotting to blow up a fuel depot outside Phnom Penh with anti-tank weapons.

Strength

Exact strength is unknown, but totals probably never have exceeded 100 armed fighters.

Location/Area of Operation

Northeastern Cambodia near the Thai border, and the United States.

External Aid

U.S.-based leadership collects funds from the Cambodian-American community.

Communist Party of India (Maoist)

a.k.a. Maoist Communist Center of India (MCCI) and People's War (PW)

Description

The Indian groups known as the Maoist Communist Center of India and People's War (a.k.a. People's War Group) joined in September 2004 to form the Communist Party of India (Maoist), or CPI (Maoist). The MCCI was originally formed in the early 1970s, while People's War (PW) was founded in 1975. Both groups are referred to as Naxalites, after the West Bengal village where a revolutionary radical Left movement originated in 1967. The new organization continues to employ violence to achieve its goals of peasant revolution, abolition of class hierarchies, and expansion of Maoist-controlled "liberated zones," eventually leading to the creation of an independent "Maoist" state. The CPI (Maoist) reportedly has a significant cadre of women. Important leaders include Ganapati (the PW leader from Andhra Pradesh), Pramod Mishra, Uma Shankar, and P.N.G. (alias Nathuni Mistry, arrested by Jharkhand police in 2002).

Activities

Prior to its consolidation with the PW, the MCCI ran a virtual parallel government in remote areas, where it collected a "tax" from villagers and, in turn, provided infrastructure improvements such as building hospitals, schools, and irrigation projects. It ran a parallel court system wherein allegedly corrupt block development officials and landlords—frequent MCCI targets—were punished by amputation and even death. People's War conducted a low-intensity insurgency that included attempted political assassination, theft of weapons from police stations, kidnapping police officers, assaulting civilians, extorting money from construction firms, and vandalizing the property of multinational corporations. Together the two groups were reportedly responsible for the deaths of up to 170 civilians and police a year. The group conducted two major attacks in 2005. In June, some 500 members attacked a village in Uttar Pradesh, killing several local policemen, destroying buildings, and seizing weapons. In November, an estimated 300 members attacked a prison in Bihar, killing two people, freeing more than 300 inmates, and abducting 30 landowners belonging to a group opposed to the Naxalites.

Strength

Although difficult to assess with any accuracy, media reports and local authorities suggest the CPI's (Maoist) membership may be as high as 31,000, including both hard-core militants and dedicated sympathizers.

Location/Area of Operation

The CPI (Maoist), which is believed to be enlarging the scope of its influence, operates in the Indian states of Andhra Pradesh, Orissa, Jharkhand, Bihar, Chhattisgarh, and parts of West Bengal. It also has a presence on the Bihar-Nepal border.

External Aid

The CPI (Maoist) has loose links to other Maoist groups in the region, including the Communist Party of Nepal (Maoist), but does not appear dependent on outside sources of support. The MCCI was a founding member of the Coordination Committee of Maoist Parties and Organizations of South Asia (CCOMPOSA).

Communist Party of Nepal (Maoist) (CPN/M)[2,3]

Description

The Communist Party of Nepal (Maoist) insurgency grew out of the radicalization and fragmentation of left-wing parties following Nepal's transition to democracy in 1990. The United People's Front, a coalition of left-wing parties, participated in the elections of 1991, but the Maoist wing failed to win the required minimum number of votes, leading to its exclusion from voter lists in the elections of 1994 and prompting the group to launch the insurgency in 1996. The CPN/M's ultimate objective is the overthrow of the Nepalese government and the establishment of a Maoist state. On October 31, 2003, the United States designated Nepal's Maoists under E.O. 13224 for terrorist activity.

Activities

The Maoists have used traditional guerrilla warfare tactics and engage in murder, torture, arson, sabotage, extortion, child conscription, kidnapping, bombings, and assassinations to intimidate and coerce the populace. In 2002, Maoists claimed responsibility for assassinating two Nepalese U.S. Embassy guards, citing anti-Maoist spying, and in a press statement threatened foreign embassies, including the U.S. Mission, to deter foreign support for the Nepalese government. Maoists are suspected in the September 2004 bombing at the American Cultural Center in Kathmandu. The attack, which caused no injuries and only minor damage, marked the first time the Maoists had damaged U.S. Government property. The Maoists entered into peace talks with the government in 2001 and 2003, but negotiations failed after a few months. In 2005, the group announced a unilateral cease-fire

[2] Listed on the Terrorist Exclusion List.
[3] Designated under Exclusion Order 13224.

in September, and entered into an alliance with the seven-party alliance of opposition political parties in November.

Strength

Approximately several thousand full-time members.

Location/Area of Operation

Operations are conducted throughout Nepal. Press reports indicate some Nepalese Maoist leaders reside in India.

External Aid

None.

Democratic Forces for the Liberation of Rwanda (FDLR)

a.k.a. Army for the Liberation of Rwanda (ALIR); a.k.a. FAR/Interahamwe

Description

In 2001, the Democratic Forces for the Liberation of Rwanda (FDLR) supplanted the Army for the Liberation of Rwanda (ALIR), the armed branch of the Party for the Liberation of Rwanda (PALIR). ALIR was formed from the merger of the Armed Forces of Rwanda (FAR), the army of the ethnic Hutu-dominated Rwandan regime that orchestrated the genocide of over 500,000 Tutsis and regime opponents in 1994, and Interahamwe, the civilian militia force that carried out much of the killing. This occurred after the two groups were forced from Rwanda into the Democratic Republic of the Congo (DRC, then Zaire) that year. Though directly tied to those who organized and carried out the genocide, identified ALIR/FDLR leaders are not thought to have played a role in the killing. They have worked to build bridges to other opponents of the Kigali regime, including ethnic Tutsis.

Activities

ALIR sought to topple Rwanda's Tutsi-dominated government, reinstitute Hutu domination, and, possibly, complete the genocide. In 1996, a message—allegedly from the ALIR—threatened to kill the U.S. Ambassador to Rwanda and other U.S. citizens. In 1999, ALIR guerrillas critical of U.S.-UK support for the Rwandan regime kidnapped and killed eight foreign tourists, including two U.S. citizens, in a game park on the DRC-Uganda border. Three suspects in the attack are in U.S. custody awaiting trial. In the 1998-2002 Congolese war, the ALIR/FDLR was allied with Kinshasa against the Rwandan invaders. ALIR/FDLR's political wing mainly has sought to topple the Kigali regime via an alliance with Tutsi regime opponents. It established the ADRN Igihango alliance in 2002, but this has not resonated politically in Rwanda. In March 2005, FDLR representatives announced a willingness to cease military actions and return to Rwanda. FDLR denounced the genocide, committed to a political struggle rather than a military one, and indicated it would voluntarily demobilize and repatriate. No large-scale FDLR repatriation to Rwanda has occurred, however, owing to FDLR concerns about security and the "political space" it would be allowed in Rwanda.

Strength

Exact strength is unknown, but an estimated 8,000 to 10,000 FDLR guerrillas operate in the eastern DRC close to the Rwandan border. In 2003, the United Nations, with Rwandan assistance, repatriated close to 1,500 FDLR combatants from the DRC. A senior FDLR military commander returned to Rwanda in November 2003 and has been working with Kigali to encourage the return of his comrades.

Location/Area of Operation

Mostly in the eastern Democratic Republic of the Congo.

External Aid

The Government of the Democratic Republic of the Congo provided training, arms, and supplies to ALIR forces to combat Rwandan armed forces that invaded the DRC in 1998. Kinshasa halted that support in 2002, though allegations persist of continued support from several local Congolese warlords and militias, including the Mai Mai.

East Turkistan Islamic Movement (ETIM)[132]

Description

The East Turkistan Islamic Movement (ETIM) is a small Islamic extremist group linked to al- Qaida and the international jihadist movement. It is the most militant of the ethnic Uighur separatist groups pursuing an independent "Eastern Turkistan," an area that would include Turkey, Kazakhstan, Kyrgyzstan, Uzbekistan, Pakistan, Afghanistan, and Western China's Xinjiang Uighur Autonomous Region. On September 12, 2002, the group was designated under E.O. 13224 for its terrorist activity. ETIM is also listed by the UN 1267 al-Qaida/Taliban/Usama bin Laden Sanctions Committee for its associations with al-Qaida.

---

[1] Listed on the UN 1267 Committee List.
[3] Designated under Exclusion Order 13224.
[2] Listed on the Terrorist Exclusion List.

Activites

ETIM militants fought alongside al-Qaida and Taliban forces in Afghanistan during Operation Enduring Freedom. In October 2003, Pakistani soldiers killed ETIM leader Hassan Makhsum during raids on al-Qaida-associated compounds in western Pakistan. U.S. and Chinese government information suggests that ETIM is responsible for various terrorist acts inside and outside China. In May 2002, two ETIM members were deported to China from Kyrgyzstan for plotting to attack the U.S. Embassy in Kyrgyzstan as well as other U.S. interests abroad.

Strength

Unknown. Only a small minority of ethnic Uighurs supports the Xinjiang independence movement or the formation of an independent Eastern Turkistan.

Location/Area of Operation

Afghanistan, China, Kyrgyzstan, and Pakistan.

External Aid

ETIM has received training and financial assistance from al-Qaida.

First of October Antifascist Resistance Group (GRAPO); Grupo de Resistencia Anti-Fascista Primero de Octubre

Description

GRAPO was formed in 1975 as the armed wing of the illegal Communist Party of Spain during the Franco era. It advocates the overthrow of the Spanish government and its replacement with a Marxist-Leninist regime. GRAPO is vehemently anti-American, seeks the removal of all U.S. military forces from Spanish territory, and has conducted and attempted several attacks against U.S. targets since 1977. The group issued a communiqué following the September 11, 2001, attacks in the United States, expressing its satisfaction that "symbols of imperialist power" were decimated and affirming that "the war" has only just begun. Spanish authorities believed they had nearly eradicated GRAPO, but a joint Spanish, French, and Italian police operation in October 2005 that resulted in the arrest of two GRAPO members led observers to speculate that the group may be reconstituting itself. GRAPO in a November 2006 internal publication announced that it was trying to find new members and resources but admitted it was having difficulty reorganizing because of sporadic arrests that continued well into 2006. The group was designated under E.O. 13224 in December 2001.

Activities

GRAPO suffered setbacks in 2004, with several members and sympathizers arrested and sentences upheld or handed down in the appellate case for GRAPO militants arrested in Paris in 2000. Press reports indicate that as of mid-2006, about 30 people connected with the terrorist group were in prison. The group's operations traditionally have been designed to cause material damage and gain publicity rather than inflict casualties, but the terrorists have conducted lethal bombings and close-range assassinations; GRAPO has killed more than 90 persons and injured more than 200 since its formation. GRAPO claimed responsibility for the murder in Zaragoza on 6 February 2006 of a Spanish businesswoman. Members of the group also have been charged with engaging in extortion and for carrying out a series of bank robberies in recent years.

Strength

Fewer than two-dozen activists remain. Police have made periodic large-scale arrests of GRAPO members, crippling the organization and forcing it into lengthy rebuilding periods. In 2002, Spanish and French authorities arrested 22 suspected members, including some of the group's reconstituted leadership. More members have been arrested in the past three years.

Location/Area of Operation

Spain.

External Aid

None.

Harakat ul-Jihad-I-Islami (HUJI)[2]

a.k.a Movement of Islamic Holy War.

Description

HUJI, a Sunni extremist group that follows the Deobandi tradition of Islam, was founded in 1980 in Afghanistan to fight in the jihad against the Soviets. It also is affiliated with the Jamiat Ulema-i-Islam's Fazlur Rehman faction (JUI-F) of the extremist religious party Jamiat Ulema-i-Islam (JUI). The group, led by Qari Saifullah Akhtar and chief commander Amin Rabbani, is made up primarily of Pakistanis and foreign Islamists who are fighting for the liberation of Jammu and Kashmir and its accession to Pakistan.

---

[2] Listed on the Terrorist Exclusion List.

Activities

The group has conducted a number of operations against Indian military targets in Jammu and Kashmir. It is linked to the Kashmiri militant group al-Faran that kidnapped five Western tourists in Jammu and Kashmir in July 1995; one was killed in August 1995, and the other four reportedly were killed in December of the same year.

Strength

Exact numbers are unknown, but there may be several hundred members in Kashmir.

Location/Area of Operation

Pakistan and Kashmir. Trained members in Afghanistan until fall of 2001.

External Aid

Specific sources of external aid are unknown.

Harakat-ul-Jihad-I-Islami/Bangladesh (HUJI-B)

Description

The goal of HUJI-B is to establish Islamic rule in Bangladesh. Bangladeshi veterans of the war against the Soviets in Afghanistan are the group's core membership. HUJI-B has connections to the Pakistani militant groups Harakat ul-Jihad-I-Islami (HUJI) and Harakat ul-Mujahedin (HUM), which advocate similar objectives in Pakistan and Jammu and Kashmir. The leaders of HUJI-B and HUM both signed the February 1998 fatwa sponsored by Usama bin Ladin that declared American civilians to be legitimate targets for attack.

Activities

HUJI-B was accused of stabbing a senior Bangladeshi journalist in November 2000 for making a documentary on the plight of Hindus in Bangladesh. HUJI-B and its detained leader, Mufti Hannan, are suspected in the assassination attempt in July 2000 of Bangladeshi Prime Minister Sheikh Hasina.

Strength

Unknown. Some estimates of HUJI-B cadre strength suggest several thousand members.

Location/Area of Operation

The group operates in Bangladesh.

External Aid

HUJI-B funding comes from a variety of sources. Several international Islamic NGOs, including the South African-based Servants of Suffering Humanity, may have funneled money to Bangladeshi militant groups, including HUJI-B. HUJI-B also can draw funding from militant madrassa leaders and teachers in Bangladesh.

Hizb-I Islami Gulbuddin (HIG)

Description

Gulbuddin Hikmatyar founded Hizb-I Islami Gulbuddin (HIG) as a faction of the Hizb-I Islami party in 1977, and it was one of the major mujahedin groups in the jihad against the Soviet occupation of Afghanistan. Hikmatyar has long-established links with Usama bin Ladin. In the early 1990s, Hikmatyar ran several terrorist training camps in Afghanistan and was a pioneer in sending mercenary fighters to other Islamic conflicts. Hikmatyar offered to shelter bin Ladin after the latter fled Sudan in 1996 and has consistently offered public support for him since the 9/11 attacks. Hikmatyar has issued regular statements on the need for Afghans to reject the international community's presence in their country. In 2005, he responded to protests against Danish cartoons of the prophet Mohammad with a new call for the expulsion of international troops from Afghanistan.

Activities

HIG has staged small attacks in its attempt to force the international community to withdraw from Afghanistan, overthrow the Afghan government, and establish an Islamic state. U.S. troops have encountered regular violence in Konar, the area of Afghanistan in which HIG is most active, which has occasionally led to U.S. casualties, and it is likely that HIG is responsible for at least some of this violence.

Strength

Unknown, but possibly could have hundreds of veteran fighters on which to call.

Location/ Area of Operation

Eastern Afghanistan, particularly Konar and Nurestan Provinces, and adjacent areas of Pakistan's tribal areas.

External Aid

Unknown.

Hizbul-Mujahedin (HM)

Description

Hizbul-Mujahedin (HM) is the largest Kashmiri militant group, and was founded in 1989. It officially supports the liberation of Jammu and Kashmir and its accession to Pakistan, although some members favor independence. The group is the militant wing of Pakistan's largest Islamic political party, the Jamaat-i-Islami, and targets Indian security forces and politicians in Jammu and Kashmir. It reportedly operated in Afghanistan in the mid-1990s and trained with the Afghan Hizb-I Islami Gulbuddin (HIG) in Afghanistan until the Taliban takeover. The group, led by Syed Salahuddin, is composed primarily of ethnic Kashmiris.

Activities

HM has conducted a number of operations against Indian military targets in Jammu and Kashmir. The group also occasionally strikes at civilian targets, but has not engaged in terrorist acts outside India. HM claimed responsibility for numerous attacks within Kashmir in 2006.

Strength

Exact numbers are unknown, but estimates range from several hundred to possibly as many as 1,000 members.

Location/Area of Operation

Jammu, Kashmir, and Pakistan.

External Aid

Specific sources of external aid are unknown.

Irish National Liberation Army (INLA)

Description

The INLA is a terrorist group formed in 1975 as the military wing of the Irish Republican Socialist Party (IRSP), which split from the Official IRA (OIRA) because of OIRA's cease-fire in 1972. The group's primary aim is to end British rule in Northern Ireland, force British troops out of the province, and unite Ireland's 32 counties into a Marxist-Leninist revolutionary state. It is responsible for some of the most notorious killings of "The Troubles," including the bombing of a Ballykelly pub that killed 17 people in 1982. Bloody internal feuding has repeatedly torn the INLA. The INLA announced a cease-fire in August 1998 but continues to carry out occasional attacks and punishment beatings.

Activities

The INLA has been active in Belfast and the border areas of Northern Ireland, where it has conducted bombings, assassinations, kidnappings, hijackings, extortion, and robberies. It is also involved in drug trafficking. On occasion, it has provided advance warning to police of its attacks. Targets include the British military, Northern Ireland security forces, and Loyalist paramilitary groups. The INLA did not join the IRA's September 2005 weapons decommissioning, but continues to observe a cease-fire because, in the words of its leadership in 2003, a return to armed struggle is "not a viable option at this time." However, the group continues to recruit members and was responsible for a 2005 arson attack against the home of a local official.

Strength

Unclear, but probably fewer than 50 hardcore activists. Police counterterrorist operations and internal feuding have reduced the group's strength and capabilities.

Location/Area of Operation

Northern Ireland and the Irish Republic. Does not have a significant established presence on the UK mainland.

External Aid

Suspected in the past of receiving funds and arms from sympathizers in the United States.

Irish Republican Army (IRA)

a.k.a. Provisional Irish Republican Army (PIRA); the Provos

Description

Formed in 1969 as the clandestine armed wing of the political movement Sinn Fein, the IRA is devoted both to removing British forces from Northern Ireland and to unifying Ireland. The IRA conducted attacks until its cease-fire in 1997 and agreed to disarm as part of the 1998 Belfast Agreement, which established the basis for peace in Northern Ireland. Dissension within the IRA over support for the Northern Ireland peace process resulted in the formation of two more radical splinter groups: Continuity IRA (CIRA) in 1995, and the Real IRA (RIRA) in 1997. The IRA, sometimes referred to as the PIRA to distinguish it from RIRA and CIRA, is organized into small, tightly-knit cells under the leadership of the Army Council.

Activities

Traditional IRA activities have included bombings, assassinations, kidnappings, punishment beatings, extortion, smuggling, and robberies. Before the cease-fire in 1997, the group had conducted bombing campaigns on various targets in Northern Ireland and Great Britain, including senior British government officials, civilians, police, and British military targets. In August 2002, three suspected IRA members were arrested in Colombia on charges of helping the Revolutionary Armed Forces of Colombia (FARC) improve its explosives capabilities; the men subsequently escaped from prison and appeared in Ireland in 2005. Irish police have questioned the men but have filed no charges. Colombia has requested their extradition, which is unlikely, since Ireland has no extradition treaty with Colombia.

In July 2005, a spokesperson for the IRA made a statement calling for an end to all forms of IRA illegal activity. This statement was confirmed in September 2005 by the Independent International Commission on Decommissioning's announcement that the IRA had met its commitments to put all arms beyond use. The Independent Monitoring Commission (IMC) also reported that since the September decommissioning the IRA has shown no evidence of training and recruiting terrorists or an intent to return to violence. There have been indications of IRA members using violence in 2006; however, the IMC reports that these incidents were not sanctioned by IRA leadership. The IRA has yet to abandon its extensive criminal activities, which reportedly provide the IRA and the political party Sinn Fein with millions of dollars each year.

Strength

Several hundred members and several thousand sympathizers, despite the defection of some members to RIRA and CIRA.

Local/Area of Operation

Northern Ireland, Irish Republic, Great Britain, and Europe.

External Aid

In the past, the IRA has received aid from a variety of groups and countries, and considerable training and arms from Libya and the PLO. It is suspected of receiving funds, arms, and other terrorist-related materiel from sympathizers in the United States. In addition to the apparent contact with the FARC, similarities in operations suggest the IRA has links to the ETA.

Islamic Army of Aden (IAA)[1,2,3]

a.k.a. Aden-Abyan Islamic Army (AAIA)

1 Listed on the UN 1267 Committee List.
2 Listed on the Terrorist Exclusion List.
3 Designated under Exclusion Order 13224.

Description

The Islamic Army of Aden (IAA) emerged publicly in mid-1998 when the group released a series of communiqués that expressed support for Usama bin Ladin and called for the overthrow of the Yemeni government and for operations against U.S. and other Western interests in Yemen. IAA was first designated under E.O. 13224 in September 2001.

Activities

The IAA, a group with established connections to al-Qaida and whose membership includes veteran fighters from the Soviet-Afghan war, in the past has engaged in small-scale operations such as bombings, kidnappings, and small arms attacks to further its agenda. In June 2003, the group reportedly was behind an attack against a medical convoy in the Abyan Governorate. Yemeni authorities responded with a raid on a suspected IAA facility that killed several individuals and captured others, including Khalid al-Nabi al-Yazidi, the group's leader. The IAA's previous involvement in terrorist attacks includes the throwing of a grenade into the British Embassy compound in Sanaa in October 2000. In 2001, Yemeni authorities found an IAA member and three associates responsible for that attack. In December 1998, the group kidnapped 16 British, American, and Australian tourists near Mudiyah in southern Yemen. The group's involvement in a 2003 attack against the medical convoy and reports that its leader was released from prison in October 2003 suggest that the IAA, or at least elements of the group, may remain active. However, Yemeni officials previously have claimed that IAA is operationally defunct, and the group has not claimed any attacks since 2003.

Strength

Not known.

Location/Area of Operation

Operates in the southern governorates of Yemen, primarily Aden and Abyan.

External Aid

Not known.

Islamic Great Eastern Raiders-Front (IBDA-C)

Description

The Islamic Great Eastern Raiders-Front (IBDA-C) is a Sunni Salafist group that supports Islamic rule in Turkey, is sympathetic to al-Qaida, and believes that Turkey's present secular leadership is "illegal." It has been known to cooperate with various opposition elements in Turkey in attempts to destabilize the country's political structure. The group supports the establishment of a "pure Islamic" state to replace the present "corrupt" Turkish regime that is cooperating with the West. Its primary goal is the establishment of the Federative Islamic State, a goal backed by armed terrorist attacks primarily against civilian targets. It has been active since the mid-1970s.

Activities

IBDA-C has engaged in activities that minimize personal risk, such as bombings, throwing Molotov cocktails, and sabotage. The group has announced its actions and targets in publications to its members, who are free to launch independent attacks. IBDA-C typically has attacked civilian targets, including churches, charities, minority-affiliated targets, television transmitters, newspapers, pro-secular journalists, Ataturk statues, taverns, banks, clubs, and tobacco shops. One of IBDA-C's more renowned attacks was the killing of 37 people in a firebomb attack in July 1993 on a hotel in Sivas. In May 2004, Turkish police indicted seven members of the group for the assassination of retired Colonel Ihsan Guven, including the alleged leader of the "Dost" (Friend) sect, and his wife. Turkish police believe that IBDA-C has also claimed responsibility for attacks carried out by other groups in order to elevate its image. Turkish government crackdowns continued into 2006. In a May operation, the government arrested 18 members.

Strength

Unknown.

Location/Area of Operation

Turkey.

External Aid

Unknown.

Islamic International Peacekeeping Brigade (IIPB)[132]

Description

The IIPB is a terrorist group affiliated with the Chechen separatist movement demanding a single Islamic state in the North Caucasus. In 1998

[1] Listed on the UN 1267 Committee List.
[3] Designated under Exclusion Order 13224.
[2] Listed on the Terrorist Exclusion List.

Chechen extremist leader Shamil Basayev established the IIPB, consisting of Chechens, Arabs, and other foreign fighters, which he led with Saudi-born mujahedin leader Ibn al-Khattab until the latter's death in March 2002. In July 2006, Basayev himself was killed by Russian forces. The IIPB was one of three groups affiliated with Chechen guerrillas that seized Moscow's Dubrovka Theater and took more than 700 hostages in October 2002. While this group has not been identified by the mujahedin media as conducting attacks since its designation three years ago, those Arab mujahedin still operating in Chechnya now fall under the command of Abu Hafs al-Urduni, who assumed the IIPB leadership in April 2004 after the death of Khattab's successor, Abu al-Walid. IIPB was designated under E.O. 13224 in February 2003 and listed by the UN al-Qaida/Taliban Sanctions Committee for its associations with al-Qaida.

Activities

The IIPB has engaged in terrorist and guerilla operations against Russian forces, pro-Russian Chechen forces, and Chechen non-combatants.

Strength

At its peak, up to 400 fighters, including as many as 100 Arabs and other foreign fighters, but almost certainly has suffered significant attrition.

Location/Area of Operation

Primarily in Russia and adjacent areas of the North Caucasus, particularly in the mountainous south of Chechnya, with major logistical activities in Georgia, Azerbaijan, and Turkey.

External Aid

The IIPB and its Arab leaders appear to be a primary conduit for Islamic funding of the Chechen guerrillas, in part through links to al-Qaida-related financiers on the Arabian Peninsula.

Jamaatul-Mujahedin Bangladesh (JMB)

Description

JMB is a Bangladeshi Islamic extremist group dedicated to the use of violence to achieve its objective of a state based on Islamic law. JMB, which emerged in the late 1990s, has been associated with several bombings during the past several years. The Bangladeshi government banned the group in February 2005.

Activities

On August 17, 2005, JMB claimed responsibility for nearly 500 simultaneous explosions throughout Bangladesh. Subsequent bombings, possibly involving suicide bombers, targeted judges, police, government offices, traditional folk festivals and cultural groups, and local non-governmental organizations. The Bangladeshi government has captured several of the group's most important leaders.

Strength

Estimates range as high as 11,000.

Location/Area of Operation

Bangladesh.

External Aid

JMB probably also receives some support from persons of Bangladeshi origin living in Europe and the Middle East.

Jamiat ul-Mujahedin (JUM)[2]

Description

The JUM is a small pro-Pakistan militant group formed in Jammu and Kashmir in 1990 that seeks to unite Jammu and Kashmir with Pakistan. Followers are mostly Kashmiris, but the group includes some Pakistanis.

Activities

Has conducted a number of operations against Indian military and political targets in Jammu and Kashmir, including two grenade attacks in 2004.

Strength

Unknown.

Location/Area of Operation

Jammu, Kashmir, and Pakistan.

External Aid

Unknown.

---

[2] Listed on the Terrorist Exclusion List.

Japanese Red Army (JRA)[2]

a.k.a. Anti-Imperialist International Brigade (AIIB)

Description

The JRA is an international terrorist group formed around 1970 after breaking away from the Japanese Communist League—Red Army Faction. The JRA's historical goal has been to overthrow the Japanese government and monarchy and to help foment world revolution. The JRA's leader, Fusako Shigenobu, claimed that the forefront of the battle against international imperialism was in Palestine, and in the early 1970s she led her small group to the Middle East. After her arrest in November 2000, Shigenobu announced she intended to pursue her goals using a legitimate political party rather than revolutionary violence, and the group apparently disbanded in April 2001.

Activities

During the 1970s, the JRA carried out a series of attacks around the world, including the 1972 massacre at Lod Airport in Israel, two Japanese airliner hijackings, an attempted takeover of the U.S. Embassy in Kuala Lumpur, and the 1974 seizure of the French Embassy in The Hague, in which the ambassador was among the hostages. During the late 1980s, the JRA began to single out American targets and used car bombs and rockets in attempted attacks on U.S. Embassies in Jakarta, Rome, and Madrid. In April 1988, JRA operative Yu Kikumura was arrested with explosives on the New Jersey Turnpike, apparently planning an attack to coincide with the bombing of a USO club in Naples, a suspected JRA operation that killed five, including a U.S. servicewoman. Kikimura was convicted of the charges and is serving a lengthy prison sentence in the United States. JRA operative Tsutomu Shirosaki, captured in 1996, is also jailed in the United States. In 2000, Lebanon deported four members it arrested in 1997 to Japan, but granted a fifth operative, Kozo Okamoto, political asylum. Longtime leader Shigenobu was arrested in November 2000 and faced charges of terrorism and passport fraud. In February 2006, Shingenobu was sentenced to 20 years in prison for coordinating the 1974 French embassy siege. Four JRA members remain in North Korea following their involvement in an airline hijacking in 1970; five of their family members returned to Japan in 2004.

Strength

At its peak, the group claimed to have 30 to 40 members.

Location/Area of Operation

Possibly in Asia.

[2] Listed on the Terrorist Exclusion List.

External Aid

Unknown.

Kumpulan Mujahedin Malaysia (KMM)

a.k.a. Kumpulan Militan Malaysia

Description

Kumpulan Mujahedin Malaysia (KMM) favors the overthrow of the Malaysian government and the creation of an Islamic state comprising Malaysia, Indonesia, and the southern Philippines (and Southern Thailand). Malaysian authorities believe an extremist wing of the KMM has engaged in terrorist acts and has close ties to the regional terrorist organization Jemaah Islamiya (JI). Key JI leaders, including the group's spiritual head, Abu Bakar Bashir, and JI operational leader Hambali, reportedly had great influence over KMM members. The Government of Singapore asserts that a Singaporean JI member assisted the KMM in buying a boat to support jihad activities in Indonesia.

Activities

Malaysia continues to hold a number of KMM members under the Internal Security Act for activities deemed threatening to Malaysia's national security, including planning to wage jihad, possession of weaponry, bombings, robberies, the murder of a former state assembly member, and planning attacks on foreigners, including U.S. citizens. A number of those detained also are believed to be members of Jemaah Islamiya. Several of the arrested KMM militants reportedly have undergone military training in Afghanistan, and some fought with the Afghan mujahedin during the war against the former Soviet Union. Some members allegedly have ties to Islamic extremist organizations in Indonesia and the Philippines. One alleged KMM member was sentenced to 10 years in prison for unlawful possession of firearms, explosives, and ammunition; eight other alleged members in detention since 2001 were later released in July and November 2004; three others were freed in November 2005. In March 2004, alleged KMM leader Nik Adli Nik Abdul Aziz and other suspected KMM members went on a hunger strike as part of an unsuccessful bid for freedom, but the Malaysian court in September 2004 rejected their applications for a writ of habeas corpus. In September 2005, detention orders for Aziz and eight other alleged KMM members were extended for another two years. The Malaysian government is confident that the arrests of KMM leaders have crippled the organization and rendered it incapable of engaging in militant activities. In May 2004, Malaysian officials denied Thailand's charge that the KMM was involved in the Muslim separatist movement in southern Thailand.

Strength

KMM's current membership is unknown.

Location/Area of Operation

The KMM is reported to have networks in the Malaysian states of Perak, Johor, Kedah, Selangor, Terengganu, and Kelantan. They also operate in Kuala Lumpur. The KMM has ties to radical Indonesian Islamic groups.

External Aid

Largely unknown, probably self-financing.

Lord's Resistance Army (LRA)[2]

Description

The LRA, founded in 1987, succeeded the ethnic Acholi-dominated Holy Spirit Movement and other insurgent groups. LRA leader Joseph Kony has called for the overthrow of the Ugandan government and its replacement with a regime run on the basis of the Ten Commandments. More frequently, however, he has spoken of the liberation and honor of the Acholi people, whom he sees as oppressed by the "foreign" government of Ugandan President Museveni. Kony is the LRA's undisputed leader. He claims to have supernatural powers and to receive messages from spirits, which he uses to formulate the LRA's strategy.

Activities

Since the early 1990s, the LRA has kidnapped some 20,000 Ugandan children, mostly ethnic Acholi, to replenish its ranks. Kony despises Acholi elders for having given up the fight against Museveni and relies on abducted children who can be brutally indoctrinated to fight for the LRA. The LRA kidnaps children and adult civilians to become soldiers, porters, and "wives" for LRA leaders. The LRA prefers to attack camps for internally displaced persons and other civilian targets, avoiding direct engagement with the Ugandan military. The LRA stepped up its activities from 2002 to 2004 after the Ugandan army, with the Sudanese government's permission, attacked LRA positions inside Sudan. By late 2003, the number of internally displaced persons had doubled to 1.4 million, and the LRA had pushed deep into non-Acholi areas where it had never previously operated. During 2004, a combination of military pressure, offers of amnesty, and several rounds of negotiation markedly degraded LRA capabilities due to death, desertion, and defection of senior commanders. In October 2005, the International Criminal Court (ICC) issued arrest warrants for

[2] Listed on the Terrorist Exclusion List.

Kony and four other top LRA leaders. Since February 2006, the Government of Southern Sudan has been holding peace talks between the LRA and the Ugandan government.

Strength

Estimated at 500 to 700 fighters.

Location/Area of Operation

Northern Uganda, southern Sudan, and northeast Democratic Republic of the Congo.

External Aid

Although the LRA has been supported by the Government of Sudan in the past, the Sudanese now appear to be cooperating with the Government of Uganda in a campaign to eliminate LRA sanctuaries in Sudan.

Loyalist Volunteer Force (LVF)

Description

An extreme Loyalist group formed in 1996 as a faction of the Ulster Volunteer Force (UVF), the LVF did not emerge publicly until 1997. It is composed largely of UVF hardliners who have sought to prevent a political settlement with Irish nationalists in Northern Ireland by attacking Catholic politicians, civilians, and Protestant politicians who endorse the Northern Ireland peace process. LVF occasionally uses the Red Hand Defenders as a cover name for its actions but has also called for the group's disbandment. In October 2001, the British government ruled the LVF had broken the cease-fire it declared in 1998 after linking the group to the murder of a journalist. According to the Independent International Commission on Decommissioning, the LVF decommissioned a small amount of weapons in December 1998, but it has not repeated this gesture. The LVF was designated under E.O. 13224 in December 2001.

Activities

The group conducts bombings, kidnappings, and close-quarter shooting attacks. It finances its activities with drug money and other criminal activities. LVF attacks have been particularly vicious; the group has murdered numerous Catholic civilians with no political or paramilitary affiliations, including an 18-year-old Catholic girl in July 1997 because she had a Protestant boyfriend. LVF terrorists also have conducted successful attacks against Irish targets in Irish border towns. From 2000 to August 2005, the LVF engaged in a violent feud with other Loyalists, which left several men dead. In October 2005, the group said that it would stand down its "military units," but the Independent Monitoring Commission has no evidence of the LVF disbanding.

Strength

Small, perhaps dozens of active members.

Location/Area of Operation

Northern Ireland and Ireland.

External Aid

None.

New Red Brigades/Communist Combatant Party (BR/PCC)[2]

a.k.a. Brigate Rosse/Partito Comunista Combattente

Description

This Marxist-Leninist group is a successor to the Red Brigades, active in the 1970s and 1980s. In addition to ideology, both groups share the same symbol, a five-pointed star inside a circle. The group is opposed to Italy's foreign and labor policies and to NATO.

Activities

In 2003, Italian authorities captured at least seven members of the BR/PCC, dealing the terrorist group a severe blow to its operational effectiveness, and the group continued to suffer setbacks in 2005 and 2006, with its leadership in prison, key suspects convicted and sentenced, and additional arrests made. In June 2005, a Rome court sentenced five BR/PCC members to life in prison for the 2002 assassination of Labor Ministry external adviser Marco Biagi. One month later, three of the five also were found guilty of the assassination of Labor Ministry external adviser Massimo D'Antona in 1999, again incurring a life sentence. An additional nine BR/PCC suspects were sentenced to between four and nine years, and some convicted members provided valuable information to Italian authorities, leading to additional arrests. In December 2005, an Italian judge refused to pardon Adriano Sofri, leader of Continuous Struggle (Lotta Continua), a precursor movement to the Red Brigades, whose life sentence was suspended for health reasons. Italian authorities in early December 2006 arrested Fabio Matteini, suspected of trying to recruit new members in an effort to revive the group. The BR/PCC in recent years has financed its activities in part through armed robberies.

[2] Listed on the Terrorist Exclusion List.

Strength

Fewer than 20.

Location/Area of Operation

Italy.

External Aid

Has obtained weapons from abroad.

People Against Gangsterism and Drugs (PAGAD)

a.k.a. Muslims Against Global Oppression; Muslims Against Illegitimate Leaders

Description

People Against Gangsterism and Drugs (PAGAD) and its ally Qibla (an Islamic fundamentalist group that favors political Islam and takes an anti-U.S. and anti-Israel stance), view the South African government as a threat to Islamic values. The two groups work to promote a greater political voice for South African Muslims. PAGAD has used front names such as Muslims Against Global Oppression and Muslims Against Illegitimate Leaders when launching anti-Western protests and campaigns.

Activities

PAGAD formed in November 1995 as a vigilante group in reaction to crime in some neighborhoods of Cape Town. In September 1996, a change in the group's leadership resulted in a change in the group's goal, and it began to support violent jihad to establish an Islamic state. Between 1996 and 2000, PAGAD conducted a total of 189 bomb attacks, including nine bombings in the western Cape that caused serious injuries. PAGAD's targets included South African authorities, moderate Muslims, synagogues, gay nightclubs, tourist attractions, and Western-associated restaurants. PAGAD is believed to have masterminded the bombing on August 1998 of the Cape Town Planet Hollywood and the 2000 attack on a New York Bagel restaurant in Cape Town. Since 2001, PAGAD's violent activities have been severely curtailed by law enforcement and prosecutorial efforts against leading members of the organization. Qibla leadership has organized demonstrations against visiting U.S. dignitaries and other protests, but the extent of PAGAD's involvement is uncertain.

Strength

Early estimates were several hundred members. Current operational strength is unknown, but probably vastly diminished.

Location/Area of Operation

Operates mainly in the Cape Town area.

External Aid

May have ties to international Islamic extremists.

Rajah Solaiman Movement (RSM)

Description

The RSM is a Philippines-based Islamic extremist group comprising Christian converts to Islam, many of whom had embraced extremist Islamic ideology while working in the Middle East. RSM promotes the use of violence and terrorism against Philippine Christians and Westerners with the aim of turning the Philippines into an Islamic state. The group is named after Rajah Solaiman, the last indigenous Muslim ruler of Manila before Spanish rule began in the 16th century.

Activities

The RSM has assisted with the terrorist plots of the Abu Sayyaf Group (ASG) in Manila and other areas in the northern Philippines. It was involved in ASG's bombing of SuperFerry 14 in February 2004, and the February 2005 Valentine's Day bombings, according to Philippine security officials. In 2005 the RSM suffered several major setbacks when in March, Philippine security forces seized more than 1,300 pounds of explosives from an RSM safe house in metropolitan Manila, and in October, Philippine intelligence agents arrested RSM leader Ahmad Santos in Zamboanga City and charged him with plotting to bomb high profile targets, including the U.S. Embassy in Manila. Two months later, Philippine security forces arrested another RSM leader in Zamboanga City. Philippine officials subsequently claimed that debriefing captives helped them thwart an alleged RSM plot to conduct attacks in Manila during the Christmas 2005 holiday season. In late 2006, another RSM leader, Feliciano de los Reyes was arrested.

Strength

The exact number of members in the RSM is unknown, but the group likely has fewer than 50 members.

Location/Area of Operation

The RSM operates throughout the Philippines and maintains a significant presence in metropolitan Manila. Some RSM operatives trained alongside members of the Abu Sayyaf Group and other militants in the southern Philippines.

External Aid

The Abu Sayyaf Group and Jemaah Islamiya have provided training, funds, and operational assistance to the RSM. Some Middle East-based non-governmental organizations and other sympathizers also may provide funds to the RSM.

Red Hand Defenders (RHD)

Description

The RHD is a terrorist group formed in 1998 and composed largely of Protestant hardliners from Loyalist groups observing a cease-fire. RHD seeks to prevent a political settlement with Irish nationalists by attacking Catholic civilian interests in Northern Ireland.

In January 2002, the group announced all staff at Catholic schools in Belfast and Catholic postal workers were legitimate targets. Despite calls in February 2002 by the Ulster Defense Association (UDA), Ulster Freedom Fighters (UFF), and Loyalist Volunteer Force (LVF) to announce its disbandment, RHD continued to make threats and issue claims of responsibility. RHD is a cover name often used by elements of the banned UDA and LVF. RHD was designated under E.O. 13224 in December 2001.

Activities

In early 2003, the RHD claimed responsibility for killing two UDA members as a result of what is described as Loyalist internecine warfare. It also claimed responsibility for a bomb that was left in the offices of Republican Sinn Fein in West Belfast, although the device was defused and no one was injured. In recent years, the group has carried out numerous pipe bombings and arson attacks against "soft" civilian targets such as homes, churches, and private businesses. In January 2002, the group bombed the home of a prison official in North Belfast. Twice in 2002 the group claimed responsibility for attacks—the murder of a Catholic postman and a Catholic teenager—that were later claimed by the UDA-UFF, further blurring distinctions between the groups. In 2001, RHD claimed responsibility for killing five persons.

Strength

Up to 20 members, some of whom have experience in terrorist tactics and bombmaking. Police arrested one member in June 2001 for making a hoax bomb threat.

Location/Area of Operation

Northern Ireland.

External Aid

None.

Revolutionary Proletarian Initiative Nuclei (NIPR)

Description

The NIPR is a clandestine leftist extremist group that appeared in Rome in 2000. It adopted the logo of the Red Brigades of the 1970s and 1980s, an encircled five point star, for its declarations. NIPR opposes Italy's foreign and labor policies. The group has targeted property interests rather than personnel in its attacks.

Activities

The NIPR has not claimed responsibility for any attacks since an April 2001 bomb attack on a building housing a U.S.-Italian relations association and an international affairs institute in Rome's historic center. The NIPR claimed to have carried out a bombing in May 2000 in Rome at an oversight committee facility for implementation of the law on strikes in public services.

Strength

Fewer than 20 members.

Location/Area of Operation

Mainly in Rome, Milan, Lazio, and Tuscany.

External Aid

None evident.

Revolutionary Struggle (RS)

Description

RS is a radical leftist group that is anti-Greek establishment and ideologically aligns itself with the Revolutionary Organization 17 November.

Activities

RS is widely regarded as the most dangerous indigenous Greek terrorist group still active and has been linked to attacks against Americans. RS first became known when the group conducted a bombing in 2003 against the courthouse where trials of alleged 17 November members were occurring. In 2004, the group detonated four improvised explosive devices at a police station in Athens. These two attacks were notable for their apparent attempts to target and kill first responders, the first time a Greek terrorist group had used this tactic. RS claimed responsibility for a large explosion in December 2005 in Constitution Square in the center of Athens, apparently targeting the Ministry of National Economy, injuring three and badly damaging the facade of a post office and other buildings. The group claimed responsibility for a bomb explosion in May 2006, near the residence of former Minister of Public Order Giorgos Voulgarakis. The remotely detonated bomb was placed next to a school along the minister's usual route to work and exploded just minutes before he was due to pass. The explosion wrecked several cars but caused no injuries. RS also claimed responsibility for a rocket-propelled-grenade (RPG) attack against the U.S. Embassy on January 12, 2007. The attack occurred early in the morning when few Embassy personnel were working and there were no injuries, but the RPG damaged a room at the front of the Embassy.

Strength

Likely less than 50 members.

Location/Area of Operation

Athens, Greece.

External Aid

Unknown.

Riyadus-Salikhin Reconnaissance and Sabotage Battalion of Chechen Martyrs (RSRSBCM)[123]

Description

Riyadus-Salikhin Reconnaissance and Sabotage Battalion of Chechen Martyrs (RSRSBCM), led by Chechen extremist Shamil Basayev, uses terrorism as part of an effort to secure an independent Muslim state in the North Caucasus. Basayev claimed the group was responsible for the Beslan school hostage crisis of September 2004, which culminated in the deaths of about 330 people; simultaneous suicide bombings aboard two Russian civilian airliners in August 2004; and a third suicide bombing outside a Moscow subway that same month. The group has not mounted a terrorist attack since the Beslan operation. The RSRSBCM, whose name translates into English as "Requirements for Getting into Paradise," was not known to Western observers before October 2002, when it participated in the seizure of the Dubrovka Theater in Moscow. The group was designated under E.O. 13224 in February 2003. The group's viability is in question since its leader Shamil Basayev was killed by Russian forces in July 2006.

[1] Listed on the UN 1267 Committee List.
[2] Listed on the Terrorist Exclusion List.
[3] Designated under Exclusion Order 13224.

Activities

RSRSBCM has primarily engaged in terrorist and guerilla operations against Russian forces, pro-Russian Chechen forces, and Russian and Chechen non-combatants.

Strength

Probably no more than 50 fighters at any given time.

Location/Area of Operation

Primarily Russia.

External Aid

May receive some external assistance from foreign mujahedin.

Sipah-I-Sahaba/Pakistan (SSP)

a.k.a. Millat-I-Islami Pakistan

Description

The Sipah-I-Sahaba/Pakistan (SSP) is a Sunni sectarian group that follows the Deobandi school. Violently anti-Shia, the SSP emerged in central Punjab in the mid-1980s as a response to the Iranian revolution. Pakistani President Musharraf banned the SSP in January 2002. In August 2002, the SSP renamed itself Millat-i-Islami Pakistan, and Musharraf re-banned the group in November 2003. The SSP also has operated as a political party, winning seats in Pakistan's National Assembly.

Activities

The group's activities range from organizing political rallies calling for Shia to be declared non-Muslims to assassinating prominent Shia leaders. The group was responsible for attacks on Shia worshippers in May 2004, when at least 50 people were killed.

Strength

The SSP may have approximately 3,000 to 6,000 trained activists who carry out various kinds of sectarian activities.

Location/Area of Operation

The SSP has influence in all four provinces of Pakistan. It is considered to be one of the most powerful sectarian groups in the country.

External Aid

The SSP reportedly receives significant funding from Saudi Arabia and wealthy private donors in Pakistan. Funds also are acquired from other sources, including other Sunni extremist groups, madrassas, and contributions by political groups.

Special Purpose Islamic Regiment (SPIR)[1 2 3]

Description

The SPIR is one of three Chechen-affiliated terrorist groups that furnished personnel to carry out the seizure of the Dubrovka Theater in Moscow in October 2002. The SPIR has had at least seven commanders since it was founded in the late 1990s. Movsar Barayev, who led and was killed during the theater standoff, was the first publicly identified leader. The group continues to conduct guerrilla operations in Chechnya under its current leader, Amir Aslan, whose true identity is not known. SPIR was designated under E.O. 13224 in February 2003. In 2006, SPIR continued to target official Russian targets and Chechen elements it believe to be sympathetic to Russia.

Activities

SPIR has primarily engaged in guerrilla operations against Russian forces. Has also been involved in various hostage and ransom operations, including the execution of ethnic Chechens who have cooperated with Russian authorities.

Strength

Probably no more than 100 fighters at any given time.

Location/Area of Operation

Primarily Russia.

External Aid

May receive some external assistance from foreign mujahedin.

Al-Tawhid w'al Jihad (TWJ)

a.k.a. Tawhid Islamic Brigades; al-Tawhid Wa al-Jihad; Monotheism and Jihad Organization

---

1 Listed on the UN 1267 Committee List.
2 Listed on the Terrorist Exclusion List.
3 Designated under Exclusion Order 13224.

Description

The TWJ is an Egypt-based Islamic extremist group motivated by Cairo's harsh treatment of the Bedouin community and difficult economic conditions in the Sinai. This group is comprised of radicalized Sinai Bedouin, criminals, and smugglers who use their knowledge of the rugged Sinai terrain and their compartmented cell structure to attack Western and Israeli tourist targets.

Activities

The TWJ has conducted bombings and suicide attacks, such as attacks at Taba in October 2004, Sharm ash Shaykh in July 2005, Dhahab in April 2006, and against the Multinational Force and Observers (MFO) in August 2005 and April 2006.

Strength

Unknown. Egyptian security services have killed or captured many high-ranking TWJ members during the past two years.

Location/Area of Operation

Sinai, Gaza.

External Aid

Unknown.

Tunisian Combatant Group (TCG)[1 2 3]

a.k.a. Jama'a Combattante Tunisienne

Description

The Tunisian Combatant Group (TCG), also known as the Jama'a Combattante Tunisienne, seeks to establish an Islamic regime in Tunisia and has targeted U.S. and Western interests. The group is an offshoot of the banned Tunisian Islamist movement, an-Nahda. Founded around 2000 by Tarek Maaroufi and Saifallah Ben Hassine, the TCG has drawn members from the Tunisian diaspora in Europe and elsewhere. It has lost some of its leadership, but may still exist, particularly in Western Europe. Belgian authorities arrested Maaroufi in late 2001 and sentenced him to six years in prison in 2003 for his role in the assassination of anti-Taliban commander Ahmed Shah Massoud two days before 9/11. The TCG was designated

[1] Listed on the UN 1267 Committee List.
[2] Listed on the Terrorist Exclusion List.
[3] Designated under Exclusion Order 13224.

under E.O. 13224 in October 2002. Historically, the group has been associated with al-Qaida as well. Members also have ties to other North African extremist groups. The TCG was designated for sanctions under UNSCR 1333 in December 2000.

Activities

Tunisians associated with the TCG are part of the support network of the broader international terrorist movement. According to European press reports, TCG members or affiliates in the past have engaged in trafficking falsified documents and recruiting for terror training camps in Afghanistan. Some TCG associates were suspected of planning an attack against the United States, Algerian, and Tunisian diplomatic missions in Rome in April 2001. Some members reportedly maintain ties to the Algerian Salafist Group for Preaching and Combat.

Strength

Unknown.

Location/Area of Operation

Western Europe and Afghanistan.

External Aid

Unknown.

Tupac Amaru Revolutionary Movement (MRTA)

Description

MRTA is a traditional Marxist-Leninist revolutionary movement formed in 1983 from remnants of the Movement of the Revolutionary Left, a Peruvian insurgent group active in the 1960s. It aims to establish a Marxist regime and to rid Peru of all imperialist elements, primarily U.S. and Japanese influence. Peru's counterterrorist program has diminished the group's ability to conduct terrorist attacks, and the MRTA has suffered from infighting, the imprisonment or deaths of senior leaders, and the loss of leftist support.

Activities

MRTA previously conducted bombings, kidnappings, ambushes, and assassinations, but recent activity has fallen drastically. In December 1996, 14 MRTA members occupied the Japanese Ambassador's residence in Lima and held 72 hostages for more than four months. Peruvian forces stormed the residence in April 1997, rescuing all but one of the remaining hostages and killing all 14 group members, including the remaining leaders. The group has not conducted a significant terrorist operation since and appears more focused on obtaining the release of imprisoned MRTA members, although there are reports of low-level rebuilding efforts.

Strength

Believed to be no more than 100 members, consisting largely of young fighters who lack leadership skills and experience.

Location/Area of Operation

Peru, with supporters throughout Latin America and Western Europe. Many exiled members live in Bolivia.

External Aid

None.

Tehrik Nefaz-I-Shariat Muhammad (TNSM)

Description

Maulawi Sufi Muhammed (now imprisoned) established TNSM in May 1989 in the former Malakand District of the Northwest Frontier Province (NWFP) of Pakistan with the goal of instituting strict Islamic law in the region because they believe the government failed to institute Sharia law in the NWFP. The group held massive rallies in 1994 and effectively shut down the Malakand District. The uprising ended after the Pakistani government agreed to implement Sharia law in the Malakand District. Islamabad banned the group in 2002 in response to TNSM's deployment of fighters to Afghanistan to fight with the Taliban. Since Sufi Muhammad's arrest in early 2002, the leadership of the group has been in flux. Both Maulawi Faqir Muhammad and Maulawi Fazlullah-Sufi Muhammad's son-in-law-have been mentioned as possible leaders of the group. Faqir Muhammad in November 2006 publicly pledged to continue the jihad in Afghanistan under Taliban leader Mullah Omar.

Activites

TNSM is a party to 2006 peace negotiations with Pakistan. Prior to the peace negotiations, the Pakistani government released nine prisoners associated with TNSM, to include Faqir Muhammad's brother and two senior clerics. On October 28, 2006, TNSM staged an anti-U.S. rally and vowed to continue to support the Taliban but agreed not to shelter foreigners. On October 30, 2006, a madrassa suspected of hosting a terrorist training camp was destroyed in a counterterrorism operation and Pakistani forces killed Maulana Liaqat, the madrassa's director and deputy for the group. At a protest rally following the operation, Faqir Muhammad declared he would continue to wage jihad, but he renewed his pledge to abide by the peace accords and not attack the Pakistani government. Faqir also denied reports that al-Qaida deputy leader Ayman al-Zawahiri was present at the madrassa. Press reports alleged TNSM was responsible for a suicide bombing on November 8 that killed 35 soldiers in Dargai, Pakistan, although the group did not claim responsibility. Pakistan security agencies have reopened investigations on members following this attack. Newspaper announcements requested certain members to appear in court and face charges filed against them under anti-terrorism laws.

Strength

Exact numbers are unknown; however, TNSM has recruited very high numbers of fighters in the past (in the thousands) and has also held demonstrations attended by several thousand people.

Location/Area of Operation

Eastern Afghanistan, Northern Pakistan—particularly Bajaur Agency and Malakand District.

External Aid

TNSM was founded to pursue the implementation of Sharia in the NWFP and stongly supports the Taliban. The group has also been linked to al-Qaida, especially through Faqir Muhammad who has stated that he would welcome Ayman al-Zawahiri and Usama Bin Ladin if they were to come to his area.

Turkish Hizballah

Description

Turkish Hizballah is a Kurdish Sunni Islamic terrorist organization that arose in the early 1980s in response to the Kurdistan Workers' Party (PKK)'s secularist approach of establishing an independent Kurdistan. Turkish Hizballah spent its first 10 years fighting the PKK, accusing the group of atrocities against Muslims in southeastern Turkey, where Turkish Hizballah seeks to establish an independent Islamic state.

Activities

Beginning in the mid-1990s, Turkish Hizballah, which is unrelated to Lebanese Hizballah, expanded its target base and modus operandi from killing PKK militants to conducting low-level bombings against liquor stores, bordellos, and other establishments the organization considered "anti-Islamic." In January 2000, Turkish security forces killed Huseyin Velioglu, the leader of Turkish Hizballah, in a shootout at a safe house in Istanbul. The incident sparked a year-long series of counterterrorist operations against the group that resulted in the detention of some 2,000 individuals; authorities arrested several hundred of them on criminal charges. At the same time, police recovered nearly 70 bodies of Turkish and Kurdish businessmen and journalists whom Turkish Hizballah had tortured and brutally murdered during the mid-to-late 1990s. The group began targeting official Turkish interests in January 2001, when its operatives assassinated the Diyarbakir police chief in the group's most sophisticated operation to date. Turkish Hizballah has not conducted a major operation since 2001, and probably is focusing at present on recruitment, fundraising, and reorganization.

Strength

Possibly a few hundred members and several thousand supporters.

Location/Area of Operation

Primarily the Diyarbakir region of southeastern Turkey.

External Aid

It is widely believed that Turkey's security apparatus originally backed Turkish Hizballah to help the Turkish government combat the PKK. Alternative views are that the Turkish government ignored Turkish Hizballah activities because its primary targets were PKK members and supporters, or that the government simply had to prioritize scarce resources and was unable to wage war on both groups simultaneously. Allegations of collusion have never been laid to rest, and the Government of Turkey continues to issue denials. Turkish Hizballah also is suspected of having ties with Iran, although there is not sufficient evidence to establish a link.

Ulster Defense Association/Ulster Freedom Fighters (UDA/UFF)

Description

The Ulster Defense Association (UDA), the largest Loyalist paramilitary group in Northern Ireland, was formed in 1971 as an umbrella organization for Loyalist paramilitary groups such as the Ulster Freedom Fighters (UFF). Today, the UFF constitutes almost the entire UDA membership. The UDA/UFF declared a series of cease-fires between 1994 and 1998. In September 2001, the UDA/UFF's Inner Council withdrew its support for Northern Ireland's Good Friday Agreement. The following month, after a series of murders, bombings, and street violence, the British government ruled the UDA/UFF's cease-fire defunct. The dissolution of the organization's political wing, the Ulster Democratic Party, soon followed. In January 2002, however, the UDA created the Ulster Political Research Group to serve in a similar capacity. In October 2006, a splinter group of the UDA, calling itself Beyond Conflict, publicly announced its mission to assist former UDA members to disengage from the conflict and develop dialogue with local neighborhoods. Designated under E.O. 13224 in December 2001.

Activities

The UDA/UFF has evolved into a criminal organization deeply involved in drug trafficking and other moneymaking criminal activities through six largely independent "brigades." It also has been involved in murder, shootings, arson, assaults, and exiling. According to the Independent Monitoring Commission (IMC), "the UDA has the capacity to launch serious, if crude, attacks." Some UDA activities of a sectarian nature directed at the Catholic community are aimed at so-called "soft" targets, and often have taken place at the interface between the Protestant and Catholic communities, especially in Belfast.

Strength

Estimates vary from 2,000 to 5,000 members, with several hundred active in paramilitary operations.

Location/Area of Operation

Northern Ireland.

External Aid

Probably obtains weapons from abroad.

Ulster Volunteer Force (UVF)

Description

The UVF is a Loyalist terrorist group formed in 1966 to oppose liberal reforms in Northern Ireland that members feared would lead to unification of Ireland. The group adopted the name of an earlier organization formed in 1912 to combat Home Rule for Ireland. The UVF's goal is to maintain Northern Ireland's status as part of the United Kingdom; to that end, it has killed some 550 persons since 1966. The UVF and its offshoots have been responsible for some of the most vicious attacks of "The Troubles", including horrific sectarian killings like those perpetrated in the 1970s by the UVF-affiliated "Shankill Butchers." In October 1994, the Combined Loyalist Military Command, which included the UVF, declared a cease-fire, and the

UVF's political wing, the Progressive Unionist Party, has played an active role in the peace process. Despite the cease-fire, the organization has been involved in a series of bloody feuds with other Loyalist paramilitary organizations, although the UVF is considering a stand-down similar to that of the Irish Republican Army. The Red Hand Defenders is linked to the UVF.

Activities

The UVF has been active in Belfast and the border areas of Northern Ireland, where it has carried out bombings, assassinations, kidnappings, hijackings, extortion, and robberies. UVF members have been linked to recent racial attacks on minorities; however, the UVF leadership reportedly did not authorize these assaults. On occasion, it has provided advance warning to police of its attacks. Targets include nationalist civilians, Republican paramilitary groups, and, on occasion, rival Loyalist paramilitary groups. The UVF is a relatively disciplined organization with a centralized command. The Independent Monitoring Commission has said that UVF members were responsible for the attempted murder in 2006 of Mark Haddock, a former UVF member turned police informant, and main suspect in the 1997 murder of Raymond McCord. Additionally, UVF members are suspected of murdering one individual and attempting to murder another, but the IMC assesses these actions were not sanctioned by UVF leadership.

Strength

Unclear, but probably several hundred supporters, with a smaller number of hard-core activists. Police counterterrorist operations and internal feuding have reduced the group's strength and capabilities.

Location/Area of Operation

Northern Ireland. Some support on the UK mainland.

External Aid

Suspected in the past of receiving funds and arms from sympathizers overseas.

United Liberation Front of Assam (ULFA)

Description

Northeast India's most prominent insurgent group, ULFA, an ethnic secessionist organization in the Indian state of Assam, which borders Bangladesh and Bhutan, was founded in 1979 at Rang Ghar, during anti-foreigner agitation organized by the state's powerful students' union. The group's objective is an independent Assam. ULFA enjoyed widespread support in upper Assam in its initial years, especially from 1985 to 1992. ULFA's kidnappings, killings, and extortion led New Delhi to ban the group and start a military offensive against it in 1990, which forced it to go underground. ULFA began to lose popularity in the late 1990s after it increasingly targeted civilians, including a prominent NGO activist. It lost further support for its anti-Indian stand during the 1999 Kargil conflict. In recent years, the group has been in decline, losing popular support and suffering from aggressive counterinsurgency operations by Indian security forces. The Royal Bhutan Army's attack on ULFA camps in Bhutan in 2003, and the suspension of operations by Bodo tribal insurgent groups in Assam, also contributed to the group's decline. Despite the ban on the group, New Delhi held official talks with ULFA's representative Peace Consultative Group in October 2005, which apparently have had little effect on dampening ULFA's operations against business and government targets in 2006.

Activities

ULFA trains, finances, and equips its cadres for a "liberation struggle", while extortion helps finance military training and weapons purchases. ULFA conducts hit-and-run operations on security forces in Assam, selective assassinations, and explosions in public places. During the 1980s and 1990s, ULFA undertook a series of abductions and murders, particularly of businessmen. In 2000, ULFA assassinated an Assam state minister. In 2003, ULFA killed more than 60 "outsiders" in Assam, mainly residents of the bordering state of Bihar. Some important ULFA functionaries surrendered in Assam, but incidents of violence continue, although of a lesser magnitude than in the past. In 2004, ULFA started targeting civilians and killed some 14 people in August that year.

Strength

ULFA's earlier strength of more than 3,000 dropped following the December 2003 attack on its camps in Bhutan. Total cadre strength now is estimated at several hundred, plus supporters providing safe houses and logistical and intelligence assistance.

Location/Area of Operation

ULFA is active in the state of Assam, and members transit and periodically conduct operations in parts of the neighboring states of Arunachal Pradesh, Meghalaya, and Nagaland. All ULFA camps in Bhutan are reportedly demolished.

External Aid

ULFA reportedly procures and trades in arms with other Northeast Indian groups.

Chapter 7
Legislative Requirements and Key Terms

Country Reports on Terrorism 2006 is submitted in compliance with Title 22 of the United States Code, Section 2656f (the "Act"), which requires the Department of State to provide Congress a full and complete annual report on terrorism for those countries and groups meeting the criteria of the Act. Statutory excerpts relating to the terms used in this report and a discussion of the interpretation and application of those terms in this report are included below.

Excerpts and Summary of Key Statutory Terms

Section 2656f(a) of Title 22 of the United States Code states as follows:

(a) . . . The Secretary of State shall transmit to the Speaker of the House of Representatives and the Committee on Foreign Relations of the Senate, by April 30 of each year, a full and complete report providing—

(1) (A) detailed assessments with respect to each foreign country—

(i) in which acts of international terrorism occurred which were, in the opinion of the Secretary, of major significance;

(ii) about which the Congress was notified during the preceding five years pursuant to Section 2405(j) of the Export Administration Act of 1979; and

(iii) which the Secretary determines should be the subject of such report; and

(B) detailed assessments with respect to each foreign country whose territory is being used as a sanctuary for terrorist organizations;

(2) all relevant information about the activities during the preceding year of any terrorist group, and any umbrella group under which such terrorist group falls, known to be responsible for the kidnapping or death of an American citizen during the preceding five years, any terrorist group known to have obtained or developed, or to have attempted to obtain or develop, weapons of mass destruction, any terrorist group known to be financed by countries about which Congress was notified during the preceding year pursuant to section 2405(j) of the Export Administration Act of 1979, any group designated by the Secretary as a foreign terrorist organization under section 219 of the Immigration and Nationality Act (8 U.S.C. 1189), and any other known international terrorist group which the Secretary determines should be the subject of such report;

(3) *with respect to each foreign country from which the United States Government has sought cooperation during the previous five years in the investigation or prosecution of an act of international terrorism against United States citizens or interests, information on—*

  (A) *the extent to which the government of the foreign country is cooperating with the United States Government in apprehending, convicting, and punishing the individual or individuals responsible for the act; and*

  (B) *the extent to which the government of the foreign country is cooperating in preventing further acts of terrorism against United States citizens in the foreign country; and*

(4) *with respect to each foreign country from which the United States Government has sought cooperation during the previous five years in the prevention of an act of international terrorism against such citizens or interests, the information described in paragraph (3)(B).*

Section 2656f(d) of Title 22 of the United States Code defines certain key terms used in Section 2656f(a) as follows:

(1) the term "international terrorism" means terrorism involving citizens or the territory of more than one country;

(2) the term "terrorism" means premeditated, politically motivated violence perpetrated against non-combatant targets by subnational groups or clandestine agents; and

(3) the term "terrorist group" means any group practicing, or which has significant subgroups which practice, international terrorism.

The "7120 Report."

Section 2656f(b) requires the Department of State, to the extent feasible, to provide Congress an update of the information contained in the report required to be transmitted to Congress under Section 7120(b) of the 9/11 Commission Implementation Act of 2004 (also known as the Intelligence Reform and Terrorist Prevention Act of 2004). The 7120 Report forms a part of the annual *Country Reports on Terrorism* but was provided under separate cover in 2004 and 2005. In *Country Reports on Terrorism 2006,* we have integrated the terrorist sanctuary reporting required under Sections 2656f(a)(1)(B) and (b)(2), with the information required under Section 7120(b).

Interpretation and Application of Key Terms

For purposes of this report, the terms "international terrorism," "terrorism," and "terrorist group" have the definitions assigned to them in 22 USC. 2656f(d) (see above). The term "non-combatant," which is referred to but not defined in 22 USC. 2656f(d)(2), is interpreted to mean, in addition to civilians, military personnel (whether or not armed or on duty) who are not deployed in a war zone or a war-like setting.

It should be noted that 22 USC 2656f(d) is one of many U.S. statutes and international legal instruments that concern terrorism and acts of violence, many of which use definitions for terrorism and related terms that are different from those used in this report. The interpretation and application of defined and related terms concerning terrorism in this report is therefore specific to the statutory and other requirements of the report, and is not intended to express the views of the U.S. government on how these terms should be interpreted or applied for any other purpose. Accordingly, there is not necessarily any correlation between the interpretation of terms such as "non-combatant" for purposes of this report and the meanings ascribed to similar terms pursuant to the law of war (which encapsulates the obligations of states and individuals with respect to their activities in situations of armed conflict).

Statistical Information

Pursuant to 22 USC § 2656f(b), this report must contain "to the extent practicable, complete statistical information on the number of individuals, including United States citizens and dual nationals, killed, injured, or kidnapped by each terrorist group during the preceding calendar year." This requirement is satisfied through the inclusion of a statistical annex to the report that sets out statistical information provided by the National Counterterrorism Center (NCTC). The statistical annex includes a discussion of the methodology employed by NCTC in compiling the relevant data.

This report does not contain statistical information specifically concerning combatants. The focus of the terrorism report, as is clear from the definition of terrorism, is on violence against noncombatant targets. Further, it would not be practicable to provide such statistics, as the government does not maintain—and would have great difficulty maintaining—statistics that distinguish between incidents against combatants by terrorist groups and by others, including insurgents, in Iraq and Afghanistan.

Contextual Reporting

Adverse mention in this report of individual members of any political, social, ethnic, religious, or national population is not meant to imply that all members of that population are terrorists. Indeed, terrorists rarely represent anything other than a tiny fraction of such larger populations. It is terrorist groups—and their actions—that are the focus of this report.

Furthermore, terrorist acts are part of a larger phenomenon of violence inspired by a cause, and at times the line between the two can become difficult to draw. This report includes some discretionary information in an effort to relate terrorist events to the larger context in which they occur, and to give a feel for the conflicts that spawn violence. Thus, this report will discuss terrorist acts as well as other violent incidents that are not necessarily international terrorism and therefore are not subject to the statutory reporting requirement.

National Counterterrorism Center: Annex of Statistical Information

April 13, 2007

FOREWORD

Consistent with its statutory mission to serve as the U.S. Government's knowledgebank on international terrorism, the National Counterterrorism Center (NCTC) is providing the Department of State with required statistical information to assist in the satisfaction of its reporting requirements under Section 2656f of title 22 of the U.S. Code. The statistical information included in this Annex to the 2006 Country Reports on Terrorism is drawn from the data NCTC maintains on the www.nctc.gov website.

Section 2656f(b) of Title 22 of the U.S. Code requires the State Department to include in its annual report on terrorism "to the extent practicable, complete statistical information on the number of individuals, including United States citizens and dual nationals, killed, injured, or kidnapped by each terrorist group during the preceding calendar year." While NCTC keeps statistics on the annual number of incidents of "terrorism," its ability to track the specific groups responsible for each incident involving killings, kidnappings, and injuries is significantly limited by the availability of reliable open source information, particularly for events involving small numbers of casualties. Moreover, specific details about victims, damage, perpetrators, and other incident elements are frequently not fully reported in open source information.

- The statistical material in this report, therefore, is drawn from the incidents of "terrorism" that occurred in 2006 as reported in open sources information, which is the most comprehensive body of information available to NCTC for compiling data that it can provide to satisfy the above-referenced statistical requirements.

In deriving its figures for incidents of terrorism, NCTC in 2005 adopted the definition of "terrorism" that appears in the 22 U.S.C. § 2656f(d)(2), i.e., "premeditated, politically motivated violence perpetrated against noncombatant targets by subnational groups or clandestine agents."

- Through 2004 NCTC compiled statistical data on the basis of a more limited methodology tied to the definition of "international terrorism," which is also contained in 22 U.S.C. § 2656f.
- Because of the change in methodology, 2006 data is only comparable to 2005 data compiled by NCTC, the highlights of which are contained in the 2005 *Country Reports on Terrorism*.
- Subject to changes in reporting statutes, NCTC anticipates that future statistics provided by it will continue to be tied to the broader definition of "terrorism."

To record and update incident records NCTC has continued to post information in the repository for the U.S. Government's database on terrorist incidents, the Worldwide Incidents Tracking System (WITS) that was unveiled in 2005. A data management system with a more comprehensive dataset than those used in previous years, WITS is accessible on the NCTC website at www.nctc.gov for the public to have an open and transparent view of the NCTC data. NCTC will insure that the data posted to the website is updated as often as necessary by regularly posting information about new or prior incidents.

Considerations for Interpreting the Data

NCTC cautions against placing too much emphasis on any single set of incident data to gauge success or failure against the forces of terrorism. Furthermore, NCTC does not believe that a simple comparison of the total number of incidents from year to year provides a meaningful measure.

- Tallying incident data necessarily involves relying exclusively on frequently incomplete and ambiguous information-information for these statistics is not derived from federal government collection programs created or operated specifically to obtain incidents data. The quality, accuracy, and volume of incident open source reporting can vary greatly from country to country. As a result, determining whether an incident meets the NCTC criteria for a terrorist incident is often difficult and highly subjective. This is particularly true if the incident does not involve mass casualties because little information is typically available on these incidents that usually are not subject to heavy media coverage. Furthermore, in the parts of the world where there is little press coverage and little non-governmental organization presence, terrorist incidents go unreported.
- Incident tallies exclusively do not provide a complete picture of the magnitude or seriousness of the terrorism challenge confronting a country or region. For example, that 50 percent of the incidents in the NCTC database involve no loss of life would be only one factor for assessing the danger of terrorism globally. Moreover, different factors

weigh more heavily than others in assessing the dangers posed by terrorism. For example, an attack that kills 100 civilians is likely to be considered more alarming than an attack that damages a pipeline but harms no one; however, each attack is simply tallied as one incident.

- Counting protocols matter and inevitably require judgment calls that may have an impact on results. For example, NCTC protocols dictate that events identified as simultaneous and coordinated would be recorded as one incident, as would be attacks that subsequently targeted first-responders. For instance, on the morning of August 17, 2005, there were approximately 450 small bomb attacks in Bangladesh, and because they were coordinated according to a central plan, NCTC counted them as a single incident. Other valid counting protocols would register these attacks as 450 separate attacks.
- Analyzing incident data from year-to-year to identify trends and notable deviations in the data is problematic, and not meaningful in most cases. The availability, quality, and depth of open source reporting vary making it hard to isolate whether a rise or fall of a particular data element from one year to the next is due to an increase or decrease of this open source reporting or whether actual events are behind the change in the data.

Despite these limitations, tracking and analyzing incidents can help us understand some important characteristics about terrorism, including the geographic distribution of incidents and information about the perpetrators, their victims, and other details about an attack. Year-to-year changes in the gross number of incidents across the globe, however, may tell us little about the international community's effectiveness either for preventing these incidents, or for reducing the capacity of terrorists to advance their agenda through violence against the innocent.

Methodology Utilized to Compile NCTC's Database of Terrorist Incidents

For compiling 2005 results, NCTC, working with a panel of terrorism experts, adopted a revised methodology for counting terrorist incidents, basing it on the broader statutory definition of "*terrorism*" rather than that of "*international terrorism*,"[1] on which the NCTC based its incident counting in previous years. For 2006, we continued using this broader definition of "terrorism" and overall this broader definition and improvements in cataloging have resulted in a larger, more comprehensive set of incident data, all of which can now be found on NCTC's website, www.nctc.gov.

[1] Users who wish to determine the number of incidents of "international terrorism" (i.e., incidents that involve the territory or citizens of two or more countries) will find these incidents included in the WITS database.

The data provided on the website is based on the statutory definition set forth in the *Developing Statistical Information* section to this Annex. Accordingly, the incidents NCTC has catalogued in the database are those that, based on available open source information, meet the criteria for "premeditated, politically motivated violence perpetrated against noncombatant targets by subnational groups or clandestine agents." Determination of what constitutes an incident of terrorism, however, is sometimes based on incomplete information and may be open to interpretation. The perpetrator's specific motivation, whether political or otherwise, is not always clear, nor is the perpetrator's identity always evident. Moreover, additional information may become available over time, affecting the accuracy of initial judgments about incidents. Users of this database should therefore recognize that expert opinions may differ on whether a particular incident constitutes terrorism or some other form of political violence.

NCTC has made every effort to limit the degree of subjectivity involved in the judgments. In the interests of transparency NCTC has adopted counting rules that require that terrorists must have initiated and executed the attack for it to be included in the database; foiled attacks, as well as hoaxes, are not included in the database. Spontaneous (i.e. non-premeditated) hate crimes without intent to cause mass casualties are excluded to the greatest extent practicable.

What is a "noncombatant"?

Under the statutory definition of *terrorism* that NCTC uses to compile its database, the victim must be a "noncombatant." However, that term is left open to interpretation by the statute. For the purposes of the WITS database, the term "combatant" was interpreted to mean military, paramilitary, militia, and police under military command and control, in specific areas or regions where war zones or war-like settings exist. Further distinctions were drawn depending on the particular country involved and the role played by the military and police, e.g., where national security forces are indistinguishable from police and/or military forces. Noncombatants therefore included civilians and civilian police and military assets outside of war zones and war-like settings. Diplomatic assets, including personnel, embassies, consulates, and other facilities, were also considered noncombatant targets.

Although only acts of violence against noncombatant targets were counted as terrorism incidents for purposes of the WITS database, if those incidents also resulted in the death of combatant victims, all victims (combatant and noncombatant) were tallied. In an incident where combatants were the target of the event, non-combatants who were incidentally harmed were designated "collateral" and the incident excluded from the posted data set.

For example, if terrorists attacked a military base in Iraq and wounded one civilian bystander, that victim would be deemed collateral, and the incident would not be counted.

In the cases of Iraq and Afghanistan, it is particularly difficult to gather comprehensive information about all incidents and to distinguish terrorism from the numerous other forms of violence, including crime and sectarian violence, in light of imperfect information. The distinction between terrorism and insurgency in Iraq is especially challenging, as Iraqis participate in the al-Qaida in Iraq and other terrorists network as well as in tribal and sectarian violence. Therefore, some combatants may be included as victims in some incidents when their presence was incidental to an attack intended for noncombatants. We note, however, that because of the difficulty in gathering data on Iraq and Afghanistan, the dataset does not provide a comprehensive account of all incidents of terrorism in these two countries.

What is "politically motivated violence"?

The statutory definition also requires the attack to be "politically motivated." NCTC has adopted a series of counting rules to assist in the data compilation. Any life threatening attack or kidnapping by any "Foreign Terrorist Organization" or group appearing on the list of "Other Organizations of Concern" is deemed politically motivated. Similarly, any serious attack by any organization or individual against a Government/Diplomatic official or a Government/Diplomatic building is deemed politically motivated and is therefore considered terrorism. On the other hand, any attack that is primarily criminal or economic in nature or is an instance of mob violence is considered not to be "politically motivated." Similarly, any terrorist organization actions that are primarily intended to enable future terrorist attacks (robbing a bank or selling narcotics for the purpose of raising money, for example) are not considered terrorism.

In between these relatively clear-cut cases, there is a degree of subjectivity. In general, NCTC counting rules consider that attacks by unknown perpetrators against either unknown victims or infrastructure are not demonstrably political and therefore are not terrorism. However, there are exceptions to this general rule: if such an attack occurs in areas in which there is significant insurgency, unrest, or political instability, the attack may be considered terrorism; or if the attack occurs in a region free of such political violence, but involves something more than a shooting (for instance, improvised explosive device, beheading, etc.), the attack may, depending on the circumstances, be considered terrorism. Finally, if low level attacks against noncombatant targets begin to suggest the existence of a chronic problem, the attacks may be considered terrorism.

Incidents of Terrorism Worldwide[2]

	2005	2006
Incidents of terrorism worldwide	11,153	14,338
Incidents resulting in death, injury, or kidnapping of at least one individual	8,028	11,170
Incidents resulting in death of at least one individual	5,135	7,332
—Incidents resulting in the death of zero individuals	6,018	7,007
—Incidents resulting in the death of only one individual	2,881	4,091
—Incidents resulting in the death of at least 10 individuals	228	291
Incidents resulting in the injury of at least one individual	3,838	5,718
Incidents resulting in the kidnapping of at least one individual	1,152	1,334
Individuals worldwide killed, injured or kidnapped as a result of incidents of terrorism	74,217	74,543
—Individuals worldwide killed as a result of incidents of terrorism	14,618	20,498
—Individuals worldwide injured as a result of incidents of terrorism	24,761	38,191
—Individuals worldwide kidnapped as a result of incidents of terrorism	34,838	15,854

Incidents of Terrorism in Iraq and Afghanistan[2]

	2005	2006
Incidents of terrorism in Iraq	3,468	6,630
Incidents in Iraq resulting in death, injury, or kidnapping of at least one individual	2,834	6,026
Individuals in Iraq killed, injured, or kidnapped as a result of incidents of terrorism	20,685	38,813
Incidents of terrorism in Afghanistan	491	749
Incidents in Afghanistan resulting in death, injury, or kidnapping of at least one individual	366	555
Individuals in Afghanistan killed, injured, or kidnapped as a result of incidents of terrorism	1,540	2,943

[2] In all cases limited to incidents targeting noncombatants. The 2005 numbers were updated since last year's publication. Updates are available on the Worldwide Incidents Tracking System at <www.nctc.gov>

NCTC Observations Related to Terrorist Incidents Statistical Material

Approximately 14,000 terrorist attacks occurred in various countries during 2006, resulting in over 20,000 deaths. Compared to 2005, attacks rose by 3,000, a 25 percent increase in 2006 while deaths rose by 5,800, a 40 percent increase. As was the case last year, by far the largest number of reported terrorist incidents and deaths occurred in the Near East and South Asia. These two regions also were the locations for 90 percent of all the 290 high casualty attacks that killed 10 or more people-only a total of five high casualty attacks occurred in Europe-Eurasia, East Asia-Pacific, and the Western Hemisphere.

- Of the 14,000 reported attacks, 45 percent-about 6600-of them occurred in Iraq where approximately 13,000 fatalities-65 percent of the worldwide total-were reported for 2006.
- Violence against non-combatants in eastern and sub-Saharan Africa, particularly related to attacks associated with turmoil in or near Sudan and Nigeria, rose 65 percent in 2006, rising to 420 from the approximately 253 attacks reported for 2005.
- The 749 attacks in Afghanistan during 2006 are over 50 percent more than the 491 attacks reported for 2005 as fighting intensified during the past year.
- The number of reported incidents in 2006 fell for Europe and Eurasia by 15 percent from 2005, for South Asia by 10 percent, and for the Western Hemisphere by 5 percent. No high casualty attacks occurred in Western Europe, and only two occurred in Southeast Asia, in the southern Philippines. There were no high casualty attacks and 95 percent fewer victims of terror in 2006 in Indonesia that was attributable, at least in part, to enhanced Indonesian security measures.

The number injured during terrorist incidents rose substantially in 2006, as compared with 2005, by 54 percent, with most of the rise stemming from a doubling of the reported number of injuries in Iraq since 2005. Although kidnappings in Iraq during 2006 rose sharply by 300 percent, kidnappings overall declined by more than 50 percent in 2006 due to a large drop of approximately 22,000 kidnappings in Nepal where peace discussions during the year apparently curtailed hostage taking.

Attackers

The perpetrators of over 9,000 terrorist attacks in 2006 could not be determined from open source information. Of the remaining incidents, as many as 290 various subnational groups-many of them well-known foreign terrorist organizations-or clandestine agents were connected to an attack in various ways, including as a claimant, as the accused, and as the confirmed perpetrator. In most instances, open source reporting contains little confirmed or corroborating information that identifies the organizations or individuals responsible for a terrorist attack. In many reports, attackers are alleged to be tied to local or well-known terrorist groups but there is little subsequent reporting that verifies these connections. Moreover, pinpointing attackers becomes even more difficult as extremist groups splinter or merge with others, make false claims, or deny allegations.

- According to open source reports, Sunni extremists, more than any other subnational group, claimed they conducted the largest number of incidents with the highest casualty totals.
- Sunni extremists in various countries carried out about the same number of high fatality attacks in 2006 but with deadlier results, and were involved in more kidnappings than these extremists reportedly carried out in 2005.

Although no terrorist attack occurred last year that approached the sophistication of planning and preparations that were characteristic of the 9/11 attacks, open source reporting alleges that al-Qaida leaders played an important role in steering the airline hijacking plot in the United Kingdom that was disrupted in August. Reporting points to a steadfast al-Qaida that is planning attacks in northwest Pakistan, and was able to expand its propaganda campaign in 2006 to invigorate supporters, win converts, and gain recruits while its al-Qaida in Iraq associates and other linked groups carried out several successful attacks.

- Al-Qaida in the Arabian Peninsula conducted the first-ever terrorist attack against a Saudi Arabia oil facility at the major oil processing plant at Abqaiq on 24 February 2006. Security forces, suffering a few casualties, prevented the attackers from damaging processing capabilities.
- According to open sources, al-Qaida senior leadership approved the merger with the Salafist Group for Preaching and Combat (GSPC), which conducted its first attack against a US target at La Trappe, Algeria on 10 December. The GSPC remotely detonated a bomb that struck a bus and wounded one of the US passengers who worked for a US company, and subsequently the attackers used small arms to fire bullets at the bus, killing or wounding 9 non-US civilians.

Types of Attacks

As was the case in 2005, in 2006 most attacks were perpetrated by terrorists applying conventional fighting methods that included using bombs and weapons, such as small arms. However, technology continues to empower terrorist and effective methods of attack continue to be developed by them to offset countermeasures. Terrorists continued their practice of coordinated attacks that included secondary attacks on first responders at attack sites, and they uniquely configured weapons and other materials to create improvised explosive devices.

- While bombing incidents increased by 30 percent from those in 2005, the death tolls in these incidents during 2006 rose by 39 percent and injuries by 45 percent. The use of suicide bombing attacks overall fell 12 percent, most notably in the use of suicide car bombers. However, suicide bombers operating outside of vehicles increased by 25 percent, and the ability of these attackers to penetrate large concentrations of people and then detonate their explosives probably accounted for the increase in lethality of bombings in 2006.
- A new CBRN terrorist attack method in Iraq emerged in 2006. According to an Iraqi Interior Ministry explosive expert, a large vehicle-borne IED (VBIED) attack that included chemicals in Sadr City on 23 November signaled a dangerous strategic shift in tactics for 2007 that features the use of chemical weapons.

Victims and Targets of Attacks

As was the case in 2005, Muslims again bore a substantial share of being the victims of terrorist attacks in 2006.

- Approximately 58,000 individuals worldwide were either killed or injured by terrorist attacks in 2006. Based upon a combination of reporting and demographic analysis of the countries involved, well over 50 percent of the victims were Muslims, and most were victims of attacks in Iraq.

Open source reporting identifies approximately 70 percent of the 58,000 killed or injured victims of terror as simply civilians, and therefore actual tallies of significant types of victims cannot be specifically determined. However, the reporting does yield some insights about the demographics of these victims.

- Government officials such as leaders, police, department personnel, paramilitary personnel such as guards, were reported 20 percent more often, rising from approximately 9,500 in 2005 to just over 11,200 in 2006. More specifically, police victims were reported more often, their total rising more than 20 percent, from over 6,500 in 2005 to over 8,200 in 2006.
- More killings of educators were reported in 2006; 148 deaths were highlighted in 2006 reporting as compared to 96 last year. Reporting of student victims increased over 320 percent to over 430 either killed or injured in attacks, and reports of teachers as victims also increased by over 45 percent reaching 214 either killed or injured in attacks.

- Children were also reported more often as victims in 2006, up by more than 80 percent, with over 1,800 children either killed or injured in terrorist attacks.
- More attacks involving journalists were reported, an increased of 5 percent, yet in those attacks more journalist deaths and injuries were reported in 2006, an increase of 20 percent.

In addition to the human toll, 19,500 facilities were struck or were the target during terrorist attacks last year. For both 2005 and 2006, the most common types of properties damaged or destroyed during an incident were vehicles and residences, which were hit in about 27 and 12 percent of the incidents in each year, respectively. The percentage of incidents that included other types of property damage or destruction, such as those associated with energy, transportation, education, government, and other enterprises, remain unchanged at single digit levels with a few notable exceptions.

- Approximately 350 Mosques were targeted or struck during an attack in 2006, in most cases by Islamic extremists, representing over a three-fold increase from 2005. The attack against the Shia Golden Dome Mosque in Iraq, attributed to al-Qaida in Iraq, triggered a watershed of escalating sectarian violence in Iraq.
- Fewer incidents involved civil aircraft and airports, resulting in less damage to either one in 2006.
- Electoral polling stations saw over an 80 percent drop in attacks by terrorists in 2006.

An Academic's Perspective of Statistical Data

"In this short note, which was invited by NCTC, I highlight some of the challenges encountered in producing credible data on terrorist incidents. The WITS database strikes me as a particularly useful resource to use to evaluate trends in terrorist activity, to infer patterns in terrorists' methods in order to take the best possible precautions, and to test hypotheses concerning the causes of terrorism. With these applications in mind, there are three areas in which the WITS data deserve particular attention: Definition, measurement and significance. The definition is missing two important pieces, whether or not an attack is international or domestic, and political violence 'usually intended to influence an audience.' Measurement of the error rate in the WITS data is important to understand. Statistical techniques used by other government statistical agencies could be adopted to measure the rate of error, comprehensiveness, and consistency of the WITS data. These measures will facilitate use of the WITS data by researchers and highlight areas where the data are weak. Providing measures of significance of events (e.g., a terrorist Richter scale running from 1 to 5) and coder confidence would be particularly useful. The collection and provision of data like the WITS is a quintessential public good, and NCTC is the most appropriate government agency to collect such data."

Alan B. Krueger
Princeton University
April 11, 2007

The full letter of Dr. Krueger is available in the *2006 NCTC Report on Terrorist Incidents*, available via the Internet at www.nctc.gov.

Terrorism Deaths, Injuries, Kidnappings of Private U.S. Citizens, 2006[3]

Provided by the Bureau of Consular Affairs, U.S. Department of State

The term "Private U.S. Citizen" refers to any U.S. citizen not acting in an official capacity on behalf of the U.S. Government; therefore these figures do not include, for example, U.S. military personnel killed or injured in a terrorism-related incident while on active duty or employees of the Department of State and other federal agencies. Members of U.S. Government employees' households are considered private U.S. citizens.

Although every effort was made to include all terrorism-related deaths and injuries involving private U.S. citizens, the figures below reflect only those cases reported to, or known by, the U.S. Department of State, and may not reflect actual numbers of injured, which may not always be reported depending on their severity. As NCTC also notes, in the cases of Iraq and Afghanistan, it is particularly difficult to gather comprehensive information about all incidents and to distinguish terrorism from the numerous other forms of violence.

U.S. citizens worldwide killed as a result of incidents of terrorism: 28

U.S. citizens worldwide injured as a result of incidents of terrorism: 27

U.S. citizens worldwide kidnapped as a result of incidents of terrorism: 12

TERRORISM DEATHS OF PRIVATE U.S. CITIZENS IN 2006 (BY COUNTRY)

Country	Date of Death	Number	Location
Afghanistan	May 18, 2006	1	Islam Qal, Herat, Afghanistan
	December 6, 2006	2	Kandahar, Afghanistan
Iraq	January 6, 2006	1	Nasiriyah, Iraq
	January 16, 2006	1	Baghdad, Iraq

[3] In all cases limited to incidents targeting noncombatants.

Country	Date of Death	Number	Location
	January 18, 2006	2	Basrah, Iraq
	February 11, 2006	1	Baghdad, Iraq
	March 9, 2006	1	Baghdad, Iraq
	March 14, 2006	1	Tal Afar, Iraq
	March 20, 2006	1	Baghdad, Iraq
	May 3, 2006	1	Tallil, Iraq
	May 7, 2006	1	Balad-Tahwilla, Iraq
	May 8, 2006	1	Near Rustamiyah, Iraq
	August 17, 2006	1	North of Tallil, Iraq
	August 18, 2006	1	Baghdad, Iraq
	August 28, 2006	1	Baji, Iraq
	September 17, 2006	1	Hawijah, Iraq
	September 22, 2006	1	Basrah, Iraq
	October 4, 2006	1	Baghdad, Iraq
	October 11, 2006	1	Tikrit, Iraq
	October 22, 2006	1	Baghdad, Iraq
	November 2, 2006	1	Baghdad, Iraq
	November 13, 2006	1	Baghdad, Iraq
	December 21, 2006	1	Baghdad, Iraq
Israel, Gaza, and the West Bank	May 14, 2006	1	Tel Aviv, Israel
Pakistan	March 2, 2006	1	Karachi, Pakistan
Thailand	September 16, 2006	1	Hat Yai, Thailand

TERRORISM INJURIES OF PRIVATE U.S. CITIZENS IN 2006 (BY COUNTRY)			
Country	**Date of Death**	**Number**	**Location**
Afghanistan	April 7, 2006	2	Lashkargar Province, Afghanistan
	May 18, 2006	2	Islam Qal, Herat, Afghanistan

Country	Date of Death	Number	Location
Algeria	December 10, 2006	1	Algiers, Algeria
Egypt	April 24, 2006	5	Dahab, Sinai, Egypt
India	July 11, 2006	1	Srinagar, India
	August 16, 2006	5	Imphal, India
Iraq	January 18, 2006	1	Basrah, Iraq
	January 29, 2006	1	Taji, Iraq
	May 18, 2006	2	Herat, Iraq
	May 29, 2006	1	Baghdad, Iraq
	October 24, 2006	1	Keokuk, Iraq
	December 21, 2006	1	Baghdad, Iraq
Israel, Gaza, and the West Bank	April 17, 2006	1	Tel Aviv, Israel
	October 11, 2006	1	Nobles, the West Bank
Russia	January 11, 2006	1	Moscow, Russia
Thailand	September 16, 2006	1	Hat Yai, Thailand

TERRORISM KIDNAPPINGS OF PRIVATE U.S. CITIZENS IN 2006 (BY COUNTRY)			
Country	**Date of Death**	**Number**	**Location**
Afghanistan	March 30, 2006*	1	Near Gresham, Afghanistan
Iraq	March 30, 2006*	1	Baghdad, Iraq
	July 9, 2006*	1	Baghdad, Iraq
	August 5, 2006*	1	Baghdad, Iraq
	November 16, 2006	4	Aswan, Iraq
Israel, Gaza, and the West Bank	June 10, 2006*	1	Nobles, the West Bank
	August 27, 2006*	1	Gaza City, Gaza
Nigeria	January 30, 2006*	1	Offshore the Niger Delta, Nigeria
	August 23, 2006*	1	Port Harcourt, Nigeria
* Date rescued/released.			

International Conventions and Protocols on Terrorism

1. Convention on Offences and Certain Other Acts Committed On Board Aircraft

Signed in Tokyo on September 14, 1963.

Convention entered into force on December 4, 1969.

Status: 180 Parties

2. Convention for the Suppression of Unlawful Seizure of Aircraft

Signed in The Hague on December 16, 1970.

Convention entered into force on October 14, 1971.

Status: 181 Parties

3. Convention for the Suppression of Unlawful Acts Against the Safety of Civil Aviation

Signed in Montreal on September 23, 1971.

Convention entered into force on January 26, 1973.

Status: 183 Parties

4. Convention on the Prevention and Punishment of Crimes against Internationally Protected Persons, including Diplomatic Agents

Adopted in New York on December 14, 1973.

Convention entered into force on February 20, 1977.

Status: 159 Parties

5. International Convention Against the Taking of Hostages

Adopted in New York on December 17, 1979.

Convention entered into force on June 3, 1983.

Status: 153 Parties

6. Convention on the Physical Protection of Nuclear Material

Signed in Vienna on October 26, 1979.

Convention entered into force on February 8, 1987.

Status: 116 Parties

7. Protocol for the Suppression of Unlawful Acts of Violence at Airports Serving International Civil Aviation, Supplementary to the Convention for the Suppression of Unlawful Acts against the Safety of Civil Aviation

Done in Montreal on September 23, 1971.

Signed in Montreal on February 24, 1988.

Protocol entered into force on August 6, 1989.

Status: 156 Parties

8. Convention for the Suppression of Unlawful Acts Against the Safety of Maritime Navigation

Done in Rome on March 10, 1988.

Convention entered into force on March 1, 1992.

Status: 134 Parties

9. Protocol for the Suppression of Unlawful Acts Against the Safety of Fixed Platforms Located on the Continental Shelf

Done in Rome on March 10, 1988.

Protocol entered into force on March 1, 1992.

Status: 123 Parties

10. Convention on the Maz rking of Plastic Explosives for the Purpose of Detection

Done in Montreal on March 1, 1991.

Convention entered into force on June 21, 1998.

Status: 123 Parties

11. International Convention for the Suppression of Terrorist Bombings

Adopted in New York on December 15, 1997.

Convention entered into force on May 23, 2001.

Status: 145 Parties

12. International Convention for the Suppression of the Financing of Terrorism

Adopted in New York on December 9, 1999.

Convention entered into force on April 10, 2002.

Status: 150 Parties

13. International Convention for the Suppression of Acts of Nuclear Terrorism

Adopted in New York on April 13, 2005.

Not yet entered into force (open for signatures from September 14, 2005 until December 31, 2006).

Status: 100 signatories, no ratifications

Country/ Instrument	1 Aircraft Conv.	2 Unlawful Seizure Conv.	3 Civil Aviation Conv.	4 Diplo Agents Conv.	5 Hostage Taking Conv.	6 Nuclear Mat. Conv.
Afghanistan	15/04/ 1977	29/08/ 1979	26/09/ 1984	24/09/ 2003	24/09/ 2003	12/09/ 2003
Albania	01/12/ 1997	21/10/ 1997	21/10/ 1997	22/01/ 2002	22/01/ 2002	05/03/ 2002
Algeria	12/10/ 1995	06/10/ 1995	06/10/ 1995	07/11/ 2000	18/12/ 1996	30/04/ 2003
Andorra	17/05/ 2006	23/09/ 2004	22/05/ 2006	23/09/ 2004	23/09/ 2004	27/06/ 2006
Angola	24/02/ 1998	12/03/ 1998	12/03/ 1998			
Antigua and Barbuda	19/07/ 1985	22/07/ 1985	22/07/ 1985	19/07/ 1993	06/08/ 1986	04/08/ 1993
Argentina	23/07/ 1971	11/09/ 1972	26/11/ 1973	18/03/ 1982	18/09/ 1991	06/04/ 1989
Armenia	23/01/ 2003	10/09/ 2002	10/09/ 2002	18/05/ 1994	16/03/ 2004	24/08/ 1993
Australia	22/06/ 1970	09/11/ 1972	12/07/ 1973	20/06/ 1977	21/05/ 1990	22/09/ 1987
Austria	07/02/ 1974	11/02/ 1974	11/02/ 1974	03/08/ 1977	22/08/ 1986	22/12/ 1988
Azerbaijan	05/02/ 2004	03/03/ 2000	15/03/ 2000	02/04/ 2001	29/02/ 2000	19/01/ 2004
Bahamas	12/06/ 1975	13/08/ 1976	27/12/ 1984	22/07/ 1986	04/06/ 1981	25/10/ 2005
Bahrain	09/02/ 1984	20/02/ 1984	20/02/ 1984	16/09/ 2005	16/09/ 2005	12/02/ 1996
Bangladesh	25/07/ 1978	28/06/ 1978	28/06/ 1978	20/05/ 2005	20/05/ 2005	11/05/ 2005
Barbados	04/04/ 1972	02/04/ 1973	06/08/ 1976	26/10/ 1979	09/03/ 1981	12/09/ 2002
Belarus	03/02/ 1988	30/12/ 1971	31/01/ 1973	05/02/ 1976	01/07/ 1987	09/09/ 1993
Belgium	06/08/ 1970	24/08/ 1973	13/08/ 1976	19/05/ 2004	16/04/ 1999	06/09/ 1991
Belize	19/05/ 1998	10/06/ 1998	10/06/ 1998	14/11/ 2001	14/11/ 2001	10/06/ 1998
Benin	30/03/ 2004	13/03/ 1972	19/04/ 2004	31/07/ 2003	31/07/ 2003	19/04/ 2004

7 Airport Protection Protocol	8 Maritime Conv.	9 Fixed Platforms Protocol	10 Plastic Explosive Conv.	11 Terrorist Bombings Conv.	12 Terrorist Financing Conv.	13 Nuclear Terrorism Conv.
23/09/ 2003	23/09/ 2003	01/10/ 2003	24/09/ 2003	24/09/ 2003		
29/04/ 2002	19/06/ 2002	19/06/ 2002	20/10/ 2004	22/01/ 2002	10/04/ 2002	
05/11/ 1995	11/02/ 1998	N/A	14/11/ 1996	08/11/ 2001	08/11/ 2001	
22/05/ 2006	N/A	N/A	17/05/ 2006	23/09/ 2004		
11/03/ 2002						
12/02/ 1992	17/08/ 1993	26/11/ 2003	08/03/ 1999	25/09/ 2003	22/08/ 2005	
10/09/ 2002	08/06/ 2005	08/06/ 2005	22/07/ 2005	16/03/ 2004	16/03/ 2004	
23/10/ 1990	19/02/ 1993	19/02/ 1993	09/08/ 2002	26/09/ 2002		
28/12/ 1989	28/12/ 1989	28/12/ 1989	31/05/ 1999	06/09/ 2000	15/04/ 2002	14/09/ 2006
23/03/ 2000	26/01/ 2004	26/01/ 2004	04/07/ 2000	02/04/ 2001	26/10/ 2001	
25/10/ 2005	01/11/ 2005					
21/10/ 2005	21/10/ 2005	30/01/ 1996	21/09/ 2004	21/09/ 2004		
27/06/ 2005	09/06/ 2005	09/06/ 2005	16/08/ 2005	20/05/ 2005	26/08/ 2005	
06/05/ 1994	06/05/ 1994	12/09/ 2002	18/09/ 2002	18/09/ 2002		
01/05/ 1989	04/12/ 2002	04/12/ 2002	06/02/ 2002	01/10/ 2001	06/10/ 2004	
20/04/ 1999	11/04/ 2005	11/04/ 2005	20/05/ 2005	17/05/ 2004		
14/11/ 2001	01/12/ 2003					
31/08/ 2006	N/A	30/03/ 2004	31/07/ 2003	30/08/ 2004		

Country/ Instrument	1 Aircraft Conv.	2 Unlawful Seizure Conv.	3 Civil Aviation Conv.	4 Diplo Agents Conv.	5 Hostage Taking Conv.	6 Nuclear Mat. Conv.
Bhutan	25/01/ 1989	28/12/ 1988	28/12/ 1988	16/01/ 1989	31/08/ 1981	26/08/ 2005
Bolivia	05/07/ 1979	18/07/ 1979	18/07/ 1979	22/01/ 2002	07/01/ 2002	24/01/ 2002
Bosnia and Herzegovina	07/03/ 1995	15/08/ 1994	15/08/ 1994	01/09/ 1993	01/09/ 1993	30/06/ 1998
Botswana	16/01/ 1979	28/12/ 1978	28/12/ 1978	25/10/ 2000	08/09/ 2000	19/09/ 2000
Brazil	14/01/ 1970	14/01/ 1972	24/07/ 1972	07/06/ 1999	08/03/ 2000	17/10/ 1985
Brunei Darussalam	23/05/ 1986	16/04/ 1986	16/04/ 1986	13/11/ 1997	18/10/ 1988	20/12/ 2000
Bulgaria	28/09/ 1989	19/05/ 1971	28/03/ 1973	18/07/ 1974	10/03/ 1988	10/04/ 1984
Burkina Faso	06/06/ 1969	19/10/ 1987	19/10/ 1987	01/10/ 2003	01/10/ 2003	13/01/ 2004
Burundi	14/07/ 1971	11/02/ 1999	17/12/ 1980			
Cambodia	22/10/ 1996	08/11/ 1996	08/11/ 1996	27/07/ 2006	27/07/ 2006	04/08/ 2006
Cameroon	24/03/ 1988	14/04/ 1988	11/07/ 1973	08/06/ 1992	09/03/ 1988	29/06/ 2004
Canada	07/11/ 1969	20/06/ 1972	19/06/ 1972	04/08/ 1976	04/12/ 1985	21/03/ 1986
Cape Verde	04/10/ 1989	20/10/ 1977	20/10/ 1977	10/09/ 2002	10/09/ 2002	12/09/ 2002
Central African Rep	11/06/ 1991	01/07/ 1991	01/07/ 1991	01/07/ 1991		
Chad	30/06/ 1970	12/07/ 1972	12/07/ 1972	01/11/ 2006		
Chile	24/01/ 1974	02/02/ 1972	28/02/ 1974	21/01/ 1977	12/11/ 1981	27/04/ 1994
China	14/11/ 1978	10/09/ 1980	10/09/ 1980	05/08/ 1987	26/01/ 1993	10/01/ 1989
Colombia	06/07/ 1973	03/07/ 1973	04/12/ 1974	16/01/ 1996	14/04/ 2005	28/03/ 2003
Comoros	23/05/ 1991	01/08/ 1991	01/08/ 1991	25/09/ 2003	25/09/ 2003	25/09/ 2003

7 Airport Protection Protocol	8 Maritime Conv.	9 Fixed Platforms Protocol	10 Plastic Explosive Conv.	11 Terrorist Bombings Conv.	12 Terrorist Financing Conv.	13 Nuclear Terrorism Conv.
26/08/ 2005	22/03/ 2004					
01/02/ 2002	13/02/ 2002	13/02/ 2002	01/02/ 2002	22/01/ 2002	07/01/ 2002	
15/08/ 1994	28/07/ 2003	28/07/ 2003	03/05/ 2004	11/08/ 2003	10/06/ 2003	
30/10/ 2000	14/09/ 2000	14/09/ 2000	19/09/ 2000	08/09/ 2000	08/09/ 2000	
09/05/ 1997	25/10/ 2005	25/10/ 2005	04/10/ 2001	23/08/ 2002	16/09/ 2005	
04/12/ 2003	04/12/ 2003	14/03/ 2002	04/12/ 2002			
26/03/ 1991	08/07/ 1999	08/07/ 1999	08/09/ 1999	12/02/ 2002	15/04/ 2002	17/03/ 2006
08/12/ 1998	15/01/ 2004	14/01/ 2004	07/07/ 2004	01/10/ 2003	01/10/ 2003	
08/11/ 1996	18/08/ 2006	31/07/ 2006	12/12/ 2005			
13/03/ 2003	03/06/ 1998	21/03/ 2005	06/02/ 2006			
02/08/ 1993	18/06/ 1993	18/06/ 1993	29/11/ 1996	03/04/ 2002	19/02/ 2002	
03/01/ 2003	03/01/ 2003	04/11/ 2002	10/05/ 2002	10/05/ 2002		
15/08/ 1989	22/04/ 1994	22/04/ 1994	02/08/ 2000	10/11/ 2001	10/11/ 2001	
05/03/ 1999	20/08/ 1991	20/08/ 1991	13/11/ 2001	19/04/ 2006		
14/01/ 2004	14/09/ 2004	14/09/ 2004				
25/09/ 2003						

Country/ Instrument	1 Aircraft Conv.	2 Unlawful Seizure Conv.	3 Civil Aviation Conv.	4 Diplo Agents Conv.	5 Hostage Taking Conv.	6 Nuclear Mat. Conv.
Congo	13/11/ 1978	24/11/ 1989	19/03/ 1987			
Congo (Democratic Republic of)	20/07/ 1977	06/07/ 1977	06/07/ 1977	25/07/ 1977	21/09/ 2004	28/10/ 2005
Cook Islands	12/04/ 2005	14/04/ 2005	14/04/ 2005	14/04/ 2005	04/03/ 2004	
Costa Rica	24/10/ 1972	09/07/ 1971	21/09/ 1973	02/11/ 1977	24/01/ 2003	02/05/ 2003
Côte d'Ivoire	03/06/ 1970	09/01/ 1973	09/01/ 1973	13/03/ 2002	22/08/ 1989	13/03/ 2002
Croatia	05/10/ 1993	08/06/ 1993	08/06/ 1993	12/10/ 1992	23/09/ 2003	29/09/ 1992
Cuba	12/02/ 2001	27/11/ 2001	31/10/ 2001	10/06/ 1998	15/11/ 2001	26/09/ 1997
Cyprus	31/05/ 1972	05/07/ 1972	27/07/ 1973	24/12/ 1975	13/09/ 1991	23/07/ 1998
Czech Republic	25/03/ 1993	14/11/ 1994	14/11/ 1994	22/02/ 1993	22/02/ 1993	24/03/ 1993
Denmark	17/01/ 1967	17/10/ 1972	17/01/ 1973	01/07/ 1975	11/08/ 1987	06/09/ 1991
Djibouti	10/06/ 1992	24/11/ 1992	24/11/ 1992	01/06/ 2004	01/06/ 2004	22/06/ 2004
Dominica	26/07/ 2005	26/07/ 2005	24/09/ 2004	09/09/ 1986	08/11/ 2004	26/07/ 2005
Dominican Republic	03/12/ 1970	22/06/ 1978	28/11/ 1973	08/07/ 1977		
Ecuador	03/12/ 1969	14/06/ 1971	12/01/ 1977	12/03/ 1975	02/05/ 1988	17/01/ 1996
Egypt	12/02/ 1975	28/02/ 1975	20/05/ 1975	25/06/ 1986	02/10/ 1981	25/07/ 2000
El Salvador	13/02/ 1980	16/01/ 1973	25/09/ 1979	08/08/ 1980	12/02/ 1981	15/12/ 2006
Equatorial Guinea	27/02/ 1991	02/01/ 1991	02/01/ 1991	07/02/ 2003	07/02/ 2003	24/11/ 2003
Eritrea	01/12/ 1994					
Estonia	31/12/ 1993	22/12/ 1993	22/12/ 1993	21/10/ 1991	08/03/ 2002	09/05/ 1994

7 Airport Protection Protocol	8 Maritime Conv.	9 Fixed Platforms Protocol	10 Plastic Explosive Conv.	11 Terrorist Bombings Conv.	12 Terrorist Financing Conv.	13 Nuclear Terrorism Conv.
22/04/ 2003	25/03/ 2003	25/03/ 2003	12/07/ 2005	20/09/ 2001	24/01/ 2003	
13/03/ 2002						
08/06/ 1993	18/08/ 2005	18/08/ 2005	24/02/ 2005	02/06/ 2005	01/12/ 2003	11/09/ 2006
31/10/ 2001	20/11/ 2001	20/11/ 2001	30/11/ 2001	15/11/ 2001	15/11/ 2001	
23/04/ 2002	02/02/ 2000	02/02/ 2000	20/09/ 2002	24/01/ 2001	30/11/ 2001	
25/03/ 1993	10/12/ 2004	10/12/ 2004	25/03/ 1993	06/09/ 2000	27/12/ 2005	25/07/ 2006
23/11/ 1989	25/08/ 1995	25/08/ 1995	05/10/ 1998	31/08/ 2001	27/08/ 2002	
11/06/ 2004	09/06/ 2004	09/06/ 2004	11/06/ 2004	01/06/ 2004	13/03/ 2006	
31/08/ 2001	12/10/ 2004	24/09/ 2004	24/09/ 2004			
04/03/ 2004	10/03/ 2003	10/03/ 2003	15/12/ 1995	09/12/ 2003		
08/01/ 1993	08/01/ 1993	19/07/ 1993	09/08/ 2005	01/03/ 2005		
08/04/ 1998	07/12/ 2000	07/12/ 2000	18/02/ 2000	15/05/ 2003	15/05/ 2003	N/A
14/01/ 2004	15/01/ 2004	15/01/ 2004	07/02/ 2003	07/02/ 2003		
22/12/ 1993	15/02/ 2002	28/01/ 2004	05/03/ 1996	10/04/ 2002	22/05/ 2002	

Country/ Instrument	1 Aircraft Conv.	2 Unlawful Seizure Conv.	3 Civil Aviation Conv.	4 Diplo Agents Conv.	5 Hostage Taking Conv.	6 Nuclear Mat. Conv.
Ethiopia	27/03/ 1979	26/03/ 1979	26/03/ 1979	16/04/ 2003	16/04/ 2003	15/12/ 1999
Fiji	31/01/ 1972	27/07/ 1972	05/03/ 1973	21/09/ 1992		
Finland	02/04/ 1971	15/12/ 1971	13/07/ 1973	31/10/ 1978	14/04/ 1983	22/09/ 1989
France	11/09/ 1970	18/09/ 1972	30/06/ 1976	26/08/ 2003	09/06/ 2000	06/09/ 1991
Gabon	14/01/ 1970	14/07/ 1971	29/06/ 1976	14/10/ 1981	19/04/ 2005	13/08/ 2003
Gambia	04/01/ 1979	28/11/ 1978	28/11/ 1978	16/06/ 2000	01/11/ 1991	20/06/ 2000
Georgia	16/06/ 1994	20/04/ 1994	20/04/ 1994	18/02/ 2004	18/02/ 2004	07/09/ 2006
Germany	16/12/ 1969	11/10/ 1974	03/02/ 1978	25/01/ 1977	15/12/ 1980	06/09/ 1991
Ghana	02/01/ 1974	12/12/ 1973	12/12/ 1973	25/04/ 1975	10/11/ 1987	16/10/ 2002
Greece	31/05/ 1971	20/09/ 1973	15/01/ 1974	03/07/ 1984	18/06/ 1987	06/09/ 1991
Grenada	28/08/ 1978	10/08/ 1978	10/08/ 1978	13/12/ 2001	10/12/ 1990	09/01/ 2002
Guatemala	17/11/ 1970	16/05/ 1979	19/10/ 1978	18/01/ 1983	11/03/ 1983	23/04/ 1985
Guinea	18/01/ 1994	02/05/ 1984	02/05/ 1984	22/12/ 2004	22/12/ 2004	29/11/ 2005
Guinea- Bissau	20/08/ 1976	20/08/ 1976				
Guyana	20/12/ 1972	21/12/ 1972	21/12/ 1972	19/06/ 2002	30/01/ 2003	30/01/ 2003
Haiti	26/04/ 1984	09/05/ 1984	09/05/ 1984	25/08/ 1980	17/05/ 1989	
Holy See						
Honduras	08/04/ 1987	13/04/ 1987	13/04/ 1987	29/01/ 2003	01/06/ 1981	28/01/ 2004
Hungary	03/12/ 1970	13/08/ 1971	27/12/ 1972	26/03/ 1975	02/09/ 1987	04/05/ 1984
Iceland	16/03/ 1970	29/06/ 1973	29/06/ 1973	02/08/ 1977	06/07/ 1981	18/06/ 2002

7 Airport Protection Protocol	8 Maritime Conv.	9 Fixed Platforms Protocol	10 Plastic Explosive Conv.	11 Terrorist Bombings Conv.	12 Terrorist Financing Conv.	13 Nuclear Terrorism Conv.
16/04/2003						
03/04/1998	12/11/1998	28/04/2000	05/12/2001	28/05/2002	28/06/2002	
06/09/1989	02/12/1991	02/12/1991	21/05/1997	19/08/1999	07/01/2002	
10/03/2005	10/03/2005					
15/02/1999	11/08/2006	N/A	25/04/2000	18/02/2004	27/09/2002	
25/04/1994	06/11/1990	06/11/1990	17/12/1998	23/04/2003	17/06/2004	
15/07/1997	01/11/2002	01/11/2002	22/04/1998	06/09/2002	06/09/2002	
25/04/1991	11/06/1993	11/06/1993	30/10/1995	27/05/2003	16/04/2004	
15/01/2002	09/01/2002	09/01/2002	15/01/2002	13/12/2001	13/12/2001	
11/10/1994	26/11/1997	12/02/2002	12/02/2002			
01/10/1998	01/02/2005	01/02/2005	23/01/2004	07/09/2000	14/07/2003	
20/01/2004	17/05/2005	17/05/2005	18/02/2004	25/03/2003	25/03/2003	
07/09/1988	09/11/1989	09/11/1989	11/01/1994	13/11/2001	14/10/2002	
09/05/1990	28/05/2002	28/05/2002	24/05/2002	15/04/2002	15/04/2002	

Country/ Instrument	1 Aircraft Conv.	2 Unlawful Seizure Conv.	3 Civil Aviation Conv.	4 Diplo Agents Conv.	5 Hostage Taking Conv.	6 Nuclear Mat. Conv.
India	22/07/ 1975	12/11/ 1982	12/11/ 1982	11/04/ 1978	07/09/ 1994	12/03/ 2002
Indonesia	07/09/ 1976	27/08/ 1976	27/08/ 1976	05/11/ 1986	29/06/ 2006	29/06/ 2006
Iran (Islamic Republic of)	28/06/ 1976	25/01/ 1972	10/07/ 1973	12/07/ 1978	20/11/ 2006	14/02/ 2002
Iraq	15/05/ 1974	03/12/ 1971	10/09/ 1974	28/02/ 1978	31/01/ 1990	
Ireland	14/11/ 1975	24/11/ 1975	12/10/ 1976	30/06/ 2005	30/06/ 2005	06/09/ 1991
Israel	19/09/ 1969	16/08/ 1971	30/06/ 1972	31/07/ 1980	N/A	22/01/ 2002
Italy	18/10/ 1968	19/02/ 1974	19/02/ 1974	30/08/ 1985	20/03/ 1986	06/09/ 1991
Jamaica	16/09/ 1983	15/09/ 1983	15/09/ 1983	21/09/ 1978	09/08/ 2005	16/08/ 2005
Japan	26/05/ 1970	19/04/ 1971	12/06/ 1974	08/06/ 1987	08/06/ 1987	28/10/ 1988
Jordan	03/05/ 1973	18/11/ 1971	13/02/ 1973	18/12/ 1984	19/02/ 1986	18/09/ 1992
Kazakhstan	18/05/ 1995	04/04/ 1995	04/04/ 1995	21/02/ 1996	21/02/ 1996	02/09/ 2005
Kenya	22/06/ 1970	11/01/ 1977	11/01/ 1977	16/11/ 2001	08/12/ 1981	11/02/ 2002
Kiribati	15/09/ 2005	15/09/ 2005	17/11/ 2005	17/11/ 2005	15/09/ 2005	15/09/ 2005
Korea (Democratic Republic of)	09/05/ 1983	28/04/ 1983	13/08/ 1980	01/12/ 1982	12/11/ 2001	19/07/ 1995
Korea (Republic of)	19/02/ 1971	18/01/ 1973	02/08/ 1973	25/05/ 1983	04/05/ 1983	07/04/ 1982
Kuwait	27/11/ 1979	25/05/ 1979	23/11/ 1979	01/03/ 1989	06/02/ 1989	23/04/ 2004
Kyrgyzstan	28/02/ 2000	25/02/ 2000	25/02/ 2000	02/10/ 2003	02/10/ 2003	28/02/ 2000
Lao People's Democratic	23/10/ 1972	06/04/ 1989	06/04/ 1989	22/08/ 2002	22/08/ 2002	07/10/ 2002
Latvia	10/06/ 1997	23/10/ 1998	13/04/ 1997	14/04/ 1992	14/11/ 2002	06/11/ 2002

7 Airport Protection Protocol	8 Maritime Conv.	9 Fixed Platforms Protocol	10 Plastic Explosive Conv.	11 Terrorist Bombings Conv.	12 Terrorist Financing Conv.	13 Nuclear Terrorism Conv.
22/03/ 1995	15/10/ 1999	15/10/ 1999	16/11/ 1999	22/09/ 1999	22/04/ 2003	01/12/ 2006
26/07/ 1991	10/09/ 2004	10/09/ 2004	15/07/ 2003	30/06/ 2005	30/06/ 2005	
02/04/ 1993	10/02/ 2003	10/02/ 2003				
13/03/ 1990	26/01/ 1990	26/01/ 1990	26/09/ 2002	16/04/ 2003	27/03/ 2003	
18/08/ 2005	17/08/ 2005	19/08/ 2005	18/08/ 2005	09/08/ 2005	16/09/ 2005	
24/04/ 1998	24/04/ 1998	24/04/ 1998	26/09/ 1997	16/11/ 2001	11/06/ 2002	
02/07/ 2004	02/07/ 2004	23/05/ 1996	28/08/ 2003			
18/05/ 1995	24/11/ 2003	24/11/ 2003	18/05/ 1995	06/11/ 2002	24/02/ 2003	
05/10/ 1995	21/01/ 2002	21/01/ 2002	22/10/ 2002	16/11/ 2001	27/06/ 2003	13/04/ 2006
27/06/ 1990	14/05/ 2003	10/06/ 2003	02/01/ 2002	17/02/ 2004	17/02/ 2004	
08/03/ 1989	30/06/ 2003	30/06/ 2003	18/03/ 1996	19/04/ 2004		
14/07/ 2000	01/05/ 2001	02/10/ 2003				
22/08/ 2002						
13/04/ 1997	04/12/ 2002	04/12/ 2002	17/08/ 1999	25/11/ 2002	14/11/ 2002	25/07/ 2006

Country/ Instrument	1 Aircraft Conv.	2 Unlawful Seizure Conv.	3 Civil Aviation Conv.	4 Diplo Agents Conv.	5 Hostage Taking Conv.	6 Nuclear Mat. Conv.
Lebanon	11/06/ 1974	10/08/ 1973	23/12/ 1977	03/06/ 1997	04/12/ 1997	16/12/ 1997
Lesotho	28/04/ 1972	27/07/ 1978	27/07/ 1978	05/11/ 1980	12/11/ 2001	12/11/ 2001
Liberia	10/03/ 2003	01/02/ 1982	01/02/ 1982	30/09/ 1975	05/03/ 2003	10/03/ 2003
Libyan Arab Jamahiriya	21/06/ 1972	04/10/ 1978	19/02/ 1974	25/09/ 2000	25/09/ 1998	18/10/ 2000
Liechtenstein	26/02/ 2001	23/02/ 2001	23/02/ 2001	28/11/ 1994	28/11/ 1994	25/11/ 1986
Lithuania	21/11/ 1996	04/12/ 1996	04/12/ 1996	23/10/ 2002	02/01/ 2001	07/12/ 1993
Luxembourg	21/09/ 1972	22/11/ 1978	18/05/ 1982	10/05/ 2006	29/04/ 1991	06/09/ 1991
Macedonia (FYROM)	30/08/ 1994	07/01/ 1998	04/01/ 1995	12/03/ 1998	12/03/ 1998	20/09/ 1996
Madagascar	02/12/ 1969	18/11/ 1986	18/11/ 1986	24/09/ 2003	24/09/ 2003	28/10/ 2003
Malawi	28/12/ 1972	21/12/ 1972	21/12/ 1972	14/03/ 1977	17/03/ 1986	11/08/ 2003
Malaysia	05/03/ 1985	04/05/ 1985	04/05/ 1985	24/09/ 2003	08/09/ 2006	24/09/ 2003
Maldives	28/09/ 1987	01/09/ 1987	01/09/ 1987	21/08/ 1990	22/03/ 1999	22/03/ 1999
Mali	31/05/ 1971	29/09/ 1971	24/08/ 1972	12/04/ 2002	08/02/ 1990	07/05/ 2002
Malta	28/06/ 1991	14/06/ 1991	14/06/ 1991	11/11/ 2001	11/11/ 2001	16/10/ 2003
Marshall Islands	15/05/ 1989	31/05/ 1989	31/05/ 1989	27/01/ 2003	27/01/ 2003	07/02/ 2003
Mauritania	30/06/ 1977	01/11/ 1978	01/11/ 1978	09/02/ 1998	13/03/ 1998	08/07/ 2003
Mauritius	05/04/ 1983	25/04/ 1983	25/04/ 1983	24/09/ 2003	17/10/ 1980	17/08/ 1989
Mexico	18/03/ 1969	19/07/ 1972	12/09/ 1974	22/04/ 1980	28/04/ 1987	04/04/ 1988
Micronesia (Federated States of)	19/03/ 2003	06/07/ 2004	06/07/ 2004	19/03/ 2003	10/02/ 2003	23/09/ 2002

7 Airport Protection Protocol	8 Maritime Conv.	9 Fixed Platforms Protocol	10 Plastic Explosive Conv.	11 Terrorist Bombings Conv.	12 Terrorist Financing Conv.	13 Nuclear Terrorism Conv.
27/05/ 1996	16/12/ 1994	16/12/ 1994	26/11/ 1997	13/11/ 2006		
05/10/ 1995	05/10/ 1995	05/03/ 2003	05/03/ 2003			
26/07/ 1996	08/08/ 2002	08/08/ 2002	10/10/ 2002	22/09/ 2000	09/07/ 2002	19/07/ 2006
26/02/ 2001	08/11/ 2002	08/11/ 2002	04/12/ 2002	26/11/ 2002	09/07/ 2003	
04/12/ 1996	30/01/ 2003	30/01/ 2003	21/11/ 1996	17/03/ 2004	20/02/ 2003	
14/11/ 2003	06/11/ 2006	06/02/ 2004	05/11/ 2003			
04/01/ 1995	21/09/ 1998	30/08/ 2004	30/08/ 2004			
30/03/ 1998	15/09/ 2006	N/A	23/12/ 2003	24/09/ 2003	24/09/ 2003	
11/08/ 2003						
07/09/ 2000	20/04/ 2004					
31/10/ 1990	29/04/ 2002	29/04/ 2002	28/09/ 2000	28/03/ 2002	28/03/ 2002	
14/06/ 1991	20/11/ 2001	20/11/ 2001	15/11/ 1994	11/11/ 2001	11/11/ 2001	
30/05/ 1989	29/11/ 1994	16/10/ 1995	06/02/ 2003	27/01/ 2003	27/01/ 2003	
30/04/ 2003	30/04/ 2003					
03/08/ 2004	03/08/ 2004	24/01/ 2003	14/12/ 2004			
11/10/ 1990	13/05/ 1994	13/05/ 1994	09/04/ 1992	20/01/ 2003	20/01/ 2003	27/06/ 2006
23/09/ 2002						

Country/ Instrument	1 Aircraft Conv.	2 Unlawful Seizure Conv.	3 Civil Aviation Conv.	4 Diplo Agents Conv.	5 Hostage Taking Conv.	6 Nuclear Mat. Conv.
Moldova (Republic of)	20/06/ 1997	21/05/ 1997	21/05/ 1997	08/09/ 1997	10/10/ 2002	07/05/ 1998
Monaco	02/06/ 1983	03/06/ 1983	03/06/ 1983	27/11/ 2002	16/10/ 2001	09/08/ 1996
Mongolia	24/07/ 1990	08/10/ 1971	14/09/ 1972	08/08/ 1975	09/06/ 1992	28/05/ 1986
Montenegro	23/10/ 2006	23/10/ 2006	N/A	23/10/ 2006	23/10/ 2006	
Morocco	21/10/ 1975	24/10/ 1975	24/10/ 1975	09/01/ 2002	23/08/ 2002	15/02/ 2002
Mozambique	06/01/ 2003	16/01/ 2003	16/01/ 2003	14/01/ 2003	14/01/ 2003	03/03/ 2003
Myanmar	23/05/ 1996	22/05/ 1996	22/05/ 1996	04/06/ 2004	04/06/ 2004	22/05/ 1996
Namibia	19/12/ 2005	04/11/ 2005	04/11/ 2005	02/10/ 2002	04/11/ 2005	10/07/ 2004
Nauru	17/05/ 1984	17/05/ 1984	17/05/ 1984	02/08/ 2005	02/08/ 2005	12/08/ 2005
Nepal	15/01/ 1979	11/01/ 1979	11/01/ 1979	09/03/ 1990	09/03/ 1990	
Netherlands	14/11/ 1969	27/08/ 1973	27/08/ 1973	06/12/ 1988	06/12/ 1988	06/09/ 1991
New Zealand	12/02/ 1974	12/02/ 1974	12/02/ 1974	12/11/ 1985	12/11/ 1985	19/12/ 2003
Nicaragua	24/08/ 1973	06/11/ 1973	06/11/ 1973	10/03/ 1975	24/09/ 2003	10/12/ 2004
Niger	27/06/ 1969	15/10/ 1971	01/09/ 1972	17/06/ 1985	26/10/ 2004	19/08/ 2004
Nigeria	07/04/ 1970	03/07/ 1973	03/07/ 1973	25/03/ 2003	24/02/ 2004	10/05/ 2002
Niue						
Norway	17/01/ 1967	23/08/ 1971	01/08/ 1973	28/04/ 1980	02/07/ 1981	15/08/ 1985
Oman	09/02/ 1977	02/02/ 1977	02/02/ 1977	22/03/ 1988	22/07/ 1988	11/06/ 2003
Pakistan	11/09/ 1973	28/11/ 1973	24/01/ 1974	29/03/ 1976	08/09/ 2000	12/09/ 2000
Palau	12/10/ 1995	03/08/ 1995	03/08/ 1995	14/11/ 2001	14/11/ 2001	12/10/ 1995

7 Airport Protection Protocol	8 Maritime Conv.	9 Fixed Platforms Protocol	10 Plastic Explosive Conv.	11 Terrorist Bombings Conv.	12 Terrorist Financing Conv.	13 Nuclear Terrorism Conv.
20/06/ 1997	11/10/ 2005	11/10/ 2005	01/12/ 1997	10/10/ 2002	10/10/ 2002	
22/12/ 1993	25/01/ 2002	25/01/ 2002	14/05/ 1998	06/09/ 2001	10/11/ 2001	
22/09/ 1999	22/11/ 2005	22/11/ 2005	22/09/ 1999	07/09/ 2000	25/02/ 2004	06/10/ 2006
08/01/ 2002	08/01/ 2002	26/05/ 1999	19/09/ 2002			
16/01/ 2003	08/01/ 2003	08/01/ 2003	15/03/ 2006	14/01/ 2003	14/01/ 2003	
19/09/ 2003	19/09/ 2003	01/09/ 2004	12/11/ 2001	16/08/ 2006		
07/09/ 2005						
19/09/ 2005	11/08/ 2005	11/08/ 2005	03/04/ 2006	02/08/ 2005	24/05/ 2005	
11/07/ 1995	05/03/ 1992	05/03/ 1992	04/05/ 1998	07/02/ 2002	07/02/ 2002	
02/08/ 1999	10/06/ 1999	10/06/ 1999	19/12/ 2003	04/11/ 2002	04/11/ 2002	
25/04/ 2002	10/01/ 2006	17/01/ 2003	14/11/ 2002			
30/08/ 2006	26/10/ 2004	30/09/ 2004				
16/06/ 2003						
29/05/ 1990	18/04/ 1991	18/04/ 1991	09/07/ 1992	20/09/ 1999	15/07/ 2002	
27/11/ 1992	24/09/ 1990	24/09/ 1990	13/12/ 2001	N/A		
26/09/ 2000	20/09/ 2000	20/09/ 2000	13/08/ 2002			
04/12/ 2001	04/12/ 2001	30/11/ 2001	14/11/ 2001	14/11/ 2001		

Country/ Instrument	1 Aircraft Conv.	2 Unlawful Seizure Conv.	3 Civil Aviation Conv.	4 Diplo Agents Conv.	5 Hostage Taking Conv.	6 Nuclear Mat. Conv.
Panama	16/11/ 1970	10/03/ 1972	24/04/ 1972	17/06/ 1980	19/08/ 1982	01/04/ 1999
Papua New Guinea	15/12/ 1975	15/12/ 1975	15/12/ 1975	30/09/ 2003	30/09/ 2003	11/07/ 2002
Paraguay	09/08/ 1971	04/02/ 1972	05/03/ 1974	24/11/ 1975	22/09/ 2004	06/02/ 1985
Peru	12/05/ 1978	28/04/ 1978	28/04/ 1978	25/04/ 1978	06/07/ 2001	11/01/ 1995
Philippines	26/11/ 1965	26/03/ 1973	26/03/ 1973	26/11/ 1976	14/10/ 1980	22/09/ 1981
Poland	19/03/ 1971	21/03/ 1972	28/01/ 1975	14/12/ 1982	25/05/ 2000	05/10/ 1983
Portugal	25/11/ 1964	27/11/ 1972	15/01/ 1973	11/09/ 1995	06/07/ 1984	06/09/ 1991
Qatar	06/08/ 1981	26/08/ 1981	26/08/ 1981	03/03/ 1997	09/03/ 2004	17/06/ 2003
Romania	15/02/ 1974	10/07/ 1972	15/08/ 1975	15/08/ 1978	17/05/ 1990	23/11/ 1993
Russian Federation	03/02/ 1988	24/09/ 1971	19/02/ 1973	15/01/ 1976	11/06/ 1987	25/05/ 1983
Rwanda	17/05/ 1971	03/11/ 1987	03/11/ 1987	29/11/ 1977	13/05/ 2002	16/05/ 2002
Saint Kitts and Nevis	17/01/ 1991	17/01/ 2002	09/05/ 2002	16/11/ 2001	16/11/ 2001	
Saint Lucia	31/10/ 1983	08/11/ 1983	08/11/ 1983	11/06/ 1990	20/05/ 2004	20/05/ 2004
Saint Vincent & Grenadines	18/11/ 1991	29/11/ 1991	29/11/ 1991	12/09/ 2000	12/09/ 2000	29/11/ 1991
Samoa	09/07/ 1998	09/07/ 1998	09/07/ 1998	09/07/ 1998	18/05/ 2004	09/07/ 1998
San Marino	12/03/ 2002	12/03/ 2002				
Sao Tome and Principe	04/05/ 2006	08/05/ 2006	08/05/ 2006	12/04/ 2006	23/08/ 2006	08/05/ 2006
Saudi Arabia	21/11/ 1969	14/06/ 1974	14/06/ 1974	01/03/ 2004	08/01/ 1991	21/02/ 1989
Senegal	09/03/ 1972	03/02/ 1978	03/02/ 1978	07/04/ 2006	10/03/ 1987	03/11/ 2003
Serbia	06/09/ 2001	23/07/ 2001	23/07/ 2001	12/03/ 2001	12/03/ 2001	06/09/ 2001

7 Airport Protection Protocol	8 Maritime Conv.	9 Fixed Platforms Protocol	10 Plastic Explosive Conv.	11 Terrorist Bombings Conv.	12 Terrorist Financing Conv.	13 Nuclear Terrorism Conv.
10/04/ 1996	03/07/ 2002	03/07/ 2002	12/04/ 1996	05/03/ 1999	03/07/ 2002	
30/09/ 2003	30/09/ 2003					
23/07/ 2002	12/11/ 2004	12/11/ 2004	15/10/ 2004	22/09/ 2004	30/11/ 2004	
07/06/ 1989	19/07/ 2001	19/07/ 2001	07/02/ 1996	10/11/ 2001	10/11/ 2001	
17/12/ 2003	06/01/ 2004	06/01/ 2004	17/12/ 2003	07/01/ 2004	07/01/ 2004	
12/08/ 2004	25/06/ 1991	25/06/ 1991	26/09/ 2006	03/02/ 2004	26/09/ 2003	
18/12/ 2001	05/01/ 1996	05/01/ 1996	09/10/ 2002	10/11/ 2001	18/10/ 2002	
18/09/ 2003	18/09/ 2003	09/11/ 1998				
03/09/ 1998	02/06/ 1993	02/06/ 1993	21/09/ 1998	29/07/ 2004	09/01/ 2003	
31/03/ 1989	04/05/ 2001	04/05/ 2001	08/05/ 2001	27/11/ 2002		
13/05/ 2002	13/05/ 2002					
09/10/ 2001	09/10/ 2001	15/09/ 2005	28/03/ 2002			
27/09/ 2002						
05/05/ 2006	N/A	12/04/ 2006	12/04/ 2006			
02/02/ 2006	02/02/ 2006	11/07/ 1996				
24/03/ 2003	09/08/ 2004	09/08/ 2004	11/02/ 2004	27/10/ 2003	24/09/ 2004	
10/05/ 2004	02/03/ 2005	22/06/ 2006	31/07/ 2003	10/10/ 2002	26/09/ 2006	

Country/ Instrument	1 Aircraft Conv.	2 Unlawful Seizure Conv.	3 Civil Aviation Conv.	4 Diplo Agents Conv.	5 Hostage Taking Conv.	6 Nuclear Mat. Conv.
Seychelles	04/01/ 1979	29/12/ 1978	29/12/ 1978	29/05/ 1980	12/11/ 2003	13/08/ 2003
Sierra Leone	09/11/ 1970	13/11/ 1974	20/09/ 1979	26/09/ 2003	26/09/ 2003	26/09/ 2003
Singapore	01/03/ 1971	12/04/ 1978	12/04/ 1978	22/11/ 1996	03/02/ 2004	20/01/ 2003
Slovakia	20/03/ 1995	13/12/ 1995	06/03/ 1995	28/05/ 1993	28/05/ 1993	10/02/ 1993
Slovenia	18/12/ 1992	27/05/ 1992	27/05/ 1992	06/07/ 1992	06/07/ 1992	07/07/ 1992
Solomon Islands	23/03/ 1982	13/04/ 1982				
Somalia						
South Africa	26/05/ 1972	30/05/ 1972	30/05/ 1972	23/09/ 2003	23/09/ 2003	21/09/ 1998
Spain	01/10/ 1969	30/10/ 1972	30/10/ 1972	08/08/ 1985	26/03/ 1984	06/09/ 1991
Sri Lanka	30/05/ 1978	30/05/ 1978	30/05/ 1978	27/02/ 1991	08/09/ 2000	11/02/ 1997
Sudan	25/05/ 2000	18/01/ 1979	18/01/ 1979	10/10/ 1994	19/06/ 1990	18/05/ 2000
Suriname	10/09/ 1979	27/10/ 1978	27/10/ 1978	05/11/ 1981	27/03/ 2003	27/03/ 2003
Swaziland	15/11/ 1999	27/12/ 1999	27/12/ 1999	04/04/ 2003	04/04/ 2003	17/04/ 2003
Sweden	17/01/ 1967	07/07/ 1971	10/07/ 1973	01/07/ 1975	15/01/ 1981	01/08/ 1980
Switzerland	21/12/ 1970	14/09/ 1971	17/01/ 1978	05/03/ 1985	05/03/ 1985	09/01/ 1987
Syrian Arab Republic	31/07/ 1980	10/07/ 1980	10/07/ 1980	25/04/ 1988	18/07/ 2002	24/03/ 2003
Tajikistan	20/03/ 1996	29/02/ 1996	29/02/ 1996	19/10/ 2001	06/05/ 2002	11/07/ 1996
Thailand	06/03/ 1972	16/05/ 1978	16/05/ 1978	14/05/ 1996	25/01/ 2006	29/09/ 2004
Timor-Leste						
Togo	26/07/ 1971	09/02/ 1979	09/02/ 1979	30/12/ 1980	25/07/ 1986	07/06/ 2006

7 Airport Protection Protocol	8 Maritime Conv.	9 Fixed Platforms Protocol	10 Plastic Explosive Conv.	11 Terrorist Bombings Conv.	12 Terrorist Financing Conv.	13 Nuclear Terrorism Conv.
21/05/ 2004	24/01/ 1989	24/01/ 1989	14/08/ 2003	22/08/ 2003	30/03/ 2004	09/01/ 2006
26/09/ 2003						
30/12/ 2002						
20/03/ 1995	08/12/ 2000	08/12/ 2000	20/03/ 1995	08/12/ 2000	13/09/ 2002	23/03/ 2006
27/05/ 1992	18/07/ 2003	18/07/ 2003	05/06/ 2000	25/09/ 2003	23/09/ 2004	
08/07/ 2005	08/07/ 2005	01/12/ 1999	01/05/ 2003	01/05/ 2003		
08/05/ 1991	07/07/ 1989	07/07/ 1989	31/05/ 1994	30/04/ 1999	09/04/ 2002	
04/09/ 2000	11/10/ 2001	23/03/ 1999	08/09/ 2000			
15/05/ 2000	22/05/ 2000	22/05/ 2000	25/05/ 2000	08/09/ 2000	05/05/ 2003	
17/04/ 2003	17/04/ 2003	13/05/ 2003	04/04/ 2003	04/04/ 2003		
26/07/ 1990	13/09/ 1990	13/09/ 1990	06/09/ 2001	06/06/ 2002		
09/10/ 1990	12/03/ 1993	12/03/ 1993	03/04/ 1995	23/09/ 2003	23/09/ 2003	
24/03/ 2003	29/09/ 2004	24/04/ 2005				
29/02/ 1996	12/08/ 2005	12/08/ 2005	18/07/ 2006	29/07/ 2002	16/07/ 2004	
09/02/ 1990	10/03/ 2003	10/03/ 2003	22/07/ 2003	10/03/ 2003	10/03/ 2003	

Country/ Instrument	1 Aircraft Conv.	2 Unlawful Seizure Conv.	3 Civil Aviation Conv.	4 Diplo Agents Conv.	5 Hostage Taking Conv.	6 Nuclear Mat. Conv.
Tonga	13/02/ 2002	21/02/ 1977	21/02/ 1977	09/12/ 2002	09/12/ 2002	24/01/ 2003
Trinidad and Tobago	09/02/ 1972	31/01/ 1972	09/02/ 1972	15/06/ 1979	01/04/ 1981	25/04/ 2001
Tunisia	25/02/ 1975	16/11/ 1981	16/11/ 1981	21/01/ 1977	18/06/ 1997	08/04/ 1993
Turkey	17/12/ 1975	17/04/ 1973	23/12/ 1975	11/06/ 1981	15/08/ 1989	27/02/ 1985
Turkmenistan	30/06/ 1999	25/05/ 1999	25/05/ 1999	25/06/ 1999	25/07/ 1999	07/01/ 2005
Tuvalu	02/12/ 2005					
Uganda	25/06/ 1982	27/03/ 1972	19/07/ 1982	05/11/ 2003	05/11/ 2003	10/12/ 2003
Ukraine	29/02/ 1988	21/02/ 1972	26/01/ 1973	20/01/ 1976	19/06/ 1987	06/07/ 1993
United Arab Emirates	16/04/ 1981	10/04/ 1981	10/04/ 1981	25/02/ 2003	24/09/ 2003	16/10/ 2003
United Kingdom	29/11/ 1968	22/12/ 1971	25/10/ 1973	02/05/ 1979	22/12/ 1982	06/09/ 1991
United Republic of Tanzania	12/08/ 1983	09/08/ 1983	09/08/ 1983	22/01/ 2003	24/05/ 2006	09/03/ 2004
United States of America	05/09/ 1969	14/09/ 1971	01/11/ 1972	26/10/ 1976	07/12/ 1984	13/12/ 1982
Uruguay	26/01/ 1977	12/01/ 1977	12/01/ 1977	13/06/ 1978	04/03/ 2003	24/10/ 2003
Uzbekistan	31/07/ 1995	07/02/ 1994	07/02/ 1994	19/01/ 1998	19/01/ 1998	09/02/ 1998
Vanuatu	31/01/ 1989	22/02/ 1989	06/11/ 1989	09/11/ 2005	18/02/ 1999	18/02/ 1999
Venezuela	04/02/ 1983	07/07/ 1983	21/11/ 1983	19/04/ 2005	13/12/ 1988	23/09/ 2003
Viet Nam	10/10/ 1979	17/09/ 1979	17/09/ 1979	02/05/ 2002	25/08/ 1999	12/07/ 2002
Yemen	26/09/ 1986	29/09/ 1986	29/09/ 1986	09/02/ 1987	14/07/ 2000	05/01/ 2007
Zambia	14/09/ 1971	03/03/ 1987	03/03/ 1987	31/05/ 1995		

7 Airport Protection Protocol	8 Maritime Conv.	9 Fixed Platforms Protocol	10 Plastic Explosive Conv.	11 Terrorist Bombings Conv.	12 Terrorist Financing Conv.	13 Nuclear Terrorism Conv.
10/12/ 2002	06/12/ 2002	06/12/ 2002	10/12/ 2002	09/12/ 2002	09/12/ 2002	
03/04/ 2001	27/07/ 1989	27/07/ 1989	03/04/ 2001	02/04/ 2001		
07/06/ 1994	06/03/ 1998	06/03/ 1998	28/05/ 1997	22/04/ 2005	10/06/ 2003	
07/07/ 1989	06/03/ 1998	06/03/ 1998	14/12/ 1994	30/05/ 2002	28/06/ 2002	
25/05/ 1999	08/06/ 1999	08/06/ 1999	14/01/ 2005	25/06/ 1999	07/01/ 2005	22/09/ 2005
17/03/ 1994	11/11/ 2003	02/07/ 2004	05/11/ 2003	05/11/ 2003		
03/01/ 1990	21/04/ 1994	21/04/ 1994	18/03/ 1999	26/03/ 2002	06/12/ 2002	
09/03/ 1989	15/09/ 2005	15/09/ 2005	21/12/ 1992	23/09/ 2005	23/09/ 2005	
15/11/ 1990	03/05/ 1991	03/05/ 1991	28/04/ 1997	07/03/ 2001	07/03/ 2001	
11/05/ 2005	11/02/ 2003	22/01/ 2003	22/01/ 2003			
19/10/ 1994	06/12/ 1994	06/12/ 1994	09/04/ 1997	26/06/ 2002	26/06/ 2002	
03/12/ 1998	10/08/ 2001	10/08/ 2001	14/06/ 2001	10/11/ 2001	08/01/ 2004	
07/02/ 1994	25/09/ 2000	25/09/ 2000	09/06/ 1999	30/11/ 1998	09/07/ 2001	
25/01/ 2006	31/10/ 2005					
23/09/ 2003						
12/07/ 2002	25/09/ 2002					
30/06/ 2000	30/06/ 2000	23/04/ 2001				

Frank C. Urbancic, Acting Coordinator for Counterterrorism; Russ Travers, Deputy Director of the National Counterterrorism Center

Washington, DC
April 30, 2007

(4:15 p.m. EST)

2006 Country Reports

MR. CASEY: Well, good afternoon, everyone. I congratulate you on—those of you who are now attending your third or fourth briefing of the day, if you include the gaggle from this morning. We wanted to have this opportunity to have two of our officials talk with you today and talk to you in a little more detail about the Country Reports on Terrorism that most of you, I see, have in front of you. We've got some additional information here from NCTC to share with you as well.

Once again, we'll have with us this afternoon our Acting Coordinator for Counterterrorism Mr. Frank Urbancic as well as, in a repeat performance from years past, Russ Travers, who as I think you all know is one of the Deputy Directors over at NCTC.

So, Frank, let me turn the podium over to you and Russ.

MR. URBANCIC: Thanks very much. Thanks. I do have a couple of opening remarks to introduce the report. I'll go through them, and then of course we'll be happy to take your questions after—Russ has got a few points to make as well.

Besides meeting the congressional requirements, the 2006 Report aims to inform, to stimulate constructive debate and to enhance our collective dynamic understanding of the global terrorist threat. It should serve as a reference tool to inform policy makers, the American public and our international partners about our efforts, progress and challenges in the war on terrorism.

As background and introduction, I would note that the Country Reports of 2006 begin with a strategic assessment to illustrate trends and to gage our progress. We are very pleased to note that cooperative international efforts have produced genuine security improvements, particularly in securing borders and transportation, in enhancing document security, in disrupting terrorist financing and in restricting the movement of terrorists.

Working with allies and partners across the world through coordination and information sharing, we have created a less permissive operating environment for terrorists, keeping leaders on the move or hiding. We've degraded their ability to plan and mount attacks. This has contributed to reduced terrorist operational capabilities and detention or deaths of numerous key terrorist leaders.

It's also important to note our shared successes, not to take credit for them but to demonstrate results. The longer we fight terrorism, the better we get at inflicting serious setbacks on our adversaries. Despite this undeniable progress, serious challenges do remain. There's no question about that. The number of incidents increased overall, largely due to terrorist attacks in Iraq and Afghanistan. The perpetrators of these terrorist acts do not represent nation-states and they have no authority, neither do they have any desire, to sign any sort of peace accord with us. As we've said before, this is not the kind of war where you can measure success with conventional numbers. We cannot aspire to a single decisive battle that will break the enemy's back, nor for a hoped—nor can we hope for a signed peace accord to mark victory.

The Report also underscores the barbaric nature that the extremists we are fighting pose for us. The vast majority of the victims were innocent civilians and a majority of them were Muslims. Attacks on children were up more than 80 percent, if you can imagine, with more than 1,800 children killed or injured in terrorist attacks in last—in 2006. The terrorists also targeted workers essential to civilized society. They targeted police. They targeted government leaders. They targeted teachers. They targeted journalists. The international community is working together to confront these extremists because they threaten the right of people everywhere to live in peaceful, just, secure neighborhoods and countries.

On al-Qaida, although we have captured or killed numerous senior al-Qaida operatives, al-Qaida's core elements are resilient and they remain the most immediate national security threat to the United States. They are a significant security challenge to the entire international community as well and they are so recognized. Al-Qaida is highly adaptive. It quickly evolves new methods in response to our countermeasures, and we have to develop countermeasures to those countermeasures.

The international community's success in disrupting terrorist leadership and operational capacity has led al-Qaida to focus greater efforts on misinformation and anti-Western propaganda. What they can't get by force, they want to take by lies. This trend accelerated in 2006 with al-Qaida exploiting the grievances of local groups and attempting to portray itself at the vanguard of a global movement. Al-Qaida openly describes itself as a transnational guerilla movement; it applies classic insurgent strategies at the global level. Through intermediaries, web-based propaganda and subversion of immigrant expatriate populations; al-Qaida inspires local cells to carry on attacks, thus circumventing the need to insert a team across borders or clandestinely to transfer funds and materiel. The 2004 Madrid bombings, the London attacks of 2005 and the thwarted August 2006 attempt to attack passenger jets operating from British airports included elements of this approach.

We have in the Report a section on state sponsors of terrorism. Much of this will not be of surprise to you, unfortunately. Al-Qaida is not the only challenge. Certain states continue to sponsor terrorism and Iran remains at the head of that list. Iran continues to threaten its neighbors. It continues to destabilize Iraq by providing weapons, training, advice and funding to select Iraqi militants. And as the President has said, some of the most powerful improvised explosive devices, IEDs that we are seeing now in Iraq today, include components that came from Iran.

Iran has also expanded its lethal assistance and funding for militant organizations, most notably Hezbollah, Palestinian Islamic Jihad and Hamas. And these all oppose reinvigorated Arab-Israeli peace efforts.

Iranian defiance of UN Security Council resolutions by providing weapons and assistance to Hezbollah demonstrates that Tehran continues to be the most dangerous enabler of terrorism in that region.

In addition, Syria, both directly and in coordination with Hezbollah, has attempted to undermine the democratically elected Government of Lebanon and to roll back progress toward democratization in the Middle East as a whole. Foreign fighters and terrorists continue to transit Syria's borders into Iraq. Syria also continues to provide political and material support to Hezbollah and political support to Palestinian terrorist groups, including the Palestinian Islamic Jihad and Hamas, who base their external leadership in Damascus.

Finally, state sponsors of terrorism pose a potentially grave weapons of mass destruction threat. A WMD program in the hands of a state sponsor of terrorism could easily enable a terrorist organization to acquire sophisticated WMD. Thus, state sponsors of terrorism deserve special attention and they are getting it as potential facilitators of WMD terrorism.

This year's Report also includes a discussion of terrorist safe havens. Safe havens allow terrorists to organize and operate with relative impunity because of challenging geography, because of limited governance capacity, limited political will or other reasons. Whatever the reason, physical safe havens provides security for terrorist leaders and they allow them to plan acts of terrorism around the world. Areas of concern include the Trans-Sahara, Somalia, the Sulawesi/ Sulu Seas, the Afghanistan-Pakistan border. This unfortunately isn't an exhaustive list, but it's illustrative.

Because of the importance of safe havens to terrorists' operational success, the United States is working with our many partners around the world to strengthen counterterrorism capabilities and to build and sustain democratic, well-governed states that respond to the needs of their people while they also control effectively their sovereign national territory. Unfortunately, problem areas do remain.

On Iraq, most of the increase in terrorist attacks in 2006 did take place in Iraq. Much of the increase is due to the spike in violence in Iraq in the aftermath of the bombings of the Al-Askariya Mosque, one of the holiest Shia Muslim sites. And a paramount strategic objective in Iraq and the regions is prevent al-Qaida—that's our objective—its affiliates and other terrorists from enjoying safe haven in Al Anbar or anywhere else in Iraq. Groups such as al-Qaida in Iraq, that's the AQI; Ansar al-Islam, the AI; or the Ansar al-Sunna, the AS; as well as the Kurdistan Workers' Party, the PKK, as it's formerly known and which we continue to use as a shorthand; view Iraq as potential safe haven and they are attempting to make that into a reality.

Iraq, however, is an ally in the war on terror. Developing Iraq's security forces will require further training and resources before they can address effectively the terrorist groups already operating within Iraq's borders without further international assistance. Iraq's intelligence services continued to improve in both competency and confidence in 2006 and they require additional support before they can identify and respond adequately to internal and external terrorist threats in the future.

The international community's support is critical to ensure the Government of Iraq's plans to reduce violence, to improve services and to increase economic opportunities are successful. Prospects for increasing stability in Iraq will depend on the extent to which the Iraqi Government and political leaders can establish effective national institutions that transcend sectarian or ethnic interests. The Government of Iraq must continue to authorize its security forces to pursue extremist elements of all kinds. Success will also depend on the extent of the international support to the Government of Iraq to do so, the extent to which extremists, most notably the AQI, can be defeated in their attempt to foment inter-sectarian struggle between Shia and Sunnis, and the extent to which Iraq's neighbors, especially Iran and Syria, can be persuaded to stop the flow of militants' ammunitions across their borders.

In Pakistan, the Federally Administered Tribal Areas, the FATA of Pakistan, have become safe haven for al-Qaida terrorists and other extremist insurgents since the fall of the Taliban in December 2001. Despite Pakistan's effort to eliminate threats and to establish effective governance in the FATA, these tribal areas continue to be terrorist safe havens and sources of instability for Pakistan and its neighbors.

The Pakistani Government maintains approximately 80,000 troops, including army and Frontier Corps units along the Afghanistan border. The U.S. plans to help modernize and increase the capacity of the Frontier Corps so that they can become a more effective force. Pakistan Army and Frontier Corps units have targeted and raided al-Qaida and other militant safe havens in the FATA. The failure of the tribal leaders in the FATA to fulfill their promises to the government under the terms of the North Waziristan agreements which were signed in September led to additional insurgent infiltration into Afghanistan.

For our part, the State Department recognizes that military actions alone do not eliminate the terrorist threat. And we are working through the Regional Strategic Initiative with Ambassadors and interagency representatives in key terrorist countries of operation to assess the threat and to devise collaborative strategies, action plans and policy recommendations. We employ all the tools of state craft to establish long-term measures to marginalize terrorists.

Our strategy is aimed over the long term. With time our goal and regional cooperative efforts will reduce the terrorist capacity to harm us and our partners on a local security and development assistance will build—I'm sorry—to harm us and our partners, while local security and development assistance will build our partners' capacity.

Once partner capacity exceeds the threat, the need for close U.S. engagement and support will diminish and the threat will be reduced to a level that our partners can manage for themselves. As of December 2006, RSI strategy groups were already in place for Southeast Asia, Iraq and its neighbors, the eastern Mediterranean, the western Mediterranean and East Africa. In 2007 we have already organized a strategy session with our ambassadors in the Trans-Sahara, while new sessions are scheduled for South Asia and Latin America later this year, in addition to the groups that will continue functioning and that are already established.

Our strategy to defeat terrorists is structured at multiple levels: a global campaign to counter violent extremism and disrupt terrorist networks; a series of regional collaborative efforts to deny terrorists safe havens; numerous bilateral security and development assistance programs which are designed to build liberal institutions, support law enforcement and the rule of law; to address political and economic injustice; and to develop military and security capacity.

This enhances our partners' capacity to resist the terrorist threat and to address conditions that terrorists exploit. You'll find in the report as well, as in past years, regional overviews and reports on terrorists—the terrorist situation in individual countries. We note progress and a lack of progress where appropriate. Examples include: (a) Afghanistan, which remains threatened by the Taliban, insurgents and religious extremists; (b) close cooperation between Pakistani, British and United States law enforcement agencies which expose the August London Heathrow bomb plot; (c) the capture of Abu Faraj al-Libbi which disrupted contacts in the Middle East and North Africa, the death of Ayman al-Zawahiri's lieutenants in January in Pakistan; (d) the 2006—in 2006 the Canadians disrupted a major extremist plot on their own territory and arrested 17 individuals in Toronto and; (e) in March the Australians arrested three suspected terrorists in Melbourne as part of an ongoing counterterrorism operation which disrupted a significant threat to that community.

We must measure counterterrorism success in the broadest perspective. While killing and capturing key terrorist actors is fundamental in combating terrorism, these actions do not eliminate the threat. We must also seek to build trusted networks of governments, private citizens and organizations, multilateral institutions, and business groups that will work collaboratively to defeat the threat from violent extremism and its radical ideology. Such networks, over time, help wean at-risk populations away from subversive manipulation by terrorists and they create mechanisms to address people's needs and grievances, thus marginalizing the terrorists.

I'll refer you to the report for any additional specifics that you might like, but I'll cut it short here to take some questions after Russ Travers has had a chance to talk about the methodology and the numbers because we don't want to confuse you with what we've done. Thank you very much.

MR. TRAVERS: Thanks, Frank. What I will do is give you kind of a quick overview, a high level on what we counted, how we counted matters for 2006. I would emphasize that there's a great deal more material on the nctc.gov website. That'll give you a sense of the methodology. It gives you, actually, a search engine against which you can look at all of the incidents if you're so inclined.

Next please, John.

I don't want this to be a methodology brief, but a couple important points. There are over a hundred definitions of terrorism according to political scientists. To avoid any controversy, we focused on the statutory definitions. Up through 2004, we used the definition there of international terrorism and that specifically emphasizes citizens or territory of more than one country. What we found was that there were some very important incidents that didn't get counted so that in 2005, we made a switch and we're now using a much broader definition of terrorism.

If you think about the key parameters, it's attacks against noncombatants for political reasons. And so it's an extraordinarily broad definition and as a result, what we've seen is that the incident totals have grown from a few hundred to well over 10,000.

Next please, John.

Since we've made the definitional switch, we have two full years of data for 2005 and 2006. Bottom lines, as Frank indicated, the incidents have grown from about 11,000 in '05 to something—or 14,000 in '06. Fatalities up from about 14.5 thousand to about 20.5 thousand. Total victims actually in '05 and '06; that is, killed, wounded and kidnapped, about 74,000 in both years.

Two very important points: There is absolutely no question that cataloguing incidents over time can help give you some significant trends with relationship to what's going on in the terrorism problem. However, we are very convinced that trying to combine global totals on a year-by-year basis doesn't tell you very much. Why? Because embedded in a global total would be, for instance, the FARC in Colombia, ETA in Spain, the Maoists in Nepal, Lord's Resistance Army in Africa, and al-Qaida and all the Sunni affiliates. Simply adding all of those categories together just doesn't tell you very much and as Frank said, numbers can never be the total metric for terrorism. I see some of you having trouble looking at these. You've got—your packages actually have got the full set of viewgraphs in the materials.

Next, please, John.

So we have to boil it down a little bit. What you see here is a regional breakout. The first point I would make is that terrorism is a tactic used around the globe. Here you've got in the dark color '05, in the red color '06 data. As you can see in the combination of the Near East and South Asia accounts for about 80 percent of the total. I mentioned that the total terrorist incidents have gone up from about 11,000 to 14,000. As you can see, most of that growth occurs in the Near East and most of that is accounted for by Iraq and I'll get into that here in a second. The rest of the world is relatively flat. There are some puts and takes and I'll walk you through those very quickly as we burrow down into countries.

Next please.

We'll look at Iraq first. The lower left-hand box will give you a sense of both incidents and fatalities as they grew from '05 to '06. And as a share of the total worldwide incidents, Iraq accounted for just under half of the total incidents and about two-thirds of the total fatalities. The top graph gives you a sense of what was going on month by month in Iraq. The light blue incidents with the scale on the left would be incident totals and the darker color will give you suicide bombings on the right.

Frank alluded to the bombing of the Golden Mosque on the 22nd of February and as he suggested, after that, you can see how the incident totals grew significantly across Iraq. Of somewhat interest, I think, might be the issue of suicide bombings. And you can see in the first six months of the year, suicide bombings are actually quite low relative to the second six months.

We don't know exactly why, but a couple of possibilities: You may recall that in the middle of 2005, Zawahiri admonished Zarqawi about indiscriminate bombings of Shia. That may be manifest in the first six months of the year, it may be because we were able to interdict suicide pipeline. Irrespective what was going on, quite clearly, there was a decision in—sometime in the spring of last year to try to incite sectarian violence and suicide bombings increased dramatically in the second half of the year.

Next please.

With respect to the rest of the world, the lower left-hand graph again will show you the fatalities and incident totals: relatively flat. We'll get into some of the specifics, but working our way from left to right, obviously no major attacks in the United States. There were, according to Consular Affairs, 28 American citizens that were killed overseas. In the Western Hemisphere, Colombia was the—certainly had the most terrorist incidents, about 750. That's very close to what we saw in 2005.

In the Middle East, Israel was up dramatically in terms of increased rocket attacks in Israel, although suicide bombings was down in Israel to very small numbers last year. There were no major attacks in either Jordan or Saudi Arabia.

Europe and Russia, nothing to compare to the July 7th bombings in the UK and Europe, and similarly nothing like what we've seen in previous years for the bombings in Chechnya and Russia over the last several years.

In Africa, the Algerian Salafist Group for Preaching and Combat, GSPC, merged with al-Qaida in the fall and we saw the first attacks against Western and U.S. interests, and that presaged also what we've seen here over the last several months.

In South Africa, a number of locations in Sub-Saharan Africa, there were additional numbers of attacks. I will tell you that the data for that part of the world is the most suspect of anyplace in the world.

In South Asia, Afghan attacks were up by about 60 percent. Pakistan and India both had fewer attacks. And in the Far East, Indonesia for the first time in several years had no major attack. We've seen attacks there every fall over the last several years until last year. In Philippines, attacks were up somewhat. In Thailand, attacks were down somewhat.

I would call your attention to that lower right-hand box; numerous plots either disrupted or just fizzled. An important point: If, as Frank suggested, the attacks in the UK, if the air plot had occurred, we'd been giving you a very different brief today. So the difference between success and failure can be very, very close.

Next, please.

In terms of types of attacks, on the left-hand side you see a pie chart that breaks out the different ways in which terrorists conducted their attacks. This looks very similar to 2005. Roughly half of all incidents were armed attacks and roughly a quarter were bombings and then the other quarter broken out in the various categories.

On the right-hand side, suicide bombings. As I mentioned, they were down last year from '05 and that's largely because of the first six months in Iraq being down. However, Afghanistan went up dramatically, by about a factor of five or six. And again, this is only attacks against noncombatants. We don't track military attacks in Afghanistan or Iraq.

Next, please.

And finally, with respect to victims, as I mentioned at the outset, about 74,000 victims—that's killed, wounded and kidnapped. In terms of fatalities themselves, a couple of key data points. As I mentioned, 28 Americans killed. Like last year, Muslims bore a disproportionate share of the attacks. Of the 20,000 fatalities, certainly something over half of all fatalities worldwide were Muslims, largely at the hands of other Islamic extremists.

Other categories, as it suggests there on the chart, several thousand police officers—and Frank gave you some numbers—many hundreds of children and teachers and press and so forth. So many categories. These are undoubtedly low. They were only the indications we get from reporting. The numbers are undoubtedly higher.

And finally, let me close with one more warning about just using gross total numbers. The chart on the right gives you a graph of fatality ranges and the number of people that were actually killed by—broken out by incidents. The chart there, as you can see on the right-hand side, like last year, over half of all incidents had no fatalities whatsoever, whereas you can see on the far left-hand chart, something less than 300 incidents accounted for over one-third of all fatalities. So it was—on the left-hand side you're getting a sense of just how many fatalities were caused by individual incidents.

So with that, I'd be happy to stop and turn it back over to Frank.

QUESTION: Let me ask just some numerical questions to start. Can you give us the figures for the number of terrorism-related fatalities in Iraq in 2006 versus 2005 and in Afghanistan in 2006 versus 2005? I don't believe they're in there. There's one rough estimate of about 13,000 for Iraq. But taking your point that one shouldn't just use gross numbers; can you give us the precise numbers for fatalities for Iraq and Afghanistan and the five comparatives?

MR. TRAVERS: I can. Why do you—we've got other questions, I'll come back to this and we can get those for you. Sure.

QUESTION: Okay. Great. And then the second question that I had was looking at the fact—and this may be for you, sir—looking at the fact that the majority of deaths clearly occurred in Iraq, do you believe that the war in Iraq ultimately has been good for the effort to reduce terrorism generally?

MR. URBANCIC: You know, if the battle against terrorism isn't in Iraq, it's going to be somewhere else. It started out in Afghanistan. The terrorists are looking for places where they can operate and that's what they're doing. So we can fight them in Iraq, we can fight them somewhere else. The fact is they are there and they're going to find other ungoverned spaces and they're doing that and they're expanding—they're expanding their scope. So yes, I mean, Iraq is at least a relatively friendly place. The people of Iraq are deserving people and they deserve better and it's good for us to help them.

I can start.

QUESTION: Yeah. Can I just—I have another numbers question, and that is—and then I have another one. Why did you choose to say there was a 25 percent increase in the number of attacks when, in fact, the percentage is slightly higher than that—almost 29 percent?

MR. TRAVERS: You will have slightly different numbers here in the book because the information cutoff—I mean, these numbers change. As you'll find out, the '05 numbers that we have are different than the '05 numbers that were in country reports. I don't know what you've got there exactly.

QUESTION: It's the same in the report and in your—in this little fact sheet. You have incidents growing from 11,153 to 14,338, which I believe is about a 28.5 percent increase. And yet the copy—these say 25 percent. I'm just curious as to why you used the lower 25 percent figure, as opposed to—

MR. TRAVERS: Probably it points to the art, not science, aspect of this, as you suggest. I also said I think that Iraq counted for half of the total incidents. In reality, it's closer to 45 percent. So I mean, what we're trying to do is give you an order of magnitude on these numbers.

QUESTION: Can you then—and this is the non-number question. What is it that has made a—that has turned a 25 percent or 28.5 percent increase—why has that resulted in a 40 percent or 40.2 percent jump in fatalities?

MR. URBANCIC: Well, I mean, that —

QUESTION: That is an exponentially larger —

MR. URBANCIC: I'll go back to that, but if we could start out, we would like to emphasize the text of this report. We're mandated to produce the numbers and we're happy to do that and Russ is doing an extremely competent job. But I really wouldn't want to get involved in a discussion about. 2 percent versus.6 percent. So just—I'd beware of that—

QUESTION: That's fine, but it's not.2 percent. It is 3.5 percent.

MR. URBANCIC: Okay. But I'd just like to get that out there. We'd like to talk about the text. That's our primary focus on this.

And the terrorists, there's no question, are intelligent people and they learn from each other. They learn from each other—they watch each other. The people in Afghanistan are watching the people in Iraq. The people in Iraq are watching the people elsewhere, and there's a snowball effect and they work through the internet. They communicate. They're working on all kinds of nasty things. The IEDs are being perfected. There's no question that they're learning. So I mean, I think that's the basic reason. They're efficient people. They're evil people. They have finances and they have contacts. But we have to continue to fight them.

Sir.

QUESTION: What is it that's kept Iraq from being included in the list of safe havens? Well, I mean, you say, I mean, the language on Iraq in the safe haven chapter is almost identical to last year, although the situation seems to have evolved quite a bit. Why is Iraq not considered a safe haven for terrorists?

MR. URBANCIC: Well, it's a potential safe haven this year. And we simply looked at the assessment according to the definition that we use, which is broader than the statutory assessment or the statutory definition. For 2006, that's where we came out. That does not mean that we're not worried about al-Qaida in Iraq. It doesn't mean that we're not worried about the PKK in Iraq. We very seriously are and we're watching it very carefully.

So again, don't be misled by distinctions that don't really count. We are very concerned about the fact that the terrorists want to use Iraq as a safe haven and they're working as hard as they can to turn it into an actual safe haven. There's no question about that.

QUESTION: And why today is it not a safe haven?

MR. URBANCIC: Well, the report addresses 2006. The situation is serious and we're watching it. I mean, there's no question that they are increasing their capabilities.

Sir.

QUESTION: Frank, you said that—I think it was your wording—attacks on children were up more than 80 percent. I was wondering if you could elaborate on that. I mean, are there instances where they were actually singling out busloads of kids? Are you talking about large-scale bombings that were indiscriminate? Is there a trend where they're targeting children?

MR. URBANCIC: So far, thank God, children themselves by and large have not been targets, but the indiscriminate attacks lead to a great increase in—well, they're all innocent, but in the deaths of very, very vulnerable populations.

MR. TRAVERS: Do we get the two different (inaudible)?

MR. URBANCIC: Do you have that?

MR. TRAVERS: Afghanistan in '05 was 684 dead. In '06, 1,040. Iraq, 8,262 up to 13,340.

QUESTION: Thank you.

QUESTION: So Iraq, the first one you gave us?

MR. TRAVERS: Iraq, 8,262.

MR. URBANCIC: Sir.

QUESTION: Mr. Coordinator, do you consider November 17 terrorist organization closed once and for all or is still active since in your report the picture is not clear?

MR. URBANCIC: Well, we hope it's closed.

QUESTION: You don't know if it is or not?

MR. URBANCIC: The actual—if I need a legal response to that, let me get back to you. But there are—the situation—there are, you know, various groups bleeding back and forth into other ones. Let me back to you on that.

QUESTION: So it's not clear yet?

MR. URBANCIC: Let me just get back to you with a more specific answer.

QUESTION: One more question. In your report you are saying that the entire Republic of Cyprus, the Kurdish organization PKK maintain an active presence for the first time. Question: Based on which information you are claiming that since it's very well known, as you said earlier, that PKK members are stationed in northern Iraq and making the Turks very angry?

MR. URBANCIC: Making the Turks very angry. The PKK is—I'm sorry?

QUESTION: About Cyprus, you are saying in the report that for the first time you note very active PKK members in Cyprus. And I was wondering on what did you base this information?

MR. URBANCIC: As you may know, the United States is running—is working actively against the PKK. General Ralston is working the trilateral part with the Turks, the United States and the Iraqi Government. And I, in fact, am leading the part of Western Europe. And what we are finding as we work more and more with our West European allies is that the PKK is like an octopus. It has a head—actually, it has multiple heads in various West European countries and it has tentacles that go throughout West Europe and leading far into East Europe for that matter.

It's a criminal organization in addition to its terrorist aspects and it has money-laundering operations. It has trafficking-in-persons operations. It has operations that would—we would recognize here as basic mafia type operations. And so I think it's not surprising to find them operating in any particular West European country. We are working now to raise both the effectiveness of the counterterrorist threat—our counterterrorist response to the PKK threat in Western Europe and to raise the consciousness and the understanding of the Europeans of the threat that the PKK poses.

QUESTION: Including Cyprus? That's my question.

MR. URBANCIC: Including Cyprus. Cyprus is part of our East European RSI.

Sir.

QUESTION: Yes. On North Korea.

MR. URBANCIC: Our embassy in Cyprus, not the government of Cyprus.

QUESTION: Yeah. North Korea is still on the state sponsors list. What are they going to need to do to get themselves off that finally?

MR. URBANCIC: As you may know, we have an agreement or we reached an agreement this year, so it's not technically covered, although it's in the 2006 report. We have an agreement with the North Koreans that we will take initial steps. This is a—coming off that list is quite a long process. You may recall how long it took us to work on Libya. The same types of things the North Koreans will have to do. But the first initial steps are what's—are what we're committed to. This is not a decision to take them off. It's just a decision to begin the process to begin the discussion.

QUESTION: Okay, because there are specific points.

MR. URBANCIC: That's right.

QUESTION: You know, the question of abductees, the question of the Japanese Red Army.

MR. URBANCIC: That's right.

QUESTION: Are they going to have to address each and every one of those?

MR. URBANCIC: Yes.

QUESTION: So just to follow up on North Korea, could you explain the reasoning why the entry of North Korea this year is much shorter in comparison to the previous years? There's a lot of detail that's been omitted. And the language seems a bit softer also when you say Japanese nationals believed to have been abducted rather than just Japanese nationals who were abducted.

MR. URBANCIC: The Country Reports on Terrorism provides the Department of State's annual statutorily mandated assessment of trends in international terrorism. There are numerous mechanisms that the North Koreans have to meet, but as part of the six-party process to resolve the North Korean nuclear threat the United States agreed on February 13th, 2007 to initial actions, as I mentioned before, to begin the process of removing the designation of the DPRK as a state sponsor of terrorism.

As part of the six-party process we also have begun the process, but there's no timetable set. And the language in the report therefore changes each year to reflect developments in that year. This is technically actually a little out of place since it happened in 2007. And just to alert you, probably the language will be different in 2007 as well—not to predict anything, but across the board, we change the language as developments occur.

QUESTION: So you felt it was reasonable to omit a lot of the detail, especially regarding the Japanese abductees this year in relation to what happened in February of this year?

MR. URBANCIC: Actually, the discussion of 2007, to be quite frank, is simply to be more complete. It does not change what happened in 2006, obviously.

Sir.

QUESTION: I have a question on North Korea. In the text you mentioned about Red Army first and then comes to the abduction issues. And in the previous years in the report, the abduction comes first and Red Army is added at the end. What the reason for the change? I don't recall any particular incident regarding the Red Army?

MR. TRAVERS: I would just urge you not to read too much into this. I think if you just read the—read what it says, it will be complete.

Sir.

QUESTION: So if Pakistan is a safe haven for terrorists and also in the chapter here you are saying that President Karzai also complaining that you have to go after terrorists and terrorism beyond Afghanistan, those who are training and arming and financing and terrorist camps and here I'm referring to Pakistan. And they also have an 80,000-person army on the border. Why can't we control terrorism into Pakistan from Pakistan or

Afghanistan when they are sending terrorism around the globe, and also why don't we have yet Usama bin Laden or his deputy with 80,000 army?

MR. URBANCIC: Okay. Pakistan is an ally in the war on terror. Afghanistan is an ally on the war on terror—in the war on terror. The problem that we have is the border, which neither has complete control over on either side. We are working very strongly with those allies to help them establish control in those areas. That, I think, is the key.

The border area is what we're talking about. There are multiple ways that this has to be addressed. It has to be addressed on the economic side. It has to be addressed on the military side. It also has to be addressed on the social side. And we are acutely aware of both the limitations and the great stress—to the great progress and the great efforts that the government of both Pakistan and Afghanistan have made. We're very pleased that Presidents Karzai and Musharraf were able to meet in Turkey, just finished up, and this is also something that we hope we'll be able to build on in the future.

QUESTION: Just a quick follow-up.

MR. CASEY: We have time for a couple more, so Goyal —

QUESTION: Just a quick one. Sir, I understand that General Musharraf has been ally and also President Karzai as far as global war on terrorism and with the U.S. But at the same time, U.S. has its army there in the area and they have not been allowed to search for Usama bin Laden or go beyond the border. Are you expecting anything, because since they have failed to help the U.S. beyond what they have done so far, are you expecting that now U.S. army may have to take action to find those who are most wanted here in the U.S. and around the globe?

MR. URBANCIC: Well, I certainly—I don't want to speculate on military operations, but I can say that we are working as closely as we can and we have very good cooperation not only with President Musharraf but with the Government of Pakistan, and we anticipate that we will continue to have. As situations evolve, we will have to deal with those situations.

MR. CASEY: Michele.

QUESTION: I just have a very basic question. Why shouldn't Americans look at this report and members of Congress look at this report, the numbers and the analysis, and come to the conclusion that we're losing this war on terrorism?

MR. URBANCIC: Well, for several reasons. First of all, I mean, people who want to draw conclusions or who have prejudgments, they will draw those conclusions. We are working as hard as we can to defeat the terrorists. We have to continue to do that. The situation on the ground—the terrorists are not omnipotent and they are not almighty and they have suffered real losses. We've been very successful against their leadership. We've been very successful in disrupting many of their networks. Not all of the things that we've been successful in doing have been able to be made public, but there are great successes that are out there.

But these people are intelligent and they want spectacular successes against us and they have been able to achieve some of those.

MR. CASEY: Thanks a lot.

MR. URBANCIC: Thank you.

2007/350

C. TERRORIST PRECURSOR CRIMES

TERRORIST PRECURSOR CRIMES: ISSUES AND OPTIONS FOR CONGRESS

CRS Report for Congress

May 24, 2007

Commentary

Terrorist Precursor Crimes: Issues and Options for Congress provides an excellent overview of an issue set that has received far too little attention. The report points out that terrorist groups all require funding, operations security, and coercive power. To meet those fundamental needs, terrorist organizations engage in criminal activity; therefore, they commit an array of "precursor crimes" to facilitate their ultimate acts of terror. The precursor crimes may be committed in the furtherance of overall campaign objectives or to support a particular attack. The key question posed by the CRS report is what can be done, at all levels of government, to identify and thwart such precursor crimes, and where prevention fails, to bring the perpetrators to justice, thus eliminating terrorism capacity over time.

Importantly, the report points out that many of the precursor crimes are committed in wealthy Western countries, especially fundraising crimes. Such crimes include fraud schemes, petty crimes, identity and immigration crimes, counterfeiting of goods and money, illegal drug sales, and illegal weapons dealing. Perhaps the most serious impediment to preventing or prosecuting precursor crimes is that they are not comprehended to be such and, therefore, do not command the law enforcement priority they deserve. The commission of precursor crimes by terrorist groups and sympathizers within the United States presents serious problems and challenges for U.S. law enforcement and intelligence agencies, at all levels of government. Congress, in its role of overseeing federal agencies, is in a position to assist and empower those responsible for terrorist precursor crime investigations and intelligence efforts. Congress has passed several important measures to do so, but more is required.

For example, more work needs to be done to ensure that many disparate federal agencies, with differing bureaucratic cultures, coordinate effectively with each other. Furthermore, Congress should require the Executive Branch to develop and implement an actual interagency strategy for preventing precursor crimes and prosecuting perpetrators. Beyond that, however, the CRS report correctly points out that efforts to prevent and prosecute precursor crimes must extend down to state, local, and tribal (SLT) levels. That is because agencies at those levels are well positioned to assist in the identification and investigation of terrorist precursor crimes. In fact, one could argue that the bulk of the effort should reside at those levels. This will require federal, state, local, and tribal investigative and law enforcement cooperation never before achieved, in a systematic manner.

Notwithstanding the multi-level governmental approach required to thwart precursor crimes, there is much the U.S. Congress can do to promote a coordinated, integrated, and synchronized effort. It can provide an example for SLT governments by reviewing and modifying federal laws for enforcement and prosecution of precursor crimes; fund counterterrorism programs that span levels of government; and promote information-sharing through its oversight of federal agencies engaged in preventing and prosecuting precursor crimes. To do so, Congress must have a thorough appreciation of the issues involved.

The CRS report summarizes issues such as the adequacy of existing terrorism material support statutes; the sufficiency of the manner in which they are interpreted and utilized for prosecutions; the role the private sector plays in identifying, reporting, and helping in the prosecution of fraud schemes, including credit card fraud, coupon fraud, and benefits fraud; and the role and effectiveness of the banking and financial sector in identifying and thwarting terrorist financing. The most serious weakness in the CRS report's analysis is its inadequate discussion of the limitations of law enforcement approaches in preventing rather than prosecuting precursor crimes, after they have occurred.

Law enforcement is reactive; a proactive approach is needed to deny terrorists the means by which to execute attacks. Law enforcement relies on the deterrent effect of the probability of punishment for criminal activity. Terrorists commit precursor crimes based on one of two calculations. Either they see the probability of arrest and punishment to be acceptably low, or they believe the value of the terrorist act will exceed the cost of punishment, even if the cost is life imprisonment or death. Therefore, while law enforcement initiatives are necessary, they are not sufficient, and Congress must look beyond them.

The CRS report does note that the Federal Bureau of Investigation (FBI) has begun to transition into a more prevention-focused, intelligence-driven agency in order to combat terrorism. The CRS report raises questions regarding the need for other agencies to enhance their ability to detect and deter terrorism. It questions whether there is a consistent approach in dealing with precursor crimes that suggests an effective formula for collecting intelligence vice law enforcement information. It also asks if precursor crimes committed in the United States, or by U.S. citizens abroad, are afforded the proper investigative priority. The report presents evidence to suggest that the answers to these questions are generally negative. However, recent congressional testimony indicates that intelligence-sharing and coordination in general have been improving between the various federal intelligence and law enforcement agencies involved in counterterrorism.

The CRS report candidly assesses that the various SLT roles in intelligence collection and investigation of precursor crimes are not as integrated with federal efforts as they should be. The report correctly points out that the agencies responsible for counterterrorism should include SLT law enforcement partners. However, the CRS report also acknowledges that disagreement exists over the roles various SLT assets should play and how to institutionalize counterterrorism efforts within the various organizations. Still, the CRS report correctly assesses the forte of the SLTs to be their ability to identify terrorist precursor crimes. They have the requisite skills and legal authority to investigate and prosecute precursor crimes, have the capacity to do so, and are most familiar with their jurisdictions.

Therefore, the SLTs are "well-positioned to serve as "scouts" in that they can effectively develop information on crimes, activities, and organizations that support terrorist organizations, as part of their normal work routines. Much potential exists to increase their involvement in identifying precursor crimes through training programs or exercises and by increasing their access to current precursor crime intelligence, trends, and *modus operandi*. To those ends, the CRS report notes, SLT agencies can utilize homeland security grant monies to fund training, but appropriate training must be developed and made available. Presently, the CRS report notes that there are few federally certified courses available to SLT agencies that specifically focus on terrorist precursor crimes.

The CRS report correctly concludes that coordination of federal and SLT efforts requires greater emphasis. Policies, protocols, and standard operating procedures need to be established to describe and prescribe how federal and SLT agencies interact. Specifically, when should SLT agencies contact federal agencies to report a suspected precursor crime? Once the report is made, what is the relationship between the federal investigating agency and the reporting SLT agency with respect to case investigation and prosecution? What are the civil rights understandings between the different levels of government and purposes for investigations? How are the various investigative levels educated on the myriad regulations that apply to the investigations? These are thorny questions that must be addressed if SLT agencies are to be brought to bear to assist effectively in the prevention and prosecution of precursor crimes.

DOCUMENT NO. 3

TERRORIST PRECURSOR CRIMES: ISSUES AND OPTIONS FOR CONGRESS

CRS Report
RL34014

May 24, 2007

Siobhan O'Neil
Analyst in Domestic Security and Intelligence
Domestic Social Policy Division

Summary

Terrorist groups, regardless of ideological ilk, geographical location, or organizational structure, have certain basic needs in common: funding, security, operatives/support, propaganda, and means and/or appearance of force. In order to meet these needs, terrorists engage in a series of activities, some of which are legal, many of which are not. Terrorist precursor crimes, offenses committed to facilitate a particular attack or promote a terrorist campaign's objectives, are thought to be often carried out far away from the primary theater of conflict associated with a terrorist group. Much of the precursor activity, especially with regard to crimes conducted for the purpose of fundraising, takes place in wealthy Western countries, including the United States. Precursor crimes, known and/or alleged, include various fraud schemes, petty crime, identity and immigration crimes, the counterfeit of goods, narcotics trade, and illegal weapons procurement, amongst others. The implications of domestically occurring terrorist precursor crimes on the current threat environment, and specifically the United State's security posture, are not fully understood.

It does appear, however, that the likely presence of terrorist groups or their sympathizers conducting precursor crimes within the United States presents a series of unique problems and challenges for U.S. law enforcement and intelligence communities' counterterrorism programs, many of which have important implications for Congress. As Congress conducts oversight of the federal agencies engaged in terrorist precursor crime investigations and intelligence efforts, this phenomenon and U.S. efforts to identify, investigate, and counter it may be of particular concern. One such issue is how these agencies coordinate with one another on the issue of terrorist precursor crimes and whether there is an across-agency strategy on how to deal with such activity. Beyond the federal government agencies, there are numerous state, local, and tribal (SLT) agencies that are well positioned to assist in the identification and investigation of terrorist precursor crimes, but it is often unclear, and at the very least inconsistent, how these agencies are incorporated into existing efforts. In addition to oversight, there are potential budgetary and legislative issues related to terrorist precursor crimes that are of interest to Congress. This report will not be updated.

Introduction

Irrespective of ideology or strategic goals, all terrorist groups have several basic needs in common: funding, security, operatives/support, propaganda, and means and/or appearance of force. In order to meet these needs, terrorists engage in a series of activities, some of which are legal, many of which are not, including various fraud schemes, petty crime, identity and immigration crimes, the counterfeit of goods, narcotics trade, and illegal weapons procurement, amongst others.[1] Terrorist precursor crimes can be defined as unlawful acts undertaken to facilitate a terrorist attack or to support a terrorist campaign. Many terrorist precursor crimes are carried out far away from the primary theater of conflict associated with a particular terrorist group. Much of the precursor activity, especially with regard to crimes conducted for the purpose of fundraising, is thought to take place in wealthy Western countries, including the United States.

This report provides an overview of the types of terrorist precursor crimes known, and/or alleged, to have been employed by individuals and/or groups in the United States. The report highlights issues related to the breadth of this activity in the United States, as well as the opportunities for intelligence collection and law enforcement-related countermeasures.

The report presents an analysis of the implications of domestically occurring terrorist precursor crimes for U.S. security. The presence of terrorist groups or terrorist sympathizers within the United States possibly conducting precursor crimes presents a series of unique problems and challenges.

[1] It is important to note that not all the individuals and/or groups that engage in the illegal activities listed in this report are terrorists or have a nexus to terrorism. Indeed, it is more likely that a very small percentage of individuals engaged in such activity are involved in terrorism. The purpose of this report is to highlight some of those precursor crimes known to be utilized and/or favored by terrorist elements in order to facilitate their attacks and/or other strategic objectives.

Unfortunately, there does not appear to be a consensus with regard to some of the fundamental questions associated with this issue: How does the presence of precursor activity affect the current threat environment? What is the current approach for dealing with terrorist precursor crimes? How effective are current efforts and what are areas for improvement?

The report's scope is largely limited to terrorist precursor crime occurring domestically, although some foreign examples are mentioned to demonstrate the importance of this issue and the extent terrorist groups are engaged in criminal activity to forward their agendas. It is beyond the scope of this report, however, to address each of the myriad national security policy implications associated with this issue. Thus, one area, the role of federal, state, and local agencies in addressing domestic, terrorist precursor crimes, is examined in greater detail.

Increase in Precursor Criminal Activity: Causes

According to numerous terrorism scholars and analysts, there are indications that terrorists are increasingly relying on non-terroristic, precursor crimes to facilitate their terrorist attacks and/or further their terrorist campaign.[2] Additionally, it appears that terrorist groups are diversifying and expanding the variety of crimes they commit.[3] The cause for the increase in pre-attack criminal activity may be due to the following four factors:

- the decline in state sponsorship;
- the amateurization and decentralization of terror;
- enhanced counterterrorism measures,
- and changing terrorist demographics (i.e. shifts in ideology, strategy, and capabilities).

It is important to note that not all groups and not all members and/or supporters of such groups engage in such activity. There are some groups that appear adverse to conducting criminal acts in order to facilitate their objectives out of ideological concerns. Some may avoid criminal activity out of logistical concerns, for example criminal activity may be viewed as a liability, enhancing the potential for detection and apprehension of operatives. In other instances, criminal activity may be isolated within a particular strata or division of a group, in order to protect key operatives, spokesmen,

[2] The Canadian Security Intelligence Service's (CSIS) Integrated Threat Assessment Centre (ITAC) "Actual and Potential Links Between Terrorism and Criminality," Trends in Terrorism Series, Volume 2006-5, available at [http://www.csis-scrs.gc.ca/en/itac/itacdocs/2006-5.asp], accessed on May 4, 2007.

[3] Ibid.

and charismatic leaders from potential detection. There are instances where a group's involvement in precursor crimes remains the subject of debate.[4]

Decline in State Sponsorship

State sponsorship of terrorism has dramatically decreased since the 1970s and 1980's when Dan Byman estimates that "almost every important terrorist group had some ties to at least one supportive government."[5] The manner and extent of state sponsorship have changed significantly over the last several decades. By Byman's assessment, of the 36 terrorist groups the U.S. State Department had labeled with Foreign Terrorist Organization (FTO) status by 2002, "twenty had enjoyed significant state support at one point in history" and of that 20, only nine still maintained a state sponsor.[6] Coinciding with the end of the Cold War there was a shift in the manner and volume of state sponsorship which forced many groups to identify other sources of revenue.[7]

Some terrorist groups turned to legitimate investments and business opportunities. Much attention has been paid to al Qaeda's business dealings in Sudan in the early 1990s. According to Jean-Charles Brisard who testified before the Senate Banking Committee in 2003, Osama bin Laden invested in and/or operated a bank, several import-export firms, several agricultural companies and a construction company with connections to his family's bin Laden construction conglomerate, while living in Sudan between 1991 and 1996.[8] As with many groups, al Qaeda used an amalgam

---

[4] Al Qaeda's purported tie to Afghan opium provides an interesting example. There have been numerous assertions in the press that the group was heavily involved in its production and trade. However, David Kaplan of US News and World Report cites counterterrorism officials who call those assertions "flat wrong," claiming, "long ago, al Qaeda strategists reasoned that drug trafficking would expose them to possible detection. . .[and since] they don't trust many of the big drug barons . . . [they] encouraged their members not to get involved with them"—David E. Kaplan, "Paying for Terror: How Jihadist Groups are Using Organized-Crime Tactics—and Profits—to Finance Attacks on Targets Around the Globe," US News and World Report, December 5, 2005. If this account is accurate, al Qaeda's choice may have been borne of logistical security concerns and a lack of acute need for funds. Yet, there are reports suggesting that while al Qaeda has not actively joined in on the opium trade, it has increasingly utilized the smuggling routes used to move opium from Afghanistan to neighboring countries and beyond. In 2004, media reports suggested "recent U.S. Navy seizures in the Persian Gulf of several small boats carrying heroin and hashish along with alleged Al Qaeda operatives offered the first firm indication of a link between the terrorist network and drug trafficking"—Liz Sly, "Opium Cash Fuels Terror, Experts Say; Taliban, Al Qaeda Profit from Trade in Afghanistan," Chicago Tribune, February 9, 2004. Again, logistical concerns regarding the safe movement of operatives may have driven al Qaeda into this marriage of convenience, if they are indeed involved in the opium trade and/or utilizing related smuggling routes.

[5] Dan Byman, *Deadly Connections: States that Sponsor Terrorism*, (Cambridge, UK: Cambridge University Press, 2005), 1, henceforth referred to as Byman, *Deadly Connections*.

[6] Ibid., 3.

[7] However, Byman says that some groups continue to receive significant financial support from state sponsors (i.e. Hezbollah from Iran). Many groups receive other kinds of support today other than money: operational/training, arms/logistics, diplomatic backing, help with organization, ideological direction, and sanctuary. Byman, *Deadly Connections*, Chapter 3.

[8] Jean-Charles Brisard, "Prepared Testimony of Jean-Charles Brisard International Expert on Terrorism Financing, Lead Investigator, 911 Lawsuit CEO, JCB Consulting International, Testimony before the Senate Committee on Banking, Housing and Urban Affairs, October 22, 2003, Federal News Service.

of means, both legal and illegal, to raise funds and facilitate its activity. Reportedly, numerous groups rely heavily on a wide range of crimes to facilitate their goals, including Hezbollah, the Irish Republican Army (IRA), Abu Sayyaf, the Liberation Tigers of Tamil Eelam (LTTE) and the Revolutionary Armed Forces of Colombia (FARC), among many others.[9]

Amateurization of Terror

As terrorism has become more decentralized over the last decade, with groups adopting less hierarchical, cell networks and the proliferation of technology, information, and inspiration to support autonomous terror, there has been a proliferation of smaller, autonomous (or semi-autonomous) cells.[10] Such groups often have fewer concrete links to larger, more organized terrorist groups and thus limited access to organized, large-scale fundraising mechanisms. In addition, many of these smaller cells mount more limited and less sophisticated attacks, which require less infrastructure, expertise, and expensive weaponry. Thus, amateur terrorists are likely to require significantly fewer funds. For example, while the September 11th attacks are estimated to have cost approximately $400,000–$500,000,[11] the July 7, 2005 London bombings are estimated to have cost between several hundred and £ 8,000 (approximately $15,600).[12] This is not a phenomenon limited to Britain. It appears that small, semi-autonomous terrorist cells in many countries have discovered that they are capable of conducting violently disruptive activities without extensive outside financial and/or logistical support, and, as such, numerous cells appear to have turned to precursor criminal activities to do just that.[13]

---

9 See for example Oded Lowenheim, "Transnational Criminal Organizations and Security: The Case Against Inflating the Threat," in *International Journal*, Vol. 57 No.4/Autumn 2002, available from [http://www.lexis.com], accessed on April 23, 2007.

10 Exactly how autonomous these newer, smaller terrorist cells are remains debated. Some, like Bruce Hoffman, have argued that "ongoing investigations increasingly suggest that recent terrorist threats and attacks—the foiled 2004 plan to stage simultaneous suicide attacks in the United States, the 2005 suicide bus and subway bombings in London and the August 2006 plot to blow up 10 planes over the Atlantic—were all coordinated in some way by Al Qaeda and not by homegrown terror groups." Bruce Hoffman, "Remember Al Qaeda? They're baaack: Defeating Osama bin Laden's resurgent terrorist network requires far more than military might," Los Angeles Times, February 20, 2007. While these new cells, like the one that perpetrated the 2005 London transit bombings, may have connections to, and in some cases may have been in part trained, funded, or directed, by 'corporate' al Qaeda, there is clearly a distinction between this type of cell and those that were handpicked and directly managed by al Qaeda's upper-level leadership. The former are clearly part of a more decentralized, inspired cell network of like-minded believers who see themselves as part of the global jihad, even if they don't have the same level of involvement with the professional terrorist cadre.

11 The National Commission on Terrorist Attacks on the United States, The Final Report of the National Commission on Terrorist Attacks on the United States, Official Government Edition, available from [http://www.9-11commission.gov/], accessed on October 30, 2006, 169.

12 Quoting British police officials, BBC, *London Bombs Cost Just Hundreds*, January 3, 2006 available from [http://news.bbc.co.uk/], accessed on October 30, 2006, and quoting Home Secretary John Reid, BBC, *Resourcing Blamed Over July Bombs*, May 11, 2006 available from [http://news.bbc.co.uk/] accessed on October 30, 2006.

13 There are examples of terrorist cells that funded their activities through their own wages and savings and/or a combination thereof with petty crime.

Enhanced Counterterrorism Measures

Enhanced counterterrorism measures, especially with regard to freezing certain charity and front business holdings, additional regulations within the banking sector, and monitoring money remittances may have caused terrorist elements to utilize different techniques for fundraising and money laundering. One notable example of a possible causal relationship is the result of the U.S. law enforcement crackdown on the Irish Republican Army's (IRA) American-based fundraising activities, which some experts have cited as the driving cause of the IRA's turn to criminal activity to fill that void and continue to fund its initiatives.[14] In the last three decades, the IRA is reported to have been involved in everything from protection/extortion rackets, bank robbery, tax evasion, construction fraud, weapons and explosives running, to cigarette/narcotics smuggling.

Shift in Threat Environment

The terrorist threat environment has changed significantly since the dawn of modern international terrorism in 1968. For example, the number of terrorist groups with primarily religious objectives has risen dramatically, the lethality of terrorism has increased, and the number of groups that are no longer satisfied with limited, symbolic violence—but rather seek to cause large-scale carnage—has increased. This altered terrorist demographic may help to explain why terrorist groups today are increasingly reliant on precursor crimes.

At that time—the height of the Cold War—the terrorist threat environment was thought to be dominated by "left-wing, revolutionary Marxist-Leninist ideological organizations."[15] In 1968, according to data from the RAND/St. Andrew's Terrorism Chronology,[16] eight of the 11 identifiable terrorist organizations could be classified as such and the other three were Palestinian ethno-nationalist groups. Due to their state sponsorship and concern that such activity would tarnish the statesman-like image they created for themselves, many of these groups did not engage in significant criminal activity. Today, groups with predominately religious or religio-nationalist

---

[14] For example, Mark Hamm, *Crimes Committed by Terrorist Groups: Theory, Research, and Prevention*, September 2005, available from [http://www.ncjrs.gov/pdffiles1/nij/grants/211203.pdf], accessed on November 14, 2006, 5.

[15] Bruce Hoffman, *Inside Terrorism*, (London: Indigo, 1999), 90, henceforth referred to as Hoffman, *Inside Terrorism*.

[16] According to a 1998–1999 RAND publication, "The RAND-St. Andrews Chronology of International Terrorism is a computerized database of international terrorist incidents that have occurred worldwide from 1968 to the present. The chronology has been continuously maintained since 1972, first by RAND and since 1994 by the Centre for the Study of Terrorism and Political Violence at the University of St. Andrews, Scotland." Bruce Hoffman, "Old Madness, New Methods: Revival of Religious Terrorism Begs for Broader U.S. Policy Review," Rand Review, Winter1998-1999, Vol. 22, No. 2, available from [http://www.rand.org/publications/randreview/issues/rrwinter98.9.pdf], accessed on April 23, 2007.

ideologies dominate the current threat environment. For example, in 1968, none of the identifiable 11 terrorist groups was predominately religious in nature, but by 1995, 26 of the 56 (46%) known, active international terrorist groups in the RAND/St. Andrews database could be classified as religious.[17] As of October 2005, the State Department had designated 42 groups as Foreign Terrorist Organizations (FTOs), of which at least 21 (50%) could be classified as religious terrorist groups.[18]

Somewhat counterintuitively, many of the terrorist groups that are religious in nature are involved in precursor criminal activity, even when said activity is expressly prohibited in religious scripture.[19] Potential rationalizations for this activity could include First, any action that is undertaken in pursuit of the group's ultimate cause is deemed permissible. For example, numerous Islamist terrorist groups promote the use of suicide bombing as a legitimate tactic in jihad despite the explicit condemnation of suicide in the Quran.

Second, sometimes criminal activity allows groups to achieve two goals simultaneously—generate funds and harm their enemies. This is iterated by the purported comments of Abu Bakar Bashir, spiritual leader of the al Qaeda-linked Jemaah Islamiyah (JI), an Islamist group in Indonesia. When questioned about JI's involvement in a series of jewelry store robberies believed to have financed the 2002 Bali Bombings, Bashir purportedly commented, "You can take their blood; then why not take their property?"[20] This sentiment is echoed by Baz Mohammad, the Taliban-linked narcotics kingpin who was extradited to the United States in 2005. According to the indictment issued by the U.S. Attorney's Office, "in or about 1990, Baz Mohammad met with members of the Baz Mohammad Organization in his Karachi, Pakistan, residence and told them that selling heroin in the United States was a 'jihad' because they were taking the Americans' money at the same time the heroin they were paying for was killing them."[21]

---

17 Hoffman, *Inside Terrorism*, 91.

18 ". . . having aims and motivations reflecting a predominate religious character or influence."—Ibid. 90. & U.S. State Department, "Fact Sheet: Foreign Terrorist Organizations (FTOs)," October 11, 2005, U.S. State Department Website available from [http://www.state.gov], accessed on June 14, 2006.

19 For example, the IRA, a political terrorist organization with religious overtones, conducted numerous violent acts and other crimes over several decades, even though these ran contrary to Catholic dogma. Another example is the numerous jihadi groups that promote a Salafist school of Islam and a literal reading of the Quran, and yet utilize suicide bombings, even though suicide is explicitly prohibited in the Quran.

20 David E. Kaplan, "Paying for Terror: How Jihadist Groups are Using Organized-Crime Tactics — and Profits—to Finance Attacks on Targets Around the Globe," US News and World Report, December 5, 2005, henceforth referred to as Kaplan, "Paying for Terror."

21 United States Attorney Southern District of New York, "United States Announces Historic Extradition of Taliban-linked Afghan Narco-terrorism to New York," Press Release, October 24, 2005, available from [http://www.usdoj.gov/usao/nys/pressreleases/] accessed on November 8, 2006.

Examples of Terrorist Precursor Activity in the United States

Although they often engage in many of the same activities, and despite the fact that terrorist attacks are ultimately criminal acts, most terrorists fundamentally differ from other criminals. It can be argued the latter are primarily driven by need, greed, and opportunity, while most terrorists are predominately driven by ideology. Terrorists may commit crimes because of that ideology or in support of more immediate logistical needs to support the group's long-term strategic ideological goal(s). Terrorists commit crimes in order to raise funds, hide their activities, and facilitate recruitment, propaganda efforts, and pre-operational planning. The following is an overview of known terrorist precursor crimes that occurred within the United States.[22]

Front Businesses and Charities

Terrorist groups often set up front organizations to raise and launder money, recruit new members, and/or provide ideological and rhetorical support for the organization's cause. These front entities have taken the form of businesses, charities, and other non-governmental organizations. For example, in December 2001, then U.S. Treasury Secretary Paul O'Neill announced that the U.S. government had shut down three HAMAS-controlled organizations and frozen their assets in the United States.[23] In the Treasury Department press release, two of the organizations, the al Aqsa bank and the Beit al Mal bank, were described as not "just banks that unknowingly administer accounts for terrorists. They are direct arms of HAMAS, established and used to do HAMAS business."[24]

A third entity that had its assets frozen, the Holy Land Foundation for Relief and Development (HLF), described itself as a charity dedicated to "prevent or alleviate human suffering arising out of conflict or natural disaster, with the core of our efforts spotlighting the Palestinian refugees in Jordan, Lebanon, and Palestine."[25] The Treasury Department, however,

[22] Many of the successfully prosecuted cases and/or allegations of terrorist precursor criminal activity could fall under the category of white collar crime. As this report demonstrates, terrorists have engaged in a wide variety of criminal activities, ranging from low-level 'street' crime to sophisticated white-collar crimes. However, there is not enough publicly available data from which to draw definitive quantitative conclusions regarding the breakdown of types of domestic precursor crimes. In general, it appears that larger, 'professional' groups are more likely to be able to engage in sophisticated, white collar crimes, while smaller terrorist cells that lack extensive links to such groups and whose members have little 'formal terrorist training' are more likely to engage in less sophisticated, smaller-scale criminal enterprises.

[23] U.S. Treasury Department, "Statement of Secretary Paul O'Neill on the Blocking of Hamas Financiers' Assets," Press Release, PO-837, December 4, 2001, available from [http://www.treas.gov], accessed on November 20, 2006.

[24] Ibid.

[25] Holy Land Foundation, "A Message from the President," Holy Land Foundation Website archived by the Library of Congress, available from [http://memory.loc.gov/911/index.html], accessed on November 27, 2006.

disagreed, stating "The Holy Land Foundation masquerades as a charity, while its primary purpose is to fund HAMAS."[26] To date, several people have pled guilty to or been convicted of providing material support to a terrorist organization for their work with HLF, including Mohamed Shorbagi,[27] Bayan Elashi, Ghassan Elashi, Basman Elashi, and their company, Infocom.[28] They are currently serving sentences related to those convictions. Ghassan Elashi and seven other co-defendants, are scheduled to go to trial again in July 16, 2007 in a case styled U.S. v. Holy Land Foundation for Relief and Development, et al.[29] The allegations in this case include transferring millions of dollars to HAMAS, other HAMAS front entities and individual Palestinian families "who had a relative 'martyred' or jailed as a result of terrorist activities."[30]

Counterfeiting Money

Another method terrorists have used to generate funds is counterfeiting. In 2005, Gale Nettles was convicted for his role in a plot to bomb the Dirksen Federal Building in Chicago.[31] Although his plot seemingly started as a lone wolf enterprise against the federal government, Nettles eventually conspired with an undercover FBI agent he believed was working with al Qaeda. Nettles was found guilty however of selling, exchanging, transferring and delivering false, forged, counterfeited and altered U.S. Federal Reserve notes. Nettles attempted to use counterfeit monies and the sale of counterfeit monies to procure the bomb-making materials for his attack.[32] Nettles was acquitted of the charge of "fraudulently making, forging and counterfeiting U.S. Federal Reserve notes with the intent that the same be passed as genuine," despite presented evidence that the counterfeit bills he used were actually created in his apartment and a prior history creating counterfeit monies.[33]

---

[26] U.S. Treasury Department, "Statement of Secretary Paul O'Neill on the Blocking of HAMAS Financiers' Assets."

[27] United States Attorney's Office, "Rome, Georgia Resident Pleads Guilty to Material Support of Foreign Terrorist Group: Local Businessman and Imam Provided Money to HAMAS," Press Release, October 13, 2006, available from [http://www.usdoj.gov/usao/gan/press/2006/10-13-06.pdf] accessed on November 27, 2006.

[28] United States Attorney's Office, Northern District of Texas, "Infocom Corporation and its Operators Sentenced in Federal Court: Elashi Brothers Convicted for Doing Business with Terrorist," Press Release, October 13, 2006, available from [http://www.usdoj.gov/usao/txn] accessed on November 27, 2006.

[29] United States v. Holy Land Foundation for Relief and Development et al., (N.D. Tex. Updated May 2007) Criminal Docket for Case #: 3:04-cr-00240 All Defendants.

[30] United States v. Holy Land Foundation for Relief and Development et al., (N.D. Tex. November 2005) (No. 3:04-CR-240-G), Superseding Indictment.

[31] United States v. Nettles, 400 F. Supp. 2d 1084, (N.D. Ill. November 2005).

[32] Ibid.

[33] Nettles was convicted of counterfeiting U.S. Federal Reserve notes in September 2002, for which he served two years time at the Federal Correctional Institute in Yazoo City, Mississippi. Ibid.

Counterfeit Goods

One of the crimes used with increasing frequency by a variety of terrorist organizations is the sale of counterfeit goods. In March 2006, Imad Hammoud and several of his associates were indicted for operating a multi-million dollar cigarette trafficking ring to benefit the terrorist group Hezbollah.[34] Between 1996 and 2002, Hammoud and his associates allegedly purchased low- and non-taxed cigarettes in North Carolina, Kentucky and on Indian reservations, outfitted them with counterfeit tax stamps and resold them in the high cigarette tax states of New York and Michigan. The operation allegedly was eventually expanded to other goods, to include counterfeit Viagra pills and stolen goods such as infant formula and toilet paper.[35] It is charged that the operation directed sums towards Hezbollah and charged customers a "Resistance Tax" above the black market price, which went to Hezbollah.[36] To date, Hammoud and 19 of his known associates have been indicted on a combination of RICO, smuggling, counterfeit tax charges related to their roles in the operation—several have been convicted or pled guilty, some are appealing their convictions, and some are at other stages of the legal system.[37]

This is just one of numerous counterfeit cases with a purported nexus to terrorism. Intelligence analysts have also warned that terrorist groups are making profits off everything from counterfeit handbags to illegally reproduced video games. In testimony before the House Committee on International Relations in 2003, Interpol's Secretary General stated that the link between organized crime and counterfeit goods (also known as intellectual property crime) was long established, but announced that the international law enforcement body was "sounding the alarm that Intellectual Property Crime is becoming the preferred method of funding for a number of terrorist groups."[38]

Narcotics

Narcotics reportedly are one of the most profitable terrorist fundraising commodities. According to the United Nations (UN) Office on Drugs and Crime, in 2003, the "value of the global illicit drug market for the year 2003 was estimated at U.S. $13 billion at the production level, at $94 billion at the wholesale level (taking seizures into account), and at U.S. $322 billion

---

[34] United States v. Imad Mohamad-Musbah Hammoud, et al., (E.D. Mich. March 2006), Indictment.
[35] Ibid.
[36] Ibid.
[37] United States v. Haydous, (E.D. Mich. Updated May 2007), Criminal Docket for Case#:2:03-cr-80406-GER-RSW All Defendants.
[38] Ronald K. Noble, "The links between intellectual property crime and terrorist financing" Testimony before the U.S. House Committee on International Relations, July 16th 2003, available from [http://www.interpol.int/Public/ICPO/speeches/SG20030716.asp], accessed on March 30, 2007.

based on retail prices and taking seizures and other losses into account."[39] Significant portions of several illicit drug markets, including the South American cocaine trade, the Afghan opium market, and the Moroccan Hashish trade, are believed by some observers in the law enforcement community to be closely intertwined with terrorist campaigns.

Terrorist groups across the ideological spectrum have become involved in the narcotics trade at various stages. Some groups are involved in the initial stages, growing coca or opium crops or taxing those farmers that grow them. Other groups provide protected smuggling routes for hefty fees. Still other, usually smaller groups, are active in the distribution stage, selling drugs on the street to generate funds.

In 2006, Elkin Alberto Arroyave-Ruiz, Edgar Fernando Blanco-Puerta, and Uwe Jensen were convicted for their role in a $25 million dollar weapons-for-drugs deal to provide material support for Autodefensas Unidos de Colombia (known by the acronym AUC or in English as the United Self-Defense Forces of Colombia), a paramilitary organization designated as a FTO by the U.S. State Department. The group brokered a deal with an FBI confidential informant to trade four to five tons of cocaine for prohibited weapons. The U.S. District Court in Houston found all three guilty of conspiracy to possess cocaine with intent to distribute and material support for a foreign terrorist organization. Ruiz received a life sentence for his role in the drugs for weapons plot, Puerta and Jensen received 15 and 14 years respectively.[40]

Smuggling and Import/Export Violations

In 2004, the Department of State (DOS) announced that in coordination with the Secretary of Homeland Security and the Attorney General, the Human Smuggling and Trafficking Center was being reestablished to combat threats emanating from human smuggling, trafficking of persons and clandestine terrorist travel.[41] The United Nations estimates that "human smuggling has grown to a $10 billion per year global criminal industry."[42] According to DOS, there are "an estimated 800,000 to 900,000 individuals trafficked across international borders each year. The U.S. Government estimates 18,000 to 20,000 victims are trafficked to the United States annually."[43]

---

39 United Nations Office on Drugs and Crime, "2005 World Drug Report, Volume 1: Analysis," available from [http://www.unodc.org/pdf/WDR_2005/volume_1_chap2.pdf], 127.

40 United States v. Carlos Ali Romero Varela et al., (S.D. Tex. November 2002) (No. 4:02-cr-0074). According to (United States v. Varela, (S.D. Texas updated April 2007) Criminal Docket for Case #: 4:02-cr-00714 All Defendants and Case#:4:02-cr00714-4), Puerta and Ruiz have since entered appeals.

41 Department of State, "Human Smuggling and Trafficking Center (HSTC) Charter," Press Release, May 2004, available from [http://www.state.gov], accessed on December 2, 2006.

42 Ibid.

43 Ibid.

Human smuggling is not currently considered one of the primary finance generating enterprises utilized by terrorists, however, several intelligence and law enforcement agencies have warned that "terrorist organizations have tapped or will tap into this global criminal infrastructure. Alien smugglers and fraudulent document providers use their skills to facilitate the movement of terrorists across international borders."[44]

There has been at least one purported case in the United States. In November 2002, an indictment against Salim Boughader-Mucharrafille for multiple counts of human smuggling was filed in U.S. district court.[45] Boughader-Mucharrafille reportedly pled guilty to two counts of human trafficking in March 2003 and served most of a year-long prison term.[46] Upon his release from prison and return to Mexico, he was immediately re-arrested. In May 2006, a Mexican judge reportedly sentenced Boughader-Mucharrafille to fourteen years in prison for his role in the smuggling ring and on organized crime charges.[47] The 9/11 Commission Staff Report on Terrorist Travel cites an Immigration and Naturalization Services (INS) background paper and Central Intelligence Agency (CIA) analytic report that claim Boughader-Mucharrafille smuggled at least 200 "Lebanese nationals sympathetic to Hamas and Hezbollah into the United States" from Mexico.[48] According to press reports, Boughader-Mucharrafille admitted that one of the individuals he helped smuggle into the United States worked for al Minar, Hezbollah's television station.[49] There also has been speculation that terrorists may utilize human smuggling/trafficking as a means to generate funds.

In addition to the criminal enterprises such as operating narcotics cartels and smuggling operations, terrorists worldwide appear to have increasingly become involved in street crime to finance their activities. This phenomenon may be the result of the increasing decentralization and amateurization of terror. Street crimes known to have been utilized domestically by terrorists include violent crimes such as armed robbery and small-scale scams such as individual credit card fraud, to name a few.

44 Ibid.

45 United States v. Salim Boughader-Mucharrafille et al., (S.D. Cal. November 2002) (No. 3048W).

46 Sandra Dibble, "Judge in Mexico City Sentences Smuggling-ring Leader to 14 years," The San Diego Union-Tribune, May 23, 2006, LOCAL; Pg. B-2.

47 Ibid.

48 Thomas R. Eldridge, Susan Ginsburg, Walter T. Hempel II, Janice L. Kephart, Kelly Moore and Joanne M. Accolla and Alice Falk, *9/11 and Terrorist Travel: Staff Report of the National Commission on Terrorist Attacks Upon the United States*, available from [http://www.9-11commission.gov], accessed on November 28, 2006, 67.

49 Pauline Arrillaga and Olga R. Rodriguez, "AP Investigation: Smuggler pipelines channel illegal immigrants into U.S. from nations with terror ties," The Associated Press, June 29, 2005.

Robbery/Theft

According to an October 2005 indictment issued by the U.S. District Court for the Central District of California, Kevin James, a prison inmate who founded the radical group Jamiyyat Ul-Islam Is-Saheeh (JIS), recruited and directed followers to conduct attacks on U.S. military, Jewish and Israeli venues in the Los Angeles area.[50] It is charged that specific targets JIS intended to strike included U.S. military recruiting stations, synagogues, El Al airlines operations, and the Israeli Consulate.[51] To finance the operation, two JIS members, Gregory Patterson and Hammad Samana, allegedly conducted a series of twelve armed robberies at California gas stations from May 30–July 5, 2005.[52] A pretrial status conference is set for August 13, 2007.[53]

In addition to funding, there are instances where domestic terrorists have used robberies to procure weaponry to use in attacks. Timothy McVeigh and Terry Nichols conducted two robberies: One in Kansas in October 1994 (where they stole explosives from a storage locker) and another in Arkansas in November 1994 (when they robbed a firearms dealer).[54]

Fraud (Credit Card, Benefits, Food Stamps, etc.)

There are numerous examples of terrorists using a variety of fraud schemes to raise funds, including credit card fraud, coupon and food stamps fraud, and benefits fraud. A 2006 case in the United States involved Karim Koubriti and his codefendant Ahmed Hannon, who were found guilty of mail fraud, insurance fraud and material support of terrorism in connection with his 'economic jihad' scheme to defraud the Titan Insurance Company.[55] In this case, Koubriti and Hannon apparently falsely claimed to have been injured in a car accident and then filed a false insurance claim with Titan. Koubriti and Hannon provided fictitious invoices for medical bills, lost wages as well as mileage and services accrued due to the purported injuries.[56]

---

50 United States v. Kevin James et al., (C.D. Cal. October 2005) Grand Jury Indictment.

51 Ibid.

52 Ibid.

53 United States v. James, et al. (C.D. CA updated May 2007) Criminal Docket for Case#: 8:05-cr-00214-CJC-ALL.

54 United States v. Timothy James McVeigh and Terry Lynn Nichols, (W.D. Okla. August 1995) (No. CR95-110), Grand Jury Indictment.

55 United States v. Koubriti, 435 F. Supp. 2d 666, (E.D. Mich. 2006). Koubriti and Hannon were previously indicted as part of a Detroit-based terror cell purportedly preparing to conduct attacks in the United States and abroad. Previously, Koubriti had been found guilty of providing material support to a terrorist group and Hannon had been found guilty of identification forgery, but these convictions were overturned in 2004 when the lead prosecutor and star witness were accused of mishandling evidence and providing false testimony, respectively. Koubriti and Hannon were also linked to Abdel-Ilah Elmardoudi who is referenced in the "Phone Scams and Cell Phone Activity" section of this report.

56 United States v. Koubriti, 435 F. Supp. 2d 666, (E.D. Mich. 2006).

Koubriti's motivation was two fold—"to commit fraud in order to both support terrorist activities and to 'cause economic harm to U.S. businesses'."[57]

Many experts believe terrorists are becoming more creative in their fraud schemes. According to media reports, "one enterprising pair of jihadists in Germany hoped to fund a suicide mission to Iraq by taking out nearly $1 million in life insurance and staging the death of one in a faked traffic accident."[58] Insurance fraud is just one of many fraud schemes utilized by terrorist elements. In 2005, Matthew Levitt testified before the Senate Committee on Homeland Security and Governmental Affairs that there have been indications that terrorist elements have funded activities through credit card fraud, welfare fraud, coupon fraud, stealing and reselling baby formula, and food stamps fraud.[59] In his testimony, Levitt cited "U.S. officials [who] believe "a substantial portion" of the estimated millions of dollars raised by Middle Eastern terrorist groups comes from the $20 million to $30 million annually brought in by the illicit scam industry in America."[60]

Phone Scams and Cell Phone Activity

Terrorists apparently have used a variety of cell phone scams to fund and facilitate their activities. Some of these scams and bulk purchases of prepaid cell phones have received particular attention by the media and law enforcement in recent years.[61] In August 2006, Abdel-Ilah Elmardoudi was convicted for operating a phone card "shoulder surfing" scheme in which he stole hundreds of telephone calling-card numbers from unsuspecting travelers at the Minneapolis-St. Paul International Airport and then "supplied them to overseas callers who used them" to make a total of $745,000 in international calls from Egypt, Kuwait, East Africa, the Philippines, the Middle East, and the Balkans.[62] The end use of any funds generated by his calling card schemes are unclear.

Elmardoudi was one of four Detroit-area men arrested in the wake of the September 11th attacks who were allegedly part of a cell plotting to conduct attacks against the MGM Grand in Las Vegas, NV, Disneyland in Anaheim, CA, a U.S. military base in Incerlik, Turkey and a hospital in

---

57 Ibid.

58 Kaplan, "Paying for Terror."

59 Matthew Levitt, "Terrorists, Criminals, and Counterfeit Goods," Statement before the Senate Committee on Homeland Security and Governmental Affairs, May 25, 2005, CQ Congressional Testimony, available from [http://www.lexis.com], accessed on April 10, 2007.

60 Ibid.

61 Arthur H. Rotstein, "DPS issues advisory concerning prepaid cell phone purchases," *The Associated Press State & Local Wire*, August 16, 2006, available from [http://www.lexis.com], accessed on April 23, 2007.

62 Office of the U.S. Attorney, District of Minnesota, "Minneapolis Man Sentenced on Federal Fraud Charges," press release, September 25, 2006, available from [http://www.usdoj.gov/usao/mn], accessed on November 9, 2006.

Amman, Jordan.[63] Elmardoudi and an accomplice, Karim Koubriti, were convicted of material support, but these convictions were overturned. A third defendant was convicted on identification fraud charges and the fourth defendant was cleared of all charges.[64]

Beyond calling card surfing, there has been increasing concern amongst law enforcement and intelligence officials that terrorist elements could use pay-as-you-go cell phones for both operational and fundraising purposes. Given the anonymity they provide compared to other cell phone plans, analysts fear they could be used by terrorists to communicate clandestinely or to hinder investigations when they are used as detonators or Global Positioning System (GPS) devices within improvised explosive devices. There have been numerous suspicious incidents regarding the resale of such phones reported throughout the United States.[65] There have been several arrests around the country related to suspicious purchases of cell phones. In some cases terrorism charges were initially filed against the defendants, such as in Michigan and Ohio, but were dropped.[66]

Bribery

In addition to engaging in illegal activities to facilitate weapons procurement, safe travel, and funds, terrorists may attempt to reduce the scrutiny they receive from the law enforcement and intelligence communities. It is alleged that between 2003 and August 2006, several individuals, including men identified as Fnu Lnu, Murugesu Vinayagamoorthy, Vijayshanthar Patpanathan, Gaspar Raj Maria Paulian, Namasivaya Viswanathan, and Nachimuthu Socrates, were involved in multiple counts of criminal activity in support of the Liberation Tigers of Tamil Eelam (LTTE), a Sri Lankan group designated by the U.S. State Department as a FTO.[67] According to the indictment, the men are alleged not only to have provided material support for the LTTE, but also to have conspired to bribe U.S. government officials in an effort to have the LTTE removed from the State Department's

---

[63] United States v. Koubriti et al., (E.D. Mich 2002) (No. 01-80778), Indictment.

[64] In 2004, Elmardoudi and Koubriti's convictions were overturned when it was discovered that the lead federal prosecutor in the case had withheld evidence from the defense and a Department of State special agent involved in the case provided false testimony. Department of Justice, "Former Federal Prosecutor, State Department Agent Indicted for Obstruction of Justice and Presenting False Evidence in Terrorism Trial, " DOJ press release, March 29, 2006, available from [http://www.usdoj.gov] accessed on December 4, 2006.

[65] According to press reports, DHS and FBI issued an alert in 2006 regarding a potential terrorist nexus with suspicious bulk cell phone purchases. Mike Wagner, "'Like gold for terrorists'," The Columbus Dispatch (Ohio), August 16, 2006.

[66] Associated Press, "Authorities Back Off Accusing Bulk Cell Phone Buyers in Ohio and Michigan of Direct Terror Link," August 15, 2006.

[67] United States v. FNU LNU et al, (E.D. N.Y. January 2007) (No. 2006R01615) Indictment.

Foreign Terrorist Organization (FTO) list.[68] Initial oral arguments in the case are expected to begin in June 2007.[69]

Immigration and Identity Crimes

In an effort to hide their identity, terrorists commit a range of identity, document, and immigration offenses. In order to conceal her well known face so as to commit additional skyjackings, Leila Khaled, an accomplished Popular Front for the Liberation of Palestine (PFLP) terrorist who was part of the team that hijacked TWA flight 840 in 1969, reportedly underwent several plastic surgeries.[70] The 9/11 hijackers committed a wide variety of immigration offenses in order to enter the United States. The 9/11 Commission Staff Report on terrorist travel concludes: The 19 hijackers used 364 aliases,[71] several had fraudulently altered their passports,[72] two hijackers lied on their visa applications, and several violated the terms of their visas.[73]

Incitement

To date, there are few, if any, examples of individuals convicted for inciting violence on behalf of a terrorist group in the United States, despite widespread terrorist propaganda campaigns aimed at encouraging followers and like-minded extremists to take action both at home and abroad, as will be discussed below. This may be due to the difficulty of successfully proving criminal intent to incite violence by our legal standards.

It is evident that over the last decade terrorist groups have increasingly utilized a decentralized, leaderless-resistence[74] organizational structure.

---

68 Ibid.

69 United States v. Thavaraja et al, (E.D. N.Y. updated May 2007) Criminal Docket for Case#: 1:06-cr-00616-RJD-6

70 The Guardian staff reporters, "'I made the Ring from a Bullet and the Pin of a Hand Grenade': When Palestinian Liberation Fighter Leila Khaled, right, Hijacked her first Plane in 1969, She Became the International Pin-up of Armed Struggle. Then She Underwent Cosmetic Surgery so She could do it Again. Thirty years on, She talks to Katharine Viner about Being a Woman at War," The Guardian (London), January 26, 2001.

71 'to include variations of their names and noms de guerre,' The National Commission on Terrorist Attacks Upon the United States, "9/11 and Terrorist Travel," 1.

72 Passports of two of the 9/11 hijackers were found after the attacks to have been "manipulated in a fraudulent manner. They contained fraudulent entry-exit stamps (or cachets) probably inserted by al Qaeda travel document forgers to hide travel to Afghanistan for terrorist training. Our analysis of their travel patterns suggests that several more hijackers whose passports did not survive the attacks were likely to have had similar false stamps in their passports." Ibid.

73 Ibid., 1-5.

74 According to Simson L. Garfinkel, "Leaderless Resistance applies specifically to groups that employ cells and that lack bidirectional vertical command links—that is, groups without leaders." Rather than receiving commands, independent cells and like-minded individuals act alone, based on their interpretation of a symbolic leader's pronouncements often circulated by propaganda, the internet, and other media. This style has been adopted by numerous terrorist and extremist organizations, including groups operating domestically, notably some of the anti-abortion extremist groups, environmental and animal rights extremist groups, and white supremacists. This strategy is associated

Concomitantly, groups have increasingly adopted methods of training and instruction that ultimately rely on inciting others to action through media channels. By its own proclamation, al Qaeda fancies itself the ultimate inciter, proclaiming to be the "pioneering vanguard" for the Islamist jihad against the West.[75] The group's founder Abdullah Azzam saw the role of the group as the "vanguard who would radicalize and mobilize those Muslims that had hitherto rejected their extremist message."[76] Intelligence analysts have long worried that al Qaeda's fatwas, internet messages, and video- and audio-tapes were attempts to incite its followers and sympathizers to action.

One good example of incitement related to terrorism is found in the UK, with the conviction of Abu Hamza al-Masri. Al Masri served as the imam of the Finsbury Park Mosque, which boasts shoe bomber Richard Reid and "20th hijacker" Zacarias Moussaoui as former regular attendees. Al Masri was notorious for the vitriol he preached and his threats against Christians, Jews and Westerners. In February 2006, al Masri was convicted of 11 charges related to inciting racial hatred and soliciting murder.[77] Al Masri's incitement efforts are not atypical, and may be indicative of a growing trend among Islamist terrorist elements. Many training manuals and attack instructions are posted on Jihadi websites, alongside virulent threats against the West, which intelligence analysts credit for facilitating and inspiring non-connected would-be jihadis to action.

In the United States, there is a long history of leaderless resistence-style organizations that utilize vitriolic rhetoric and instructions for action which opponents claim are clear efforts to incite followers to violence. Many of the single-issue domestic extremist groups operating currently in the United States (including environmental, animal rights or anti-abortion groups) have adopted such structures. However, many of these groups have been careful with regard to their language and defend their material as protected by First Amendment and not criminal incitement.

In the United States, there are numerous instances where environmental and animal rights extremists have provided instructions on how to construct weapons or conduct attacks (e.g. How to build an incendiary device that can flatten a two story building). Some have provided home addresses and contact information for individuals the movement considers enemies

---

with Louis Beam, who attributed its origins to Col. Ulius Loius Amoss, but adapted it to pursue his white supremacist agenda. (See Simson L. Garfinkel, "Leaderless Resistance Today," First Monday, Volume 8, No. 3, March 2003, available from [http://www.firstmonday.org/issues/issue8_3/garfinkel/], accessed on May 15, 2007.

75 Rohan Gunaratna, "The Post-Madrid Face of al Qaeda," Washington Quarterly, available from [http://www.twq.com] accessed on August 27, 2006.

76 Ibid.

77 BBC staff, "Abu Hamza Loses Race-hate Appeal," BBC, November 28, 2006, available from [http://www.bbc.co.uk] accessed on December 12, 2006.

with encouragement for supporters to express their outrage. In one case, Planned Parenthood successfully sued the American Coalition of Life Activists (ACLA) for its role in inciting attacks on doctors who perform abortions in 1999 in a civil case.[78] ACLA created wanted posters for doctors that performed abortions. Subsequently, one of its members posted the information on his website and struck through the names when those doctors were killed or greyed out the names when they were maimed by anti-abortion extremists.

Training

There have been reported cases where terrorist elements have conducted paramilitary training exercises in the United States or attended training abroad to prepare for terrorist activities against the United States. Several individuals, dubbed the "Portland Seven," were convicted on terrorist material support charges after they apparently conducted martial arts and weapons training in anticipation of mounting jihad against the United States.[79] A group purportedly tied to the Pakistani terrorist organization Laskhar-e-Toiba conducted paintball training for similar purposes in Northern Virginia in 2000.[80]

In other cases, individuals went abroad in search of jihad training. In April 2006, Hamid Hayat was convicted of providing material support to terrorists after he was found to have attended a jihadi training camp in Pakistan for a period of time between October 2003 and November 2004.[81] The Department of Justice asserted that following his training, Hayat returned to the United States "to wage jihad upon receipt of orders."[82]

According to the United Nations, there is a convergence of organized crime and ideologically driven terrorist groups. Antonio Maria Costa, a UN official with the Office on Drugs and Crime, reportedly believes the "world is seeing

---

[78] Planned Parenthood v. American Coalition of Life Activists, 41 F. Supp. 2d 1130, 1999, U.S. District Court for the District of Oregon.

[79] October Martinique Lewis, Ahmed Bilal, Muhammad Bilal, Maher "Mike" Hawash, Jeffery Leon Battle, Patrice Lumumbard Ford and Habis Abdulla al Saoub "all named in the 15-count superseding indictment that included charges of conspiracy to levy war against the United States, conspiracy to provide material support and resources to al Qaeda, conspiracy to contribute services to al Qaeda and the Taliban, conspiracy to possess and discharge firearms in furtherance of crimes of violence, possessing firearms in furtherance of crimes of violence and money laundering." All, except Habis Abdulla al Saoub, who was killed in Afghanistan in 2003, are currently serving sentences for their role in this conspiracy. Department of Justice, "October Martinique Lewis Pleads Guilty to Money Laundering Charges in 'Portland Cell' Case," Press Release, September 26, 2004, available from [http://www.usdoj.gov/opa/pr/2003/September/03_crm_532.htm], accessed on November 10, 2006.

[80] United States v. Masoud Khan et al., 309 F. Supp. 2d 789, (D. Or. 1999) *aff'd* 290 F.3d 1058 (9th Cir. 2002), *cert denied* 539 U.D. 958 (2003).

[81] Department of Justice, "Hamid Hayat Convicted of Terrorism Charges," Press Release, April 25, 2006, available from [http://www.usdoj.gov] accessed on November 2, 2006.

[82] Ibid.

the birth of a new hybrid of organized-crime-terrorist organizations."[83] For example, media reports suggest that "Jihadists have penetrated as much as a third of the $12.5 billion Moroccan hashish trade."[84] According to the Brussels-based World Customs Organization, "counterfeiting is one of the fastest growing industries in the world with an estimated market worth more than [$]500 billion each year, or 7 percent of global trade!," the illegal profits of which often go to fund terrorist organizations.[85]

Extent of Terrorist Precursor Criminal Activity in the United States

While there have been few comprehensive empirical studies to gauge the extent of terrorist precursor criminal activity in the United States to date, largely due to the lack of data, there are some indications that such activities may be widespread. As previously mentioned, there are numerous reports that suggest terrorist precursor criminal activity is occurring across the globe, with criminal trends emerging within each region. Some analysts have suggested that terrorist precursor crime may be even worse in the United States given the high per capita income of its citizenry, open society, and the presence of numerous terrorist groups with a known presence in the United States,[86] as well as large expatriate communities that foreign terrorists may attempt to tap.

One of the only attempts to provide a comprehensive review of terrorist activity within the United States is the American Terrorism Study (Study), which chronicles individuals convicted of terrorist-related offences in the United States as the result of an official FBI terrorism/domestic security investigation.[87] The Study categorizes specific activities and conducts trend analysis. The Study, based on a limited data set,[88] found that approximately

83 Kaplan, "Paying for Terror."

84 Ibid.

85 World Customs Organization, "En route towards the future, Council 2006," Special Report, No. 51, October 2006, available form [http://www.wcoomd.org], accessed on December 17, 2006, 20.

86 Steven Emerson, *American Jihad: The Terrorists Living Amongst Us*, (New York: Free Press, 2003), & Dale Watson, Section Chief for International Terrorism Operations, FBI, "Hearing on Foreign Terrorists in America," Testimony before the Senate Committee on Judiciary Subcommittee on Technology, Terrorism, and Government Information, February 24, 1998, FDCH Political Transcripts, available from [http://www.lexis.com], accessed on April 10, 2007.

87 Brent Smith and Kelly R. Damphouse, *The American Terrorism Study Data* (Fayetteville, AR: University of Arkansas).

88 The authors of the American Terrorism Study acknowledge their research is limited to a relatively small data set: only the information that is available regarding individuals who were successfully convicted of terrorist crimes in the United States as the outcome of a FBI-led terrorism investigation. This Study was initially funded by a National Institute of Justice (NIJ) grant (1999-2000, Grant #1999-IJCX-0005) and later supported by the Oklahoma City National Memorial Institute for the Prevention of Terrorism(MIPT) (Grant #106-113-200064). The authors relied on court records. As such, intelligence regarding terrorist precursor crimes, individuals who were acquitted or never brought to trial on specific terrorist charges, and/or individuals who were convicted but not due to a FBI case were left out of this data set. However, this is one of the only extensive quantitative analyses on domestic terrorist activity in the United States to date. The Study includes information on 447 indictees charged with 2,851 counts from 1978–1999. This represents an estimated 75% of all federal terrorism indictments

one-third of the various activities that terrorists engage in to facilitate attacks were criminal.[89]

Division of Labor within Terrorist Organizations

The organizational structure related to terrorist precursor criminal activity in the United States (i.e., the breakdown of labor within a terrorist group or cell with regard to criminal enterprises) may influence which countermeasures are most effective. Some larger, more experienced terrorist groups are structured in such a way that fundraising, recruitment, and operational activities are delegated to separate divisions.[90] Organizations like HAMAS separate their ideological and military wings, a move that provides spiritual leaders like the former Sheikh Yassin an air of plausible deniability about attacks and shields them from potential arrest and prosecution for involvement in these activities. In analogous organizations, criminal acts may be carried out by low-level supporters or operatives who are ostracized from the group's leadership in an effort to shield the latter from potential exposure to law enforcement. However, there are always exceptions to the rule. For example, the Charlotte, NC-based Hezbollah cell that was engaged in a multi-million dollar cigarette smuggling ring reportedly "responded directly to Sheikh Abbas Haraki, a senior Hezbollah military commander in South Beirut."[91]

It is likely that within smaller more amateur terrorist cells, direct interaction with leadership increases, compartmentalization of duty decreases, and a more even distribution of preoperational duties is adopted. For example, Ahmed Ressam (the would-be Millennium bomber) and his group of like-minded jihadis were reported to all be involved in a series of criminal activities, to include credit card fraud, pick pocketing, shoplifting, and stealing identity documents for resale to mujahideen.[92] Given the

from this period. The author of this report acknowledges that there are other research initiatives that examine terrorist activity in the United States, however, many of those studies rely on open source data and related media reports. For the purposes of this report, the latter were not included.

89 Brent L. Smith, Kelly R. Damphouse, Paxton Roberts, *Pre-Incident Indicators of Terrorist Incidents: The Identification of Behavioral, Geographic and Temporal Patters of Preparatory Conduct* (Washington DC: Department of Justice, March 2006), 33.

90 For example, the 9/11 Commission found that al Qaeda is organized into several committees, each with distinct missions and responsibilities. For example, the Military Committee is responsible for "proposing targets, gathering ideas for and supporting operations and managing training camps," whereas, the Finance Committee is responsible for "fundraising and budgetary support for training camps, housing costs, living expenses, travel, and the movement of money allocated to operations." 9/11 Commission, "Overview of the Enemy: Staff Statement No. 15," available from [http://www.9-11commission.gov/staff_statements/staff_statement_15.pdf], accessed on May 1, 2007, 3.

91 Matthew A. Levitt, "Islamic Extremism in Europe," Statement before the House Committee on International Relations, Subcommittee on Europe, April 27, 2005 available from [http://www.cq.com], accessed on November 1, 2006.

92 Hal Bernton, Mike Carter, David Heath and James Neff, "The Terrorist Within: The Story Behind One Man's Holy War Against America, Chapter 6—It Takes a Thief," A Special Report, *The Seattle Times*, June 23-July 7, 2002, available from [http://seattletimes.nwsource.com], accessed on November 2, 2006.

differences among groups and individual cells, identifying terrorist precursor activity will not serve as a universal counterterrorism panacea. Such an approach may be extremely effective against some groups (those heavily involved in criminal activity) but less effective against others (those not involved, or not significantly involved, in criminal activity). The same goes for types of operatives: entry-level members assigned to fundraising efforts may engage in criminal activities on a greater scale then high-level commanders, potentially rendering the former more vulnerable to capture than the latter.

In addition to division of labor, decentralization of the flow of funds and goods may further frustrate interception and intelligence efforts. It has been suggested that some terrorist groups are careful about co-mingling funds and thus separate funds intended for different general purposes (e.g. training vs. operations vs. propaganda, etc). Some may separate funds for specific operations in an attempt to protect those channels from discovery or leading to a greater discovery by the security officials. This practice may frustrate law enforcement and intelligence efforts to identify and thwart future activity and/or link plots or acts to specific groups. Ultimately, a group's or cell's approach to precursor crimes can impact how the United States designs effective countermeasures.

Potential for Identification and Infiltration

To some extent, terrorist precursor criminal activity actually may provide additional opportunities for detecting the groups that engage in such activity. Each criminal act (as well as non-criminal operational support actions) in which terrorists engage has the potential to expose the elements that perform it. Furthermore, demonstrated criminal intent and/or evidence of criminal activity provides justification for intelligence and investigation efforts. Precursor criminal activity also provides opportunities to thwart not just individuals but potentially large parts of the terrorist group. According to congressional testimony, the FBI utilizes the Enterprise Theory of Investigation (ETI) when investigating criminal enterprises, especially those involved in human smuggling and human trafficking.[93] ETI is an "intelligence driven investigative technique which seeks to identify the full scope of a criminal organization,"[94] in contrast to an approach that focuses on the arrest and prosecution of individual members of a larger network involved in criminal acts. It is unclear if the FBI and its field offices, as well as the other organizations in the law enforcement and intelligence communities whose work deals with these terrorist precursor crimes,

[93] "Statement of Chris Swecker," submitted to the U.S. House of Representatives Committee on Homeland Security Subcommittee on Management, Integration and Oversight, March 8, 2006, available from [http://www.fbi.gov/congress/congress06/swecker030806.htm], accessed on April 3, 2007.

[94] Ibid.

vigorously and comprehensively employ enterprise-focused approaches to terrorist precursor crime investigations. Whether an investigation is narrowly or broadly focused could potentially influence terrorist behavior and, as such, impact future efforts to uncover terrorist activity in the United States.

Some might argue that exposing terrorist engagement in criminal activity could potentially discredit a terrorist group in the eyes of its supporters. However, as more terrorist organizations turn to criminal activity to fund and facilitate their agenda, and as their supporters increasingly accept such justifications, there is a distinct possibility that such an approach could have negative consequences. For example, groups could become more clandestine in their activities or adopt new techniques and novel scams, making it difficult for law enforcement and intelligence agencies to identify them. There are indications to suggest that thwarting a group's ability to engage in criminal activities aimed at fundraising, recruiting, training, and arming could potentially weaken the organization and eventually cripple it to the point where it is no longer a threat.

Precursor Crimes for Fundraising and Longevity of Terror Campaigns

Margaret Thatcher is attributed with saying that it is necessary to starve terrorists of the oxygen of publicity on which they depend, in order to reduce the threat they pose. There is some research that suggests that it is just as important to cut off funding. James Fearon has researched the longevity of civil wars and concludes that civil wars last longer when rebels have access to finances generated from contraband goods like narcotics and gems.[95] Some of the conflicts he examined, specifically the Colombian civil war, are dominated by organizations that blur the lines between terrorists, criminal gangs, and guerrilla organizations, like Revolutionary Armed Forces of Colombia (Fuerzas Armadas Revolucionarias de Colombia, or FARC) and United Self-Defense Forces of Colombia (Autodefensas Unidas de Colombia, or AUC).[96] Fearon's theory may have implications beyond civil wars, and specifically for the longevity of terrorist campaigns. Indeed, Bruce Hoffman has argued that when comparing the relative longevity of ethno-nationalist campaigns to those run by left- and right-wing terrorist groups, the former's resilience is "doubtless a product of the relative ease with which they are able to draw sustenance and support from an existing constituency. . . ."[97] A cursory review of some of the longest

[95] James D. Fearon, "Why Do Some Civil Wars Last so Much Longer than Others?" available from [http://www.stanford.edu/group.ethnic/], accessed on October 25, 2006, 11.
[96] Both FARC and AUC are designated as Foreign Terrorist Organizations (FTOs) by the U.S. government, U.S. State Department, "Foreign Terrorist Organizations (FTOs," Fact Sheet, October 11, 2005, available from [http://www.state.gov/s/ct/rls/fs/37191.htm], accessed on January 20, 2007.
[97] Hoffman, *Inside Terrorism*, 171.

terrorist campaigns of the latter half of the 20th century through today finds numerous well financed organizations, relative to their terrorist peers, to include al Qaeda, Palestine Liberation Organization (PLO), Irish Republican Army (IRA), FARC, Hezbollah, amongst many others.

In addition to longevity, some claim that there is a correlation between a group's level of finances and its ability to cause mass destruction. While overall, access to technology and technical information, as well as creative deployment, has allowed modestly-funded terrorist groups to conduct medium- to large-scale attacks, there appears to be a positive correlation between extensive funding and the potential for mass destruction. The most catastrophic attacks and attack plots have traditionally been hatched by the best financed groups of our time, like Aum Shinrykio[98] and al Qaeda.[99] These groups have demonstrated an interest in Chemical, Biological, Radiological, and/or Nuclear (CBRN) weapons, and appear willing to pay large sums to obtain deadly agents/material and the scientific expertise to generate them. There are claims, which vary in credibility, regarding al Qaeda's CBRN programs, including multiple attempts to obtain fissile material; discovery of labs and videotapes in Afghanistan suggesting production and/or experimentation with chemical weapons; and attack plots that sought to deploy CBRN.[100] RAND estimates on the cost of al Qaeda's CBRN programs and the numerous al Qaeda "scams involving the sale of radiological waste and other non-weapons-grade material"[101] run into the millions of dollars.[102] In addition to its chemical and biological programs—which produced nerve agents sarin and VX—"throughout the 1990s, Aum Shinrikyo tried without success to hire Russian

[98] Aum Shinrikyo (Aum), categorized by the U.S. government as a FTO, is the Japanese cult that aimed to "take over Japan and then the world, but over time it began to emphasize the imminence of the end of the world." U.S. State Department, Country Reports on Terrorism, updated April 30, 2007, available from [http://www.state.gov/s/ct/rls/crt/2006/82738.htm], accessed on May 1, 2007. In an effort to spark Armageddon, Aum launched a sarin gas attack on the Tokyo subway system in March 1995. At the time of the attack, Aum was estimated to have over $1.4 billion dollars in assets, "Threats to America: Are We Prepared?" Testimony of James K. Campbell, CDR U.S. Navy before the Senate Judiciary Subcommittee on Technology, Terrorism and Government Information and the Senate Select Committee on Intelligence on Chemical and Biological Weapons, April 22, 1998,available from [http://www.lexis.com], accessed on May 3, 2007.

[99] In 2002, the United Nations, citing numerous government officials and terrorism experts, estimated that al Qaeda's financial portfolio was "around $30 million, although some have put the figure as high as $300 million." United Nations, "Second Report of the Monitoring Group Established Pursuant to Security Council Resolution 1363 (2001) and Extended by Resolution 1390 (2002)," available from [http://www.un.org/Docs/sc/committees/1267/1050E02.pdf], accessed on May 2, 2007.

[100] Center for Nonproliferation Studies, "Chart: Al-Qaida's WMD Activities," Weapons of Mass Destruction Terrorism Research Program, Updated May 13, 2005, available from [http://cns.miis.edu/pubs/other/sjm_cht.htm], accessed on February 13, 2007. These claims vary in reliability and degree of corroboration, however there are several well documented allegations made by reputable sources and government officials.

[101] RAND, "Combating Nuclear Terrorism: Lessons from Aum Shinrikyo, Al Qaeda, and the Kinshasa Reactor," Research Brief, Project Air Force, available from [http://www.rand.org/pubs/research_briefs/RB165/RAND_RB165.pdf], accessed on February 14, 2007.

[102] Ibid.

nuclear experts, to purchase Russian nuclear technology and data, to mine uranium, and to steal sensitive nuclear power plant information."[103]

An anecdotal story regarding the arrest of 1993 World Trade Center bomb mastermind Ramzi Yousef lends some credence for the apparent correlation between funding and mass destructive capability. As U.S. federal agents flew with Yousef over Manhattan as they escorted him back to the United States after he was arrested in Pakistan, one of the FBI officials reportedly asked Yousef to look out the window and commented that the twin towers were " still standing" despite Yousef's efforts to bring them down.[104] Yousef purportedly retorted, "They wouldn't be if I had enough money and explosives."[105]

Precursor Crimes' Effect on Threat Environment

More generally, the question of how the domestic occurrence of terrorist precursor crimes alters the threat environment has not been answered. Beyond potentially providing funds that could be directly used to finance an attack on a U.S. target, how does precursor criminal activity affect the threat to the United States? There are two conflicting schools of thought: The first, the 'don't-bite-the-hand-that feeds-you' theory suggests terrorist groups engaged in fundraising and other logistical support activities in the United States are unlikely to mount attacks within that country's borders for fear of losing lucrative funding streams. A contrasting approach, the 'presence-equals-threat' theory, suggests that the groups fundraising or providing support functions within the country present a viable and immediate threat to the United States as those support networks could easily go operational.

The 'don't-bite-the-hand-that-feeds-you' theory may explain why anti-American Islamist groups with a presence in the United States, such as HAMAS and Hezbollah, have avoided attacking targets in the United States to date. This leads one to ask, if U.S. funding channels were to dry up, would groups present in the United States become more willing to conduct attacks on our soil? Irrespective of funding levels, are there issues that might cause such a group to determine that the cost of attacking the United States on its own soil was in its strategic interest? And if so, are the cells currently operating in the United States capable of carrying out operations?

It is important to consider the fundamental questions surrounding terrorist precursor crimes before charting a counterterrorism strategy that deals

[103] Ibid.

[104] Simon Reeve, *The New Jackals: Ramzi Yousef, Osama bin Laden and the Future of Terrorism*, (Boston: Northeastern University Press, 1999), 109.

[105] Ibid.

with this activity. The following strategic questions are worthy of further consideration:

- What is our national strategy for dealing with terrorist predicate crimes, do we have a coherent strategy, or do individual agencies approach this issue differently?
- What metrics are used to measure the success of U.S. strategy(ies) for terrorist precursor activity?
- Is that strategy(s) effective? Are there unintended consequences that actually work against the strategy's stated goals?

Implications for Congress

The existence of domestic terrorist precursor criminal activity has myriad, far-reaching implications. The presence of terrorist precursor activity within U.S. borders has relevance for areas of congressional oversight and interest, such as existing laws for enforcement and prosecution of precursor crimes; funding of various counterterrorism programs; and oversight of numerous agencies engaged in such activity to ensure coordination.

Issues directly related to the terrorist precursor crime phenomenon include concerns whether existing terrorism material support statutes and the way they are interpreted and utilized are sufficient for effectively prosecuting individuals who conduct terrorist precursor crimes. Another related issue is the role the private sector role plays in identifying, reporting, and helping facilitate the prosecution of fraud schemes, many of which may be utilized by terrorist groups to raise funds, including credit card fraud, coupon fraud, and benefits fraud. Furthermore, the question of the role and the effectiveness of the banking and financial sector in identifying and thwarting terrorist financing is an important issue. It is beyond the scope of this report, however, to explore each of these topics in-depth. The next section provides a single, narrow prism through which to examine the congressional implications of terrorist precursor criminal activity: the identification of terrorist precursor criminal activity by agencies at all levels of government and the subsequent collection of intelligence on and investigation of such activity.

Federal Role in Intelligence/Investigation of Precursor Crimes

Traditionally, federal intelligence agencies were primarily responsible for counterterrorism. Since the September 11th terrorist attacks, however, there have been changes to that approach, and additional federal agencies have become closely involved in counterterrorism activities. For instance, the FBI has begun to transition into a more prevention-focused, intelligence-driven agency in order to combat terrorism. As agencies continue to enhance their ability to detect and deter terrorism several questions are raised: Do they utilize a consistent approach in dealing with precursor crimes? If so, what is the accepted formula for collecting intelligence vs. enforcement? Are precursor crimes that are committed in the United States or by U.S. residents/citizens abroad a priority for these agencies? What is their assessment of the breadth and diversity of criminal activity terrorist groups are engaging in within the United States? Which groups are the most active in the United States?

Testimony at congressional hearings in recent years suggests that intelligence sharing and coordination in general has been improving between the various intelligence and law enforcement agencies involved in counterterrorism. Specifically with regard to terrorist precursor criminal activity in the United States, this issue may be worth further examination. Is there a coherent strategy for dealing with precursor crimes across agencies? Have agencies made sufficient progress coordinating with other agencies on individual cases related to terrorist precursor crimes? Are additional congressional measures needed to ensure the effective coordination of terrorist pre-cursor crimes strategy amongst disparate agencies?

Based on information available, it is unclear whether there is a coordinated, federal-wide strategy for approaching terrorist precursor crimes occurring within the United States. A similar question relates to the intelligence and law enforcement communities' assessment of how the presence of such activity affects the security environment.

SLT Role in Intelligence/Investigation of Precursor Crimes

Since the September 11th attacks, there appears to be consensus that the stakeholders responsible for counterterrorism need to be expanded to include nontraditional partners, such as state, local, and tribal (SLT) law enforcement, amongst others. There is far less agreement over what kind of role SLT forces should play or how to further incorporate counterterrorism efforts into their daily duties. Given the proliferation of proposed players, many of which have overlapping jurisdictions, the issue of defining the 'lanes in the road' amongst federal, state, local, and tribal law enforcement and intelligence agencies begs further examination.

Of all the terrorism prevention roles that have been discussed for SLT agencies, identifying terrorist precursor crimes is perhaps the most natural. Given their existing skill sets, legal authority to investigate and prosecute such offenses, sheer numbers,[106] and intimate familiarity with their jurisdictions, SLT personnel are "well-positioned to develop information

[106] According to the most recent, publicly-available statistics from the Department of Justice's Bureau of Statistics, there were nearly 800,000 sworn law enforcement officers in the United States in 2000. Only 88,496, (11%) worked for federal agencies while approximately 711,000 (89%) were state, local and tribal law enforcement officers. U.S. Department of Justice, "Law Enforcement Statistics,"

on crimes, activities, and organizations that support terrorist organizations" during the course of their normal duties.[107] Further issues include What is the current level of involvement of SLT agencies in identifying terrorist precursor activities? Are there appropriate ways to strengthen that involvement through additional training programs or exercises? Do SLT agencies have access to current intelligence regarding precursor criminal trends and other terrorist modus operandi that could assist them in identifying such activity within their own jurisdictions?

SLT agencies can utilize homeland security grant monies to fund such training, but the availability of training is unclear. There appear to be few, if any, federally certified courses available to SLT agencies that specifically focus on terrorist precursor crimes. That said, there are numerous classes that examine pre-incident indicators and other terrorism-related trends that may address the precursor crime issue.

With regards to overall integration of SLT agencies in the area of terrorist precursor crime investigation and intelligence efforts, anecdotal information suggests it is likely that progress in these three areas varies significantly from agency to agency. Given the importance of preventing future attacks and the potential role SLT agencies could play in identifying terrorist precursor activities within their communities, Congress may further examine the role that SLT agencies play in identifying and thwarting terrorist precursor crimes.

Coordination of Federal and SLT Efforts

It is also important to examine the intersection between counterterrorism efforts conducted at various levels of government and/or the potential for such involvement. How do federal agencies currently engage SLT agencies in this area? At what point do SLT agencies contact federal agencies when they believe they have identified a nexus to terrorism in the course of examining criminal activity? What happens next: Is the case taken over by federal agencies or is it worked in concert? Moreover, do current regulations on collecting intelligence, at each level of government, provide sufficient protections for civil rights while ensuring appropriate leverage for agencies working on counterterrorism? Have relevant agencies at all levels of government received adequate training on these regulations and do they fully understand what they do and do not prevent the agency from doing?

U.S. Department of Justice Website, available from [http://www.ojp.usdoj.gov], accessed on April 29, 2006.

107 K. Jack Riley, Gregory F. Treverton, Jeremy M. Wilson and Lois M. Davis, *State and Local Intelligence in the War on Terrorism*. Santa Monica, CA: RAND Co, 2005, 1.

As demonstrated by the wealth of questions generated by examining just one aspect of terrorist precursor crimes, their identification and subsequent investigation, several areas deserve further attention. The challenge posed by domestic terrorist precursor crimes is complex. For example, on occasion, seemingly straightforward countermeasures applied to terrorist precursor activity may have resulted in unintended and unforeseen consequences. In some cases, well-intentioned countermeasures could actually exacerbate some terrorist threats and/or result in relatively few benefits given their overall cost.[108]

In addition to the complexity of the problem at hand, the complexity of the U.S. counterstrategy, as demonstrated by the sheer number of agencies involved, can be daunting. There are numerous agencies involved in the U.S. countermeasures, many with overlapping legal and geographic jurisdictions. This oversight issue may require additional attention at a level of detail beyond the scope of this report.

[108] For example, scholars, and media sources have recently questioned the effectiveness of anti-money laundering strategies. Several recent studies suggest that such regulations are ineffective, and increasingly so given the cost/benefit ratio and increasing electronic nature of the financial industry. For example, Mariano-Florentino Cuellar argues that the fight against money laundering "delivers less than what it promises," in the article "The Tenuous Relationship between the Fight Against Money Laundering and the Disruption of Criminal Finance," *Journal of Criminal Law and Criminology*, Winter 2003. In October 2005, the editors of the Economist suggested that post-9/11 efforts to thwart terrorist financing via regulation may have cost billions of dollars, while "yield[ing] depressingly few tangible results." "Looking in the Wrong Places: Hindering Flows Across International Financial Networks is Costly and Does Not Stop Terrorists' Primary Activity,"*The Economist*, October 20, 2005, Print Edition.

D. NATIONAL INTELLIGENCE ESTIMATE: THE TERRORIST THREAT TO THE US HOMELAND

NATIONAL INTELLIGENCE ESTIMATE: THE TERRORIST THREAT TO THE US HOMELAND

July 2007

Commentary

The unclassified extract of the *National Intelligence Estimate of the Terrorist Threat to the U.S. Homeland* presented in this volume was one of the seminal terrorist intelligence documents produced in 2007. A presentation of intelligence on terrorism would be incomplete absent its inclusion. National Intelligence Estimates (NIEs) are the most important intelligence judgments issued by what is referred to as the Intelligence Community (IC). The NIEs provide policymakers and strategists key judgments about the likely course of future events and identify implications for U.S. policy. NIEs are collaborative products, in that they are produced and vetted among many different organizations comprising the IC. The NIEs are reviewed by the National Intelligence Board (NIB), which is chaired by the DNI and is composed of the heads of relevant IC agencies. Various agencies have the opportunity to state the level of confidence they have in the predictions they offer for the NIEs. The DNI or his representative briefs the NIEs to the President or his representative and senior policymakers.

The *National Intelligence Estimate of the Terrorist Threat to the U.S. Homeland* offers several key judgments. First, worldwide counterterrorism efforts over the past five years have constrained the ability of al-Qaeda to attack the U.S. homeland again and have led terrorist groups to perceive the homeland as a harder target to strike than on 9/11. Nonetheless, the NIE warns that this level of international cooperation may wane as 9/11 becomes a more distant memory and perceptions of the threat diverge. Consequently, the U.S. homeland will face a persistent and evolving terrorist threat, deriving mainly from Islamic terrorist groups and cells, especially al-Qaeda. Additionally, such groups will continue to adapt and improve their capabilities. The notion of a continuing, if not increasing, threat by al-Qaeda and affiliated movements, AQAM as they are called, is not universally accepted. As previously mentioned, many analysts believe that AQAM leadership has been placed so much on the run, that concerns about personal security constrain their ability to plot and execute major attacks.

That argument notwithstanding, the NIE goes on to warn that the United States is in a heightened threat environment brought about by al-Qaeda, which remains the most serious terrorist threat to the U.S. homeland. The NIE claims that al-Qaeda leadership continues to plan sensational attacks and encourages other Sunni extremists to join its cause. The NIE claims a resurgent al-Qaeda safely ensconced in Pakistan's Federally Administered Tribal Areas (FATA), with operational lieutenants and top leadership intact and functional. The NIE does not provide convincing evidence to support this claim, leaving one to wonder if such evidence is contained in the full, classified version.

By far the most worrisome key judgment offered by the NIE is that al-Qaeda will continue to try to acquire chemical, biological, radiological, or nuclear material and would not hesitate to use them if it develops what it deems is sufficient capability. This finding includes a suite of threats. A chemical attack could produce hundreds of casualties as could a radiological, or "dirty bomb" attack. However, most analysts consider those types of attacks manageable. An attack by a nuclear weapon of any appreciable yield, or a well planned and executed biological attack, however, could be utterly devastating. The unpredictability of the opaque indigenous nuclear weapons programs of North Korea, Iran, and Pakistan, coupled with the possibility that some tactical nuclear weapons of the Former Soviet Union could find their way onto the black market, combine to make this key judgment of the NIE one that should garner top priority in U.S. counter- and anti-terrorism planning. As suggested earlier, many analysts posit that only the probability of tracing a nuclear weapon back to its source country has kept such a weapon out of the hands of terrorists.

The NIE also observes that the ability to detect broader and more diverse terrorist plotting in an increasingly Internetted global community is increasingly challenging and will complicate U.S. defensive efforts immensely. Success will require greater understanding of how to evaluate local activities in relation to strategic threat information and more sophisticated identification of indicators of terrorist activity in the midst of countless legitimate interactions. The NIE quite reasonably assesses that globalization trends and technological communications advances will assist in the formation of virtual affiliations that pursue common causes, even without common leadership or formal organization. Furthermore, the NIE also prudently assesses that the spread of radical Internet sites, increasingly aggressive anti-U.S. rhetoric and actions, and the growing number of radical, self-generating cells in western countries indicate that the radical and violent segment of the West's Muslim population is expanding, including in the United States.

A careful reading of the entire unclassified NIE can provide insights into the political context within which the NIE was prepared. Additionally, it can point toward U.S. priorities for intelligence collection and disruption of planned terrorist activities.

DOCUMENT NO. 4

NATIONAL INTELLIGENCE ESTIMATE: THE TERRORIST THREAT TO THE US HOMELAND

Office of the Director of National Intelligence
National Security Council

July 2007

Office of the Director of National Intelligence

The Director of National Intelligence serves as the head of the Intelligence Community (IC), overseeing and directing the implementation of the National Intelligence Program and acting as the principal advisor to the President, the National Security Council, and the Homeland Security Council for intelligence matters.

The Office of the Director of National Intelligence is charged with:

- Integrating the domestic and foreign dimensions of US intelligence so that there are no gaps in our understanding of threats to our national security;
- Bringing more depth and accuracy to intelligence analysis; and
- Ensuring that US intelligence resources generate future capabilities as well as present results.

National Intelligence Council

Since its formation in 1973, the National Intelligence Council (NIC) has served as a bridge between the intelligence and policy communities, a source of deep substantive expertise on critical national security issues, and as a focal point for Intelligence Community collaboration. The NIC's key goal is to provide policymakers with the best, unvarnished, and unbiased information. Its primary functions are to:

- Support the DNI in his role as Principal Intelligence Advisor to the President and other senior policymakers.

- Lead the Intelligence Community's effort to produce National Intelligence Estimates (NIEs) and other NIC products that address key national security concerns.
- Provide a focal point for policymakers, warfighters, and Congressional leaders to task the Intelligence Community for answers to important questions.
- Reach out to nongovernment experts in academia and the private sector—and use alternative analyses and new analytic tools—to broaden and deepen the Intelligence Community's perspective.

NIEs are the DNI's most authoritative written judgments concerning national security issues. They contain the coordinated judgments of the Intelligence Community regarding the likely course of future events.

National Intelligence Estimates and the Nie Process

National Intelligence Estimates (NIEs) are the Intelligence Community's (IC) most authoritative written judgments on national security issues and designed to help US civilian and military leaders develop policies to protect US national security interests. NIEs usually provide information on the current state of play but are primarily "estimative"—that is, they make judgments about the likely course of future events and identify the implications for US policy.

The NIEs are typically requested by senior civilian and military policymakers, Congressional leaders and at times are initiated by the National Intelligence Council (NIC). Before a NIE is drafted, the relevant National Intelligence Officer is responsible for producing a concept paper, or terms of reference (TOR), and circulates it throughout the Intelligence Community for comment. The TOR defines the key estimative questions, determines drafting responsibilities, and sets the drafting and publication schedule. One or more IC analysts are usually assigned to produce the initial text. The NIC then meets to critique the draft before it is circulated to the broader IC. Representatives from the relevant IC agencies meet to hone and coordinate line-by-line the full text of the NIE. Working with their Agencies, representatives also assign the level of confidence they have in key judgments. IC representatives discuss the quality of sources with collectors, and the National Clandestine Service vets the sources used to ensure the draft does not include any that have been recalled or otherwise seriously questioned.

All NIEs are reviewed by National Intelligence Board, which is chaired by the DNI and is composed of the heads of relevant IC agencies. Once approved by the NIB, NIEs are briefed to the President and senior policymakers. The whole process of producing NIEs normally takes at least several months.

The NIC has undertaken a number of steps to improve the NIE process under the DNI. These steps are in accordance with the goals and recommendations set out in the Senate Select Committee on Intelligence and WMD Commission reports and the 2004 Intelligence Reform and Prevention of Terrorism Act. Most notably, over the last two years the IC has:

- ***Created new procedures to integrate formal reviews of source reporting and technical judgments.*** The Director of CIA, as the National HUMINT Manager, as well as the Directors of NSA, NGA, and DIA and the Assistant Secretary/INR are now required to submit formal assessments that highlight the strengths, weaknesses, and overall credibility of their sources used in developing the critical judgments of the NIE.
- ***Applied more rigorous standards.*** A textbox is incorporated into all NIEs that explains what we mean by such terms as "we judge" and that clarifies the difference between judgments of likelihood and confidence levels. We have made a concerted effort to not only highlight differences among agencies but to explain the reasons for such differences and to display them prominently in the Key Judgments.

The US Homeland Threat Estimate: How it Was Produced

The Estimate, Terrorist Threats to the US Homeland, followed the standard process for producing National Intelligence Estimates (NIEs), including a thorough review of sourcing, in-depth Community coordination, the use of alternative analysis, and review by outside experts. Starting in October 2006, the NIC organized a series of roundtables with IC experts to scope out terms of reference (TOR) for the Estimate. Drafters from throughout the Community contributed to the draft. In May, a draft was submitted to IC officers in advance of a series of coordination meetings that spanned several days. The National Clandestine Service, FBI, and other IC collection officers reviewed the text for the reliability and proper use of the sourcing. As part of the normal coordination process, analysts had the opportunity—and were encouraged—to register "dissents" and provide alternative analysis. Reactions by the two outside experts who read the final product were highlighted in the text. The National Intelligence Board, composed of the heads of the 16 IC agencies and chaired by the ODNI, reviewed and approved the Estimate on 21 June. As with other NIEs, it is being distributed to senior Administration officials and Members of Congress.

What We Mean When We Say: An Explanation of Estimative Language

When we use words such as "we judge" or "we assess"—terms we use synonymously— as well as "we estimate," "likely" or "indicate," we are trying to convey an analytical assessment or judgment. These assessments, which are based on incomplete or at times fragmentary information are not a fact, proof, or knowledge. Some analytical judgments are based directly on collected information; others rest on previous judgments, which serve as building blocks. In either type of judgment, we do not have "evidence" that shows something to be a fact or that definitively links two items or issues.

Intelligence judgments pertaining to likelihood are intended to reflect the Community's sense of the probability of a development or event. Assigning precise numerical ratings to such judgments would imply more rigor than we intend. The chart below provides a rough idea of the relationship of terms to each other.

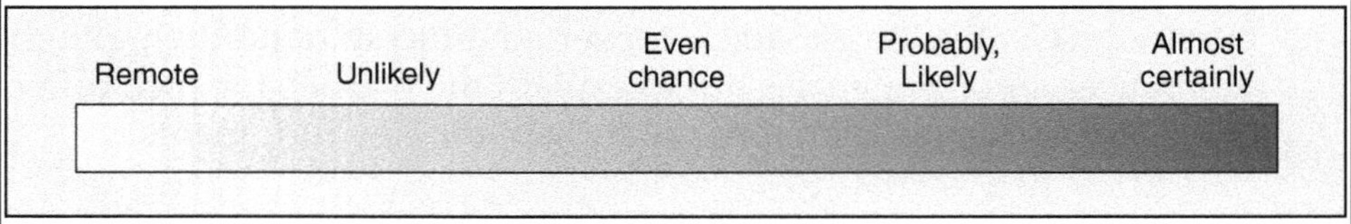

We do not intend the term "unlikely" to imply an event will not happen. We use "probably" and "likely" to indicate there is a greater than even chance. We use words such as "we cannot dismiss," "we cannot rule out," and "we cannot discount" to reflect an unlikely—or even remote—event whose consequences are such it warrants mentioning. Words such as "may be" and "suggest" are used to reflect situations in which we are unable to assess the likelihood generally because relevant information is nonexistent, sketchy, or fragmented.

In addition to using words within a judgment to convey degrees of likelihood, we also ascribe "high," "moderate," or "low" confidence levels based on the scope and quality of information supporting our judgments.

- "High confidence" generally indicates our judgments are based on high-quality information and/or the nature of the issue makes it possible to render a solid judgment.
- "Moderate confidence" generally means the information is interpreted in various ways, we have alternative views, or the information is credible and plausible but not corroborated sufficiently to warrant a higher level of confidence.
- "Low confidence" generally means the information is scant, questionable, or very fragmented and it is difficult to make solid analytic inferences, or we have significant concerns or problems with the sources.

Key Judgments

We judge the US Homeland will face a persistent and evolving terrorist threat over the next three years. The main threat comes from Islamic terrorist groups and cells, especially al-Qa'ida, driven by their undiminished intent to attack the Homeland and a continued effort by these terrorist groups to adapt and improve their capabilities.

We assess that greatly increased worldwide counterterrorism efforts over the past five years have constrained the ability of al-Qa'ida to attack the US Homeland again and have led terrorist groups to perceive the Homeland as a harder target to strike than on 9/11. These measures have helped disrupt known plots against the United States since 9/11.

- We are concerned, however, that this level of international cooperation may wane as 9/11 becomes a more distant memory and perceptions of the threat diverge.

Al-Qa'ida is and will remain the most serious terrorist threat to the Homeland, as its central leadership continues to plan high-impact plots, while pushing others in extremist Sunni communities to mimic its efforts and to supplement its capabilities. We assess the group has protected or regenerated key elements of its Homeland attack capability, including: a safehaven in the Pakistan Federally Administered Tribal Areas (FATA), operational lieutenants, and its top leadership. Although we have discovered only a handful of individuals in the United States with ties to al-Qa'ida senior leadership since 9/11, we judge that al-Qa'ida will intensify its efforts to put operatives here.

- As a result, we judge that the United States currently is in a heightened threat environment.

We assess that al-Qa'ida will continue to enhance its capabilities to attack the Homeland through greater cooperation with regional terrorist groups. Of note, we assess that al-Qa'ida will probably seek to leverage the contacts and capabilities of al-Qa'ida in Iraq (AQI), its most visible and capable affiliate and the only one known to have expressed a desire to attack the Homeland. In addition, we assess that its association with AQI helps al-Qa'ida to energize the broader Sunni extremist community, raise resources, and to recruit and indoctrinate operatives, including for Homeland attacks.

We assess that al-Qa'ida's Homeland plotting is likely to continue to focus on prominent political, economic, and infrastructure targets with the goal of producing mass casualties, visually dramatic destruction, significant economic aftershocks, and/or fear among the US population. The group is proficient with conventional small arms and improvised explosive devices, and is innovative in creating new capabilities and overcoming security obstacles.

- We assess that al-Qa'ida will continue to try to acquire and employ chemical, biological, radiological, or nuclear material in attacks and would not hesitate to use them if it develops what it deems is sufficient capability.

We assess Lebanese Hizballah, which has conducted anti-US attacks outside the United States in the past, may be more likely to consider attacking the Homeland over the next three years if it perceives the United States as posing a direct threat to the group or Iran.

We assess that the spread of radical—especially Salafi—Internet sites, increasingly aggressive anti-US rhetoric and actions, and the growing number of radical, self-generating cells in Western countries indicate that the radical and violent segment of the West's Muslim population is expanding, including in the United States. The arrest and prosecution by US law enforcement of a small number of violent Islamic extremists inside the United States—who are becoming more connected ideologically, virtually, and/or in a physical sense to the global extremist movement—points to the possibility that others may become sufficiently radicalized that they will view the use of violence here as legitimate. We assess that this internal Muslim terrorist threat is not likely to be as severe as it is in Europe, however.

We assess that other, non-Muslim terrorist groups—often referred to as "single-issue" groups by the FBI—probably will conduct attacks over the next three years given their violent histories, but we assess this violence is likely to be on a small scale.

We assess that globalization trends and recent technological advances will continue to enable even small numbers of alienated people to find and connect with one another, justify and intensify their anger, and mobilize resources to attack—all without requiring a centralized terrorist organization, training camp, or leader.

- The ability to detect broader and more diverse terrorist plotting in this environment will challenge current US defensive efforts and the tools we use to detect and disrupt plots. It will also require greater understanding of how suspect activities at the local level relate to strategic threat information and how best to identify indicators of terrorist activity in the midst of legitimate interactions.

E. CONGRESSIONAL TESTIMONY: CONFRONTING THE TERRORIST THREAT TO THE HOMELAND

CONGRESSIONAL TESTIMONY BEFORE THE SENATE HOMELAND SECURITY AND GOVERNMENTAL AFFAIRS COMMITTEE

Hearing on Confronting the Terrorist Threat to the Homeland:Six Years after 9/11

10 September 2007

Statement for the Record of J. Michael McConnell
Director of National Intelligence
and
John Scott Redd
Vice Admiral, U.S. Navy (Retired)
Director, National Counterterrorism Center

Commentary

The statements for the record provided in this volume add texture to the July 2007 NIE discussed above. The Director of National Intelligence (DNI) begins his statement with a discussion of the findings of the NIE, reminding the committee that an NIE is the most authoritative written judgment of the Intelligence Community (IC) on a particular subject. He then used the quality of the NIE to suggest that many improvements to the IC have been made since September 11, 2001. He first discusses intelligence reforms that moved the IC away from its lingering Cold War structure.

It is a truism that although the Cold War ended in 1989, the U.S. IC retained its Cold War habiliments into the 21st century. The IC was imprudently downsized during the last decade of the 20th century, when it should have been transformed. It needed a national-level intelligence apparatus to manage the IC effectively and synthesize vast amounts of information in order to produce timely, relevant, all-source intelligence. Traditional "stovepipes" of information within agencies had to be eliminated and replaced with new collaboration and coordination protocols. In short, the IC needed to be managed as an enterprise.

Since 9/11, the IC has made many changes in the way it conducts intelligence, law enforcement, homeland security, diplomatic, and defense support. Its major accomplishments fall into four main areas: restructuring the IC to meet 21st century challenges; improving analysis through cross-agency integration and technical initiatives; developing a collaborative IC that provides the right information to the right people at the right time; and building a dynamic intelligence enterprise that promotes diversity to gain and sustain a competitive advantage against U.S. adversaries.

Vice Admiral (Ret) Redd began by addressing the role that the National Counterterrorism Center (NCTC) plays in detecting, disrupting, and deterring the threat of terrorism against U.S. interests both at home and abroad. He points out that the NCTC performs two significant functions in support of the Global War Against Terrorists. The center's intelligence efforts support the DNI. However, the NCTC also has a "Strategic Operational Planning" role. In that role, the Director of the NCTC reports to the President as the senior leader responsible for developing the U.S. Government's overall war plan for the Global War Against Terrorists. VADM (Ret) Redd first addresses NCTC improvements in accomplishing its intelligence mission and then turns to a discussion of the planning mission.

Improved approaches to accomplishing the intelligence mission include performance of all-source, integrated analysis; production of a daily Threat Matrix and twice daily Situation Reports; analysis coordinated IC-wide; use of an *Analytic Framework for Counterterrorism* that focuses on the four counterterrorism mission areas of Tactical Offense, Tactical Defense, Strategic Offense, and Strategic Defense; improved information sharing within the federal government, states, local governments, and tribal governments; bringing together departments and agencies to discuss current threats; and comprehensive watchlisting of individuals of concern.

The NCTC fosters greater interagency collaboration, by coordinating routinely with the larger counterterrorism intelligence community so that all parts of the IC work toward a coherent, cohesive counterterrorism vision. The NCTC practices a systematic "lessons learned" process to improve the efficacy and efficiency of its efforts. Finally, the NCTC created the "Terrorist Identities Datamart Environment (TIDE)," that includes, to the extent permitted by law, all information the U.S. government possesses on the identities of individuals suspected to have been involved in international terrorism.

In its Strategic Operational Planning (SOP) role for the Global War Against Terrorists, the NCTC performs a wide spectrum of planning functions. It strives to connect interagency policy and strategy to tactical operations. Essentially, SOP takes interagency planning to a more detailed level than done in the past, at least at the national level. The NCTC leads the interagency planning effort to bring all elements of national power to bear in the Global War Against Terrorists. Deliberate planning involves planning, implementation, and assessment. The NCTC is building processes for all three phases.

The statements by these two former naval officers describe an IC with capabilities superior to the separate and fragmented capabilities that existed on September 11, 2001. A careful reading of the statements provides many insights into the United States' new approaches to information acquisition, intelligence production, collaboration, and intelligence dissemination.

DOCUMENT NO. 5

CONFRONTING THE TERRORIST THREAT TO THE HOMELAND: SIX YEARS AFTER 9/11

Hearing Before the
Senate Homeland Security and Governmental Affairs Committee

September 10, 2007

Statement for the Record of J. Michael McConnell
Director of National Intelligence

Chairman Lieberman, Ranking Member Collins, and members of the Senate Committee on Homeland Security and Government Affairs: Thank you for your invitation to appear before the committee to provide a status report on the nation's efforts to confront terrorist threats to the nation and to describe the implementation of institutional reforms mandated by Congress and by Presidential directive since September 11, 2001.

It is my privilege to be accompanied by Michael Chertoff, Secretary of Homeland Security, Robert Mueller, Director of the Federal Bureau of Investigation, and Vice Admiral John Scott Redd, Director of the National Counterterrorism Center.

Terrorist Threat to the U.S. Homeland

I would like to begin my statement with a discussion of the findings of the July 2007 National Intelligence Estimate (NIE) on the Terrorist Threat to the U.S. Homeland. An NIE is the most authoritative written judgment of the Intelligence Community (IC) on a particular subject and a declassified version of this NIE's key judgments was made available on the Internet. It assessed the following:

- The US Homeland will face a persistent and evolving terrorist threat over the next three years. The main threat comes from Islamic terrorist groups and cells, especially al-Qa'ida, driven by their undiminished intent to attack the Homeland and a continued effort by these terrorist groups to adapt and improve their capabilities.

- Greatly increased worldwide counterterrorism efforts over the past five years have constrained the ability of al-Qa'ida to attack the US Homeland again and have led terrorist groups to perceive the Homeland as a harder target to strike than on 9/11.
- We are concerned, however, that this level of international cooperation may wane as 9/11 becomes a more distant memory and perceptions of the threat diverge.
- Al-Qa'ida is and will remain the most serious terrorist threat to the Homeland, as its central leadership continues to plan high-impact plots, while pushing others in extremist Sunni communities to mimic its efforts and to supplement its capabilities. We assess the group has protected or regenerated key elements of its Homeland attack capability, including: a safehaven in the Pakistan Federally Administered Tribal Areas (FATA), operational lieutenants, and its top leadership. Although we have discovered only a handful of individuals in the United States with ties to al-Qa'ida senior leadership since 9/11, we judge that al-Qa'ida will intensify its efforts to put operatives here.
- As a result, we judge that the United States currently is in a heightened threat environment.
- We assess that al-Qa'ida will continue to enhance its capabilities to attack the Homeland through greater cooperation with regional terrorist groups. Of note, we assess that al-Qa'ida will probably seek to leverage the contacts and capabilities of al-Qa'ida in Iraq.
- We assess that al-Qa'ida's Homeland plotting is likely to continue to focus on prominent political, economic, and infrastructure targets with the goal of producing mass casualties, visually dramatic destruction, significant economic aftershocks, and/or fear among the US population.
- We assess that al-Qa'ida will continue to try to acquire and employ chemical, biological, radiological, or nuclear material in attacks and would not hesitate to use them if it develops what it deems is sufficient capability.
- We assess Lebanese Hizballah, which has conducted anti-US attacks outside the United States in the past, may be more likely to consider attacking the Homeland over the next three years if it perceives the United States as posing a direct threat to the group or Iran.
- We assess that the spread of radical—especially Salafi—Internet sites, increasingly aggressive anti-US rhetoric and actions, and the growing number of radical, self-generating cells in Western countries indicate that the radical and violent segment of the West's Muslim population is expanding, including in the United States.

- We assess that other, non-Muslim terrorist groups probably will conduct attacks over the next three years given their violent histories, but we assess this violence is likely to be on a small scale.
- We assess that globalization trends and recent technological advances will continue to enable even small numbers of alienated people to find and connect with one another, justify and intensify their anger, and mobilize resources to attack—all without requiring a centralized terrorist organization, training camp, or leader.

The analytic effort that culminated in this NIE was strengthened by many of the intelligence reforms realized since September 11.

Intelligence Reforms Since 9/11

I turn now to the transformation we have undertaken in the IC to meet the challenges of today and the threats of tomorrow.

The Intelligence Community has made significant strides in addressing the underlying deficiencies exposed by the attacks of 9/11. This morning, I would like to first highlight a few of the flaws in America's intelligence system that existed before 9/11; second, detail the steps we have taken thus far to build a stronger Community; and, finally, turn our gaze to initiatives that will further these reforms.

Generally speaking, before 9/11 America's Intelligence Community was structured to win the Cold War—a traditional struggle between two great powers. The Community was downsized during the 1990s and while it consisted of over a dozen agencies with unique mandates and competencies, we lacked a national-level intelligence apparatus to manage effectively the Community and synthesize information from across the government to support a host of customers— policymakers, warfighters, and law enforcement officials—with various, and often competing, requirements. This construct led often to the "stovepiping" of information within agencies that guarded their cultures and their secrets. Data was provided on a "need to know" basis. "Information sharing" was considered more an exposure to foreign espionage than a path to a smarter intelligence enterprise. Accordingly, analysts in one agency were not encouraged to work with analysts in others. There were few processes in place to collaborate, share lessons learned and best practices, and manage the Community as an enterprise.

In the past, policy barriers also prevented the government from attracting young people of promise with the skills and backgrounds needed to strengthen our national defense. Too often, agencies became so focused on protecting sources and methods that they made it nearly impossible for first- and second-generation Americans to serve the intelligence enterprise.

This was a serious deficiency that denied the country the efforts of those with the language fluencies, political, scientific, and technical skills, and cultural insights that we need to bolster our workforce and improve our intelligence.

Structurally, the Community was also largely divided between domestic and foreign intelligence.

The end of the Cold War and the advance of globalization enabled the acceleration of threats stemming from international terrorism, weapons of mass destruction (WMD) proliferation, failed states, and illegal drug trafficking. These threats, among others, move at increasing speeds due to technology and across geographic and organizational boundaries, blurring the distinction between foreign and domestic, and between strategic and tactical events. As we witnessed on 9/11, radical extremist movements continue to use global terrorism to further their causes by attacking innocent people without regard to national boundaries and state and non-state actors continue to demonstrate their intent to acquire WMD through illicit means.

To confront today's threats, we have made many changes in the way we conduct intelligence, law enforcement, homeland security, diplomatic, and defense activities. Implementing the Intelligence Reform and Terrorism Prevention Act of 2004 (IRTPA) along with the recommendations from various in-depth studies— such as the 9/11 Commission Report, the WMD Commission Report, internal Executive Branch reviews and reports by both houses of Congress—the Community received direction and the mandate and many of the tools needed to build an effective, results-oriented enterprise. The Intelligence Reform Act provided a mechanism for overhauling the IC by providing a new office, the Office of the Director of National Intelligence (ODNI), with the tools and mandate to unify and direct the efforts of our 16 intelligence agencies.

With these new mechanisms, we are working to forge an integrated Intelligence Community that spans the historical divide between foreign and domestic intelligence efforts. Far from being a buzz word, integration means ensuring that our various specialized intelligence missions operate as a single enterprise. An integrated and collaborative Community is a critical advance because no single agency has the capacity to evaluate all available information— lest we forget that over one billion pieces of data are collected by America's intelligence agencies everyday.

While we recognize that much more must be accomplished, the professionals of the Intelligence Community take pride in the notable progress we have made over the past six years. I would like to describe our accomplishments thus far in four main areas: our efforts to **structure** the Intelligence Community to meet 21st century challenges; **improve** analysis through cross-agency integration and technical initiatives; develop a **collaborative** Community that provides the right information to the right people at the right time; and **build** a dynamic intelligence enterprise that promotes diversity to gain and sustain a competitive advantage against our adversaries.

Structuring the IC

The principal legacy of the IRTPA was the establishment of the office of the Director of National Intelligence with assigned responsibilities to serve as the chief intelligence advisor to the President and National and Homeland Security Councils and to head the IC to ensure closer coordination and integration. The DNI is afforded responsibility to determine the National Intelligence Program and significant authority over personnel policy. In a larger sense, the creation of the DNI allows one person to see across the wide American Intelligence Community, identify gaps, and promote a strategic, unified vision.

I will leave to my colleagues with me here today the discussion of the specifics of their efforts, but I would like to highlight the key structural changes, in addition to the establishment of the ODNI, that have been undertaken since 9/11.

Working closely with the Department of Justice and the FBI, we supported the creation of the FBI's National Security Branch to integrate the FBI's counterterrorism, counterintelligence, WMD, and intelligence programs. We also supported the creation of Field Intelligence Groups in every FBI field office—a major steps in the FBI's effort to transform itself into a preeminent domestic counterterrorism agency. Furthermore, the Executive Assistant Director of the National Security Branch now works closely with me and my leadership team, ensuring close coordination on addressing the FBI's intelligence mission.

We established the National Counterterrorism Center (NCTC), the government's hub for all strategic level counterterrorism intelligence assessments, which draws on collected terrorist intelligence from agencies across the U.S. Government with access to more than 30 different networks carrying more than 80 unique data sources to produce integrated analysis on terrorist plots against U.S. interests at home and abroad. This kind of fusion is conducted nowhere else in government—and it was only an aspiration prior to 9/11.

The results are tangible. NCTC produces a daily threat matrix and situation reports that are the Community standard for current intelligence awareness. In addition, NCTC hosts three video teleconferences daily to discuss the threat matrix and situation reports to ensure the intelligence agencies and organizations see all urgent counterterrorism information.

We also established the National Counterproliferation Center (NCPC), the mission manager for counterproliferation, which has developed integrated and creative strategies against some of the nation's highest priority targets, including "gap attacks" (focused strategies against longstanding intelligence gaps), "over the horizon" studies to address potential future counterproliferation threats, and specialized projects on priority issues such as the Counterterrorism-Counterproliferation Nexus.

ODNI Mission Managers for high-priority topics, such as North Korea, Iran, counterintelligence, and Cuba and Venezuela, have also made considerable progress by identifying intelligence priorities, gaps, and requirements and engaging in strategic planning and collection management in the larger context of other intelligence collection and analytical priorities.

In the last few months, we also established an Executive Committee (EXCOM) to advise the DNI in the discharge of his responsibility for the coordination of all intelligence activities that constitute the domestic and foreign intelligence efforts of the country. This EXCOM is composed of the heads of all major intelligence producers and consumers and provides a biweekly forum for the key stakeholders to gather and provide common guidance on the development, implementation, and evaluation of activities of the IC.

Within the past six months, we also named a Deputy Director of National Intelligence (DDNI) for Acquisition to enhance the efficiency and effectiveness of our acquisitions. The DDNI for Acquisition has drafted a strategy to improve the acquisition process and recommended modifications to acquisition authorities. We are also in the process of standing up the Intelligence Advanced Research Projects Activity to create synergy and innovation across the IC by harnessing technology in new ways to create strategic advantage.

These three initiatives were highlighted by the Intelligence Community's 100 Day Plan for Integration and Collaboration, which we launched in April and concluded in August. The 100 Day Plan identified 24 specific initiatives and tasks to be accomplished on a rigorous timeline; of those 24, 17 tasks were achieved in that timeframe and the remaining tasks are scheduled to be met in the coming weeks. The Plan was designed to build on the successes so far—many of which I will discuss here—and to jumpstart further efforts. Initiatives were aligned to six integration and transformation focus areas:

1. Create a Culture of Collaboration
2. Foster Collection and Analytic Transformation
3. Build Acquisition Excellence and Technology Leadership
4. Modernize Business Practices
5. Accelerate Information Sharing
6. Clarify and Align DNI's Authorities.

I have discussed the specifics of this Plan in other forums and will not detail it today, although I note that the focus on accountability and achieving identified targets has given a renewed emphasis to transforming the Community and executing these reform initiatives. I will speak again of our planning process at the conclusion of my testimony.

Improving Analysis

Cross-Agency Integration

Two of the main goals of intelligence reform are to build a sense of community among foreign, military, and domestic intelligence agencies and, through that kind of collaboration, improve the quality of analysis. For greater collaboration to occur, however, analysts must be able to identify and contact peers and counterparts working on related topics.

Prior to the creation of the ODNI, analysts had no easy way to obtain contact information on analysts from other agencies. Today, they have the Analysts Yellow Pages. Launched in February 2006, the Analysts Yellow Pages is a classified, web-based phonebook and a single stop for obtaining contact information on analysts in all IC agencies. It is accessible on the Joint World-wide Intelligence Communications System and allows users to search for analysts across the Intelligence Community by name, by intelligence topic, country, or non-state actor, or by agency. Search results provide contact information including name, agency, phone number, and email address. Our ODNI Chief Information Officer (CIO) is developing a common method to identify, in perpetuity, all the individuals across the IC.

The Information Sharing Environment

Created by IRTPA, the Program Manager for the Information Sharing Environment (PM-ISE), operating in coordination with the interagency under guidelines issued by the President and statutory authority—a well as with strong support from this Committee—has led the charge with our state, local, tribal, private sector, and foreign partners to transform government-wide terrorism-related information sharing policies, processes, procedures, and most important,workplace cultures, to normalize the sharing of terrorism-related information as part of how we do business.

Section 1016 of the IRTPA and as amended by the 9/11 Commission Act of 2007, established the Office of the Program Manager and provided it with government-wide authority to plan, oversee and manage the ISE. The ISE is a trusted partnership among all levels of government that facilitates the sharing of information relating to terrorism. Creating the ISE is not about building a massive new information system; it is policies, processes/protocols and technology that enable the sharing of this information among Federal, State, local, tribal, private sector entities and our foreign partners.

To guide efforts to establish the ISE and implement the requirements of Section 1016 of IRTPA, on December 16, 2005, the President issued a Memorandum to the Heads of Executive Departments and Agencies on the *Guidelines and Requirements in Support of the Information Sharing Environment*. In this Memorandum the President prioritized efforts that he believes are most critical to the development of the ISE and assigned to relevant Cabinet officials the responsibility for resolving some of the more complicated issues associated with information sharing.

The PM-ISE in consultation with the Information Sharing Council, State, local, and tribal governments, and private sector partners have made significant progress against the President's priorities in the following areas:

- Development of proposed Common Terrorism Information Sharing Standards (CTISS). The CTISS program develops and issues functional standards that document the rules, conditions, guidelines, and characteristics of business processes, production methods, and products supporting terrorism-related information sharing. (Presidential Guideline 1)
- Establishment of a Federally-sponsored interagency capability in the NCTC to enable the production and dissemination of Federally-coordinated terrorism-related information to state, local, and tribal authorities and the private sector. (Presidential Guideline 2)
- Establishment of a national, integrated network of State and major urban area fusion centers that optimizes our capacity to better support the information needs of State and local authorities, as well as efforts to gather, analyze, and share locally generated information in a manner that protects the information privacy and legal rights of Americans. (Presidential Guideline 2)
- Development of the *Presidential Guideline 3 Report: Standardize Procedures for Sensitive but Unclassified (SBU) Information*. The Report will recommend to the President a new Controlled Unclassified Information (CUI) Framework for rationalizing, standardizing, and simplifying procedures for SBU information in the ISE. (Presidential Guideline 3)
- A repository of information on over 400 unclassified and SBU international information sharing agreements with foreign governments. (Presidential Guideline 4)
- PM-ISE publication of ISE Privacy Guidelines, including development of an implementation guide for Federal agencies. (Presidential Guideline 5)

Although the effort to implement the ISE is well underway, it is essential that implementation activities take place within a broader strategic context of enhancing our Nation's ability to combat terrorism. The ultimate goal is not simply information sharing for the sake of sharing information. The objective is to improve our national capacity to protect the nation from future attack.

Information Sharing Initiatives within the IC

Initiatives in support of information sharing specifically within the IC include the efforts of the CIO and the ODNI Analysis directorate, to profoundly change how IC components collaborate with each other. We have integrated Internet technologies into the Intelligence Community's secure and unclassified Intranets, giving individuals the ability to collaborate as groups, peer-to-peer, and in self-identified teams. We are also developing virtual communities of analysts who can securely exchange ideas and expertise across organizational boundaries. Through our pilot Library of National Intelligence initiative, we are providing analysts across the Community a searchable database of disseminated Intelligence products. In a later phase, even if a particular user does not have the clearances to review a desired document, he or she will (in most cases) be advised of the product's existence and offered the opportunity to request access to it.

And analysts are also increasingly using interactive, classified blogs and wikis, much as the tech-savvy, collaboration-minded user would outside the Community. Intellipedia, the IC's version of Wikipedia, and "A-Space" a common workspace environment likened in the press to the commercial website "MySpace," are perhaps the best-known examples. Such tools enable experts from different disciplines to pool their knowledge, form virtual teams, and quickly make complete intelligence assessments.

Efforts to improve collaboration do not stop at the water's edge—literally. Under CIO auspices, we have created the capability for US persons to communicate via email with their Allied counterparts overseas. The solution does not require special networks or equipment but has dramatically changed our capability to share information in a timely manner. The Allied Collaborative Shared Services program and email projects have improved how the US Intelligence Community shares intelligence with our partners.

The underlying principle here is a simple one: no one has a monopoly on truth.

Much the same principle animates our engagement with outside professionals who can challenge our analytic assumptions, provide deep knowledge, insights, and new ways of thinking. Through the Analytic Outreach Initiative, ODNI is expanding networking opportunities for IC analysts and encouraging them to tap expertise on key issues wherever it resides through conferences, seminars, workshops, and exchanges. These outside experts—whether academics, business people, journalists, technical experts, or retired intelligence officers—contribute to proof and validation exercises and to lessons learned processes. They also provide a critical surge capability, especially in areas where IC resources are slim.

We have also taken steps to safeguard the impartiality of our analytic products. As mandated by the IRTPA, the ODNI established an Assistant Deputy for Analytic Integrity and Standards, who serves as the focal point for analysts who wish to raise concerns regarding politicization, bias, or the lack of objectivity, appropriate alternative analysis, or dissenting views in intelligence products. The Office of Analytic Integrity and Standards challenges the IC to evaluate its work and enforce standard that will produce the best possible analytic product for our customers. The AIS is also promoting the use of diverse analytic methodologies. For example, AIS has developed an Introductory Analysis course for new IC analysts, who will receive instruction in critical skills, establish contacts in other agencies, and gain better appreciation of the diversity within the IC.

Many of these improvements would be of little use if they did not reach our customers, including the policymakers of this Committee. Specifically, you may have noticed the qualitative improvements to our National Intelligence Estimates, the IC's most authoritative written judgment on a particular subject. Specifically, NIE Key Judgments no longer contain a list of conclusions but are written to explore more thoroughly the implications of our critical underlying conclusions. Appendices and annexes now provide full transparency of their analytic judgments through the careful identification of sources and intelligence gaps, and by "showing our homework"—essentially, describing the analytic train of reasoning we use to arrive at our conclusions. The main text now highlights the full range of analytic judgments and their implications, bringing dissenting opinions to the fore so policymakers have the benefit of the full picture. We applied many of these lessons learned to the NIE on Homeland Security Threats that I discussed earlier.

Developing a Collaborative Community with a Responsibility to Provide

In the years since 9/11, multiple studies have attributed our inability to prevent the terrorist attacks to the inability or unwillingness of government organizations to share critical information and intelligence fully and effectively. Our success in preventing future attacks depends upon our ability to gather, analyze, and share information and intelligence regarding those who would do us more harm. The intelligence and information sharing structures that enabled the winning of the Cold War need greater flexibility and resilience to confront today's threats from transnational terrorists. Most important, the long-standing policy of only allowing officials access to intelligence on a "need to know" basis should be abandoned for a mindset guided by a "responsibility to provide" intelligence to policymakers, warfighters, and analysts, while still ensuring the protection of sources and methods.

In short, those responsible for combating terrorism must have access to timely and accurate information regarding our adversaries. We must:

- Identify rapidly both immediate and long-term threats;
- Identify persons involved in terrorism-related activities; and
- Implement information-driven and risk-based detection, prevention, deterrence, attribution, response, protection, and emergency management efforts.

Accomplishments Thus Far

In the aftermath of 9/11, our Nation began the historic transformation aimed at preventing future attacks and improving our ability to protect and defend our people and institutions at home and abroad. As a result, we are now better informed of terrorist intentions and plans and better prepared to detect, prevent, and respond to their actions. Improved intelligence collection and analysis has helped paint a more complete picture of the threat, and more robust information sharing has provided us a greater capacity for coordinated and integrated action. Several information sharing successes since 9/11 include the following:

- The enactment of the "USA PATRIOT Act" helped remove barriers that once restricted the effective sharing of information and coordination between the law enforcement and intelligence communities.
- The establishment of the Department of Homeland Security (DHS) and DHS's Office of Intelligence and Analysis has enhanced the sharing of information between federal, state, and local government agencies, and the private sector which in turn has enhanced our ability to detect, identify, understand, and assess terrorist threats both to and vulnerabilities of the homeland to better protect our Nation's critical infrastructure, integrate our emergency response networks, and link state and federal governments. The Chief Intelligence Officer of DHS is now responsible for integrating the intelligence activities of that Department, providing overall guidance on homeland security-specific issues.
- The Terrorist Screening Center was created to consolidate terrorist watch lists and provide around the clock operational support for federal and other government law enforcement personnel across the country.
- The growth and maturation of the 101 Joint Terrorism Task Forces (JTTF) in major jurisdictions throughout the United States, with support from Field Intelligence Groups (FIGs), has substantially contributed to improved terrorism-related information sharing and operational capabilities at the state and municipal levels.

Through these and other efforts, the United States and its coalition partners have made significant strides against al-Qa'ida, its affiliates, and others who threaten us. Collaboration and information sharing have helped limit the ability of al-Qa'ida and like-minded terrorist groups to operate. We have uncovered and eliminated numerous threats to our citizens and to our friends and allies. We have disrupted terrorist plots, arrested operatives, captured or killed senior leaders, and strengthened the capacity of the Nation to confront and defeat our adversaries.

Building a Dynamic Intelligence Enterprise

Joint Duty

Building a collaborative intelligence enterprise goes beyond merely sharing information. It also means fostering a new, Intelligence Community-wide culture without destroying the unique perspectives and capabilities of each agency. In this effort, the IC has a useful model in the Defense Department, which was revolutionized by the Goldwater-Nichols Act of 1986. That Act unified the military establishment and laid the foundations for a "joint" military by establishing incentives for interservice collaboration (such as requiring a joint duty assignment to achieve flag rank) and promoting joint training and development).

Recently, we took a dramatic step toward realizing a similar bedrock shift within the Intelligence Community. Through the authorities granted to the DNI by the IRTPA, I signed a directive mandating civilian joint duty for intelligence officers across the IC. This was a key accomplishment of our 100 Day Plan. Now, if an up-and-coming officer aspires to the senior-ranks of the Community, he or she will have to serve a tour of duty at a different agency during his or her career. The experience provides the officer with a broader perspective and brings the Community a long ways toward the collaborative and unified ideal.

Recruitment Initiatives

Since the establishment of the ODNI, we have been working vigorously to recruit intelligence officers with the backgrounds and skills that will strengthen our security.

The Intelligence Community's 100 Day Plan for Integration and Collaboration highlighted the need to recruit and retain first- and second-generation Americans with diverse background, critical language skills, and a nuanced understanding of foreign cultures to strengthen the nation's security. In accordance with initiatives specified in this Plan, the ODNI hosted an inaugural IC Heritage Summit and the first IC Leadership Colloquium in June 2007, beginning a dialogue with national and regional Heritage Community organizations and internal IC affinity groups and special emphasis program leaders. The results from these two events, and the feedback from the external and internal groups, were the foundation for developing the first IC Heritage Community Recruitment, Hiring, and Retention Strategy for first- and second-generation Americans. These groups, as well as our legacy communities, provide a rich pool of diverse talent that has not been consistently tapped into as a source to enable the IC to more accurately reflect the "face" of the American people.

In addition, we have established a formal Intelligence Community Recruiting Subcommittee, consisting of IC Agency Recruitment organizations, that meets regularly to discuss common issues, share best-practices and recruiting successes, plan annual IC collaborative recruiting events, network with leading external recruiting companies and consultants, and recommend solutions to individual IC Agency challenges.

We also developed a centrally funded IC corporate recruiting strategy to recruit collaboratively at national- or high-priority IC target events. Since 2005, the number of events at which we have recruited has more than doubled from 10 to about 25. We pursue a wide-range of applicants by recruiting at a broad array of national career fairs and conferences, including those hosted by: the Society of Hispanic Professional Engineers (SHPE), the National Society of Black Engineers, the American Indian Science and Engineering Society, the Thurgood Marshall Leadership Institute, Women for Hire, and Asian Diversity Career Expos. The IC is also a major sponsor of SHPE and events for the Careers for the Disabled.

Since the enactment of the IRTPA, the IC has established an IC-wide resume database that allows the sharing of resumes from collaborative events and IC Agency referrals and allows recruiters to search for highly-qualified applicants, especially those with desirable backgrounds or language fluencies.

We also established an annual campaign to recruit students from universities deemed Centers for Academic Excellence (CAE). The IC CAE program was established in 2004 to increase the diversity of the IC's applicant pool for entry-level professional positions. The program provides technical and financial support to a diverse cohort of ten specially-selected American colleges and universities so they can develop and deliver degree programs that prepare their graduates for IC jobs in the sciences, information systems and technology, regional studies, and foreign languages.

These initiatives will require follow-on implementation to recruit and hire personnel with the backgrounds and skills considered essential to improve the diversity and ability of the IC workforce, but with continued emphasis and support from the Administration and the Congress, I believe we are well positioned to succeed.

Focused Emphasis on Diversity

I would like to make special mention of the strong support we have received from the Congress in our efforts to diversify our workforce. Representative Silvestre Reyes, Chairman of the House Permanent Select Committee on Intelligence (HPSCI), has, in particular, worked closely with us to promote the recruitment of traditionally underrepresented groups. Chairman Reyes and I both addressed the first IC-wide Affinity Group and Special Emphasis Program Leadership Colloquium in June 2007, and the Chairman hosted a panel on diversity and the Intelligence Community last month in El Paso, Texas with Jose A. Rodriguez, the outgoing director of the CIA's National Clandestine Service.

We have also completed the first IC EEO and Diversity Strategy (Five-Year Plan for 2007-2012) as a priority initiative in our 100 Day Plan, responding to the HPSCI mark draft language and addressing a fundamental need to ensure that the IC workplace continues to be characterized by fairness and equality. Without such assurance, we cannot expect to attract and retain a workforce that looks like America and can operate in a global threat environment. Furthermore, our IC hiring and promotion practices must at least equal, and preferably surpass, other government agencies in transparency and equity if the American people are to willingly extend to us the latitude absolutely necessary to protect our nation.

Security Reform

The recruitment and hiring of first- and second-generation Americans brings into sharp relief a weakness that has plagued the Intelligence Community for decades: the onerous security clearance process required to work in the IC. The IRTPA mandated the reformation of security clearance procedures, and it remains one of our top priorities.

As someone who has worked in the private sector and been exposed to the other side of the security clearance process, I can speak from experience of the frustration that often accompanies lengthy and seemingly unnecessary delays in getting individuals cleared for duty.

Accordingly, we identified security clearance reform as a top priority for the 100 Day Plan and established a Tiger Team at the ODNI Special Security Center to lead this crucial reform. We are undertaking this security reform initiative jointly with the Department of Defense. We have designed a transformed clearance process and developed a plan to assess the validity of this process.

The comprehensive reform of the security clearance process remains our ultimate goal in order to deliver high-assurance security clearances, fairly, efficiently, and at the lowest possible cost. The new process will be based upon end-to-end automation, new sources of data, analytical research, and best practices. Some of these pieces already exist in the Community but they need to be integrated into a single process.

Foreign Language Initiatives

To build a strong foundation for the future of the Intelligence Community, we must also increase foreign language capacity among our workforce and support the study of languages among America's youth. To that end, ODNI is sponsoring a major Intelligence Community study of how to optimize foreign language staffing, taking into account language and proficiency requirements, retention, training, and cost, and comparing the roles played by civilian, military, and contractor personnel in performing foreign language tasks. The study is being conducted by the RAND Corporation and initial results are expected in 2008.

The ODNI also purchased a Community license for on-line language training software in 150 languages. All IC personnel will be able to utilize this resource. We are also supporting several research projects to improve the effectiveness of foreign language training, including evaluations of both commercially-developed and government-sponsored on-line language training programs.

Furthermore, ODNI has initiated a new collaborative program, called the Language Education and Resources Network to share best teaching practices and learning materials in critical languages developed in language schools throughout the U.S. government. Major workshops have been held in Chinese and Arabic, with additional workshops planned in Persian, Hindi, Urdu, and Korean within the next year.

We have also sponsored conferences and facilitated information sharing to enhance key capabilities in human language technology, such as machine translation and content extraction. ODNI is developing a Human Language Technology Roadmap, to guide and prioritize investment across the IC.

To fill critical gaps, ODNI is spearheading an initiative to create temporary hiring billets, to speed up the on-boarding process for applicants with outstanding foreign language skills, including heritage community applicants. Temporary billets could be used to hire personnel who are awaiting clearance and allow them to work in unclassified settings, such as open source research, or to permit placement of personnel who have been cleared, but for whom no permanent billet is immediately available.

Finally, ODNI—in partnership with the National Security Agency—leads STARTALK, a new program in summer language education. A part of a Presidential initiative to improve critical language skills, STARTALK will provide funding for programs in over 20 states and Washington D.C. to educate both students and language teachers. The classes focus on Arabic or Chinese and range from week-long tutorials to nine-week immersions.

Through this program, hundreds of young people will receive education that will enrich their lives, enhance their futures, and strengthen our nation's global competitiveness— yielding substantial returns for an initial investment of only five million dollars.

Looking to the Future

The passage of the IRTPA and the creation of the DNI were important steps toward building an integrated and collaborative Intelligence Community that is well positioned to defend the nation—but they must be part of a larger reform effort.

To support the IC vision of integration and collaboration we initiated a deliberate planning process based on the principles of transparency, accountability, deadlines, and deliverables. The first phase of these efforts—the recently completed 100 Day Plan—was designed to jump-start the process and build momentum. The next phase—the 500 Day Plan—is intended to sustain and accelerate that energy with an expanded set of initiatives and a greater level of participation. This latter plan was developed through a Community-wide effort beginning last May through the use of working groups, blogs, and wikis to solicit input from the Community. During our coordination process, we identified several core priorities and over 30 supporting initiatives. The core initiatives represent major long term impact projects that will be monitored and reported on a biweekly basis to my office and reviewed by the EXCOM monthly; they represent "major muscle movements"—something required for this transformational effort.

The 500 Day Plan will be executed through cross-organizational and Community-wide engagement and collaboration. Working groups for each initiative will include key stakeholders from throughout the Community. It is through implementation of these initiatives that the IC will continue to increase its efficiency and effectiveness and further meet the national security challenges of the 21st century.

Protect America Act of 2007

Finally, I would like to make note of an issue on which I hope the Congress takes action in the coming months. The recent enactment of the Protect America Act of 2007 provided a necessary update to the Foreign Intelligence Surveillance Act (FISA). This critical legislation has already assisted the IC in closing a critical gap in the IC's ability to provide warning of threats to the country. This Act sunsets in less than six months, and I believe that making its changes permanent will be an important step toward ensuring the protection of our Nation. Importantly, the Act provides for meaningful oversight of activities. The Department of Justice's National Security Division, IC general counsel offices, and the ODNI Civil Liberties and

Privacy Office, in addition to existing oversight mechanisms within the IC, will all be involved in overseeing implementation of the Act's authorities.

I am committed to keeping the Congress fully and currently informed of how this Act has improved the ability of the Intelligence Community to protect the country and look forward to working with the Congress to obtain lasting FISA modernization.

Conclusion

In closing, we have come a long way over the past six years developing a more integrated, more collaborative intelligence enterprise, and I believe the result has been a stronger Community better positioned to know the world and anticipate surprise. While we have seen success in our efforts to **structure** the Intelligence Community to meet 21st century challenges; **improve** analysis; develop a **collaborative** Community that provides the right information to the right people at the right time; and **build** a dynamic intelligence enterprise that promotes diversity to gain and sustain a competitive advantage against our adversaries, our work is far from done.

With your support, I look forward to building a legacy of reform that will outlast our own time and provide for the protection of the Republic in the decades to come.

Mr. Chairman, this concludes my remarks. I welcome any questions you may have. Thank you.

Statement for the Record
by
The Honorable John Scott Redd
Director, National Counterterrorism Center (NCTC) to the United States Senate Committee on Homeland Security and Governmental Affairs

Chairman Lieberman, Ranking Member Collins, distinguished members of the Committee, thank you for the opportunity to testify before you today on our nation's efforts to confront the terrorist threat to the homeland since 9/11.

Since 9/11, sweeping legislative and organizational changes—many of which are attributable to this committee—have fundamentally altered how we protect and defend U.S. interests at home and abroad against terrorism. In particular, the U.S. Government has made substantial progress in building our counterterrorism (CT) capability, developing a strategy based on a detailed understanding of al-Qa'ida and the global movement of violent extremists, and reorganizing the government to remedy the shortfalls revealed by the 9/11 attacks. I will discuss some of these developments with you today.

None of what I will say should be understood to mean that we do not continue to face real and significant challenges. We must continue to improve our intelligence collection on the hardest targets. We must continue to mature our coordination with state and local officials so that the federal government supports their efforts and benefits from their many capabilities. We must better coordinate departmental efforts to counter radicalization both at home and abroad. And we must ensure that departmental planning and budgeting is done in a manner consistent with a U.S. Government-wide effort to counter the terrorist threat we face now and are likely to face in the future.

I would like to briefly review the role NCTC is playing, and will play, to further sustain this progress through enhancing the U.S. Government's capability to detect, disrupt, and deter the threat of terrorism against U.S. interests both at home and abroad.

Today, as directed by the Intelligence Reform and Terrorism Prevention Act (IRTPA), NCTC performs two significant functions in the War on Terror. The first, Intelligence, is a familiar one and one in which I report to the DNI. The second is Strategic Operational Planning. As you are well aware, in this second role I report to the President and am responsible for producing the U.S. Government's overall War Plan for the War on Terror (WOT).

In both roles, NCTC's work is truly an interagency effort. We are part of the ODNI and benefit from his authorities. Our staff includes some 400 U.S. Government employees, the vast majority of whom are on rotation from one of 16 federal departments and agencies, including CIA, DoD, and FBI. This rotational structure is deliberate and embodies the model of "Joint Duty" that has proven so successful within the Department of Defense. By bringing so many departments and agencies together at NCTC, we are able to capitalize on the diverse talents and perspectives that only a truly joint workforce can provide.

I would now like to highlight just a few of the areas in which we've seen improvement over the last few years. I'll speak first to the changes in intelligence and then to those related to strategic operational planning.

In the intelligence area, we have made significant progress translating into action the lessons learned from 9/11 and WMD Commissions. An effective intelligence enterprise requires analysis, information sharing, and interagency collaboration, and NCTC continues to lead the counterterrorism community in all three areas.

Analysis. Analysis is at the heart of the counterterrorism intelligence process, and therefore also at the center of NCTC's mission. Our officers involved in the analytical process understand that their insights and judgments may figure directly in the defense of our nation and our allies. Analysis literally *counters terrorism:* it surveys the battlefield, identifies enemy forces and their intentions, and lays the groundwork for an effective offense and defense that use every instrument of national power—from military force to public diplomacy, and everything in between.

NCTC's analytic mission, as defined by IRTPA, is a broad one. As the primary organization in the United States Government for integrating and analyzing all intelligence pertaining to terrorism, with the exception of purely domestic terrorism, our mandate crosses the foreign and domestic divide, and requires us to support the full spectrum of intelligence customers. Central to performing this critical responsibility is providing all of our analysts with intelligence from throughout the U.S. Government. This is, as you know well, a revolutionary concept within the Intelligence Community. But today that concept is reality at NCTC; analysts can and do see sensitive intelligence from the CIA, FBI, Department of Defense, Department of Homeland Security, and other organizations.

This base of knowledge enables us to provide our customers with all-source, integrated analysis. NCTC, in collaboration with a wide array of government partners, generates a spectrum of integrated, analytic products—tailored to the needs and interests of our customers, including the President, Departments and Agencies, and the Congress. Our products range from immediate reports providing situational awareness about largely unevaluated intelligence—for example a daily Threat Matrix and twice daily Situation Reports—to in-depth finished intelligence such as the National Terrorism Bulletin and the President's Daily Brief. Significantly, virtually all of these reports for senior policy makers are coordinated by NCTC, as the DNI's Mission Manager. The purpose of that is to ensure that differing views are not only represented, but that they are also put in context.

NCTC's analytic efforts are not just focused on today's most pressing issue. While we spend significant time analyzing current threat streams to ensure that policy makers are kept fully informed, we also analyze longer-term trends in homegrown terrorism, radicalization, terrorists' use of the Internet, and future terrorists' tactics and weapons. In short, we seek to inform on the full range of terrorism topics.

One of the ways in which we ensure policymakers are informed by the best intelligence possible is to provide Intelligence Community-wide coordinated analysis that includes different agencies' views when such differences exist. The Interagency Intelligence Committee on Terrorism (IICT) serves as our primary forum to do this. Although the IICT existed before 9/11, it has expanded and improved its activities since that time. The chairmanship has also been elevated so it rests with the Director of NCTC. We take very seriously our responsibility to ensure that IICT products fully and faithfully represent dissenting views—should they exist—among agencies.

Finally, NCTC—in conjunction with the DNI—has over the past year sought to best leverage the Intelligence Community's finite analytic resources for counterterrorism. One important corollary to this is to avoid having every agency cover the same issues. To that end, we have identified agency-specific missions, designated lead responsibility for subject areas, and ensured appropriate competitive analysis so that the Intelligence Community is not single-threaded on important issues. This alignment, called the *Analytic Framework for Counterterrorism,* is a tangible recognition that not every agency can cover every topic all the time—and that to try to do so would not serve the U.S. Government well.

The Analytic Framework is focused on four counterterrorism mission areas:

- **Tactical Offense:** Analysis supporting direct action against the terrorist enemy—led by department and agency analytic elements.
- **Tactical Defense:** Analytic warnings of planned terrorist attacks and operations—led by NCTC, and Defense Intelligence Agency (DIA) in the case of threats to U.S. military targets.
- **Strategic Offense:** Analysis to guide national policy and policymakers in countering violent extremism and radical ideology as a threat to our way of life—led by NCTC.
- **Strategic Defense:** Analysis supportive of efforts to reduce our vulnerability to terrorist attacks and future terrorist capabilities—led by NCTC for strategic warnings, and relevant departments and agencies for vulnerability assessments.

One immediate impact of the Framework's adoption has been the shift of some CIA resources to NCTC so that the former can focus on operational support and the latter can concentrate on strategic analysis, such as the "War of Ideas."

Information Sharing. Let me now turn to the second critical piece of our intelligence enterprise—information sharing. NCTC is committed to sharing information quickly, effectively, and consistently.

Under the IRTPA, NCTC has the responsibility "to ensure that agencies, as appropriate, have access to and receive all-source intelligence products needed to execute their counterterrorism plans or perform independent, alternative analysis," and "to ensure that such agencies receive intelligence needed to accomplish their assigned activities." Today I'll highlight four of our principal efforts: sharing intelligence within the federal government, sharing intelligence with state, local, and tribal governments; bringing together departments and agencies to discuss current threats; and, comprehensive watchlisting of individuals of concern.

At the core of our mission is ensuring that all our federal partners have the intelligence they need. Prior to 9/11 there was no comprehensive place to go if an analyst or operator wanted to find all disseminated terrorism intelligence available to the U.S. Government. Today, NCTC Online (NOL) allows more than 60 U.S. Government elements to share information electronically. It serves as a key classified repository and collaboration tool, reaching intelligence, law enforcement, defense, homeland security, foreign affairs and other federal organizations with a counterterrorism mission. It now hosts more than 8,000 authorized users and holds over seven million terrorism documents.

NOL is also available at different levels of classification. This means that even if users are not permitted to see everything, they can automatically see those materials that fit their security clearances. And this capability is particularly important in helping us with the next information sharing initiative—sharing with state, local, and tribal officials.

NCTC's information sharing responsibilities go beyond that of the Federal Government. IRTPA states that the Director of NCTC is responsible for "supporting the Department of Justice and the Department of Homeland Security, and other appropriate agencies, in fulfillment of their responsibilities to disseminate terrorism information to State and local governments." More recently, with the recent passage of the *Implementing Recommendations of the 9/11 Commission Act of 2007,* NCTC has been given additional responsibilities to tailor CT-related information and products for timely passage to state, local, and tribal governments.

As initially proposed as part of the President's ISE Guideline implementation and later directed by the legislation, we are working with FBI, DHS, the Program Manager for the Information Sharing Environment and state and local officials to establish, within NCTC, the Interagency Threat Assessment and Coordination Group (ITACG). Led by a DHS detailee, with a deputy from FBI, this group will provide additional counsel and subject matter expertise to the federal Intelligence Community and facilitate the sharing of intelligence products tailored to the needs of state, local and tribal entities. It will further strengthen the overall national counterterrorism and homeland security effort.

Our information sharing responsibilities also require us to facilitate robust interagency communication about ongoing operations and events. NCTC chairs regular video teleconferences to maintain U.S. Government-wide situational awareness. Intelligence, law enforcement, homeland security, military, and diplomatic officials from roughly 17 U.S. Government organizations come together three times a day, seven days a week, 365 days a year, to exchange information and collaborate on response options. This is a fundamental change: Before 9/11, there was no routine mechanism to maintain situational awareness across the U.S. Government.

Finally, NCTC also plays a pivotal role in the terrorist watchlisting process. For the past four-plus years, NCTC has served as the U.S. Government's central repository for information on international terrorist identities, known as the "Terrorist Identities Datamart Environment," or TIDE for short. The TIDE database includes, to the extent permitted by law, all information the U.S. Government possesses on the identities of individuals known or appropriately suspected to be or to have been involved in activities constituting, in preparation for, in aid of, or related to international terrorism.

The establishment of TIDE marked a major milestone in the nation's CT effort, compiling into one database information on all known and suspected international terrorists. Before 9/11, watchlisting efforts were spread across multiple databases managed by multiple agencies, a significant vulnerability in the nation's efforts to defend against terrorist attack.

Each day, TIDE sends the FBI's Terrorist Screening Center (TSC) a sensitive but unclassified subset of terrorist identifiers to populate the U.S. Government's consolidated watchlist. This consolidated watchlist, in turn, supports efforts to screen, detect, and interdict the travel of known and suspected terrorists here and overseas. These screening efforts encompass the work of consular officers at embassies, Customs and Border Protection (CBP) personnel, law enforcement organizations across the United States, and foreign and domestic air carriers that fly to the United States. So today, an applicant for a State Department visa is checked against the watchlist at a consulate overseas. At U.S. ports of entry, a border crosser's passport, visa, or driver's license is also checked against the CBP's subset of the consolidated watchlist. And at a routine traffic encounter inside the United States, a suspect's identity is checked against the Terrorist Screening Database (TSDB) through the National Crime Information Center. Finally, airline screening personnel review passenger lists for all flights traveling to the United States to identify individuals who are believed to be a threat to civil aviation or the homeland or who should have additional screening prior to boarding a plane.

Examples of the types of activity that warrant an individual's entry into TIDE and terrorist screening systems include:

- Commission of an international terrorist activity;
- Preparation for or planning of international terrorist activity;
- Collection of information on potential targets for international terrorist activity;
- Collection or solicitation of funds or other items of value on behalf of international terrorist organizations or activity;
- Recruitment of members into international terrorist organizations;
- Provision of material support (e.g., safe houses, transportation, communications, funds, false documentation, weapons, or training) to international terrorist organizations; and,
- Membership in or representation of an international terrorist organization.

While the number of names contained in TIDE has grown since its inception in 2003 from approximately 100,000 to over 500,000, this figure represents every identity associated with individuals entered in the database. This distinction is significant because of the multiple aliases and name variants of terrorism suspects. As a result, the number of actual individuals recorded in TIDE is closer to 400,000. And although TIDE continues to grow, individuals' names are also regularly removed when it is determined that they no longer meet the criteria for inclusion. As a result, more than 10,000 names were removed from TIDE in 2006.

Interagency Collaboration. You will note that NCTC's analytic and information sharing efforts are but a part of the larger CT intelligence effort. Let me now turn, then, to the third piece of NCTC's support for CT intelligence—its coordination of the larger counterterrorism intelligence community. As the DNI's "Mission Manager" for counterterrorism, I am responsible for ensuring that all parts of Intelligence Community work toward a coherent, cohesive counterterrorism vision. Let me give you some of examples of IC-wide efforts that NCTC is leading.

First, NCTC orchestrates the counterterrorism National Collection Plan, which identifies information needs and requirements, assesses collector capabilities, and feeds CT requirements into the collection mechanisms. Second, NCTC has conducted the first-ever comprehensive CT analytic workforce analysis. In March of this year, we published *The Counterterrorism Analytic Posture of the Intelligence Community: A Baseline Report*, which gives us a foundation for evaluating the Community of today and developing recommendations for how to position the Community of tomorrow. The results are now being used to implement improved training and retention plans for the Intelligence Community. We have also developed a systematic "lessons learned" process to capture best practices to improve the efficacy and efficiency of our efforts. We believe that by creating mechanisms to conduct lessons learned studies the CT Community has, over the past year, taken significant steps towards fostering a culture of learning

Thus far I have addressed NCTC's intelligence responsibilities; I would like to turn now to our second role—Strategic Operational Planning (SOP) for the War on Terror.

SOP involves a wide spectrum of planning functions. It bridges the gap between coordinated interagency policy and strategy and tactical operations by departments and agencies to implement that strategy. Essentially, SOP takes interagency planning to a new and much more granular level than we have historically undertaken as a government.

In this role we lead an interagency planning effort that brings all elements of national power to bear in the War on Terror. That includes the full weight of our diplomatic, financial, military, intelligence, homeland security and law enforcement activities. The strategic operational planning effort is new to the U.S. Government. It involves a three-part continuous process: planning, implementation and assessment. NCTC is leading an interagency effort to build processes for all three phases. We've completed the first phase of planning by the CT community, and we're now in the process of guiding the implementation of the plan and assessing its effectiveness.

NCTC's planning efforts span a spectrum from strategic, deliberate planning to more dynamic planning.

The National Implementation Plan (NIP), which was approved by the President in June 2006, is the keystone document for our strategic—or deliberate—planning. The N!P is truly an unprecedented effort to bring together disparate parts of the U.S. Government that have a role in countering terrorism. Building on the President's unclassified National Strategy for Countering Terrorism (NSCT), it incorporates five years of planning, analysis, operations, and successes in the War on Terror. Each of the strategic objectives is further divided into specific tasks assig-ned to a Cabinet-level officer for action and other Cabinet officers for support.

The primary value added of the NIP is that it provides a comprehensive, coordinated plan of action that clearly assigns responsibility, sets priorities, illuminates areas of coordination, and provides a framework for assessing success and, ultimately, assigning resources.

In the spectrum of plans, the NIP is overarching and strategic, both in the scope of tasks it contains and the planning process that it initiates for the

U.S. Government. Other interagency strategic operational plans have a more focused functional or regional scope—such as the National Strategy to Combat Terrorist Travel—but follow the same process of planning, implementing, assessing, and adjusting.

At the more tactical end of the planning process are dynamic planning efforts, including those established to address emerging threat streams—for example what we have assessed to be the current heightened strategic threat window. For this reason, the White House directed NCTC to establish and lead an Interagency Task Force (ITF) to develop additional options and measures to increase intelligence collection and disrupt potential al-Qa'ida planning. Although led by NCTC, the ITF comprises a core group of representatives from the departments and agencies with the greatest responsibility for implementing new activities in the near term—including the Departments of Defense, State, Homeland Security and Justice.

Each week senior White House and Departmental officials review the actions proposed by the ITF, consider alternative options, and provide further direction on particular activities or measures recommended by the task force. Although I am unable to publicly describe specific actions taken by any single agency or department without undermining their effectiveness, I can report that the ITF has implemented a number of coordinated offensive and defensive measures designed to decrease the likelihood of a successful terrorist attack against the United States and our interests abroad. In addition, the ITF is continuously evaluating intelligence to recommend the most appropriate actions, assess ongoing operations, and ensure that U.S. Government resources are aligned to most effectively address the threat.

After we have developed a plan to address a specific CT issue or challenge, and taken it through NSC's policy approval process, we move into the implementation phase. NCTC's role in this implementation process is not directive; as clearly delineated in the IRTPA, we do not tell agencies and departments how to do their jobs or when to execute specific actions. Instead, the legislation charges us with the "interagency coordination of operational activities." In practice this means monitoring the key elements of the plan to ensure execution by the relevant departments and agencies. It means working through the obstacles to implementation that inevitably arise. It means identifying the gaps in the plan that are only apparent when execution begins or when the enemy adapts to ongoing activities. Finally, it means highlighting resource issues so that we can match our limited resources to our most urgent CT priorities.

The strategic planning process is less than glamorous. However, as the former Director for Strategic Plans and Policy (DJ-5) for the Joint Staff, I believe it is absolutely critical to the long term success of our government as we prosecute the long war on terror. It is, in short, a revolutionary new way of doing business for the U.S. Government.

Throughout this process, all of our SOP efforts are designed to provide the context and the connective tissue to link the President's CT strategy with the operations and activities on the front lines of the War on Terror.

In closing, I would reiterate that we have come a long way in the last two years as a Center and in the last several years as a Community despite our continued challenges, six years after 9/11,1 believe the United States is better prepared to fight this war than at any time in our history. Let me list seven reasons why I believe that.

First, our intelligence is better. Terrorists are clearly a difficult target, but our collection, analysis and production are significantly improved.

Second, we have made major strides in information sharing—in getting that intelligence to the people who need it.

Third, we have taken the fight to the enemy and achieved significant successes in the field. Thousands of terrorists have been taken off the field of battle and dozens of plots have been disrupted.

Fourth, we are attacking every element of the terrorist life cycle, including travel and finance.

Fifth, this is not only an American effort. We are working more closely and more effectively with a greater number of allies around the world to defeat the terrorists.

Sixth, and of special interest to this committee, we have taken significant steps to make the homeland a hostile place for terrorists to enter and operate.

Finally, through a new strategic planning effort, we are laying the groundwork to take the efforts already underway to a new level of integration and effectiveness.

All of this means we are safer than we were on September 11, 2001.

But we are not safe. Nor are we likely to be for a generation or more. We are in a long war, and we face an enemy that is adaptable, dangerous, and persistent and who always has a vote. While we have won many battles since 9/11, there are many battles yet to be fought and setbacks are certain to come along the way.

Thank you. This concludes my remarks.

F. TERRORISM 2002–2005

TERRORISM 2002–2005

Department of Justice
Federal Bureau of Investigation

Commentary

The next document in this section is the Federal Bureau of Investigation's (FBI) report on publicly acknowledged terrorist incidents and preventions that occurred on U.S. territory during the years 2002 through 2005. The report omits criminal incidents not designated as terrorism by the FBI but discusses major FBI investigations overseas and identifies significant events and program developments relevant to U.S. counterterrorism efforts. The report concludes with a summary of the history of the FBI's counterterrorism program. The report is not intended to be a comprehensive annual review of worldwide terrorist activity. For that information the reader is directed to the National Counterterrorism Center at www.nctc.gov and the Terrorism Knowledge Base compiled by the Memorial Institute for the Prevention of Terrorism at www.tkb.org.

The report states at the outset that in accordance with U.S. counterterrorism policy, the FBI considers terrorists to be criminals. The FBI, therefore, seeks to prevent terrorism but also to apprehend and prosecute terrorists. FBI investigations are conducted in accordance with *The Attorney General's Guidelines on General Crimes, Racketeering Enterprise, and Terrorism Enterprise Investigations.* These guidelines are important in that they set forth the predication threshold and limits for investigations of U.S. persons who reside in the United States, who are not acting on behalf of a foreign power, and who may be conducting criminal activities in support of terrorist objectives.

The report notes that the FBI conducts international terrorism investigations in accordance with *The Attorney General Guidelines for FBI Foreign Intelligence Collection and Foreign Counterintelligence Investigations.* These guidelines set forth the predication level and limits for investigating U.S. persons or foreign nationals in the United States who are targeting national security interests on behalf of a foreign power. Terrorism is not a separately codified crime. Law enforcement agencies apply existing criminal statutes as the bases for apprehending suspected terrorists, who are provided the constitutional rights afforded to other criminals. That said, the reader is referred to Volume 90 of this series' discussion of National Security Letters.

Interestingly, as the FBI report points out, there is no single, universally accepted definition of terrorism. The *Code of Federal Regulations* (CFR) defines it the as "the unlawful use of force and violence against persons or property to intimidate or coerce a government, the civilian population, or any segment thereof, in furtherance of political or social objectives" (28 C.F.R. Section 0.85). The FBI further describes terrorism as either domestic or international, depending on the origin, base, and objectives of the terrorist organization. For the purpose of its report, the FBI defines domestic terrorism as the unlawful use, or threatened use, of force or violence by a group or individual based and operating entirely within the United States or Puerto Rico without foreign direction and committed against persons or property to intimidate or coerce a government, the civilian population, or any segment thereof in furtherance of political or social objectives.

The FBI defines international terrorism as violent acts or acts dangerous to human life that are a violation of the criminal laws of the United States or any state, or that would be a criminal violation if committed within the jurisdiction of the United States or any state. These acts appear to be intended to intimidate or coerce a civilian population, influence the policy of a government by intimidation or coercion, or affect the conduct of a government by assassination or kidnapping. International terrorist acts occur outside the United States or transcend national boundaries in terms of the means by which they are accomplished, the persons they appear intended to coerce or intimidate, or the locale in which their perpetrators operate or seek asylum.

Both FBI definitions of terrorism are somewhat narrow, in that they do not encompass the use of terror tactics by individuals or groups that have no political or social agendas. For example, many gangs and organized crime syndicates employ the tactic of terror to achieve economic gains. In many cases the severity of their tactics exceeds that of organizations seeking political or social change. The question is, what is the evil that counterterrorism efforts seek to remove? Is it the striving for political or social change, or is it the indiscriminant but sensational use of extreme violence to accomplish one's objectives, whatever they may be. Many astute analysts suggest it is the latter, and the definition of terrorism should not hinge on the purposes for which the abominable tactic is used.

The FBI report divides terrorist-related activity into two categories, incidents and preventions. A terrorist incident is a violent act or an act dangerous to human life, in violation of the criminal laws of the United States, or of any state, to intimidate or coerce a government, the civilian population, or any segment thereof, in furtherance of political or social objectives.

A terrorism prevention, on the other hand, is a documented instance in which a violent act by a known or suspected terrorist group or individual with the means and a proven propensity for violence is successfully interdicted through investigative activity. Therefore, reporting those who have been prosecuted for terrorist incidents alone would not be a complete measure of effectiveness of FBI counterterrorism efforts. The prevention of terrorist incidents is arguably an even more important measure. Of course, often there is considerable difficulty associated with determining conclusively why something did not happen.

The FBI report highlights significant terrorism-related events in the United States and selected FBI investigative efforts overseas that occurred during 2002 through 2005 and provides a wide range of statistical data, to provide an historical framework for the examination of contemporary terrorism issues. It reports that domestic extremists carried out the majority of terrorist incidents during the period. Most were committed by special interest extremists active in the animal rights and environmental movements. They typically targeted materials and facilities rather than persons. The sole international terrorist incident in the United States recorded for this long period (2002–2005) involved an attack at the El Al ticket counter at Los Angeles International Airport, which claimed the lives of two victims.

Eight of the 14 terrorism preventions reported for 2002 through 2005 stemmed from right-wing extremists such as militias, white supremacists, constitutionalists, tax protestors, and anti-abortionists. The rest involved an anarchist who sought to bomb a U.S. Coast Guard station; a plot to attack an Islamic center in Florida; a plot by a prison-originated Muslim convert group to attack U.S. military, Jewish, and Israeli targets; and supporters of foreign terrorists who planned attacks within the United States.

The report states that FBI counterterrorism initiatives since the 9/11 terrorist attack have focused on preventing future attacks through the timely gathering, analysis, and dissemination of information; the facilitation of appropriate sharing of terrorism-related information between federal, state, and local partners; and the advancement of intelligence and law enforcement partnerships worldwide. These are themes found in every document presented in this volume and comprise the suite of objectives toward which U.S. policy changes have focused.

The report summarizes significant organizational changes, including creation of the National Joint Terrorism Task Force; establishment of the Foreign Terrorist Tracking Task Force; consolidation of government terrorist watch lists into the Terrorist Screening Center; creation of the U.S. Department of Homeland Security; and restructuring of the U.S. Intelligence Community under the newly created Office of the Director of National Intelligence. These and other federal initiatives are discussed in greater detail in the concluding *In Focus* retrospective of the FBI's counterterrorism program.

The FBI report stresses the importance of information sharing; attacking every element of the terrorist life cycle, including travel and finance; working with an ever-increasing number of partners around the world to defeat terrorists; making the U.S. homeland a very hostile place for terrorists to enter and operate; and better integrating efforts to achieve greater effectiveness. This report is important in that it provides a counterterrorism assessment from a law enforcement agency's perspective. As suggested in the discussion of National Security Letters in Volume 90, that perspective is unique and not understood or appreciated by all.

DOCUMENT NO. 6

TERRORISM 2002–2005

FBI Report

November 2007

Foreword

Since the mid-1980s, the FBI has published *Terrorism in the United States,* an unclassified annual report summarizing terrorist activities in this country. While this publication provided an overview of the terrorist threat in the United States and its territories, its limited scope proved inadequate for conveying either the breadth or width of the terrorist threat facing U.S. interests or the scale of the FBI's response to terrorism worldwide. To better reflect the nature of the threat and the international scope of our response, the FBI expanded the focus of its annual terrorism report in the 2000/2001 edition to include discussion of FBI investigations overseas and renamed the series *Terrorism.*

This second edition of *Terrorism* provides an overview of the terrorist incidents and preventions designated by the FBI as having taken place in the United States and its territories during the years 2002 through 2005 and that are matters of public record. This publication does not include those incidents which the Bureau classifies under criminal rather than terrorism investigations. In addition, the report discusses major FBI investigations overseas and identifies significant events—including legislative actions, prosecutorial updates, and program developments—relevant to U.S. counterterrorism efforts. The report concludes with an "In Focus" article summarizing the history of the FBI's counterterrorism program.

While the discussion of international terrorism provides a more complete overview of FBI terrorism investigations into acts involving U.S. interests around the world, *Terrorism* is not intended as a comprehensive annual review of worldwide terrorist activity. The chronological incidents, charts, and figures included in *Terrorism 2002–2005* reflect only those incidents identified in the *Terrorism/ Terrorism in the United* States series. For more complete listings of worldwide terrorist incidents, see the Worldwide

Incidents Tracking System maintained by the National Counterterrorism Center at *www.nctc.gov* and the Terrorism Knowledge Base compiled by the Memorial Institute for the Prevention of Terrorism at *www.tkb.org*.

The FBI hopes you will find *Terrorism 2002–2005* to be a helpful resource and thanks you for your interest in the FBI's Counterterrorism Program. A full-text and graphics version of this issue, as well as recent back issues of *Terrorism* and *Terrorism in the United* States, are available for on-line reference on the FBI home page at *www.fbi.gov*.

Federal Bureau of Investigation
Counterterrorism Division

FBI Policy and Guidelines

In accordance with U.S. counterterrorism policy, the FBI considers terrorists to be criminals. FBI efforts in countering terrorist threats are multifaceted. Information obtained through FBI investigations is analyzed and used to prevent terrorist activity and, whenever possible, to effect the arrest and prosecution of potential perpetrators. FBI investigations are initiated in accordance with the following guidelines:

- Domestic terrorism investigations are conducted in accordance with *The* Attorney *General's Guidelines on General Crimes, Racketeering Enterprise, and Terrorism Enterprise Investigations.* These guidelines set forth the predication threshold and limits for investigations of U.S. persons who reside in the United States, who are not acting on behalf of a foreign power, and who may be conducting criminal activities in support of terrorist objectives.
- International terrorism investigations are conducted in accordance with *The Attorney General Guidelines for FBI Foreign Intelligence Collection and Foreign Gounterintelligence Investigations.* These guidelines set forth the predication level and limits for investigating U.S. persons or foreign nationals in the United States who are targeting national security interests on behalf of a foreign power.

Although various Executive Orders, Presidential Decision Directives, and congressional statutes address the issue of terrorism, there is no single federal law specifically making terrorism a crime. Terrorists are arrested and convicted under existing criminal statutes. All suspected terrorists placed under arrest are provided access to legal counsel and normal judicial procedure, including Fifth Amendment guarantees.

Definitions

There is no single, universally accepted, definition of terrorism. Terrorism is defined in the *Code of Federal Regulations* as "the unlawful use of force and violence against persons or property to intimidate or coerce a government, the civilian population, or any segment thereof, in furtherance of political or social objectives" (28 C.F.R. Section 0.85).

The FBI further describes terrorism as either domestic or international, depending on the origin, base, and objectives of the terrorist organization. For the purpose of this report, the FBI will use the following definitions:

- Domestic terrorism is the unlawful use, or threatened use, of force or violence by a group or individual based and operating entirely within the United States or Puerto Rico without foreign direction committed against persons or property to intimidate or coerce a government, the civilian population, or any segment thereof in furtherance of political or social objectives.
- International terrorism involves violent acts or acts dangerous to human life that are a violation of the criminal laws of the United States or any state, or that would be a criminal violation if committed within the jurisdiction of the United States or any state. These acts appear to be intended to intimidate or coerce a civilian population, influence the policy of a government by intimidation or coercion, or affect the conduct of a government by assassination or kidnapping. International terrorist acts occur outside the United States or transcend national boundaries in terms of the means by which they are accomplished, the persons they appear intended to coerce or intimidate, or the locale in which their perpetrators operate or seek asylum.

The FBI Divides Terrorist-related Activity into Two Categories:

- A terrorist *incident* is a violent act or an act dangerous to human life, in violation of the criminal laws of the United States, or of any state, to intimidate or coerce a government, the civilian population, or any segment thereof, in furtherance of political or social objectives.
- A terrorism *prevention* is a documented instance in which a violent act by a known or suspected terrorist group or individual with the means and a proven propensity for violence is successfully interdicted through investigative activity.

Note

The FBI investigates terrorism-related matters without regard to race, religion, national origin, or gender. Reference to individual members of any political, ethnic, or religious group in this report is not meant to imply that all members of that group are terrorists. Terrorists represent a small criminal minority in any larger social context.

Introduction

This edition of *Terrorism* highlights significant terrorism-related events in the United States and selected FBI investigative efforts overseas that occurred during the years 2002 through 2005. Additionally, this report provides a wide range of statistical data relating to terrorism in the United States during the past two decades. This material is presented to provide readers with an historical framework for the examination of contemporary terrorism issues.

In keeping with a longstanding trend, domestic extremists carried out the majority of terrorist incidents during this period. Twenty three of the 24 recorded terrorist incidents were perpetrated by domestic terrorists. With the exception of a white supremacist's firebombing of a synagogue in Oklahoma City, Oklahoma, all of the domestic terrorist incidents were committed by special interest extremists active in the animal rights and environmental movements. The acts committed by these extremists typically targeted materials and facilities rather than persons. The sole international terrorist incident in the United States recorded for this period involved an attack at the El Al ticket counter at Los Angeles International Airport, which claimed the lives of two victims.

The terrorism preventions for 2002 through 2005 present a more diverse threat picture. Eight of the 14 recorded terrorism preventions stemmed from right-wing extremism, and included disruptions to plotting by individuals involved with the militia, white supremacist, constitutionalist and tax protestor, and anti-abortion movements. The remaining preventions included disruptions to plotting by an anarchist in Bellingham, Washington, who sought to bomb a U.S. Coast Guard station; a plot to attack an Islamic center in Pinellis Park, Florida; and a plot by prison-originated, Muslim convert group to attack U.S. military, Jewish, and Israeli targets in the greater Los Angeles area. In addition, three preventions involved individuals who sought to provide material support to foreign terrorist organizations, including al-Qa'ida, for attacks within the United States.

Whereas the violent global jihadist movement manifested itself primarily in terrorism preventions in the United States from 2002 through 2005, internationally the movement claimed major attacks against U.S. and Western targets that resulted in American casualties. Most of these incidents were perpetrated by regional jihadist groups operating in primarily Muslim countries, and included attacks committed by Indonesia-based Jemaah Islamiya and al-Qa'ida in the Arabian Peninsula. The coordinated suicide bombing of London's mass transit system by homegrown jihadists, however, brought the violent jihadist movement and the tactic of suicide bombing to a major European capital.

In addition to these incidents and preventions, the years 2002 through 2005 saw the resolutions to high-profile prosecutions in the fight against terrorism. These included the October 4, 2002, sentencing of John Walker Lindh to 20 years in prison for conspiring with the Taliban to kill U.S. citizens; the January 30, 2003, sentencing of Richard Colvin Reid to life in prison for attempting to bomb a transcontinental flight using a shoe bomb; the December 2003 sentencings of the Lackawanna Six terror cell members, who received prison terms ranging from seven to 10 years for providing material support or resources to al-Qa'ida; the sentencings in 2003 and 2004 of members of a Portland terrorist cell, who received prison terms ranging from three to 18 years for plotting to provide assistance to the Taliban and al-Qa'ida in fighting against U.S. troops in Afghanistan; the September 29, 2004, sentencing in Yemeni court of six individuals for their roles in the *USS Cole* bombing, two of whom received the death penalty; the April 6, 2005, sentencing of Matthew Hale, leader of the white supremacist Creativity Movement, to 40 years in prison for solicitation of violence and obstruction of justice; the July 18, 2005, sentencing of Eric Robert Rudolph to life in prison for perpetrating several bombings, including the Centennial Olympic Park bombing in Atlanta, Georgia; the April 26, 2005, sentencing of Ali Al-Timimi to life in prison for encouraging others to receive military training from the designated foreign terrorist organization Lashkar-e-Tayyiba to fight U.S. troops in Afghanistan; and the August 30, 2005, sentencing of white supremacist Sean Michael Gillespie to 39 years for the synagogue firebombing in Oklahoma City.

FBI counterterrorism initiatives since the 9/11 terrorist attack have focused on preventing future attacks through the timely gathering, analysis, and dissemination of information; the facilitation of appropriate sharing of terrorism-related information between federal, state, and local partners; and the advancement of intelligence and law enforcement partnerships worldwide. FBI and U.S. counterterrorism organizational changes from 2002 through 2005 include the creation of the National Joint Terrorism Task Force; the establishment of the Foreign Terrorist Tracking Task Force; the consolidation of government terrorist watch lists into the Terrorist Screening Center; the creation of the U.S. Department of Homeland Security; and the restructuring of the U.S. Intelligence Community under the newly created Office of the Director of National Intelligence. These and other federal initiatives are discussed in greater detail in the concluding In Focus retrospective of the FBI's counterterrorism program.

2002 In Review

The FBI recorded seven domestic terrorist incidents, one international terrorist incident, and one terrorism prevention in 2002. The seven domestic terrorism incidents included a string of attacks over a period of several months claimed by special interest movements. These attacks are attributed either solely to the Earth Liberation Front (ELF), an extremist environmental movement active in the United States during the past 20 years, or jointly to the ELF and the Animal Liberation Front, an extremist animal rights movement that has carried out numerous terrorist attacks since 1987. The international terrorist incident involved fatal shootings at the El Al ticket counter at Los Angeles International Airport.

In the one terrorism prevention, law enforcement in Florida exposed a plot to attack Islamic facilities in the United States in response to international events, including the September 11 attacks.

Two deaths resulted from terrorist activity carried out in the United States in 2002.

A major international terrorist incident during 2002 involved the October 12 bombing of the Kuta Beach nightclub area on Bali, Indonesia. The attack, carried out by the Jemaah Islamiya, a terrorist organization active in Southeast Asia, resulted in 202 deaths, including those of seven Americans.

2002 Terrorist Incidents

MARCH 2002–NOVEMBER 2002
Vandalism and Arson
Erie, Harborcreek, and Warren, Pennsylvania
(*Six acts of Domestic Terrorism*)

Between March 2002 and November 2002, a series of animal rights and ecoterrorism incidents occurred in Erie, Harborcreek, and Warren, Pennsylvania. On March 18, 2002, Pennsylvania State Police discovered heavy equipment used to clear trees at a construction site in Erie, Pennsylvania, spray painted with the statements "ELF, in the protection of mother earth," and "Stop Deforestation." On March 24, 2002, police responded to the same construction site, where a large hydraulic crane had been set on fire, causing approximately $500,000 in damage. A facsimile, purportedly from ELF, claimed responsibility for the arson and vandalism. ELF also claimed responsibility for an August 11, 2002, arson on the U.S. Forestry Scientific Laboratory in Warren, Pennsylvania.

In separate incidents in May and September 2002, unknown subjects released approximately 250 mink from a fur farm in Harborcreek, Pennsylvania. On November 26, 2002, the barn on the same Harborcreek fur farm was destroyed by arson. On the ELF Web site, ELF and ALF jointly claimed responsibility for these mink releases and the arson. On August 11, 2002, unknown individuals committed arson on the U.S. Forestry Scientific Laboratory in Warren, Pennsylvania.

JULY 4, 2002
Attack on El Al Ticket Counter in Los Angeles International Airport
Los Angeles, California
(One act of International Terrorism)

On July 4, 2002, Hesham Mohamed Ali Hedayat began shooting randomly while standing in line at the ticket counter of El Al Israeli National Airlines at the Los Angeles International Airport. During the attack, an El Al ticketing agent and a bystander were killed. Hedayat was subsequently killed by an El Al security officer. A worldwide investigation determined that Hadayat's religious and political beliefs were the primary motivation for the attack, and not personal revenge. Following these investigative findings, this case was officially designated as an act of international terrorism.

AUGUST–OCTOBER 2002
Vandalism and Destruction of Property
Henrico County, Virginia Goochland County, Virginia
(*One act of Domestic Terrorism*)

During the period of August–November 2002, Aaron L. Linas, John B. Wade, and Adam V. Blackwell carried out several acts of vandalism and destruction of private property, in apparent acts of environmental terrorism. Many of these acts were attributed to the Earth Liberation Front (ELF).

On several days in August 2002, the individuals damaged 12 construction vehicles at a construction site in Goochland, Virginia, by pouring sugar into the gas tanks. The individuals also vandalized two homes under construction in the area, writing the word "sprawl" on one of the homes.

In September 2002, the individuals vandalized construction vehicles in Henrico County, Virginia, and attempted to burn a backhoe and construction crane. On September 28, 2002, 25 sport utility vehicles (SUVs) were damaged at an Henrico County Ford Dealership, including the etching of the letters "ELF" and "SUV into some of the vehicles. Also in September, vandalism occurred at two fast food restaurants. A Jeep Liberty was also damaged, and the vandals left a note on the vehicle stating "SUVs are killing the world" and "Earth Liberation Front."

In October of 2002, vandals claiming to be part of ELF apparently used an axe to damage three SUVs parked in the River Lake Colony subdivision of Henrico County, Virginia. Notes were left on all of the vehicles claiming the attack was an effort to raise environmental and political awareness.

Linas, Wade, and Blackwell pled guilty to conspiracy to commit these acts and were subsequently convicted and sentenced to three years and six months, three years and one month, and 10 months in federal prison, respectively, and ordered to divide the total restitution payment of $204,021.86 between them.

2002 Terrorism Preventions

AUGUST 22, 2002
Planned Attack against Islamic Center of Pinellas County
Pinellas Park, Florida
(Prevention of one act of Domestic Terrorism)

On August 22, 2002, police in Pinellas County, Florida, responding to a domestic dispute detained Robert J. Goldstein after finding nume-rous weapons and explosives and a "mission statement" threatening to attack Islamic facilities in the United States. Goldstein was later arrested and charged with weapons violations and an attempt to des-troy property. Michael Wallace Hardee, Samuel V. Shannahan III, and Goldstein's wife, Kristi Goldstein, were also arrested and charged in connection with the plot. An investigation revealed that the intended target of Goldstein's planned attack was the Islamic Center of Pinellas County, in Pinellas Park, Florida, and that the attack had been planned to coincide with the first anniversary of the September 11, 2001, terrorist attack. Investigators also determined that Goldstein intended to target the Islamic Center in perceived retaliation for Palestinian suicide bombings in Israel. The four pled guilty in the Middle District of Florida to their roles in the plotting, and in 2003 received federal prison sentences ranging from three years to Robert Goldstein's 12 years and seven months.

2002 Significant Events

JANUARY 19, 2002
Kathleen Ann Soliah Sentenced

On January 19, 2002, Kathleen Ann Soliah was sentenced to two consecutive 10 years to life terms for her role in a 1975 car bombing plot associated with the Symbionese Liberation Army. On October 31, 2001, Soliah pled guilty to two counts related to the car bombing plot. Soliah remained a fugitive for 23 years until her arrest on June 16, 1999, when she was living under the alias Sara Jane Olsen.

MARCH 14, 2002
Appeal Denied in the Pan Am 103 Bombing Case

On March 14, 2002, an appeal filed by Abdel Basset Ali Al-Megrahi, seeking to overturn his conviction of bombing Pan Am flight 103 over Lockerbie, Scotland, was denied. Al-Megrahi had filed the appeal at the Scottish Court of Appeal in Camp Zeist, The Netherlands. Al-Megrahi was convicted on January 31, 2001, for the 1988 bombing, which killed the 259 passengers of the flight and 11 individuals on the ground. Al-Megrahi was sentenced to life in prison.

JUNE 15, 2002
Donald Rudolph Sentenced for 1999 Propane Plot

On June 15, 2002, Donald Rudolph was sentenced to five years in prison for his role in a plot to destroy a propane storage facility near Elk Grove, California. Rudolph had pled guilty on January 19, 2001, to withholding knowledge of a conspiracy to use a weapon of mass destruction in connection with the propane plot.

The plot to attack the propane storage facility was disrupted on December 3, 1999, when members of the Sacramento Joint Terrorism Task Force arrested Kevin Ray Patterson and Charles Dennis Kiles. Patterson, Kiles, and Rudolph were associated with an antigovernment group active in the central region of the state. When arrested, Patterson and Kiles were in possession of a detonation cord, blasting caps, grenade hulls, and various chemicals—including ammonium nitrate—and numerous weapons. Patterson and Kiles were convicted in May 2002 for conspiracy to use a weapon of mass destruction and conspiracy to use a destructive device.

OCTOBER 12, 2002
Nightclub Bombing
Bali, Indonesia

On October 12, 2002, three bombs, including a large vehicle bomb and a possible suicide bomber, devastated a nightclub area at Kuta Beach on the Indonesian island of Bali. The blasts killed 202 people, including seven Americans, and injured as many as 350. Most of those killed and injured were foreign tourists. This bombing has been attributed to members of the Jemaah Islamiya (JI) terrorist organization, a Southeast Asian-based terrorist network with links to al-Qa'ida, which allegedly helped finance the attack. The Bali bombing may have been carried out in response to audiotaped appeals from al-Qa'ida leader Usama Bin Ladin and his senior deputy Ayman al-Zawahiri broadcast on the al-Jazeera network beginning on October 6, 2002, that urged renewed attacks on U.S. and Western interests.

The FBI joined several other international antiterror agencies to assist Indonesia in the investigation of the attack. The investigation has yielded approximately 30 convictions overseas; including three suspects sentenced to death after being convicted of planning and carrying out the bombing. Notable among the convictions is Muslim cleric Abu Bakar Bashir, who is suspected of being the spiritual leader of JI. Bashir was sentenced in March 2003 to 30 months in prison for his part in the criminal conspiracy leading to the attack, although he was cleared of charges of planning a terrorist attack.

Investigators believe JI militants Noordin Mohammad Top and bomb-maker Azahari Husin were the masterminds behind the Bali nightclub attacks and several other Southeast Asian terrorist attacks. Husin was killed by Indonesian police during a shootout on November 9, 2005, in East Java, Indonesia. Top remained a fugitive at the end of 2005.

On October 23, 2002, President George W. Bush designated JI as a Specially Designated Global Terrorist (SDGT) under Executive Order 13224. Investigation into the Bali bombing is ongoing.

JUNE 21, 2002
Two Smugglers Convicted in Terror Financing Case

On June 21, 2002, Mohamad Hammoud and Chawki Hammoud were convicted for their roles in a Charlotte, North Carolina-based, cigarette smuggling ring with ties to terrorism financing. Both men were convicted of cigarette smuggling, money laundering, racketeering, and credit card fraud. Mohamad Hammoud was also convicted of providing financial support to Hizballah, a designated foreign terrorist organization believed to have received financing through Hammoud's smuggling enterprise. Chawki Hammoud was not found guilty of Hizballah ties.

JUNE 21, 2002
FBI Fly Team Established

On June 21, 2002, FBI Director Mueller announced the creation of the Fly Team in the Counterterrorism Division to enhance the Bureau's capabilities in the areas of counterterrorism and intelligence collection. The Fly Team deploys rapidly and proactively worldwide on missions to identify and prevent acts of terrorism, respond to crisis incidents, and pursue the arrests and prosecutions of terrorists who have engaged in or aided and abetted those who engaged in acts of terrorism.

JULY 2002
Creation of National Joint Terrorism Task Force

In July of 2002, the National Joint Terrorism Task Force (NJTTF) was created by order of the Director of the FBI. The NJTTF, staffed by representatives from 40 federal, state, and local agencies, is tasked with coordinating the flow of information between its participating entities and the Joint Terrorism Task Forces (JTTFs) located in FBI field offices and resident agencies across the country.

OCTOBER 4, 2002
John Walker Lindh Sentenced

On October 4, 2002, U.S. citizen John Walker Lindh was sentenced to 20 years in prison after pleading guilty in July to terrorism charges related to his association with the Taliban in Afghanistan. In February, a grand jury in the Eastern District of Virginia indicted Lindh on 10 counts, charging him as an al-Qa'ida-trained terrorist who conspired with the Taliban to kill U.S. citizens. In addition to criminal charges that had previously been levied against Lindh, the indictment added charges of conspiracy to contribute services to al-Qa'ida, contributing services to al-Qa'ida, conspiracy to supply services to the Taliban, and weapons charges.

NOVEMBER 25, 2002
Signing of the Homeland Security Act of 2002

On November 25, 2002, President Bush signed House Resolution 5005, the Homeland Security Act of 2002, officially establishing the U.S. Department of Homeland Security. The act combined various government agencies dealing with transportation, border, and other security issues from the U.S. Departments of Justice, Defense, Treasury, and Commerce into a single cabinet department, consolidating the U.S. government's homeland security efforts.

2003 In Review

In 2003, the FBI recorded six terrorist incidents and five terrorism preventions. Domestic terrorists, specifically animal rights and environmental extremists, were responsible for each of the six incidents. Three of the incidents were perpetrated by followers of the Earth Liberation Front extremist movement and involved acts of arson or vandalism and destruction of property. The other three incidents were perpetrated by extremists within the animal rights movement, and included and act of vandalism claimed by the Animal Liberation Front, and two bombings at businesses affiliated with Huntingdon Life Sciences, a frequent target of the extreme animal rights movement.

Each of the five preventions involved domestic terrorist organizations or extremists. These included a white supremacist in Pennsylvania, who planned attacks against abortion clinics and minority targets; a constitutionalist and tax protestor in Idaho, who attempted to arrange for the murders of federal persons involved in a tax evasion case against him; an individual in Texas associated with antigovernment militia members, who was found in possession of heavy weaponry, sodium cyanide, and plans to weaponize sodium cyanide; an anarchist, who planned to bomb a U.S. Coast Guard; and an anti-abortion extremist in Florida, who planned to bomb abortion clinics.

No deaths or serious injuries resulted from terrorist activity carried out in the United States in 2003.

Major international terrorist incidents involving U.S. casualties included two attacks stemming from the violent global jihadist movement. In Riyadh, Saudi Arabia, al-Qa'ida operatives conducted coordinated assaults on three residential compounds housing Western workers. Nine of the 35 people killed in the attack were Americans. In addition, Jemaah Islamiya bombed the JW Marriott Hotel in Jakarta, Indonesia. The attack resulted in 11 fatalities and 144 injuries, including injuries to two U.S. citizens.

2003 Terrorist Incidents

JANUARY 1, 2003
Arson
Girard, Pennsylvania
(One act of Domestic Terrorism)

On January 1, 2003, an unknown individual(s) set two pickup trucks and one sport utility vehicle on fire at a car dealership in Girard, Pennsylvania, causing $96,000 in damages. This arson followed the series of environmental and animal rights extremist incidents in northwest Pennsylvania discussed in the preceding 2002 terrorist incidents section. ELF claimed responsibility for the arson.

MARCH 3, 2003
Vandalism
Chico, California
(One act of Domestic Terrorism)

On March 3, 2003, an unknown number of individuals placed two one-gallon jugs filled with kerosene near a McDonald's restaurant in Chico, California, and vandalized the restaurant with graffiti. The graffiti included statements such as "Animal Liberation Front," "Meat is Murder," and "Species Equality." Two communiques were discovered claiming responsibility for the attack. Robert Brooks and Harjit Singh Gill were convicted in the Eastern District of California for making false statements to a grand jury in connection with the attack, and, in June 2005, received sentences of a $500 fine and 36 months probation, respectively.

AUGUST 1, 2003
SEPTEMBER 19, 2003
Arson
San Diego, California
(One act of Domestic Terrorism)

On August 1, 2003, the San Diego Fire Department and San Diego Police Department responded to an arson fire at the Garden Condominium, a five-story, 206-unit condominium complex under construction in the University Town Center area of San Diego. The fire caused an estimated $20 million in damages to the building and surrounding construction equipment. Investigators found graffiti at the site implicating Earth Liberation Front (ELF) extremists with the incident, including the message "IF YOU BUILD IT—WE WILL BURN IT. THE ELF'S ARE MAD.

On September 19, 2003, two other new home sites were also set on fire, with similar messages left at the scene. The fires destroyed four homes and damaged two others, causing an estimated loss of $3 million. The August 1 and September 19 arson incidents remain under investigation.

MAY 12, 2003
Bombings of Residential Compounds
Riyadh, Saudi Arabia

On the evening of May 12, 2003, al-Qa'ida operatives assaulted three residential compounds in Riyadh, Saudi Arabia, that house Western guest workers. At least fifteen assailants in six vehicles-two vehicles at each location-participated in the attacks against the Al-Hamra Oasis Village, Jedawal compound, and Vinnell Company compound located in suburban Riyadh. After breaching manned security barriers at two of the three sites, the attackers detonated vehicle-borne improvised explosive devices (VBIEDs) in the compounds, killing 35 people, including nine Americans, and injuring nearly 200 others. This assault followed a string of al-Qa'ida operations, including the August 7, 1998, East African embassy bombings; the October 12, 2000, bombing of the USS Cole in Aden, Yemen; the September 11, 2001, attack in the United States; and attacks on November 28, 2002, carried out against primarily Israeli targets in Mombasa, Kenya, involving simultaneous attacks against multiple targets.

The May 12 attack reflected a high degree of planning, pre-operational surveillance, and coordination among teams—traditional hallmarks of al-Qa'ida operations. It also reflected a highly refined approach to suicide bombings that may have incorporated lessons learned from the 1998 U.S. embassy bombings and other attacks. Preliminary investigation indicates that operatives traveling in lead vehicles attacked guards at each of the sites with small arms fire and hand grenades to quickly breach gates and other security measures to gain access to the compounds. Once inside the compounds, assailants may also have fired weapons to draw the attention of residents to window areas to maximize casualties.

The FBI and foreign partners have identified approximately 30 individuals thought to be involved in the planning and execution of the attack. Nearly all of these individuals have been killed or arrested by Saudi security forces.

AUGUST 5, 2003
Bombing of JW Marriott Hotel
Jakarta, Indonesia

On the afternoon of August 5, 2003, a vehicle-borne improvised explosive device (VBIED) exploded in front of the JW Marriott Hotel located in Mega Kuningan, South Jakarta, Indonesia. The blast killed 11 people, not including the suicide bomber, and injured 144 others, including two U.S. citizens. The blast caused extensive damage to the hotel and an adjacent office building.

Investigation by the Indonesian National Police, the Australian Federal Police, and the FBI traced responsibility for the bombing to Jemaah Islamiyah (Jl), a transnational Southeast Asian terrorist organization based in Indonesia with close links to al-Qa'ida, which helped to finance the bombing.

The international investigation has identified over 30 individuals involved in the conspiracy to bomb the JW Marriott Hotel in Jakarta. Witness testimony has identified Noordin Mohammed Top as the leader of the operation and Dr. Azahari Husin as the bombmaker. Approximately 30 of the conspirators have been arrested, tried, and convicted in Indonesian courts and have received prison sentences ranging from three to 14 years. Husin was killed by Indonesian police during a Shootout on November 9, 2005, in East Java, Indonesia. Top remained a fugitive at the end of 2005.

The investigation into the bombing of the JW Marriott Hotel in Jakarta is ongoing.

AUGUST 22, 2003
Vandalism and Destruction of Property
West Covina, California
(One act of Domestic Terrorism)

On August 22, 2003, individuals associated with the Earth Liberation Front (ELF) carried out acts of vandalism in the Los Angeles, California, area, damaging roughly 125 vehicles and one commercial building. Much of the damage was caused by spray-painted graffiti, although in two cases, individuals set fire to sport utility vehicles (SUVs). Some of the graffiti associated SUVs with "terrorism." On April 18, 2005, William Jensen Cottrell was sentenced to eight years and four months in federal prison and fined $3.5 million for the incident. Two other suspects in the attack—Tyler Johnson and Michie Oe—remained at large at the end of 2005.

AUGUST 28, 2003
Bombing
Emeryville, California
(One act of Domestic Terrorism)

On August 28, 2003, an improvised explosive device (IED) was detonated near the front door of Chiron Life Science Center in Emeryville, California, causing damage to the building. A second device detonated in another Chiron building shortly after first responders arrived at the scene, also damaging the building and the surrounding area. Chiron had previously received harassing e-mails, telephone calls, and faxes, and some Chiron employees had been harassed at their residences. Chiron, an animal testing laboratory, is associated with Huntingdon Life Sciences (HLS). HLS, and individuals and companies associated with it, have regularly been targeted by animal rights extremists. Daniel Andreas San Diego is suspected of having carried out the bombing and remained a fugitive at the end of 2005.

SEPTEMBER 26, 2003
Bombing
Pleasanton, California
(One act of Domestic Terrorism)

On September 26, 2003, an improvised explosive device was detonated at Shaklee Corporation in Pleasanton, California. Shaklee Corporation is a subsidiary of Yamanouchi Pharmaceutical Co. Ltd., which has been targeted by animal rights extremists in the past. Daniel Andreas San Diego is suspected of having carried out this bombing and the August 28, 2003, bombing at Chiron Life Science Center. San Diego remained a fugitive at the end of 2005.

2003 Terrorism Preventions

FEBRUARY 13, 2003
Planned Attacks on Abortion Clinics and Minority Targets
Amwell Township, Pennsylvania
(Prevention of one act of Domestic Terrorism)

On February 13, 2003, law enforcement officials arrested David Wayne Hull, a long-time member and self-professed leader of the White Knights of the Ku Klux Klan (KKK). Hull had been exploding pipe bombs on his property in Amwell Township, Pennsylvania, had built and detonated improvised explosive devices (IEDs) during KKK events, and was recorded instructing individuals on how to place IEDs to cause maximum damage. Hull had also made threats against minorities and abortion clinics. Hull was indicted in March 2003 for firearms charges, witness tampering, and instructing persons on procedures for creating destructive devices. A jury in the Western District of Pennsylvania convicted Hull on seven counts of the ten-count indictment. On February 25, 2005, Hull was sentenced to 12 years in prison, followed by three years of probation.

APRIL 4, 2003
Planned Murder Plots against Federal Judge, AUSA, and IRS Agent
Grangeville, Idaho
(Prevention of one act of Domestic Terrorism)

On April 4, 2003, the FBI arrested David Roland Hinkson, a constitutionalist and tax protestor, for attempting to arrange the murders of a federal judge, an Assistant U.S. Attorney, and an IRS Agent whom he blamed for his legal problems regarding a tax evasion case against him. Between December 2002 and March 2003, Hinkson offered two individuals $10,000 for committing all three murders. On January 27, 2005, Hinkson was found guilty on three counts of solicitation to commit murder after a three week jury trial in Boise, Idaho. On June 3, 2005, Hinkson was sentenced to 43 years in federal prison.

APRIL 10, 2003
Planned Cyanide Attack
Tyler, Texas
(Prevention of one act of Domestic Terrorism)

On April 10, 2003, the FBI arrested William Joseph Krar for fraud-related charges stemming from his attempt to deliver numerous false identification badges—including a United Nations Observer Badges, Defense Intelligence Agency identification, and a Federal Concealed Weapons Permit—to Edward Feltus, a member of the New Jersey Militia. Krar had also been identified as a potential weapons supplier associated with extremist militia activities. In a search of Krar's Texas residence at the time of his arrest, FBI investigators found firearms, explosives, blasting caps, machine guns, over 100,000 rounds of ammunition, approximately 800 grams of sodium cyanide, and plans to weaponize the sodium cyanide. Krar and a co-conspirator, Judith Bruey, pled guilty to federal weapons charges, and in May 2004 were sentenced to 135 months and 57 months in federal custody, respectively. Feltus pled guilty to aiding and abetting the transportation of false IDs, and was sentenced in May 2004 to 18 months probation and fined $1,500.

JUNE 9, 2003
Planned Bombing of a U.S. Coast Guard Facility
Bellingham, Washington
(Prevention of one act of Domestic Terrorism)

On June 9, 2003, the FBI arrested Paul Douglas Revak for plotting to bomb a U.S. Coast Guard facility in Bellingham, Washington. Revak, who had previously declared himself to be an anarchist, was reportedly attempting to precipitate a revolution in the United States and had discussed the targeting of several nearby military installations. Revak was arrested when he negotiated with an undercover FBI employee for the purchase of explosive device components. Under a plea agreement, Revak was charged with threatening to use a weapon of mass destruction and sentenced to five years' probation.

NOVEMBER 11, 2003
Planned Bombings of Abortion Clinics
Miami, Florida
(Prevention of one act of Domestic Terrorism)

On November 11, 2003, Stephen John Jordi was arrested in Miami, Florida, for plotting to attack several abortion clinics. Jordi had openly discussed his intentions to attack abortion clinics, had expressed solidarity with anti-abortion extremists, and had associated with individuals from the anti-abortion extremist group Army of God. Jordi set out potential targets and a specific time frame for the attacks, and had cased and videotaped numerous Miami-area abortion clinics. He had also purchased several items to carry out the attack, including containers of gasoline and propane, flares, starting fluid, and a silencer purchased from an FBI source. Jordi was indicted on November 15, 2003, for attempting to damage and destroy property used in interstate commerce, distribution of information relating to the manufacture or use of explosive or destructive devices, and possession of a firearm that was not registered to him. On July 8, 2004, a federal judge in Miami sentenced Jordi to five years in prison.

2003 Significant Events

JANUARY 30, 2003
Richard C. Reid Sentenced

On January 30, 2003, Richard Colvin Reid was sentenced to life in prison for his December 2001 attempt to bomb American Airlines flight 63 with an explosive device concealed in his shoe. Reid had been indicted on January 16, 2002, on nine terrorism-related counts, and pled guilty on October 4, 2002.

FEBRUARY 14, 2003
Kathleen Ann Soliah Sentenced

On February 14, 2003, Kathleen Ann Soliah, a former member of the Symbionese Liberation Army (SLA) serving time for her role in a 1975 car bombing plot, was sentenced for the 1975 murder of Myrna Opsahl. Soliah received six years added to the sentence she was already serving, after pleading guilty on November 7, 2002, for her role in the 1975 SLA bank robbery that killed Opsahl.

FEBRUARY 19, 2003

Arrests and Indictments of Palestinian Islamic Jihad Members

On February 19, 2003, four members of the Palestinian Islamic Jihad (PIJ) terrorist organization—Sami Amin al-Arian, Sameeh Hammoudeh, Hatim Naji Fariz, and Ghassan Zayed Ballut—were arrested and charged with operating a racketeering enterprise from 1984 to 2003 in support of violence. The indictment, which was unsealed on February 20, 2003, also charged the individuals with "conspiracy within the United States to kill and maim persons abroad, conspiracy to provide material support and resources to PIJ, conspiracy to violate emergency economic sanctions," extortion, perjury, obstruction of justice, and immigration fraud. Four other individuals were also charged under the same indictment—Ramadan Abduallah Shallah, Bashir Musa Mohammed Nafi, Mohammed Tasir Hassan Al-Khatib, and Abd Al Aziz Awda—but were overseas and remained fugitives at the end of 2005.

FEBRUARY 28, 2003

Cigarette Smugglers Sentenced in Terror Financing Case

On February 28, 2003, Mohamad and Chawki Hammoud were sentenced to prison terms for their roles in a Charlotte, North Carolina-based, cigarette smuggling ring with ties to terrorist financing. Both men were convicted of cigarette smuggling, money laundering, racketeering, and credit card fraud. Mohamad Hammoud, who was found guilty of providing support to Hizballah in addition to smuggling charges, was given a maximum 155-year prison sentence. Chawki Hammoud, who was convicted in the smuggling case but was not found to have ties to Hizballah, was sentenced to 51 months in prison.

MARCH 1, 2003

Capture of Khalid Shaykh Mohammed

On March 1, 2003, counterterrorism forces in Pakistan captured Khalid Shaykh Mohammed, an al-Qa'ida operational commander and the man believed to have been the mastermind of the September 11, 2001, attack. Shaykh Mohammed is also believed to have played a role in a number of other attacks and planned attacks, including the 2002 bombings in Bali, Indonesia, the 2000 bombing of the *USS Cole* in Yemen, and a 1995 plot to blow up multiple U.S. commercial airliners.

APRIL 14, 2003

Plea Agreement for Earnest James Ujaama

On April 14, 2003, Earnest James Ujaama pled guilty in Seattle federal court to conspiring to provide goods and services to the Taliban in Afghanistan. As part of the plea agreement, federal prosecutors dropped charges alleging that Ujaama had plotted to establish a terrorist training camp in Bly, Oregon. In return, Ujaama was sentenced to 24 months in prison.

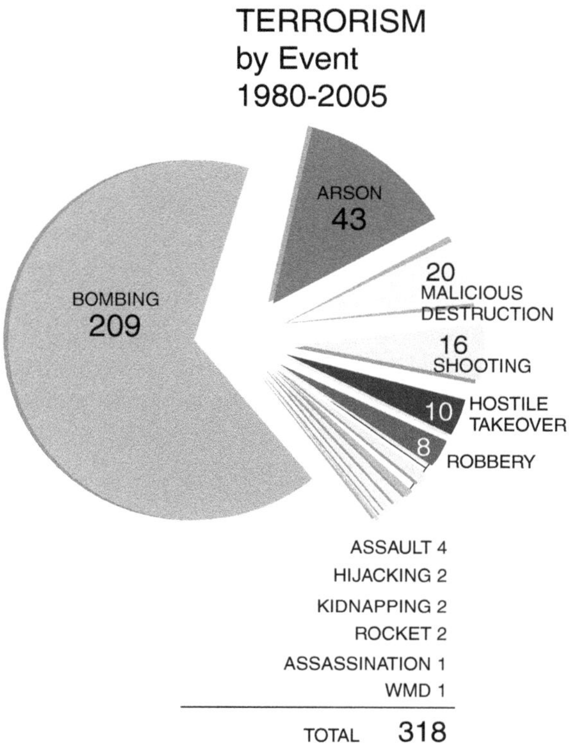

AUGUST 18, 2003
Sentencing of Enaam Arnaout

On August 18, 2003, Enaam Arnaout, the director of Benevolence International Foundation, was sentenced to 11 years in federal prison after pleading guilty on February 10, 2003, to terrorism-related racketeering conspiracy charges. Arnaout had been indicted on October 9, 2002, for conspiracy to fraudulently obtain charitable donations in order to provide financial assistance to al-Qa'ida and other organizations engaged in violence and terrorism. The indictment charged Arnaout with conspiracy to engage in racketeering, conspiracy to provide material support to terrorists, money laundering, mail fraud, and wire fraud in his attempt to fraudulently use the charitable contributions of Muslim Americans, U.S. corporations, and other donors to support terrorism overseas. Benevolence International Foundation was registered as a tax-exempt charitable organization; Arnaout allegedly used it as a racketeering enterprise.

AUGUST–DECEMBER 2003
Plea Agreements and Sentencing for Portland Terror Cell Suspects

Between August and December 2003, six of seven members of a Portland, Oregon-based terrorist cell pled guilty to terrorism-related charges. The six were indicted in October 2002 for conspiracy to provide assistance to Taliban and al-Qa'ida forces by planning to travel to fight U.S. troops stationed in Afghanistan. Charges against the seventh defendant, Habis Al Saoub, were dismissed after he was killed in Pakistan by Pakistani troops on October 3, 2003.

On August 6, 2003, Maher Hawash pled guilty to conspiracy to supply services to the Taliban. On September 18, 2003, brothers Ahmed and Muhammad Bilal pled guilty to federal weapons charges and conspiracy to contribute services to the Taliban. On September 26, 2003, October Martinique Lewis, the ex-wife of Jeffrey Leon Battle, pled guilty to money laundering for the purpose of assisting Battle in willfully supplying services to the Taliban. On October 16, 2003, Battle and Patrice Lumumba Ford pled guilty to seditious conspiracy. Prison sentences for cell members taken into custody ranged from three to 18 years.

OCTOBER 7, 2003

Sentencing of Raymond Anthony Sandoval

On October 7, 2003, a U.S. District judge in New Mexico sentenced Raymond Anthony Sandoval to 84 months incarceration and to make restitution payment of $3 million for having initiated the June 1998 Oso Complex wildfire near Espanola, New Mexico, and attempting to bomb the Santa Fe, New Mexico, offices of the Forest Guardians environmentalist group on March 19, 1999. On June 25, 2003, Sandoval pled guilty to charges of manufacturing a destructive device, possession of an unregistered firearm, arson on federal land, and willfully injuring property of the United States. Law enforcement officers with the FBI, U.S. Forest Service, and Espanola, New Mexico Police arrested Sandoval on February 14, 2003.

OCTOBER 28, 2003

lyman Faris Sentenced for Material Support to al-Qa'ida

On October 28, 2003, a federal court in the Eastern District of Virginia sentenced U.S. citizen lyman Faris (aka Mohammed Rauf) to 20 years in prison. Faris had been charged with conspiracy and providing material support to al-Qa'ida and pled guilty on May 1, 2003. According to the indictment and plea, Faris conducted casing of a New York City bridge and researched and provided information on U.S. targets to al-Qa'ida.

DECEMBER 2003

Sentencing of Lackawanna Six Terror Cell Members

In December 2003, Faysal Galab, Shafal Mosed, Yahya Goba, Sahim Alwan, Yasein Taher, and Mukhtar Albakri received federal prison sentences ranging from seven to 10 years after pleading guilty to providing material support or resources to al-Qa'ida. The six individuals, who resided in Lackawanna, New York, traveled to Afghanistan in the summer of 2001 to attend the al-Farooq terrorist training camp near Kandahar. Attendees were present at this camp for a period of up to two months and received terrorism training; several of the men were also present for a speech by Usama Bin Ladin. They were arrested in September of 2002 for providing material support or resources to a designated foreign terrorist organization.

2004 In Review

The FBI recorded five terrorist incidents and five terrorism preventions in 2004. Domestic extremists were responsible for each incident. Three of the incidents involved possible associates of the Earth Liberation Front environmental extremist movement, who used incendiary devices against car dealerships, construction sites and housing developments. In a fourth incident, associates of the Animal Liberation Front conducted two attacks against an animal science facility on the campus of Brigham Young University, which resulted in more than $75,000 in damages. Another incident involved a white supremacist affiliated with Aryan Nations who firebombed a synagogue in Oklahoma City, Oklahoma.

In the first terrorism prevention, law enforcement officers in Birmingham, Alabama, arrested two men in possession of multiple fire-arms, bomb-making literature, components of an improvised explosive device, and literature related to the Waco and Ruby Ridge incidents, as well as photographs of serial bomber Eric Rudolph. The second terrorism prevention involved the same white supremacist arrested in 2004 for firebombing an Oklahoma City synagogue, and for whom further investigation uncovered his intention to commit additional attacks against minorities. The third prevention involved a plot by extremist members of the Montana-based Project 7 Militia to kidnap and assassinate local judges, law enforcement officers, and their family members. The fourth prevention involved a Chicago-area man attempting to sell ammonium nitrate to an individual purportedly associated with a foreign terrorist organization. The fifth prevention involved the arrest of a man in Tennessee who wanted to obtain nuclear or chemical materials to blow up a courthouse.

No deaths or serious injuries resulted from terrorist activity carried out in the United States in 2004.

Among the major international terrorist incidents during 2004, al-Qa'ida conducted a series of terrorist attacks in Saudi Arabia against economic and diplomatic targets through kidnapings, murders, and suicide attacks using small groups of operatives. The attacks resulted in 36 deaths, including the deaths of six Americans, and over two dozen injuries, including those to four Americans. Another major incident involved the coordinated bombing of the train system in Madrid, Spain, by terrorists affiliated with the violent global jihadist movement. A total of 10 bombs detonated during the March 11 morning rush hour in Madrid, killing 191 persons and injuring more the 1,400. Although this incident did not result in any American casualties and is not elsewhere summarized in this report, the Madrid bombing is significant in showing the extension of global jihadist violence outside of predominantly Muslim nations.

2004 Terrorist Incidents

JANUARY 19, 2004
Arson
Henrico County, Virginia
(One act of Domestic Terrorism)

On January 19, 2004, Henrico County Fire Department officials discovered four Molotov cocktails that had been used to commit arson on a Ford car dealership. One Molotov cocktail scorched a vehicle in the dealership. Investigators on the scene also discovered a BMW on which the letters "XXX" were spray-painted. A business neighboring the dealership had the letters "XELFX" spray-painted on it. Christopher Kyle Salmon and Timothy Ryan Kennedy were convicted of attempted arson. Salmon was sentenced to 24 months in prison, two years of probation, and $500 restitution. Kennedy was sentenced to 25 months in prison, two years of probation, and $500 restitution.

APRIL 1, 2004
Arson
Oklahoma City, Oklahoma
(One act of Domestic Terrorism)

On April 1, 2004, Sean Michael Gillespie used a Molotov cocktail to firebomb the Temple B'nai Israel in Oklahoma City, Oklahoma. The attack caused mostly smoke damage to the synagogue. Gillespie committed the arson as a target of opportunity when he could not locate for a similar attack the address of a person he presumed to be Jewish, whose name he had randomly discovered in a phone book. On April 16, 2004, the FBI arrested Gillespie for the firebombing. A search of Gillespie's residence and truck revealed two videotapes, a baseball bat, brass knuckles, and a stun gun. One of the videotapes clearly implicates Gillespie in the firebombing of the synagogue. Gillespie had claimed association with the Aryan Nations and stated that he was proud of his actions. On April 26, 2005, Gillespie was convicted on charges related to the possession and use of an explosive device and on August 30, 2005, was sentenced to 39 years in prison.

APRIL 20, 2004
Vandalism and Arson
Snohomish, Washington
(One act of Domestic Terrorism)

In the early morning of April 20, 2004, two new homes were destroyed and another was damaged by arson, and an improvised incendiary device (IID) was found inside a fourth home at a new housing development in the Lobo Ridge area of Snohomish, Washington. The causes of the arson incidents are believed to be IIDs of the type recovered, consisting of jugs with duct-taped fuses and filled with flammable liquid. Approximately 20 miles away from the arson location, six containers of flammable liquid, duct tape, matches, and fuse like material were found by a contractor. The containers were found at the end of an uninhabited cul-de-sac of another new housing development along with graffiti that read "Consider these 13 as a warning. Walk on the edge. Green equals no burn all others are fair game. Bush is a rapist. ELF."

On April 21, 2004, three additional IIDs were found in a new construction subdivision several miles from where the previous day's incidents had occurred. The devices, which were ignited but failed to completely burn, resulted in no damage to the homes. The devices were similar to those found earlier. No note or claim of responsibility was found at this scene. The discovery of these three devices brought the total number of IIDs to 13, corresponding to the number warned of in the original ELF graffiti.

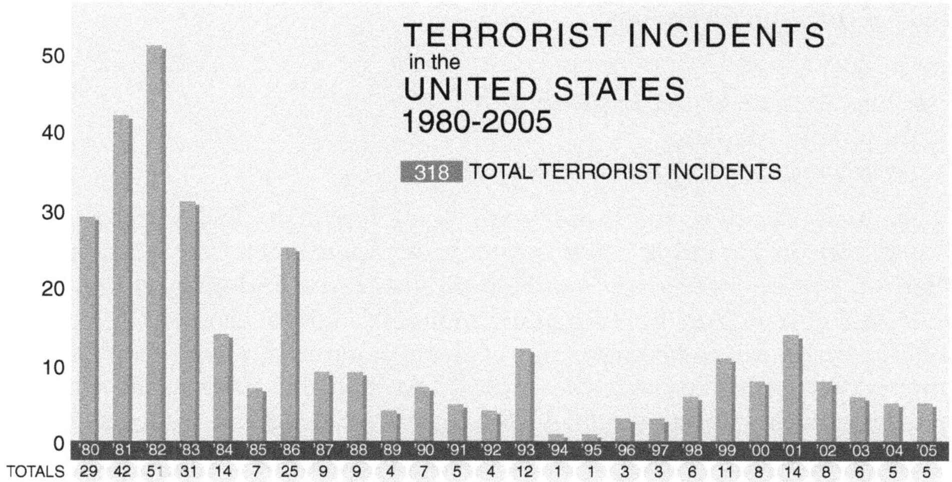

MAY–JULY, 2004
Vandalism and Arson
Provo, Utah
(One act of Domestic Terrorism)

On July 8, 2004, an arson occurred at the Ellsworth Farm animal science facility on the campus of Brigham Young University. The building was also vandalized and the walls spray painted with the phrases "ALF," "war is on," "you are the terrorists," and "this will never end." Damages from the fire and vandalism were estimated at over $75,000. Two related vandalism incidents attributed to the Animal Liberation Front (ALF) occurred at the same facility in May 2004. Harrison Burrows and Joshua Demmitt confessed to the July arson and May incidents. In January 2005 Burrows and Demmitt were each sentenced to 30 months in federal prison.

DECEMBER 27, 2004
Attempted Arson
Lincoln, California
(One act of Domestic Terrorism)

On December 27, 2004, four incendiary devices were placed in two homes under construction in Lincoln, California. However, the devices failed to function as intended. The site contained Earth Liberation Front (ELF)-related graffiti on one of the homes as well as the letters "ELF" on the cul-de-sac where the homes were located. Members of the Sacramento Joint Terrorism Task Force arrested Ryan Lewis, Eva Holland, Lili Holland, and Jeremiah Colcleasure in connection with the incident. The four were convicted of arson and Colcleasure, Holland, and Holland were each sentenced to two years in federal prison; Lewis received a six year prison sentence for his role in this incident and for arsons that took place in early 2005.

2004 Terrorism Preventions

JANUARY 20, 2004
Planned Attacks Using Explosives
Birmingham, Alabama
(Prevention of one act of Domestic Terrorism)

On January 20, 2004, the Birmingham Joint Terrorism Task Force arrested David Nelson Hemphill for possession of pipe bombs and a homemade silencer. Subsequent searches of Hemphill's person and property revealed a .45-caliber handgun, bomb-making materials, antigovernment and bomb-making literature, and components of an ammonium nitrate fuel oil (ANFO) improvised explosive device. Hemphill admitted that prior to his arrest he had been trying to construct ANFO bombs. Hemphill's associate, Bruce Stephen Metzler, was also arrested. A search of Metzler's person and property revealed two .22-caliber handguns, a .233-caliber rifle, a .308-caliber assault rifle, a single- barrel shotgun, a .38-caliber revolver, literature related to the Waco and Ruby Ridge incidents, and photographs of an abortion clinic bombed by serial bomber Eric Rudolph. Also located were two empty 20 mm military ammunition containers, wire end caps, fuses, gunpowder, and a partially constructed silencer. Hemphill and Metzler pled guilty to weapons charges. On January 25, 2005, Hemphill was sentenced in the Southern District of Alabama to 23 months in prison followed by 24 months supervised release. On September 22, 2004, Metzler was sentenced to probation.

MAY–DECEMBER 2004

Attacks by Al-Qa'ida in the Arabian Peninsula

Yanbu, Al Khobar, Riyadh, and Jeddah, Saudi Arabia

Early attacks by al-Qa'ida regional affiliate al-Qa'ida in the Arabian Peninsula (AQAP)—such as the May 12,2003, coordinated bombings of three residential compounds in Riyadh, Saudi Arabia—focused on large mass-casualty events using vehicle-borne improvised explosive devices. After April 2004, AQAP changed tactics to include individual kidnappings, murders, and attacks against economic and diplomatic facilities using small teams of suicide operatives. Attacks by AQAP operatives that used these tactics and involved U.S. citizens or interests during 2004 include:

- On May 1, 2004, four gunmen drove into the ABB Lummus Global Compound at the Yanbu Petrochemical plant in Yanbu, Saudi Arabia. In the attack that followed, the assail ants killed six ABB Lummus employees, including two Americans.
- On May 29, 2004, gunmen made a coordinated attack against Western and oil-infrastructure targets in Al Khobar, Saudi Arabia, including the Arab Petroleum Investments Corporation/Royal Dutch Shell compound, the Al Rushaid Petroleum Center, and the Oasis housing compound. The assailants killed 22 people in the attack, including one American, and wounded more than two dozen others, including four Americans.
- On June 8, 2004, gunmen fatally shot U.S. citizen Robert Corgan Jacobs, an employee of military training contractor Vinnell Arabia, as he walked from his car to his private residence in the al-Khalij section of Riyadh, Saudi Arabia.
- On June 12, 2004, three assailants fatally shot U.S. citizen Kenneth Raymond Scroggs as he returned from work to his residence in the Malaz District of Riyadh. Scroggs worked for Advanced Electronics, a Saudi business involved in the development of Apache Attack Helicopter systems.

- On June 12, 2004, U.S. citizen Paul Marshal Johnson, Jr., an employee of Advanced Electronics, was kidnaped in Riyadh. Johnson was killed by his captors six days later.
- On December 6, 2004, five armed assailants breached the U.S. consulate compound in Jeddah, Saudi Arabia. The terrorists were killed before gaining entrance to the consulate building. Five U.S. consulate Foreign Service Nationals died in the attack.

In response to these incidents, the FBI deployed investigative teams to assist Saudi authorities. Law enforcement actions have resulted in the deaths or capture of many of the perpetrators, including AQAP leader Abd al-Aziz al-Muqrin, who was killed in a shoot-out with Saudi authorities in June 2004.

APRIL 16, 2004
Planned Attacks against Minorities
Oklahoma City, Oklahoma
(Prevention of one act of Domestic Terrorism)

As noted in 2004 Terrorist Incidents, the FBI arrested Sean Michael Gillespie on April 16, 2004, for having firebombed the Temple B'nai Israel in Oklahoma City, Oklahoma. The attack against the synagogue in Oklahoma City was likely the first of a series of unspecified attacks Gillespie intended to commit. Following Gillespie's arrest, a search of his residence revealed a videotape containing surveillance of a Las Vegas synagogue and a statement by Gillespie that he was on a "mission for the white race," which was to involve a cross-country spree of unspecified terrorist acts. Concern for future attacks was also supported by Gillespie's admission following his arrest to having previously committed random acts of vandalism and violence against minorities.

MAY 6, 2004
Convictions of Project 7 Militia Extremists
Flathead County, Montana
(Prevention of one act of Domestic Terrorism)

On May 6, 2004, several extremist members of the Project 7 Militia were arrested following an extensive investigation into the group by FBI, Bureau of Alcohol, Tobacco, and Firearms, and local police. Investigation had identified leader David Burgert and five other members of the Project 7 Militia as having committed various violations of federal law in furtherance of violent plans targeting law enforcement officers and other government officials. Burgert, along with Tracy Brockway, James Day, John Slater, and Steven Morey, pled guilty to various federal weapons charges, including possession of machine guns and other illegal weapons as well as conspiracy to possess illegal weapons. On November 12, 2004, Burgert received an 87 month prison sentence for his role in the plotting. In early 2005, the four other members who entered guilty pleas received sentences ranging from 18 to 37 months in federal prison. A sixth subject, Larry Chezem, was convicted in a federal trial of conspiracy and was sentenced on September 30, 2005, to 15 months in prison.

AUGUST 5, 2004
Planned Attacks against Federal Buildings
Chicago, Illinois
(Prevention of one act of Domestic Terrorism)

On August 5, 2004, the FBI arrested Gale William Nettles in connection with his attempted sale of a half ton of ammonium nitrate to an undercover agent purportedly associated with a foreign terrorist organization. The FBI also had information that Nettles intended to use ammonium nitrate to bomb Chicago's Dirksen Federal Office Building. Nettles planned to counterfeit U.S. currency in order to earn money to purchase bomb components for his attack. On September 15, 2005, Nettles was found guilty of attempting to bomb the Dirksen Building and awaited sentencing at the end of 2005.

OCTOBER 25, 2004
Planned Attacks against Federal or State Courthouse
Memphis, Tennessee
(Prevention of one act of Domestic Terrorism)

On October 25, 2004, Demetrius Van Crocker was arrested in Jackson, Tennessee, for attempting to obtain C-4 explosives and Sarin nerve gas from an undercover FBI agent. Van Crocker was planning to use these materials to blow up a federal or state courthouse in furtherance of his hatred toward the U.S. and State of Tennessee governments. Van Crocker's federal trial on chemical weapons and explosives violations was pending at the end of 2005.

2004 Significant Events

FEBRUARY 9, 2004
Final Sentencings in Portland Terror Cell Case

On February 9, 2004, three men affiliated with a terrorist cell in Portland, Oregon, were given prison sentences. Maher Hawash received a seven-year prison sentence, while two of his co-conspirators, Ahmed and Mohammed Bilal, were sentenced to ten and eight years in prison, respectively. The three men, along with three other suspects, pled guilty in 2003 to conspiracy to provide services to the Taliban and conspiracy to use firearms in a crime of violence. Several of these individuals had planned to travel to Afghanistan to fight alongside the Taliban against U.S. and Coalition forces. Three other Portland cell members were sentenced in 2003.

MARCH THROUGH APRIL 2004
"Virginia Jihad" Members Convicted and Sentenced

On April 9, 2004, Randall T. Royer and Ibrahim Ahmed al-Hamdi were sentenced to 20 years and 15 years in prison, respectively, for their roles in an alleged "Virginia Jihad" terrorist cell, which conducted weapons training in Virginia. On March 4, 2004, Masoud Khan, Seifullah Chapman, and Hammad Abdur-Raheem, three other cell members arrested in the case, were convicted on conspiracy and weapons charges. Two other men, Yong Ki Kwon and Khwarja Mahmood Hasan, pled guilty in the case, and testified that they had attended a training camp associated with the terrorist group Lashkar-e-Tayyiba with the intention of fighting on the side of the Taliban against U.S. forces in Afghanistan. The remaining two members of the group were not convicted. A federal judge acquitted Sabri Benkhala on March 9, 2004, and the case against Caliph Basha Ibn Abdur-Raheem was dismissed.

APRIL 26, 2004
Sentencing of Symbionese Liberation Army Member

On April 26, 2004, Symbionese Liberation Army (SLA) member James William Kilgore was sentenced to 48 months in prison for several bombings in California in 1975. Kilgore was also sentenced to six months in prison for passport fraud charges. Kilgore was arrested in Cape Town, South Africa, in 2002 and was indicted for multiple murders, possession of an explosives device, and other charges in conjunction with his membership in the SLA, an organization that sought to overthrow the U.S. government in the 1970s.

JUNE 2, 2004
Mohammed Junaid Babar Guilty Plea

On April 10, 2004, the FBI arrested naturalized U.S. citizen Mohammed Junaid Babar in New York City for his suspected role in providing material support to al-Qa'ida that included support for a terrorist plot to blow up pubs, train stations, and restaurants in the United Kingdom. This arrest followed police actions by British authorities, who, in late March 2004, arrested eight British citizens and seized approximately 1,320 pounds of ammonium nitrate from a self-storage warehouse in west London in connection with the same plot. On June 2, 2004, Junaid Babar pled guilty in the Southern District of New York to five counts of conspiring to provide material support to al-Qa'ida. Sentencing for Junaid Babar was pending at the end of 2005.

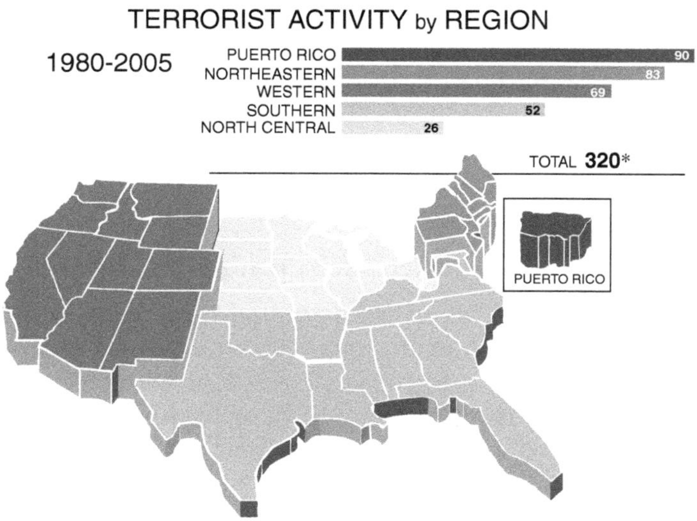

* Although designated as a single act of international terrorism, the aircraft attacks of September 11, 2001, have been designated as one terrorist incident in the Northeastern region and one terrorist incident in the Southern region for the purposes of this graph. Similarly, although the anthrax mailings that occurred from September through November 2001 have been categorized as a single act of terrorism, the incidents have been designated as one terrorist incident in the Northeastern region and one terrorist incident in the Southern region for the purposes of this graph.

JUNE 10, 2004
Nuradin M. Abdi Indicted

On June 10, 2004, a federal grand jury indicted Nuradin M. Abdi on terrorism charges. The four-count indictment included charges of conspiracy to provide material support to terrorists; conspiracy to provide material support to al Qa'ida, a designated foreign terrorist organization; fraud and misuse of documents; and fraudulent use of travel documents. Abdi, a Somali national living in the United States, is believed to have misrepresented his reasons for travel on a federal government form, claiming he intended to travel to Germany and Saudi Arabia for religious and family reasons when he actually planned to travel to Ethiopia for terrorism training. Abdi allegedly conspired to blow up a shopping mall in the Columbus, Ohio, area and engaged in explosives instruction in preparation for this plot. Abdi is also accused of obtaining refugee asylum status through false means. The indictment was originally filed under seal and was unsealed on June 14, 2005.

JULY 26, 2004
***The 9/11 Commission Report* Published**

On July 26, 2004, the National Commission on Terrorist Attacks Upon the United States issued its final report on the September 11, 2001, attack. The report accounted for the circumstances surrounding the attack and provided recommendations for change. The FBI had submitted to the commission the "Report to the National Commission on Terrorist Attacks Upon the United States: The FBI's Counterterrorism Program Since September 2001" on April 14, 2004. This report covers the FBI's efforts to improve its counterterrorism capabilities since the attacks of September 11 and supplemented the testimony of several senior FBI officials.

AUGUST 19, 2004

Indictment of HAMAS Associates for Criminal Enterprise

On August 19, 2004, the FBI arrested Muhammad Salah, of Chicago, and Abdelhaleem Ashqar, of Washington, D.C., and issued an arrest warrant for Mousa Abu Marzook, a former U.S. resident who currently resides in Damascus, Syria, and is considered to be a fugitive from justice. These arrest actions followed an indictment by a federal grand jury in Chicago that alleged the three participated in a 15-year racketeering conspiracy in the United States and abroad by joining with 20 identified co-conspirators and others in illegally conducting the affairs of the foreign terrorist organization HAMAS. The indictment, which for the first time identifies HAMAS as a criminal enterprise, alleges that Salah, Ashqar, and Marzook provided money and personnel to HAMAS at a time when HAMAS was engaging in terrorist attacks. Although the defendants were not charged with direct participation in violence, these attacks resulted in the deaths of Israeli military personnel and civilians, as well as American and other foreign nationals in Israel and the West Bank. Trial for the defendants was pending at the end of 2005.

SEPTEMBER 22, 2004

Nevada Chapter Leader of Aryan Nations Arrested for Sending Threatening Letters

In December 2003, Steven Joseph Holten, the Nevada Chapter leader for Aryan Nations (AN), began a letter-writing campaign announcing the existence of AN in Nevada and condemning the actions of certain federal, media, and Jewish institutions. Many of the letters contained specific threats to the recipients. On September 22, 2004, FBI agents in Reno arrested Holten. On November 29, 2004, Holten pled guilty to mailing threatening communications through interstate commerce. On March 28, 2005, Holten was sentenced to ten months in prison, three years of supervised release, and a mandatory $100 fine.

SEPTEMBER 29, 2004

Sentencings in USS Cole Bombing

On September 29, 2004, a Yemeni court sentenced Abd al-Rahim al-Nashiri and Jamal al-Badawi to death for their roles in the October 12, 2000, bombing of the *USS Cole* in the Port of Aden, Yemen. Four other men were given prison sentences, ranging from five to 10 years, for their roles in the attack.

Seventeen American sailors were killed and more than 40 were injured in the October 12, 2000 bombing of the *USS Cole,* in which two suicide terrorists pulled a small, bomb-laden boat alongside the U.S. destroyer and detonated their explosives. Al-Badawi was also charged with a similar, failed attack against the *USS The Sullivans* in January 2000.

DECEMBER 8, 2004

Signing of the Intelligence Reform and Terrorism Prevention Act of 2004

On December 8, 2004, President Bush signed into law the Intelligence Reform and Terrorism Prevention Act of 2004 (IRTPA). In direct response to the recommendations of the 9/11 Commission, IRTPA instituted reforms to the Foreign Intelligence Surveillance Act and modified material support statutes for prosecuting terrorists. Among its many organizational provisions, IRTPA created the Office of the Director of National Intelligence; established the Director of National Intelligence as the head of the U.S. Intelligence Community; and instituted the joint-agency National Count-erterrorism Center as the primary entity for analyzing intelligence pertaining to transnational terrorism.

DECEMBER 13, 2004

Yemeni Terror Suspects Indicted

On December 13, 2004, a federal grand jury in the Eastern District of New York indicted two Yemeni nationals, Sheik Mohammad Ali Hassan Al-Moayad and Mohammed Mohsen Yahya Zayed, for conspiracy and attempt to provide material support to al-Qa'ida and HAMAS. Al-Moayad allegedly supported *mujahideen* around the world, and is believed to have provided money and equipment to al-Qa'ida and raised funds through a Brooklyn mosque for terrorism financing.

2005 In Review

In 2005, the FBI recorded five terrorist incidents and three terrorism preventions. All of the incidents involved arson or attempted arson. Domestic terrorists associated with the Earth Liberation Front were responsible for three of the incidents, which targeted commercial and residential construction sites. The other two incidents targeted the residences of persons involved with animal research. One of these incidents was claimed by the Animal Liberation Front, and the other is possibly attributable to animal rights extremists as well.

Separate preventions in Houston, Texas, and Pocatello, Idaho, involved individuals who sought to provide material support or resources to al-Qa'ida. A third prevention involved a group that formed in a Los Angeles prison, which adopted a jihadist ideology and was preparing to commit terrorist acts in the United States in furtherance of the violent global jihadist movement.

No deaths or serious injuries resulted from terrorist activity carried out in the United States in 2005.

A major international terrorist incident in 2005 involved the coordinated suicide bombing of the transit system in London, United Kingdom. The attack, carried out by British citizens affiliated with the violent global jihadist movement, resulted in 52 deaths and approximately 700 injuries. One American died in the attack and four others were injured.

2005 Terrorist Incidents

JANUARY–FEBRUARY 2005
Arson and Attempted Arson
Auburn and Sutter Creek, California
(One act of Domestic Terrorism)

On January 12, 2005, five intact incendiary devices were discovered at a commercial construction site in Auburn, California. On January 21, 2005, a letter was sent to four newspapers claiming responsibility for the attempted arson by the Earth Liberation Front (ELF).

On February 7, 2005, an arson was reported at an apartment complex in Sutter Creek, California. Fire officials discovered seven partially burned incendiary devices placed in five buildings of the apartment complex. Graffiti found at the site included "ELF" and "We Will Win" in red paint. Sprinkler systems installed in the buildings extinguished six of the seven devices and first responders extinguished the seventh. Damage was estimated at $50,000.

Ryan Daniel Lewis was convicted of arson and attempted arson involving these collective incidents as well as a December 27, 2004, incident in Lincoln, California. On March 17, 2005, Lewis was sentenced to a 72-month prison term followed by three years of supervised release.

JULY 7, 2005

Bombing of London Transportation System

London, United Kingdom

On July 7, 2005, a series of coordinated suicide bomb blasts struck London's transport system during morning rush hour. Beginning at 8:50 a.m. three bombs exploded within 50 seconds of each other on three London Underground trains, and a fourth bomb exploded on a bus nearly an hour later at 9:47 a.m. in London's Tavistock Square. Fifty-two people were killed and approximately 700 injured in the bombing. Among the casualties were one American killed and four wounded.

> The four suicide bombers were British citizens; three had been born in the United Kingdom, and the fourth had been born in Jamaica. The British citizenship of the bombers and the lack of strong ties between them and an international terrorist group illustrate the potential threat of "homegrown" terrorists as perpetrators of future attacks.

APRIL 13, 2005
Arson
Sammamish, Washington
(One act of Domestic Terrorism)

In the early morning of April 13, 2005, arson occurred at a nearly completed residence under construction in Sammamish, Washington, and an intact improvised incendiary device (IID) was discovered in a second residence under construction nearby. The IID in the first residence was located in the garage, which was destroyed by the fire. The second IID—a plastic, two-liter bottle filled with fuel and using an improvised igniter—had been placed under debris in the kitchen nook. The device had been activated but did not fully ignite. In addition a bedsheet with the wording, "Where are all the trees? Burn rapist burn. ELF," had been placed outside the second residence.

JULY 7,2005
Attempted Arson
Los Angeles, California
(One act of Domestic Terrorism)

In the early morning of July 7, 2005, fire officials responded to a vehicle fire in the driveway of a private residence in Los Angeles, California. In extinguishing the fire, authorities recovered a partially melted, plastic gasoline container from behind the vehicle's left front wheel. The car belonged to a representative for the Animal Care Technicians Union, which represents employees for the Los Angeles Animal Services (LAAS). LAAS and its affiliates have been targeted by local animal rights extremists, and the LAAS union representative had been placed on a "targets" list of indivi-duals profiled by extremists for "direct actions." The incident remains under investigation.

SEPTEMBER 16, 2005
Attempted Arson
Los Angeles, California
(One act of Domestic Terrorism)

On September 16, 2005, fire officials responded to a fire at the high-rise condominium home of the director of Los Angeles Animal Services, after residents observed smoke coming from a recyclables/janitorial closet. First responders recovered an improvised incendiary device consisting of a four-inch-long tube labeled "TOXIC" and using a cigarette as a fuse. The device, which had been placed next to a stack of newspapers in the recycling/janitorial closet, had malfunctioned and only scorched the concrete floor of the closet. The Animal Liberation Front claimed responsibility for this incident.

NOVEMBER 20, 2005
Arson
Hagerstown, Maryland
(*One act of Domestic Terrorism*)

In the early morning of November 20, 2005, five townhomes under construction were set on fire at the Hagers Crossing Development in Hagerstown, Maryland. Fire officials investigating the scene determined that kerosene was used as the accelerant in the arson. The blaze damaged or destroyed five units in two buildings. The Earth Liberation Front claimed responsibility for the fire.

OCTOBER 1, 2005
Kuta and Jimbaran Bombings
Bali, Indonesia

On October 1, 2005, three suicide bombers affiliated with the Jemaah Islamiya (Jl) terrorist organization used improvised explosive devices to conduct attacks against targets in the towns of Kutu and Jimbaran, outside the provincial capital of Denpasar, on the island of Bali, Indonesia. The bombers, who either wore vests or carried backpacks containing the explosives, targeted the Raja Restaurant in Kuta Square, the Nyoman Cafe in Jimbaran Beach, and the Mandega Cafe also in Jimbaran Beach and located across from the Four Seasons and Intercontinental Hotels.

The bombings killed 22 persons and injured 102. The FBI reported that those injured included a family of six U.S. and Indonesian dual national individuals, who were dining at the Raja Restaurant in Kuta.

On November 9, 2005, officers from the Indonesian National Police, working on leads from the October 1st bombing, conducted a number of law enforcement operations throughout the island of Java, Indonesia. These operations resulted in the arrests of a number of Jl associates and the death of Jl bomb-maker Azahari Husin. Husin was one of the most wanted terrorists in Southeast Asia and was a suspect in both the Kuta and Jimbaran bombing operation and the October 12, 2002, bombing of a Balinese nightclub.

2005 Terrorism Preventions

MAY 20, 2005
Attempt to Build and Sell Explosives
Houston, Texas
(Prevention of one act of Terrorism)

On May 20, 2005, FBI Special Agents arrested Ronald Allen Grecula following an arranged meeting with undercover officers. During the meeting, Grecula presented his design for a bomb, which he allegedly understood would be used by al-Qa'ida to kill Americans. On June 16, 2005, the U.S. District Court, Southern District of Texas, indicted Grecula on one count of providing material support or resources to a designated foreign terrorist organization. The indictment stemmed from information that indicated Grecula intended to build and sell a bomb to a terrorist organization for use against the United States.

JULY 5, 2005
Disruption of Plot to Attack Military and Jewish Targets
Los Angeles County, California
(Prevention of one act of International Terrorism)

On July 5, 2005, officers with the Torrance (California) Police Department arrested Levar Washington and Gregory Patterson during a commercial armed robbery in progress at a Los Angeles area gas station. Their arrest, and subsequent local and FBI investigation, revealed that Washington and Patterson were conducting the armed robberies to raise money for an alleged terrorist plot targeting U.S. military facilities, Israeli government facilities, and Jewish synagogues in the greater Los Angeles area. FBI investigation determined that Washington and Patterson were part of a Muslim convert organization, Jam'iyyat Ul-Islam Is-Sa-heeh ("Authentic Assembly of Islam"), or JIS, allegedly founded in prison by inmate Kevin James in 1997. The FBI identified James, Washington, Patterson—all U.S. citizens—and Hammad Samana, a Permanent Resident Alien of Pakistani origin, as the primary members of JIS. Samana was arrested on August 1, 2005.

On August 31, 2005, a federal grand jury in Santa Ana, California, indicted James, Washington, Patterson, and Samana for their alleged roles in the terrorist plot on charges of conspiracy to levy war against the U.S. government through terrorism and conspiracy to possess and discharge firearms in furtherance of crimes of violence. Washington, Patterson, and Samana were also charged with conspiracy to kill members of the U.S. government uniformed services and conspiracy to kill foreign officials. Washington and Patterson were further charged with interference with commerce by robbery and using and carrying a firearm in connection with a crime of violence.

DECEMBER 5, 2005
Planned Attacks Against Pipeline Systems
Pocatello, Idaho
(Prevention of one act of International Terrorism)

On December 5, 2005, Michael Curtis Reynolds was arrested at a motel near Pocatello, Idaho, after arranging to meet a purported al-Qa'ida contact. Reynolds offered to assist al-Qa'ida in engaging in acts of terrorism within the United States by identifying targets, planning terrorist attacks, and describing bomb-making methods. Reynolds sought to carry out violent attacks against pipeline systems and energy facilities in an effort to reduce energy reserves, create environmental hazards, and increase anxiety. Reynolds sought payment for supplying his assistance and continuing work on behalf of al-Qa'ida. Reynolds has been charged with attempting to provide material support to a foreign terrorist organization.

2005 Significant Events

FEBRUARY 10, 2005
Associates of Imprisoned Sheikh Convicted

On February 10, 2005, a federal jury in Manhattan convicted Lynne Stewart, an attorney representing Sheik Omar Abdul Rahman the "Blind Sheikh"; Mohammed Yousry, a translator for Rahman's attorneys; and Ahmed Abdel Sattar, a follower of Rahman in New York, on charges including providing and concealing the provision of material support or resources to terrorists. Rahman, who was convicted of a 1993 conspiracy to bomb several New York City landmarks, is the spiritual leader of the Egyptian-based terrorist organization Al-Gama Al-Islamiya.

FEBRUARY 17, 2005
Indictment against the Al-Haramain Islamic Foundation

On February 17, 2005, a federal grand jury returned a three-count indictment against the Ashland, Oregon-based Al-Haramain Islamic Foundation, Inc., and two of its officers on charges of conspiring to defraud the U.S. government and concealing their intent by filing a false tax return and failing to acknowledge they were transporting funds out of the United States. The charges of conspiracy to defraud the United States, tax fraud, and currency smuggling revolve around a $150,000 transaction apparently intended for the benefit of Chechen *mujahideen*.

MARCH 1, 2005
Kourani Pleads Guilty

On March 1, 2005, Mahmoud Youssef Kourani pled guilty to one count of conspiracy to provide material support to the designated foreign terrorist organization Hizballah. The guilty plea came in response to meetings

Kourani hosted at his home, during which a guest speaker from Lebanon solicited donations to Hizballah's "orphans of martyrs" program to benefit the families of Hizballah members killed in action. Kourani was sentenced on June 14, 2005, to a 54-month prison term to be followed by his removal upon release.

MARCH 10, 2005

Al-Moayed and Zayed Convicted

On March 10, 2005, a federal jury convicted Yemeni cleric Mohamed Al-Moayed and Mohammed Zayed on charges of providing and conspiring to provide material support and resources to al-Qa'ida and HAMAS. Tape-recorded statements from Al-Moayad indicated that he was engaged in providing money to support *mujahideen* fighters in Afghanistan, Chechnya, and Kashmir. Al-Moayed and Zayed were arrested in Germany in January 2003 and charged with providing, and conspiring to provide, material support to terrorism. On July 28, 2005, Al-Moayed was sentenced to a 75-year prison term; Zayed was sentenced to a 45-year prison term.

APRIL 6, 2005

Hale Sentenced

On April 6, 2005, Matthew Hale, leader of the white supremacist Creativity Movement was sentenced to 40 years in prison. Hale had been convicted on three counts of obstruction of justice and soliciting the murder of Joan Lefkow, a federal judge in Chicago. Hale was arrested on January 8, 2003, for attempting to arrange the murder of Judge Lefkow, who had previously upheld a ruling against Hale in a trademark infringement case.

APRIL 13, 2005

Elashi Brothers Convicted

On April 13, 2005, a federal jury convicted Bayan Elashi, Basman Elashi, Ghassan Elashi, and the Infocom Corporation of conspiring and sending money to co-defendant Mousa Abu Marzook, an investor in Infocom and a self-admitted leader of HAMAS. In 1995, the U.S. Department of Treasury named HAMAS a specially designated terrorist organization, making it illegal for any U.S. person or entity to conduct business with HAMAS or its representatives.

APRIL 22, 2005

Guilty Plea of Zacarias Moussaoui

On April 22, 2005, Zacarias Moussaoui pled guilty to six charges related to his participation in the 9/11 conspiracy. Moussaoui admitted he had trained with al-Qa'ida in Afghanistan; had communicated directly with Usama Bin Ladin; and had been personally selected by Bin Ladin to participate in an operation to fly hijacked airplanes into American buildings, and who approved him to attack the White House.

APRIL 26, 2005
Ali Al-Timimi Convicted

On April 26, 2005, Ali Al-Timimi was convicted on all charges brought against him in connection with the "Virginia Jihad" case. Al-Timimi, a spiritual leader at a mosque in Northern Virginia, encouraged other individuals to go to Pakistan to receive military training from Lashkar-e-Tayyiba, a designated foreign terrorist organization, in order to fight U.S. troops in Afghanistan. Al-Timimi was sentenced to life in prison.

APRIL 27, 2005
Hemant Lakhani Convicted

On April 27, 2005, a federal jury in the District of New Jersey convicted British national Hemant Lakhani on charges of attempting to sell shoulder-fired missiles to what he thought was a terrorist group intent on shooting down U.S. airliners. Lakhani was arrested following an undercover sting operation involving agents from several nations. Lakhani was sentenced on September 11, 2005, to 47 years in prison.

JULY 7, 2005
Clayton Lee Waagner Sentenced

On July 7, 2005, anti-abortion extremist Clayton Lee Waagner was sentenced in the Southern District of Ohio to 19 years in federal prison for acts of violence he committed against abortion clinics in 2003 and for sending hoax anthrax letters to several reproductive health clinics in 2001.

JULY 18, 2005
Rudolph Sentenced

On July 18, 2005, a federal judge in Birmingham, Alabama, sentenced convicted bomber Eric Robert Rudolph to life in prison for the 1998 bombing of a Birmingham family planning clinic that killed a police officer and critically injured a nurse. On May 31, 2003, Rudolph had been arrested and charged with the clinic bombing as well as the bombing of Centennial Olympic Park in Atlanta, Georgia, two bombings at the Sandy Springs Professional Office Building near Atlanta, and two bombings at the Otherside Lounge in Atlanta. Rudolph pled guilty to the charges in April 2005.

JULY 26, 2005
Aref Ahmed Sentenced

On July 26, 2005, a federal judge in Buffalo, New York, sentenced Yemeni-American businessman Aref Ahmed to three years' imprisonment for his role in a cigarette-smuggling operation that may have been linked to terrorist activity. According to federal prosecutors, Ahmed gave $14,000 to five members of the Lackawanna Six to facilitate their travel to and attendance at a terrorist training camp. Members of the Lackawanna Six were charged with conspiring, providing, and attempting to provide material support to al-Qa'ida based upon their travel to Afghanistan to train in the al-Farooq camp operated by al-Qa'ida.

JULY 27, 2005
Ressam Sentenced

On July 27, 2005, Ahmed Ressam was sentenced to 22 years in prison for conspiracy to commit an international terrorist act and smuggling explosives. Ressam had been arrested on December 14, 1999, in Port Angeles, Washington, as he attempted to smuggle explosives into the United States for use in the Millennium Bombing plot against Los Angeles International Airport.

AUGUST 8, 2005
Carlos E. Gamarra-Murillo Sentenced

On August 8, 2005, Carlos Gamarra-Murillo was sentenced in U.S. District Court in Tampa, Florida, to 25 years' imprisonment for brokering and exporting defense articles without a license and providing material support to a foreign terrorist organization. Gamarra-Murillo attempted to supply the Colombian-based FARC with 4,000 grenades and 200 firearms.

AUGUST 25, 2005
Qureshi Sentenced

On August 25, 2005, Mohammed Salman Farooq Qureshi was sentenced in the Western District of Louisiana to four years of federal incarceration. On February 11, 2005, Qureshi pled guilty to making false statements to the FBI and provided information that established Qureshi's connections to and contacts with al-Qa'ida member Wadih El Hage. In addition, Qureshi provided information about his activities and financial support of the non-governmental organization Help Africa People, which was believed to have been used by El Hage and others in connection with the attacks on the U.S. embassies in Kenya and Tanzania.

NOVEMBER 8, 2005
Young Sentenced

On November 8, 2005, a federal judge in Madison, Wisconsin, sentenced Peter Daniel Young to 24 months in prison following his September 2, 2005, guilty plea to one count of conspiracy and one count of animal enterprise terrorism. Young and Justin C. Samuel had been indicted by a grand jury for actions in releasing thousands of mink from three Wisconsin farms in late 1997. Samuel was extradited from Belgium and later pled guilty to two counts of animal enterprise terrorism on November 3, 2000. Young remained a federal fugitive until his capture by the San Jose Police Department in San Jose, California, on March 21, 2005.

NOVEMBER 22, 2005
Jose Padilla Indicted

On November 22, 2005, a federal grand jury in Miami, Florida, indicted Jose Padilla on charges of conspiring to "murder, kidnap and maim persons" overseas and providing material support to terrorists as part of a North American terrorist support cell. Padilla was arrested in Chicago on May 8, 2002. He allegedly trained with al-Qa'ida while on travel in Afghanistan and Pakistan during 2001.

NOVEMBER 22, 2005
Ahmad Abu Ali Convicted of Terrorist Plots

On November 22, 2005, a federal jury in the Eastern District of Virginia convicted Ahmad Abu Ali on all counts of an indictment charging him with terrorism offenses of providing material support and resources to al-Qa'ida and conspiracy to commit air piracy and conspiracy to destroy aircraft. An investigation revealed that Ali had sought out and joined an al-Qai'da cell in Medina, Saudi Arabia, where he received training in weapons, explosives, and document forgery. He, along with other members of the cell, began to develop plans for several terrorist attacks against the United States, including a plot to assassinate President Bush.

NOVEMBER 23, 2005
Paracha Convicted

On November 23, 2005, a federal jury in the Southern District of New York convicted Uzair Paracha, a Pakistani national with permanent resident alien status in the United States, on charges of providing material support to al-Qa'ida. Evidence at trial proved that Paracha agreed with his father, Saifullah Paracha, and al-Qa'ida members Majid Kahn and Ammar Al-Baluchi to provide material support to al-Qa'ida by trying to help Kahn reenter the United States to commit a terrorist act. The elder Paracha was in custody at the U.S. military prison in Guantanamo Bay, Cuba, at the end of 2005.

DECEMBER 5, 2005
"Operation Backfire" Arrests

On December 7, 2005, the following individuals were taken into federal custody on arson charges stemming from a series of approximately 25 criminal actions that occurred from 1996 to 2001 in a major investigation collectively referred to as Operation Backfire: Stanislas Meyerhoff (Charlottesville, Virginia), Kevin Tubbs (Springfield, Oregon), Daniel McGowan (New York, New York), Chelsea Gerlach (Portland, Oregon), Sarah Kendall Harvey (Flagstaff, Arizona), and William Rodgers (Prescott, Arizona). Rodgers later committed suicide while in state custody on December 22, 2005. Meyerhoff and McGowan were also charged with multiple counts of use of an incendiary device. Darren Thurston, a Canadian citizen, was arrested on immigration charges in connection with the case. In addition, Grand Jury subpoenas were issued to Jennifer Adrian, Joseph Dibee, Frank Winbigler, Shannon Urich, Suzanne Savoie, Jonathan Paul, and Jennifer Kolar. The location of Dibee and another suspect, Josephine Overaker, were unknown at the end of 2005.

The subjects of the Backfire investigation are suspected of having committed a series of arsons in Oregon, Washington, Colorado, Wyoming, and California on behalf of the Animal Liberation Front and Earth Liberation Front. Among the most significant of these actions were the October 19, 1998, Vail Ski Resort arson in Vail, Colorado, that resulted in an estimated $26 million in damage, and the May 21, 2001, destruction by arson of the University of Washington's Center for Urban Horticulture, that resulted in an estimated $3 million in damage. Other targets included U.S. Forest Service ranger stations, BLM wild-horse facilities, meat-processing companies, lumber companies, and a high-tension power line. Members of the group allegedly committed the attacks using improvised incendiary devices made from milk jugs, petroleum products, and homemade timers. Federal, state, and local law enforcement agencies participating in these investigations include the FBI, Bureau of Alcohol, Tobacco, Firearms, and Explosives, U.S. Forest Service, Bureau of Land Management, Oregon State Police, Eugene Police Department, and Portland Police Bureau. Additional arrests are expected in the ongoing investigation.

Conclusion

The preceding summary of terrorism-related events and investigations offers a picture of the FBI's response to domestic and international terrorism from 2002 through 2005. In keeping with a longstanding trend, domestic extremists carried out the majority of terrorist incidents during this period. Twenty three of the 24 recorded terrorist incidents were perpetrated by domestic terrorists. With the exception of white supremacist Sean Michael Gillespie's firebombing of a synagogue in Oklahoma City, Oklahoma, all of the domestic terrorist incidents were committed by special interest extremists active in the animal rights and environmental movements. The acts committed by these extremists typically targeted materials and facilities rather than persons. The sole international terrorist incident in the United States recorded for this period involved the attack by Hesham Hedayet, who fatally shot two people at the El Al ticket counter at Los Angeles International Airport.

The terrorist preventions for 2002 through 2005 paint a more diverse threat picture. Eight of the 14 recorded terrorist preventions stemmed from right-wing extremism, and included disruptions to plotting by individuals involved with the militia, white supremacist, constitutionalist and tax protestor, and anti-abortion movements. The remaining preventions included disruptions to plotting by an anarchist in Bellingham, Washington, who sought to bomb a U.S. Coast Guard station; a plot to attack an Islamic center in Pinellis Park, Florida; and a plot by prison-originated, Muslim convert group to attack U.S. military, Jewish, and Israeli targets in the greater Los Angeles area. In addition, three preventions involved individuals who sought to provide material support to foreign terrorist organizations, including al-Qa'ida, for attacks within the United States.

Whereas the violent, global jihadist movement manifested itself primarily in terrorist preventions in the United States from 2002 through 2005, internationally the movement claimed major attacks against U.S. and Western targets that resulted in American casualties. Most of these incidents were perpetrated by regional jihadist groups operating in primarily Muslim countries, including attacks perpetrated by Indonesia-based Jemaah Islamiya and al-Qa'ida in the Arabian Peninsula. The coordinated suicide bombing of London's mass transit system by homegrown jihadists, however, brought the violent jihadist movement and the tactic of suicide bombing to the heart of a major European capital.

In addition to these incidents and preventions, the years 2002 through 2005 saw the resolutions to high-profile prosecutions in the fight against terrorism. These included the December 2003 sentencing of the Lackawanna Six terror cell members, who received prison terms ranging from 7 to 10 years for providing material support or resources to al-Qa'ida; the October 4, 2002, sentencing of John Walker Lindh to 20 years in prison for conspiring with the Taliban to kill U.S. citizens; the January 30, 2003, sentencing of Richard Colvin Reid to life in prison for attempting to bomb a transcontinental flight using a shoe bomb; the sentencings in 2003 and 2004 of members of a Portland terrorist cell, who received prison terms ranging from 3 to 18 years for plotting to provide assistance to the Taliban and al-Qa'ida in fighting against U.S. troops in Afghanistan; the September 29, 2004, sentencing in Yemeni court of six individuals for their roles in the bombing of the USS Cole bombing, two of whom received the death penalty; the April 6, 2005, sentencing of Matthew Hale, leader of the white supremacist Creativity Movement, to 40 years in prison for solicitation of violence and obstruction of justice; the April 22, 2005, guilty plea of Zacaraias Moussaoui to his role in the 9/11 attack; the July 18, 2005, sentencing of Eric Robert Rudolph to life in prison for perpetrating several bombings, including the Centennial Olympic Park bombing in Atlanta, Georgia; the April 26, 2005, sentencing of Ali Al-Timimi to life in prison for encouraging others to receive military training from the designated foreign terrorist organization Lashkar-e-Tayyiba, to fight U.S. troops in Afghanistan; and the August 30, 2005, sentencing of white supremacist Sean Michael Gillespie to 39 years for firebombing a synagogue in Oklahoma City, Oklahoma.

FBI counterterrorism initiatives since the 9/11 terrorist attack have focused on preventing future attacks through the timely gathering, analysis, and dissemination of information; the facilitation of appropriate sharing of terrorism-related information between federal, state, and local partners; and the advancement of intelligence and law enforcement partnerships worldwide. FBI and U.S. counterterrorism organizational changes from 2002 through 2005 include the creation of the National Joint Terrorism Task Force; the establishment of the Foreign Terrorist Tracking Task Force; the establishment of the U.S. Department of Homeland Security through the signing of the Homeland Security Act; and the consolidation of government terrorist watch lists into the Terrorist Screening Center. In direct response to recommendations made by the 9/11 Commission, the Intelligence Reform and Terrorism Prevention Act of 2004 created the Office of the Director of National Intelligence, established the Director of National Intelligence as the head of the U.S. Intelligence Community, and instituted the National Counterterrorism Center as the primary federal entity for analyzing intelligence pertaining to transnational terrorism. These and other FBI and government initiatives are discussed in greater detail in the following In Focus retrospective of the FBI's counterterrorism program.

In Focus

Historical Overview of the Fbi's Counterterrorism Program

Introduction

From its inception the FBI's counterterrorism program has had a mission to prevent planned acts of terrorism and, should a terrorist act occur, to mount a swift investigative response. During the first 75 years after the Bureau's founding in 1908, the terrorist threat to the United States came primarily from domestic sources. In recent decades, however, the problem of terrorism has developed into an international and global concern, and the FBI's counterterrorism program has evolved significantly as its counterterrorism responsibilities have increased. As a result, the FBI has steadily improved its ability to assess and counter the dynamic variety of domestic and international terrorist threats. The following summary provides a brief discussion of the definition of terrorism, followed by an historical overview of the FBI's counterterrorism efforts—from discrete, ad hoc responses to terrorist threats to its current top priority status—through a retrospective of the formative events and legislative initiatives that have contributed to its development.

Terrorism: Definitions

Terrorism is not always self-evident. On July 4, 2002, Egyptian national Hesham Mohamed Hadayet shot and killed two people and wounded a

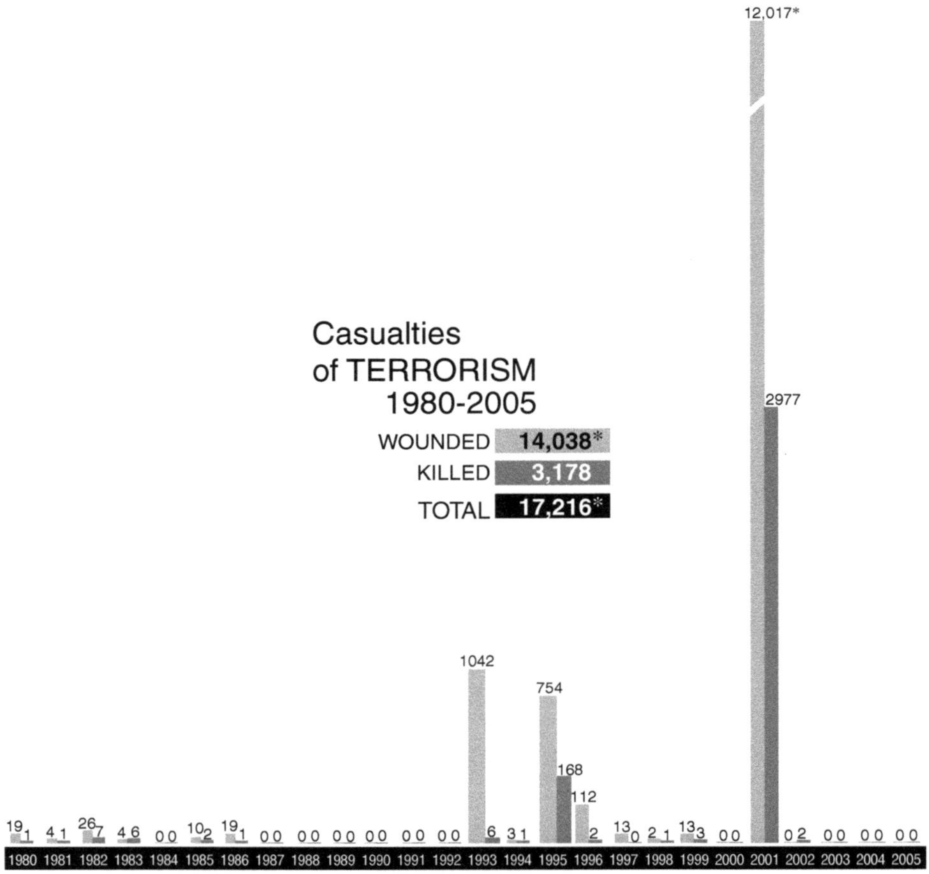

* The FBI uses 12,017 as an estimate for the number of those injured as a result of the September 11 attack; the exact number is unknown. Seventeen persons were infacted by and recovered from exposure to the anthrax mailings during September-November 2001.

third person at Los Angeles International Airport's El Al ticket counter before he was himself fatally shot by an airline security guard. Nine months later, on April 12, 2003, the U.S. Department of Justice publicly declared the shootings by Hadayet an act of terrorism. The FBI's investigation into the incident led to the conclusion that Hadayet, while unconnected to a formal terrorist organization, had committed an act of terrorism based upon his intention to advance the Palestinian cause in the Israel-Palestine conflict through the killing of civilians and the targeting of an airline owned by the Government of Israel. This case shows that investigation of an incident is sometimes necessary to determine motives or objectives behind a crime that would lead to its consideration as an act of terrorism. Beyond any consolation that understanding the nature of a crime can bring to survivors, to declare an incident a terrorist act is also to invoke a set of laws and punishments under which the incident may then be prosecuted.

Over the past several decades, the United States has begun to articulate terrorism as a distinctive category of criminal activity. The United States Code (USC) uses several definitions of terrorism that address specific legal situations, all of which have entered into the legal lexicon only since the 1970s. The FBI subdivides the terrorist threat facing the United States into the broad categories of international and domestic terrorism, each of which involves violent acts intended to intimidate or coerce a civilian population, or influence the policy or conduct of a government by mass destruction, assassination, or kidnapping. In cases of international terrorism, these acts transcend national boundaries in terms of the means by which they are accomplished, the persons they intend to intimidate, or the locale in which perpetrators operate (18 USC § 2331(1)). In cases of domestic terrorism, the FBI defines the source of coercion as a group or individual based and operating entirely within the United States, or its territories, without foreign direction (18 USC § 2331(5)). These legal definitions revolve around terrorism as coercion—as a violent means to a political end.

Another incident unrelated to terrorism provides comparative insight into the nature of terrorism. On the morning of February 21, 2003, an oil tanker exploded while unloading at a Staten Island oil depot. The blast killed two mariners and critically injured a third. News of the explosion sent prices on the New York Stock Exchange sharply lower on the assumption that a major terrorist incident had occurred. When details emerged in subsequent hours that revealed the explosion to have occurred accidentally, however, the stock market quickly recovered. The public anxiety and relief exhibited in the drop and recovery of trading on the stock exchange highlight two features of terrorism not otherwise covered by the legal definitions, and which to some extent reveal terrorism to be more about the intention than the violence behind the act. What the accident shared with terrorist acts was its dramatic impact. By virtue of its accidental nature, however, the explosion lacked the premeditated intent to do harm that marks terrorist attacks. The publicity and motivation associated with terrorism contribute to the anxiety a population can experience from an attack and also help to identify terrorism as an act of propaganda by which extremists bring notoriety to their causes.

In his September 20, 2001, Address to a Joint Session of Congress and the American People, President Bush assured his audience that in the present conflict with terrorism, violence would be met with "patient justice." The struggle against terrorism—especially that currently waged against al-Qa'ida—is one of endurance, and it is one in which the FBI is prepared to engage with unflagging persistence. Although the preeminent mission of protecting the United States from terrorist attack is changing the character of the FBI as a whole, an abiding strength of the FBI remains its tradition of excellence in vigorously investigating and prosecuting criminal acts. These traditional pursuits are essential to the disruption of terrorist activities, the dismantling of terrorist organizations, and, consequently, the prevention of future terrorist attacks. By combining a willingness to innovate with its traditional law enforcement responsibilities, the FBI continues to evolve in order to counter the varied forms of terrorism that threaten the interests and security of the United States.

Countering Domestic Terror (1908–1982)

Terrorism Trends

There are five traditional means by which the U.S. government fights terrorism: diplomacy, economic sanctions, military options, covert intelligence operations, and law enforcement action. The last two of these engage the resources of the FBI. Throughout its history, the FBI has directed the emphasis of its resources toward the most pressing national security and criminal activities affecting the country. Founded in 1908, the Bureau inherited subversive domestic political threats, including anarchism and communism, as concerns. Following the U.S. entry into World War I, the Bureau became the principle counterintelligence agency in the United States and, following the war, the investigation of a series of domestic terrorist bombings were the focus of its activities. These activities were eventually eclipsed by the property and violent crimes of the 1920s and early 1930s gangster era. World War II and the subsequent Cold War greatly increased the FBI's role in international affairs and counterintelligence. The Civil Rights Movement and the Vietnam War of the 1960s and early 1970s provoked criminal responses both from reactionary groups, such as the Ku Klux Klan, and antiwar extremists, such as the Weather Underground, respectively. Following strong criticism of FBI domestic security efforts by Congress in the mid-1970s, the Bureau's focus on domestic subversion gave way to new emphasis on organized crime and other criminal matters in the late 1970s and early 1980s.

Prior to the early 1980s, the FBI's terrorism-related investigations were dominated by domestic concerns. During the period from 1908 to 1982, the FBI dealt with two broad categories of domestic terrorism: right- and left-wing extremist groups. In the period between World War I and World War II, the domestic threat primarily came from right-wing groups, like the Ku Klux Klan, which often adhered to principles of racial supremacy or embraced antigovernment and antiregulatory beliefs in favor of individual freedoms. The FBI had little jurisdiction over these groups. In one case, the Bureau successfully developed a case against a ranking Klan official based on his violation of a law against interstate prostitution; there were no significant federal laws that forbade the Klan's terrorist activities at that time. The passage of significant civil rights legislation in the 1960s enabled the FBI to more effectively target the Klan and support successful prosecutions of Klan members for terrorist crimes.

Beginning in the 1950s, the most serious domestic terrorist threat shifted to leftist-oriented extremist groups that generally professed a revolutionary socialist doctrine and viewed themselves as protectors of the people against the adverse effects of capitalism and U.S. foreign policies. Some of the more sensational terrorist events during this latter period included the November 1, 1950, attempted assassination of President Truman at Blair House by two members of the National Party of Puerto Rico. On March 1, 1954, members of the same group opened fire on a session of the U.S. House of Representatives, injuring five congressmen. The 1958 commandeering of a Cuban airliner in flight from Miami inaugurated a decade of hijackings by Cuban revolutionaries.

During the 1970s and 1980s, Croatian nationalists and the anti-Castro Cuban group Omega 7 arose as prominent terrorist threats. Leftist groups, however, continued to remain active during these decades and committed numerous bombings, including the prominent March 1, 1971, bombing of the U.S. Senate building and the January 29, 1975, bombing of the U.S. State Department building, both attributed to the Weather Underground, and the January 24, 1975, bombing of Fraunces Tavern on Wall Street by the Armed Forces for Puerto Rican National Liberation (FALN) that resulted in four deaths and 53 people injured. The threat from leftist groups receded by the late 1980s as law enforcement dismantled their infrastructures. The dissolution of the communist Soviet Union in December 1991 into the democratic Russian Federation with a free market economy further deprived many of these groups of their ideological foundation and patronage.

Legislative Action

In this earliest period of FBI counterterrorism responses, there were few strong legislative tools available to handle the terrorist threats facing the United States. The 1917 Espionage Act and 1918 Sabotage Act addressed domestic subversion during wartime, but had no significant peacetime extension. Alien anarchists were apprehended and removed under various immigration statutes. National Security Action Memorandum 177, signed by President Kennedy on August 7, 1962, enhanced the U.S. government's foreign police training program, which has come to include counterterrorism measures. The Organized Crime Control Act of 1970 bears upon terrorism issues as they relate to the importation, manufacture, distribution, and storage of explosive materials (18 USC §§ 842-844). The Antihijacking Act of 1974 is noteworthy because it was the first law to specifically address an issue intimately connected to terrorism. And on April 10, 1982, President Reagan signed National Security Directive 30 (NSD 30), which gave lead agency counterterrorism responsibilities and crisis management in terrorist attacks to the FBI under the U.S. Department of Justice.

FBI Initiatives

In the decades leading up to the 1980s, the FBI had not yet begun to structure its resources in terrorism-specific terms. Following two significant anarchist bombing attacks in the spring of 1919, the U.S. Department of Justice established a General Intelligence Division, headed by J. Edgar Hoover, to gather and analyze intelligence concerning communist, anarchist, and other radical threats in the United States. In 1920, the General Intelligence Division was incorporated into what was then known as the Bureau of Investigation. Hoover continued to head the division and was appointed the Bureau's Assistant Director under Director William Burns (1922–24), a position he held until his own appointment as Director, a position he held from 1924 to 1972. Discontinued at that time, the division was re-established in 1935 to monitor communist and fascist activities.

The General Intelligence Division went through several name changes during the 1940s and 1950s—the National Defense Division in 1940, the Security Division in 1942, and the Domestic Security Division in 1951—that tended to reflect the FBI's responsibilities for domestic security. Until 1973, this division oversaw the FBI's responsibilities for domestic security, counterintelligence, and counterterrorism. In 1973, in response to criticism of FBI programs to disrupt radical groups, the Domestic Security Division was split into a General Investigative Division and an Intelligence Division. In 1977 the newly created Criminal Investigative Division assumed domestic terrorism responsibilities on the principle that investigations into domestic radical groups were predicated upon criminal activity. In 1982, in response to NSD 30, Director William H. Webster (1978–87) named counterterrorism an FBI priority program.[1] The responsibilities for counter-terrorism continued to reside in the Criminal Investigative Division, which developed a Terrorism Section comprised of a domestic unit and several international counterterrorism units.

Like the early acts of legislation that have since served as the foundation for terrorism-related amendments, the FBI initiated several programs over this period that have come to play significant roles in its evolving counterterrorism efforts. One innovation during this early period was the deployment of forensic specialists to the site of an investigation. The first incarnation of this rapid deployment capability was the Disaster Squad established on June 24, 1940, to assist civilian authorities in identifying persons killed in a Virginia plane crash. Since then, these deployment capabilities have expanded to other areas of FBI operations including the Hostage Rescue Team, the Rapid Deployment Teams, and the Fly Team,

[1] The designation of "Priority Programs" began under the management reform initiated by Director Clarence M. Kelley (1973–78) to focus FBI resources on the most pressing matters. At the time, these included white collar crime, organized crime, and foreign counterintelligence. Counterterrorism became a Priority Program in 1982.

which support counterterrorism operations, as well as the Laboratory Division's Evidence Response Teams and Hazardous Materials Response Teams, which support forensic investigations.

In the middle of the 20th century, the FBI also laid the foundations for coordinating investigations and sharing information with international law enforcement and intelligence partners when it established its Legal Attache, or "Legat" program. The origins of the Legat program lie in the FBI's early intelligence responsibilities. On June 24, 1940, prior to the United States' involvement in World War II, President Roosevelt issued a directive for the FBI to assume responsibility for countering Axis movements in the Western Hemisphere and gathering intelligence about other developments in that sphere of responsibility. In response, Director Hoover created the Special Intelligence Service (SIS) within the FBI. The effort was successful both in gathering intelligence and countering Axis intelligence activities. In 1946, President Truman terminated the SIS and reassigned its duties to the newly created Central Intelligence Group, later renamed the Central Intelligence Agency, as part of his centralization of foreign intelligence collection. The FBI, however, was allowed to maintain a number of its liaison offices in order to communicate with foreign police and intelligence services. By January 1953, FBI Legats operated in U.S. embassies in London, Paris, Madrid, Havana, Mexico City, and Rio de Janeiro. The number of Legat offices has continued to grow in recognition of their valued assistance in tracking terrorist threats and bringing investigative resources swiftly to bear on terrorist and other incidents overseas.

Cooperation among law enforcement and intelligence agencies is now widely recognized as essential to a comprehensive plan to prevent and respond to terrorism. Internationally, in order to create a corps of advocates for best law enforcement practices worldwide, in 1935 the Bureau began training law enforcement officers from foreign countries at its National Academy in Quantico, Virginia. Domestically, the FBI operationally cooperates with other law enforcement agencies in part through Joint Terrorism Task Forces (JTTFs), whose strength lies in combining the national and international investigative resources of the FBI with the street-level expertise of state and local law enforcement agencies. The first JTTF was formed in New York City in 1980 in response to domestic terrorism threats posed by such organizations as the Puerto Rican separatist group FALN and the anti-Castro Cuban group Omega 7.

The Emergence of International Terrorism (1983–1992)

Terrorism Trends

For the decade from 1983–1992, major acts of terrorism against U.S. interests took place overseas. The FBI recognized state-sponsored and autonomous terrorist organizations as the two significant sources of international terrorism. Both types of organizations remain threats today.

State-sponsored terrorism refers to those countries that violate international law by using terrorism as a tool of foreign policy.[2] One of the most infamous acts of state-sponsored terrorism during this period occurred on December 21, 1988, with the bombing of Pan Am flight 103 in mid-air over Lockerbie, Scotland. The bombing killed all 259 people aboard the Boeing 747 aircraft and 11 people on the ground. In November 1991, following an extensive investigation by the FBI and other U.S. and foreign police authorities, a U.S. grand jury indicted two Libyan intelligence officers for the crime. The two were tried in the Netherlands under Scottish law. On January 31, 2001, the court acquitted one of the officers due to insufficient evidence, but convicted the other officer, Abdel Basset Ali al-Megrahi, of murder and issued him a mandatory life sentence. In August 2003 the Government of Libya agreed to pay $2.7 billion in restitution to the families of the victims.

Foreign terrorist organizations (FTOs) are autonomous, generally transnational groups that maintain their own personnel, infrastructures, financial arrangements, and training facilities. FTOs are often formed to pursue nationalistic agendas that can span the political spectrum, and their operational capabilities range from organizations with extremely limited resources and memberships of fewer than 100, to others with thousands of supporters and substantial sources of aid. FTOs committed two major bombings in 1983 and a series of prominent hijackings in the decade that followed, drawing legislative and law enforcement attention to international terrorism. On April 18, 1983, members of Lebanese Hizballah bombed the U.S. Embassy in Beirut, Lebanon. The attack resulted in 63 deaths, including those of 17 U.S. citizens. Six months later, on October 23, Hizballah bombed the U.S. Marine barracks in Beirut. The blast killed 301, of whom 241 were U.S. Marines. Hijackings during the 1980s, most notably committed by Hizballah[3] and the Abu Nidal Organization in the Middle East and South Asia, targeted U.S. airliners, or American citizens on foreign carriers, and frequently resulted in extended hostage situations and civilian fatalities.

Although international terrorism against U.S. interests took place overseas during this period, the FBI began investigations into the use of the United States as a staging area or source of arms for terrorist operations and activities overseas. An example of this is the 1990 conviction in Boston court of two U.S. citizens and a citizen of the Republic of Ireland of conspiracy to violate the Arms Export Control Act and of conspiracy to injure and destroy

[2] At the end of 2005, the U.S. Department of State designated six nations—Cuba, Iran, Libya, North Korea, Sudan, and Syria—as state sponsors of terrorism. The U.S. Department of State formally removed Iraq from the list of state sponsors of terrorism on October 20, 2004.

[3] Since its founding in 1982, Hizballah's numerous anti-U.S. attacks overseas made it responsible for the deaths of more Americans than any other terrorist group in the world prior to September 11, 2001.

foreign property. Until their arrest in 1989, these individuals had engaged in the research and development of an anti-helicopter missile system for use by the Provisional Irish Republican Army in its attacks against British targets in Northern Ireland and elsewhere.

Legislative Action

In the mid-1980s Congress passed several legislative initiatives that expanded the FBI's jurisdiction to include U.S. interests overseas. The Comprehensive Crime Control Act of 1984 gave the FBI jurisdiction to pursue terrorists who have taken Americans hostage, regardless of where the incident occurred. Also in 1984, the Act to Combat International Terrorism established the Rewards for Justice Program, authorizing the Secretary of State to issue rewards of up to $5 million for information that prevents or favorably resolves acts of international terrorism against U.S. persons or property worldwide. The Omnibus Diplomatic Security and Antiterrorism Act of August 27, 1986, expanded the FBI's jurisdiction to include homicide or violence against U.S. citizens abroad. The Biological Weapons Anti-Terrorism Act of 1989 granted federal jurisdiction with respect to developing, transferring, and possessing biological weapons.

FBI Initiatives

The FBI's international responsibilities had been increasing in the decades leading up to the 1980s as drug trafficking, organized crime, and terrorism investigations frequently crossed national boundaries. With respect to international liaison activities, in 1983 Congress authorized the U.S. Department of State's Antiterrorism Assistance Program as part of a major initiative against international terrorism. As part of this program the FBI began to provide counterterrorism training to law enforcement and security personnel of selected friendly foreign governments at the FBI Academy at Quantico. This training served both to strengthen bilateral ties and to increase respect for human rights by sharing with civilian authorities modern, humane, and effective counterterrorism techniques.

Another significant development within the Bureau resulted from an incident during the 1972 Summer Olympic Games held in Munich, Germany, in which Palestinian gunmen associated with the terrorist group Black September took 11 Israeli athletes hostage in the Olympic Village. The gunmen killed their captives in the rescue attempt that followed. This incident led the FBI to anticipate the possibility of a similar international act of terrorism during the 1984 Summer Olympics to be held in Los Angeles. In 1983 the FBI began training its Hostage Rescue Team (HRT), which was in operation by the start of the games. Based at the FBI Academy at Quantico, the HRT has the mission of responding within four hours of notification by the Director or his designate to any extraordinary hostage crisis occurring within the United States.

Since its inception, the HRT has been deployed in support of FBI terrorism, violent criminal, foreign counterintelligence, and other investigations.

Recognizing the importance of warning as a component in the FBI's efforts to prevent acts of terrorism, on October 13, 1989, the FBI established the Terrorist Threat Warning System (TTWS) for the dissemination of terrorist threat information to the U.S. Intelligence Community[4] and state and local law enforcement agencies.[5]

The Globalization Of Terrorism (1993–2001)

Terrorism Trends

Until the 1990s, terrorist targets had historically been selected for reasons of their vulnerability and symbolism. Indiscrimination generally remained an unintended consequence of terrorist attacks. During the 1990s, however, the nature of domestic and international terrorism underwent recognizable changes in tactics and methodologies as terrorists aimed to inflict massive and indiscriminate casualties upon civilian populations. The terrorist trend toward higher levels of casualties came at a time when interest was growing among domestic and international extremists in weapons of mass destruction (WMD). The movement toward acquiring and using WMD became a reality on March 20, 1995, when the Japanese group Aum Shinrikyo launched a series of sarin nerve gas attacks in Tokyo's subway system. The incidents resulted in 12 deaths and approximately 5,000 exposures. The FBI provided investigative assistance to Japanese law enforcement and intelligence agencies in response to the incident. These attacks suggested the wide range of weapons available to contemporary terrorists and raised the specter of a similar attack in the United States.

Another trend during this period altered the paradigm that only international terrorists operating outside of the United States committed major acts of terrorism. With respect to domestic terrorism, left-wing political groups and *special interest terrorism*—that is, terrorism committed by extremists who use violence to compel society to change its attitudes about specific causes—asserted themselves during the 1990s. Anarchists reemerged in the United States during this period and caused much of the criminal disruption during the 1999 World Trade Organization meeting in Seattle. The majority of domestic terrorism incidents from 1993 to 2001 were attributable to the left-wing special interest movements the Animal Liberation Front (ALF) and the Earth Liberation Front (ELF). Right-wing extremism,

---

4 The "U.S. Intelligence Community" refers to those Executive Branch organizations engaged in U.S. national intelligence efforts. The Community includes the Central Intelligence Agency, National Security Agency, Defense Intelligence Agency, intelligence elements of the departments of Defense, State, Treasury, Energy, Homeland Security, and the FBI (CIA, *Factbook on Intelligence*, 2006).

5 On January 4, 1999, the FBI integrated the TTWS into the National Threat Warning System (NTWS).

however, primarily in the form of domestic militias and conservative special interest causes, began to overtake left-wing extremism as the most dangerous, if not the most prolific, domestic terrorist threat to the country during the 1990s. In contrast to the ALF and the ELF, which have pursued a philosophy that avoids physical violence in favor of acts of property damage that cause their victims economic harm, right-wing extremists pursued a qualitatively different method of operation by targeting people.

The April 19, 1995, bombing of the Alfred P. Murrah Federal Building in Oklahoma City, Oklahoma, brought the threat of right-wing terrorism to the forefront of American law enforcement attention. The Oklahoma City bombing, which killed 168 people and injured 642 others, was an extreme manifestation of a grass-roots antigovernment movement that became prominent during the 1990s. Several factors fueled the growth of this movement, including the passage of gun control legislation, fears of increased United Nations involvement in domestic affairs, and several confrontations between members of right-wing groups and law enforcement officers at Waco, Texas, and Ruby Ridge, Idaho. These confrontations inspired Timothy McVeigh and Terry Nichols to carry out the Oklahoma City bombing, which coincided with the second anniversary of the destruction of the Branch Davidian compound near Waco. The FBI aggressively pursued the prosecutions of McVeigh and Nichols, and the two were eventually convicted for their roles in the bombing. McVeigh was executed on June 11, 2001, marking the first federal execution in 38 years.

The motivations behind another series of bombings in the mid-1990s illustrate the increasing prominence of terrorism in support of conservative special interest causes during this decade. On July 27, 1996, an explosion in Olympic Centennial Park killed two and injured 112 during the closing days of the Summer Olympics held in Atlanta, Georgia. Early the next year, two more bombings occurred: the first, on January 16, 1997, at a Birmingham, Alabama, health clinic; the second, on February 21, 1997, at the Otherside Lounge, a nightclub patronized by Atlanta's gay community. These latter bombings were distinctive in that the terrorist used secondary explosive devices with an apparent intent to target emergency responders. On May 31, 2003, Top Ten Fugitive Eric Robert Rudolph was arrested in North Carolina on suspicion of having committed the bombings; Rudolph pled guilty to these attacks and received a life sentence for his crimes.

The bombings in Oklahoma City, Atlanta, and Birmingham also brought an awareness of a new type of threat from those who may be sympathetic to extreme political or social ideologies, but who commit acts of violence outside of the auspices of structured terrorist organizations or without the prior approval or knowledge of these groups' leaders. The roles of McVeigh and Nichols in the Oklahoma City bombing, and the bombings by Rudolph, exemplify the FBI's "lone offender" category of terrorist for those who engage in terrorist activities free from organizational guidance.

With respect to international terrorism, terrorist organizations, sometimes with state sponsorship, continued to attack U.S. military targets overseas. A November 13, 1995, truck bomb killed seven people, including five Americans, and injured at least 34 U.S. citizens at the Office of the Program Manager/Saudi Arabian National Guard building in Riyadh, Saudi Arabia. Seven months later, on June 25, 1996, members of Saudi Hizballah bombed the Khobar Towers in Dhahran, Saudi Arabia, where Western military personnel resided. The explosion killed 19 U.S. service personnel and injured over 350 others. These bombings highlighted force protection issues, to which the U.S. government responded by "hardening" its official establishments overseas.

During the 1990s, the U.S. Intelligence Community began to recognize a trend in international terrorism away from state sponsors of terrorism and FTOs to those of loosely affiliated extremists, whose ad hoc, autonomous nature tended to shield them from infiltration and disruption. This new aspect of international terrorism first presented itself in the February 26, 1993, bombing of New York City's World Trade Center. The blast killed six people, injured more than 1,000, and caused millions of dollars in damage. In a subsequent plot based out of the Philippines, the New York bombing's operational mastermind, Ramzi Ahmed Yousef, along with two co-conspirators, planned to destroy simultaneously as many as 12 American jumbo jets in flight over the Pacific. Yousef conducted a trial run of the "Manila Air" plot on December 11, 1994, when a test explosive killed a Japanese businessman on board a Philippine airliner in flight to Tokyo. A few months later, on February 7, 1995, Yousef was apprehended in Islamabad, Pakistan, by Pakistani officials who were working with FBI assistance and rendered back to the United States. In January 1998, Yousef was sentenced to 240 years plus a life sentence in prison for his roles in the 1993 World Trade Center bombing and the "Manila Air" plot.

By the late 1990s, the interwoven violence and self-perpetuating nature of terrorism, in which a terrorist act in one location can elicit a sympathetic response elsewhere, regardless of national boundaries, became apparent. An example of the web of terrorism can be seen in the events involving Shayk Omar Abdel Rahman, the spiritual leader of Egypt's Al-Gama'a al-Islamiyya (AGAI) militant group. Investigation into the World Trade Center bombing uncovered unrelated plotting by Shayk Rahman and his followers to bomb landmarks throughout New York City in the summer of 1993 and to assassinate Egyptian President Hosni Mubarak during a visit to New York in 1994. In January 1996 Shayk Rahman and nine co-conspirators were convicted of the plots, and Shayk Rahman himself received a life sentence plus 55 years. On November 17, 1997, six AGAI members killed 58 foreign tourists at the Temple of Hatshepsut near Luxor, Egypt. Although no Americans were among the victims, the attack was intended to apply pressure on the United States to release Shayk Rahman from incarceration. The web-like nature of terrorism underscores the need for vigilance and international cooperation in countering terrorist groups. While the serial plotting of Shayk Rahman highlights the importance of relentlessly pursuing the arrest and prosecution of individual terrorists in order to prevent them from perpetrating future acts, the related attack near Luxor underscores the importance of a cooperative international effort to control terrorism.

As a result of the plots by Ramzi Yousef and Shayk Rahman, the FBI began to focus investigative attention on the then-emerging phenomenon of Sunni extremism and its operational manifestation in loosely affiliated groups devoted to violent international jihad. The international jihad movement, which interprets jihad ("struggle") in militant terms, is composed of individuals of varying nationalities, ethnicities, and terrorist group affiliations. These individuals find common purpose in seeking to establish states ruled by *sharia* (conservative Islamic) law and free of Western influence. As precedent, Afghanistan's resistance to the Soviet invasion of 1979 attracted foreign fighters, who viewed their participation in the regional conflict as a defense both of their Muslim brethren and of Islam. The Soviet Union's eventual withdrawal from Afghanistan in 1989 led to the establishment of Afghanistan's Taliban regime and inspired former Arab-Afghan *mujahidin* ("holy warriors") to focus their zeal upon other international conflicts that involved Muslim populations. This globalization of violent jihad contributed to the globalization of terrorist groups, which recruited *mujahidin* to engage in militant struggle with operations that transcended national boundaries.

Influenced by radical leaders such as Usama Bin Ladin, former Arab-Afghan *mujahidin* integrated into the international terrorist infrastructure known as al-Qa'ida ("the Root"). In the early 1990s the al-Qa'ida network began issuing *fatwahs* (religious opinions based upon Islamic law) to its members and associates calling for the deposition of the Saudi monarchy and the forced removal of U.S. and other Western forces from the Arabian Peninsula. Bin Ladin first stated his declaration of war against the United States in a twelve-page *banyan* ("statement") issued on August 22, 1996, in which he offered a "final warning" for all American troops to leave the land of the "Two Holy Places" (Mecca and Medina in Saudi Arabia) or else face military action by the same people who drove the Soviets out of Afghanistan. Bin Ladin's rhetoric since then, including a 1998 statement urging Muslims to "kill the Americans and their allies-civilians and military," revealed a steady shift toward greater indiscrimination in al-Qa'ida's targeting.

With the exception of the 1995 Oklahoma City bombing, the major terrorist acts or attempts against U.S. interests leading into the 21st century stemmed from militant Islamic jihad, guided directly or indirectly by al-Qa'ida. These include the following:

- On August 7, 1998, al-Qa'ida operatives carried out near-simultaneous bombings of the U.S. embassies in Nairobi, Kenya, and Dar es Salaam, Tanzania. These attacks, which took place against targets considered "soft" and in low-threat countries, resulted in 224 deaths and 5,722 injuries. The small number of Americans among the casualties (12 dead and seven wounded) highlighted the indiscriminate nature of, and collateral damage inflicted by, large-scale terrorist attacks even when directed against specific targets.
- On December 14, 1999, U.S. border guards at Port Angeles, Washington, arrested Ahmed Ressam as he attempted to smuggle explosives into the United States from Canada. Investigation by the FBI and other domestic and foreign law enforcement agencies revealed that Ressam had attended al-Qa'ida training camps in Afghanistan and was part of an Algerian terrorist cell based in Canada that had plotted to detonate explosives at Los Angeles International Airport.
- On October 12, 2000, in the port of Aden, Yemen, pilots of a bomb-laden boat pulled alongside the *USS Cole* at midship and detonated their explo sives in a suicide attack against the destroyer, killing 17 and injuring at least 40 crew members. Investigation revealed that the incident followed an unsuccessful attack on January 3, 2000, against the *USS The Sullivans*. The alleged conspirators in the *Sullivans* and *Cole* attacks were al-Qa'ida opera tives who trained in its terrorist camps in Afghanistan during the 1990s. The *Cole* bombing highlighted al-Qa'ida's resolve and revealed the network's resourcefulness and ingenuity in developing asymmetrical tactics to strike a more powerful and technologically more advanced target.

Legislative Action

Motivated by the World Trade Center and Oklahoma City bombings, the U.S. government took a number of executive and legislative steps that directed the focus of future law enforcement activity to include prevention before an incident, as well as the apprehension and conviction of those responsible after an incident has occurred.

On June 21, 1995, President Clinton issued Presidential Decision Directive 39 (PDD 39), which clarified the FBI's designation as the lead U.S. government agency for dealing with terrorism against Americans in the United States and overseas. On April 24, 1996, the U.S. government passed the Anti-Terrorism and Effective Death Penalty Act (AEDPA), which addressed domestic terrorism by increasing the protection afforded to federal workers and expanding criminal statutes relating to explosives. The AEDPA's most significant contributions, however, concerned the expansion of the FBI's investigative authority into international acts of terrorism and the activities of international terrorist groups as they occurred within the United States. These contributions included provisions addressing the prevention of entry into and deportation of alien terrorists from the United States and the prosecution of those who provide material support to a designated terrorist organization.

In a reflection of the changing dynamics of terrorism, the U.S. government responded legislatively and administratively to the WMD threat. In 1996 the passage of the Defense Against Weapons of Mass Destruction Act—also known as the Nunn-Lugar-Domenici Program after the three senators who sponsored the legislation—established first-responder training. On May 28, 1998, President Clinton issued Presidential Decision Directives 62 and 63 (PDDs 62 and 63). PDD 62 established guidelines for FBI-led interagency cooperation in the detection, prevention, and consequence management of terrorist incidents involving WMD. PDD 63 set objectives for protecting the nation's infrastructure from attack. On October 16, 1998, Congress established the interagency National Domestic Preparedness Office at FBI Headquarters to coordinate federal assistance programs and to streamline the process of delivering that assistance to state and local communities in the event of a catastrophic terrorist attack.

FBI Initiatives

During the 1990s, the FBI's counterterrorism program underwent several organizational transformations that led to the eventual creation of a Counterterrorism Division within the Bureau. On March 18, 1994, the Intelligence Division was renamed the National Security Division, retaining foreign counterintelligence responsibilities and taking over the Criminal Investigative Division's domestic and international terrorism responsibilities. In 1998, the FBI established a strategic plan that set flexible investigative priorities within a three-tiered structure: Tier 1 for criminal and intelligence matters—including terrorism—that threatened national or economic security; Tier 2 for offenses that involved criminal enterprises, public corruption, and violations of civil rights; and Tier 3 for violations that affected individual property. The priority given to counterterrorism was reflected in FBI Director Louis J. Freeh's (1993–2001) October 29, 1999, transfer of the National Security Division's counterterrorism components into two new complementary divisions—the Counterterrorism Division and the Investigative Services Division—that took responsibility for most of the old division's operational and analytical functions, respectively.

The FBI's liaison activities also evolved during this period. Domestically, the New York JTTF took part in several high-profile terrorism-related investigations in the mid-1990s. Its proven value led to the expansion of the JTTF program to other field offices and spurred an increase in the participation of federal, state, and local member agencies in the task forces. In 1996, JTTFs received executive endorsement when President Clinton issued PDD 39 authorizing the Bureau to provide a coordinated law enforcement effort. PDDs 62 and 63 led to the establishment of the multi-agency Domestic Emergency Support Team (DEST), coordinated by the FBI and deployed by the FBI Director.[6] On November 20, 1998, a technologically upgraded Strategic Information and Operations Center (SIOC) opened at FBI Headquarters to manage and monitor major events and crises, including those requiring a counterterrorism response.[7]

The bombings of the World Trade Center, the Khobar Towers, and the East African embassies made clear the importance of international cooperation in investigations of international acts of terrorism. As part of its cooperative efforts with international law enforcement, Director Freeh expanded the number of Legat offices to 42 by the spring of 2001. The FBI also took lead-agency responsibility for establishing the International Law Enforcement Academy (ILEA) to provide professional law enforcement education to foreign nationals overseas including counterterrorism components; the first ILEA opened in 1994 in Budapest, Hungary.

Until the last decade of the 20th century, criminal threats within the United States set a domestic agenda for the FBI. The East African embassy bombings, however, elevated al-Qa'ida to the highest priority of FBI counterterrorism. On November 4, 1998, Usama Bin Ladin was indicted for his role in the embassy bombings, and the U.S. Department of State issued an unprecedented $5 million reward for his apprehension.[8] In April 1999 the FBI placed Bin Ladin on its Ten Most Wanted Fugitives List, and in the same year established a dedicated Bin Ladin Unit at FBI Headquarters.

In 1998, the FBI formalized its ability to respond to international terrorist incidents by creating Rapid Deployment Teams (RDTs), which swiftly bring investigative personnel and resources to attack sites where an FBI presence

6 The FBI also participates in the Foreign Emergency Support Team (FEST) coordinated by the U.S. Department of State.

7 SIOC was originally conceived in 1987 in response to prison riots at Oakdale, Louisiana, and Atlanta, Georgia. These concurrent incidents suggested the need to provide integrated support to FBI field offices in major crises. SIOC first became operational under the aegis of the Criminal Investigative Division on January 20, 1989, in time for the inauguration of the elder President Bush. In subsequent years, management of SIOC transferred to the Investigative Services Division and the Critical Incident Response Group before being integrated into the Counterterrorism Division in April 2003.

8 Four al-Qa'ida members have received life sentences for conspiring to kill Americans in the East African embassy bombings. Two other suspects await trial, and 16 others, including Usama Bin Ladin, stand indicted.

is otherwise wanting or in need of augmentation. These teams are capable of organizing and establishing field command posts, forensically exploring crime scenes, and conducting criminal investigations. By March 28, 2001, the FBI had established five RDTs in four of its major field offices.

"Cyberterrorism," or the use of cyber tools to shut down critical national infrastructures for the purpose of coercing or intimidating a government or civilian population, emerged as a threat at the end of the last century. While terrorist groups have not yet employed cyber tools as a weapon against critical U.S. infrastructures, their acquisition of computer expertise and reliance on information technology to formulate plans, raise funds, spread propaganda, and engage in secure communications represent clear warning signs. In 1996 the FBI established the Computer Investigation and Infrastructure Threat Center (CIITC) at FBI Headquarters. On February 26, 1998, President Clinton expanded CIITC into the multi-agency National Infrastructure Protection Center (NIPC), to serve as the focal point for the government's effort to warn of and respond to domestic and international cyber intrusions.[9]

The "War on Terrorism" (September 11, 2001 -Present)

Terrorism Trends

Beginning in the late 1950s the most serious terrorist threat to U.S. civil aviation came in the form of hijackings of commercial aircraft. In these incidents, the aircraft provided hijackers both transportation to diverted destinations and a ready supply of hostages for leverage in their negotiations with government authorities. By the late 1980s—as seen in the 1988 bombing of Pan Am flight 103 over Lockerbie, Scotland, and in the prevented "Manila Air" plot of 1994—the threat to civil aviation began to include the targeting of commercial aircraft and their passengers and crews for destruction.

On the morning of September 11, 2001, al-Qa'ida directed its ruthless ingenuity toward the further exploitation of civil aviation when 19 of its operatives hijacked four U.S. commercial airliners for use as suicide weapons against selected political, military, and economic targets on the U.S. East Coast. The hijackers used knives, boxcutters, and possibly pepper spray to commandeer the aircraft. Three of the aircraft struck their targets, destroying the Twin Towers of the World Trade Center in New York City and badly damaging the Pentagon in Arlington, Virginia. The fourth aircraft crashed into a remote field in Stonycreek Township, Pennsylvania, as passengers

[9] NIPC now operates under the aegis of the Department of Homeland Security. In December 2001, Director Robert S. Mueller III approved creation of the FBI's Cyber Division to address cyber investigations formerly addressed by the Counterterrorism and Criminal Investigative Divisions.

attempted to regain control of the airplane. All of the passengers on each of the aircraft were killed in the attack, as were more than 2,500 people in the Twin Towers and the Pentagon. In total, 2,972 people died in the September 11 attack, making it the most deadly act of terrorism ever committed.[10] The September 11 attack also marked the first known suicide terrorist attack carried out in the United States since the FBI began keeping terrorist records.

The threat of terrorism is expected to continue from both international and domestic sources. Internationally, at least two operational trends are evident in the militant Islamic jihad movement. First is a preference for high-casualty, high-profile attacks directed against lower-risk, unofficial, so-called "soft" targets, as traditional military and diplomatic targets become increasingly hardened. Second, the dissolution of much of al-Qa'ida's structure by international military and law enforcement efforts has resulted in the dispersal of its multinational trainees to pursue their own regional agendas. The following terrorist incidents from September 11, 2001, through 2005 may involve both trends:

- On October 12, 2002, a nightclub bombing on the Indonesian island of Bali killed approximately 200 people, including seven Americans, and on August 5, 2003, a bombing of the JW Marriott Hotel in Jakarta, Indonesia, resulted in 15 deaths. Both of these bombings have been attributed to members of the Jemaah Islamiyya terrorist organization, a Southeast Asian-based terrorist network with links to al-Qa'ida.
- On May 12 and November 9, 2003, al-Qa'ida operatives conducted bombings of residential compounds that housed Western workers in Riyadh, Saudi Arabia. The first incident claimed dozens of lives and injured nearly 200 others. The second resulted in 18 deaths and over 120 injuries.
- On May 16, 2003, five nearly simultaneous explosions in Casablanca, Morocco, killed 41 people and injured approximately 100 others. Although no definitive evidence links al-Qa'ida to the bombings in Casablanca, the Sunni extremist group responsible for this attack may have al-Qa'ida ties.
- On March 11, 2004, a series of 10 bombs detonated on four commuter trains in Madrid, Spain. The near simultaneous explosions killed 191 people and injured more than 1,400 others. Spanish police have traced responsibility for the attack to Moroccan Islamic militants with ties to al-Qa'ida.

[10] This number does not include the 19 hijackers, all of whom died in the attack.

- On July 7, 2005, four coordinated bomb blasts struck London's public transit system during the morning rush hour. Fifty-two people were killed and approximately 700 injured in the attack, including the death of one American and the wounding of four others. The London bombing was distinctive in having involved "homegrown" jihadist terrorists operating in a Western, predominantly non-Muslim country.

The use of WMD against civilian targets represents the most serious potential international and domestic terrorism threat facing the United States today and provides a glimpse into emerging terrorist scenarios of the 21st century. A variety of intelligence reporting indicates that al-Qa'ida has energetically sought to acquire and experiment with biological, chemical, and radiological weapons of mass destruction. The January 2003 arrests in the United Kingdom of Algerian extremists suspected of producing the biological toxin ricin exemplifies the interest some Islamic militants have in the operational use of such agents. In April 2004, Jordanian authorities disrupted a plot by Islamic extremists to generate a cloud of cyanide gas in Amman.

Ricin and the bacterial agent anthrax are emerging as the most prevalent agents involved in WMD investigations. Prior to the fall of 2001, there had been no criminal cases involving the actual use of anthrax in the United States. In September and October of that year, however, several anthrax-tainted letters were received in Florida, New York, New Jersey, Connecticut, and the District of Columbia. The contaminations resulted in five fatalities and 22 infections. On February 2, 2004, in an incident for which no threat was made or threat letter identified, ricin was discovered on the automated mail opening system used in the Washington, D.C., office of U.S. Senate Majority Leader William Frist. Both the anthrax mailings of 2001 and the 2004 ricin incident remain under investigation by the FBI, and their connection to domestic or international terrorism has not been determined.

Legislative Action

In his September 20, 2001, address to a Joint Session of Congress and the American people, President Bush declared a war to disrupt global terrorism, beginning with al-Qa'ida. The war on terrorism has included military action to overthrow Afghanistan's Taliban government and Sadaam Hussein's Baathist regime in Iraq, as well as a multifaceted campaign involving diplomacy, economic sanctions, covert intelligence operations, and law enforcement action. In the weeks immediately following the September 11, 2001, attack, Congress and the President enacted legislation and policies intended to minimize the possibility of another catastrophic act of terrorism from occurring on U.S. soil.

On October 26, 2001, Congress passed the Uniting and Strengthening America by Providing Appropriate Tools Required to Interrupt and Obstruct

Terrorism Act of 2001 (USA PATRIOT Act), which includes changes to national security authorities, criminal and immigration laws, and money-laundering and victim assistance statutes. In making these modifications to existing laws, Congress intended to strengthen the capabilities of federal law enforcement in the fight against terrorism while simultaneously protecting civil liberties. The USA PATRIOT Act improved the processes by which federal law enforcement officials obtain legal authority for conducting surveillance and allowed for greater information sharing between criminal investigators and intelligence collectors. The act modified the definition of terrorism as a federal crime to include several offenses likely to be committed by terrorists, including certain computer crimes and a number of violent crimes involving aircraft. New federal offenses include attacks on mass transportation systems, vehicles, facilities, or passengers; harboring or concealing persons who have committed or are about to commit an act of terrorism; expansion of the prohibition against providing material support or resources to terrorists; and possessing a biological agent or toxin of a type or in a quantity that is not reasonably justified for specifically defined purposes. Additionally, the inclusion of the International Money Laundering Abatement and Financial Anti-Terrorism Act of 2001 into the USA PATRIOT Act significantly increased the United States' ability to combat the financing of terrorism.

On October 29, 2001, President Bush issued Homeland Security Presidential Directive No. 2 (HSPD-2). Among its provisions, HSPD-2 offers federal guidance for keeping foreign terrorists and their supporters out of the United States through entry denial, removal, and prosecution.

On November 27, 2002, Congress and the President created the National Commission on Terrorist Attacks Upon the United States (Public Law 107-306) with a mandate "to investigate 'facts and circumstances relating to the terrorist attacks of September 11, 2001,' including those relating to intelligence agencies, law enforcement agencies, diplomacy, immigration issues and border control, the flow of assets to terrorist organizations, commercial aviation, the role of congressional oversight and resource allocation," and other relevant areas.[11]

On July 22, 2004, the 9/11 Commission published a summary of its investigative findings along with recommendations designed to guard against future attacks. In response to this report, President Bush signed into law on December 8 the Intelligence Reform and Terrorism Prevention Act of 2004 (IRTPA). This act instituted reforms to FISA and modifications to material support statutes for prosecuting terrorists. The IRTPA also created the Office of the Director of National Intelligence and established the Director

[11] National Commission on Terrorist Attacks Upon the United States, *The 9/11 Commission Report* (New York: W.W. Norton & Co., 2004), preface, xv.

of National Intelligence (DNI) as the head of the U.S. Intelligence Community. In addition, the act created the National Counter Proliferation Center to oversee the Intelligence Community's efforts against the proliferation of weapons of mass destruction; the Joint Intelligence Community Council to assist the DNI in establishing a collective national intelligence effort; the Privacy and Civil Liberties Oversight Board within the Executive Office; and instituted the joint-agency National Counterterrorism Center as the primary entity for analyzing intelligence pertaining to transnational terrorism.

FBI Initiatives

Director Robert S. Mueller III (2001-present) took office in the FBI on September 4, 2001, with an agenda to restructure the Bureau and upgrade its technology. Seven days later, the September 11 terrorist attack gave greater urgency to this agenda and focused it on the prevention of future terrorist attacks. On May 29, 2002, Director Mueller formally elevated counterterrorism and the prevention of future terrorist attacks against U.S. interests to the FBI's preeminent mission. In response to this mandate, the FBI moved away from its traditional field-oriented approach to setting priorities and managing cases, to a more centralized national approach in which counterterrorism was the overriding priority in every field office and all international counterterrorism cases were managed centrally by FBI Headquarters. The shift of resources to meet this new priority has resulted in a significant structural reorganization at the FBI that includes a greatly expanded counterterrorism program.

FBI Priorities

Three factors influence the ranking of priorities: the significance of the threat to the security of the United States; the priority the American public places upon the threat; and the degree to which addressing the threat falls most exclusively within the FBI's jurisdiction. In executing the following priorities, the FBI produces and uses intelligence to protect the nation from threats and to bring to justice those who violate the law.

1. Protect the United States from terrorist attack.
2. Protect the United States against foreign intelligence operations and espionage.
3. Protect the United States against cyber-based attacks and high-technology crimes.
4. Combat public corruption at all levels.

5. Protect civil rights.
6. Combat transnational and national criminal organizations and enterprises.
7. Combat major white-collar crime.
8. Combat significant violent crime.
9. Support federal, state, municipal, and international partners.
10. Upgrade technology to successfully perform the FBI's mission.

As the top priority, counterterrorism receives first consideration throughout the Bureau in the allocation of funding, physical space, resources, and the hiring and training of personnel.

The current shape of the Counterterrorism Division reflects the complexity of terrorism as the United States currently faces it, with branches, sections, and units that focus upon domestic terrorism, different global regions of international terrorist activity, and terrorists' methods of operation, finance, and communication. This reorganization supports the Bureau's current strategic mission of preventing terrorist attacks while preserving the civil liberties of all American citizens. This strategic mission also identifies the Bureau's law enforcement and domestic intelligence leadership roles within the U.S. Intelligence Community. In these leadership capacities, the FBI defines the domestic and international terrorism threats to the Homeland, contributes to the Intelligence Community in its evaluation of those threats, and provides investigative and crisis response in the event a terrorist attack does occur. Many of the organizational changes, developments in strategic mission, and the initiatives discussed below anticipated the recommendations made in July 2004, when the 9/11 Commission published its endorsement of the FBI's continuing role in terrorism prevention and urged the Bureau to institutionalize and cultivate its expertise in intelligence and national security.[12]

Focus On Prevention

One of the most effective weapons in the prevention of terrorist attacks involves the gathering, analysis, and dissemination of intelligence and the full integration of that intelligence into investigations, operations, and crisis response. To this end, in December 2001, the FBI merged the counterterrorism analytical activities of the Investigative Services Division into the

[12] National Commission on Terrorist Attacks upon the United States, *The 9/11 Commission Report*, 423-27.

Counterterrorism Division and established the Office of Intelligence to cultivate the division's analytical workforce and develop information-sharing policies. In response to the IRTPA and a subsequent Presidential directive, the FBI redesignated the Office of Intelligence as the Directorate of Intelligence and, in September 2005, incorporated it into the newly created National Security Branch, which oversees all of the Bureau's national intelligence programs, projects, activities, and workforce.

Domestically through its field offices, and internationally through its Legat offices, the FBI has a significant infrastructure in place by which to gather intelligence. Although the FBI has traditionally employed its intelligence analysts in "tactical," or case-specific support capacities, the mandate to prevent acts of terrorism has led the FBI to develop a professional corps of analysts who study broader terrorism trends and assess priority threats at the "strategic," or predictive, level. In 2002, the Counterterrorism Division established an Analytical Branch to develop actionable and strategic intelligence for FBI field offices, the U.S. Intelligence Community, and domestic and international law enforcement partners. In September 2003, the FBI established Field Intelligence Groups in each of its field offices to analyze and direct the collection of information, and ensure its appropriate dissemination.

Focus on Partnerships

The timely two-way flow of information between appropriate federal, state, and local partners is a key element in dismantling terrorist organizations and eliminating threats. Whereas the primary consumer of FBI intelligence used to be its field offices, FBI agents and analysts now regularly communicate with the larger U.S. Intelligence Community and other federal agencies, law enforcement partners at the state and local levels, and private and public sectors of society. At the federal level, a new, multiagency National Joint Terrorism Task Force (NJTTF) was integrated into the Counterterrorism Division at FBI Headquarters in June 2002. Staffed by representatives from more than 40 federal, state, and local agencies, the NJTTF coordinates the flow of information between its participating entities and over 100 JTTFs that were in place nationwide by the end of 2005. In addition, the FBI details agents and analysts to numerous federal agencies, including the CIA, National Security Agency, National Security Council, Defense Intelligence Agency, Department of Homeland Security, and the National Counterterrorism Center (NCTC).[13]

In response to HSPD-2, the Attorney General established the Foreign Terrorist Tracking Task Force (FTTTF) to track and identify terrorists and,

[13] The Terrorist Threat Integration Center (TTIC) was established by presidential directive and became operational on May 1, 2003. NCTC replaced TTIC on December 6, 2004.

on August 6, 2002, consolidated the task force into the FBI. In addition to its federal agency participants, the FTTTF maintains a close liaison with foreign intelligence and law enforcement services. In another terrorist tracking initiative, on September 16, 2003, the President directed the Attorney General, Secretary of Homeland Security, Secretary of State, and Director of Central Intelligence to develop the Terrorist Screening Center (TSC) to consolidate information from terrorist watch lists and provide 24-hour, seven-day-a-week operational support for law enforcement, consular officers, and other officials. The TSC began operations on December 1, 2003.

An example of interagency cooperation led by the FBI involves the analysis of improvised explosive devices (IEDs)—a technology used in most of the terrorist attacks against U.S. citizens and interests during the past five years. These explosives often reflect the unique characteristics, or signature, of the terrorist organizations or individuals who made them. In December 2003 the FBI Laboratory began preliminary operations of the Terrorist Explosive Device Analytical Center (TEDAC) to coordinate and manage a national effort to gather and analyze information on IEDs recovered both inside and outside the United States. TEDAC uses the knowledge gained from its analysis to assist in the investigation of terrorist bombing attacks, to develop countermeasures to defeat IEDs, and to train first-responders in terrorist IED techniques.

Shortly after the events of September 11, 2001, the FBI undertook several initiatives to integrate state and local law enforcement into counterterrorism operations. On February 27, 2002, the Counterterrorism Division issued its first weekly FBI Intelligence Bulletin to provide actionable terrorism-related intelligence to law enforcement partners. The Bulletin currently reaches more than 60 federal agencies, all FBI field offices and Legats, and more than 18,000 state and local law enforcement agencies through secure communication systems.[14] Since September 11, 2001, the Counterterrorism Division has also disseminated Intelligence Assessments and several thousand Information Intelligence Reports to the U.S. Intelligence Community and appropriate state and local law enforcement entities. In spring 2002 the FBI created the Office of Law Enforcement Coordination (OLEC) as a liaison between the Bureau and other law enforcement organizations. In response to a USA PATRIOT Act mandate, the FBI has participated with other federal agencies in the State and Local Anti-Terrorism Training initiative (SLATT), which has raised the level of counterterrorism expertise and developed professional relationships among law enforcement partners.

[14] Beginning on August 6, 2004, the FBI began routinely disseminating bulletins jointly with the U.S. Department of Homeland Security.

Global Focus

The investigation into the September 11, 2001, attack—which at its height involved more than 7,000 FBI agents and support personnel, including approximately 700 personnel deployed overseas—underscored the global nature of terrorism and the ability of terrorists to plan, finance, and conduct operations in a variety of countries around the world. The transition in recent decades from terrorism as a primarily domestic concern to one of global implications has led the FBI to develop its intelligence and law enforcement partnerships worldwide.

This has led to new initiatives and the cultivation of old ones, including the continued expansion of the Legat program and the offering of counterterrorism training to international law enforcement agencies at the National Academy at Quantico and International Law Enforcement Academies in Budapest, Hungary; Bangkok, Thailand; and Gaborone, Botswana. Other venues of international cooperation include FBI participation in the Group of 8, the Organization of American States, the NATO alliance, and chairing the International Association of Chiefs of Police Committee on Terrorism.

In October 2001 the FBI established a Most Wanted Terrorists List to engage the international public's assistance in the war on terrorism. Set at 22 names, this list places a "global spotlight" on indicted terrorist suspects. Those who initially occupied the list took part in the 1985 hijacking of TWA flight 847, the 1993 World Trade Center bombing, the "Manila Air" plot, the bombing of Khobar Towers, and the U.S. embassy bombings in East Africa. Usama Bin Ladin occupies a place on this list and on that of the FBI's list of Top Ten Most Wanted Fugitives.

Conclusion

During the first 75 years of its history the FBI encountered a predominantly domestic terrorist threat that underlay larger criminal trends. Between the World Wars, this threat came primarily from right-wing extremists, then shifted to left-wing, socialist-oriented groups beginning in the 1950s and continuing into the 1980s. In the early 1980s, international terrorism-sponsored primarily by states or organizations-began to impact US interests overseas and led to legislation that extended the FBI's responsibilities to cover terrorist threats originating outside the United States and its territories. The 1990s saw a new era of domestic and international terrorism in which terrorists sought to inflict massive and indiscriminate casualties upon civilian populations. This threat grew as terrorists began to seek out unconventional weapons and weapons of mass destruction. The 1990s also saw the rise of terrorism pursued by loosely-affiliated extremists, with examples ranging from terrorists involved with domestic special interest causes to militants engaged in international jihad. These terrorism trends combined into the September 11, 2001, attack that has set in motion an international effort to counter the global terrorist threat and elevated counterterrorism to the FBI's preeminent mission.

In his September 20, 2001, Address to a Joint Session of Congress and the American People, President Bush assured his audience that in the present conflict with terrorism, violence would be met with "patient justice." The struggle against terrorism—especially that currently waged against al-Qa'ida—is one of endurance, and it is one in which the FBI is prepared to engage with unflagging persistence. Although the preeminent mission of protecting the United States from terrorist attack is changing the character of the FBI as a whole, an abiding strength of the FBI remains its tradition of excellence in vigorously investigating and prosecuting criminal acts. These traditional pursuits are essential to the disruption of terrorist activities, the dismantling of terrorist organizations, and, consequently, the prevention of future terrorist attacks. By combining a willingness to innovate with its traditional law enforcement responsibilities, the FBI continues to evolve in order to counter the varied forms of terrorism that threaten the interests and security of the United States.

Updates

To ensure that the most current terrorism-related information is available to the American public, the FBI continually evaluates, and, when investigation warrants, updates terrorism statistics presented in the *Terrorism* series. In this issue, the following two acts, which were committed during 1998 and 1999, have been added to the concluding chronological summary of terrorist incidents.

JUNE 27, 1998
Oso Complex Fire
Espanola, New Mexico
(One act of Domestic Terrorism)

On June 27, 1998, a wildfire originated by arson began in the Espanola Ranger District, 10 miles northwest of Espanola, New Mexico. Known as the Oso Complex Fire, the blaze reached within eight miles of Los Alamos and burned a total of 5,185 forested acres, including on Santa Fe National Forest and Santa Clara Pueblo lands. The cost to suppress the fire was $3,433,983. In November 1998, the Albuquerque Journal received a letter claiming the wildfire on behalf of a local militia group, the Minutemen, as a statement against the killing of gray wolves. Associates of the group are suspected of arsons and threats targeting federal and state land use and environmental advocacy groups over apparent disagreements with environmental causes during the late 1990s.

MARCH 19, 1999
Pipe Bombing
Santa Fe, New Mexico
(One act of Domestic Terrorism)

On March 19, 1999, a pipe bomb improvised explosive device (IED) was discovered in a mailbox at Forest Guardians in Santa Fe, New Mexico. The pipe bomb failed to detonate apparently because the cigarette intended to initiate the IED burned out before igniting the fuse. Forest Guardians is a nonprofit group devoted to stopping commercial logging in national forests, and other environmental issues.

On February 14, 2003, law enforcement officers with the FBI, U.S. Forest Service, and Espanola, New Mexico Police arrested Raymond Anthony Sandoval for setting the June 27, 1998, Oso Complex Fire and the attempted March 19, 1999, Forest Guardians bombing. On June 25, 2003, Sandoval pled guilty to manufacturing a destructive device, possession of an unregistered firearm, arson on federal land, and willfully injuring property of the United States. On October 7, 2003, Sandoval, was sentenced to 84 months incarceration and ordered to make restitution payment of $3 million.

The following Chronological Summary includes all of the terrorist incidents recorded in the *Terrorism/Terrorism in the United States* series. The statistical information contained in the following summary supports the graphs and charts presented in this publication.

Chronological Summary of Terrorist Incidents in the United States 1980–2005

Date	Location	Incident Type	Perpetrator	Killed	Injured
1-7-80	San Juan, PR	Pipe Bombing	Anti-Communist Alliance		
1-13-80	New York, NY	Bombing	Omega 7		4
1-13-80	Miami, FL	Bombing	Omega 7		
1-19-80	San Juan, PR	Bombing	Omega 7		
3-12-80	Hato Rey, PR	Armed Assault	Ejercito Popular Boricua Macheteros		
3-15-80	Chicago, IL	Hostile Takeovers (2)	Armed Forces of National Liberation		
3-17-80	New York, NY	Bombing	Croatian Freedom Fighters		3
3-25-80	New York, NY	Attempted Bombing	Omega 7		

Date	Location	Incident Type	Perpetrator	Killed	Injured
4-19-80	Chattanooga, TN	Shooting	Justice Knights of the Ku Klux Klan		4
4-30-80	New York, NY	Assault	Revolutionary Communist Party		
6-3-80	Washington, DC	Bombing	Croatian Freedom Fighters		
6-3-80	New York, NY	Bombing	Croatian Freedom Fighters		
7-14-80	Dorato, PR San Juan, PR	Multiple Bombings (2)	Organization of Volunteers for the Puerto Rico Revolution		
7-14-80	Ponce, PR Mayaguez, PR	Multiple Arsons (2)	Organization of Volunteers for the Puerto Rico Revolution		
7-22-80	Hato Rey, PR Santurce, PR Rio Piedras, PR	Multiple Bombings (4)	Revolutionary Commandos of the People, Ready and at War		
8-20-80	Berkeley, CA	Pipe Bombing	Iranian Free Army		2
9-11-80	New York, NY	Shooting	Omega 7	1	
10-7-80	New York, NY	Attempted Bombing	International Committee Against Nazism		
10-12-80	New York, NY	Bombing	Justice Commandos of the Armenian Genocide		4
10-12-80	Hollywood, CA	Bombing	Justice Commandos of the Armenian Genocide		1
10-14-80	Fort Collins, CO	Shooting	Libyan Revolutionary Committee		1
12-21-80	New York, NY	Pipe Bombing	Armed Forces of Popular Resistance		
12-30-80	Hialeah, FL	Attempted Bombing	Omega 7		
1-8-81	Santurce, PR Ponce, PR Rio Piedras, PR	Multiple Incendiary Bombings (3)	People's Revolutionary Commandos		

Date	Location	Incident Type	Perpetrator	Killed	Injured
1-12-81	San Juan, PR	Bombing	Ejercito Popular Boricua Macheteros		
1-23-81	New York City, NY	Bombing	Croatian Freedom Fighters		
1-26-81	San Francisco, CA	Bombing	Jewish Defense League/American Revenge Committee		
2-2-81	Los Angeles, CA	Attempted Bombing	October 3		
2-9-81	Eugene, OR	Assault	Revolutionary Communist Youth Brigade		
2-22-81	Hollywood, CA	Bombing	Armenian Secret Army for the Liberation of Armenia		
3-15-81	San Juan, PR	Attempted Bombing	Armed Forces of Popular Resistance		
4-21-81	Santurce, PR	Robbery	Ejercito Popular Boricua Macheteros		
4-27-81	Washington, DC	Incendiary Bombing	Iranian Patriotic Army		
5/16–18/81	New York City, NY	Multiple Bombings (5)	Puerto Rican Armed Resistance	1	
6-25-81	Torrance, CA	Incendiary Bombing	Jewish Defenders		
6-26-81	Los Angeles, CA	Bombing	June 9 Organization		
7-30-81	New York City, NY	Hostile Takeover	Libyan Students		
8-7-81	Washington, DC	Hostile Takeover	People's Mujahedin Organization of Iran		3
8-20-81	Washington, DC	Arson	Black Brigade		
8-20-81	Los Angeles, CA	Bombing	June 9 Organization		
8-27-81	Carolina, PR	Bombing	Grupo Estrella		
8-31-81	New York City, NY	Hostile Takeover	Jewish Defense League		
9/3-4/81	New York City, NY	Multiple Bombings (2)	Jewish Defense League		

Date	Location	Incident Type	Perpetrator	Killed	Injured
9-9-81	Washington, DC	Assault	Concerned Sierra Leone Nationals		
9-11-81	Miami, FL	Multiple Bombings (2)	Omega 7		
9-12-81	New York City, NY	Bombing	Omega 7		
9-22-81	Schenectady, NY	Bombing	Communist Workers Party		
9-24-81	Miami, FL	Attempted Bombing	Omega 7		
10-1-81	Hollywood, CA	Bombing	Armenian Secret Army for the Liberation of Armenia		
10-25-81	New York City, NY	Incendiary Bombing	Jewish Defense League		
11-11-81	Santurce, PR	Bombing	Ejercito Popular Boricua Macheteros		
11-14-81	Glen Cove, NY	Shooting	Unaffiliated Extremists		
11-20-81	Los Angeles, CA	Bombing	Justice Commandos of the Armenian Genocide		
11-27-81	Fort Buchanan, PR	Shooting	National Liberation Movement		1
11-27-81	Santurce, PR Condado, PR	Multiple Bombings (2)	Ejercito Popular Boricua Macheteros		
12-24-81	New York City, NY	Attempted Pipe Bombing	Jewish Defense League		
1-28-82	Los Angeles, CA	Shooting	Justice Commandos of the Armenian Genocide	1	
2-19-82	Miami, FL	Multiple Bombings (2)	Omega 7		
2-19-82	Washington, DC	Bombing	Jewish Defense League		

Date	Location	Incident Type	Perpetrator	Killed	Injured
2-21-82	Rio Piedras, PR	Pipe Bombing	Antonia Martinez Student Commandos		
2-28-82	New York City, NY	Multiple Bombings (4)	Armed Forces of National Liberation		
3-22-82	Cambridge, MA	Bombing	Justice Commandos of the Armenian Genocide		
4-5-82	Brooklyn, NY	Arson	Jewish Defense League	1	7
4-28-82	New York City, NY	Multiple Bombings (2)	Jewish Defense League		
4-29-82	San Juan, PR Bayamon, PR	Multiple Bombings (2)	Provisional Coordinating Committee of the Labor Self-Defense Group		
4-29-82	San Juan, PR	Shooting	Provisional Coordinating Committee of the Labor Self-Defense Group		
5-4-82	Somerville, MA	Shooting	Justice Commandos of the Armenian Genocide	1	
5-16-82	San Juan, PR	Shooting	Ejercito Popular Boricua Macheteros/ Group for the Liberation of Vieques	1	3
5-17-82	Union City, NJ	Incendiary Bombing	Omega 7		
5-19-82	Villa Sin Miedo, PR	Shooting	Ejercito Popular Boricua Macheteros	1	12
5-20-82	San Juan, PR	Attempted Bombing	Ejercito Popular Boricua Macheteros		
5-25-82	San German, PR	Kidnapping	Grupo Estrella		1
5-30-82	Van Nuys, CA	Attempted Bombing	Armenian Secret Army for the Liberation of Armenia		

Date	Location	Incident Type	Perpetrator	Killed	Injured
6-10-82	Carolina, PR	Multiple Bombings (3)	Armed Forces of Popular Resistance		
7-4-82	New York City, NY Astoria, NY	Multiple Pipe Bombings (2)	Croatian Freedom Fighters		
7-5-82	New York City, NY	Multiple Pipe Bombings (2)	Jewish Defense League		
8-20-82	Old San Juan, PR	Bombing	Armed Forces of National Liberation		
9-1-82	Naranjito, PR	Attempted Bombing	Ejercito Popular Boricua Macheteros		
9-2-82	Miami, FL	Bombing	Omega 7		
9-8-82	Chicago, IL	Bombing	Omega 7		
9-20-82	New York City, NY	Bombing	Armed Forces of National Liberation		
9-25-82	Miami, FL	Attempted Bombing	Omega 7		
10-15-82	Washington, DC	Hostile Takeover	Islamic Extremists		
10-22-82	Philadelphia, PA	Attempted Bombing	Justice Commandos of the Armenian Genocide		
11-4-82	New York City, NY	Smoke Bombing	Jewish Defense League		
11-16-82	Carolina, PR	Multiple Robberies (2)	Ejercito Popular Boricua Macheteros	1	
12-8-82	Washington, DC	Attempted Bombing	Norman David Mayer	1	
12-16-82	Elmont, NY	Multiple Bombings (2)	United Freedom Front		
12-21-82	New York City, NY	Attempted Pipe Bombing	Jewish Defense League		
12-22-82	McLean, VA	Hostile Takeover	People of Omar		
12-31-82	New York City, NY	Multiple Bombings (5)	Armed Forces of National Liberation		3
1/11-12/83	Miami, FL	Multiple Bombings (3)	Omega 7		
1 -28-83	New York City, NY	Bombing	Revolutionary Fighting Group		

Date	Location	Incident Type	Perpetrator	Killed	Injured
2-13-83	Medina, ND	Shooting	Sheriff's Posse Comitatus	2	4
2-15-83	Killeen, TX	Hijacking	Hossein Olya		
2-19-83	Washington, DC	Pipe Bombing	Jewish Defense League		
3-20-83	San Antonio, TX	Bombing	Republic of Revolutionary		
4-26-83	Washington, DC	Bombing	Armed Resistance Unit		
4-27-83	Miami, FL	Attempted Bombings (4)	Haitian Extremists		
4-29-83	Rio Piedras, PR	Hostile Takeover	Ejercito Popluar Boricua Macheteros		
5-12-83	Uniondale, NY	Bombing	United Freedom Front		
5-13-83	New York City, NY	Bombing	United Freedom Front		
5-27-83	Miami, FL	Bombing	Omega 7		
7-8-83	Miami, FL	Kidnapping	Ejercito Revolucionario Del Pueblo		
7-15-83	Rio Piedras, PR	Robbery	Ejercito Popular Boricua Macheteros	1	
8-8-83	Detroit, Ml	Attempted Incendiary Bombing	Fuqra		
8-8-83	Detroit, Ml	Shooting	Fuqra	1	
8-9-83	Detroit, Ml	Arson	Fuqra	2	
8-16-83	Los Angeles, CA	Hostile Takeover	Carlos Martinez		
8-18-83	Washington, DC	Bombing	Armed Resistance Unit		
8-21-83	New York City, NY	Bombing	United Freedom Front		
8-27-83	Washington, DC	Incendiary Bombing	Unknown		
10-12-83	Miami, FL	Pipe Bombing	Omega 7		

Date	Location	Incident Type	Perpetrator	Killed	Injured
10-30-83	Hato Rey, PR	Rocket Attack	Ejercito Popular Boricua Macheteros		
11-7-83	Washington, DC	Bombing	Armed Resistance Unit		
12/13-14/83	East Meadow, NY New York City, NY	Multiple Bombings (2)	United Freedom Front		
1 -29-84	New York City, NY	Bombing	United Freedom Front		
2-23-84	New York City, NY	Bombing	Jewish Direct Action		
3-19-84	Harrison, NY	Bombing	United Freedom Front		
4-5-84	New York City, NY	Bombing	Red Guerrilla Resistance		
4-20-84	Washington, DC	Bombing	Red Guerrilla Resistance		
5-9-84	New York City, NY	Attempted Assassination	Bashir Baesho		
8-22-84	Melville, NY	Bombing	United Freedom Front		
9-26-84	New York City, NY	Bombing	Red Guerrilla Resistance		
9-26-84	Mount Pleasant, NY	Bombing	United Freedom Front		
12-10-84	Levittown, PR Rio Piedras, PR Ponce, PR Mayaguez, PR Cayey, PR	Multiple Bombings (5)	Organization of Volunteers for the Puerto Rican Revolution		
1-25-85	Old San Juan, PR	Rocket Attack	Ejercito Popular Boricua Macheteros/ Organization of Volunteers for the Puerto Rican Revolution		
2-23-85	New York City, NY	Bombing	Red Guerrilla Resistance		

Date	Location	Incident Type	Perpetrator	Killed	Injured
5-15-85	Northridge, CA	Pipe Bombing	Jewish Defense League		
8-15-85	Paterson, NJ	Bombing	Jewish Defense League	1	1
9-6-85	Brentwood, NY	Bombing	Jewish Defense League		1
10-11-85	Santa Ana, CA	Bombing	Jewish Defense League	1	7
11-6-85	Bayamon, PR	Shooting	Organization of Volunteers for the Puerto Rican Revolution		1
1-6-86	Cidra, PR Toa Baja, PR Guanica, PR Santurce, PR	Multiple Bombings (4)	Ejercito Revolucionario Clandestino/ National Revolutionary Front of Puerto Rico		
3-17-86	Ponce, PR	Attempted Bombing	Commando Rojo		
4-14-86	Rio Piedras, PR	Bombing	Organization of Volunteers for the Puerto Rican Revolution		
4-29-86	San Juan, PR	Shooting	Organization of Volunteers for the Puerto Rican Revolution	1	1
5-14-86	Phoenix, AZ	Sabotage	Earth First Organization		
9-2-86	New York City, NY	Tear Gas Bombing	Jewish Defense League		17
9-15-86	Coeur d'Alene, ID	Pipe Bombing	Aryan Nations		
9-29-86	Coeur d'Alene, ID	Multiple Bombings (4)	Aryan Nations		
10-20-86	New York City, NY	Incendiary Bombing	Jewish Defense League		

Date	Location	Incident Type	Perpetrator	Killed	Injured
10-28-86	Bayamon, PR Fajardo, PR Mayaguez, PR Aguadilla, PR Santurce, PR Fort Buchanan, PR	Multiple Bombings (7)	Ejercito Popular Boricua Macheteros		1
11-4-86	Puerta De Tierra, PR	Attempted Bombing	Ejercito Popular Boricua Macheteros		
12-28-86	Yauco, PR Guayama, PR	Multiple Bombings (2)	Ejercito Popular Boricua Macheteros		
4-16-87	Davis, CA	Arson	Animal Liberation Front		
5-25-87	Caguas, PR Carolina, PR Mayaguez, PR Cidra, PR Aibonita, PR Ponce, PR	Multiple Bombings (7)	Guerrilla Forces of Liberation		
11-9-87	Flagstaff, AZ	Sabotage	Evan Mecham Eco-Terrorist International Conspiracy		
1-12-88	Rio Piedras, PR	Multiple Incendiary Bombings (2)	Pedro Albizu Campos Revolutionary Forces		
5-26-88	Coral Gables, FL	Bombing	Organization Alliance of Cuban Intransigence		
7-22-88	Caguas, PR	Pipe Bombing	Ejercito Popular Boricua Macheteros		
9-19-88	Los Angeles, CA	Bombing	Up the IRS, Inc.		
9-25-88	Grand Canyon, AZ	Sabotage	Evan Mecham Eco-Terrorist International Conspiracy		
10-25-88	Flagstaff, AZ	Sabotage	Evan Mecham Eco-Terrorist International Conspiracy		

Date	Location	Incident Type	Perpetrator	Killed	Injured
11-1-88	Rio Piedras, PR	Multiple Bombings (2)	Pedro Albizu Campos Revolutionary Forces		
4-3-89	Tucson, AZ	Arson	Animal Liberation Front		
6-19-89	Bayamon, PR	Multiple Bombings (2)	Ejercito Popular Boricua Macheteros		
7/3-4/89	Lubbock, TX	Malicious Destruction of Property	Animal Liberation Front		
1-12-90	Santurce, PR Carolina, PR	Multiple Pipe Bombings (2)	Eugenio Maria de Hostos International Brigade of the Pedro Albizu Campos Revolutionary Forces		
2-22-90	Los Angeles, CA	Bombing	Up the IRS, Inc.		
4-22-90	Santa Cruz County, CA	Malicious Destruction of Property	Earth Night Action Group		
5-27-90	Mayaguez, PR	Arson	Unknown Puerto Rican Group		
9-17-90	Arecibo, PR Vega Baja, PR	Multiple Bombings (2)	Pedro Albizu Group Revolutionary Forces		
2-3-91	Mayaguez, PR	Arson	Popular Liberation Army		
2-18-91	Sabana Grande, PR	Arson	Popular Liberation Army		
3-17-91	Carolina, PR	Arson	Unknown Puerto Rican Group		
4-1-91	Fresno, CA	Bombing	Popular Liberation Army		
7-6-91	Punta Borinquen, PR	Bombing	Popular Liberation Army		
4-5-92	New York, NY	Hostile Takeover	Mujahedin-E-Khalq		

Date	Location	Incident Type	Perpetrator	Killed	Injured
11-19-92	Urbana, IL	Attempted Firebombing	Mexican Revolutionary Movement		
12-10-92	Chicago, IL	Car Fire and Attempted Firebombing (2)	Boricua Revolutionary Front		
2-26-93	New York, NY	Car Bombing	International Islamist Extremists	6	1042
7/20-22/93	Tacoma, WA	Multiple Bombings (2)	American Front Skinheads		
11/27-28/93	Chicago, IL	Firebombings (9)	Animal Liberation Front		
3-1-94	New York, NY	Shooting	Rashid Najib Baz	1	3
4-19-95	Oklahoma City, OK	Truck Bombing	Timothy McVeigh and Terry Nichols (Michael Fortier found guilty of failing to alert authorities of plot)	168	754
4-1-96	Spokane, WA	Pipe Bombing/ Bank Robbery	Spokane Bank Robbers		
7-12-96	Spokane, WA	Pipe Bombing/ Bank Robbery	Spokane Bank Robbers		
7-27-96	Atlanta, GA	Pipe Bombing	Eric Robert Rudolph	2	112
1 -2-97	Washington, DC Leavenworth, KS	Letter Bombing (Counted as 1 incident)	Unknown		
1-16-97	Atlanta, GA	Bombing of Abortion Clinic	Eric Robert Rudolph		8
2-21-97	Atlanta, GA	Bombing of Alternative Lifestyle Nightclub	Eric Robert Rudolph		5
1-29-98	Birmingham, AL	Bombing of Reproductive Services Clinic	Eric Robert Rudolph	1	1

Date	Location	Incident Type	Perpetrator	Killed	Injured
3-31-98	Arecibo, PR	Bombing of Superaqueduct Construction Project	Ejercito Popular Boricua Macheteros		
6-9-98	Rio Piedras, PR	Bombing of Bank Branch Office	Ejercito Popular Boricua Macheteros		
6-25-98	Santa Isabel, PR	Bombing of Bank Branch Office	Ejercito Popular Boricua Macheteros suspected		1
6-27-98	Espanola, NM	Arson	Raymond Anthony Sandoval		
10-19-98	Vail, CO	Arson Fire at Ski Resort	Earth Liberation Front		
3-19-99	Santa Fe, NM	Attempted Bombing	Raymond Anthony Sandoval		
3-27-99	Franklin Township, NJ	Bombing of Circus Vehicles	Animal Liberation Front		
4-5-99	Minneapolis-St. Paul, MN	Malicious Destruction and Theft	Animal Liberation Front		
5-9-99	Eugene, OR	Bombing	Animal Liberation Front		
7/2-4/99	Chicago, IL Skokie, IL Northbrook, IL Bloomington, IN	Multiple Shootings	Benjamin Nathaniel Smith	2	8
8-10-99	Granada Hills, CA	Multiple Shootings	Buford O'Neal Furrow	1	5
8/28-29/99	Orange, CA	Malicious Destruction and Theft	Animal Liberation Front		
10-24-99	Bellingham, WA	Malicious Destruction and Theft	Animal Liberation Front		
11-20-99	Puyallup, WA	Malicious Destruction	Animal Liberation Front		
12-25-99	Monmouth, OR	Arson	Earth Liberation Front		
12-31-99	East Lansing, MI	Arson	Earth Liberation Front		

Date	Location	Incident Type	Perpetrator	Killed	Injured
1-3-00	Petaluma, CA	Incendiary Attack	Animal Liberation Front		
1-15-00	Petaluma, CA	Incendiary Attack	Animal Liberation Front		
1-22-00	Bloomington, IN	Arson	Earth Liberation Front		
5-7-00	Olympia, WA	Arson	Revenge of the Trees		
7-2-00	North Vernon, IN	Arson	Animal Liberation Front		
7-20-00	Rhinelander. Wl	Vandalism	Earth Liberation Front		
12-1-00	Phoenix, AZ	Multiple Arsons	Mark Warren Sands		
12/9-30/00	Suffolk County, Long Island, NY	Multiple Arsons	Earth Liberation Front		
1-2-01	Glendale, OR	Arson	Earth Liberation Front		
2-20-01	Visalia, CA	Arson	Earth Liberation Front		
3-9-01	Culpeper, VA	Tree Spiking	Earth Liberation Front		
3-30-01	Eugene, OR	Arson	Earth Liberation Front		
4-15-01	Portland, OR	Arson	Earth Liberation Front		
5-17-01	Harrisburg, PA	Bank Robbery	Clayton Lee Waagner		
5-21-01	Seattle, WA	Arson	Earth Liberation Front		
5-21-01	Clatskanie, OR	Arson	Earth Liberation Front		
7-24-01	Stateline, NV	Destruction of Property	Earth Liberation Front		
9-9-01	Morgantown, WV	Bank Robbery	Clayton Lee Waagner		
9-11-01	New York, NY Washington, DC New Cumberland, PA	Aircraft Attack	Al-Qa'ida	2972	est. 12000

Date	Location	Incident Type	Perpetrator	Killed	Injured
9/01-11/01	New York, NY Washington, DC Lantana, FL	*Bacillus anthracis* Mailings	Unknown	5	17
10-14-01	Litchfield, CA	Arson	Earth Liberation Front		
11-12-01	San Diego, CA	Burglary and Vandalism	Animal Liberation Front		
3-18-02	Erie, PA	Vandalism	Earth Liberation Front		
3-24-02	Erie, PA	Arson	Earth Liberation Front		
5/11-12/02	Harborcreek, PA	Vandalism/ Destruction of Property	Earth Liberation Front/ Animal Liberation Front		
7-4-02	Los Angeles, CA	Shooting	Hesham Mohamed AN Hedayat	2	
8/02-10/02	Henrico and Goochland Counties, VA	Vandalism and Destruction of Property	Earth Liberation Front		
8-11-02	Warren, PA	Arson	Earth Liberation Front		
9/15-16/02	Harborcreek, PA	Vandalism/ Destruction of Property	Earth Liberation Front/ Animal Liberation Front		
11-26-02	Harborcreek, PA	Arson	Earth Liberation Front/ Animal Liberation Front		
1-1-03	Girard, PA	Arson	Earth Liberation Front		
3-3-03	Chico, CA	Vandalism	Animal Liberation Front		
8/03-9/03	San Diego, CA	Arson	Earth Liberation Front		
8-22-03	West Covina, CA	Vandalism and Destruction of Property	Earth Liberation Front		
8-28-03	Emeryville, CA	Bombing	Daniel Andreas San Diego suspected		
9-26-03	Pleasanton, CA	Bombing	Daniel Andreas San Diego suspected		

Date	Location	Incident Type	Perpetrator	Killed	Injured
1-19-04	Henrico County, VA	Arson	Earth Liberation Front suspected		
4-1-04	Oklahoma City, OK	Arson	Sean Michael Gillespie/Aryan Nations		
4-20-04	Redmond, WA	Vandalism and Arson	Earth Liberation Front		
5/04-7/04	Provo, UT	Vandalism and Arson	Animal Liberation Front		
12-27-04	Lincoln, CA	Attempted Arson	Earth Liberation Front		
1/05-2/05	Auburn, CA Sutter Creek, CA	Attempted Arson and Arson	Earth Liberation Front		
4-13-05	Sammanish, WA	Arson	Earth Liberation Front		
7-7-05	Los Angeles, CA	Attempted Arson	Animal rights extremists suspected		
9-16-05	Los Angeles, CA	Attempted Arson	Animal Liberation Front		
11-20-05	Hagerstown, MD	Arson	Earth Liberation Front		

G. BOTNETS, CYBERCRIME, AND CYBERTERRORISM

BOTNETS, CYBERCRIME, AND CYBERTERRORISM: VULNERABILITIES AND POLICY ISSUES FOR CONGRESS

CRS Report for Congress

November 15, 2007

Commentary

In the spring of 2007, Estonian government computers suffered debilitating attacks by what many believe were political protestors. The protestors may have hired the expertise of cybercriminals to execute the attack. U.S. Department of Defense (DOD) experts opine that similar cyberattacks from individuals, groups, and countries will increasingly target economic, political, and military organizations in the future. This volume includes the CRS Report *Botnets, Cybercrime, and Cyberterrorism: Vulnerabilities and Policy Issues for Congress* to provide a more complete picture of the terrorist threat the United States and other advanced countries will face in the future.

The report correctly states that cybercrime is becoming more organized and established as a transnational business, and that highly skilled cyberwarriors are available in the marketplace today. Those with a criminal propensity have connected with drug traffickers and terrorists to form the cyberterror threat. Cyberterror could be used as a precursor crime to extort money to fund more conventional terrorist attacks. Alternatively, it could be used to damage the U.S. economy to an extent that compromises national security. The tools available to the cyberterrorist constantly become more sophisticated, and effective defenses become more difficult to achieve.

This CRS report discusses options now open to nation states, extremists, or terrorist groups for obtaining malicious technical services from cybercriminals to meet political or military objectives. The report also describes the possible effects of a coordinated cyberattack against the U.S. critical infrastructure. The Internet is an open system that cannot be closed. The U.S. military, because of the authority it exercises over its component parts, has gone far to close its sensitive systems to unofficial access, but malicious penetration still occurs. Other government and non-government entities that provide essential and critical public and commercial services do not have that degree of control over the information systems upon which performance of their respective functions rely.

Future cyberterrorism attempts may conflate military and civilian targets. The CRS report points out that past incidents of conventional terrorism have already been linked with cybercrime, and that computer vulnerabilities may make government and civilian critical infrastructure systems seem attractive as targets for cyberattack. The report explores the possible connections between cybercriminals and terrorist groups that want to damage the U.S. economy or other national security interests and examines the hypothetical effects that would result from a coordinated cyberattack against the U.S. critical infrastructure, including use of cybercrime tools that could possibly take advantage of openly publicized cyber vulnerabilities.

The report also describes possible trends in cybercrime, in that malicious Internet websites and identity theft might be linked to attempts at conventional terrorist activity. The report suggests that Congress should make the examination of the cyberterrorism threat a priority and poses specific issues for Congress to consider.

DOCUMENT NO. 7

BOTNETS, CYBERCRIME, AND CYBERTERRORISM: VULNERABILITIES AND POLICY ISSUES FOR CONGRESS

CRS Report
RL32114

November 15, 2007

Clay Wilson
Specialist in Technology and National Security
Foreign Affairs, Defense, and Trade Division

Summary

Cybercrime is becoming more organized and established as a transnational business. High technology online skills are now available for rent to a variety of customers, possibly including nation states, or individuals and groups that could secretly represent terrorist groups. The increased use of automated attack tools by cybercriminals has overwhelmed some current methodologies used for tracking Internet cyberattacks, and vulnerabilities of the U.S. critical infrastructure, which are acknowledged openly in publications, could possibly attract cyberattacks to extort money, or damage the U.S. economy to affect national security.

In April and May 2007, NATO and the United States sent computer security experts to Estonia to help that nation recover from cyberattacks directed against government computer systems, and to analyze the methods used and determine the source of the attacks.[1] Some security experts suspect that political protestors may have rented the services of cybercriminals, possibly a large network of infected PCs, called a "botnet," to help disrupt the computer systems of the Estonian government. DOD officials have also indicated that similar cyberattacks from individuals and countries

[1] Larry Greenemeier, "Estonian Attacks Raise Concern Over Cyber 'Nuclear Winter,'" *Information Week*, May 24, 2007, at [http://www.informationweek.com/news/showArticle. jhtml?articleID=199701774].

targeting economic, political, and military organizations may increase in the future.[2]

Cybercriminals have reportedly made alliances with drug traffickers in Afghanistan, the Middle East, and elsewhere where profitable illegal activities are used to support terrorist groups. In addition, designs for cybercrime botnets are becoming more sophisticated, and future botnet architectures may be more resistant to computer security countermeasures.[3]

This report discusses options now open to nation states, extremists, or terrorist groups for obtaining malicious technical services from cybercriminals to meet political or military objectives, and describes the possible effects of a coordinated cyberattack against the U.S. critical infrastructure. This report will be updated as events warrant.

Introduction

The U.S. military is supported partly by civilian high technology services and products, most often in the form of communications systems and computer software.[4] In future conflicts that involve cyberwarfare between nations, the distinction between U.S. military and civilian targets may be blurred and civilian computer systems may increasingly be seen as viable targets vulnerable to attack by adversaries.[5]

Computer networking technology has also blurred the boundaries between cyberwarfare, cybercrime, and cyberterrorism. Officials in government and industry now say that cybercrime and cyberattack services available for hire from criminal organizations are a growing threat to national security as well as to the U.S. economy.[6] New and sophisticated cybercrime tools could operate to allow a nation state or terrorist group to remain unidentified while they direct cyberattacks through the Internet.[7] Many experts

---

[2] Jeanne Meserve, "Official: International Hackers Going After U.S. Networks," CNN.com, October 19, 2007, [http://www.cnn.com/2007/US/10/19/cyber.threats/index.html]. Sebastian Sprenger, "Maj. Gen. Lord Is a Groundbreaker," *Federal Computer Week*, October 15, 2007, vol. 21, no. 34, p. 44.

[3] Tom Espiner, "Security Expert: Storm Botnet 'Services' Could Be Sold," CnetNews.com, October 16, 2007, [http://www.news.com/Security-expert-Storm-botnet-services-could-besold/2100-7349_3-6213781.html]. Dan Sullivan, "P2P Botnets Increasingly Sophisticated, Realtime-Websecurity," April 18, 2007, [http://www.realtime-websecurity.com/articles_and_analysis/2007/04/p2p_botnets_increasingly_sophi.html].

[4] Dan Kuehl, professor at the National Defense University School of Information Warfare and Strategy, has pointed out that a high percentage of U.S. military messages flow through commercial communications channels, and this reliance creates a vulnerability during conflict. Eric Naef, "Wanja," *Infocon Magazine*, October 2003, [http://www.iwar.org.uk/infocon/io-kuehl.htm].

[5] Sebastian Sprenger, "Maj. Gen. Lord Is a Groundbreaker," *Federal Computer Week*, October 15, 2007, vol. 21, no. 34, p. 44.

[6] James Lewis, testimony before the House Committee on Homeland Security, Subcommittee on Emerging Threats, Cybersecurity, and Science and Technology, April 15, 2007.

[7] Tim Greene, "Storm Worm Strikes Back at Security Pros," NetworkWorld.com, October 24, 2007, at [http://www.networkworld.com/news/2007/102407-storm-worm-security.html?nlhtsec=1022securityalert4&&nladname=102507securityal].

point out that past incidents of conventional terrorism have already been linked with cybercrime, and that computer vulnerabilities may make government and civilian critical infrastructure systems seem attractive as targets for cyberattack.[8] Some experts argue that the government of Estonia may have already experienced this type of cyberattack directed against their systems and websites in April, 2007.

This report explores the possible connections between cybercriminals and terrorist groups that want to damage the U.S. economy or national security interests. The report also examines the effects of a coordinated cyberattack against the U.S. critical infrastructure, including use of cybercrime tools that could possibly take advantage of openly-publicized cyber vulnerabilities. Trends in cybercrime are described, showing how malicious Internet websites, and other cybercrimes such as identity theft are linked to conventional terrorist activity.

Congress may wish to explore the possible effects on the U.S. economy and on the U.S. military that could result from a coordinated attack against civilian and military computers and communications systems, whether due to cybercrime or cyberterrorism. Congress may also wish to explore the difficulties associated with establishing doctrine for selecting an appropriate military or law enforcement response after such an attack.

Background

It is clear that terrorist groups are using computers and the Internet to further goals associated with spreading terrorism. This can be seen in the way that extremists are creating and using numerous Internet websites for recruitment and fund raising activities, and for Jihad training purposes. Several criminals who have recently been convicted of cybercrimes used their technical skills to acquire stolen credit card information in order to finance other conventional terrorist activities.[9] It is possible that as criminals and terrorist groups explore more ways to work together, a new type of threat may emerge where extremists gain access to the powerful network tools now used by cybercriminals to steal personal information, or to disrupt computer systems that support services through the Internet.

---

[8] Brian Krebs, "Three Worked the Web to Help Terrorists," *The Washington Post*, July 6, 2007, p. D01. Walsh, *Terrorism on the Cheap*. Rollie Lal, "Terrorists and Organized Crime Join Forces," *International Herald Tribune*, May 25, 2005, at [http://www.iht.com/articles/2005/05/23/opinion/edlal.php]. Barbara Porter, "Forum Links Organized Crime and Terrorism," *By George!*, summer 2004, at [http://www2.gwu.edu/~bygeorge/060804/crimeterrorism.html].

[9] Gregory Crabb, "U.S. Postal Service Global Investigations," and Yuval Ben-Itzhak, "CTO Finjan," Presentation at the Gartner IT Security Summit 2007, Washington, DC, June 4, 2007.

Three Basic Methods for Disrupting Computer Systems

There are several effective methods for disrupting computer systems. This report focuses on the method known as cyberattack, or computer network attack (CNA), which uses malicious computer code to disrupt computer processing, or steal data. A brief description of three different methods are shown here. However, as technology changes, future distinctions between these methods may begin to blur.

An attack against computers may (1) disrupt equipment and hardware reliability, (2) change processing logic, or (3) steal or corrupt data.[10] The methods discussed here are chosen based on the technology asset against which each attack mode is directed, and the effects each method can produce. The assets affected or effects produced can sometimes overlap for different attack methods.

- Conventional kinetic weapons can be directed against computer equipment, a computer facility, or transmission lines to create a physical attack that disrupts the reliability of equipment.
- The power of electromagnetic energy, most commonly in the form of an electromagnetic pulse (EMP), can be used to create an electronic attack (EA) directed against computer equipment or data transmissions. By overheating circuitry or jamming communications, EA disrupts the reliability of equipment and the integrity of data.[11]
- Malicious code can be used to create a cyberattack, or computer network attack (CNA), directed against computer processing code, instruction logic, or data. The code can generate a stream of malicious network packets that can disrupt data or logic through exploiting a vulnerability in computer software, or a weakness in the computer security practices of an organization. This type of cyberattack can disrupt the reliability of equipment, the integrity of data, and the confidentiality of communications.

Cyberattack, Cybercrime, and Cyberterrorism

Labeling a "cyberattack" as "cybercrime" or "cyberterrorism" is problematic because of the difficulty determining with certainty the identity, intent, or the political motivations of an attacker.[12] "Cybercrime" can be very broad in scope, and may sometimes involve more factors than just a

---

[10] All methods of computer attack are within the current capabilities of several nations. See CRS Report RL31787, *Information Operations and Cyberwar: Capabilities and Related Policy Issues*, by Clay Wilson.

[11] For more on electromagnetic weapons, see CRS Report RL32544, *High Altitude Electromagnetic Pulse (HEMP) and High Power Microwave (HPM) Devices: Threat Assessments*, by Clay Wilson.

[12] Serge Krasavin, *What is Cyberterrorism?* Computer Crime Research Center, April 23, 2004, [http://www.crime-research.org/analytics/Krasavin/].

computer hack. "Cyberterrorism" is often equated with the use of malicious code. However, a "cyberterrorism" event may also sometimes depend on the presence of other factors beyond just a "cyberattack."

Definitions for Cyberterrorism

Various definitions exist for the term "cyberterrorism", just as various definitions exist for the term "terrorism."[13] Security expert Dorothy Denning defines cyberterrorism as ". . . politically motivated hacking operations intended to cause grave harm such as loss of life or severe economic damage."[14] The Federal Emergency Management Agency (FEMA) defines cyberterrorism as "unlawful attacks and threats of attack against computers, networks, and the information stored therein when done to intimidate or coerce a government or its people in furtherance of political or social objectives."[15]

Others indicate that a physical attack that destroys computerized nodes for critical infrastructures, such as the Internet, telecommunications, or the electric power grid, without ever touching a keyboard, can also contribute to, or be labeled as cyberterrorism.[16] Thus, it is possible that if a computer facility were deliberately attacked for political purposes, all three methods described above (physical attack, EA, and cyberattack) might contribute to, or be labeled as "cyberterrorism."

Definitions for Cybercrime

Cybercrime is crime that is enabled by, or that targets computers. Some argue there is no agreed-upon definition for "cybercrime" because "cyberspace" is just a new specific instrument used to help commit crimes that are not new at all. Cybercrime can involve theft of intellectual property, a violation of patent, trade secret, or copyright laws. However, cybercrime also includes attacks against computers to deliberately disrupt processing, or may include espionage to make unauthorized copies of classified data. If a terrorist group were to launch a cyberattack to cause harm, such an act also fits within the definition of a cybercrime. The primary difference between a cyberattack to commit a crime or to commit terror is found in the

[13] Under 22 USC, Section 2656, "terrorism" is defined as premeditated, politically motivated violence perpetrated against noncombatant targets by sub national groups or clandestine agents, usually intended to influence an audience. The United States has employed this definition of terrorism for statistical and analytical purposes since 1983. U.S. Department of State, 2002, *Patterns of Global Terrorism, 2003*, [http://www.state.gov/s/ct/rls/pgtrpt/2001/html/10220.htm].

[14] Dorothy Denning, "Activism, Hactivism, and Cyberterrorism: The Internet as a tool for Influencing Foreign Policy," in John Arquilla and David Ronfeldt, eds., *Networks and Netwars*, (Rand 2001), p. 241. Dorothy Denning, *Is Cyber War Next?* Social Science Research Council, November 2001, at [http://www.ssrc.org/sept11/essays/denning.htm].

[15] [http://www.fema.gov/pdf/onp/toolkit_app_d.pdf].

[16] Dan Verton, "A Definition of Cyber-terrorism", *Computerworld*, August 11, 2003, [http://www.computerworld.com/securitytopics/security/story/0,10801,83843,00.html].

intent of the attacker, and it is possible for actions under both labels to overlap.

Botnets

Botnets are becoming a major tool for cybercrime, partly because they can be designed to very effectively disrupt targeted computer systems in different ways, and because a malicious user, without possessing strong technical skills, can initiate these disruptive effects in cyberspace by simply renting botnet services from a cybercriminal.[17] Botnets, or "Bot Networks," are made up of vast numbers of compromised computers that have been infected with malicious code, and can be remotely-controlled through commands sent via the Internet. Hundreds or thousands of these infected computers can operate in concert to disrupt or block Internet traffic for targeted victims, harvest information, or to distribute spam, viruses, or other malicious code. Botnets have been described as the "Swiss Army knives of the underground economy" because they are so versatile.

Botnet designers, or "botmasters", can reportedly make large sums of money by marketing their technical services. For example, Jeanson Ancheta, a 21-year-old hacker and member of a group called the "Botmaster Underground", reportedlymade more than $100,000 from different Internet Advertising companies who paid him to download specially-designed malicious adware code onto more than 400,000 vulnerable PCs he had secretly infected and taken over. He also made tens of thousands more dollars renting his 400,000-unit "botnet herd" to other companies that used them to send out spam, viruses, and other malicious code on the Internet. In 2006, Ancheta was sentenced to five years in prison.[18]

Botnet code was originally distributed as infected email attachments, but as users have grown more cautious, cybercriminals have turned to other methods. When users click to view a spam message, botnet code can be secretly installed on the users' PC. A website may be unknowingly infected with malicious code in the form of an ordinary-looking advertisement banner, or may include a link to an infected website. Clicking on any of these may install botnet code. Or, botnet code can be silently uploaded, even if the user takes no action while viewing the website, merely through some un-patched vulnerability that may exist in the browser. Firewalls and antivirus software do not necessarily inspect all data that is downloaded through browsers. Some bot software can even disable antivirus security

---

[17] Jeanne Meserve, "Official: International Hackers Going After U.S. Networks," CNN.com, October 19, 2007, [http://www.cnn.com/2007/US/10/19/cyber.threats/index.html]. Sebastian Sprenger, "Maj. Gen. Lord Is a Groundbreaker," *Federal Computer Week*, October 15, 2007, vol. 21, no. 34, p. 44.

[18] Bob Keefe, "PC Security Still More of a Wish than a Promise," *The Atlanta Journal*, February 3, 2007, p. 1A.

before infecting the PC. Once a PC has been infected, the malicious software establishes a secret communications link to a remote "botmaster" in preparation to receive new commands to attack a specific target. Meanwhile, the malicious code may also automatically probe the infected PC for personal data, or may log keystrokes, and transmit the information to the botmaster.

The Shadowserver Foundation is an organization that monitors the number of command and control servers on the Internet, which indicates the number of bot networks that are being controlled online at a given time. From November 2006 through May 2007, approximately 1,400 command and control servers were found to be active on the Internet. The number of individual infected drones that are controlled by these 1,400 servers reportedly grew from half a million to more than 3 million from March to May 2007. Symantec, another security organization, reported that it detected 6 million bot-infected computers in the second half of 2006.[19]

Some botnet owners reportedly rent their huge networks for US $200 to $300 an hour, and botnets are becoming the weapon of choice for fraud and extortion.[20] Newer methods are evolving for distributing "bot" software that may make it even more difficult in the future for law enforcement to identify and locate the originating "botmaster." Some studies show that authors of software for botnets are increasingly using modern, open-source techniques for software development, including the collaboration of multiple authors for the initial design, new releases to fix bugs in the malicious code, and development of software modules that make portions of the code reusable for newer versions of malicious software designed for different purposes. This increase in collaboration among hackers mirrors the professional code development techniques now used to create commercial software products, and is expected to make future botnets even more robust and reliable. This, in turn, is expected to help increase the demand for malware services in future years.[21]

Traditionally, botnets organize themselves in an hierarchical manner, with a central command and control location (sometimes dynamic) for the botmaster. This central command location is useful to security professionals because it offers a possible central point of failure for the botnet. However, in the near future, security experts believe that attackers may use new botnet architectures that are more sophisticated, and more difficult to detect and trace. One class of botnet architecture that is beginning to emerge uses

[19] Julie Bort, "Attack of the Killer Bots," *Network World*, Jul 2/9, 2007, p. 29.

[20] Susan MacLean, "Report warns of Organized Cyber Crime," *ItWorldCanada*, August 26, 2005, [http://www.itworldcanada.com/a/IT-Focus/39c78aa4-df47-4231-a083-ddd1ab8985 fb.html].

[21] McAfee Virtual Criminology Report: Organized Crime and the Internet, December 2006, [http://www.sigma.com.pl/pliki/albums/userpics/10007/Virtual_Criminology_Report_ 2006.pdf].

peer-to-peer protocol[22], which, because of its decentralized control design, is expected to be more resistant to strategies for countering its disruptive effects.[23] For example, some experts reportedly argue that a well-designed peer-to-peer botnet may be nearly impossible to shut down as a whole because it may provide anonymity to the controller, who can appear as just another node in the bot network.[24]

Estonia, 2007

In the Spring of 2007, government computer systems in Estonia experienced a sustained cyberattack that has been labeled by various observers as cyberwarfare, or cyberterror, or cybercrime. On April 27, officials in Estonia moved a Soviet-era war memorial commemorating an unknown Russian who died fighting the Nazis. The move stirred emotions, and led to rioting by ethnic Russians, and the blockading of the Estonian Embassy in Moscow. The event also marked the beginning of a series of large and sustained Distributed Denial-Of-Service (DDOS) attacks launched against several Estonian national websites, including government ministries and the prime minister's Reform Party.[25]

In the early days of the cyberattack, government websites that normally receive around 1,000 visits a day reportedly were receiving 2,000 visits every second. This caused the repeated shut down of some websites for several hours at a time or longer, according to Estonian officials.[26] The attacks, which flooded computers and servers and blocked legitimate users, were described as crippling, owing to Estonia's high dependence on information technology, but limited resources for managing their infrastructure. Security experts say that the cyberattacks against Estonia were unusual because the rate of the packet attack was very high, and the series of attacks lasted weeks, rather than hour or days, which is more commonly

---

[22] Gnutella emerged as the first fully decentralized peer-to-peer protocol in 2000, and was used on the Internet to share and swap music files in MP3 compression format. The music industry was often frustrated in their efforts to counter this peer-to-peer technology because it could not identify a main controlling source. Since then, several other peer-to-peer protocols have been developed.

[23] Symantec, *Trojan.Peacomm: Building a Peer-to-Peer Botnet*, 2007, [http://www.symantec.com/enterprise/security_response/weblog/2007/01/trojanpeacomm_building_a_peert.html]. Matthew Broersma, *Peer-to-Peer Botnets a New and Growing Threat*, CSO Online, April 17, 2007, [http://www2.csoonline.com/blog_view.html?CID=32852]. Julian B. Grizzard et. al., *Peer-to-Peer Botnets: Overview and Case Study*, 2007, [http://www.usenix.org/events/hotbots07/tech/full_papers/grizzard/grizzard_html/]. Reinier Schoof and Ralph Koning, *Detecting Peer-to-Peer Botnets*, February 4, 2007, [http://staff.science.uva.nl/~delaat/sne-2006-2007/p17/report.pdf].

[24] Tom Espiner, "Security Expert: Storm Botnet 'services' Could Be Sold," CnetNews.com, October 16, 2007, [http://www.news.com/Security-expert-Storm-botnet-services-could-be-sold/2100-7349_3-6213781.html]. Robert Lemos, *Bot software looks to improve peerage*, The Register, May 4, 2006, [http://www.theregister.co.uk/2006/05/04/nugache_p2p_ botnet/].

[25] Robert Vamosi, "Cyberattack in Estonia—What It Really Means," CnetNews.com, May 29, 2007, at [http://news.com.com/Cyberattack+in+Estonia-what+it+really+means/2008-7349_3-6186751.html].

[26] Christopher Rhoads, "Cyber Attack Vexes Estonia, Poses Debate," *The Wall Street Journal*, May 18, 2007, p. A6.

seen for a denial of service attack.[27] Eventually, NATO and the United States sent computer security experts to Estonia to help recover from the attacks, and to analyze the methods used and attempt to determine the source of the attacks.

This event can serve to illustrate how computer network technology has blurred the boundaries between crime, warfare, and terrorism. A persistent problem during and after any cyberattack is accurate identification of the attacker, by finding out whether it was sponsored by a nation, or was the independent work of a few unconnected individuals, or was initiated by a group to instill frustration and fear by damaging the computerized infrastructure and economy. The uncertainty of not knowing the initiator also affects the decision about whom should ultimately become a target for retaliation, and whether the response should come from law enforcement or the military.

Initially, the Russian government was blamed by Estonian officials for the cyberattacks, and there were charges of cyberwarfare. Other observers argued that the cyberattack involved collusion between the Russian government and transnational cybercriminals who made their large botnets available for short-term rent, either to individuals or to larger groups. They argue that as the rented time expired, the intensity of the persistent cyberattacks against Estonia also began to fall off.[28] However, not all security experts agree, and it remains unclear at this time whether the cyberattacks were sanctioned or initiated by the Russian government, or if a criminal botnet was actually involved.

After some investigation, network analysts later concluded that the cyberattacks targeting Estonia were not a concerted attack, but instead were the product of spontaneous anger from a loose federation of separate attackers. Technical data showed that sources of the attack were worldwide rather than concentrated in a few locations. The computer code that caused the DDOS attack was posted and shared in many Russian language chat rooms, where the moving of the war memorial was a very emotional topic for discussion. These analysts state that although access to various Estonian government agencies was blocked by the malicious code, there was no apparent attempt to target national critical infrastructure other than internet resources, and no extortion demands were made. Their analysis thus far concluded that there was no Russian government connection to the attacks against Estonia.[29] However, investigation into the incident continues, and officials from the United States view some aspects of the event as

[27] Carolyn Marsan, "Examining the Reality of Cyberwar in Wake of Estonian Attacks," *Network World*, August 27, 2007, vol. 24, no. 33, p. 24.

[28] Iain Thomson, "Russia 'Hired Botnets' for Estonia Cyber-War," *Computing*, [http://www.computing.co.uk/vnunet/news/2191082/claims-russia-hired-botnets].

[29] Heise Security, *Estonian DDoS—a final analysis*, [http://www.heise-security.co.uk/news/print/90461].

a possible model for future cyberwarfare or cyberterrorism directed against a nation state.

Other Trends in Cybercrime Methods

Cybercrime is usually conducted through a connection to the Internet, but can also involve unauthorized removal of data on small, portable flash drive storage devices. Cybercrime, usually in the form of network hacking, has involved persons with strong technical skills, often motivated by the desire to gain popularity among their technology peers. However, the growing trend is now to profit from these network cyberattacks by targeting specific systems, often through collaboration among criminals and technical experts. The motives that drive these cybercriminal groups now may differ from those of their paying customers, who may possess little or no technical skills.

New technologies continue to outpace policy for law enforcement. Problems of coordination among agencies of different countries, along with conflicting national policies about crime in cyberspace, work to the advantage of cybercriminals who can choose to operate from geographic locations where penalties for some forms of cybercrime may not yet exist. Sophisticated tools for cyberattack can now be found for sale or for rent on the Internet, where highly-organized underground cybercrime businesses host websites that advertise a variety of disruptive software products and malicious technical services. High-end cybercrime groups use standard software business development techniques to keep their products updated with the latest anti-security features, and seek to recruit new and talented software engineering students into their organizations.

Where illicit profits are potentially very large, some high-end criminal groups have reportedly adopted standard IT business practices to systematically develop more efficient and effective computer code for cybercrime. Studies also show that organized crime groups now actively recruit college engineering graduates and technical expert members of computer societies, and sponsor them to attend more information technology (IT) courses to further their technical expertise. However, in some cases, targeted students may not realize that a criminal organization is behind the recruitment offer.[30]

Cyberattacks are increasingly designed to silently steal information without leaving behind any damage that would be noticed by a user. These types of attacks attempt to escape detection in order to remain on host systems for longer periods of time. It is also expected that as mobile

[30] McAfee Virtual Criminology Report: Organized Crime and the Internet, December 2006, [http://www.sigma.com.pl/pliki/albums/userpics/10007/Virtual_Criminology_Report_ 2006.pdf].

communication devices are incorporated more into everyday life, they will be increasingly targeted in the future for attack by cybercriminals.[31]

Malicious Code Hosted on websites

Malicious code, such as viruses or Trojan Horses, are used to infect a computer to make it available for takeover and remote control. Malicious code can infect a computer if the user opens an email attachment, or clicks an innocent-looking link on a website. For example, users who visited the popular MySpace and YouTube websites in 2005, and who lacked important software security patches, reportedly may have had their PCs infected if they clicked on a banner advertisement which silently installed malicious code on their computers to log keystrokes or capture sensitive data. During the first half of 2006, the Microsoft Security Team reported that it had removed 10 million pieces of malicious software from nearly 4 million computers and web servers.[32] Recently, analysts at Google tested several million web pages for the presence of malicious software, and determined that 4.5 million of the web pages examined were suspicious in nature. After further testing of the 4.5 million web pages, over 1 million were found to launch downloads of malicious software, and more than two thirds of those programs were "bot" software that, among other things, collected data on banking transactions and then emailed the information to a temporary email account.[33]

Researchers at the San Jose, Calif.-based security firm, Finjan Inc., after reviewing security data from the first quarter of 2007, found that more malware is hosted on servers in countries such as the U.S. and U.K., than in other countries with less developed e-crime law enforcement policies. Findings from the Finjan 2007 Web Security Trends Report are based on an analysis of more than 10 million unique websites from Internet traffic recorded in the UK, and include the following:

- Attacks that involve the use of code obfuscation through diverse randomization techniques are growing more numerous and complex, making them virtually invisible to pattern-matching/signature-based methods in use by traditional antivirus products.

[31] A web crawler (also known as a Web spider or Web robot) is a program or automated script that browses the World Wide Web in a methodical, automated manner. Web crawlers are mainly used to create a copy of all the visited pages for later processing by a search engine that will index the downloaded pages to provide fast searches. Wikipedia, [http://en.wikipedia.org/wiki/Web_crawler].

[32] Elise Ackerman, "Hackers' Infections Slither Onto Web Sites," *The Mercury News*, January 3, 2007, p. 1.

[33] Jeff Hecht, "Web Browsers Are New Frontline in Internet War," *NewScientistTech*, May 5, 2007, [http://www.newscientisttech.com/article.ns?id=mg19426026.000&print=true]. Niels Provos et. al., *The Ghost in the Browser: Analysis of Web-based Malware*, Google, Inc., [http://www.usenix.org/events/hotbots07/tech/full_papers/provos/provos.pdf].

- Criminals are displaying an increasing level of sophistication when embedding malicious code within legitimate content with less dependence on outlaw servers in unregulated countries.

Finjan found that 90% of the websites examined containing malware resided on servers located in the U.S. or U.K. "The results of this study shatter the myth that malicious code is primarily being hosted in countries where e-crime laws are less developed," Finjan CTO Yuval Ben-Itzhak reportedly stated.[34]

Identity Theft

Botnets and other examples of malicious code can operate to assist cybercriminals with identity theft. Current FBI estimates are that identity theft costs American businesses and consumers $50 billion a year. Individual users are often lured into clicking on tempting links that are found in email or when visiting websites. Clicking on titles such as "Buy Rolex watches cheap," or "Check out my new Photos," can take advantage of web browser vulnerabilities to place malicious software onto a users system which allows a cybercriminal to gather personal information from the user's computer.

Malicious code can scan a victim's computer for sensitive information, such as name, address, place and date of birth, social security number, mother's maiden name, and telephone number. Full identities obtained this way are bought and sold in online markets. False identity documents can then be created from this information using home equipment such as a digital camera, color printer, and laminating device, to make official-looking driver's licences, birth certificates, reference letters, and bank statements.[35]

Identity theft involving thousands of victims is also enabled by inadequate computer security practices within organizations.[36] MasterCard International reported that in 2005 more than 40 million credit card numbers belonging to U.S. consumers were accessed by computer hackers.[37] Some of

---

[34] Finjan, Inc., *Web Security Trends Report, Q2 2007*, [http://www.finjan.com/Content.aspx?id=827].

[35] Lou Bobson, "Identity Theft Ruining Lives," *The Sunday Mail*, May 20, 2007, p. 62.

[36] On April 12, 2005, personal information, such as Social Security Numbers for 310,000 U.S. citizens, may have been stolen in a data security breach that involved 59 instances of unauthorized access into its corporate databases using stolen passwords. Boston College reported in March 2005 that a hacker had gained unauthorized access to computer database records with personal information for up to 106,000 alumni, and in the same month, Chico State University of California, reported that its databases had been breached containing the names and Social Security numbers for as many as 59,000 current and former students. David Bank and Christopher Conkey, "New Safeguards for Your Privacy," *The Wall Street Journal*, March 24, 2005, p. D1.

[37] Jonathan Krim and Michael Barbaro, "40 Million Credit Card Numbers Hacked," *Washington Post*, June 18, 2005, p. A01. See also the report by the U.S. House of Representatives Homeland Security Committee, July 1, 2005, raising concerns about potential ties between identity theft victims and terrorism. Caitlin Harrington, "Terrorists Can Exploit Identity Theft, Report From House Democrats Says," *CQ Homeland Security*, July 1, 2005.

these account numbers were reportedly being sold on a Russian website, and some consumers have reported fraudulent charges on their statements. Officials at the UFJ bank in Japan reportedly stated that some of that bank's customers may also have become victims of fraud related to theft of the MasterCard information.[38] In June 2006, officials from the U.S. Department of Energy acknowledged that names and personal information belonging to more than 1,500 employees of the National Nuclear Security Administration (NNSA) had been stolen in a network intrusion that apparently took place starting in 2004. The NNSA did not discover the security breach until one year after it had occurred.[39]

Some sources report that stolen credit card numbers and bank account information are traded online in a highly structured arrangement, involving buyers, sellers, intermediaries, and service industries. Services include offering to conveniently change the billing address of a theft victim, through manipulation of stolen PINs or passwords. Observers estimated that in 2005 such services for each stolen MasterCard number cost between $42 and $72.[40] Other news articles report that, in 2007, a stolen credit card number sells online for only $1, and a complete identity, including a U.S. bank account number, credit-card number, date of birth, and a government-issued ID number now sells for just $14 to $18.[41]

As of January 2007, 35 states have enacted data security laws requiring businesses that have experienced an intrusion involving possible identity theft to notify persons affected, and to improve security for protection of restricted data. However, existing federal and state laws that impose obligations on information owners, may require harmonization to provide protections that are more uniform.[42]

Cyber Espionage

Cyber espionage involves the unauthorized probing to test a target computer's configuration or evaluate its system defenses, or the unauthorized viewing and copying of data files. However, should a terrorist group, nation, or other organization use computer hacking techniques for political or economic motives, their deliberate intrusions may also qualify them, additionally, as cybercriminals. If there is disagreement about this, it is

---

38 BBC News, "Japan Cardholders 'Hit' by Theft," June 21, 2005, at [http://news.bbc.co.uk/1/hi/business/4114252.stm].

39 Dawn Onley and Patience Wait, "DOD's Efforts to Stave off Nation-State Cyberattacks Begin with China," *Government Computer News*, August 21, 2006.

40 CCRC staff, *Russia, Biggest Ever Credit Card Scam*, Computer Crime Research Center, July 8, 2005, at [http://www.crime-research.org/news/08.07.2005/1349/].

41 David Hayes, "A Dollar goes a Long Way in Swiping Private Data," *The Kansas City Star*, March 20, 2007, p. 1.

42 For more information about laws related to identity theft, see CRS Report RL34120, *Information Security and Data Breach Notification Safeguards*, by Gina Marie Stevens.

likely because technology has outpaced policy for labeling actions in cyberspace. In fact, industrial cyber espionage may now be considered a necessary part of global economic competition, and secretly monitoring the computerized functions and capabilities of potential adversary countries may also be considered essential for national defense.[43]

U.S. counterintelligence officials reportedly have stated that about 140 different foreign intelligence organizations regularly attempt to hack into the computer systems of U.S. government agencies and U.S. companies. Cyber espionage, which enables the exfiltration of massive amounts of information electronically, has now transformed the nature of counterintelligence, by enabling a reduced reliance on conventional spying operations.[44] The Internet, including satellite links and wireless local networks, now offers new, low cost and low risk opportunities for espionage. In 2001, a Special Committee of Inquiry established by the European parliament accused the United States of using its Echelon electronic spy network to engage in industrial espionage against European businesses. Echelon was reportedly set up in 1971 as an electronic monitoring system during the Cold War. European-Union member Britain helps operate the system, which includes listening posts in Canada, Australia, and New Zealand. Echelon is described as a global spy system reportedly capable of intercepting wireless phone calls, e-mail, and fax messages made from almost any location around the world.[45]

The European parliament Special Committee reported that information gathered on Echelon may have helped the United States beat the European Airbus Consortium in selling aircraft to Saudi Arabia in 1994.[46] In 1995, France expelled five American diplomats and other officials, reportedly including the Paris station chief for the CIA, because of suspected industrial espionage activities linked to Echelon.[47]

The State Department denied that the U.S. government was engaged in industrial espionage. However, former director of the U.S. Central Intelligence Agency, James Woolsey, has reportedly justified the possibility of

[43] U.S. intelligence officials, speaking on background, explained that they have routinely penetrated potential enemies' computer networks. These officials claim that thousands of attacks have taken place and sensitive information was stolen. John Stanton, "Rules of Cyber War Baffle U.S. Government Agencies," *National Defense*, February 2000, [http://www.nationaldefensemagazine.org/issues/2000/Feb/Rules.htm].

[44] Jeanne Meserve, "Official: International Hackers Going after U.S. Netoworks," CNN.com, October 19, 2007, [http://www.cnn.com/2007/US/10/19/cyber.threats/index. html].

[45] Martin Asser, "Echelon: Big brother without a cause?" BBC News, July 6, 2000, [http://news.bbc.co.uk/1/hi/world/europe/820758.stm].

[46] Ron Pemstein, "Europe Spy System," GlobalSecurity.org, March 30, 2000, [http://www.globalsecurity.org/intell/library/news/2000/03/000330-echelon1.htm]. Paul Meller, "European Parliament Adopts 'Echelon' Report," CNN.com, September 7, 2001, [http://archives.cnn.com/2001/TECH/internet/09/07/echelon.report.idg/].

[47] Chris Marsden, "European Union to Investigate US-Run Satellite Spy Network," World Socialist Website, July 10, 2000, [http://www.wsws.org/articles/2000/jul2000/eche-j10.shtml].

Figure 1: Diagram of Purported Echelon Spy System

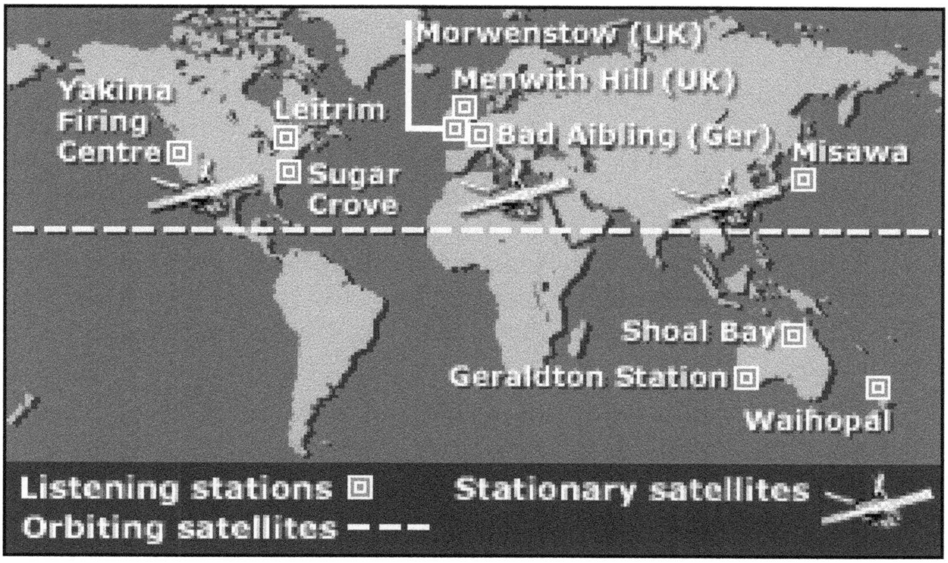

Source: BBC News, July 6, 2000, at [http://news.bbc.co.uk/1/hi/world/europe/820758.stm].

industrial espionage by the United States on the basis of the use of bribery by European companies. Officials of the European parliament reportedly expressed outrage about the justification, while not denying that bribery is sometimes used to make sales.[48]

Some government officials warn that criminals now sell or rent malicious code tools for cyber espionage, and the risk for damage to U.S. national security due to cyber espionage conducted by other countries is great. One industry official, arguing for stronger government agency computer security practices, stated that, "If gangs of foreigners broke into the State or Commerce Departments and carried off dozens of file cabinets, there would

[48] European Parliament resolution on the existence of a global system for the interception of private and commercial communications (ECHELON interception system) (2001/2098(INI)), European Parliament approved on September 5, 2001, by 367 votes for, 159 against, and 39 abstentions, [http://www.cyber-rights.org/interception/echelon/European_parliament_resolution.htm]. Gerhard SCHMID *Report on the existence of a global system for the interception of private and commercial communications (ECHELON interception system)*, Doc.: A5-0264/2001, May 9, 2001, [http://www.statewatch.org/ news/2001/sep/ 02echelon.htm]. James Woolsey, *Intelligence Gathering and Democracies: The Issue of Economic and Industrial Espionage*, Federation of American Scientists, March 7, 2000, [http://ftp.fas.org/irp/ news/2000/03/wool0300.htm].

be a crisis. When the same thing happens in cyberspace, we shrug it off as another of those annoying computer glitches we must live with."[49]

In 2003, a series of cyberattacks designed to copy sensitive data files was launched against DOD systems, and the computers belonging to DOD contractors. The cyber espionage attack apparently went undetected for many months. This series of cyberattacks was labeled "Titan Rain," and was suspected by DOD investigators to have originated in China. The attacks were directed against the U.S. Defense Information Systems Agency (DISA), the U.S. Redstone Arsenal, the Army Space and Strategic Defense Installation, and several computer systems critical to military logistics. Although no classified systems reportedly were breached, many files were copied containing information that is sensitive and subject to U.S. export-control laws.

In 2006, an extended cyberattack against the U.S. Naval War College in Newport, Rhode Island, prompted officials to disconnect the entire campus from the Internet.[50] A similar attack against the Pentagon in 2007 led officials to temporarily disconnect part of the unclassified network from the Internet. DOD officials acknowledge that the Global Information Grid, which is the main network for the U.S. military, experiences more than three million daily scans by unknown potential intruders.[51]

Accurate attribution is important when considering whether to retaliate using military force or police action. Some DOD officials have indicated that the majority of cyber attacks against DOD and U.S. civilian agency systems are suspected to originate in China, and these attacks are consistently more numerous and sophisticated than cyberattacks from other malicious actors. The motives appear to be primarily cyber espionage against civilian agencies, DOD contractors, and DOD systems. The espionage involves unauthorized access to files containing sensitive industrial technology, and unauthorized research into DOD operations. Some attacks included attempts to implant malicious code into computer systems for future use by intruders.[52]

Security experts warn that all U.S. federal agencies should now be aware that in cyberspace some malicious actors consider that no boundaries exist between military and civilian targets. According to an August 2005 computer

---

[49] James Lewis, testimony before the House Committee on Homeland Security, Subcommittee on Emerging Threats, Cybersecurity, and Science and Technology, April 15, 2007.

[50] Chris Johnson, Naval War College Network, "Web Site Back Up Following Intrusion," *Inside the Navy*, December 18, 2006.

[51] Some estimates say that up to 90% of computer software used in China is pirated, and thus open to hijack through computer viruses. James Lewis, *Computer Espionage, Titan Rain and China*, Center for Strategic and International Studies, December 14, 2005.

[52] Josh Rogin, "Cyber officials: Chinese hackers attack 'anything and everything,'" FCW.com, Febrary 13, 2007, [http://www.fcw.com/article97658-02-13-07-Web&print Layout].

security report by IBM, more than 237 million overall security attacks were reported globally during the first half of that year.[53] Government agencies were targeted the most, reporting more than 54 million attacks, while manufacturing ranked second with 36 million attacks, financial services ranked third with approximately 34 million, and healthcare received more than 17 million attacks. The most frequent targets for these attacks, all occurring in the first half of 2005, were government agencies and industries in the United States (12 million), followed by New Zealand (1.2 million), and China (1 million). These figures likely represent an underestimation, given that most security analysts agree that the number of incidents reported are only a small fraction of the total number of attacks that actually occur.

Terrorism Linked to Cybercrime

The proportion of cybercrime that can be directly or indirectly attributed to terrorists is difficult to determine. However, linkages do exist between terrorist groups and criminals that allow terror networks to expand internationally through leveraging the computer resources, money laundering activities, or transit routes operated by criminals. For example, the 2005 U.K. subway and bus bombings, and the attempted car bombings in 2007, also in the U.K., provide evidence that groups of terrorists are already secretly active within countries with large communication networks and computerized infrastructures, plus a large, highly skilled IT workforce. London police officials reportedly believe that terrorists obtained high-quality explosives used for the 2005 U.K. bombings through criminal groups based in Eastern Europe.[54]

A recent trial in the U.K. revealed a significant link between Islamic terrorist groups and cybercrime. In June 2007, three British residents, Tariq al-Daour, Waseem Mughal, and Younes Tsouli, pled guilty, and were sentenced for using the Internet to incite murder. The men had used stolen credit card information at online web stores to purchase items to assist fellow jihadists in the field—items such as night vision goggles, tents, global positioning satellite devices, and hundreds of prepaid cell phones, and more than 250 airline tickets, through using 110 different stolen credit cards. Another 72 stolen credit cards were used to register over 180 Internet web domains at 95 different web hosting companies. The group also laundered money charged to more than 130 stolen credit cards through online

[53] The Global Business Security Index reports worldwide trends in computer security from incidents that are collected and analyzed by IBM and other security organizations. IBM press release, *IBM Report: Government, Financial Services and Manufacturing Sectors Top Targets of Security Attacks in First Half of 2005*, IBM, August 2, 2005.

[54] Walsh, *Terrorism on the Cheap*. Rollie Lal, "Terrorists and Organized Crime Join Forces," *International Herald Tribune*, May 25, 2005, at [http://www.iht.com/articles/2005/05/23/opinion/edlal.php]. Barbara Porter, "Forum Links Organized Crime and Terrorism," *By George!* summer 2004 [http://www2.gwu.edu/~bygeorge/060804/crimeterrorism.html].

gambling websites. In all, the trio made fraudulent charges totaling more than $3.5 million from a database containing 37,000 stolen credit card numbers, including account holders' names and addresses, dates of birth, credit balances, and credit limits.[55]

Cybercriminals have made alliances with drug traffickers in Afghanistan, the Middle East, and elsewhere where illegal drug funds or other profitable activities such as credit card theft, are used to support terrorist groups.[56] Drug traffickers are reportedly among the most widespread users of encryption for Internet messaging, and are able to hire high-level computer specialists to help evade law enforcement, coordinate shipments of drugs, and launder money. Regions with major narcotics markets, such as Western Europe and North America, also possess optimal technology infrastructure and open commercial nodes that increasingly serve the transnational trafficking needs of both criminal and terrorist groups.[57] Officials of the U.S. Drug Enforcement Agency (DEA), reported in 2003 that 14 of the 36 groups found on the U.S. State Department's list of foreign terrorist organizations were also involved in drug trafficking. A 2002 report by the Federal Research Division at the Library of Congress, revealed a "growing involvement of Islamic terrorist and extremists groups in drug trafficking", and limited evidence of cooperation between different terrorist groups involving both drug trafficking and trafficking in arms.[58] Consequently, DEA officials reportedly argued that the war on drugs and the war against terrorism are and should be linked.[59]

State Department officials, at a Senate hearing in March 2002, also indicated that some terrorist groups may be using drug trafficking as a way to gain financing while simultaneously weakening their enemies in the West through exploiting their desire for addictive drugs.[60] The poppy crop in

---

55 Brian Krebs, "Three Worked the Web to Help Terrorists," *The Washington Post*, July 6, 2007, p. D01.

56 Peter Bergen, "The Taliban, Regrouped and Rearmed," *The Washington Post*, September 10, 2006, p. B1. Helen Cooper, "NATO Chief Says More Troops Are Needed in Afghanistan," *The New York Times*, September 22, 2006, p. 10.

57 Glenn Curtis and Tara Karacan, *The Nexus Among Terrorists, Narcotics Traffickers, Weapons Proliferators, and Organized Crime Networks in Western Europe*, a study prepared by the Federal Research Division, Library of Congress, December 2002, p. 22, at [http://www.loc.gov/rr/frd/pdf-files/WestEurope_NEXUS.pdf].

58 L. Berry, G.E. Curtis, R.A. Hudson, and N. A. Kollars, *A Global Overview of Narcotics-Funded Terrorist and Other Extremist Groups*, Federal Research Division, Library of Congress, Washington, DC, May 2002.

59 Authorization for coordinating the federal war on drugs expired on September 30, 2003. For more information, see CRS Report RL32352, *War on Drugs: Reauthorization of the Office of National Drug Control Policy*, by Mark Eddy. Also, see D.C. Préfontaine, QC and Yvon Dandurand, *Terrorism and Organized Crime Reflections on an Illusive Link and its Implication for Criminal Law Reform*, International Society for Criminal Law Reform Annual Meeting—Montreal, August 8—12, Workshop D-3 Security Measures and Links to Organized Crime, August 11, 2004, at [http://www.icclr.law.ubc.ca/Publications/Reports/International%20Society%20Paper%20of%20Terrorism.pdf].

60 Rand Beers and Francis X. Taylor, U.S. State Department, *Narco-Terror: The Worldwide Connection Between Drugs and Terror*, testimony before the U.S. Senate Judiciary Committee, Subcommittee on Technology, Terrorism, and Government Information, March 13, 2002.

Afghanistan reportedly supplies resin to produce over 90 percent of the world's heroin, supporting a drug trade estimated at $3.1 billion. Reports indicate that money from drug trafficking in Afghanistan is used to help fund terrorist and insurgent groups that operate in that country. Subsequently, U.S. intelligence reports in 2007 have stated that "Al Qaeda in Afghanistan" has been revitalized and restored to its pre-September 11, 2001 operation levels, and may now be in a better position to strike Western countries.[61]

Drug traffickers have the financial clout to hire computer specialists with skills for using technologies which make Internet messages hard or impossible to decipher, and which allow terrorist organizations to transcend borders and operate internationally with less chance of detection. Many highly trained technical specialists that make themselves available for hire originally come from the countries of the former Soviet Union and the Indian subcontinent. Some of these technical specialists reportedly will not work for criminal or terrorist organizations willingly, but may be misled or unaware of their employers' political objectives. Still, others will agree to provide assistance because other well-paid legitimate employment is scarce in their region.[62]

Terrorist Groups linked to Hackers

Links between computer hackers and terrorists, or terrorist-sponsoring nations may be difficult to confirm. Membership in the most highly-skilled computer hacker groups is sometimes very exclusive and limited to individuals who develop, demonstrate, and share only with each other, their most closely-guarded set of sophisticated hacker tools. These exclusive hacker groups do not seek attention because maintaining secrecy allows them to operate more effectively. Some hacker groups may also have political interests that are supra-national, or based on religion, or other socio-political ideologies, while other hacker groups may be motivated by profit, or linked to organized crime, and may be willing to sell their computer services, regardless of the political interests involved.

Information about computer vulnerabilities is now for sale online in a hackers' "black market". For example, a list of 5,000 addresses of computers that have already been infected with spyware and which are waiting to be remotely controlled as part of an automated "bot network" reportedly

[61] Matthew Lee and Katherine Shrader, *Al-Qaida has rebuilt, U.S. intel warns*, Associated Press, July 12, 2007, [http://news.yahoo.com/s/ap/20070712/ap_on_go_pr_wh/us_terror_ threat_32;_ylt=AuUR r2eP8AhBrfHyTOdw714Gw_IE]. Associated Press, "Afghanistan's poppy crop could yield more than 2006's record haul, UN says," International Herald Tribune, June 25, 2007, [http://www.iht.com/articles/ap/2007/06/25/asia/AS-GEN-Afghan-Drugs.php].

[62] Louise Shelly, *Organized Crime, Cybercrime and Terrorism*, Computer Crime Research Center, September 27, 2004, [http://www.crime-research.org/articles/Terrorism_Cybercrime/].

can be obtained for about $150 to $500. Prices for information about computer vulnerabilities for which no software patch yet exists reportedly range from $1,000 to $5,000. Purchasers of this information are often organized crime groups, various foreign governments, and companies that deal in spam.[63]

Terrorist Capabilities for Cyberattack

Some experts estimate that advanced or structured cyberattacks against multiple systems and networks, including target surveillance and testing of sophisticated new hacker tools, might require from two to four years of preparation, while a complex coordinated cyberattack, causing mass disruption against integrated, heterogeneous systems may require 6 to 10 years of preparation.[64] This characteristic, where hackers devote much time to detailed and extensive planning before launching a cyberattack, has also been described as a "hallmark" of previous physical terrorist attacks and bombings launched by Al Qaeda.

It is difficult to determine the level of interest, or the capabilities of international terrorist groups to launch an effective cyberattack. A 1999 report by The Center for the Study of Terrorism and Irregular Warfare at the Naval Postgraduate School concluded that it is likely that any severe cyberattacks experienced in the near future by industrialized nations will be used by terrorist groups simply to supplement the more traditional physical terrorist attacks.[65]

Some observers have stated that Al Qaeda does not see cyberattack as important for achieving its goals, preferring attacks which inflict human casualties.[66] Other observers believe that the groups most likely to consider and employ cyberattack and cyberterrorism are the terrorist groups operating in post-industrial societies (such as Europe and the United States), rather than international terrorist groups that operate in developing regions where there is limited access to high technology.

However, other sources report that Al Qaeda has taken steps to improve organizational secrecy through more active and sophisticated use of technology,

---

[63] Hackers sell their information anonymously through secretive websites. Bob Francis, "Know Thy Hacker," *Infoworld*, January 28, 2005 at [http://www.infoworld.com/article/05/01/28/05O Psecadvise_1.html].

[64] Dorothy Denning, "Levels of Cyberterror Capability: Terrorists and the Internet," [http://www.cs.georgetown.edu/~denning/infosec/Denning-Cyberterror-SRI.ppt], presentation, and Zack Phillips, "Homeland Tech Shop Wants to Jump-Start Cybersecurity Ideas," *CQ Homeland Security*, September 14, 2004 at [http://homeland.cq.com/hs/display.do?docid=1330150&sourcetype=31&binderName=news-all].

[65] Report was published in 1999, available at [http://www.nps.navy.mil/ctiw/reports/].

[66] The Ashland Institute for Strategic Studies has observed that Al Qaeda is more fixated on physical threats than electronic ones. John Swartz, "Cyberterror Impact, Defense Under Scrutiny," *USA Today*, August 3, 2004, p. 2B.

and evidence suggests that Al Qaeda terrorists used the Internet extensively to plan their operations for September 11, 2001.[67] In past years, Al Qaeda groups reportedly used new Internet-based telephone services to communicate with other terrorist cells overseas. Khalid Shaikh Mohammed, one of the masterminds of the attack against the World Trade Center, reportedly used special Internet chat software to communicate with at least two airline hijackers. Ramzi Yousef, who was sentenced to life imprisonment for the previous bombing of the World Trade Center, had trained as an electrical engineer, and had planned to use sophisticated electronics to detonate bombs on 12 U.S. airliners departing from Asia for the United States. He also used sophisticated encryption to protect his data and to prevent law enforcement from reading his plans should he be captured.[68]

Tighter physical security measures now widely in place throughout the United States may encourage terrorist groups in the future to explore cyberattack as way to lower the risk of detection for their operations.[69] However, other security observers believe that terrorist organizations might be reluctant to launch a cyberattack because it would result in less immediate drama and have a lower psychological impact than a more conventional bombing attack. These observers believe that unless a cyberattack can be made to result in actual physical damage or bloodshed, it will never be considered as serious as a nuclear, biological, or chemical terrorist attack.[70]

Possible Effects of a Coordinated Cyberattack

In March 2007, researchers at Idaho National Laboratories (INL) conducted an experiment labeled the "Aurora Generator Test" to demonstrate the results of a simulated cyberattack on a power network. In a video released by the Department of Homeland Security, a power generator turbine, similar to many now in use throughout the United States, is forced to overheat and shut down dramatically, after receiving malicious commands from a hacker. The researchers at INL were investigating results of a possible cyberattack directed against a vulnerability that, reportedly, has since been fixed.[71] The video, however, implied that other multiple power generators sharing similar cyber vulnerabilities could potentially be disabled the same way.

---

[67] David Kaplan, "Playing Offense: The Inside Story of How U.S. Terrorist Hunters Are Going after Al Qaeda," *U.S. News & World Report*, June 2, 2003, pp. 19–29.

[68] Robert Windrem, "9/11 Detainee: Attack Scaled Back," September 21, 2003, [http://www.msnbc.com/news/969759.asp].

[69] "Terrorism: An Introduction," April 4, 2003 at [http://www.terrorismanswers.com/terrorism].

[70] James Lewis, "Assessing the Risks of Cyber Terrorism, Cyber War and Other Cyber Threats," December 2002 at [http://www.csis.org/tech/0211_lewis.pdf].

[71] Robert Lemos, *DHS Video Shows Potential Impact of Cyberattack*, SecurityFocus.com, September 27, 2007, [http://www.securityfocus.com/brief/597].

In July 2002, the U.S. Naval War College hosted a war game called "Digital Pearl Harbor" to develop a scenario for a coordinated cyberterrorism event, where mock attacks by computer security experts against critical infrastructure systems simulated state-sponsored cyberwarfare. The simulated cyberattacks determined that the most vulnerable infrastructure computer systems were the Internet itself, and the computer systems that are part of the financial infrastructure.[72] It was also determined that attempts to cripple the U.S. telecommunications infrastructure would be unsuccessful because built-in system redundancy would prevent damage from becoming too widespread. The conclusion of the exercise was that a "Digital Pearl Harbor" in the United States was only a slight possibility.[73]

However, in 2002, a major vulnerability was discovered in switching equipment software that threatened the infrastructure for major portions of the Internet. A flaw in the Simple Network Management Protocol (SNMP) would have enabled attackers to take over Internet routers and cripple network telecommunications equipment globally. Network and equipment vendors worldwide raced quickly to fix their products before the problem could be exploited by hackers, with possible worldwide consequences. U.S. government officials also reportedly made efforts to keep information about this major vulnerability quiet until after the needed repairs were implemented on vulnerable Internet systems.[74] According to an assessment reportedly written by the FBI, the security flaw could have been exploited to cause many serious problems, such as bringing down widespread

[72] At the annual conference of the Center for Conflict Studies, Phil Williams, Director of the Program on Terrorism and Trans-National Crime and the University of Pittsburgh, said an attack on the global financial system would likely focus on key nodes in the U.S. financial infrastructure: Fedwire and Fednet. Fedwire is the financial funds transfer system that exchanges money among U.S. banks, while Fednet is the electronic network that handles the transactions. The system has one primary installation and three backups. "You can find out on the Internet where the backups are. If those could be taken out by a mix of cyber and physical activities, the U.S. economy would basically come to a halt," Williams said. "If the takedown were to include the international funds transfer networks CHIPS and SWIFT then the entire global economy could be thrown into chaos." George Butters, "Expect Terrorist Attacks on Global Financial System," October 10, 2003 at [http://www.theregister.co.uk/content/55/33269.html].

[73] The simulation involved more than 100 participants. Gartner, Inc., "Cyberattacks: The Results of the Gartner/U.S. Naval War College Simulation," July 2002, at [http://www3.gartner.com/2_events/audioconferences/dph/dph.html.] War game participants were divided into cells, and devised attacks against the electrical power grid, telecommunications infrastructure, the Internet and the financial services sector. It was determined that "peer-to-peer networking," a special method of communicating where every PC used commonly available software to act as both a server and a client, posed a potentially critical threat to the Internet itself. William Jackson, "War College Calls Digital Pearl Harbor Doable," *Government Computer News*, August 23, 2002, at [http://www.gcn.com/vol1_no1/daily-updates/19792-1.html].

[74] The vulnerability was found in Abstract Syntax Notation One (ASN.1) encoding, and was extremely widespread. Ellen Messmer, "President's Advisor Predicts Cyber-catastrophes Unless Security Improves," *Network World Fusion*, July 9, 2002 at [http://www.nwfusion.com/news/2002/0709schmidt.html].

telephone networks and also halting control information exchanged between ground and aircraft flight control systems.[75]

Security experts agree that a coordinated cyberattack could be used to amplify the effects of a conventional terrorist attack, including a nuclear, biological, or chemical (NBC) attack. However, many of these same experts disagree about the damaging effects that might result from an attack directed against control computers that operate the U.S. critical infrastructure. Some observers have stated that because of U.S. dependency on computer technology, such attacks may have the potential to create economic damage on a large scale, while other observers have stated that U.S. infrastructure systems are resilient and would possibly recover easily, thus avoiding any severe or catastrophic effects.

While describing possible offensive tactics for military cyber operations, DOD officials reportedly stated that the U.S. could confuse enemies by using cyberattack to open floodgates, control traffic lights, or scramble the banking systems in other countries.[76] Likewise, some of China's military journals speculate that cyberattacks could disable American financial markets. China, however, is almost as dependent on these U.S. markets as the United States, and might possibly suffer even more from such a disruption to finances. As to using cyberattack against other U.S. critical infrastructures, the amount of potential damage that could be inflicted might be relatively trivial compared to the costs of discovery, if engaged in by a nation state. However, this constraint does not apply to non-state actors like Al Qaeda, thus making cyberattack a potentially useful tool for those groups who reject the global market economy.[77]

SCADA Vulnerabilities

Supervisory Control And Data Acquisition (SCADA) systems are the computers that monitor and regulate the operations of most critical infrastructure industries (such as the companies that manage the power grid). These SCADA computers automatically monitor and adjust switching, manufacturing, and other process control activities, based on digitized feedback data gathered by sensors. These control systems are often placed in remote locations, are frequently unmanned, and are accessed only periodically by engineers or technical staff via telecommunications links. However, for more efficiency, these communication links are increasingly connected to corporate administrative local area networks, or directly to the Internet.

[75] Barton Gellman, "Cyber-Attacks by Al Qaeda Feared," *Washington Post*, June 27, 2002, p. A01.

[76] Sebastian Sprenger, "Maj.Gen. Lord Is a Groundbreaker," *Federal Computer Week*, October 15, 2007, vol. 21, no. 34, pp. 44–45.

[77] James Lewis, "Assessing the Risks of Cyber Terrorism, Cyber War and Other Cyber Threats," December 2002, at [http://www.csis.org/tech/0211_lewis.pdf].

Some experts believe that the importance of SCADA systems for controlling the critical infrastructure may make them an attractive target for terrorists.[78] Many SCADA systems also now operate using Commercial-Off-The-Shelf (COTS) software, which some observers believe are inadequately protected against a cyberattack. These SCADA systems are thought to remain persistently vulnerable to cyberattack because many organizations that operate them have not paid proper attention to these systems' unique computer security needs.[79]

The following example may serve to illustrate the possible vulnerability of control systems and highlight cybersecurity issues that could arise for infrastructure computers when SCADA controls are interconnected with office networks. In August 2003, the "Slammer"Internet computer worm was able to corrupt for five hours the computer control systems at the Davis-Besse nuclear power plant located in Ohio (fortunately, the power plant was closed and off-line when the cyberattack occurred). The computer worm was able to successfully penetrate systems in the Davis-Besse power plant control room largely because the business network for its corporate offices was found to have multiple connections to the Internet that bypassed the control room firewall.[80]

Other observers, however, suggest that SCADA systems and the critical infrastructure are more robust and resilient than early theorists of cyberterror have stated, and that the infrastructure would likely recover rapidly from a cyberterrorism attack. They cite, for example, that water system failures, power outages, air traffic disruptions, and other scenarios resembling possible cyberterrorism often occur as routine events, and rarely affect national security, even marginally. System failures due to storms routinely occur at the regional level, where service may often be denied to customers for hours or days. Technical experts who understand the

---

[78] Proprietary systems are unique, custom built software products intended for installation on a few (or a single) computers, and their uniqueness makes them a less attractive target for hackers. They are less attractive because finding a security vulnerability takes time, and a hacker may usually not consider it worth their while to invest the pre-operative surveillance and research needed to attack a proprietary system on a single computer. Widely used Commercial-Off-The-Shelf (COTS) software products, on the other hand, are more attractive to hackers because a single security vulnerability, once discovered in a COTS product, may be embedded in numerous computers that have the same COTS software product installed.

[79] Industrial computers sometimes have operating requirements that differ from business or office computers. For example, monitoring a chemical process, or a telephone microwave tower may require 24-hour continuous availability for a critical industrial computer. Even though industrial systems may operate using COTS software (see above), it may be economically difficult to justify suspending the operation of an industrial SCADA computer on a regular basis to take time to install every new security software patch. See interview with Michael Vatis, director of the Institute for Security Technology Studies related to counterterrorism and cybersecurity. Sharon Gaudin, "Security Experts: U.S. Companies Unprepared for Cyber Terror," *Datamation*, July 19, 2002 at [http://itmanagement. earthweb. com/secu/article.php/1429851]. Also, Government Accountability Office, *Information Security: Further Efforts Needed to Fully Implement Statutory Requirements in DOD*, GAO-03-1037T, July 24, 2003, p. 8.

[80] Kevin Poulsen, "Slammer Worm Crashed Ohio Nuke Plant Network," *Security Focus*, August 19, 2003, at [http://www.securityfocus.com/news/6767].

systems would work to restore functions as quickly as possible. Cyberterrorists would need to attack multiple targets simultaneously for long periods of time to gradually create terror, achieve strategic goals, or to have any noticeable effects on national security.[81]

For more information about SCADA systems, see CRS Report RL31534, *Critical Infrastructure: Control Systems and the Terrorist Threat*, by Dana A. Shea.

Unpredictable Interactions Between Infrastructures

An important area that is not fully understood concerns the unpredictable interactions between computer systems that operate the different U.S. infrastructures. The concern is that numerous interdependencies (where downstream systems may rely on receiving good data through stable links with upstream computers) could possibly build to a cascade of effects that are unpredictable in how they might affect national security.[82] For example, while the "Blaster" worm was disrupting Internet computers over several days in August 2003, some security experts suggest that slowness of communication links, caused by Blaster worm network congestion, may have contributed to the Eastern United States power blackout that occurred simultaneously on August 14. The computer worm could have degraded the performance of several communications links between data centers normally used to send warnings to other utility managers downstream on the power grid.[83]

Civilian Technology that Supports DOD

DOD uses Commercial-Off-The-Shelf (COTS) hardware and software products in core information technology administrative functions, and also in the combat systems of all services, as for example, in the integrated warfare systems for nuclear aircraft carriers.[84] DOD favors the use of COTS

---

81 Scott Nance, "Debunking Fears: Exercise Finds 'Digital Pearl Harbor' Risk Small," *Defense Week*, April 7, 2003 at [http://www.kingpublishing.com/publications/dw/].

82 The most expensive natural disaster in U.S. history, Hurricane Andrew, is reported to have caused $25 billion in damage, while the Love Bug virus is estimated to have cost computer users around the world somewhere between $3 billion and $15 billion. However, the Love Bug virus was created and launched by a single university student in the Philippines, relying on inexpensive computer equipment. Christopher Miller, *GAO Review of Weapon Systems Software*, March 3, 2003, e-mail communication, MillerC@gao.gov.

83 Network congestion caused by the Blaster worm reportedly delayed the exchange of critical power grid control data across the public telecommunications network, which could have hampered the operators' ability to prevent the cascading effect of the blackout. Dan Verton, "Blaster Worm Linked to Severity of Blackout," *Computerworld*, August 29, 2003, [http://www.computerworld.com/printthis/2003/0,4814,84510,00.html.].

84 Some ships of the U.S. Navy use Windows software. Bill Murray, "Navy Carrier to Run Win 2000," *GCN.com*, September 11, 2000, [http://www.gcn.com/vol19_no27/dod/2868-1.html]. Major U.K. naval systems defense contractor, BAE Systems, also took the decision to standardize future development on Microsoft Windows. John Lettice, "OSS Torpedoed: Royal Navy Will Run on Windows

products in order to take advantage of technological innovation, product flexibility and standardization, and resulting contract cost-effectiveness. Nevertheless, DOD officials and others have stated that COTS products are lacking in security, and that strengthening the security of those products to meet military requirements may be too difficult and costly for most COTS vendors. To improve security, DOD Information Assurance practices require deploying several layers of additional protective measures around COTS military systems to make them more difficult for enemy cyberattackers to penetrate.[85]

However, on two separate occasions in 2004, viruses reportedly infiltrated two top-secret computer systems at the Army Space and Missile Defense Command. It is not clear how the viruses penetrated the military systems, or what the effects were. Also, contrary to security policy requirements, the compromised computers reportedly lacked basic anti virus software protection.[86] Security experts have noted that no matter how much protection is given to computers, hackers are always creating new ways to defeat those protective measures.[87]

Why Cyberattacks Are Successful

Networked computers with exposed vulnerabilities may be disrupted or taken over by a hacker, or by automated malicious code. Botnets opportunistically scan the Internet to find and infect computer systems that are poorly configured, or lack current software security patches. Compromised computers are taken over to become slaves in a "botnet", which can include thousands of compromised computers that are remotely controlled to collect sensitive information from each victim's PC, or to collectively attack as a swarm against other targeted computers.

Even computers that have updated software and the newest security patches may still be vulnerable to a type of cyberattack known as a "Zero-Day exploit." This may occur if a computer hacker discovers a new software vulnerability and launches a malicious attack to infect computers before a security patch can be created by the software vendor and distributed to protect users. Zero-day vulnerabilities in increasingly complex software are regularly discovered by computer hackers. Recent news articles report that zero-day vulnerabilities are now available at online

for Warships," *Register*, September 6, 2004 at [http://www.theregister.co.uk/2004/09/06/ams_goes_windows_for_warships/].

85 Patience Wait, "Defense IT Security Can't Rest on COTS," *GCN.com*, September 27, 2004, at [http://www.gcn.com/23_29/news/27422-1.html].

86 Dawn Onley, "Army Urged to Step Up IT Security Focus," *GCN.com*, September 2, 2004, at [http://www.gcn.com/vol1_no1/daily-updates/27138-1.html].

87 Patience Wait, "Defense IT Security Can't Rest on COTS," *GCN.com*, September27, 2004, at [http://www.gcn.com/23_29/news/27422-1.html].

auctions, where buyers and sellers negotiate with timed bidding periods and minimum starting prices. This allows newly-discovered computer security vulnerabilities to be sold quickly to the highest bidder. Computer security expert Terri Forslof, of Tipping Point, has reportedly said that such practices will ". . . increase the perceived value of vulnerabilities, and the good guys already have trouble competing with the money you can get on the black market."[88]

The Insider Threat

A major threat for organizations is the ease with which data can now be copied and carried outside using a variety of portable storage devices, such as small flash drives. Newer high-density memory stick technology reportedly allows installed computer applications to be run entirely from the flash drive. This means that the entire contents of a PC could possibly be copied to and stored on a small, easily portable, and easily concealed media device.[89]

Employees with access to sensitive information systems can initiate threats in the form of malicious code inserted into software that is being developed either locally, or under offshore contracting arrangements. For example, in January 2003, 20 employees of subcontractors working in the United States at the Sikorsky Aircraft Corporation were arrested for possession of false identification used to obtain security access to facilities containing restricted and sensitive military technology. All of the defendants pleaded guilty and have been sentenced, except for one individual who was convicted at trial on April 19, 2004.[90]

Persistence of Computer System Vulnerabilities

Vulnerabilities in software and computer system configurations provide entry points for a cyberattack. Vulnerabilities persist largely as a result of poor security practices and procedures, inadequate training in computer security, or technical errors in software products.[91] Inadequate resources devoted to staffing the security function may also contribute to poor security practices. Home PC users often have little or no training in best practices for effectively securing home networks and equipment.

---

[88] Tim Green, *Web Site auctions software vulnerabilities to highest bidder*, Network World, August 8, 2007.

[89] McAfee Virtual Criminology Report: Organized Crime and the Internet, December 2006, [http://www.sigma.com.pl/pliki/albums/userpics/10007/Virtual_Criminology_Report_ 2006.pdf].

[90] U.S. Attorneys Office, District of Connecticut, at [http://www.usdoj.gov/usao/ct/attf. html].

[91] The SANS Institute, in cooperation with the National Infrastructure Protection Center (NIPC), publishes an annual list of the 10 most commonly exploited vulnerabilities for Windows systems and for Unix systems. *The SANS/FBI Twenty Most Critical Internet Security Vulnerabilities, 2003*, SANS, April 15, 2003 at [http://www.sans.org/top20/].

Errors in New Software Products

Vendors for Commercial-Off-The-Shelf software (COTS) are often criticized for releasing new products with errors that create the computer system vulnerabilities.[92] Richard Clarke, former White House cyberspace advisor until 2003, has reportedly said that many commercial software products have poorly written, or poorly configured security features.[93] In response to such criticism, the software industry reportedly has made new efforts to design products with architectures that are more secure. For example, Microsoft has created a special Security Response Center and now works with DOD and with industry and government leaders to improve security features in its new products. However, many software industry representatives reportedly agree that no matter what investment is made to improve software security, there will continue to be vulnerabilities in future software because products are becoming increasingly more complex.[94]

Inadequate Resources

Although software vendors periodically release fixes or upgrades to solve newly discovered security problems, an important software security patch might not get scheduled for installation on an organization's computers until several weeks or months after the patch is available.[95] The job may be too time-consuming, too complex, or too low a priority for the system administration staff. With increased software complexity comes the introduction of more vulnerabilities, so system maintenance is never-ending. Sometimes the security patch itself may disrupt the computer when

---

92 In September 2003, Microsoft Corporation announced three new critical flaws in its latest Windows operating systems software. Security experts predicted that computer hackers may possibly exploit these new vulnerabilities by releasing more attack programs, such as the "Blaster worm" that recently targeted other Windows vulnerabilities causing widespread disruption on the Internet. Jaikumar Vijayan, "Attacks on New Windows Flaws Expected Soon," *Computerworld*, September 15, 2003, vol. 37, no. 37, p. 1.

93 Agencies operating national security systems must purchase software products from a list of lab-tested and evaluated products in a program that requires vendors to submit software for review in an accredited lab, a process (known as certification and accreditation under the Common Criteria, a testing program run by the National Information Assurance Partnership) that often takes a year and costs several thousand dollars. The review requirement previously has been limited to military national security software, however, the administration has stated that the government will undertake a review of the program in 2003 to "possibly extend" it as a new requirement for civilian agencies. Ellen Messmer, White House issue "National Strategy to Secure Cyberspace," *Network World Fusion*, February 14, 2003, [http://www.nwfusion.com/news/2003/0214ntlstrategy.html].

94 Scott Charney, Chief Security Strategist, Microsoft, Statement before the House Committee on Armed Services, Terrorism, Unconventional Threats and Capabilities Subcommittee, *Information Technology in the 21st Century Battlespace*, hearing, July 24, 2003, p. 9.

95 A survey of 2000 PC users found that 42% had not downloaded the vendor patch to ward off the recent Blaster worm attack, 23% said they do not regularly download software updates, 21% do not update their anti-virus signatures, and 70% said they were not notified by their companies about the urgent threat due to the Blaster worm. Jaikumar Vijayan, "IT Managers Say They Are Being Worn Down by Wave of Attacks," *Computerworld*, August 25, 2003, vol. 37, no. 34, p. 1.

installed, forcing the system administrator to take additional time to adjust the computer to accept the new patch. To avoid such disruption, a security patch may first require testing on a separate isolated network before it is distributed for installation on all other regular networked computers.

Because of such delays, the computer security patches installed in many organizations may lag considerably behind the current cyberthreat situation. Whenever delays are allowed to persist in private organizations, in government agencies, or among PC users at home, computer vulnerabilities that are widely reported may remain unprotected, leaving networks open to possible attack for long periods of time.

Future Attractiveness of Critical Infrastructure Systems

There has yet been no published evidence showing a widespread focus by cybercriminals on attacking the control systems that operate the U.S. civilian critical infrastructure. Disabling infrastructure controls for communications, electrical distribution or other infrastructure systems, is often described as a likely scenario to amplify the effects of a simultaneous conventional terrorist attack involving explosives.

However, in 2006, at a security discussion in Williamsburg, Virginia, a government analyst reportedly stated that criminal extortion schemes may have already occurred, where cyberattackers have exploited control system vulnerabilities for economic gain. And, in December 2006, malicious software that automatically scans for control system vulnerabilities reportedly was made available on the Internet for use by cybercriminals. This scanner software reportedly can enable individuals with little knowledge about infrastructure control systems to locate a SCADA computer connected to the Internet, and quickly identify its security vulnerabilities.

The Idaho National Laboratory is tasked to study and report on technology risks associated with infrastructure control systems. Past studies have shown that many, if not most, automated control systems are connected to the Internet, or connected to corporate administrative systems that are connected to the Internet, and are currently vulnerable to a cyberattack. And, because many of these infrastructure SCADA systems were not originally designed with security as a priority, in many cases, new security controls cannot now be easily implemented to reduce the known security vulnerabilities.[96] Following past trends, where hackers and cybercriminals have taken advantage of easy vulnerabilities, some analysts now predict that we

[96] Testimony of Aaron Turner, House Committee on Homeland Security, Subcommittee on Emerging Threats, Cybersecurity and Science & Technology, Hearing on "Cyber Insecurity: Hackers are Penetrating Federal Systems and Critical Infrastructure," April 19, 2007, [http://homeland.house.gov/SiteDocuments/20070419153130-95132.pdf].

may gradually see new instances where cybercriminals exploit vulnerabilities in critical infrastructure control systems.[97]

Measuring Cybercrime

New, automated attack methods have outpaced current methods for tracking the number and severity of cyberattacks and cybercrime intrusions. For example, according to a study by the Cooperative Association for Internet Data Analysis (CAIDA), on January 25, 2003, the SQL Slammer worm (also known as "Sapphire") automatically spread to infect more than 90% of vulnerable computers worldwide within 10 minutes of its release on the Internet, making it the fastest-spreading computer worm in history. As the study reports, the Slammer worm doubled in size every 8.5 seconds and achieved its full scanning rate (55 million scans per second) after about 3 minutes. It caused considerable harm through network outages which led to numerous canceled airline flights and automated teller machine (ATM) failures.[98]

The use of automated tools for cybercrime has had a dramatic affect on the Computer Emergency Response Team/ Coordinating Center (CERT/CC). In 2004, CERT/CC announced that it had abandoned its traditional practice of producing an annual report tracking the number of cyber intrusions recorded for each year. For many years prior to 2004, CERT/CC had maintained a database of statistics about security incidents that were reported to it anonymously by businesses and individuals worldwide. The reason given for abandoning its annual tracking report was because the widespread use of new, automated cyberattack tools had escalated the number of network attacks to such a high level, that the CERT/CC organization determined that traditional methods for counting security incidents had become meaningless as a metric for assessing the scope and effects of attacks against Internet-connected systems.[99] The CERT-CC website currently states, "Given the widespread use of automated attack tools, attacks against Internet-connected systems have become so commonplace that counts of the number of incidents reported provide little information with regard to assessing the scope and impact of attacks. Therefore, beginning in 2004, we stopped publishing the number of incidents reported."[100]

---

97 Testimony of Aaron Turner, House Committee on Homeland Security, Subcommittee on Emerging Threats, Cybersecurity and Science & Technology, Hearing on "Cyber Insecurity: Hackers are Penetrating Federal Systems and Critical Infrastructure," April 19, 2007, [http://homeland.house.gov/SiteDocuments/20070419153130-95132.pdf].

98 "Internet Worm Keeps Striking," January 27, 2003, *CBSNews.com* at [http://www.cbsnews.com/stories/2003/01/28/tech/main538200.shtml].

99 "CERT/CC Statistics 1988-2004" at [http://www.cert.org/stats/cert_stats.html].

100 CERT Coordination Center, Carnegie Mellon University, [http://www.cert.org/stats/].

The FBI estimates that all types of computer crime in the U.S. now costs industry about $400 billion, while officials in the Department of Trade and Industry in Britain say computer crime has risen by 50 percent from 2005 to 2006. As one example of costs associated with a recent computer security breach, TJX, the parent company of TJ Maxx, took a $12 million charge in its fiscal first quarter of 2008 due to the theft of more than 45 million credit and debit card numbers, starting in 2006. The money reportedly went to investigating and containing the intrusion, improving computer security, communicating with customers, and other fees. TJX estimates that, adding damages from future lawsuits, the breach may eventually cost $100 per lost record, or a total of $4.5 billion.[101]

It is estimated that only five per cent of cybercriminals are ever arrested or convicted because the anonymity associated with web activity makes them hard to catch, and the trail of evidence needed to link them to a cybercrime is hard to unravel. Studies also show that cybercrime incidents are rarely reported, especially by companies that wish to avoid negative publicity leading to possible loss of confidence by its customers. However, law enforcement officials argue that "maintaining a code of silence" won't benefit a company in the long-run. Steven Martinez, deputy assistant director for the FBI's cyber division, reportedly stated at the 2006 RSI Computer Security Conference that partnerships between law enforcement, the academic community, and the private sector are key to understanding and reducing cybercrime.[102]

Each year, the Computer Security Institute (CSI), with help from the FBI, conducts a survey of thousands of security practitioners from U.S. corporations, government agencies, financial institutions, and universities. The CSI/FBI Computer Crime and Security Survey, published annually, is perhaps the most widely-used source of information about how often computer crime occurs and how expensive these crimes can be. The 2006 survey indicated that the average financial loss reported due to security breaches was $167,713, an 18% decrease from the previous year's average loss of $203,606.

However, some observers argue that the analyses reported in the CSI/FBI survey may be questionable, because the survey methodology is not statistically valid.[103] This is because the survey is limited only to CSI members, which reduces the likelihood that respondents are a representative sample of all security practitioners, or that their employers are representative of

101 Sharon Gaudin, *Breach Costs Soar at TJX*, Information Week, May 21, 2007, p. 19.

102 Marcia Savage, "Companies Still Not Reporting Attacks, FBI Director Says," SearchSecurity.com, February 15, 2006, [http://searchsecurity.techtarget.com/originalContent/0,289142,sid14_gci1166845,00.html?bucket=NEWS&topic=299990].

103 Bill Brenner, "Security Blog Log: Has CSI/FBI Survey Jumped the Shark?" SearchSecurity.com, July 21, 2006, [http://searchsecurity.techtarget.com/columnItem/0,294698,sid14_gci1202328,00.html].

employers in general. In addition, the 2006 CSI/FBI survey points out that most companies are continuing to sweep security incidents under the rug.

With the apparent absence of statistically valid survey results concerning the financial costs of computer crime, and with an accompanying lack of clear data about the number and types of computer security incidents reported, it appears that there may be no valid way to currently understand the real scope and intensity of cybercrime. The growing use of botnets and sophisticated malicious code also suggests that the percentage of unreported cybercrime, plus the percentage undetected, may both be going up.

Problems Tracing Cybercrime

The challenge of identifying the source of attacks is complicated by the unwillingness of commercial enterprises to report attacks, owing to potential liability concerns. CERT/CC estimates that as much as 80% of all actual computer security incidents still remain unreported.[104] Law enforcement officials concede they are making little progress in tracing the profits and finances of cybercriminals. Online payment services, such as PayPal and E-Gold, enable criminals to launder their profits and exploit the shortcomings of international law enforcement. Recently, Intermix Media was fined $7.5 million in penalties for distribution of spyware which silently captures personal information from user's PCs. However, some adware and spyware purveyors reportedly can still make millions of dollars per year in profits. Many companies who distribute spyware are difficult to pursue legally because they typically also offer some legitimate services. In many cases, the finances that back cybercrimes are so distributed they are hard for law enforcement to figure out.[105]

Organized Cybercrime

Some large cybercriminal groups are transnational, with names like Shadowcrew, Carderplanet, and Darkprofits. Individuals in these groups reportedly operate from locations all over the world, working together to hack into systems, steal credit card information and sell identities, in a very highly structured, organized network.[106] Organized crime is also recruiting teenagers who indicate they feel safer doing illegal activity online than in the street. A recent report from the McAfee security organization, titled

[104] Many cyberattacks are unreported usually because the organization is unable to recognize that it has been attacked, or because the organization is reluctant to reveal publicly that it has experienced a cyberattack, Government Accountability Office, *Information Security: Further Efforts Needed to Fully Implement Statutory Requirements in DOD*, GAO-031037T, July 24, 2003, p. 6.

[105] Matt Hines, "Malware Money Though to Trace," *Eweek*, September 18, 2006, p. 14.

[106] Kevin Poulsen, "Feds Square off with Organized Cyber Crime," SecurityFocus, February 17, 2005, [http://www.securityfocus.com/news/10525].

the "Virtual Criminology Report", draws on input from Europe's leading high-tech crime units and the FBI, and suggests that criminal outfits are targeting top students from leading academic institutions and helping them acquire more of the skills needed to commit high-tech crime on a massive scale.[107]

In the future, we may see new and different modes of criminal organization evolve in cyberspace. Cyberspace frees individuals from many of the constraints that apply to activities in the physical world, and current forms of criminal organization may not transition well to online crime. Cybercrime requires less personal contact, less need for formal organization, and no need for control over a geographical territory. Therefore, some researchers argue that the classical hierarchical structures of organized crime groups may be unsuitable for organized crime on the Internet. Consequently, online criminal activity may emphasize lateral relationships and networks instead of hierarchies.[108]

Instead of assuming stable personnel configurations that can persist for years, online criminal organization may incorporate the "swarming" model, in which individuals coalesce for a limited period of time in order to conduct a specific task, or set of tasks, and afterwards go their separate ways. The task of law enforcement could therefore become much more difficult. If cybercriminals evolve into the "Mafia of the moment" or the "cartel of the day," police will lose the advantage of identifying a permanent group of participants who engage in a set of routine illicit activities, and this will only contribute to the future success of organized cybercrime.[109]

Federal Efforts to Protect Computers

The federal government has taken steps to improve its own computer security and to encourage the private sector to also adopt stronger computer security policies and practices to reduce infrastructure vulnerabilities. In 2002, the Federal Information Security Management Act (FISMA) was enacted, giving the Office of Management and Budget (OMB) responsibility for coordinating information security standards and guidelines developed by federal agencies.[110] In 2003, the National Strategy to Secure Cyberspace

---

107 Bill Brenner, "Criminals Find Safety in Cyberspace," SearchSecurity.com, December 18, 2006, [http://searchsecurity.techtarget.com/originalContent/0,289142,sid14_gci1235455,00. html?bucket=NEWS &topic=299990].

108 Council of Europe Octopus Programme, *Summary of the Organised Crime Situation Report 2004: Focus on the Threat of Cybercrime*, Strausbourg, September 6, 2004, p. 48.

109 Susan Brenner, "Organized Cybercrime? How Cyberspace May Affect the Structure of Criminal Relationships," *North Carolina Journal of Law and Technology*, 2002, [http://www.jolt.unc.edu/Vol4_I1/Web/Brenner-V4I1.htm].

110 GAO has noted that many federal agencies have not implemented security requirements for most of their systems, and must meet new requirements under FISMA. See GAO Report GAO-03-852T, *Information Security: Continued Efforts Needed to Fully Implement Statutory Requirements*, June 24, 2003.

was published by the Administration to encourage the private sector to improve computer security for the U.S. critical infrastructure through having federal agencies set an example for best security practices.[111]

The National Cyber Security Division (NCSD), within the National Protection and Programs Directorate of the Department of Homeland Security (DHS) oversees a Cyber Security Tracking, Analysis and Response Center (CSTARC), tasked with conducting analysis of cyberspace threats and vulnerabilities, issuing alerts and warnings for cyberthreats, improving information sharing, responding to major cybersecurity incidents, and aiding in national-level recovery efforts. In addition, a new Cyber Warning and Information Network (CWIN) has begun operation in 50 locations, and serves as an early warning system for cyberattacks.[112] The CWIN is engineered to be reliable and survivable, has no dependency on the Internet or the public switched network (PSN), and reportedly will not be affected if either the Internet or PSN suffer disruptions.[113]

In January 2004, the NCSD also created the National Cyber Alert System (NCAS), a coordinated national cybersecurity system that distributes information to subscribers to help identify, analyze, and prioritize emerging vulnerabilities and cyberthreats. NCAS is managed by the United States Computer Emergency Readiness Team (US-CERT), a partnership between NCSD and the private sector, and subscribers can sign up to receive notices from this new service by visiting the US-CERT website.[114]

International Convention on Cybercrime

Cybercrime is also a major international challenge, even though attitudes about what comprises a criminal act of computer wrongdoing still vary from country to country. However, the Convention on Cybercrime was adopted in 2001 by the Council of Europe, a consultative assembly of 43 countries, based in Strasbourg. The Convention, effective July 2004, is the first and only international treaty to deal with breaches of law "over the internet or other information networks." The Convention requires participating countries to update and harmonize their criminal laws against

[111] Tinabeth Burton, *ITAA Finds Much to Praise in National Cybersecurity Plan*, May 7, 2003, [http://www.findarticles.com/p/articles/mi_go1965/is_200303/ai_n7418485].

[112] Bara Vaida, "Warning Center for Cyber Attacks is Online, Official Says," *Daily Briefing*, GovExec.com, June 25, 2003.

[113] The Cyber Warning Information Network (CWIN) provides voice and data connectivity to government and industry participants in support of critical infrastructure protection, [http://www.publicsectorinstitute.net/ELetters/HomelandSecurityStrategies/Volume1 No1/CyberWarningNet Launch.lsp].

[114] [http://www.us-cert.gov/cas/].

hacking, infringements on copyrights, computer facilitated fraud, child pornography, and other illicit cyber activities.[115]

Although the United States has signed and ratified the Convention, it did not sign a separate protocol that contained provisions to criminalize xenophobia and racism on the Internet, which would raise Constitutional issues in the United States.[116] The separate protocol could be interpreted as requiring nations to imprison anyone guilty of "insulting publicly, through a computer system" certain groups of people based on characteristics such as race or ethnic origin, a requirement that could make it a crime to e-mail jokes about ethnic groups or question whether the Holocaust occurred. The Department of Justice has said that it would be unconstitutional for the United States to sign that additional protocol because of the First Amendment's guarantee of freedom of expression. The Electronic Privacy Information Center, in a June 2004 letter to the Foreign Relations Committee, objected to U.S. ratification of the Convention, because it would "create invasive investigative techniques while failing to provide meaningful privacy and civil liberties safeguards."[117]

On August 3, 2006, the U.S. Senate passed a resolution of ratification for the Convention. The United States will comply with the Convention based on existing U.S. federal law; and no new implementing legislation is expected to be required. Legal analysts say that U.S. negotiators succeeded in scrapping most objectionable provisions, thereby ensuring that the Convention tracks closely with existing U.S. laws.[118]

The Need to Improve Cybersecurity

Department of Defense (DOD) officials have stated that, while the threat of cyber attack is "less likely" to appear than conventional physical attack, it could actually prove more damaging because it could involve disruptive technology that might generate unpredictable consequences that give an adversary unexpected advantages.[119] The Homeland Security Presidential Directive 7 required that the Department of Homeland Security (DHS) coordinate efforts to protect the cybersecurity for the nation's critical infrastructure.

[115] Full text for the Convention on Cyber Crime may be found at [http://conventions.coe.int/Treaty/Commun/QueVoulezVous.asp?NT=185&CM=8&DF= 18/06/04&CL=ENG].

[116] The U.S. Senate Committee on Foreign Relations held a hearing on the Convention on June 17, 2004. CRS Report RS21208, *Cybercrime: The Council of Europe Convention*, by Kristin Archick. Estelle Durnout, *Council of Europe Ratifies Cybercrime Treaty*, ZDNet, March 22, 2004, at [http://news.zdnet.co.uk/business/legal/0,39020651,39149470,00.htm].

[117] [http://www.epic.org/privacy/intl/senateletter-061704.pdf].

[118] For more information about the Convention on Cybercrime, see CRS Report RS21208, *Cybercrime: The Council of Europe Convention*, by Kristin Archick.

[119] Advantages of EA and CNA might derive from United States reliance on a computer-controlled critical infrastructure, along with unpredictable results depending on severity of the attack. Jason Sherman, "Bracing for Modern Brands of Warfare," *Air Force Times*, September 27, 2004, [http://www.airforcetimes.com/story.php?f=1-AIRPAPER-358727. php].

This resulted in two reports in 2005, titled "Interim National Infrastructure Protection Plan," and "The National Plan for Research and Development in Support of Critical Infrastructure Protection", where DHS provided a framework for identifying and prioritizing, and protecting each infrastructure sector.

However, some observers question why, in light of the many such reports describing an urgent need to reduce cybersecurity vulnerabilities, there is not an apparent perceived sense of national urgency to close the gap between cybersecurity and the threat of cyberattack. For example, despite Federal Information Security Management Act of 2002 (FISMA), some experts argue that security remains a low priority, or is treated almost as an afterthought at some domestic federal agencies.[120] In 2007, the Government Accountability Office issued a report, titled "Critical Infrastructure Protection: Multiple Efforts to Secure Control Systems Are Under Way, but Challenges Remain," which states that cybersecurity risks have actually increased for infrastructure control systems because of the persistence of interconnections with the Internet, and continued open availability of detailed information on the technology and configuration of the control systems. The report states that no overall strategy yet exists to coordinate activities to improve computer security across federal agencies and the private sector, which owns the critical infrastructure.[121] Some observers argue that, as businesses gradually strengthen their security policies for headquarters and administrative systems, the remote systems that control critical infrastructure and manufacturing may soon be seen as easier targets of opportunity for cybercrime.

Cybercrime is obviously one of the risks of doing business in the age of the internet, but observers argue that many decision-makers may currently view it as a low-probability threat. Some researchers suggest that the numerous past reports describing the need to improve cybersecurity have not been compelling enough to make the case for dramatic and urgent action by decision-makers. Others suggest that even though relevant information is available, future possibilities are still discounted, which reduces the apparent need for present-day action. In addition, the costs of current inaction are not borne by the current decision-makers. These researchers argue that IT vendors must be willing to regard security as a product attribute that is coequal with performance and cost; IT researchers must be willing to value cybersecurity research as much as they value research for

---

120 Statement of James A. Lewis, Senior Fellow and Director, Technology and Public Policy Program, Center for Strategic and International Studies, Committee on House Oversight and Government Reform Subcommittee on Government Management, Organization, and Procurement, Subcommittee on Information Policy, Census, and National Archives, June 7, 2007.

121 GAO -08-119T, *Critical Infrastructure Protection: Multiple Efforts to Secure Control Systems are Under Way, but Challenges Remain*, October 17, 2007.

high performance or cost-effective computing; and, finally, IT purchasers must be willing to incur present-day costs in order to obtain future benefits.[122]

Issues for Congress

Policy issues for cybercrime and cyberterrorism include a need for the following:

- increase awareness about changing threats due to the growing technical skills of extremists and terrorist groups;
- develop more accurate methods for measuring the effects of cybercrime;
- help to determine appropriate responses by DOD to a cyberattack;
- examine the incentives for achieving the goals of the National Strategy to Secure Cyberspace;
- search for ways to improve the security of commercial software products;
- explore ways to increase security education and awareness for businesses and home PC users; and
- find ways for private industry and government to coordinate to protect against cyberattack.

Congress may also wish to consider ways to harmonize existing federal and state laws that require notice to persons when their personal information has been affected by a computer security breach, and that impose obligations on businesses and owners of that restricted information.[123]

Growth in Technical Capabilities of Terrorists

Seized computers belonging to Al Qaeda indicate its members are becoming more familiar with hacker tools and services that are available over the Internet.[124] Could terrorist groups find it advantageous to hire a cybercrime botnet tailored to attack specific targets, possibly including the civilian critical infrastructure of Western nations? Could cybercrime botnets, used strategically, provide a useful way for extremists to amplify the effects of a conventional terrorist attack using bombs?

---

[122] Seymour Goodman and Herber Lin, editors, Toward a Safer and More Secure Cyberspace, *Committee on Improving Cybersecurity Research in the United States, National Research Council*, 2007, pp. 261–267, [http://books.nap.edu/openbook.php?isbn=030910 3959].

[123] For more information about laws related to identity theft, see CRS Report RL34120, *Information Security and Data Breach Notification Safeguards*, by Gina Marie Stevens.

[124] Richard Clarke, "Vulnerability: What Are Al Qaeda's Capabilities?" *PBS Frontline: Cyberwar*, April 2003, at [http://www.pbs.org].

As computer-literate youth increasingly join the ranks of terrorist groups, will cyberterrorism likely become increasingly more mainstream in the future? Will a computer-literate leader bring increased awareness of the advantages of an attack on information systems, or be more receptive to suggestions from other, newer computer-literate members? Once a new tactic has won widespread media attention, will it likely motivate other rival terrorist groups to follow along the new pathway?[125]

Better Measurement of Cybercrime Trends

Experiences at CERT/CC show that statistical methods for measuring the volume and economic effects of cyberattacks may be questionable. Without sound statistical methods to accurately report the scope and effects of cybercrime, government and legal authorities will continue to have unreliable measures of the effectiveness of their policies and enforcement actions.

Figures from several computer security reports now used for measuring annual financial losses to U.S. industry due to intrusions and cybercrime are believed by some observers to be limited in scope or possibly contain statistical bias.[126] Is there a need for a more statistically reliable analysis of trends in computer security vulnerabilities and types of cyberattacks to more accurately show the costs and benefits for improving national cybersecurity? Congress may wish to encourage security experts to find more effective ways to collect data that will enable accurate analysis of trends for cyberattacks and cybercrime. Congress may also wish to encourage security researchers to find better ways to identify the initiators of cyberattacks.

DOD and Cyberattack Response

If a terrorist group were to use a cybercrime botnet to subvert computers in a third party country, such as China, to launch a cyberattack against the United States, the U.S. response to the cyberattack must be carefully considered, in order to avoid retaliating against the wrong entity. Would the resulting effects of cyberweapons used by the United States be difficult to

---

[125] Jerrold M. Post, Kevin G. Ruby, and Eric D. Shaw, "From Car Bombs to Logic Bombs: The Growing Threat From Information Terrorism," *Terrorism and Political Violence*, summer 2000, vol. 12, no. 2, pp. 97–122.

[126] A well known source of information about the costs of cyberattacks is the annual computer security survey published by the Computer Security Institute (CSI), which utilizes data collected by the FBI. However, respondents to the CSI/FBI survey of computer security issues are generally limited only to CSI members, which may create statistical bias that affects the survey findings. Recently, CSI has also conceded weaknesses in its analytical approach and has suggested that its survey of computer security vulnerabilities and incidents may be more illustrative than systematic. However, the CSI/FBI survey remains useful despite its imperfect methodology. Bruce Berkowitz and Robert W. Hahn, "Cybersecurity: Who's Watching the Store?" *Issues in Science and Technology*, spring 2003.

limit or control? Would a cyberattack response that could be attributed to the United States possibly encourage other extremists, or rogue nations, to start launching their own cyberattacks against the United States? Would an attempt by the U.S. to increase surveillance of another entity via use of cyberespionage computer code be labeled as an unprovoked attack, even if directed against the computers belonging to a terrorist group? If a terrorist group should subsequently copy, or reverse-engineer a destructive U.S. military cyberattack program, could it be used against other countries that are U.S. allies, or even turned back to attack civilian computer systems in the United States?[127] If the effects become widespread and severe, could the U.S. use of cyberweapons exceed the customary rules of military conflict, or violate international laws.[128]

Commercial electronics and communications equipment are now used extensively to support complex U.S. weapons systems, and are possibly vulnerable to cyberattack. This situation is known to our potential adversaries.[129] To what degree are military forces and national security threatened by computer security vulnerabilities that exist in commercial software systems, and how can the computer industry be encouraged to create new COTS products that are less vulnerable to cyberattack?

Incentives for the National Strategy to Secure Cyberspace

Does the National Strategy to Secure Cyberspace present clear incentives for achieving security objectives? Suggestions to increase incentives may include requiring that all software procured for federal agencies be certified under the "Common Criteria" testing program, which is now the requirement for the procurement of military software. However, industry observers point out that the software certification process is lengthy and may interfere with innovation and competitiveness in the global software market.[130]

---

[127] See CRS Report RL31787, *Information Warfare and Cyberwar: Capabilities and Related Policy Issues*, by Clay Wilson.

[128] The laws of war are international rules that have evolved to resolve practical problems relating to military conflict, such as restraints to prevent misbehavior or atrocities, and have not been legislated by an overarching central authority. The United States is party to various limiting treaties. Sometimes the introduction of new technology tends to force changes in the understanding of the laws of war. Gary Anderson and Adam Gifford, "Order Out of Anarchy: The International Law of War," *The Cato Journal*, August 2004, vol. 15, no. 1, pp. 25–36.

[129] Stanley Jakubiak and Lowell Wood, "DOD Uses Commercial Software and Equipment in Tactical Weapons," Statements before the House Military Research and Development Subcommittee, Hearing on EMP Threats to the U.S. Military and Civilian Infrastructure, October 7, 1999. House Armed Services Committee, *Commission to Assess the Threat to the United States from Electromagnetic Pulse Attack*, hearing, July 22, 2004.

[130] Agencies operating national security systems are required to purchase software products from a list of lab-tested and evaluated products in a program run by the National Information Assurance Partnership (NIAP), a joint partnership between the National Security Agency and the National Institute of Standards and Technology. The NIAP is the U.S. government program that works with organizations in a dozen other countries around the world which have endorsed the international

Should the National Strategy to Secure Cyberspace rely on voluntary action on the part of private firms, home users, universities, and government agencies to keep their networks secure, or is there a need for possible regulation to ensure best security practices? Has public response to improve computer security been slow partly because there are no regulations currently imposed?[131] Would regulation to improve computer security interfere with innovation and possibly harm U.S. competitiveness in technology markets? Two of the former cybersecurity advisers to the president have differing views: Howard Schmidt has stated that market forces, rather than the government, should determine how product technology should evolve for better cybersecurity; however, Richard Clarke has stated that the IT industry has done little on its own to improve security of its own systems and products.[132]

Improving Security of Commercial Software

Some security experts emphasize that if systems administrators received the necessary training for keeping their computer configurations secure, then computer security would greatly improve for the U.S. critical infrastructure. However, should software product vendors be required to create higher quality software products that are more secure and that need fewer patches? Could software vendors possibly increase the level of security for their products by rethinking the design, or by adding more test procedures during product development?

---

security-evaluation regimen known as the "Common Criteria." The program requires vendors to submit software for review in an accredited lab, a process that often takes a year and costs several thousand dollars. The review previously was limited to military national security software and equipment, however, the Administration has stated that the government will undertake a review of the program to "possibly extend" this software certification requirement to civilian agencies. Ellen Messmer, White House issue "National Strategy to Secure Cyberspace," *Network World Fusion*, February 14, 2003, at [http://www.nwfusion.com/news/2003/0214ntlstrategy.html].

131 Business executives may be cautious about spending for large new technology projects, such as placing new emphasis on computer security. Results from a February 2003 survey of business executives indicated that 45% of respondents believed that many large Information Technology (IT) projects are often too expensive to justify. Managers in the survey pointed to the estimated $125.9 billion spent on IT projects between 1977 and 2000 in preparation for the year 2000 (Y2K) changeover, now viewed by some as a non-event. Sources reported that some board-level executives stated that the Y2K problem was overblown and over funded then, and as a result, they are now much more cautious about future spending for any new, massive IT initiatives. Gary H. Anthes and Thomas Hoffman, "Tarnished Image," *Computerworld*, May 12, 2003, vol. 37, no. 19, p. 37.

132 Howard Schmidt points out that major technology firms now promote anti-virus software and encourage better cybersecurity practices. He stresses that market forces are causing private industry to improve security of products. Martin Kady, "Cybersecurity a Weak Link in Homeland's Armor," *CQ Weekly*, February 14, 2005. Meanwhile, Richard Clarke, who initially opposed regulation during his tenure in the Clinton and Bush administrations, now states that the IT industry only reponds to improve security of its products when regulation is threatened. William Jackson, "To Regulate or Not to Regulate? That Is the Question," *Government Computer News*, February 26, 2005.

Education and Awareness of Cyberthreats

Ultimately, reducing the threat to national security from cybercrime depends on a strong commitment by government and the private sector to follow best management practices that help improve computer security. Numerous government reports already exist that describe the threat of cybercrime and make recommendations for management practices to improve cybersecurity.

A 2004 survey done by the National Cyber Security Alliance and AOL showed that most home PC users do not have adequate protection against hackers, do not have updated antivirus software protection, and are confused about the protections they are supposed to use and how to use them.[133] How can computer security training be made available to all computer users that will keep them aware of constantly changing computer security threats, and that will encourage them to follow proper security procedures?

Coordination Between Private Sector and Government

What can be done to improve sharing of information between federal government, local governments, and the private sector to improve computer security? Effective cybersecurity requires sharing of relevant information about threats, vulnerabilities, and exploits.[134] How can the private sector obtain information from the government on specific threats which the government now considers classified, but which may help the private sector protect against cyberattack? And, how can the government obtain specific information from private industry about the number of successful computer intrusions, when companies resist reporting because they want to avoid publicity and guard their trade secrets?[135] Should cybercrime information voluntarily shared with the federal government about successful intrusions be shielded from disclosure through Freedom of Information Act requests?

How can the United States better coordinate security policies and international law to gain the cooperation of other nations to better protect against a cyberattack? Pursuit of hackers may involve a trace back through networks

---

[133] A 2004 survey of 329 PC users revealed that most computer users think they are safe but lack basic protections against viruses, spyware, hackers, and other online threats. In addition, large majorities of home computer users have been infected with viruses and spyware and remain highly vulnerable to future infections. AOL and the National Cyber Security Alliance, "Largest In-home Study of Home Computer Users Shows Major Online Threats, Perception Gap," October 2004 at [http://www.staysafeonline.info/news/NCSA-AOLIn-HomeStudyRelease.pdf].

[134] Government Accountability Office, *Homeland Security: Efforts To Improve Information Sharing Need to Be Strengthened*, GAO-03-760, August 2003.

[135] CRS Report RL30153, *Critical Infrastructures: Background, Policy and Implementation*, by John Moteff.

requiring the cooperation of many Internet Service Providers located in several different nations.[136] Pursuit is made increasingly complex if one or more of the nations involved has a legal policy or political ideology that conflicts with that of the United States.[137]

Thirty-eight countries, including the United States, participate in the Council of Europe's Convention on Cybercrime, which seeks to combat cybercrime by harmonizing national laws, improving investigative abilities, and boosting international cooperation. However, how effective will the Convention without participation of other countries where cybercriminals now operate freely? (For more on the Convention, see CRS Report RS21208, *Cybercrime: The Council of Europe Convention*, by Kristin Archick.)

Legislative Activity

H.R. 1525—The Internet Spyware (I-SPY) Prevention Act of 2007, proposes penalties for unauthorized access to computers, or the use of computers to commit crimes. On May 23, 2007, this bill was received in the Senate and referred to the Committee on the Judiciary.

H.R. 1684—The Department of Homeland Security Authorization Act for Fiscal Year 2008 establishes within the Department of Homeland Security an Office of Cybersecurity and Communications, headed by the Assistant Secretary for Cybersecurity and Communications, with responsibility for overseeing preparation, response, and reconstitution for cybersecurity and to protect communications from terrorist attacks, major disasters, and other emergencies, including large-scale disruptions.

The bill directs the Assistant Secretary to do the following:

- Establish and maintain a capability within the Department for ongoing activities to identify threats to critical information infrastructure to aid in detection of vulnerabilities and warning of potential acts of terrorism and other attacks.
- Conduct risk assessments on critical information infrastructure with respect to acts of terrorism.
- Develop a plan for the continuation of critical information operations in the event of a cyber attack.

---

[136] Trace back to identify a cyberattacker at the granular level remains problematic. Dorothy Denning, *Information Warfare and Security* (Addison-Wesley, 1999), p. 217.

[137] In Argentina, a group calling themselves the X-Team, hacked into the website of that country's Supreme Court in April 2002. The trial judge stated that the law in his country covers crime against people, things, and animals but not websites. The group on trial was declared not guilty of breaking into the website. Paul Hillbeck, "Argentine Judge Rules in Favor of Computer Hackers," February 5, 2002, at [http://www.siliconvalley.com/mld/siliconvalley/news/editorial/3070194.htm].

- Define what qualifies as a cyber incident of national significance for purposes of the National Response Plan.
- Develop a national cybersecurity awareness, training, and education program that promotes cybersecurity awareness within the Federal Government and throughout the Nation.
- Consult and coordinate with the Under Secretary for Science and Technology on cybersecurity research and development to strengthen critical information infrastructure against acts of terrorism.

On May 11, 2007, this bill was referred to the Senate Committee on Homeland Security and Governmental Affairs.

H.R. 3221—The New Direction for Energy Independence, National Security, and Consumer Protection Act proposes establishment of the Grid Modernization Commission to facilitate the adoption of Smart Grid standards, technologies, and practices across the Nation's electricity grid. The bill was passed in the House on August 4, 2007. On October 19, 2007, there was a unanimous consent request to consider H.R. 3221 in the Senate, but objection was heard.

H.R. 3237—The Smart Grid Facilitation Act of 2007, proposes to modernize the Nation's electricity transmission and distribution system to incorporate digital information and controls technology. "Smart grid" technology functions will include the ability to detect, prevent, respond to, or recover from cyber-security threats and terrorism. The new Grid Modernization Commission is directed to undertake, and update on a biannual basis, an assessment of the progress toward modernizing the electric system including cybersecurity protection for extended grid systems. On August 24, 2007, the bill was referred to House subcommittee on Energy and Environment.

H. OPEN SOURCE INTELLIGENCE (OSINT)

OPEN SOURCE INTELLIGENCE (OSINT): ISSUES FOR CONGRESS

CRS Report for Congress

December 5, 2007

Commentary

For many years, the belief among Washington policymakers has been best expressed by the saying, "If it isn't classified, it isn't worth reading." The explosion of the worldwide web and the attendant information explosion have called that maxim into question. Unclassified, "open source" information now figures prominently in intelligence analysis and policymaking, as well it should. *Open Source Intelligence (OSINT): Issues for Congress* provides an up-to-date assessment of open source information and the role it can play in formulating intelligence on terrorists.

The report correctly acknowledges that a consensus now exists that open source information must be systematically collected and is essential to the intelligence analysis process. Congress agrees and has directed the Director of National Intelligence (DNI) to establish the position of Assistant Deputy Director of National Intelligence for Open Source and the National Open Source Center. The missions assigned to the Assistant Deputy Director and the Center go beyond the performance of open source acquisition and analysis. Rather, it is to create a center that will support all agencies of the Intelligence Community (IC) to effectively exploit open sources of information. That is easier said than done. We all know there is an enormous amount of information available literally at our fingertips. But, how do agencies of the IC efficiently sift through the seemingly endless supply of data to glean only relevant information? The CRS report correctly states that the challenge is to deploy all available information sources and technologies, including cutting edge approaches, to obtain and analyze information of national security importance that is available openly.

The CRS report is a primer for the novice, as well as an assessment for the seasoned intelligence analyst. It explains that open source information is derived from newspapers, journals, radio, television, and the Internet. The report goes on to explain that intelligence analysts have routinely collected and used such information to supplement classified data, but only as a side project. Classified information has always had priority. However, recently, Congress, the 9/11 Commission, and others have called for a greater and more focused effort to collect and analyze open source information. In one sense, such an effort would be nothing more than achieving a competitive advantage in exploiting a resource available to all. Other countries, China especially, have devoted considerable resources to open source collection and analysis. To the extent China and other countries are able to leverage open source information to the United States' detriment, they achieve competitive advantages in producing intelligence. That fact points to a limitation of the CRS report; it spends little time assessing what the United States should do to reduce its vulnerability to open source collection of its sensitive information by potential adversaries.

The CRS report notes that the National Open Source Center is up and running and is training OSINT professionals throughout the IC, and that administrative mechanisms are in place to attempt a comprehensive community-wide open source effort. The report suggests, however, that not all agencies have as yet made comprehensive commitments to acquiring and using open source information, nor has the Office of the Director of National Intelligence (ODNI) taken sufficient steps to ensure that open sources are appropriately exploited. This brings up another point not sufficiently addressed in the CRS report. Many open source experts exist outside the IC, in various government and private think tanks, as well as in university faculties. The point is that IC professionals therefore do not have to do all the open source analysis themselves. Much has already been done in other fora and merely needs to be exploited.

As for OSINT funding, the CRS report suggests that Congress may have to become more deeply involved in determining the potential tradeoffs between funding the collection of secrets and funding the analysis of open source information. The report offers three arguments concerning the classified-OSINT tradeoff. The first is that policymakers simply derive less value from OSINT than from clandestinely collected secrets. Proponents of classified collection argue that while OSINT can complement, supplement and provide context for classified data, such information rarely provides insight into an adversary's plans and intentions. Intentions are critical information to policymakers, more so than observable capabilities it is argued. Therefore the priority effort must be the collection of secret information.

There are at least two problems with this line of argument. First, regardless of what intentions are suggested by a nation's or group's secret information, such intentions can change overnight, rendering the secret information collected at great cost at best obsolete and at worse misleading. Second, the claim that secret information signals with greater clarity and authority what a foreign leader may do more than openly available information is an unproven hypothesis. It is quite feasible that OSINT could prove intentions as reflected in secret information to be either impractical or intentionally misleading. Take for example Saddam Hussein's secret claim to have a nuclear weapons program.

The alternative view holds that OSINT should be considered not only as an important contextual supplement to classified data, but also as a potential source of valuable intelligence in and of itself. The CRS report presents the as-Sahab Institute, al-Qaeda's sophisticated Internet-based messaging and propaganda multimedia production facility, as an example of why open source collection and analysis are so important in today's technology-driven and globalized world. Other observers cite al-Qaeda's ability to use virtual space to recruit, proselytize, plot, and plan with impunity. The analogy is "people rob banks because that is where the money is." Intelligence officials should mine open sources because of the use being made of them by adversaries. This argument has merit but does seem to create a false dichotomy. No one is seriously arguing that OSINT should replace the collection of secret information. The challenge is to strike the correct balance, as far as resource allocation is concerned.

The CRS report characterizes the third argument as a "middle-ground" position, arguing that open source information should be used to help determine what is truly secret, so as to better focus clandestine collection efforts. The argument seems to be that before spending a lot of money or exposing agents to danger, analysts should first glean as much intelligence as they can from open sources. This narrow concept of the usefulness of OSINT could actually lead to inefficiencies, should the criteria for clandestine collection approval merely devolve to the proof of exhaustion of open sources. Experienced intelligence professionals know, intuitively in most cases, what information is available only through clandestine collection. Additionally, to collect OSINT merely for the purpose of establishing a basis for the collection of secrets would unnecessarily forego exploitation of key OSINT collected.

The CRS report very prudently states that collection and analysis of OSINT information will be ultimately judged by its contribution to the overall intelligence effort. Early indications are favorable. Collection of OSINT is generally less expensive and less risky than clandestine collection, and its use may result not only in monetary savings but also in less risk than utilizing sensitive technical and human sources. The CRS report also makes some other interesting points. OSINT may provide insights that clandestine collection cannot, such as new and innovative applications of new technologies, shifts in popular attitudes, the emergence of new political and religious movements, growing popular discontent, and burgeoning disillusionment with leadership.

The CRS report makes yet another interesting point. The debate over the relative value of open source information is occurring at a time when the global information environment is viewed by some as having reached a "post-modern" stage. In such an environment, the report states, secret information may be less important than the combination of open source information, information sharing, computer networking, and an ability to sift and analyze vast amounts of open source information. This point relates to the point made above that what appears important is the ability to achieve a competitive advantage in exploiting open source information. The CRS report provides a fascinating discussion of a very timely and important topic—the "elephant in the living room," if you will.

DOCUMENT NO. 8

OPEN SOURCE INTELLIGENCE (OSINT): ISSUES FOR CONGRESS

CRS Report
RL34270

December 5, 2007

Richard A. Best, Jr.
Specialist in National Defense
Foreign Affairs, Defense, and Trade Division
&
Alfred Cumming
Specialist in Intelligence and National Security
Foreign Affairs, Defense, and Trade Division

Summary

Open source information (OSINT) is derived from newspapers, journals, radio and television, and the Internet. Intelligence analysts have long used such information to supplement classified data, but systematically collecting open source information has not been a priority of the U.S. Intelligence Community (IC). In recent years, given changes in the international environment, there have been calls, from Congress and the 9/11 Commission among others, for a more intense and focused investment in open source collection and analysis. However, some still emphasize that the primary business of intelligence continues to be obtaining and analyzing secrets.

A consensus now exists that OSINT must be systematically collected and should constitute an essential component of analytical products. This has been recognized by various commissions and in statutes. Responding to legislative direction, the Intelligence Community has established the position of Assistant Director of National Intelligence for Open Source and created the National Open Source Center. The goal is to perform specialized OSINT acquisition and analysis functions and create a center of excellence that will support and encourage all intelligence agencies.

The effort has been only underway since late 2005 but the Center is up and running, and providing support, including training, to OSINT professionals throughout the Intelligence Community. Administrative mechanisms are in place to ensure that there is a comprehensive community-wide open source effort. It appears, however, to some observers that not all agencies have as yet made comprehensive commitments to acquiring and using open source information, nor that the ODNI has taken sufficient steps to ensure that open sources are appropriately exploited. Observers suggest that congressional oversight of the OSINT process might provide insight into current progress as well as identify areas that need modification. A particular focus of congressional interest might be potential tradeoffs between classified and open source collection to ensure that needed information is obtained in the best and most cost-effective manner. Proponents maintain that this approach helps to ensure that agents and expensive surveillance systems are focused on obtaining information that is being actively hidden.

The collection and analysis of OSINT information will be ultimately judged by its contribution to the overall intelligence effort. Collecting information from open sources is generally less expensive and less risky than collection from other intelligence sources. The use of OSINT may result not only in monetary savings but also in less risk than utilizing sensitive technical and human sources. OSINT can also provide insights into the types of developments that may not be on the priority list for other systems or may not be susceptible to collection through other intelligence approaches—innovative applications of new technologies, shifts in popular attitudes, emergence of new political and religious movements, growing popular discontent, disillusionment with leadership, etc. Supporters of OSINT maintain that the future contribution of the Intelligence Community will be enhanced by its ability to provide detailed information and incisive analyses of such developments. This report will be updated as new information becomes available.

Introduction

Although the Intelligence Community has received its share of criticism since its formal establishment in 1947, it appears such criticism has intensified since the end of the Cold War as the Community confronted a string of perhaps unprecedented challenges, including those from the dissolution of the former Soviet Union, the 9/11 terrorist attacks, and the 2003 Iraq War and its aftermath. Although each of these events triggered demands for Intelligence Community reform, perhaps no single change in the past quarter of a century can match the enduring, day-to-day challenge posed by the information revolution. Twenty five years after the development of the Internet and the personal computer, the explosive impact of the this technology-driven change continues to ripple through the Intelligence Community.

One result of this revolutionary change has been a newfound willingness on the part of the U.S. Intelligence Community to reexamine the extent to which it relies—or has failed to rely—upon open source information, which some have argued has been relegated to a "second class" status by many intelligence professionals who continue to value secret information above all else. As part of this reexamination, the Intelligence Community appears to be reassessing a number of open source issues, including the relative value of open source information compared to that of secret information; the impact and importance of the growing volumes of information unlocked by easy access to the Internet; the dampening effect that certain Community security practices may have had and may continue to be having on the use of open sources; the state of development of analytic tools necessary to effectively and efficiently collect, sift, analyze, and disseminate a vast volume of publicly available information when analysts are expected to also analyze increasingly large amounts of classified information; and, training issues relating to open source technology and techniques.

If the global information revolution has sparked debate within the Intelligence Community over the value of open source information, the ongoing jihadist terrorist threat has sharpened its focus. In underscoring the strategic and tactical importance of open source information generally, and the role of the Internet specifically, one senior policymaker recently described the Internet as being America's new open source battlefield.[1] Those who share this view tend to argue that the Intelligence Community must improve its strategic understanding of the of the jihadist threat by more effectively mining the Internet and other open sources for information. Such an effort, it is suggested, also will enable the Community to achieve a better tactical understanding of how jihadists use the Internet's web-television capabilities, chat rooms, and "news" sites, to train forces and raise money. Ultimately, these observers suggest, the United States must develop the capability to understand and influence foreign populations—"not in their council of states but in their villages and slums"—if it is to effectively counter the threat posed by jihadists. In such circumstances, it is argued, the information that should matter most to policymakers can be derived from open sources.[2]

The debate over the relative value of open source information, compared to that of classified data, is occurring at a time when the global information

[1] See comments of Francis Townsend, Assistant to the President for Homeland Security and Counterterrorism, DNI Open Source Conference, July16–17, 2007, Washington, D.C.

[2] George Parker, "Knowing the Enemy; A Reporter at Large," *The New Yorker*, December 18, 2006, p. 69.

environment is viewed by some as having reached a "post-modern" stage.[3] In such an environment, secret information may be less important than the combination of open source information, information sharing, computer networking, and an ability to sift and analyze a dizzying volume of open source information. Indeed, one former senior intelligence officer suggested that whereas the 20th century was the century of secrets, the 21st century may well prove to be the century of global information. If the Intelligence Community as a whole accepts and understands this change, according to some observers, it may gain an edge in confronting current threats, particularly those posed by terrorism.

Debate Centers on Relative Value Of Open Source

Intelligence professionals generally agree that open source information is useful and that such information should be collected and analyzed, just as is data derived from classified sources. They disagree, however, over its value relative to that of clandestinely-collected secret information, and thus the amount of time, attention, and resources that should be devoted to its collection and analysis remains in dispute. For a brief case study of open source intelligence, see Appendix.

There generally are three different prevailing views regarding the of relative value of open source information. The first holds that policymakers simply derive less value from such information than from clandestinely-collected secrets. While open source information can complement, supplement and provide context for classified data, such information, it is suggested, rarely provides insight into an adversary's plans and intentions. Policymakers tend to view such information as being critically important to policy deliberations, and attach to it the highest value. For that type of insight, it is argued, the Intelligence Community must discover and collect secrets. It therefore is entirely appropriate that the Community target the preponderance of its resources to that end. As the Director of Central Intelligence (DCI) reportedly stated in 2005, "I only have money to pay for secrets."[4]

The second view asserts that open source information should be viewed not only as an important contextual supplement to classified data, but also as a potential source of valuable intelligence, in and of itself. Proponents of this view tend to cite the as-Sahab Institute, al-Qaida's sophisticated Internet-based messaging and propaganda multimedia production facility, as an example of why open source collection and analysis is so important

[3] Stevyn Gibson, "Open Source Intelligence, An Intelligence Lifeline," *RUSI Journal*, February 2004, p. 17.
[4] See Ronald A. Marks, "Spying and the Internet," *The Washington Times*, April 25, 2005, p. A–21.

in today's technology-driven and globalized world.[5] Others cite al-Qaida's ability to use virtual space to recruit, proselytize, plot, and plan with impunity.[6] According to one observer, "al-Qaida is right on the cutting edge of the adoption of new technologies. They grab hold of the new stuff as soon as it becomes available and start using it."[7] Another commentator suggested that gaining an understanding of the inner workings of the as-Sahab Institute may provide as an effective way as any "to get close to bin Laden and Zawahiri."[8] According to one former senior intelligence who believes that the Intelligence Community continues to undervalue open source information, "[Open source information] is no longer the icing on the cake, it is the cake itself."[9]

Proponents of the third view adopt a "middle-ground" position, arguing that open source information probably will never provide the "smoking gun" about some issue or threat, but that it can be instrumental in helping analysts to better focus or "drive" clandestine collection activities by first identifying what is truly secret. Open sources therefore should be viewed as an analyst's "source of first resort." Although these adherents tend to champion the relative value of open sources, their supports appears to be measured. While generally believing that the Intelligence Community should devote additional resources to collecting and analyzing open source information, they appear wary of over-selling its value. "We don't have the confidence yet," according to one senior intelligence officer, in explaining such wariness.[10]

Historically, Open Source Has Played a Secondary Role

Although the Intelligence Community has long utilized open source information, some suggest that the Community has been slow to recognize its value, for two reasons. First, the Intelligence Community's principal mission is to discover and steal secrets; relying on open sources runs counter to that mission. Second, it is suggested that the Intelligence Community views clandestine-collected information as being more valuable because it is more difficult to collect.[11] As one observer of the Intelligence Community commented, "[Open source] was seen as irrelevant, and [the Intelligence

5 See Shaun Waterman, "As-Sahab: al Qaida's Video Production Unit," *United Press International*, September 20, 2007.

6 See Arnaud de Borchgrave, "Networked and Lethal," *The Washington Times*, September 25, 2007, p. 18.

7 Ibid.

8 Ibid.

9 Interview with former senior intelligence official, June 6, 2007.

10 See comments of Mary Katherine Graham, Deputy Director of National Intelligence/Collection, Director of National Intelligence Open Source Conference, July 16–17, 2007, Washington, D.C.

11 Amy Sands, "Integrating Open Sources into Transnational Threat Assessments," in Jennifer E. Sims and Burton Gerber, *Transforming U.S. Intelligence* (Washington: Georgetown University Press, 2005), p. 64.

Community] much preferred working with spies and satellites."[12] Because of this bias, the Intelligence Community has been viewed as supporting and investing in collecting and analyzing open sources only on the margins.

Ironically, any failure by the Intelligence Community to more fully appreciate the importance of open source information may have occurred despite some senior intelligence officers acknowledging its value at various times. For example, Sherman Kent, the Intelligence Community's legendary analyst, estimated that in peacetime 80 percent of the information policymakers needed to make decisions was available publicly.[13] Lt. Gen. Samuel V. Wilson, former director of the Defense Intelligence Agency, provided an even higher estimate, asserting, "Ninety percent of intelligence comes from open sources. The other ten percent, the clandestine work, is just the more dramatic. The real intelligence hero is Sherlock Holmes, not James Bond."[14]

Since the onset of the information revolution, and in the aftermath of the Cold War, the Intelligence Community's reliance on open source information grew as the Internet expanded and the availability of public information increased dramatically. The world also became more open. For example, in the case of Russia, it is estimated that the ratio of unclassified to classified information in the case of Russia has more than reversed from its 20:80 cold war ratio.[15]

With the end of the Cold War, the Intelligence Community's reliance on open source information also grew because it turned its attention away from the sophisticated military programs of the Soviet Union and towards the disparate threats posed by emerging post-Cold War threats. Collection strategies shifted from sophisticated surveillance satellites capable of counting tanks and missiles to the gathering of whatever information was available on rogue states and terrorist groups. Much of the information found was actually openly available but not hitherto collected and analyzed.

[12] Benjamin Wallace-Wells, "Private Jihad," *The New Yorker*, May 29, 2006, P. 38.

[13] Memorandum Respecting Section 202 (Central Intelligence Agency) of the Bill to Provide for a National Defense Establishment, Submitted by Allen W. Dulles, April 25, 1947, reprinted in U.S. Congress, 80th Congress, 1st session, Senate, Committee on Armed Services, *National Defense Establishment (Unification of the Armed Services)*, Hearings, Part 1, page 525.

[14] Donna O'Harren, "Opportunity Knocking: Open Source Intelligence For the War on Terrorism," Thesis, Naval Postgraduate School, December 2006, p. 9.

[15] See Mark M. Lowenthal, *Intelligence, From Secrets to Policy, Second Edition*, CQ Press (Washington, D.C.), 2003, p. 80. Even at the height of the Cold War, a period of time when the Intelligence Community focused much of its efforts on clandestine collection against the former Soviet Union, American intelligence analysts made time to track the publishing records of Soviet scientists. They highlighted when certain scientists stopped publishing for a period of time, concluding that any such pauses could signify that the Soviets were developing new technologies. Such pauses would trigger new targeting aimed at determining if new technology was under development. See Amy Sands, "Integrating Open Sources into Transnational Threat Assessments," in Jennifer E. Sims and Burton Gerber, *Transforming U.S. Intelligence* (Washington: Georgetown University Press, 2005), pp. 67–68.

The shift within the intelligence agencies was publicly championed by open source advocates such as Robert Steele of Open Source Solutions, who has conducted annual conferences to bring together open source experts from around the world and written extensively on the topic.[16] In addition, intelligence agencies have come to utilize and rely on electronic databases and search engines which were developed for civilian markets. Some contractors have developed software and other research tools specifically for sale to intelligence agencies.

While acknowledging that the Intelligence Community is relying more on open source information, some observers insist that the Community continues to undervalue such information while focusing most of its attention on collecting secret information. Joseph Nye, a former head of the National Intelligence Council in the 1990s, perhaps best captured the prevailing view of the Intelligence Community when he stated, "Open source intelligence is the outer pieces of the jigsaw puzzle, without which one can neither begin nor complete the puzzle . . . open source intelligence is the critical foundation for the all-source intelligence product, but it cannot ever replace the totality of the all-source effort."[17]

Some open source proponents view such information as constituting more than just the "the outer pieces of the jigsaw puzzle," but rather every bit as valuable as clandestinely-collected secrets.

Open Source Information Defined

Definitions of "open source information" have varied over time. Most simply, the term refers to information that is unclassified. It also has been defined to signify information that is derived from overt, non-clandestine or non-secret, rather than hidden or covert collection. The Intelligence Community defines open source information as that information that is publicly available material that anyone can lawfully obtain by request, purchase, or observation.[18] Thus, the acquisition of such information must conform with extant copyright requirements.

Although open source information consists of unclassified material, the Intelligence Community sometimes classifies certain open source information that it collects, including information provided by substantive outside experts, if it determines that the process by which the information is collected

[16] See Robert D. Steele, *On Intelligence: Spies and Secrecy in an Open World* (Fairfax, VA: AFCEA, 2000).

[17] Amy Sands, "Integrating Open Sources into Transnational Threat Assessments," in Jennifer E. Sims and Burton Gerber, *Transforming U.S. Intelligence* (Washington: Georgetown University Press, 2005), pp. 67–68. p. 64.

[18] Intelligence Community Directive Number 301 and P.L. 109-163, Sec. 931.

could reveal intelligence sources and methods, intelligence requirements for certain collection of intelligence, or certain policy concerns.[19]

Open source information, according to some observers, generally falls into four categories:[20] widely available data and information; targeted commercial data; individual experts; and "gray" literature, which consists of written information produced by the private sector, government, and academe that has limited availability, either because few copies are produced, existence of the material is largely unknown, or access to information is constrained.[21] Within these four categories, open source information can include:

- media such as newspaper, magazines, radio, television, and computer-based information;
- public data such as government reports, and official data such as budgets and demographics, hearings, legislative debates, press conferences, and speeches;
- information derived from professional and academic sources such as conferences, symposia, professional associations, academic papers, dissertations and theses, and experts;[22]
- commercial data such as commercial imagery; and,
- gray literature such as trip reports, working papers, discussion papers, unofficial government documents, proceedings, preprints, research reports, studies, and market surveys.[23]

Open source information also can include information, which although unclassified, could be considered company proprietary, financially sensitive, legally protected, or personally damaging.[24] With increasing frequency, it also includes information derived from Internet blogs. According to Intelligence Community officials, blogs are providing "a lot of rich information that are telling us a lot about social perspective and everything from what the general feeling is[,], to . . . people putting information on there that doesn't exist anywhere else."[25]

---

[19] Amy Sands, "Integrating Open Sources into Transnational Threat Assessments," in Jennifer E. Sims and Burton Gerber, *Transforming U.S. Intelligence* (Washington: Georgetown University Press, 2005), p. 65.

[20] Ibid, p. 65.

[21] Ibid, p. 65.

[22] See Mark M. Lowenthal, *Intelligence, From Secrets to Policy, Second Edition*, CQ Press (Washington, D.C.), 2003, p. 79.

[23] Amy Sands, "Integrating Open Sources into Transnational Threat Assessments," in Jennifer E. Sims and Burton Gerber, *Transforming U.S. Intelligence* (Washington: Georgetown University Press, 2005), pp. 64–65.

[24] Ibid, p. 65.

[25] See Bill Gertz, "CIA Mines 'Rich' Content From Blogs," *The Washington Times*, April 19, 2006, p. 4.

There continue to be misconceptions about open source information, even, it is suggested, among intelligence officials. One such misconception is that intelligence analysts rely on the Internet for most open source information. In fact, according to a 2003 published estimate, analysts derived only three to five percent of such information from Internet sources.[26] It should be noted that there could be any several reasons for this low estimate, including the lack of open source expertise; ineffective analytic tools; a lack of subject expertise; deadline pressures that prevent more extensive evaluation of Internet sources; the possibility that the Internet may not provide the best sources for certain needed information; or, some combination of these factors.

Another misconception is that open source information is free. Although such information can be collected, certainly at less expense than, for example, than that collected by satellite, the Intelligence Community, like any other consumer of various media, still must pay for access. The Community also must purchase analytic tools that enable analysts to more effectively sift open source information. And the Intelligence Community is increasing its investment in analytic tool development. For example, the Department of Defense recently awarded Johns Hopkins University a $48 million grant to develop technology that is capable of automatically translating and analyzing speech and text in multiple languages. It is generally believed that the Intelligence Community must achieve such a capability if it is to effectively collect and analyze open source information.

When does open source information become "open source intelligence?" According to the statutory definition, such information becomes "intelligence" when it is collected, exploited, and disseminated in a timely manner to an appropriate audience for the purpose of addressing a specific intelligence requirement.[27] The definition refers to "collection," even though some open source analysts prefer to use the term "acquired," arguing that analysts generally acquire previously collected and publicly available information second-hand. Most intelligence professionals, however, employ the term "collection."

Analysts Face Obstacles in Use of Open Source

Intelligence analysts confront several obstacles in making more effective use of open source information. One such obstacle—perhaps a principal one—is that many analysts lack sufficient subject matter expertise. Indeed, open source proponents assert that open source intelligence is as much about such expertise—foreign language and cultural understanding—as it

---

[26] See Mark M. Lowenthal, *Intelligence, From Secrets to Policy, Second Edition*, CQ Press (Washington, D.C.), 2003, p. 80.

[27] P.L. 109-163, Sec. 931. Intelligence Community Directive Number 301.

is about the underlying data itself, and that it would be misleading to assume that the value of such intelligence exists mostly, or solely, in the information itself.

Another such obstacle can be the analyst's own bias against open source information. Some analysts believe that such information generally is not as carefully vetted as clandestinely-collected intelligence and therefore is less creditable, and ultimately provides less value to the policymaker. Thus, driven by deadlines and confronted by large volumes of open source and classified information, analysts often choose to focus their limited time and resources on analyzing clandestine-collected intelligence. Moreover, they often receive further encouragement to do so from managers who establish priorities that favor the analysis of clandestinely-collected secrets.

Other obstacles include:

- Training. Analysts often lack the training necessary to make the most effective use of open sources.
- Internet on the desktop. An unknown number of analysts and collectors still are unable to access the Internet from their desktops. That any analyst or collector lacks Internet access leads some observers to question the Intelligence Community's commitment to more fully developing open source capabilities.
- Volume. In searching open sources, analysts confront an enormous volume of information. Identifying and analyzing information from this data stream can be daunting, and analysts must rely upon their subject matter expertise and an effective set of analytic tools to tackle the task. Volume, however, also can work in an analyst's favor. By being able to check multiple sources, an analyst is better able to assess whether a certain piece of information is deceptive, biased, or in error.
- Tools. The search for more effective analytic tools remains a challenge. Analysts continue to be overwhelmed by text searches that require examination and correlation. In addressing this problem, the Intelligence Community trying to develop visualization tools that will better enable analysts to more effectively extract and manipulate critical information from all available information sources.
- The "echo" effect. Such an effect occurs when more than one media outlet makes available the same news story. The resulting repetition can imbue a particular news item with more credibility and importance than is warranted. Given the proliferation of news sources, this phenomenon remains a continuing challenge for analysts.
- Security. According to some observers, overly rigid Intelligence Community security practices continue to limit the broader and more effective use of open source information. Certain practices—for example,

polygraph requirements and classification reviews of subsequent publications—can discourage outside experts from collaborating with Intelligence Community counterparts. Subsequently classifying information provided by outside collaborators can also undermine cooperation. Such practices have a "dampening effect," according to some critics.[28] Security officials acknowledge as much, but generally argue that security concerns must take precedence.

Intelligence Community Criticized For Not Making Greater Use of Open Source

Over the past decade, two national commissions criticized the Intelligence Community for its failure to promote the use of open source information and a third recommended that an open source center be established that would serve the Community. The commissions also criticized the Community's preferential bias with regard to classified information.

Aspin-Brown Commission

In 1996, the Aspin-Brown Commission criticized the Intelligence Community for failing to make greater use of open source information.[29] The commission, established by Congress to review the Intelligence Community's post-Cold War effectiveness, concluded that the Intelligence Community was moving too slowly to provide analysts access to open source data bases, particularly given the volume of information readily available on the Internet.

While noting that the development of open source data bases was growing, the Commission said that intelligence analysts had only limited access to such data bases. The Commission criticized the Community for an effort that it characterized as "inexplicably slow" and recommended that a computer infrastructure be established that connected intelligence analysts into open source information networks. Although the Commission did not address the issue of funding for open source, it did urge the Intelligence Community to adopt less intrusive security measures.

9/11 Commission

In contrast to the Aspin Brown Commission's more detailed treatment of the open source issue, the 9/11 Commission's final report only briefly

[28] See "Preparing for the 21st Century: An Appraisal of U.S. Intelligence," *Commission the Roles and Capabilities of the United States Intelligence Community*, March 1, 1996, p. 88. The Commission is referred to as the Aspin-Brown Commission, in recognition of the Commission's leaders, former Congressman Les Aspin and former Secretary of Defense Harold Brown.

[29] Ibid, p. 88.

mentioned the topic of open source information. Its final report contained a diagram outlining a new Intelligence Community organizational chart that proposed the establishment of an open source center within the Central Intelligence Agency (CIA)[30] but did not further explain the concept. Commissioners reportedly viewed open source information as important but lacked sufficient time to more fully explore the issue.[31]

WMD Commission

The WMD Commission, formally known as The Commission on the Intelligence Capabilities of the United States Regarding Weapons of Mass Destruction, concluded in a 2005 report that the Intelligence Community makes too little systematic use of outside experts and open source information.[32] As did its 9/11 Commission counterparts, the WMD commissioners recommended that a open source center be established within CIA.

In making this recommendation, commissioners concluded that:

> Analysts have large quantities of information from a wide variety of sources delivered to their desktops each day. Given the time constraints analysts face, it is understandable that their daily work focuses on using what's readily available—usually classified material. Clandestine sources, however, constitute only a tiny sliver of the information available on many topics of interest to the Intelligence Community. Other sources, such as traditional media, the Internet, and individuals in academia, non-governmental organizations, and business, offer vast intelligence possibilities. Regrettably, all too frequently these "non-secret" sources are undervalued and underused by the Intelligence Community.[33]

Commissioners recommended that analysts broaden their information horizons and encouraged them to expand their use of open source material, outside experts, and new and emerging technologies.

Congress Urges Creation of an Open Source Center

Following the completion of the 9/11 Commission report but in advance of the publication of the WMD Commission's final report, Congress in 2004 approved a comprehensive intelligence reform bill that included a "Sense of Congress" resolution calling for the establishment of an open source center which would collect, analyze, produce, and disseminate open-source intelligence.[34] The resolution described open source intelligence as a valuable source of such information that must be integrated into

[30] The 9/11 Commission Report, 2004.
[31] Interview with 9/11 Commission staff.
[32] The Commission on the Intelligence Capabilities of the United States Regarding Weapons of Mass Destruction, March 31, 2005, p. 389.
[33] Ibid, p. 395.
[34] Section 1052, P.L. 108-458.

the intelligence cycle to ensure that the U.S. policymakers are fully and completely informed.

Intelligence Community's Response: the Open Source Enterprise

Greater emphasis on open source information came in the wake of the Intelligence Reform and Terrorism Protection Act of 2004 (P.L. 108-458) which included the most extensive changes in intelligence organization since 1947. The act stated that open source intelligence is "a valuable source that must be integrated into the intelligence cycle to ensure that United States policymakers are fully and completely informed." It also expressed the sense of Congress that the Director of National Intelligence (DNI) should establish "an intelligence center for the purpose of coordinating the collection, analysis, production, and dissemination of open-source intelligence to elements of the intelligence community." The act asked for a report by June 30, 2005, from the DNI containing his decision on whether an open source center is advisable.

In response to this congressional direction, the Administration opted to establish a National Open Source Enterprise built around several key principles:

- the establishment of the position of Assistant Deputy Director of National Intelligence for Open Source with overall oversight responsibility of the open source effort;
- coordination by the Office of the Director of National Intelligence (ODNI) for open source funding requests in the DNI's budgetary submissions and allocations;
- the creation of a "Guild" of open source experts at an Open Source Center and by ensuring that open source competency becomes an Intelligence Community requirement;
- a single open source requirements management system to balance resources and acquisitions against priorities;
- establishment of a single open source architecture to facilitate access to a wide range of potential consumers at federal, state, local, and tribal levels; and
- creation of an entity to develop and acquire cutting-edge technologies and processes that advances efforts to acquire and utilize open source information.[35]

[35] See Office of the Director of National Intelligence, Intelligence Community Directive 301, *National Open Source Enterprise,* July 11, 2006.

General Hayden, then the Deputy DNI, described the new approach to a subcommittee of the House Permanent Select Committee on Intelligence (HPSCI) in July 2005 as setting up an "enabling function" to encourage the effective use of open source information throughout the Intelligence Community. Hayden stated:

> . . . what we're talking about is a center that has the expertise that can advise us in the community on the information technology and the policy changes that will be needed to allow every analyst in the community access to open source information.
>
> . . . we picture a kind of a SWAT team of experts that can go to a new activity or a new center or a new agency, or to meet an emerging need, to go there and say, 'Here is what open source can contribute. Let me set up these functions for you. Let me advise you along these paths.[36]

National Open Source Center (NOSC)

The unfolding of the Administration's plan to establish a National Open Source Center (NOSC) began on November 1, 2005 when the Center was officially and publicly established by the DNI. Administratively, it was placed under the management of the CIA and its organization incorporated and augmented the Foreign Broadcast Information Service (FBIS) which has provided open source products to the government and outside researchers since February 1941. According to a DNI press release, the Center's functions include "collection, analysis and research, training, and information technology management to facilitate government-wide access and use." Located in suburban Northern Virginia, the NOSC currently has several hundred full-time personnel some of whom are on temporary assignments in other agencies. Although NOSC remains under the administrative control of the CIA, the aim is to provide a center of expertise for the entire government in exploiting open source information. It can be tasked by other agencies for specific research efforts.[37]

NOSC provides translations and transcriptions of media products from around the world. NOSC translations and analytical products are currently available online in a website (*opensource.gov*) that is available to government officials. Many of these products are also available to the public or to outside experts through the World News Connection, a commercial news service.[38] The NOSC maintains a vast collection of published material in

[36] Testimony of Lt. Gen. Michael Hayden, Deputy Director of National Intelligence, to the Oversight Subcommittee of the House Permanent Select Committee on Intelligence, July 28, 2005, Federal News Service transcript.

[37] See Hamilton Bean, "The DNI's Open Source Center: An Organizational Communication Perspective," *International Journal of Intelligence and Counterintelligence*, Summer 2007; also, Robert K. Ackerman, "Intelligence Center Mines Open Sources," *Signal*, March 2006.

[38] See [http://wnc.fedworld.gov/description.html].

electronic form, including daily downloads of hundreds of newspapers and journals.[39]

The NOSC seeks to establish higher professional standards for open source collection and analysis, to create an open source "guild." Although every analyst knows about some open source materials such as the local newspaper, the rapidly expanding availability of electronic databases and a large variety of search strategies requires extensive training and skills that only IT specialists are likely to acquire in graduate schools. It is widely maintained that training in specific searching skills is cost effective as it reduces time-consuming and unproductive searches.

Use of Open Source in Government Agencies

A fundamental goal is not just to hire more open source practitioners but to alter agency cultures to ensure that use of open source information is a routine and natural component of analytical practice. Changing agency cultures is a formidable task. As one intelligence scholar has noted:

> The culture of the intelligence community tends to devalue the use of open sources except in marginal ways. In part because open sources are by definition available to the public, they remove one of the psychological benefits of being an insider with special information. Relying on classified information immediately limits those with whom an analyst can discuss issues and creates a wall between those with access and those without it. Intelligence analysts must, by law, exclude outsiders without clearance from access to classified information; but in this way they create an exclusive club that inhibits the use of relevant and potentially significant expertise. Also, as noted earlier, many intelligence analysts trust only classified information. They may put excessive confidence in such materials, perhaps in the belief that they have been closely vetted and validated during the collection process. This stamp of approval for classified information, and the bias favoring it over other sources, can cause analysts to be closed off to data emerging from researchers who use open sources.[40]

To some extent, resistance to the use of open source information may be more prevalent among analysts whose careers began during the Cold War when the focus was on secretive nation states with sophisticated military capabilities. Analysts who have entered the workforce in more recent years will have had routine access to open source information in academic

[39] Much of this information appears in online versions that is removed after a few days; NOSC performs an essential service by archiving key website publications for future reference.

[40] Amy Sands, "Integrating Open Sources into Transnational Threat Assessments," in Jennifer E. Sims and Burton Gerber, *Transforming U.S. Intelligence* (Washington: Georgetown University Press, 2005), p. 72.

environments or in previous professional assignments.[41] Thus they may be more inclined to continue routine use of open sources in conjunction with classified data.

A major component of the open source initiative has, nevertheless, been an effort to ensure that open source experts are available and utilized in all intelligence agencies and at the same time avoid unnecessary duplicative efforts. This effort has concentrated on enhancing expertise within the NOSC and in offering training for open source experts in other agencies. In many cases, however, the number of persons whose job responsibilities focus on, or include open source information to a significant degree have not been consistently identified.

The ODNI's budgetary authorities may permit decisive support to the open source effort. Dedicated open source positions at appropriate pay-grades could do much to ensure the visability of the open source effort. With information expected to be available from individual agencies and reviewed by the ODNI, budgets submitted by the DNI each year could include more detailed information on specific open source analyst positions in each agency. Congress would then have the opportunity to review these efforts through the budget process to ensure adequate, but not redundant, open source capabilities. Some argue that open source billets should be identified not only in national intelligence agencies but also in military intelligence agencies.

Information sharing, based on state-of-the-art information technology, is another important part of the effort. The Open Source Center manages this effort for the entire Intelligence Community as well as homeland defense partners at the state, local, and tribal levels. The goal is to maximize connectivity throughout the Government and to supercede separate agency-based system that have incompatible formats and extensive duplicative materials. Individual agencies may continue to maintain independent open source databases, but the goal is that they are maintained in formats that can be accessed by analysts at other agencies. The WMD Commission noted that "Information technology has made remarkable advances in recent years. The private sector (without the same kinds of security concerns as the Intelligence Community) has led the adoption of technologies that are also critical to intelligence. Two areas show particular promise: first, machine translation of foreign languages; and, second, tools designed to prioritize documents in their native language without the need for translation."[42]

---

[41] Clive Thompson, "Open-Source Spying," *New York Times Magazine*, December 3, 2006 describes the frustration felt by some newly-hired analysts coming into intelligence agencies several years ago only to discover that computer access to intelligence literature and the search engines used in intelligence agencies reflected decades-old technologies.

[42] *WMD Commission Report*, p. 396.

This effort depends heavily on the expertise and initiative of commercial enterprises to develop useful and cost-effective technologies. In 1999 the CIA developed In-Q-Tel to to provide a means for business firms to work with intelligence agencies on comparatively small contracts. The effort has been widely praised but has been largely focused on classified technologies. A similar approach, but one focused solely on unclassified open source technologies has been proposed for implementation by the ODNI.

One of the most important sources of information from non-governmental sources private sector contributors is commercial imagery that is purchased by the National Geospatial-Intelligence Agency. Commercial satellites provide extensive overhead coverage of targets throughout the world to supplement imagery from government satellites. In some cases it has also meant that overhead imagery of significant quality is available to anyone with access to the Internet. Although the background and extent of this use lies beyond the scope of this Report, the use of commercial imagery has had a major influence on the intelligence community, especially on the procurement and operation of government satellites.[43] Commercial imagery, however, is a special case as the Government is in the many cases the principle customer. For most other open source information, the U.S. Government is only an incidental customer (and in some cases an undesired one).[44]

Department of Defense (DOD)

The Defense Department has long been an important center of open source information. The Asian Studies Detachment (ASD) in Camp Zama, Japan has collected and analyzed open source information on Far Eastern topics since 1947. With the services of U.S. military personnel and Japanese civilians, the ASD translates and analyses information for military commands in the region and makes its products available to the Intelligence Community.[45] Other military commands, some not technically part of the Intelligence Community, also undertake open source collection and analysis. Although the introduction of web-based information sharing systems makes it possible to share such information with other DOD and IC users, incentives to share information have not always been present.

In the wake of the 9/11 Commission Report and during consideration of the Intelligence Reform Act of 2004, the Under Secretary of Defense for Intelligence established a working group to assess open source efforts

[43] See Richard E. Rowberg, "Commercial Remote Sensing by Satellite: Status and Issues," CRS Report RL31218.

[44] Special efforts are taken in some cases to avoid too many hits on certain websites from computers recognizable as coming from.gov addresses.

[45] See David A. Reese, "50 Years fo Excellence: ASD Forges Ahead as the Army's Premier OSINT Unit in the Pacific," *Military Intelligence Professional Bulletin*, October-December 2005.

throughout DOD. The effort resulted in the establishment of the Defense Open Source Council. The Council was tasked with establishing open source requirements and developing an open source strategy for all DOD components. In July 2005 there was a conference between FBIS (which would shortly merge into the National Open Source Center) and DOD open source officials. The conference aimed to improve support to military users, encourage information sharing, and inaugurate a long-term mutually beneficial relationship. However, many of the conference attendees reportedly concluded that open source collection is poorly funded, and the personnel involved in DOD open source efforts often lack training in media analysis and foreign language capabilities. Furthermore, it was concluded that "there is no clear external point of contact or central responsibility for [open source] support for the military."[46]

Although there is greater coordination between the NOSC and DOD offices in acquiring materials to reduce duplication, it is not clear that the inherent challenges in training intelligence personnel in open source collection and analysis have been eliminated. Although information is shared more extensively and certain open source functions have been rationalized,[47] the open source efforts are in large measure are conducted in isolation from the NOSC and even other DOD entities.

In the FY2006 the Defense Authorization Act Congress found that the Intelligence Community "has not expanded its exploitation efforts and systems to produce open-source intelligence," and directed DOD to prepare a plan for funding a "robust" open source intelligence capability under the oversight of the Under Secretary of Defense for Intelligence.[48] The legislation also mandated plans for incorporating an open source intelligence speciality into military personnel systems and for using reserve personnel to support the open source intelligence mission.

Department of Homeland Security (DHS)

DHS, which is by statute both an intelligence and a law enforcement agency, is an important consumer of open source information and potentially able to make far more extensive use of it given the disparate extent of DHS responsibilities. Currently, DHS is focusing its open source effort on working in cooperation with state and local entities. The goal is to establish open source collection with in the various component agencies of DHS, relying on the Open Source Center for technical support and training.

---

[46] Douglas Peak, "DOD and the DNI Open Source Center—Building the Partnership," *Military Intelligence Professional Bulletin*, October-December 2005, p. 16.

[47] For instance, the headlines of the leading Chinese military newspaper are now summarized by the Open Source Center rather that the ASD, freeing up resources in the latter. Ibid., p. 17.

[48] P.L. 109-163, section 931.

Charles Allen, the Assistant Secretary for Intelligence and Analysis of DHS testified in May 2006:

> We're looking at putting together a cadre of governmental specialists, as well as contractors from my office, to work as a virtual satellite bureau of the open-source center that is run by the CIA to ensure that we meet the requirements not only of the federal government for homeland security open-source information but that we also make available this information and we push it down to the states. The states also . . . have open-source things publicly and lawfully acquired that we hope to have pushed back to us.[49]

Open source acquisition and use at DHS appears to be in the formative stages, a situation similar to that existing at many agencies. There is an acceptance of the need for greater use, but the infrastructure is incomplete and observers believe that full utilization of available sources has not been obtained.

Metrics for Open Source Use

One of the key challenges to managing the use of open source is the absence of widely accepted measurements or metrics. Intelligence Community managers seek quantifable measures for day-to-day administration. Counts are made of the occasions in which open source analyses have been included in the President's Daily Brief, one of the Intelligence Community's most important products. Other products are published by the Open Source Center based solely on open source information and disseminated to intelligence analysts and outside experts. Use of the website *opensource.gov* is also monitored.

Inasmuch as open source information is used by all-source analysts in connection with information from classified sources, it is difficult to measure how much open source information contributes to a specific intelligence product. It is anticipated that open source information will increasingly be relied upon given its greater availability, the nature of issues that today's analysts must cover, and the heavier emphasis placed on it by senior intelligence leaders. The ultimate metric for the Intelligence Community is, however, the quality of analysis. Today's analysts work with the awareness that products reflecting ignorance of information contained in open sources will discredit the entire intelligence effort. This will be especially the case when intelligence products are made public and are scrutinized by knowledgeable outside experts.

---

[49] Federal News Service, Testimony of Charles Allen, Assistant Secretary, Department of Homeland Security to House Homeland Security Committee, May 24, 2006.

Congressional Oversight of Open Source: Potential Options

Congress has been an important advocate of greater use of open source information; as noted above, it created a statutory requirement for increased use of open source information. In addition to ongoing oversight, some observers suggest that there are also a number of specific issues that Congress might address to further the goal of its greater use. These issues include:

- Identifying open source activities
- Copyright issues
- Moving the NOSC to the Office of the DNI

Identifying Open Source Activities

It is not clear that there are adequate reporting mechanisms to allow Congress to evaluate the implementation of mandated open source efforts. This creates uncertainties about how the mandate is progressing. For example, while the DNI currently has the statutory authority to ensure the effective execution of the budget, including open source activities, throughout the Intelligence Community[50], the reality is that funding allocations may be affected by requirements imposed by agency heads including the DCIA. Some observers suggest that open source positions and budgets need to be effectively "fenced," or protected, to ensure that congressional mandates are implemented. This concern has been expressed in regard to open source efforts in the various agencies and even to the NOSC itself. The extent to which different priorities of CIA managerial officials and the NOSC leadership have complicated open source efforts is unknown, but oversight committees may wish to verify the current IC approach is adequately implementing the congressional open source mandate.

One way is to examine specific budget areas in which spending on open source currently can be identified. First, there are amounts indicated in budget submissions for the staff of the Deputy DNI for Open Source and, within the budget submission for the CIA, for the personnel and operations of the Open Source Center. Similar information for open source efforts in other agencies may be more difficult to identify. It is not known if relevant detailed budget information on open source efforts is included in the classified budget justification books that are presented annually to the intelligence and appropriations committees. A requirement that a Congressional Budget Justification Book (CBJB) be submitted specifically devoted to open source could provide detailed insights into open source operations and capabilities throughout the Intelligence Community. An open

[50] 118 Stat. 3645.

source CBJB would provide the information base on which more detailed open source oversight could be exercised.

Another opportunity occurs when the DNI submits to congressional intelligence committees an annual report reviewing analytical products. Arguably, these annual reports should address the use of open source information. However, oversight committees could ask for additional information on open source utilization if needed. And finally, an approach that might be considered in some situations would be a request for an alternative analysis of a specified topic solely based on open sources in order to compare it with all-source analyses. The Intelligence Reform Act specifically provided for alternative analyses[51] and, in some cases, it might be appropriate to have alternate analyses based solely on information in the public record. Such an effort could demonstrate the additive value of specific forms of classified information. If a product based on open sources was essentially consistent with an analogous analytical product based on classified sources, then the former would have the useful advantage of being more easily provided to Congress and the public.

Copyright Issues

A difficult issue for those responsible for acquiring, analyzing, and disseminating open source information within the Government is the extent to which such activities can be carried out in accordance with the provisions of laws governing copyrights. Much of the open source information acquired by intelligence agencies is in the "public domain," i.e. information for which no copyright is claimed. In other cases, as with certain commercial databases, rights to the information have been obtained by contract in accordance with usual government procurement procedures. In many other cases, however, agencies acquire copyright information without the authorization of the copyright holder (as of course millions of writers and researchers also routinely do).

In using such copyrighted information, intelligence agencies, like other users of public information, are governed by the doctrine of "fair use" (based on common law and codified in the Copyright Act of 1976 (17 USC 107)). "Fair use" permits the use of copyrighted materials without authorization from the copyright holder if certain criteria are met; these include variables such as (1) the amount and character of the use; (2) the nature of the copyrighted work; (3) the amount copied in relation to the whole copyrighted work; and (4) the effect of copying on the potential market for the copyrighted work.[52] Copyright, however, has to be claimed and defended

[51] P.L. 108-458, section 1017.

[52] Douglas Reid Weimer, "The Copyright Doctrine of Fair Use and the Internet: Case Law," CRS Report RL30495, pp.1–2.

by the copyright holder and some, if not many, would see no benefit in suing the Federal Government on such grounds. Further complications arise in regard to works published in foreign countries whose governments may or may not adhere to the Berne Convention for the Protection of Literary and Artistic Works which provides international protections for copyrighted material. A detailed analysis of the implications of copyright law on the open source intelligence effort lies beyond the scope of this Report, but it is clear that the Intelligence Community's desire to "buy it once and only once" may be in conflict with the goal of copyright holders to ensure that payment for the use of their products by multiple government agencies is not avoided.

Some may argue that Congress should consider an amendment to copyright law that would cover the open source efforts of intelligence agencies. Removing uncertainty of the extent of copyright would facilitate open source efforts and facilitate the widest possible use of the information by public officials. On the other hand, such an initiative could infringe upon the legitimate rights of copyright holders including the profits they could reasonably expect from copies sold to the many government offices.

Moving the NOSC from the CIA to the Office of the DNI

Some have proposed making the Open Source Center a component of the Office of the Director of National Intelligence (ODNI) while essentially retaining its current roles and missions. This approach would attempt to guarantee that open source resources would be managed by practitioners with significant expertise that could not be redirected for a single agency's temporary higher priority. Given the availability of information systems that extend throughout the Intelligence Community, an Open Source Center directly under the DNI arguably could meet the needs of analysts at all levels even if it had no agency homebase.

The advantage of placing the NOSC directly under the DNI would be to enhance the prestige of the open source discipline by raising its profile, fencing the funding, and ensuring its independence from shifting priorities within the CIA where human intelligence collection inevitably makes heavy and continuing demands on senior officials. As part of the ODNI, the NOSC would have more visability and arguably would be better positioned to influence the use of open source throughout the Community. A disadvantage would be the need to establish an administrative infrastructure that would to some extent duplicate that which already exists within the CIA.

Placing the NOSC within the ODNI could also facilitate the NOSC's ability to support law enforcement agencies and state, local, and tribal entities. As part of the CIA, the NOSC is constrained in collecting information that will be used for law enforcement purposes in accordance with the provisions of the National Security Act precluding CIA involvement in law enforcement activities.[53] The Intelligence Community as a whole contains, however, several intelligence agencies—the FBI and DHS—that are also law enforcement agencies and use open source information to carry out their statutory responsibilities. Arguably, placing the NOSC in the ODNI would facilitate its ability to support law enforcement agencies. For instance, collecting media accounts in foreign publications or websites that provide information about potential terrorist activities that involve persons physically present in the U.S. could arguably infringe on the statutory prohibition of CIA involvement in law enforcement functions.[54]

Alternate Approaches

Congress also has broader reaching options. The Bush Administration's approach to open source intelligence is based on establishing standards and best practices at the National Open Source Center, and encouraging through various means, greater acquisition and use of open source information by analysts in all agencies. Although there has been little opposition to this approach expressed by Members of Congress, some outside observers have advocated alternative approaches.

A more radical, approach would be to establish an Open Source Agency completely outside the Intelligence Community (in addition to the existing Open Source Center). The goal would be to provide open source information not just to intelligence analysts but to all elements of the Federal Government including congressional committees. It is envisioned that the new agency would be an independent Federal agency under the Secretary of State (and similar to the Broadcasting Board of Governors). Such an entity could also be established in the Defense Department (outside of intelligence agencies) with special responsibilities for supporting multilateral operations involving a number of countries some of whom might not be intelligence partners of the United States.

This initiative could be based on an assessment that open source information, systematically collected and analyzed, is important for all government efforts including those that cannot realisticallybe supported by the Intelligence Community. A particular advantage cited by advocates is that open source intelligence could support the conduct of U.S. public diplomacy efforts without what is considered the taint of the "secret world." In addition, there might be less concern about acquiring public information

[53] 50 USC 403-3(d)(1): the CIA "shall have no police, subpoena, or law enforcement powers or internal security functions."

[54] 50 USC 403-3(d)(1).

that included references to U.S. persons, than about intelligence agencies collecting information from all sources that included references to U.S. persons.

Proponents of this plan argue that open source information is essential for virtually all governmental functions but that the explosion of available information has not been matched by concerted efforts to acquire and analyze it. The goal would be to establish a center of expertise for the entire Federal Government and to make available to the public free universal access to all unclassified information acquired through this initiative.

At present, information provided by the NOSC is available to all government agencies, but it is designed to support the Intelligence Community. Some ask why shouldn't an "information collection and analysis" agency be established to deal with policy issues that may be of concern to other government agencies including those responsible for domestic issues? Such an effort would have to be justified on the basis of a widely perceived need and pervasive support throughout the Federal Government. This support, it seems, is not yet apparent, but advocates of a wider effort to acquire and analyze open source information may continue to make the case that it is needed to meet ongoing and emerging policy issues. It is also possible that the NOSC will become more useful as times goes on, and that its contribution will be so widely recognized that it will become a model for a larger entity that can serve all Federal organizations.

Summary

Although unclassified information has often been slighted by the Intelligence Community, a consensus now exists that open source information must be systematically collected and in fact constitutes an essential component of analytical products. This has been recognized by various commissions and by Congress in statutory language. Responding to legislative direction, the Intelligence Community has established the position of Assistant Director of National Intelligence for Open Source and the National Open Source Center. The goal is not only to perform open source acquisition and analysis functions; but also, to create a center of excellence in open source collection and analysis that will support and encourage all agencies in the Intelligence Community in the effective use of open source. The challenge is to deploy all available information sources and technologies, including cutting edge approaches, to obtain and analyze information of national security importance that is available openly.

The effort has been only underway since late 2005 but the NOSC is up and running, and providing support, including training, to open source professionals throughout the Intelligence Community. It is less clear that administrative mechanisms are in place to ensure that there is a comprehensive community-wide open source effort. It appears to observers that not all agencies have as yet made comprehensive commitments to acquiring and using open source information, nor that the ODNI has taken sufficient steps to ensure that open sources are fully exploited. Observers suggest that congressional oversight of the open source process might provide insight into current progress of Administration efforts as well as identify areas that need modification. A particular focus of congressional interest might be potential tradeoffs between classified and open source collection to ensure that needed information is obtained in the best and most cost-effective manner. The goal would be to ensure that vulnerable human agents and expensive surveillance systems are focused on obtaining information that is being actively hidden and obtainable through no other means.

Appendix: Open Source Case Study: India's 1998 Nuclear Tests

"Senator, we didn't have a clue."[55] (Response by former Director of Central Intelligence Director George Tenet in a telephone conversation with Chairman Richard Shelby in the aftermath of India's 1998 nuclear tests.)

On May 11, 1998, the Indian Government tested three nuclear devices, the first such tests in 20 years. The tests caught the U.S. Intelligence Committee by surprise. Then-Director of Central Intelligence George Tenet appointed former Admiral David Jeremiah to "examine how and why we had missed the boat so badly."[56]

In conducting his review, Jeremiah touched on a number of issues, including the availability at the time of open source information in the form of public statements made by Bharatiya Janata Party (BJP) leaders prior to the election of party leader Atal Behari Vajpayee to be India's prime minister. Those public statements indicated that the BJP was interested in exercising the nuclear option.[57]

In his final report, Jeremiah concluded:

> . . . that both the intelligence and the policy communities had an underlying mindset going into these tests that the BJP would behave as we behave. For instance, there is an assumption that the BJP platform would mirror Western political platforms. In other words, a politician is going to say something in his political platform leading up to the elections, but not necessarily follow through on the platform once he takes office and is exposed to the immensity of his problem. The BJP was dead serious . . .[58]

Others were more explicit in their criticism. Former U.S. Senator Patrick Moynihan reportedly commented, "It didn't take spies or spy-masters simply to read what Indian leaders said and to take it seriously."[59]

These and other observations suggest that if analysts had paid greater attention and attached more significance to some of the BJP's public statements about nuclear testing, the Intelligence Community might have more accurately assessed BJP intentions.

A review of the public record prior to the Indian tests, however, presents a mixed picture in this regard and arguably underscores some of the

---

[55] George Tenet, "At the Center of the Storm: My Years at the CIA," HarperCollins Publishers (New York), 2007, p. 44.

[56] George Tenet, "At the Center of the Storm: My Years at the CIA," HarperCollins Publishers (New York), 2007, p. 44.

[57] George Perkovich, "India's Nuclear Bomb," University of California Press (Berkeley), 1999, p. 405. Perkovich's book is viewed by specialists as offering the definitive, publicly available analysis of what occurred during the lead up to India's 1998 nuclear tests.

[58] See Jeremiah News Conference, June 2, 1998.

[59] Amy Sands, "Integrating Open Sources into Transnational Threat Assessments," in Jennifer E. Sims and Burton Gerber, *Transforming U.S. Intelligence* (Washington: Georgetown University Press, 2005), p. 66.

difficulties analysts confront when attempting to analyze open source information.

During the election campaign in January 1998, the BJP's foreign policy spokesman stated that his party had every intention of exercising the nuclear option if elected.[60] But in February of that year the BJP issued a campaign manifesto that suggested to some Indian analysts that the BJP might not be fully committed to conducting nuclear tests.[61] New BJP Prime Minister Vajpayee, while reportedly stating that government would keep open the option of adding a nuclear capability to its arsenal, said there was no time frame for doing so.[62] The government's defense minister further suggested there was no need to test nuclear weapons.[63]

Amid other public signs that included no indication of imminent nuclear testing, a high-level U.S. delegation met with their Indian counterparts and concluded that no such tests were imminent.

In the final analysis, open source information that was available prior to India's nuclear tests in 1998 presents a mixed if not misleading picture that presented a number of analytic challenges.

[60] George Perkovich, "India's Nuclear Bomb, University of California Press (Berkeley), 1999, p. 405.
[61] Ibid, p. 407.
[62] Ibid, p. 408.
[63] Ibid, p. 408.

I. INTELLIGENCE AUTHORIZATION ACT FOR FISCAL YEAR 2008

INTELLIGENCE AUTHORIZATION ACT FOR FISCAL YEAR 2008 (H.R. 2082)

Commentary

This volume presents the Intelligence Authorization Act of 2008 to help inform readers on the intelligence priorities of the U.S. Congress and on issues requiring resolution before the Act can become law. Although the bill was vetoed by the President and returned to Congress unsigned, it still is a must-read, if one is to understand the viewpoint of Congress with respect to intelligence support for the War. The President's veto also is presented, and his objections to the Act are discussed. Additionally, this commentary summarizes this long and complex Act.

The Act authorizes appropriations for fiscal year 2008 for intelligence and intelligence-related activities of the U.S. Government, the Community Management Account, the Central Intelligence Agency Retirement and Disability System, and for other purposes. It authorizes classified dollar amounts to be appropriated for fiscal year 2008 for intelligence and intelligence-related activities for the Office of the Director of National Intelligence, the Central Intelligence Agency, the Department of Defense, the Defense Intelligence Agency, the National Security Agency, the military departments, the Coast Guard, the Department of State, the Department of the Treasury, the Department of Energy, the Department of Justice, the Federal Bureau of Investigation, the Drug Enforcement Administration, the National Reconnaissance Office, the National Geospatial-Intelligence Agency, and the Department of Homeland Security (Sec. 101).

The Act specifies that the amounts authorized and the authorized personnel ceilings as of September 30, 2008, for such activities are those specified in the classified Schedule of Authorizations, which shall be made available to the Senate and House Appropriations Committees and the President (Sec. 102). The Act allows the DNI, with the approval of the Director of the Office of Management and Budget (OMB), to authorize employment of civilian personnel in excess of the number authorized for FY2008 (by not more than 3%) when necessary to the performance of important intelligence functions. The Act also authorizes the DNI to have Intelligence Community (IC) personnel perform activities currently performed by contractors. The Act requires notification of the congressional intelligence committees, if either action is taken (Sec. 103).

The Act also authorizes appropriations for the Intelligence Community Management Account of the DNI for FY2008, as well as for full-time personnel for elements within the account. This statute also earmarks a specified amount for the National Drug Intelligence Center (Sec. 104). The Act deems funds appropriated for an intelligence or intelligence-related activity within the National Intelligence Program for FY2008, in excess of the amount specified for such activity in the classified Schedule of Authorizations, as specifically authorized by Congress for such purposes (Sec. 105).

The Act also authorizes $262.50 million for the Central Intelligence Agency Retirement and Disability Fund (Sec. 201). It permits appropriations authorized by the Act for salary, pay, retirement, and other benefits for federal employees to be increased by such additional or supplemental amounts as may be necessary for increases in such compensation or benefits authorized by law (Sec. 301). The Act allows an officer or employee of the United States or member of the Armed Forces to be detailed in any fiscal year after 2007 to the staff of an element of the IC funded through the Community Management Account, on a reimbursable or nonreimbursable basis, as jointly agreed to by the DNI and the head of the detailing IC element, for a period not to exceed two years (Sec. 302). The Act directs the DNI to implement a multi-level security clearance system for persons proficient in foreign languages or with cultural, linguistic, or other subject matter expertise "critical to national security," and to annually report to Congress regarding the foreign language proficiency of the intelligence community (Sec. 303, Sec. 414).

The Act authorizes the DNI to grant authority to fix the rate of basic pay for one or more positions within the IC in excess of any applicable limitation, with respect to a position which requires an extremely high level of expertise and is critical to successful accomplishment of an important mission, but only to the extent necessary to recruit and retain well-qualified individuals. The Act prohibits the pay level from exceeding Level II of the Executive Schedule (Sec. 304).

The Act permits the DNI to delegate to IC heads, and IC heads to delegate to senior officials within IC elements, the authority to approve certain employee travel on common carriers. However, the Act requires the DNI to submit to the intelligence committees guidelines for determining the senior officials to whom such further delegation is authorized (Sec. 305). The Act directs the DNI to prepare and submit to the intelligence committees an annual personnel assessment for the IC that assesses the personnel levels for each IC element for the fiscal year following the fiscal year in which the assessment is submitted (Sec. 306). Additionally, the Act requires the DNI to submit a report to Congress no later than March 31, 2008, regarding the use and impact of private contractors in the intelligence community, as well as the accountability mechanisms that govern their performance

(Sec. 307). It prohibits the DNI or any IC element head from implementing a plan that provides compensation to personnel based on performance until 45 days after the DNI reports to the intelligence committees on such performance-based compensation (Sec. 308). The Act requires the DNI to submit a report to Congress no later than March 31, 2008, outlining plans to increase the recruiting, hiring, and retaining of diverse candidates (Sec. 309).

The Act also requires the DNI to conduct vulnerability assessments for major systems, which are defined as significant programs of the intelligence community with projected total development and procurement costs exceeding $500 million (Sec. 311), to present annual reports to Congress regarding the acquisition of any major systems, and to notify Congress within 60 days if development costs for any programs significantly exceed the baseline costs (Sec. 313, Sec. 314). The Act specifies that the authorization of appropriations by the Act shall not be deemed to constitute authority for the conduct of any intelligence Activity that is not otherwise authorized by the Constitution or laws of the United States (Sec. 321). The Act amends the National Security Act of 1947 to allow funds available to an intelligence committee to be reprogrammed for an intelligence activity, if the activity supports an emergent need, improves program effectiveness, or increases efficiency (Sec. 323)

The Act increases the time of potential imprisonment for disclosing the identity of undercover intelligence officers and agents from 10 to 15 years (Sec. 324). The Act extends to IC elements current federal authority to delete from federal gift listing requirements information concerning the receipt and disposition of foreign gifts and decorations, if the IC element head certifies to the Secretary of State that publication of such information could adversely affect U.S. intelligence sources or methods (Sec. 325). The Act requires the DNI to report to Congress within 45 days after the date of the enactment of the bill regarding the detention and interrogation methods used by the intelligence community (Sec. 326) and states that no person in the custody or control of an element of the intelligence community shall be "subject to any treatment or technique of interrogation not authorized by the United States Army Field Manual on Human Intelligence Collector Operations" (Sec. 327).

The Act requires all members of the Congressional intelligence committees to be fully updated on intelligence regarding the Israeli military action in Syria on September 6, 2007 (Sec. 328). The Act incorporates each requirement to submit a report to the intelligence committees that is included in the classified annex to the Act (Sec. 329). The Act amends the National Security Act of 1947 and the Intelligence Authorization Act for Fiscal Year 2003 to repeal various intelligence-related reporting requirements (Sec. 330) and replaces the CIA Director with the DNI as a member of the Transportation Security Oversight Board (Sec. 402).

The Act establishes additional duties for the DNI's Director of Science and Technology, including assisting the DNI in establishing goals for basic, applied, and advanced research to meet and execute IC technology needs and submitting an annual report to Congress on the DNI's science and technology strategy (Sec. 403). The Act designates as the head of the National Counter Proliferation Center the Director of the National Counter Proliferation Center, who shall be appointed by the DNI and who locates the Center within the Office of the DNI (Sec. 404). The Act directs the DNI to develop and report to Congress on a plan to implement, across the IC, the recommendations of a report concerning the use of energy-efficient computer servers in the United States (Sec. 405).

The Act directs the DNI to submit to the intelligence committees a classified listing of all special access programs under the National Intelligence Program (Sec. 406); requires the Director of National Intelligence to report to Congress regarding the nuclear intentions and capabilities of Iran and North Korea (Sec. 407); requires the DNI to conduct accountability reviews of IC elements or personnel in relation to significant failures or deficiencies within the IC; and establish guidelines and procedures for conducting such reviews (Sec. 408).

The Act permits the DNI to delegate to the Chief Information Officer of the IC the authority to protect intelligence sources and methods from unauthorized disclosure (Sec. 409); authorizes the DNI to expend funds, and make funds available to other federal departments and agencies, to address deficiencies or needs that arise in intelligence information access or sharing capabilities; authorizes department or agency heads to use funds made available by the DNI for such purposes; and requires annual reports, in each of FY2009-FY2012, on the distribution of such funds (Sec. 410). Furthermore, the Act authorizes the DNI to approve interagency financing of national intelligence centers established under authority of the National Security Act of 1947, as well as for boards, commissions, councils, or similar groups established by the DNI for a period not to exceed two years and requires annual reports during FY2009–FY2012 on the exercise of such authority (Sec. 411).

The Act renames the DNI's Chief Information Officer as the Chief Information Officer of the Intelligence Community (Sec. 412) and establishes an Office of the Inspector General of the IC to objectively investigate and audit the conduct of the IC (Sec. 413).

The Act requires the DNI to report annually to the intelligence committees on the foreign language proficiency of each IC element (Sec. 414); to report to Congress on the advisability of providing federal retirement benefits to U.S. citizens for their service before 1977 as employees of Air America or an associated company while such company was owned or controlled by the

U.S. government and operated or managed by the CIA (Sec. 415); to ensure that space intelligence-related issues and concerns are fully considered in carrying out IC authorities, and IC agencies give due consideration to the vulnerability assessment prepared for a given major system at all stages of architecture and system planning, development, acquisition, operation, and support of a space intelligence system (Sec. 416).

The Act exempts from search, review, publication, and the disclosure requirements of the Freedom of Information Act certain operational files in the Office of the DNI that were provided by IC elements; provides exemption exceptions; requires the DNI, at least once every ten years, to review the exempted operational files to determine whether such files, or any portion thereof, may be removed from the exemption; and provides judicial review of an allegation of the improper withholding of records through the use of such exemption (Sec. 417).

The Act makes provisions of the Federal Advisory Committee Act inapplicable to advisory committees of the Office of the DNI (Sec. 418), authorizes the DNI to prescribe regulations to exempt any system of records maintained within the Office of the DNI from certain Privacy Act requirements (Sec. 419), and repeals certain administrative authorities within the Office of the National Counterintelligence Executive (Sec. 420).

The Act requires the CIA Inspector General, at least every three years, to conduct and report to the intelligence committees on an audit of each CIA covert action (Sec. 431), makes inapplicable to the CIA director a requirement to submit to the intelligence committees an annual report on actions taken to ensure the auditability of CIA financial statements (Sec. 432), amends the Central Intelligence Agency Act of 1949 to authorize CIA protective detail personnel to make arrests without a warrant for any offense against the United States committed in their presence or when having reasonable cause to believe that the person to be arrested has committed or is committing a felony (Sec. 433), requires a report from the DNI to the intelligence committees on the exercise of such authority (Sec 434), and amends the Intelligence Authorization Act for Fiscal Year 2004 to replace the CIA director with the DNI for responsibility over the Office of Intelligence and Analysis (Sec. 435).

The Act removes the requirement that the NSA disclose to educational institutions students who are NSA employees or training program participants (Sec. 441), authorizes the NSA Director to designate NSA personnel to perform protective functions for the director and any NSA personnel designated by the director, authorizes such protective personnel to make arrests without a warrant: for any offense against the United States committed in their presence when having reasonable cause to believe that the person to be arrested has committed or is committing a felony, and requires the NSA director to report to the intelligence committees after the exercise of such authority (Sec. 442).

The Act amends the Inspector General Act of 1978 to require the heads of the National Reconnaissance Office (NRO), Defense Intelligence Agency (DIA), National Security Agency (NSA), and National Geospatial-Intelligence Agency (NGIA) to appoint an independent inspector general for their agency (thus giving such inspectors general the same information-gathering power and independence as is currently held by inspectors general of other federal agencies); allows the Secretary of Defense to prohibit the inspector general of an IC element from initiating, carrying out, or completing any audit or investigation, if the DNI or Secretary determines that the prohibition is necessary to protect vital U.S. national security interests; and requires notification of such determination to the defense and intelligence committees (Sec. 443).

The Act requires the directors of the NSA and NRO to be appointed by the President, by and with the advice and consent of the Senate (Sec. 444) and requires the NGIA, as directed by the DNI, to analyze, disseminate, and incorporate into the National System for Geospatial-Intelligence likenesses, videos, and presentations produced by ground-based platforms, including handheld or clandestine photography taken by or on behalf of human intelligence collection organizations or available as open-source information (Sec. 445).

The Act directs the Secretary of Defense, during the period beginning on the date of enactment of the Act and ending on December 31, 2008, to delegate to the NGIA director personnel security clearance authority with respect to NGIA personnel that is identical to the authority held by the NSA director over NSA personnel (Sec. 446).

As for other elements and matters, the Act includes appropriate elements of the Coast Guard and Drug Enforcement Agency (DEA) within the definition of "intelligence community" (Sec. 451); amends the Intelligence Authorization Act for Fiscal Year 2003 to extend until December 31, 2008, the final report requirement of the National Commission for the Review of the Research and Development Programs of the United States Intelligence Community (Sec. 501); and directs the DNI to report to the intelligence committees describing any authorization granted during the ten-year period ending on the date of enactment of the Act, to engage in intelligence activities related to the overthrow of a democratically elected government (Sec. 502).

The Act also amends the John Warner National Defense Authorization Act for Fiscal Year 2007 to prohibit the Secretary of the Air Force, in any fiscal year after FY2007, from retiring any U-2 aircraft unless the Secretary of Defense has made certain certifications to Congress that the U-2 aircraft no longer contribute to mitigating any gaps in intelligence, surveillance, and reconnaissance capabilities (Sec. 503); and makes technical and/or clarifying amendments to the Central Intelligence Agency Act of 1949, the National Defense Authorization Act for Fiscal Year 1991, the National Security Act of 1947, the National Security Intelligence Reform Act of 2004, the Central Intelligence Agency Act of 1949, and other specified laws (Sec. 511).

President Bush vetoed the Act on March 8, 2008, stating that it would impede the U.S. Government's efforts to protect the American people from terrorist attacks and other threats because it imposes several unnecessary and unacceptable burdens on the IC. The President's specific objections included imposition of additional Senate confirmation requirements on two national security positions, creation of an unnecessary new office of Inspector General for the IC, and requiring the IC to use only the interrogation methods authorized in the Army field manual on interrogations. Additionally, the President found two other provisions of the Act objectionable: requiring the Executive Branch to submit information to the Congress that may be constitutionally protected from disclosure, and requiring a consolidated inventory of highly sensitive special access programs (SAPs) to be submitted to the Congress.

Congress likely could accept compromises and revise the Act to address the president's concerns sufficiently to have the Act signed into law; however, the president may consider two of his objections to be nonnegotiable. One would think that Congress and the president could reach agreement on the need for Senate confirmation for the two appointees and whether an additional Inspector General is needed. However, the president is likely to stand firm on his position regarding the sharing of SAP information. The Executive Branch makes a reasonable argument that the wholesale sharing of information on SAPs would likely compromise one or more of the highly sensitive programs, to the great detriment to U.S. national security. The president also could argue that the blanket sharing of SAPs simply is not necessary and would violate the "need to know" principle. Presently, SAP information is provided to Congress on a case-by-case basis, in accordance with security clearance requirements.

The other point on which the president will not likely yield concerns the limitation of interrogation methods to those approved in the U.S. Army field manual on interrogations, FM 2-22.3, *Human Intelligence Collector Operations*, published September 6, 2006. Although the president's position on this point has been consistent and unwavering, it seems logically flawed. The Executive Branch argues, probably urged on by the DNI, that the IC is not subject to the international law of armed conflict, the body of international laws that seeks to govern and regulate warfare, at least in its traditional form. The U.S. Armed Forces conform their conduct to those laws for two fundamental reasons. First, complying with the laws is the morally correct thing to do, since they provide for the humane treatment of combatants and non-combatants swept up by war. Second, adherence to the laws provides the U.S. Armed Forces a reasonable expectation of reciprocity and a legitimate basis for prosecuting for war crimes adversaries who commit violations. The logical flaw in the Executive Branch's argument that the IC should not comply with those laws is that the underlying reasons for compliance would seem to apply to those who serve as IC interrogators as well.

The president's utilitarian argument that the use of harsher interrogation techniques is justified by their effectiveness also seems flawed. Many experts point out that information acquired through the use of harsh interrogation techniques is of questionable reliability. Other commentators see the utilitarian argument as ignoring the lessons learned by the French in "The Battle of Algiers—"that a nation should not stoop to terrorist tactics to battle terrorists, no matter how effective the tactics may prove to be. Many in Congress embrace these powerful counter-arguments to the president's objections and may be unwilling to yield. Nonetheless, Congress may be willing to reserve the fight on this issue for another day and venue and therefore remove the objectionable language from the Act.

DOCUMENT NO. 9

INTELLIGENCE AUTHORIZATION ACT FOR FISCAL YEAR 2008 (H.R. 2082)

110th Congress, Second Session

January 3, 2008

One Hundred Tenth Congress of the United States of America

At the Second Session

Begun and held at the City of Washington on Thursday, the third day of January, two thousand and eight

An Act

To authorize appropriations for fiscal year 2008 for intelligence and intelligence-related activities of the United States Government, the Community Management Account, and the Central Intelligence Agency Retirement and Disability System, and for other purposes.

Be it enacted by the Senate and House of Representatives of the United States of America in Congress assembled,

SECTION 1. SHORT TITLE; TABLE OF CONTENTS.

(a) SHORT TITLE.—This Act may be cited as the "Intelligence Authorization Act for Fiscal Year 2008".

(b) TABLE OF CONTENTS.—The table of contents for this Act is as follows:

Subtitle C—Other Matters

Sec. 321. Restriction on conduct of intelligence activities.

Sec. 322. Clarification of definition of intelligence community under the National Security Act of 1947.

Sec. 323. Modification of availability of funds for different intelligence activities.

Sec. 324. Protection of certain national security information.

Sec. 325. Extension of authority to delete information about receipt and disposition of foreign gifts and decorations.

Sec. 326. Report on compliance with the Detainee Treatment Act of 2005 and related provisions of the Military Commissions Act of 2006.

Sec. 327. Limitation on interrogation techniques.

Sec. 328. Limitation on use of funds.

Sec. 329. Incorporation of reporting requirements.

Sec. 330. Repeal of certain reporting requirements.

TITLE IV—MATTERS RELATING TO ELEMENTS OF THE INTELLIGENCE COMMUNITY

Subtitle A—Office of the Director of National Intelligence

Sec. 401. Clarification of limitation on colocation of the Office of the Director of National Intelligence.

Sec. 402. Membership of the Director of National Intelligence on the Transportation Security Oversight Board.

Sec. 403. Additional duties of the Director of Science and Technology.

Sec. 404. Leadership and location of certain offices and officials.

Sec. 405. Plan to implement recommendations of the data center energy efficiency reports.

Sec. 406. Comprehensive listing of special access programs.

Sec. 407. Reports on the nuclear programs of Iran and North Korea.

Sec. 408. Requirements for accountability reviews by the Director of National Intelligence.

Sec. 409. Modification of limitation on delegation by the Director of National Intelligence of the protection of intelligence sources and methods.

Sec. 410. Authorities for intelligence information sharing.

SEC. 2. DEFINITIONS.

In this Act:

(1) CONGRESSIONAL INTELLIGENCE COMMITTEES.—The term "congressional intelligence committees" means—

(A) the Select Committee on Intelligence of the Senate; and

(B) the Permanent Select Committee on Intelligence of the House of Representatives.

(2) ELEMENT OF THE INTELLIGENCE COMMUNITY.—The term "element of the intelligence community" means an element of the intelligence community listed in or designated under section 3(4) of the National Security Act of 1947 (50 U.S.C. 401a(4)).

(3) INTELLIGENCE COMMUNITY.—The term "intelligence community" has the meaning given that term in section 3(4) of the National Security Act of 1947 (50 U.S.C. 401a(4)).

TITLE I—BUDGET AND PERSONNEL AUTHORIZATIONS

SEC. 101. AUTHORIZATION OF APPROPRIATIONS.

Funds are hereby authorized to be appropriated for fiscal year 2008 for the conduct of the intelligence and intelligence-related activities of the following elements of the United States Government:

(1) The Office of the Director of National Intelligence.

(2) The Central Intelligence Agency.

(3) The Department of Defense.

(4) The Defense Intelligence Agency.

(5) The National Security Agency.

(6) The Department of the Army, the Department of the Navy, and the Department of the Air Force.

(7) The Coast Guard.

(8) The Department of State.

(9) The Department of the Treasury.

(10) The Department of Energy.

(11) The Department of Justice.

(12) The Federal Bureau of Investigation.

(13) The Drug Enforcement Administration.

(14) The National Reconnaissance Office.

(15) The National Geospatial-Intelligence Agency.

(16) The Department of Homeland Security.

SEC. 102. CLASSIFIED SCHEDULE OF AUTHORIZATIONS.

(a) SPECIFICATIONS OF AMOUNTS AND PERSONNEL LEVELS.— The amounts authorized to be appropriated under section 101 and, subject to section 103, the authorized personnel ceilings as of September 30, 2008, for the conduct of the intelligence activities of the elements listed in paragraphs (1) through (16) of section 101, are those specified in the classified Schedule of Authorizations prepared to accompany the conference report on the bill H.R. 2082 of the One Hundred Tenth Congress.

(b) AVAILABILITY OF CLASSIFIED SCHEDULE OF AUTHORIZATIONS.—The classified Schedule of Authorizations referred to in subsection (a) shall be made available to the Committee on Appropriations of the Senate, the Committee on Appropriations of the House of Representatives, and to the President. The President shall provide for suitable distribution of the Schedule, or of appropriate portions of the Schedule, within the executive branch.

SEC. 103. PERSONNEL CEILING ADJUSTMENTS.

(a) AUTHORITY FOR INCREASES.—With the approval of the Director of the Office of Management and Budget, the Director of National Intelligence may authorize employment of civilian personnel in excess of the number authorized for fiscal year 2008 by the classified Schedule of Authorizations referred to in section 102(a) if the Director of National Intelligence determines that such action is necessary to the performance of important intelligence functions, except that the number of personnel employed in excess of the number authorized under such section may not, for any element of the intelligence community, exceed 3 percent of the number of civilian personnel authorized under such Schedule for such element.

(b) TRANSITION TO FULL-TIME EQUIVALENCY.—

(1) TREATMENT FOR FISCAL YEAR 2008.—For fiscal year 2008, the Director of National Intelligence, in consultation with the head of each element of the intelligence community, may treat the personnel ceilings authorized under the classified Schedule of Authorizations referred to in section 102(a) as full-time equivalents.

(2) CONSIDERATION.—In exercising the authority described in paragraph (1), the Director of National Intelligence may consider the circumstances under which civilian employees are employed and accounted for at each element of the intelligence community in—

(A) a student program, trainee program, or similar program;

(B) reserve corps or equivalent status as a reemployed annuitant or other employee;

(C) a joint duty rotational assignment; or

(D) other full-time or part-time status.

(3) NOTIFICATION TO CONGRESS.—Not later than 90 days after the date of the enactment of this Act, the Director of National Intelligence shall notify the congressional intelligence committees in writing of—

(A) the policies for implementing the authorities described in paragraphs (1) and (2); and

(B) the number of all civilian personnel employed by, or anticipated to be employed by, each element of the intelligence community during fiscal year 2008 accounted for—

(i) by position;

(ii) by full-time equivalency; or

(iii) by any other method.

(4) TREATMENT FOR FISCAL YEAR 2009.—The Director of National Intelligence shall express the personnel levels for all civilian employees for each element of the intelligence community in the congressional budget justifications submitted for fiscal year 2009 as full-time equivalent positions.

(c) AUTHORITY FOR CONVERSION OF ACTIVITIES PERFORMED BY CONTRACTORS.—In addition to the authority in subsection (a), upon a determination by the head of an element of the intelligence community that activities currently being performed by contractor employees should be performed by government employees, the concurrence of the Director of National Intelligence in such determination, and the approval of the Director of the Office of Management and Budget, the Director of National Intelligence may authorize for that purpose employment of additional full-time equivalent personnel in such element of the intelligence community equal to the number that is—

(1) in the case of personnel of Office of the Director of National Intelligence, not more than 5 percent of the number of such personnel authorized for fiscal year 2008 by the classified Schedule of Authorizations referred to in section 102(a); or

(2) except as provided in paragraph (1), not more than 10 percent of the number authorized for fiscal year 2008 by the classified Schedule of Authorizations referred to in section 102(a).

(d) NOTICE TO CONGRESSIONAL INTELLIGENCE COMMITTEES.—The Director of National Intelligence shall notify the congressional intelligence committees in writing at least 15 days prior to each exercise of an authority described in subsection (a) or (c).

SEC. 104. INTELLIGENCE COMMUNITY MANAGEMENT ACCOUNT.

(a) AUTHORIZATION OF APPROPRIATIONS.—There is authorized to be appropriated for the Intelligence Community Management Account of the Director of National Intelligence for fiscal year 2008 the sum of $734,126,000. Within such amount, funds identified in the classified Schedule of Authorizations referred to in section 102(a) for advanced research and development shall remain available until September 30, 2009.

(b) AUTHORIZED PERSONNEL LEVELS.—The elements within the Intelligence Community Management Account of the Director of National Intelligence are authorized 952 full-time or full-time equivalent personnel as of September 30, 2008. Personnel serving in such elements may be permanent employees of the Office of the Director of National Intelligence or personnel detailed from other elements of the United States Government.

(c) Construction of Authorities.—The authorities available to the Director of National Intelligence under section 103 are also available to the Director for the adjustment of personnel levels within the Intelligence Community Management Account.

(d) CLASSIFIED AUTHORIZATIONS.—

(1) AUTHORIZATION OF APPROPRIATIONS.—In addition to amounts authorized to be appropriated for the Intelligence Community Management Account by subsection (a), there are authorized to be appropriated for the Community Management Account for fiscal year 2008 such additional amounts as are specified in the classified Schedule of Authorizations referred to in section 102(a). Such additional amounts for advanced research and development shall remain available until September 30, 2009.

(2) AUTHORIZATION OF PERSONNEL.—In addition to the personnel authorized by subsection (b) for elements of the Intelligence Community Management Account as of September 30, 2008, there are authorized such additional personnel for the Community Management Account as of that date as are specified in the classified Schedule of Authorizations referred to in section 102(a).

(e) NATIONAL DRUG INTELLIGENCE CENTER.—

(1) IN GENERAL.—Of the amount authorized to be appropriated in subsection (a), $39,000,000 shall be available for the National Drug Intelligence Center. Within such amount, funds provided for research, development, testing, and evaluation purposes shall remain available until September 30, 2009, and funds provided for procurement purposes shall remain available until September 30, 2010.

(2) TRANSFER OF FUNDS.—The Director of National Intelligence shall transfer to the Attorney General funds available for the National Drug Intelligence Center under paragraph (1). The Attorney General shall utilize funds so transferred for the activities of the National Drug Intelligence Center.

(3) LIMITATION.—Amounts available for the National Drug Intelligence Center may not be used for purposes of exercising police, subpoena, or law enforcement powers or internal security functions.

(4) AUTHORITY.—Notwithstanding any other provision of law, the Attorney General shall retain full authority over the operations of the National Drug Intelligence Center.

SEC. 105. SPECIFIC AUTHORIZATION OF FUNDS WITHIN THE NATIONAL INTELLIGENCE PROGRAM FOR WHICH FISCAL YEAR 2008 APPROPRIATIONS EXCEED AMOUNTS AUTHORIZED.

Funds appropriated for an intelligence or intelligence-related activity within the National Intelligence Program for fiscal year 2008 in excess of the amount specified for such activity in the classified Schedule of Authorizations referred to in section 102(a) shall be deemed to be specifically authorized by Congress for purposes of section 504(a)(3) of the National Security Act of 1947(50 U.S.C. 414(a)(3)).

TITLE II—CENTRAL INTELLIGENCE AGENCY RETIREMENT AND DISABILITY SYSTEM

SEC. 201. AUTHORIZATION OF APPROPRIATIONS.

There is authorized to be appropriated for the Central Intelligence Agency Retirement and Disability Fund for fiscal year 2008 the sum of $262,500,000.

SEC. 202. TECHNICAL MODIFICATION TO MANDATORY RETIREMENT PROVISION OF THE CENTRAL INTELLIGENCE AGENCY RETIREMENT ACT.

Subparagraph (A) of section 235(b)(1) of the Central Intelligence Agency Retirement Act (50 U.S.C. 2055(b)(1)) is amended by striking "receiving compensation under the Senior Intelligence Service pay schedule at the rate" and inserting "who is at the Senior Intelligence Service rank".

TITLE III—GENERAL INTELLIGENCE COMMUNITY MATTERS

Subtitle A—Personnel Matters

SEC. 301. INCREASE IN EMPLOYEE COMPENSATION AND BENEFITS AUTHORIZED BY LAW.

Appropriations authorized by this Act for salary, pay, retirement, and other benefits for Federal employees may be increased by such additional or supplemental amounts as may be necessary for increases in such compensation or benefits authorized by law.

SEC. 302. ENHANCED FLEXIBILITY IN NONREIMBURSABLE DETAILS TO ELEMENTS OF THE INTELLIGENCE COMMUNITY.

Except as provided in section 113 of the National Security Act of 1947 (50 U.S.C. 404h) and section 904(g)(2) of the Counterintelligence Enhancement Act of 2002 (title IX of Public Law 107–306; 50 U.S.C. 402c(g)(2)) and notwithstanding any other provision of law, in any fiscal year after fiscal year 2007 an officer or employee of the United States or member of the Armed Forces may be detailed to the staff of an element of the intelligence community funded through the Community Management Account from another element of the United States Government on a reimbursable or nonreimbursable basis, as jointly agreed to by the Director of National Intelligence and the head of the detailing element (or the designees of such officials), for a period not to exceed 2 years.

SEC. 303. MULTI-LEVEL SECURITY CLEARANCES.

(a) IN GENERAL.—Section 102A of the National Security Act of 1947 (50 U.S.C. 403–1) is amended by adding at the end the following new subsection:

> "(s) MULTI-LEVEL SECURITY CLEARANCES.—The Director of National Intelligence shall be responsible for ensuring that the elements of the intelligence community adopt a multi-level security clearance approach in order to enable the intelligence community to make more effective and efficient use of persons proficient in foreign languages or with cultural, linguistic, or other subject matter expertise that is critical to national security.".

(b) IMPLEMENTATION.—The Director of National Intelligence shall issue guidelines to the intelligence community on the implementation of subsection (s) of section 102A of the National Security Act of 1947, as added by subsection (a), not later than 180 days after the date of the enactment of this Act.

SEC. 304. PAY AUTHORITY FOR CRITICAL POSITIONS.

Section 102A of the National Security Act of 1947 (50 U.S.C. 403–1), as amended by section 303 of this Act, is further amended by adding at the end the following new subsection:

> "(t) PAY AUTHORITY FOR CRITICAL POSITIONS.—(1) Notwithstanding any pay limitation established under any other provision of law applicable to employees in elements of the intelligence community, the Director of National Intelligence may, in consultation with the Director of the Office of Personnel Management and the Director of the Office of Management and

Budget, grant authority to fix the rate of basic pay for 1 or more positions within the intelligence community at a rate in excess of any applicable limitation, subject to the provisions of this subsection. The exercise of authority so granted is at the discretion of the head of the department or agency employing the individual in a position covered by such authority, subject to the provisions of this subsection and any conditions established by the Director of National Intelligence when granting such authority.

"(2) Authority under this subsection may be granted or exercised—

"(A) only with respect to a position which requires an extremely high level of expertise and is critical to successful accomplishment of an important mission; and

"(B) only to the extent necessary to recruit or retain an individual exceptionally well qualified for the position.

"(3) A rate of basic pay may not be fixed under this subsection at a rate greater than the rate payable for level II of the Executive Schedule under section 5312 of title 5, United States Code, except upon written approval of the Director of National Intelligence or as otherwise authorized by law.

"(4) A rate of basic pay may not be fixed under this subsection at a rate greater than the rate payable for level I of the Executive Schedule under section 5311 of title 5, United States Code, except upon written approval of the President in response to a request by the Director of National Intelligence or as otherwise authorized by law.

"(5) Any grant of authority under this subsection for a position shall terminate at the discretion of the Director of National Intelligence.".

SEC. 305. DELEGATION OF AUTHORITY FOR TRAVEL ON COMMON CARRIERS FOR INTELLIGENCE COLLECTION PERSONNEL.

(a) DELEGATION OF AUTHORITY.—Section 116(b) of the National Security Act of 1947 (50 U.S.C. 404k(b)) is amended—

(1) by inserting "(1)" before "The Director";

(2) in paragraph (1), as designated by paragraph (1) of this subsection, by striking "may only delegate" and all that follows and inserting "may delegate the authority in subsection (a) to the head of any other element of the intelligence community."; and

(3) by adding at the end the following new paragraph:

"(2) The head of an element of the intelligence community to whom the authority in subsection (a) is delegated pursuant to paragraph (1) may further delegate such authority to such senior officials of such element as are specified in guidelines prescribed by the Director of National Intelligence for purposes of this paragraph.".

(b) SUBMISSION OF GUIDELINES TO CONGRESS.—Not later than 6 months after the date of the enactment of this Act, the Director of National

Intelligence shall prescribe and submit to the congressional intelligence committees the guidelines referred to in paragraph (2) of section 116(b) of the National Security Act of 1947, as added by subsection (a).

SEC. 306. ANNUAL PERSONNEL LEVEL ASSESSMENTS FOR THE INTELLIGENCE COMMUNITY.

(a) IN GENERAL.—Title V of the National Security Act of 1947 (50 U.S.C. 413 et seq.) is amended by inserting after section 506A the following new section:

"SEC. 506B. ANNUAL PERSONNEL LEVEL ASSESSMENTS FOR THE INTELLIGENCE COMMUNITY.

"(a) REQUIREMENT TO PROVIDE.—The Director of National Intelligence shall, in consultation with the head of the element of the intelligence community concerned, prepare an annual personnel level assessment for such element of the intelligence community that assesses the personnel levels for each such element for the fiscal year following the fiscal year in which the assessment is submitted.

"(b) SCHEDULE.—Each assessment required by subsection (a) shall be submitted to the congressional intelligence committees each year along with the budget submitted by the President under section 1105 of title 31, United States Code.

"(c) CONTENTS.—Each assessment required by subsection (a) submitted during a fiscal year shall contain, at a minimum, the following information for the element of the intelligence community concerned:

"(1) The budget submission for personnel costs for the upcoming fiscal year.

"(2) The dollar and percentage increase or decrease of such costs as compared to the personnel costs of the current fiscal year.

"(3) The dollar and percentage increase or decrease of such costs as compared to the personnel costs during the prior 5 fiscal years.

"(4) The number of personnel positions requested for the upcoming fiscal year.

"(5) The numerical and percentage increase or decrease of such number as compared to the number of personnel positions of the current fiscal year.

"(6) The numerical and percentage increase or decrease of such number as compared to the number of personnel positions during the prior 5 fiscal years.

"(7) The best estimate of the number and costs of contractors to be funded by the element for the upcoming fiscal year.

"(8) The numerical and percentage increase or decrease of such costs of contractors as compared to the best estimate of the costs of contractors of the current fiscal year.

"(9) The numerical and percentage increase or decrease of such costs of contractors as compared to the cost of contractors, and the number of contractors, during the prior 5 fiscal years.

"(10) A written justification for the requested personnel and contractor levels.

"(11) The number of intelligence collectors and analysts employed or contracted by each element of the intelligence community.

"(12) A list of all contractors that have been the subject of an investigation completed by the Inspector General of any element of the intelligence community during the preceding fiscal year, or are or have been the subject of an investigation by such an Inspector General during the current fiscal year.

"(13) A statement by the Director of National Intelligence that, based on current and projected funding, the element concerned will have sufficient—

"(A) internal infrastructure to support the requested personnel and contractor levels;

"(B) training resources to support the requested personnel levels; and

"(C) funding to support the administrative and operational activities of the requested personnel levels.".

(b) CLERICAL AMENDMENT.—The table of contents in the first section of that Act is amended by inserting after the item relating to section 506A the following new item:

"Sec. 506B. Annual personnel levels assessment for the intelligence community.".

SEC. 307. COMPREHENSIVE REPORT ON INTELLIGENCE COMMUNITY CONTRACTORS.

(a) REQUIREMENT FOR REPORT.—Not later than March 31, 2008, the Director of National Intelligence shall submit to the congressional intelligence committees a report describing the personal services activities performed by contractors across the intelligence community, the impact of such contractors on the intelligence community workforce, plans for conversion of contractor employment into government employment, and the accountability mechanisms that govern the performance of such contractors.

(b) CONTENT.—

(1) IN GENERAL.—The report submitted under subsection (a) shall include—

(A) a description of any relevant regulations or guidance issued by the Director of National Intelligence or the head of an element of the intelligence community relating to minimum standards required regarding the hiring, training, security clearance, and assignment of contract personnel and how those standards may differ from those for government employees performing substantially similar functions;

(B) an identification of contracts where the contractor is providing a substantially similar functions to a government employee;

(C) an assessment of costs incurred or savings achieved by awarding contracts for the performance of such functions referred to in subparagraph (B) instead of using full-time employees of the elements of the intelligence community to perform such functions;

(D) an assessment of the appropriateness of using contractors to perform the activities described in paragraph (2);

(E) an estimate of the number of contracts, and the number of personnel working under such contracts, related to the performance of activities described in paragraph (2);

(F) a comparison of the compensation of contract employees and government employees performing substantially similar functions;

(G) an analysis of the attrition of government personnel for contractor positions that provide substantially similar functions;

(H) a description of positions that will be converted from contractor employment to government employment under the authority described in section 103(c) of this Act and the justification for such conversion;

(I) an analysis of accountability mechanisms within services contracts awarded for intelligence activities by each element of the intelligence community during fiscal years 2006 and 2007;

(J) an analysis of procedures in use in the intelligence community for conducting oversight of contractors to ensure identification and prosecution of criminal violations, financial waste, fraud, or other abuses committed by contractors or contract personnel; and

(K) an identification of best practices of accountability mechanisms within services contracts.

(2) ACTIVITIES.—Activities described in this paragraph are the following:

(A) Intelligence collection.

(B) Intelligence analysis.

(C) Covert actions, including rendition, detention, and interrogation activities.

SEC. 308. REPORT ON PROPOSED PAY FOR PERFORMANCE INTELLIGENCE COMMUNITY PERSONNEL MANAGEMENT SYSTEM.

(a) PROHIBITION ON PAY FOR PERFORMANCE UNTIL REPORT.—The Director of National Intelligence and the head of an element of the intelligence community may not implement a plan that provides compensation to personnel of that element of the intelligence community based on performance until the date that is 45 days after the date on which the Director of National Intelligence submits a report for that element under subsection (b).

(b) REPORT.—The Director of National Intelligence shall submit to Congress a report on performance-based compensation for each element of the intelligence community, including, with respect to each such element—

(1) an implementation time line which includes target dates for completion of—

(A) the development of performance appraisal plans;

(B) establishment of oversight and appeal mechanisms;

(C) deployment of information technology systems;

(D) management training;

(E) employee training;

(F) compensation transition; and

(G) full operational capacity;

(2) an estimated budget for the implementation of the performance-based compensation system;

(3) an evaluation plan to monitor the implementation of the performance-based compensation system and to improve and modify such system;

(4) written standards for measuring the performance of employees;

(5) a description of the performance-based compensation system, including budget oversight mechanisms to ensure sufficient funds to pay employees for bonuses;

(6) a description of internal and external accountability mechanisms to ensure the fair treatment of employees;

(7) a plan for initial and ongoing training for senior executives, managers, and employees;

(8) a description of the role of any advisory committee or other mechanism designed to gather the input of employees relating to the creation and implementation of the system;

(9) an assessment of the impact of the performance-based compensation system on women, minorities, persons with disabilities, and veterans; and

(10) an assessment of the consistency of the plan described in subsection (a) for such element with the plans of the Director of National Intelligence for a performance-based compensation system for the intelligence community.

SEC. 309. REPORT ON PLANS TO INCREASE DIVERSITY WITHIN THE INTELLIGENCE COMMUNITY.

(a) REQUIREMENT FOR REPORT.—Not later than March 31, 2008, the Director of National Intelligence, in coordination with the heads of the elements of the intelligence community, shall submit to the congressional intelligence committees a report on the plans of each element to increase diversity within the intelligence community.

(b) CONTENT.—The report required by subsection (a) shall include specific implementation plans to increase diversity within each element of the intelligence community, including—

(1) specific implementation plans for each such element designed to achieve the goals articulated in the strategic plan of the Director of National Intelligence on equal employment opportunity and diversity;

(2) specific plans and initiatives for each such element to increase recruiting and hiring of diverse candidates;

(3) specific plans and initiatives for each such element to improve retention of diverse Federal employees at the junior, midgrade, senior, and management levels;

(4) a description of specific diversity awareness training and education programs for senior officials and managers of each such element; and

(5) a description of performance metrics to measure the success of carrying out the plans, initiatives, and programs described in paragraphs (1) through (4).

Subtitle B—Acquisition Matters

SEC. 311. VULNERABILITY ASSESSMENTS OF MAJOR SYSTEMS.

(a) IN GENERAL.—Title V of the National Security Act of 1947 (50 U.S.C. 413 et seq.), as amended by section 306 of this Act, is further amended by inserting after section 506B, as added by section 306(a), the following new section:

"VULNERABILITY ASSESSMENTS OF MAJOR SYSTEMS

"SEC. 506C. (a) INITIAL VULNERABILITY ASSESSMENTS.—The Director of National Intelligence shall conduct an initial vulnerability assessment for any major system and its significant items of supply that is proposed for inclusion in the National Intelligence Program prior to completion of Milestone B or an equivalent acquisition decision. The initial vulnerability assessment of a major system and its significant items of supply shall, at a minimum, use an analysis-based approach to—

"(1) identify vulnerabilities;

"(2) define exploitation potential;

"(3) examine the system's potential effectiveness;

"(4) determine overall vulnerability; and

"(5) make recommendations for risk reduction.

"(b) SUBSEQUENT VULNERABILITY ASSESSMENTS.—(1) The Director of National Intelligence shall conduct subsequent vulnerability assessments of each major system and its significant items of supply within the National Intelligence Program—

"(A) periodically throughout the life span of the major system;

"(B) whenever the Director determines that a change in circumstances warrants the issuance of a subsequent vulnerability assessment; or

"(C) upon the request of a congressional intelligence committee.

"(2) Any subsequent vulnerability assessment of a major system and its significant items of supply shall, at a minimum, use an analysis-based approach and, if applicable, a testing-based approach, to monitor the exploitation potential of such system and reexamine the factors described in paragraphs (1) through (5) of subsection (a).

"(c) MAJOR SYSTEM MANAGEMENT.—The Director of National Intelligence shall give due consideration to the vulnerability assessments prepared for a given major system when developing and determining the annual consolidated National Intelligence Program budget.

"(d) CONGRESSIONAL OVERSIGHT.—(1) The Director of National Intelligence shall provide to the congressional intelligence committees a copy of each vulnerability assessment conducted under subsection (a) or (b) not later than 10 days after the date of the completion of such assessment.

"(2) The Director of National Intelligence shall provide the congressional intelligence committees with a proposed schedule for subsequent vulnerability assessments of a major system under subsection (b) when providing such committees with the initial vulnerability assessment under subsection (a) of such system as required by subsection (d).

"(e) DEFINITIONS.—In this section:

"(1) The term 'items of supply'—

"(A) means any individual part, component, subassembly, assembly, or subsystem integral to a major system, and other property which may be replaced during the service life of the major system, including spare parts and replenishment parts; and

"(B) does not include packaging or labeling associated with shipment or identification of items.

"(2) The term 'major system' has the meaning given that term in section 506A(e).

"(3) The term 'Milestone B' means a decision to enter into system development and demonstration pursuant to guidance prescribed by the Director of National Intelligence.

"(4) The term 'vulnerability assessment' means the process of identifying and quantifying vulnerabilities in a major system and its significant items of supply.".

(b) CLERICAL AMENDMENT.—The table of contents in the first section of the National Security Act of 1947, as amended by section 306 of this Act, is further amended by inserting after the item relating to section 506B, as added by section 306(b), the following:

"Sec. 506C. Vulnerability assessments of major systems.".

SEC. 312. BUSINESS ENTERPRISE ARCHITECTURE AND BUSINESS SYSTEM MODERNIZATION FOR THE INTELLIGENCE COMMUNITY.

(a) BUSINESS ENTERPRISE ARCHITECTURE AND BUSINESS SYSTEM MODERNIZATION.—

(1) IN GENERAL.—Title V of the National Security Act of 1947 (50 U.S.C. 413 et seq.), as amended by sections 306 and 311 of this Act, is further amended by inserting after section 506C, as added by section 311(a), the following new section:

"INTELLIGENCE COMMUNITY BUSINESS SYSTEMS, ARCHITECTURE, ACCOUNTABILITY, AND MODERNIZATION

"SEC. 506D. (a) LIMITATION ON OBLIGATION OF FUNDS FOR INTELLIGENCE COMMUNITY BUSINESS SYSTEM MODERNIZATION.—(1) After

April 1, 2008, no funds appropriated to any element of the intelligence community may be obligated for an intelligence community business system modernization described in paragraph (2) unless—

"(A) the approval authority designated by the Director of National Intelligence under subsection (c)(2) makes the certification described in paragraph (3) with respect to the intelligence community business system modernization; and

"(B) the certification is approved by the Intelligence Community Business Systems Management Committee established under subsection (f).

"(2) An intelligence community business system modernization described in this paragraph is an intelligence community business system modernization that—

"(A) will have a total cost in excess of $1,000,000; and

"(B) will receive more than 50 percent of the funds for such cost from amounts appropriated for the National Intelligence Program.

"(3) The certification described in this paragraph for an intelligence community business system modernization is a certification, made by the approval authority designated by the Director under subsection (c)(2) to the Intelligence Community Business Systems Management Committee, that the intelligence community business system modernization—

"(A) complies with the enterprise architecture under subsection (b); or

"(B) is necessary—

"(i) to achieve a critical national security capability or address a critical requirement in an area such as safety or security; or

"(ii) to prevent a significant adverse effect on a project that is needed to achieve an essential capability, taking into consideration the alternative solutions for preventing such adverse effect.

"(4) The obligation of funds for an intelligence community business system modernization that does not comply with the requirements of this subsection shall be treated as a violation of section 1341 (a)(1)(A) of title 31, United States Code.

"(b) ENTERPRISE ARCHITECTURE FOR INTELLIGENCE COMMUNITY BUSINESS SYSTEMS.—(1) The Director of National Intelligence shall, acting through the Intelligence Community Business Systems Management Committee established under subsection (f), develop and implement an enterprise architecture to cover all intelligence community business systems, and the functions and activities supported by such business systems.

The enterprise architecture shall be sufficiently defined to effectively guide, constrain, and permit implementation of interoperable intelligence community business system solutions, consistent with applicable policies and procedures established by the Director of the Office of Management and Budget.

"(2) The enterprise architecture under paragraph (1) shall include the following:

"(A) An information infrastructure that, at a minimum, will enable the intelligence community to—

"(i) comply with all Federal accounting, financial management, and reporting requirements;

"(ii) routinely produce timely, accurate, and reliable financial information for management purposes;

"(iii) integrate budget, accounting, and program information and systems; and

"(iv) provide for the systematic measurement of performance, including the ability to produce timely, relevant, and reliable cost information.

"(B) Policies, procedures, data standards, and system interface requirements that apply uniformly throughout the intelligence community.

"(c) RESPONSIBILITIES FOR INTELLIGENCE COMMUNITY BUSINESS SYSTEM MODERNIZATION.—(1) The Director of National Intelligence shall be responsible for review, approval, and oversight of the planning, design, acquisition, deployment, operation, and maintenance of an intelligence community business system modernization if more than 50 percent of the cost of the intelligence community business system modernization is funded by amounts appropriated for the National Intelligence Program.

"(2) The Director shall designate 1 or more appropriate officials of the intelligence community to be responsible for making certifications with respect to intelligence community business system modernizations under subsection (a)(3).

"(d) INTELLIGENCE COMMUNITY BUSINESS SYSTEM INVESTMENT REVIEW.—(1) The approval authority designated under subsection (c)(2) shall establish and implement, not later than March 31, 2008, an investment review process for the review of the planning, design, acquisition, development, deployment, operation, maintenance, modernization, project cost, benefits, and risks of the intelligence community business systems for which the approval authority is responsible.

"(2) The investment review process under paragraph (1) shall—

"(A) meet the requirements of section 11312 of title 40, United States Code; and

"(B) specifically set forth the responsibilities of the approval authority under such review process.

"(3) The investment review process under paragraph (1) shall include the following elements:

"(A) Review and approval by an investment review board (consisting of appropriate representatives of the intelligence community) of each intelligence community business system as an investment before the obligation of funds for such system.

"(B) Periodic review, but not less often than annually, of every intelligence community business system investment.

"(C) Thresholds for levels of review to ensure appropriate review of intelligence community business system investments depending on the scope, complexity, and cost of the system involved.

"(D) Procedures for making certifications in accordance with the requirements of subsection (a)(3).

"(E) Mechanisms to ensure the consistency of the investment review process with applicable guidance issued by the Director of National Intelligence and the Intelligence Community Business Systems Management Committee established under subsection (f).

"(F) Common decision criteria, including standards, requirements, and priorities, for purposes of ensuring the integration of intelligence community business systems.

"(e) BUDGET INFORMATION.—For each fiscal year after fiscal year 2009, the Director of National Intelligence shall include in the materials the Director submits to Congress in support of the budget for such fiscal year that is submitted to Congress under section 1105 of title 31, United States Code, the following information:

"(1) An identification of each intelligence community business system for which funding is proposed in such budget.

"(2) An identification of all funds, by appropriation, pro posed in such budget for each such system, including—

"(A) funds for current services to operate and maintain such system; and

"(B) funds for business systems modernization identified for each specific appropriation.

"(3) For each such system, identification of approval authority designated for such system under subsection (c)(2).

"(4) The certification, if any, made under subsection (a)(3) with respect to each such system.

"(f) INTELLIGENCE COMMUNITY BUSINESS SYSTEMS MANAGEMENT COMMITTEE.—(1) The Director of National Intelligence shall establish an Intelligence Community Business Systems Management Committee (in this subsection referred to as the 'Committee').

"(2) The Committee shall—

"(A) recommend to the Director policies and procedures necessary to effectively integrate all business activities and any transformation, reform, reorganization, or process improvement initiatives undertaken within the intelligence community;

"(B) review and approve any major update of—

"(i) the enterprise architecture developed under subsection (b); and

"(ii) any plans for an intelligence community business systems modernization;

"(C) manage cross-domain integration consistent with such enterprise architecture;

"(D) be responsible for coordinating initiatives for intelligence community business system modernization to maximize benefits and minimize costs for the intelligence community, and periodically report to the Director on the status of efforts to carry out an intelligence community business system modernization;

"(E) ensure that funds are obligated for intelligence community business system modernization in a manner consistent with subsection (a); and

"(F) carry out such other duties as the Director shall specify.

"(g) RELATION TO ANNUAL REGISTRATION REQUIREMENTS.—Nothing in this section shall be construed to alter the requirements of section 8083 of the Department of Defense Appropriations Act, 2005 (Public Law 108–287; 118 Stat. 989), with regard to information technology systems (as defined in subsection (d) of such section).

"(h) RELATION TO DEFENSE BUSINESS SYSTEMS ARCHITECTURE, ACCOUNTABILITY, AND MODERNIZATION REQUIREMENTS.—An intelligence community business system that receives more than 50 percent of its funds from amounts available for the National Intelligence Program shall be exempt from the requirements of section 2222 of title 10, United States Code.

"(i) RELATION TO CLINGER-COHEN ACT.—(1) The Director of National Intelligence and the Chief Information Officer of the Intelligence Community shall fulfill the executive agency responsibilities in chapter 113 of title 40, United States Code, for any intelligence community business system that receives more than 50 percent of its funding from amounts appropriated for the National Intelligence Program.

"(2) Any intelligence community business system covered by paragraph (1) shall be exempt from the requirements of such chapter 113 that would otherwise apply to the executive agency that contains the element of the intelligence community involved.

"(j) REPORTS.—Not later than March 15 of each of the years 2009 through 2014, the Director of National Intelligence shall submit to the congressional intelligence committees a report on the compliance of the intelligence community with the requirements of this section. Each such report shall—

"(1) describe actions taken and proposed for meeting the requirements of subsection (a), including—

"(A) specific milestones and actual performance against specified performance measures, and any revision of such milestones and performance measures; and

"(B) specific actions on the intelligence community business system modernizations submitted for certification under such subsection;

"(2) identify the number of intelligence community business system modernizations that received a certification described in subsection (a)(3)(B); and

"(3) describe specific improvements in business operations and cost savings resulting from successful intelligence community business systems modernization efforts.

"(k) DEFINITIONS.—In this section:

"(1) The term 'enterprise architecture' has the meaning given that term in section 3601(4) of title 44, United States Code.

"(2) The terms 'information system' and 'information technology' have the meanings given those terms in section 11101 of title 40, United States Code.

"(3) The term 'intelligence community business system' means an information system, other than a national security system, that is operated by, for, or on behalf of the intelligence community, including financial systems, mixed systems, financial data feeder systems, and the business infrastructure capabilities shared by the systems of the business enterprise architecture that build upon the core infrastructure used to support business activities, such as acquisition, financial management, logistics, strategic planning and budgeting, installations and environment, and human resource management.

"(4) The term 'intelligence community business system modernization' means—

"(A) the acquisition or development of a new intelligence community business system; or

"(B) any significant modification or enhancement of an existing intelligence community business system (other than necessary to maintain current services).

"(5) The term 'national security system' has the meaning given that term in section 3542 of title 44, United States Code.".

(2) CLERICAL AMENDMENT.—The table of contents in the first section of that Act, as amended by sections 306 and 311 of this Act, is further amended by inserting after the item relating to section 506C, as added by section 311(b), the following new item:

"Sec. 506D. Intelligence community business systems, architecture, accountability, and modernization.".

(b) IMPLEMENTATION.—

(1) CERTAIN DUTIES.—Not later than 60 days after the date of the enactment of this Act, the Director of National Intelligence shall—

(A) complete the delegation of responsibility for the review, approval, and oversight of the planning, design, acquisition, deployment, operation, maintenance, and modernization of intelligence community business systems required by subsection (c) of section 506D of the National Security Act of 1947 (as added by subsection (a)); and

(B) designate a vice chairman and personnel to serve on the Intelligence Community Business System Management Committee established under subsection (f) of such section 506D (as so added).

(2) ENTERPRISE ARCHITECTURE.—

(A) SCHEDULE FOR DEVELOPMENT.—The Director shall develop the enterprise architecture required by subsection (b) of such section 506D (as so added) by not later than September 1, 2008.

(B) REQUIREMENT FOR IMPLEMENTATION PLAN.—In developing such enterprise architecture, the Director shall develop an implementation plan for such enterprise architecture that includes the following:

(i) An acquisition strategy for new systems that are expected to be needed to complete such enterprise architecture, including specific time-phased milestones, performance metrics, and a statement of the financial and nonfinancial resource needs.

(ii) An identification of the intelligence community business systems in operation or planned as of December 31, 2006, that will not be a part of such enterprise architecture, together with the schedule for the phased termination of the utilization of any such systems.

(iii) An identification of the intelligence community business systems in operation or planned as of December 31, 2006, that will be a part of such enterprise architecture, together with a strategy for modifying such systems to ensure that such systems comply with such enterprise architecture.

(C) SUBMISSION OF ACQUISITION STRATEGY.—The Director shall submit the acquisition strategy described in subparagraph (B)(i) to the congressional intelligence committees not later than March 1, 2008.

SEC. 313. REPORTS ON THE ACQUISITION OF MAJOR SYSTEMS.

(a) IN GENERAL.—Title V of the National Security Act of 1947 (50 U.S.C. 413 et seq.), as amended by sections 306, 311, and 312 of this Act, is further amended by inserting after section 506D, as added by section 312(a)(1), the following new section:

"REPORTS ON THE ACQUISITION OF MAJOR SYSTEMS

"SEC. 506E. (a) ANNUAL REPORTS REQUIRED.—(1) The Director of National Intelligence shall submit to the congressional intelligence committees each year, at the same time the budget of the President for the fiscal year beginning in such year is submitted to Congress pursuant to section 1105 of title 31, United States Code, a separate report on each acquisition of a major system by an element of the intelligence community.

"(2) Each report under this section shall be known as a 'Report on the Acquisition of Major Systems'.

"(b) ELEMENTS.—Each report under this section shall include, for the acquisition of a major system, information on the following:

"(1) The current total acquisition cost for such system, and the history of such cost from the date the system was first included in a report under this section to the end of the calendar quarter immediately proceeding the submittal of the report under this section.

"(2) The current development schedule for the system, including an estimate of annual development costs until development is completed.

"(3) The planned procurement schedule for the system, including the best estimate of the Director of National Intelligence of the annual costs and units to be procured until procurement is completed.

"(4) A full life-cycle cost analysis for such system.

"(5) The result of any significant test and evaluation of such major system as of the date of the submittal of such report, or, if a significant test and evaluation has not been conducted, a statement of the reasons therefor and the results of any other test and evaluation that has been conducted of such system.

"(6) The reasons for any change in acquisition cost, or schedule, for such system from the previous report under this section, if applicable.

"(7) The major contracts or subcontracts related to the major system.

"(8) If there is any cost or schedule variance under a contract referred to in paragraph (7) since the previous report under this section, the reasons for such cost or schedule variance.

"(c) DETERMINATION OF INCREASE IN COSTS.—Any determination of a percentage increase in the acquisition costs of a major system for which a report is filed under this section shall be stated in terms of constant dollars from the first fiscal year in which funds are appropriated for such contract.

"(d) DEFINITIONS.—In this section:

"(1) The term 'acquisition cost', with respect to a major system, means the amount equal to the total cost for development and procurement of, and system-specific construction for, such system.

"(2) The term 'full life-cycle cost', with respect to the acquisition of a major system, means all costs of development, procurement, construction, deployment, and operation and support for such program, without regard to funding source or management control, including costs of development and procurement required to support or utilize such system.

"(3) The term 'major contract,' with respect to a major system acquisition, means each of the 6 largest prime, associate, or government-furnished equipment contracts under the program that is in excess of $40,000,000 and that is not a firm, fixed price contract.

"(4) The term 'major system' has the meaning given that term in section 506A(e).

"(5) The term 'significant test and evaluation' means the functional or environmental testing of a major system or of the subsystems that combine to create a major system.".

(b) CLERICAL AMENDMENT.—The table of contents in the first section of that Act, as amended by sections 306, 311, and 312 of this Act, is further amended by inserting after the item relating to section 506D, as added by section 312(a)(2), the following new item:

"Sec. 506E. Reports on the acquisition of major systems.".

SEC. 314. EXCESSIVE COST GROWTH OF MAJOR SYSTEMS.

(a) NOTIFICATION.—Title V of the National Security Act of 1947, as amended by sections 306, 311, 312, and 313 of this Act, is further amended by inserting after section 506E, as added by section 313(a), the following new section:

"EXCESSIVE COST GROWTH OF MAJOR SYSTEMS

"SEC. 506F. (a) COST INCREASES OF AT LEAST 25 PERCENT.— (1)(A) On a continuing basis, and separate from the submission of any report on a major system required by section 506E of this Act, the program manager shall determine if the acquisition cost of such major system has increased by at least 25 percent as compared to the baseline cost of such major system.

"(B) Not later than 10 days after the date that a program manager determines that an increase described in subparagraph (A) has occurred, the program manager shall submit to the Director of National Intelligence notification of such increase.

"(2) (A) If, after receiving a notification described in paragraph (1)(B), the Director of National Intelligence determines that the acquisition cost of a major system has increased by at least 25 percent, the Director shall submit to the congressional intelligence committees a written notification of such determination as described in subparagraph (B), a description of the amount of the increase in the acquisition cost of such major system, and a certification as described in subparagraph (C).

"(B) The notification required by subparagraph (A) shall include—

"(i) an updated cost estimate;

"(ii) the date on which the determination covered by such notification was made;

"(iii) contract performance assessment information with respect to each significant contract or sub-contract related to such major system, including the name of the contractor, the phase of the contract at the time of the report, the percentage of work under the contract that has been completed, any change in contract cost, the percentage by which the contract is currently ahead or behind schedule, and a summary explanation of significant occurrences, such as cost and schedule variances, and the effect of such occurrences on future costs and schedules;

"(iv) the prior estimate of the full life-cycle cost for such major system, expressed in constant dollars and in current year dollars;

"(v) the current estimated full life-cycle cost of such major system, expressed in constant dollars and current year dollars;

"(vi) a statement of the reasons for any increases in the full life-cycle cost of such major system;

"(vii) the current change and the total change, in dollars and expressed as a percentage, in the full life-cycle cost applicable to such major system, stated both in constant dollars and current year dollars;

"(viii) the completion status of such major system expressed as the percentage—

"(I) of the total number of years for which funds have been appropriated for such major system compared to the number of years for which it is planned that such funds will be appropriated; and

"(II) of the amount of funds that have been appropriated for such major system compared to the total amount of such funds which it is planned will be appropriated;

"(ix) the action taken and proposed to be taken to control future cost growth of such major system; and

"(x) any changes made in the performance or schedule of such major system and the extent to which such changes have contributed to the increase in full life-cycle costs of such major system.

"(C) The certification described in this subparagraph is a written certification made by the Director and submitted to the congressional intelligence committees that—

"(i) the acquisition of such major system is essential to the national security;

"(ii) there are no alternatives to such major system that will provide equal or greater intelligence capability at equal or lesser cost to completion;

"(iii) the new estimates of the full life-cycle cost for such major system are reasonable; and

"(iv) the management structure for the acquisition of such major system is adequate to manage and control full life-cycle cost of such major system.

"(b) COST INCREASES OF AT LEAST 50 PERCENT.—(1)(A) On a continuing basis, and separate from the submission of any report on a major system required by section 506E of this Act, the program manager shall determine if the acquisition cost of such major system has increased by at least 50 percent as compared to the baseline cost of such major system.

"(B) Not later than 10 days after the date that a program manager determines that an increase described in subparagraph (A) has occurred, the program manager shall submit to the Director of National Intelligence notification of such increase.

"(2) If, after receiving a notification described in paragraph (1)(B), the Director of National Intelligence determines that the acquisition cost of a major system has increased by at least 50 percent as compared to the baseline cost of such major system, the Director shall submit to the congressional intelligence committees a written certification stating that—

"(A) the acquisition of such major system is essential to the national security;

"(B) there are no alternatives to such major system that will provide equal or greater intelligence capability at equal or lesser cost to completion;

"(C) the new estimates of the full life-cycle cost for such major system are reasonable; and

"(D) the management structure for the acquisition of such major system is adequate to manage and control the full life-cycle cost of such major system.

"(3) In addition to the certification required by paragraph (2), the Director of National Intelligence shall submit to the congressional intelligence committees an updated notification, with current accompanying information, as required by subsection (a)(2).

"(c) PROHIBITION ON OBLIGATION OF FUNDS.—(1) If a written certification required under subsection (a)(2)(A) is not submitted to the congressional intelligence committees within 60 days of the determination made under subsection (a)(1), funds appropriated for the acquisition of a major system may not be obligated for a major contract under the program. Such prohibition on the obligation of funds shall cease to apply at the end of the 30-day period of a continuous session of Congress that begins on the date on which Congress receives the notification required under subsection (a)(2)(A).

"(2) If a written certification required under subsection (b)(2) is not submitted to the congressional intelligence committees within 60 days of the determination made under subsection (b)(2), funds appropriated for the acquisition of a major system may not be obligated for a major contract under the program. Such prohibition on the obligation of funds for the acquisition of a major system shall cease to apply at the end of the 30-day period of a continuous session of Congress that begins on the date on which Congress receives the notification required under subsection (b)(3).

"(d) DEFINITIONS.—In this section:

"(1) The term 'acquisition cost' has the meaning given that term in section 506E(d).

"(2) The term 'baseline cost', with respect to a major system, means the projected acquisition cost of such system that is approved by the Director of National Intelligence at Milestone B or an equivalent acquisition decision for the development, procurement, and construction of such system. The baseline cost may be in the form of an independent cost estimate.

"(3) The term 'full life-cycle cost' has the meaning given that term in section 506E(d).

"(4) The term 'independent cost estimate' has the meaning given that term in section 506A(e).

"(5) The term 'major system' has the meaning given that term in section 506A(e).

"(6) The term 'Milestone B' means a decision to enter into system development and demonstration pursuant to guidance prescribed by the Director of National Intelligence.

"(7) The term 'program manager', with respect to a major system, means—

"(A) the head of the element of the intelligence community which is responsible for the budget, cost, schedule, and performance of the major system; or

"(B) in the case of a major system within the Office of the Director of National Intelligence, the deputy who is responsible for the budget, cost, schedule, and performance of the major system.".

(b) CLERICAL AMENDMENT.—The table of contents in the first section of that Act, as amended by sections 304, 311, 312, and 313 of this Act, is further amended by inserting after the items relating to section 506E, as added by section 313(b), the following new item:

"Sec. 506F. Excessive cost growth of major systems.".

Subtitle C—Other Matters

SEC. 321. RESTRICTION ON CONDUCT OF INTELLIGENCE ACTIVITIES.

The authorization of appropriations by this Act shall not be deemed to constitute authority for the conduct of any intelligence activity which is not otherwise authorized by the Constitution or the laws of the United States.

SEC. 322. CLARIFICATION OF DEFINITION OF INTELLIGENCE COMMUNITY UNDER THE NATIONAL SECURITY ACT OF 1947.

Subparagraph (L) of section 3(4) of the National Security Act of 1947 (50 U.S.C. 401a(4)) is amended by striking "other" the second place it appears.

SEC. 323. MODIFICATION OF AVAILABILITY OF FUNDS FOR DIFFERENT INTELLIGENCE ACTIVITIES.

Subparagraph (B) of section 504(a)(3) of the National Security Act of 1947 (50 U.S.C. 414(a)(3)) is amended to read as follows:

"(B) the use of such funds for such activity supports an emergent need, improves program effectiveness, or increases efficiency; and".

SEC. 324. PROTECTION OF CERTAIN NATIONAL SECURITY INFORMATION.

(a) INCREASE IN PENALTIES FOR DISCLOSURE OF UNDERCOVER INTELLIGENCE OFFICERS AND AGENTS.—

(1) DISCLOSURE OF AGENT AFTER ACCESS TO INFORMATION IDENTIFYING AGENT.—Subsection (a) of section 601 of the National Security Act of 1947 (50 U.S.C. 421) is amended by striking "ten years" and inserting "15 years".

(2) DISCLOSURE OF AGENT AFTER ACCESS TO CLASSIFIED INFORMATION.—Subsection (b) of such section is amended by striking "five years" and inserting "10 years".

(b) MODIFICATIONS TO ANNUAL REPORT ON PROTECTION OF INTELLIGENCE IDENTITIES.—The first sentence of section 603(a) of the National Security Act of 1947 (50 U.S.C. 423(a)) is amended by inserting "including an assessment of the need for any modification of this title for the purpose of improving legal protections for covert agents," after "measures to protect the identities of covert agents,".

SEC. 325. EXTENSION OF AUTHORITY TO DELETE INFORMATION ABOUT RECEIPT AND DISPOSITION OF FOREIGN GIFTS AND DECORATIONS.

Paragraph (4) of section 7342(f) of title 5, United States Code, is amended to read as follows:

"(4) (A) In transmitting such listings for an element of the intelligence community, the head of such element may delete the information described in subparagraph (A) or (C) of paragraph (2) or in subparagraph (A) or (C) of paragraph (3) if the head of such element certifies in writing to the Secretary of State that the publication of such information could adversely affect United States intelligence sources or methods.

"(B) Any information not provided to the Secretary of State pursuant to the authority in subparagraph (A) shall be transmitted to the Director of National Intelligence who shall keep a record of such information.

"(C) In this paragraph, the term 'element of the intelligence community' means an element of the intelligence community listed in or designated under section 3(4) of the National Security Act of 1947 (50 U.S.C. 401a(4)).".

SEC. 326. REPORT ON COMPLIANCE WITH THE DETAINEE TREATMENT ACT OF 2005 AND RELATED PROVISIONS OF THE MILITARY COMMISSIONS ACT OF 2006.

(a) REPORT REQUIRED.—Not later than 45 days after the date of the enactment of this Act, the Director of National Intelligence shall submit to the congressional intelligence committees a comprehensive report on all measures taken by the Office of the Director of National Intelligence and by each element, if any, of the intelligence community with relevant responsibilities to comply with the provisions of the Detainee Treatment Act of 2005 (title X of division A of Public Law 109–148; 119 Stat. 2739) and related provisions of the Military Commissions Act of 2006 (Public Law 109–366; 120 Stat. 2600).

(b) ELEMENTS.—The report required by subsection (a) shall include the following:

(1) A description of the detention or interrogation methods, if any, that have been determined to comply with section 1003 of the Detainee Treatment Act of 2005 (119 Stat. 2739; 42 U.S.C. 2000dd) and section 6 of the Military Commissions Act of 2006 (120 Stat. 2632; 18 U.S.C. 2441 note) (including the amendments made by such section 6), and, with respect to each such method—

(A) an identification of the official making such determination; and

(B) a statement of the basis for such determination.

(2) A description of the detention or interrogation methods, if any, whose use has been discontinued pursuant to the Detainee Treatment Act of 2005 or the Military Commission Act of 2006, and, with respect to each such method—

(A) an identification of the official making the determination to discontinue such method; and

(B) a statement of the basis for such determination.

(3) A description of any actions that have been taken to implement section 1004 of the Detainee Treatment Act of 2005 (119 Stat. 2740; 42 U.S.C. 2000dd–1), and, with respect to each such action—

(A) an identification of the official taking such action; and

(B) a statement of the basis for such action.

(4) Any other matters that the Director considers necessary to fully and currently inform the congressional intelligence committees about the implementation of the Detainee Treatment Act of 2005 and related provisions of the Military Commissions Act of 2006.

(5) An appendix containing—

(A) all guidelines for the application of the Detainee Treatment Act of 2005 and related provisions of the Military Commissions Act of 2006 to the detention or interrogation activities, if any, of any element of the intelligence community; and

(B) the legal justifications of any office of the Department of Justice about the meaning or application of the Detainee Treatment Act of 2005 or related provisions of the Military Commissions Act of 2006 with respect to the detention or interrogation activities, if any, of any element of the intelligence community.

(c) FORM.—The report required by subsection (a) shall be submitted in classified form.

(d) SUBMISSION TO THE CONGRESSIONAL ARMED SERVICES COMMITTEES.—To the extent that the report required by subsection (a) addresses an element of the intelligence community within the Department of Defense, that portion of the report, and any associated material that is necessary to make that portion understandable, shall also be submitted by the Director of National Intelligence to the congressional armed services committees.

(e) CONGRESSIONAL ARMED SERVICES COMMITTEE DEFINED.—In this section, the term "congressional armed services committees" means—

(1) the Committee on Armed Services of the Senate; and

(2) the Committee on Armed Services of the House of Representatives.

SEC. 327. LIMITATION ON INTERROGATION TECHNIQUES.

(a) LIMITATION.—No individual in the custody or under the effective control of an element of the intelligence community or instrumentality thereof, regardless of nationality or physical location, shall be subject to any treatment or technique of interrogation not authorized by the United States Army Field Manual on Human Intelligence Collector Operations.

(b) INSTRUMENTALITY DEFINED.—In this section, the term "instrumentality", with respect to an element of the intelligence community, means a contractor or subcontractor at any tier of the element of the intelligence community.

SEC. 328. LIMITATION ON USE OF FUNDS.

Not more than 30 percent of the funds authorized to be appropriated for the Expenditure Center referred to on page 157 of Volume VI, Book 1 of the Fiscal Year 2008—Fiscal Year 2009 Congressional Budget Justification, National Intelligence Program, may be obligated or expended until each member of the congressional intelligence committees has been fully and currently informed with respect to intelligence regarding a facility in Syria subject to reported military action by the State of Israel on September 6, 2007, including intelligence relating to any agent or citizen of North Korea,

Iran, or any other foreign country present at the facility, and any intelligence provided to the Federal Government by a foreign country regarding the facility (as available).

SEC. 329. INCORPORATION OF REPORTING REQUIREMENTS.

Each requirement to submit a report to the congressional intelligence committees that is included in the classified annex to this Act is hereby incorporated into this Act and is hereby made a requirement in law.

SEC. 330. REPEAL OF CERTAIN REPORTING REQUIREMENTS.

(a) ANNUAL REPORT ON INTELLIGENCE.—

(1) REPEAL.—Section 109 of the National Security Act of 1947 (50 U.S.C. 404d) is repealed.

(2) CLERICAL AMENDMENT.—The table of contents in the first section of the National Security Act of 1947 is amended by striking the item relating to section 109.

(b) ANNUAL AND SPECIAL REPORTS ON INTELLIGENCE SHARING WITH THE UNITED NATIONS.—Section 112 of the National Security Act of 1947 (50 U.S.C. 404g) is amended—

(1) by striking subsection (b); and

(2) by redesignating subsections (c), (d), and (e) as subsections (b), (c), and (d), respectively.

(c) ANNUAL CERTIFICATION ON COUNTERINTELLIGENCE INITIATIVES.—Section 1102(b) of the National Security Act of 1947 (50 U.S.C. 442a(b)) is amended—

(1) by striking "(1)"; and

(2) by striking paragraph (2).

(d) REPORT AND CERTIFICATION UNDER TERRORIST IDENTIFICATION CLASSIFICATION SYSTEM.—Section 343 of the Intelligence Authorization Act for Fiscal Year 2003 (50 U.S.C. 404n–2) is amended—

(1) by striking subsection (d); and

(2) by redesignating subsections (e), (f), (g), and (h) as subsections (d), (e), (f), and (g), respectively.

(e) ANNUAL REPORT ON COUNTERDRUG INTELLIGENCE MATTERS.—Section 826 of the Intelligence Authorization Act for Fiscal Year 2003 (Public Law 107–306; 116 Stat. 2429; 21 U.S.C. 873 note) is repealed.

(f) CONFORMING AMENDMENTS.—Section 507(a) of the National Security Act of 1947(50 U.S.C. 415b(a)) is amended—

(1) in paragraph (1)—

(A) by striking subparagraphs (A) and (B); and

(B) by redesignating subparagraphs (C) through (N) as subparagraphs (A) through (L), respectively; and

(2) in paragraph (2), by striking subparagraph (D).

TITLE IV—MATTERS RELATING TO ELEMENTS OF THE INTELLIGENCE COMMUNITY

Subtitle A—Office of the Director of National Intelligence

SEC. 401. CLARIFICATION OF LIMITATION ON COLOCATION OF THE OFFICE OF THE DIRECTOR OF NATIONAL INTELLIGENCE.

Section 103(e) of the National Security Act of 1947 (50 U.S.C. 403–3(e)) is amended—

(1) by striking "WITH" and inserting "OF HEADQUARTERS WITH HEADQUARTERS OF";

(2) by inserting "the headquarters of" before "the Office"; and

(3) by striking "any other element" and inserting "the headquarters of any other element".

SEC. 402. MEMBERSHIP OF THE DIRECTOR OF NATIONAL INTELLIGENCE ON THE TRANSPORTATION SECURITY OVERSIGHT BOARD.

Subparagraph (F) of section 115(b)(1) of title 49, United States Code, is amended to read as follows:

"(F) The Director of National Intelligence, or the Director's designee.".

SEC. 403. ADDITIONAL DUTIES OF THE DIRECTOR OF SCIENCE AND TECHNOLOGY.

Section 103E of the National Security Act of 1947 (50 U.S.C. 403–3e) is amended—

(1) in subsection (c)—

(A) by redesignating paragraph (5) as paragraph (7);

(B) in paragraph (4), by striking "and" at the end; and

(C) by inserting after paragraph (4) the following:

"(5) assist the Director in establishing goals for basic, applied, and advanced research to meet the technology needs of the intelligence community and to be executed by elements of the intelligence community by—

"(A) systematically identifying, assessing, and prioritizing the most significant intelligence challenges that require technical solutions; and

"(B) examining options to enhance the responsiveness of research programs;

"(6) submit to Congress an annual report on the science and technology strategy of the Director; and"; and

(2) in paragraph (3) of subsection (d)—

(A) by redesignating subparagraphs (A) and (B) as subparagraphs (B) and (C), respectively;

(B) in subparagraph (B), as so redesignated, by inserting "and prioritize" after "coordinate"; and

(C) by inserting before subparagraph (B), as so redesignated, the following new subparagraph:

"(A) identify basic, advanced, and applied research programs to be executed by elements of the intelligence community;".

SEC. 404. LEADERSHIP AND LOCATION OF CERTAIN OFFICES AND OFFICIALS.

(a) NATIONAL COUNTER PROLIFERATION CENTER.—Section 119A(a) of the National Security Act of 1947 (50 U.S.C. 404o- 1(a)) is amended—

(1) by striking "(a) ESTABLISHMENT.—Not later than 18 months after the date of the enactment of the National Security Intelligence Reform Act of 2004, the" and inserting the following:

"(a) IN GENERAL.—

"(1) ESTABLISHMENT.—The"; and

(2) by adding at the end the following new paragraphs:

"(2) DIRECTOR.—The head of the National Counter Proliferation Center shall be the Director of the National Counter Proliferation Center, who shall be appointed by the Director of National Intelligence.

"(3) LOCATION.—The National Counter Proliferation Center shall be located within the Office of the Director of National Intelligence.".

(b) OFFICERS.—Section 103(c) of that Act (50 U.S.C. 403–3(c)) is amended—

(1) by redesignating paragraph (9) as paragraph (13); and

(2) by inserting after paragraph (8) the following new paragraphs:

"(9) The Chief Information Officer of the Intelligence Community.

"(10) The Inspector General of the Intelligence Community.

"(11) The Director of the National Counterterrorism Center.

"(12) The Director of the National Counter Proliferation Center.".

SEC. 405. PLAN TO IMPLEMENT RECOMMENDATIONS OF THE DATA CENTER ENERGY EFFICIENCY REPORTS.

(a) PLAN.—The Director of National Intelligence shall develop a plan to implement the recommendations of the report submitted to Congress under section 1 of the Act entitled "An Act to study and promote the use of energy efficient computer servers in the United States" (Public Law 109–431; 120 Stat. 2920) across the intelligence community.

(b) REPORT.—

(1) IN GENERAL.—Not later then February 1, 2008, the Director of National Intelligence shall submit to the congressional intelligence committees a report containing the plan developed under subsection (a).

(2) FORM.—The report under paragraph (1) shall be submitted in unclassified form, but may contain a classified annex.

SEC. 406. COMPREHENSIVE LISTING OF SPECIAL ACCESS PROGRAMS.

Not later than February 1, 2008, the Director of National Intelligence shall submit to the congressional intelligence committees a classified comprehensive listing of all special access programs under the National Intelligence Program (as defined in section 3(6) of the National Security Act of 1947 (50 U.S.C. 401a(6))). Such listing may be submitted in a form or forms consistent with the protection of national security.

SEC. 407. REPORTS ON THE NUCLEAR PROGRAMS OF IRAN AND NORTH KOREA.

(a) REQUIREMENT FOR REPORTS.—Not less frequently than once during fiscal year 2008 and twice during fiscal year 2009, the Director of National Intelligence shall submit to the congressional intelligence committees a report on the intentions and capabilities of the Islamic Republic of Iran and the Democratic People's Republic of Korea, with regard to the nuclear programs of each such country.

(b) CONTENT.—Each report submitted by subsection (a) shall include, with respect of the Islamic Republic of Iran and the Democratic People's Republic of Korea—

(1) an assessment of nuclear weapons programs of each such country;

(2) an evaluation, consistent with existing reporting standards and practices, of the sources upon which the intelligence used to prepare the assessment described in paragraph (1) is based, including the number of such sources and an assessment of the reliability of each such source;

(3) a summary of any intelligence related to any such program gathered or developed since the previous report was submitted under subsection (a), including intelligence collected from both open and clandestine sources for each such country; and

(4) a discussion of any dissents, caveats, gaps in knowledge, or other information that would reduce confidence in the assessment described in paragraph (1).

(c) NATIONAL INTELLIGENCE ESTIMATE.—The Director of National Intelligence may submit a National Intelligence Estimate on the intentions and capabilities of the Islamic Republic of Iran and the Democratic People's Republic of Korea in lieu of a report required by subsection (a).

(d) FORM.—Each report submitted under subsection (a) may be submitted in classified form.

SEC. 408. REQUIREMENTS FOR ACCOUNTABILITY REVIEWS BY THE DIRECTOR OF NATIONAL INTELLIGENCE.

(a) RESPONSIBILITY OF THE DIRECTOR OF NATIONAL INTELLIGENCE.—Subsection (b) of section 102 of the National Security Act of 1947 (50 U.S.C. 403) is amended—

(1) in paragraph (2), by striking "and" at the end;

(2) in paragraph (3)—

(A) by striking "2004," and inserting "2004 (50 U.S.C. 403 note),"; and

(B) by striking the period at the end and inserting a semicolon and "and"; and

(3) by inserting after paragraph (3), the following new paragraph:

"(4) conduct accountability reviews of elements of the intelligence community and the personnel of such elements, if appropriate.".

(b) TASKING AND OTHER AUTHORITIES.—Subsection (f) of section 102A of such Act (50 U.S.C. 403–1) is amended—

(1) by redesignating paragraphs (7) and (8), as paragraphs (8) and (9), respectively; and

(2) by inserting after paragraph (6), the following new paragraph:

"(7) (A) The Director of National Intelligence shall, if the Director determines it is necessary, or may, if requested by a congressional intelligence committee, conduct accountability reviews of elements of the intelligence community or the personnel of such elements in relation to significant failures or deficiencies within the intelligence community.

"(B) The Director of National Intelligence, in consultation with the Attorney General, shall establish guidelines and procedures for conducting accountability reviews under subparagraph (A).

"(C) The requirements of this paragraph shall not limit any authority of the Director of National Intelligence under subsection (m) or with respect to supervision of the Central Intelligence Agency.".

SEC. 409. MODIFICATION OF LIMITATION ON DELEGATION BY THE DIRECTOR OF NATIONAL INTELLIGENCE OF THE PROTECTION OF INTELLIGENCE SOURCES AND METHODS.

Section 102A(i)(3) of the National Security Act of 1947 (50 U.S.C. 403–1(i)(3)) is amended by inserting before the period the following: "or the Chief Information Officer of the Intelligence Community".

SEC. 410. AUTHORITIES FOR INTELLIGENCE INFORMATION SHARING.

(a) AUTHORITIES FOR INTERAGENCY FUNDING.—Section 102A(g)(1) of the National Security Act of 1947 (50 U.S.C. 403– 1(g)(1)) is amended—

(1) in subparagraph (E), by striking "and" at the end;

(2) in subparagraph (F), by striking the period and inserting a semicolon; and

(3) by adding at the end the following new subparagraphs:

"(G) in carrying out this subsection, without regard to any other provision of law (other than this Act and the National Security Intelligence Reform Act of 2004 (title I of Public Law 108–458; 118 Stat. 3643)), expend funds and make funds available to other departments or agencies of the United States for, and direct the development and fielding of, systems of common concern related to the collection, processing, analysis, exploitation, and dissemination of intelligence information; and

"(H) for purposes of addressing critical gaps in intelligence information sharing or access capabilities, have the authority to transfer funds appropriated for a program within the National Intelligence Program to a program funded by appropriations not within the National Intelligence Program, consistent with paragraphs (3) through (7) of subsection (d).".

(b) AUTHORITIES OF HEADS OF OTHER DEPARTMENTS AND AGENCIES.—Notwithstanding any other provision of law, the head of any department or agency of the United States is authorized to receive and utilize funds made available to the department or agency by the Director of National Intelligence pursuant to section 102A(g)(1) of the National Security Act of 1947 (50 U.S.C. 403–1(g)(1)), as amended by subsection (a), and receive and utilize any system referred to in such section that is made available to the department or agency.

(c) REPORTS.—

(1) REQUIREMENT FOR REPORTS.—Not later than February 1 of each of the fiscal years 2009 through 2012, the Director of National Intelligence shall submit to the congressional intelligence committees a report detailing the distribution of funds and systems during the preceding fiscal year pursuant to subparagraph (G) or (H) of section 102A(g)(1) of the National Security Act of 1947 (50 U.S.C. 403–1(g)(1)), as added by subsection (a).

(2) CONTENT.—Each such report shall include—

(A) a listing of the agencies or departments to which such funds or systems were distributed;

(B) a description of the purpose for which such funds or systems were distributed; and

(C) a description of the expenditure of such funds, and the development, fielding, and use of such systems by the receiving agency or department.

SEC. 411. AUTHORITIES OF THE DIRECTOR OF NATIONAL INTELLIGENCE FOR INTERAGENCY FUNDING.

(a) IN GENERAL.—Section 102A of the National Security Act of 1947 (50 U.S.C. 403–1), as amended by sections 303 and 304 of this Act, is further amended by adding at the end the following new subsection:

"(u) AUTHORITIES FOR INTERAGENCY FUNDING.—(1) Notwithstanding section 1346 of title 31, United States Code, or any other provision of law prohibiting the interagency financing of activities described in subparagraph (A) or (B), upon the request of the Director of National Intelligence, any element of the intelligence community may use appropriated funds to support or participate in the interagency activities of the following:

"(A) National intelligence centers established by the Director under section 119B.

"(B) Boards, commissions, councils, committees, and similar groups that are established—

"(i) for a term of not more than 2 years; and

"(ii) by the Director.

"(2) No provision of law enacted after the date of the enactment of the Intelligence Authorization Act for Fiscal Year 2008 shall be construed to limit or supersede the authority in paragraph (1) unless such provision makes specific reference to the authority in that paragraph.".

(b) REPORTS.—Not later than February 1 of each of the fiscal years 2009 through 2012, the Director of National Intelligence shall submit to the congressional intelligence committees a report detailing the exercise of any authority pursuant to subsection (u) of section 102A of the National Security Act of 1947 (50 U.S.C. 403–1), as amended by subsection (a), during the preceding fiscal year.

SEC. 412. TITLE OF CHIEF INFORMATION OFFICER OF THE INTELLIGENCE COMMUNITY.

Section 103G of the National Security Act of 1947 (50 U.S.C. 403–3g) is amended—

(1) in subsection (a), by inserting "of the Intelligence Community" after "Chief Information Officer";

(2) in subsection (b), by inserting "of the Intelligence Community" after "Chief Information Officer";

(3) in subsection (c), by inserting "of the Intelligence Community" after "Chief Information Officer"; and

(4) in subsection (d), by inserting "of the Intelligence Community" after "Chief Information Officer" the first place it appears.

SEC. 413. INSPECTOR GENERAL OF THE INTELLIGENCE COMMUNITY.

(a) ESTABLISHMENT.—

(1) IN GENERAL.—Title I of the National Security Act of 1947 (50 U.S.C. 402 et seq.) is amended by inserting after section 103G the following new section:

"INSPECTOR GENERAL OF THE INTELLIGENCE COMMUNITY

"SEC. 103H. (a) OFFICE OF INSPECTOR GENERAL OF INTELLIGENCE COMMUNITY.—There is within the Office of the Director of National Intelligence an Office of the Inspector General of the Intelligence Community.

"(b) PURPOSE.—The purpose of the Office of the Inspector General of the Intelligence Community is to—

"(1) create an objective and effective office, appropriately accountable to Congress, to initiate and conduct independently investigations, inspections, and audits on matters within the responsibility and authority of the Director of National Intelligence;

"(2) recommend policies designed—

"(A) to promote economy, efficiency, and effectiveness in the administration and implementation of matters within the responsibility and authority of the Director of National Intelligence; and

"(B) to prevent and detect fraud and abuse in such matters;

"(3) provide a means for keeping the Director of National Intelligence fully and currently informed about—

"(A) problems and deficiencies relating to matters within the responsibility and authority of the Director of National Intelligence; and

"(B) the necessity for, and the progress of, corrective actions; and

"(4) in the manner prescribed by this section, ensure that the congressional intelligence committees are kept similarly informed of—

"(A) significant problems and deficiencies relating to matters within the responsibility and authority of the Director of National Intelligence; and

"(B) the necessity for, and the progress of, corrective actions.

"(c) INSPECTOR GENERAL OF INTELLIGENCE COMMUNITY.—(1) There is an Inspector General of the Intelligence Community, who shall be the head of the Office of the Inspector General of the Intelligence Community, who shall be appointed by the President, by and with the advice and consent of the Senate.

"(2) The nomination of an individual for appointment as Inspector General shall be made—

"(A) without regard to political affiliation;

"(B) solely on the basis of integrity, compliance with the security standards of the intelligence community, and prior experience in the field of intelligence or national security; and

"(C) on the basis of demonstrated ability in accounting, financial analysis, law, management analysis, public administration, or auditing.

"(3) The Inspector General shall report directly to and be under the general supervision of the Director of National Intelligence.

"(4) The Inspector General may be removed from office only by the President. The President shall immediately communicate in writing to the congressional intelligence committees the reasons for the removal of any individual from the position of Inspector General.

"(d) DUTIES AND RESPONSIBILITIES.—Subject to subsections (g) and (h), it shall be the duty and responsibility of the Inspector General of the Intelligence Community—

"(1) to provide policy direction for, and to plan, conduct, supervise, and coordinate independently, the investigations, inspections, and audits relating to matters within the responsibility and authority of the Director of National Intelligence to ensure they are conducted efficiently and in accordance with applicable law and regulations;

"(2) to keep the Director of National Intelligence fully and currently informed concerning violations of law and regulations, violations of civil liberties and privacy, fraud and other serious problems, abuses, and deficiencies that may occur in matters within the responsibility and authority of the Director, and to report the progress made in implementing corrective action;

"(3) to take due regard for the protection of intelligence sources and methods in the preparation of all reports issued by the Inspector General, and, to the extent consistent with the purpose and objective of such reports, take such measures as may be appropriate to minimize the disclosure of intelligence sources and methods described in such reports; and

"(4) in the execution of the duties and responsibilities under this section, to comply with generally accepted government auditing standards.

"(e) LIMITATIONS ON ACTIVITIES.—(1) The Director of National Intelligence may prohibit the Inspector General of the Intelligence Community from initiating, carrying out, or completing any investigation, inspection, or audit if the Director determines that such prohibition is necessary to protect vital national security interests of the United States.

"(2) If the Director exercises the authority under paragraph (1), the Director shall submit an appropriately classified statement of the reasons for the exercise of such authority within 7 days to the congressional intelligence committees.

"(3) The Director shall advise the Inspector General at the time a report under paragraph (2) is submitted, and, to the extent consistent with the protection of intelligence sources and methods, provide the Inspector General with a copy of such report.

"(4) The Inspector General may submit to the congressional intelligence committees any comments on a report of which the Inspector General has notice under paragraph (3) that the Inspector General considers appropriate.

"(f) AUTHORITIES.—(1) The Inspector General of the Intelligence Community shall have direct and prompt access to the Director of National Intelligence when necessary for any purpose pertaining to the performance of the duties of the Inspector General.

"(2)(A) The Inspector General shall have access to any employee, or any employee of a contractor, of any element of the intelligence community whose testimony is needed for the performance of the duties of the Inspector General.

"(B) The Inspector General shall have direct access to all records, reports, audits, reviews, documents, papers, recommendations, or other material which relate to the programs and operations with respect to which the Inspector General has responsibilities under this section.

"(C) The level of classification or compartmentation of information shall not, in and of itself, provide a sufficient rationale for denying the Inspector General access to any materials under subparagraph (B).

"(D) Failure on the part of any employee, or any employee of a contractor, of any element of the intelligence community to cooperate with the Inspector General shall be grounds for appropriate administrative actions by the Director or, on the recommendation of the Director, other appropriate officials of the intelligence community, including loss of employment or the termination of an existing contractual relationship.

"(3) The Inspector General is authorized to receive and investigate complaints or information from any person concerning the existence of an activity constituting a violation of laws, rules, or regulations, or mismanagement, gross waste of funds, abuse of authority, or a substantial and specific danger to the public health and safety. Once such complaint or information has been received from an employee of the Federal Government—

"(A) the Inspector General shall not disclose the identity of the employee without the consent of the employee, unless the Inspector General determines that such disclosure is unavoidable during the course of the investigation or the disclosure is made to an official of the Department of Justice responsible for determining whether a prosecution should be undertaken; and

"(B) no action constituting a reprisal, or threat of reprisal, for making such complaint may be taken by any employee in a position to take such actions, unless the complaint was made or the information was disclosed with the knowledge that it was false or with willful disregard for its truth or falsity.

"(4) The Inspector General shall have authority to administer to or take from any person an oath, affirmation, or affidavit, whenever necessary in the performance of the duties of the Inspector General, which oath, affirmation, or affidavit when administered or taken by or before an employee of the Office of the Inspector General of the Intelligence Community designated by the Inspector General shall have the same force and effect as if administered or taken by, or before, an officer having a seal.

"(5) (A) Except as provided in subparagraph (B), the Inspector General is authorized to require by subpoena the production of all information, documents, reports, answers, records, accounts, papers, and other data and documentary evidence necessary in the performance of the duties and responsibilities of the Inspector General.

"(B) In the case of departments, agencies, and other elements of the United States Government, the Inspector General shall obtain information, documents, reports, answers, records, accounts, papers, and other data and evidence for the purpose specified in subparagraph (A) using procedures other than by subpoenas.

"(C) The Inspector General may not issue a subpoena for, or on behalf of, any other element of the intelligence community, including the Office of the Director of National Intelligence.

"(D) In the case of contumacy or refusal to obey a subpoena issued under this paragraph, the subpoena shall be enforceable by order of any appropriate district court of the United States.

"(g) COORDINATION AMONG INSPECTORS GENERAL OF INTELLIGENCE COMMUNITY.—(1)(A) In the event of a matter within the jurisdiction of the Inspector General of the Intelligence Community that may be subject to an investigation, inspection, or audit by both the Inspector General of the Intelligence Community and an Inspector General, whether statutory or administrative, with oversight responsibility for an element or elements of the intelligence community, the Inspector General of the Intelligence Community and such other Inspector or Inspectors General shall expeditiously resolve the question of which Inspector General shall conduct such investigation, inspection, or audit.

"(B) In attempting to resolve a question under subparagraph (A), the Inspectors General concerned may request the assistance of the Intelligence Community Inspectors General Forum established under subparagraph (C). In the event of a dispute between an Inspector General within an agency or department of the United States Government and the Inspector General of the Intelligence Community that has not been resolved with the assistance of the Forum, the Inspectors General shall submit the question to the Director of National Intelligence and the head of the agency or department for resolution.

"(C) There is established the Intelligence Community Inspectors General Forum which shall consist of all statutory or administrative Inspectors General with oversight responsibility for an element or elements of the intelligence community. The Inspector General of the Intelligence Community shall serve as the chair of the Forum. The Forum shall have no administrative authority over any Inspector

General, but shall serve as a mechanism for informing its members of the work of individual members of the Forum that may be of common interest and discussing questions about jurisdiction or access to employees, employees of a contractor, records, audits, reviews, documents, recommendations, or other materials that may involve or be of assistance to more than 1 of its members.

"(2) The Inspector General conducting an investigation, inspection, or audit covered by paragraph (1) shall submit the results of such investigation, inspection, or audit to any other Inspector General, including the Inspector General of the Intelligence Community, with jurisdiction to conduct such investigation, inspection, or audit who did not conduct such investigation, inspection, or audit.

"(h) STAFF AND OTHER SUPPORT.—(1) The Inspector General of the Intelligence Community shall be provided with appropriate and adequate office space at central and field office locations, together with such equipment, office supplies, maintenance services, and communications facilities and services as may be necessary for the operation of such offices.

"(2)(A) Subject to applicable law and the policies of the Director of National Intelligence, the Inspector General shall select, appoint, and employ such officers and employees as may be necessary to carry out the functions of the Inspector General. The Inspector General shall ensure that any officer or employee so selected, appointed, or employed has security clearances appropriate for the assigned duties of such officer or employee.

"(B) In making selections under subparagraph (A), the Inspector General shall ensure that such officers and employees have the requisite training and experience to enable the Inspector General to carry out the duties of the Inspector General effectively.

"(C) In meeting the requirements of this paragraph, the Inspector General shall create within the Office of the Inspector General of the Intelligence Community a career cadre of sufficient size to provide appropriate continuity and objectivity needed for the effective performance of the duties of the Inspector General.

"(3)(A) Subject to the concurrence of the Director, the Inspector General may request such information or assistance as may be necessary for carrying out the duties and responsibilities of the Inspector General from any department, agency, or other element of the United States Government.

"(B) Upon request of the Inspector General for information or assistance under subparagraph (A), the head of the department, agency, or element concerned shall, insofar as is practicable and not in contravention of any existing statutory restriction or regulation of the department, agency, or element, furnish to the Inspector General, or to an authorized designee, such information or assistance.

"(C) The Inspector General of the Intelligence Community may, upon reasonable notice to the head of any element of the intelligence community, conduct, as authorized by this section, an investigation, inspection, or audit of such element and may enter into any place occupied by such element for purposes of the performance of the duties of the Inspector General.

"(i) REPORTS.—(1)(A) The Inspector General of the Intelligence Community shall, not later than January 31 and July 31 of each year, prepare and submit to the Director of National Intelligence a classified, and, as appropriate, unclassified semiannual report summarizing the activities of the Office of the Inspector General of the Intelligence Community during the immediately preceding 6-month period ending December 31 (of the preceding year) and June 30, respectively. The Inspector General of the Intelligence Community shall provide any portion of the report involving a component of a department of the United States Government to the head of that department simultaneously with submission of the report to the Director of National Intelligence.

"(B) Each report under this paragraph shall include, at a minimum, the following:

"(i) A list of the title or subject of each investigation, inspection, or audit conducted during the period covered by such report, including a summary of the progress of each particular investigation, inspection, or audit since the preceding report of the Inspector General under this paragraph.

"(ii) A description of significant problems, abuses, and deficiencies relating to the administration and implementation of programs and operations of the intelligence community, and in the relationships between elements of the intelligence community, identified by the Inspector General during the period covered by such report.

"(iii) A description of the recommendations for corrective or disciplinary action made by the Inspector General during the period covered by such report with respect to significant problems, abuses, or deficiencies identified in clause (ii).

"(iv) A statement whether or not corrective or disciplinary action has been completed on each significant recommendation described in previous semiannual reports, and, in a case where corrective action has been completed, a description of such corrective action.

"(v) A certification whether or not the Inspector General has had full and direct access to all information relevant to the performance of the functions of the Inspector General.

"(vi) A description of the exercise of the subpoena authority under subsection (f)(5) by the Inspector General during the period covered by such report.

"(vii) Such recommendations as the Inspector General considers appropriate for legislation to promote economy, efficiency, and effectiveness in the administration and implementation of matters within the responsibility and authority of the Director of National Intelligence, and to detect and eliminate fraud and abuse in such matters.

"(C) Not later than the 30 days after the date of receipt of a report under subparagraph (A), the Director shall transmit the report to the congressional intelligence committees together with any comments the Director considers appropriate. The Director shall transmit to the committees of the Senate and of the House of Representatives with jurisdiction over a department of the United States Government any portion of the report involving a component of such department simultaneously with submission of the report to the congressional intelligence committees.

"(2)(A) The Inspector General shall report immediately to the Director whenever the Inspector General becomes aware of particularly serious or flagrant problems, abuses, or deficiencies relating to matters within the responsibility and authority of the Director of National Intelligence.

"(B) The Director shall transmit to the congressional intelligence committees each report under subparagraph (A) within 7 calendar days of receipt of such report, together with such comments as the Director considers appropriate. The Director shall transmit to the committees of the Senate and of the House of Representatives with jurisdiction over a department of the United States Government any portion of each report under subparagraph (A) that involves a problem, abuse, or deficiency related to a component of such department simultaneously with transmission of the report to the congressional intelligence committees.

"(3) In the event that—

"(A) the Inspector General is unable to resolve any differences with the Director affecting the execution of the duties or responsibilities of the Inspector General;

"(B) an investigation, inspection, or audit carried out by the Inspector General focuses on any current or former intelligence community official who—

"(i) holds or held a position in an element of the intelligence community that is subject to appointment by the President, whether or not by and with the advice and consent of the Senate, including such a position held on an acting basis;

"(ii) holds or held a position in an element of the intelligence community, including a position held on an acting basis, that is appointed by the Director of National Intelligence; or

"(iii) holds or held a position as head of an element of the intelligence community or a position covered by subsection (b) or (c) of section 106;

"(C) a matter requires a report by the Inspector General to the Department of Justice on possible criminal conduct by a current or former official described in subparagraph (B);

"(D) the Inspector General receives notice from the Department of Justice declining or approving prosecution of possible criminal conduct of any current or former official described in subparagraph (B); or

"(E) the Inspector General, after exhausting all possible alternatives, is unable to obtain significant documentary information in the course of an investigation, inspection, or audit,

the Inspector General shall immediately notify and submit a report on such matter to the congressional intelligence committees.

"(4) Pursuant to title V, the Director shall submit to the congressional intelligence committees any report or findings and recommendations of an investigation, inspection, or audit conducted by the office which has been requested by the Chairman or Vice Chairman or Ranking Minority Member of either committee.

"(5)(A) An employee of an element of the intelligence community, an employee assigned or detailed to an element of the intelligence community, or an employee of a contractor to the intelligence community who intends to report to Congress a complaint or information with respect to an urgent concern may report such complaint or information to the Inspector General.

"(B) Not later than the end of the 14-calendar day period beginning on the date of receipt from an employee of a complaint or information under subparagraph (A), the Inspector General shall determine whether the complaint or information appears credible. Upon making such a determination, the Inspector General shall transmit to the Director a notice of that determination, together with the complaint or information.

"(C) Upon receipt of a transmittal from the Inspector General under subparagraph (B), the Director shall, within 7 calendar days of such receipt, forward such transmittal to the congressional intelligence committees, together with any comments the Director considers appropriate.

"(D)(i) If the Inspector General does not find credible under subparagraph (B) a complaint or information submitted under subparagraph (A), or does not transmit the complaint or information to the Director in accurate form under subparagraph (B), the employee (subject to clause (ii)) may submit the complaint or information to Congress by contacting either or both of the congressional intelligence committees directly.

"(ii) An employee may contact the intelligence committees directly as described in clause (i) only if the employee—

"(I) before making such a contact, furnishes to the Director, through the Inspector General, a statement of the employee's complaint or information and notice of the employee's intent to contact the congressional intelligence committees directly; and

"(II) obtains and follows from the Director, through the Inspector General, direction on how to contact the intelligence committees in accordance with appropriate security practices.

"(iii) A member or employee of 1 of the congressional intelligence committees who receives a complaint or information under clause (i) does so in that member or employee's official capacity as a member or employee of such committee.

"(E) The Inspector General shall notify an employee who reports a complaint or information to the Inspector General under this paragraph of each action taken under this paragraph with respect to the complaint or information. Such notice shall be provided not later than 3 days after any such action is taken.

"(F) An action taken by the Director or the Inspector General under this paragraph shall not be subject to judicial review.

"(G) In this paragraph, the term 'urgent concern' means any of the following:

"(i) A serious or flagrant problem, abuse, violation of law or Executive order, or deficiency relating to the funding, administration, or operation of an intelligence activity involving classified information, but does not include differences of opinions concerning public policy matters.

"(ii) A false statement to Congress, or a willful withholding from Congress, on an issue of material fact relating to the funding, administration, or operation of an intelligence activity.

"(iii) An action, including a personnel action described in section 2302(a)(2)(A) of title 5, United States Code, constituting reprisal or threat of reprisal prohibited under subsection (f)(3)(B) of this section in response to an employee's reporting an urgent concern in accordance with this paragraph.

"(H) In support of this paragraph, Congress makes the findings set forth in paragraphs (1) through (6) of section 701(b) of the

Intelligence Community Whistleblower Protection Act of 1998 (title VII of Public Law 105–272; 5 U.S.C. App. 8H note).

"(6) In accordance with section 535 of title 28, United States Code, the Inspector General shall report to the Attorney General any information, allegation, or complaint received by the Inspector General relating to violations of Federal criminal law that involves a program or operation of an element of the intelligence community, or in the relationships between the elements of the intelligence community, consistent with such guidelines as may be issued by the Attorney General pursuant to subsection (b)(2) of such section. A copy of each such report shall be furnished to the Director.

"(j) SEPARATE BUDGET ACCOUNT.—The Director of National Intelligence shall, in accordance with procedures to be issued by the Director in consultation with the congressional intelligence committees, include in the National Intelligence Program budget a separate account for the Office of Inspector General of the Intelligence Community.

"(k) CONSTRUCTION OF DUTIES REGARDING ELEMENTS OF INTELLIGENCE COMMUNITY.—Except as resolved pursuant to subsection (g), the performance by the Inspector General of the Intelligence Community of any duty, responsibility, or function regarding an element of the intelligence community shall not be construed to modify or effect the duties and responsibilities of any other Inspector General, whether statutory or administrative, having duties and responsibilities relating to such element.".

(2) CLERICAL AMENDMENT.—The table of contents in the first section of the National Security Act of 1947 is amended by inserting after the item relating to section 103G the following new item:

"Sec. 103H. Inspector General of the Intelligence Community.".

(b) REPEAL OF SUPERSEDED AUTHORITY TO ESTABLISH POSITION.—Section 8K of the Inspector General Act of 1978 (5 U.S.C. App.) is repealed.

(c) EXECUTIVE SCHEDULE LEVEL IV.—Section 5315 of title 5, United States Code, is amended by adding at the end the following new item:

"Inspector General of the Intelligence Community.".

SEC. 414. ANNUAL REPORT ON FOREIGN LANGUAGE PROFICIENCY IN THE INTELLIGENCE COMMUNITY.

(a) REPORT.—

(1) IN GENERAL.—Title V of the National Security Act of 1947 (50 U.S.C. 413 et seq.), as amended by title III of this Act, is further amended by

adding at the end the following new section:

"REPORT ON FOREIGN LANGUAGE PROFICIENCY IN THE INTELLIGENCE COMMUNITY

"SEC. 508. Not later than February 1 of each year, the Director of National Intelligence shall submit to the congressional intelligence committees a report on the proficiency in foreign languages and, if appropriate, in foreign dialects of each element of the intelligence community, including—

"(1) the number of positions authorized for such element that require foreign language proficiency and the level of proficiency required;

"(2) an estimate of the number of such positions that each element will require during the 5-year period beginning on the date of the submission of the report;

"(3) the number of positions authorized for such element that require foreign language proficiency that are filled by—

"(A) military personnel; and

"(B) civilian personnel;

"(4) the number of applicants for positions in such element in the previous fiscal year that indicated foreign language proficiency, including the foreign language indicated and the proficiency level;

"(5) the number of persons hired by such element with foreign language proficiency, including the foreign language and proficiency level;

"(6) the number of personnel of such element currently attending foreign language training, including the provider of such training;

"(7) a description of such element's efforts to recruit, hire, train, and retain personnel that are proficient in a foreign language;

"(8) an assessment of methods and models for basic, advanced, and intensive foreign language training;

"(9) for each foreign language and, where appropriate, dialect of a foreign language—

"(A) the number of positions of such element that require proficiency in the foreign language or dialect;

"(B) the number of personnel of such element that are serving in a position that—

"(i) requires proficiency in the foreign language or dialect to perform the primary duty of the position; and

"(ii) does not require proficiency in the foreign language or dialect to perform the primary duty of the position;

"(C) the number of personnel of such element rated at each level of proficiency of the Interagency Language Roundtable;

"(D) whether the number of personnel at each level of proficiency of the Interagency Language Roundtable meets the requirements of such element;

"(E) the number of personnel serving or hired to serve as linguists for such element that are not qualified as linguists under the standards of the Interagency Language Roundtable;

"(F) the number of personnel hired to serve as linguists for such element during the preceding calendar year;

"(G) the number of personnel serving as linguists that discontinued serving such element during the preceding calendar year;

"(H) the percentage of work requiring linguistic skills that is fulfilled by an ally of the United States; and

"(I) the percentage of work requiring linguistic skills that is fulfilled by contractors;

"(10) an assessment of the foreign language capacity and capabilities of the intelligence community as a whole; and

"(11) recommendations for eliminating required reports relating to foreign-language proficiency that the Director of National Intelligence considers outdated or no longer relevant.".

(2) REPORT DATE.—Section 507(a)(1) of such Act (50 U.S.C. 415b(a)(1)), as amended by section 328(f) of this Act, is further amended by adding at the end the following new subparagraph:

"(M) The annual report on foreign language proficiency in the intelligence community required by section 508.".

(b) CONFORMING AMENDMENT.—The table of contents in the first section of such Act is further amended by inserting after the item relating to section 507 the following new item:

"Sec. 508. Report on foreign language proficiency in the intelligence community.".

SEC. 415. DIRECTOR OF NATIONAL INTELLIGENCE REPORT ON RETIREMENT BENEFITS FOR FORMER EMPLOYEES OF AIR AMERICA.

(a) IN GENERAL.—Not later than 120 days after the date of the enactment of this Act, the Director of National Intelligence shall submit to Congress a report on the advisability of providing Federal retirement benefits to United States citizens for the service of such individuals before 1977 as employees of Air America or an associated company while such company was owned or controlled by the United States Government and operated or managed by the Central Intelligence Agency.

(b) REPORT ELEMENTS.—

(1) IN GENERAL.—The report required by subsection (a) shall include the following:

(A) The history of Air America and associated companies before 1977, including a description of—

(i) the relationship between such companies and the Central Intelligence Agency and other elements of the United States Government;

(ii) the workforce of such companies;

(iii) the missions performed by such companies and their employees for the United States; and

(iv) the casualties suffered by employees of such companies in the course of their employment with such companies.

(B) A description of the retirement benefits contracted for or promised to the employees of such companies before 1977, the contributions made by such employees for such benefits, the retirement benefits actually paid such employees, the entitlement of such employees to the payment of future retirement benefits, and the likelihood that former employees of such companies will receive any future retirement benefits.

(C) An assessment of the difference between—

(i) the retirement benefits that former employees of such companies have received or will receive by virtue of their employment with such companies; and

(ii) the retirement benefits that such employees would have received and in the future receive if such employees had been, or would now be, treated as employees of the United States whose services while in the employ of such companies had been or would now be credited as Federal service for the purpose of Federal retirement benefits.

(D) Any recommendations regarding the advisability of legislative action to treat employment at such companies as Federal service for the purpose of Federal retirement benefits in light of the relationship between such companies and the United States Government and the services and sacrifices of such employees to and for the United States, and if legislative action is considered advisable, a proposal for such action and an assessment of its costs.

(2) OTHER CONTENT.—The Director of National Intelligence shall include in the report any views of the Director of the Central Intelligence

Agency on the matters covered by the report that the Director of the Central Intelligence Agency considers appropriate.

(c) ASSISTANCE OF COMPTROLLER GENERAL.—The Comptroller General of the United States shall, upon the request of the Director of National Intelligence and in a manner consistent with the protection of classified information, assist the Director in the preparation of the report required by subsection (a).

(d) FORM.—The report required by subsection (a) shall be submitted in unclassified form, but may include a classified annex.

(e) DEFINITIONS.—In this section:

(1) AIR AMERICA.—The term "Air America" means Air America, Incorporated.

(2) ASSOCIATED COMPANY.—The term "associated company" means any company associated with or subsidiary to Air America, including Air Asia Company Limited and the Pacific Division of Southern Air Transport, Incorporated.

SEC. 416. SPACE INTELLIGENCE.

Section 102A of the National Security Act of 1947 (50 U.S.C. 403–1) as amended by sections 303, 304, and 411 of this Act, is further amended by adding at the end the following new subsection:

"(v) CONSIDERATION OF SPACE INTELLIGENCE.—

"(1) IN GENERAL.—The Director of National Intelligence shall require that space-intelligence related issues and concerns are fully considered in carrying out the authorities of the intelligence community under this Act and under other provisions of law, including in carrying out—

"(A) the responsibilities and authorities described under subsections (f), (h), and (q); and

"(B) the creation of policy, and in the recruitment, hiring, training, and retention of personnel.

"(2) ADDITIONAL CONSIDERATIONS.—The Director of National Intelligence shall ensure that agencies give due consideration to the vulnerability assessment prepared for a given major system, as required in section 506C of this Act, at all stages of architecture and system planning, development, acquisition, operation, and support of a space-intelligence system.".

SEC. 417. OPERATIONAL FILES IN THE OFFICE OF THE DIRECTOR OF NATIONAL INTELLIGENCE.

(a) IN GENERAL.—Title VII of the National Security Act of 1947 (50 U.S.C. 431 et seq.) is amended by adding at the end the following new section:

"OPERATIONAL FILES IN THE OFFICE OF THE DIRECTOR OF NATIONAL INTELLIGENCE

"SEC. 706. (a) RECORDS FROM EXEMPTED OPERATIONAL FILES.—(1) Any record disseminated or otherwise provided to an element of the Office of the Director of National Intelligence from the exempted operational files of elements of the intelligence community designated in accordance with this title, and any operational files created by the Office of the Director of National Intelligence that incorporate such record in accordance with subparagraph (A)(ii), shall be exempted from the provisions of section 552 of title 5, United States Code that require search, review, publication, or disclosure in connection therewith, in any instance in which—

"(A) (i) such record is shared within the Office of the Director of National Intelligence and not disseminated by that Office beyond that Office; or

"(ii) such record is incorporated into new records created by personnel of the Office of the Director of National Intelligence and maintained in operational files of the Office of the Director of National Intelligence and such record is not disseminated by that Office beyond that Office; and

"(B) the operational files from which such record has been obtained continue to remain designated as operational files exempted from section 552 of title 5, United States Code.

"(2) The operational files of the Office of the Director of National Intelligence referred to in paragraph (1)(A)(ii) shall be substantially similar in nature to the originating operational files from which the record was disseminated or provided, as such files are defined in this title.

"(3) Records disseminated or otherwise provided to the Office of the Director of National Intelligence from other elements of the intelligence community that are not protected by paragraph (1), and that are authorized to be disseminated beyond the Office of the Director of National Intelligence, shall remain subject to search and review under section 552 of title 5, United States Code, but may continue to be exempted from the publication and disclosure provisions of that section by the originating agency to the extent that such section permits.

"(4) Notwithstanding any other provision of this title, records in the exempted operational files of the Central Intelligence Agency, the National Geospatial-Intelligence Agency, the National Reconnaissance Office, the National Security Agency, or the Defense Intelligence Agency shall not be subject to the search and review provisions of section 552 of title 5, United States Code, solely because they have been disseminated to an element or elements of the Office of the Director of National Intelligence, or referenced in operational files of the Office of the Director of National Intelligence and that are not disseminated beyond the Office of the Director of National Intelligence.

"(5) Notwithstanding any other provision of this title, the incorporation of records from the operational files of the Central Intelligence Agency, the National Geospatial-Intelligence Agency, the National Reconnaissance Office, the National Security Agency, or the Defense Intelligence Agency, into operational files of the Office of the Director of National Intelligence shall not subject that record or the operational files of the Central Intelligence Agency, the National Geospatial-Intelligence Agency, the National Reconnaissance Office, the National Security Agency or the Defense Intelligence Agency to the search and review provisions of section 552 of title 5, United States Code.

"(b) OTHER RECORDS.—(1) Files in the Office of the Director of National Intelligence that are not exempted under subsection (a) of this section which contain information derived or disseminated from exempted operational files shall be subject to search and review under section 552 of title 5, United States Code.

"(2) The inclusion of information from exempted operational files in files of the Office of the Director of National Intelligence that are not exempted under subsection (a) shall not affect the exemption of the originating operational files from search, review, publication, or disclosure.

"(3) Records from exempted operational files of the Office of the Director of National Intelligence which have been disseminated to and referenced in files that are not exempted under subsection (a), and which have been returned to exempted operational files of the Office of the Director of National Intelligence for sole retention, shall be subject to search and review.

"(c) SEARCH AND REVIEW FOR CERTAIN PURPOSES.—Notwithstanding subsection (a), exempted operational files shall continue to be subject to search and review for information concerning any of the following:

"(1) United States citizens or aliens lawfully admitted for permanent residence who have requested information on themselves pursuant to the provisions of section 552 or 552a of title 5, United States Code.

"(2) Any special activity the existence of which is not exempt from disclosure under the provisions of section 552 of title 5, United States Code.

"(3) The specific subject matter of an investigation by any of the following for any impropriety, or violation of law, Executive order, or Presidential directive, in the conduct of an intelligence activity:

"(A) The Select Committee on Intelligence of the Senate.

"(B) The Permanent Select Committee on Intelligence of the House of Representatives.

"(C) The Intelligence Oversight Board.

"(D) The Department of Justice.

"(E) The Office of the Director of National Intelligence.

"(F) The Office of the Inspector General of the Intelligence Community.

"(d) DECENNIAL REVIEW OF EXEMPTED OPERATIONAL FILES.—

(1) Not less than once every 10 years, the Director of National Intelligence shall review the operational files exempted under subsection (a) to determine whether such files, or any portion of such files, may be removed from the category of exempted files.

"(2) The review required by paragraph (1) shall include consideration of the historical value or other public interest in the subject matter of the particular category of files or portions thereof and the potential for declassifying a significant part of the information contained therein.

"(3) A complainant that alleges that the Director of National Intelligence has improperly withheld records because of failure to comply with this subsection may seek judicial review in the district court of the United States of the district in which any of the parties reside, or in the District of Columbia. In such a proceeding, the court's review shall be limited to determining the following:

"(A) Whether the Director has conducted the review required by paragraph (1) before the expiration of the 10-year period beginning on the date of the enactment of the Intelligence Authorization Act for Fiscal Year 2008 or before the expiration of the 10-year period beginning on the date of the most recent review.

"(B) Whether the Director of National Intelligence, in fact, considered the criteria set forth in paragraph (2) in conducting the required review.

"(e) SUPERSEDURE OF OTHER LAWS.—The provisions of this section may not be superseded except by a provision of law that is enacted after the date of the enactment of this section and that specifically cites and repeals or modifies such provisions.

"(f) APPLICABILITY.—The Director of National Intelligence will publish a regulation listing the specific elements within the Office of the Director of National Intelligence whose records can be exempted from search and review under this section.

"(g) ALLEGATION; IMPROPER WITHHOLDING OF RECORDS; JUDICIAL REVIEW.—(1) Except as provided in paragraph (2), whenever any person who has requested agency records under section 552 of title 5, United States Code, alleges that the Office of the Director of National Intelligence has withheld records improperly because of failure to comply with any provision of this section, judicial review shall be available under the terms set forth in section 552(a)(4)(B) of title 5, United States Code.

"(2) Judicial review shall not be available in the manner provided for under paragraph (1) as follows:

"(A) In any case in which information specifically authorized under criteria established by an Executive order to be kept secret in the interests of national defense or foreign relations is filed with, or produced for, the court by the Office of the Director of National Intelligence, such information shall be examined ex parte, in camera by the court.

"(B) The court shall determine, to the fullest extent practicable, the issues of fact based on sworn written submissions of the parties.

"(C) When a complainant alleges that requested records are improperly withheld because of improper placement solely in exempted operational files, the complainant shall support such allegation with a sworn written submission based upon personal knowledge or otherwise admissible evidence.

"(D) (i) When a complainant alleges that requested records were improperly withheld because of improper exemption of operational files, the Office of the Director of National Intelligence shall meet its burden under section 552(a)(4)(B) of title 5, United States Code, by demonstrating to the court by sworn written submission that exempted operational files likely to contain responsive records currently meet the criteria set forth in subsection (a).

"(ii) The court may not order the Office of the Director of National Intelligence to review the content of any exempted operational file or files in order to make the demonstration required under clause (i), unless the complainant disputes the Office's showing with a sworn written submission based on personal knowledge or otherwise admissible evidence.

"(E) In proceedings under subparagraph (C) or (D), a party may not obtain discovery pursuant to rules 26 through 36 of the Federal Rules of Civil Procedure, except that requests for admissions may be made pursuant to rules 26 and 36.

"(F) If the court finds under this subsection that the Office of the Director of National Intelligence has improperly withheld requested records because of failure to comply with any provision of this section, the court shall order the Office to search and review the appropriate exempted operational file or files for the requested records and make such records, or portions thereof, available in accordance with the provisions of section 552 of title 5, United States Code, and such order shall be the exclusive remedy for failure to comply with this section.

"(G) If at any time following the filing of a complaint pursuant to this paragraph the Office of the Director of National Intelligence agrees to search the appropriate exempted operational file or files for the requested records, the court shall dismiss the claim based upon such complaint.".

(b) CLERICAL AMENDMENT.—The table of contents in the first section of the National Security Act of 1947 is amended by inserting after the item relating to section 705 the following new item:

"Sec. 706. Operational files in the Office of the Director of National Intelligence.".

SEC. 418. INAPPLICABILITY OF FEDERAL ADVISORY COMMITTEE ACT TO ADVISORY COMMITTEES OF THE OFFICE OF THE DIRECTOR OF NATIONAL INTELLIGENCE.

Section 4(b) of the Federal Advisory Committee Act (5 U.S.C. App.) is amended—

(1) in paragraph (1), by striking "or";

(2) in paragraph (2), by striking the period and inserting "; or"; and

(3) by adding at the end the following new paragraph:

"(3) the Office of the Director of National Intelligence.".

SEC. 419. APPLICABILITY OF THE PRIVACY ACT TO THE DIRECTOR OF NATIONAL INTELLIGENCE AND THE OFFICE OF THE DIRECTOR OF NATIONAL INTELLIGENCE.

Subsection (j) of section 552a of title 5, United States Code, is amended—

(1) in paragraph (1), by striking "or";

(2) by redesignating paragraph (2) as paragraph (3); and

(3) by inserting after paragraph (1) the following new paragraph:

"(2) maintained by the Office of the Director of National Intelligence; or".

SEC. 420. REPEAL OF CERTAIN AUTHORITIES RELATING TO THE OFFICE OF THE NATIONAL COUNTERINTELLIGENCE EXECUTIVE.

(a) REPEAL OF CERTAIN AUTHORITIES.—Section 904 of the Counterintelligence Enhancement Act of 2002 (title IX of Public Law 107–306; 50 U.S.C. 402c) is amended—

(1) by striking subsections (d), (h), (i), and (j); and

(2) by redesignating subsections (e), (f), (g), (k), (l), and (m) as subsections (d), (e), (f), (g), (h), and (i), respectively; and

(3) in subsection (f), as redesignated by paragraph (2), by striking paragraphs (3) and (4).

(b) CONFORMING AMENDMENTS.—Such section 904 is further amended—

(1) in subsection (d), as redesignated by subsection (a)(2) of this section, by striking "subsection (f)" each place it appears in paragraphs (1) and (2) and inserting "subsection (e)"; and

(2) in subsection (e), as so redesignated—

(A) in paragraph (1), by striking "subsection (e)(1)" and inserting "subsection (d)(1)"; and

(B) in paragraph (2), by striking "subsection (e)(2)" and inserting "subsection (d)(2)".

Subtitle B—Central Intelligence Agency

SEC. 431. REVIEW OF COVERT ACTION PROGRAMS BY INSPECTOR GENERAL OF THE CENTRAL INTELLIGENCE AGENCY.

(a) IN GENERAL.—Section 503 of the National Security Act of 1947 (50 U.S.C. 413b) is amended by—

(1) redesignating subsection (e) as subsection (g) and transferring such subsection to the end; and

(2) by inserting after subsection (d) the following new subsection:

"(e) INSPECTOR GENERAL AUDITS OF COVERT ACTIONS.—

"(1) IN GENERAL.—Subject to paragraph (2), the Inspector General of the Central Intelligence Agency shall conduct an audit of each covert action at least every 3 years. Such audits shall be conducted subject to the provisions of paragraphs (3) and (4) of subsection (b) of section 17 of the Central Intelligence Agency Act of 1949 (50 U.S.C. 403q).

"(2) TERMINATED, SUSPENDED PROGRAMS.—The Inspector General of the Central Intelligence Agency is not required to conduct an audit under paragraph (1) of a covert action that has been terminated or suspended if such covert action was terminated or suspended prior to the last audit of such covert action conducted by the Inspector General and has not been restarted after the date on which such audit was completed.

"(3) REPORT.—Not later than 60 days after the completion of an audit conducted pursuant to paragraph (1), the Inspector General of the Central Intelligence Agency shall submit to the congressional intelligence committees a report containing the results of such audit.".

(b) CONFORMING AMENDMENTS.—Title V of the National Security Act of 1947 (50 U.S.C. 413 et seq.) is amended—

(1) in section 501(f) (50 U.S.C. 413(f)), by striking "503(e)" and inserting "503(g)";

(2) in section 502(a)(1) (50 U.S.C. 413b(a)(1)), by striking "503(e)" and inserting "503(g)"; and

(3) in section 504(c) (50 U.S.C. 414(c)), by striking "503(e)" and inserting "503(g)".

SEC. 432. INAPPLICABILITY TO DIRECTOR OF THE CENTRAL INTELLIGENCE AGENCY OF REQUIREMENT FOR ANNUAL REPORT ON PROGRESS IN AUDITABLE FINANCIAL STATEMENTS.

Section 114A of the National Security Act of 1947 (50 U.S.C. 404i–1) is amended by striking "the Director of the Central Intelligence Agency,".

SEC. 433. ADDITIONAL FUNCTIONS AND AUTHORITIES FOR PROTECTIVE PERSONNEL OF THE CENTRAL INTELLIGENCE AGENCY.

(a) IN GENERAL.—Section 5(a)(4) of the Central Intelligence Agency Act of 1949 (50 U.S.C. 403f(a)(4)) is amended—

(1) by inserting "(A)" after "(4)";

(2) in subparagraph (A), as so designated—

(A) by striking "and the protection" and inserting "the protection"; and

(B) by striking the semicolon and inserting ", and the protection of the Director of National Intelligence and such personnel of the Office of the Director of National Intelligence as the Director of National Intelligence may designate; and"; and

(3) by adding at the end the following new subparagraph:

"(B) Authorize personnel engaged in the performance of protective functions authorized pursuant to subparagraph (A), when engaged in, and in furtherance of, the performance of such functions, to make arrests without warrant for any offense against the United States committed in the presence of such personnel, or for any felony cognizable under the laws of the United States, if such personnel have reasonable grounds to believe that the person to be arrested has committed or is committing such felony, except that any authority pursuant to this subparagraph may be exercised only in accordance with guidelines approved by the Director and the Attorney General and such personnel may not exercise any authority for the service of civil process or for the investigation of criminal offenses;".

(b) REQUIREMENT TO REPORT.—As soon as possible after the date of an exercise of authority under subparagraph (B) of section 5(a)(4) of the Central Intelligence Agency Act of 1949 (50 U.S.C. 403f(a)(4)), as added by subsection (a)(3), and not later than 10 days after such date, the Director of the Central Intelligence Agency shall submit to the congressional intelligence committees a report describing such exercise of authority.

SEC. 434. TECHNICAL AMENDMENTS RELATING TO TITLES OF CERTAIN CENTRAL INTELLIGENCE AGENCY POSITIONS.

Section 17(d)(3)(B)(ii) of the Central Intelligence Agency Act of 1949 (50 U.S.C. 403q(d)(3)(B)(ii)) is amended—

(1) in subclause (I), by striking "Executive Director" and inserting "Associate Deputy Director";

(2) in subclause (II), by striking "Deputy Director for Operations" and inserting "Director of the National Clandestine Service";

(3) in subclause (III), by striking "Deputy Director for Intelligence" and inserting "Director of Intelligence";

(4) in subclause (IV), by striking "Deputy Director for Administration" and inserting "Director of Support"; and

(5) in subclause (V), by striking "Deputy Director for Science and Technology" and inserting "Director of Science and Technology".

SEC. 435. CLARIFYING AMENDMENTS RELATING TO SECTION 105 OF THE INTELLIGENCE AUTHORIZATION ACT FOR FISCAL YEAR 2004.

Section 105(b) of the Intelligence Authorization Act for Fiscal Year 2004 (Public Law 108–177; 117 Stat. 2603; 31 U.S.C. 311 note) is amended—

(1) by striking "Director of Central Intelligence" and inserting "Director of National Intelligence"; and

(2) by inserting "or in section 313 of such title," after "subsection (a)),".

Subtitle C—Defense Intelligence Components

SEC. 441. ENHANCEMENT OF NATIONAL SECURITY AGENCY TRAINING PROGRAM.

Subsection (e) of section 16 of the National Security Agency Act of 1959 (50 U.S.C. 402 note) is amended by striking "(1) When an employee" and all that follows through "(2) Agency efforts" and inserting "Agency efforts".

SEC. 442. CODIFICATION OF AUTHORITIES OF NATIONAL SECURITY AGENCY PROTECTIVE PERSONNEL.

The National Security Agency Act of 1959 (50 U.S.C. 402 note) is amended by adding at the end the following new section:

"SEC. 21. (a) The Director of the National Security Agency is authorized to designate personnel of the National Security Agency to perform protective functions for the Director and for any personnel of the Agency designated by the Director.

"(b) (1) In the performance of protective functions under this section, personnel of the Agency designated to perform protective functions pursuant to subsection (a) are authorized, when engaged in, and in furtherance of, the performance of such functions, to make arrests without a warrant for—

"(A) any offense against the United States committed in the presence of such personnel; or

"(B) any felony cognizable under the laws of the United States if such personnel have reasonable grounds to believe that the person to be arrested has committed or is committing such felony.

"(2) The authority in paragraph (1) may be exercised only in accordance with guidelines approved by the Director and the Attorney General.

"(3) Personnel of the Agency designated to perform protective functions pursuant to subsection (a) shall not exercise any authority for the service of civil process or the investigation of criminal offenses.

"(c) Nothing in this section shall be construed to impair or otherwise affect any authority under any other provision of law relating to the performance of protective functions.

"(d) As soon as possible after the date of an exercise of authority under this section and not later than 10 days after such date, the Director shall submit to the congressional intelligence committees a report describing such exercise of authority.

"(e) In this section, the term 'congressional intelligence committees' means—

"(1) the Select Committee on Intelligence of the Senate; and

"(2) the Permanent Select Committee on Intelligence of the House of Representatives.".

SEC. 443. INSPECTOR GENERAL MATTERS.

(a) COVERAGE UNDER INSPECTOR GENERAL ACT OF 1978.—Subsection (a)(2) of section 8G of the Inspector General Act of 1978 (5 U.S.C. App. 8G) is amended—

(1) by inserting "the Defense Intelligence Agency," after "the Corporation for Public Broadcasting,";

(2) by inserting "the National Geospatial-Intelligence Agency," after "the National Endowment for the Humanities,"; and

(3) by inserting "the National Reconnaissance Office, the National Security Agency," after "the National Labor Relations Board,".

(b) CERTAIN DESIGNATIONS UNDER INSPECTOR GENERAL ACT OF 1978.—Subsection (a) of section 8H of the Inspector General Act of 1978

(5 U.S.C. App. 8H) is amended by adding at the end the following new paragraph:

"(3) The Inspectors General of the Defense Intelligence Agency, the National Geospatial-Intelligence Agency, the National Reconnaissance Office, and the National Security Agency shall be designees of the Inspector General of the Department of Defense for purposes of this section.".

(c) POWER OF HEADS OF ELEMENTS OVER INVESTIGATIONS.—Subsection (d) of section 8G of that Act—

(1) by inserting "(1)" after "(d)";

(2) in the second sentence of paragraph (1), as designated by paragraph (1) of this subsection, by striking "The head" and inserting "Except as provided in paragraph (2), the head"; and

(3) by adding at the end the following new paragraph:

"(2) (A) The Secretary of Defense, in consultation with the Director of National Intelligence, may prohibit the Inspector General of an element of the intelligence community specified in subparagraph (D) from initiating, carrying out, or completing any audit or investigation if the Secretary determines that the prohibition is necessary to protect vital national security interests of the United States.

"(B) If the Secretary exercises the authority under subparagraph (A), the Secretary shall submit to the committees of Congress specified in subparagraph (E) an appropriately classified statement of the reasons for the exercise of the authority not later than 7 days after the exercise of the authority.

"(C) At the same time the Secretary submits under subparagraph (B) a statement on the exercise of the authority in subparagraph (A) to the committees of Congress specified in subparagraph (E), the Secretary shall notify the Inspector General of such element of the submittal of such statement and, to the extent consistent with the protection of intelligence sources and methods, provide the Inspector General with a copy of such statement. The Inspector General may submit to such committees of Congress any comments on a notice or statement received by the Inspector General under this subparagraph that the Inspector General considers appropriate.

"(D) The elements of the intelligence community specified in this subparagraph are as follows:

"(i) The Defense Intelligence Agency.

"(ii) The National Geospatial-Intelligence Agency.

"(iii) The National Reconnaissance Office.

"(iv) The National Security Agency.

"(E) The committees of Congress specified in this subparagraph are—

"(i) the Committee on Armed Services and the Select Committee on Intelligence of the Senate; and

"(ii) the Committee on Armed Services and the Permanent Select Committee on Intelligence of the House of Representatives.".

SEC. 444. CONFIRMATION OF APPOINTMENT OF HEADS OF CERTAIN COMPONENTS OF THE INTELLIGENCE COMMUNITY.

(a) DIRECTOR OF NATIONAL SECURITY AGENCY.—The National Security Agency Act of 1959 (50 U.S.C. 402 note) is amended by inserting after the first section the following new section:

"SEC. 2. (a) There is a Director of the National Security Agency.

"(b) The Director of the National Security Agency shall be appointed by the President, by and with the advice and consent of the Senate.

"(c) The Director of the National Security Agency shall be the head of the National Security Agency and shall discharge such functions and duties as are provided by this Act or otherwise by law.".

(b) DIRECTOR OF NATIONAL RECONNAISSANCE OFFICE.—The Director of the National Reconnaissance Office shall be appointed by the President, by and with the advice and consent of the Senate.

(c) POSITIONS OF IMPORTANCE AND RESPONSIBILITY.—

(1) DESIGNATION OF POSITIONS.—The President may designate any of the positions referred to in paragraph (2) as positions of importance and responsibility under section 601 of title 10, United States Code.

(2) COVERED POSITIONS.—The positions referred to in this paragraph are as follows:

(A) The Director of the National Security Agency.

(B) The Director of the National Reconnaissance Office.

(d) EFFECTIVE DATE AND APPLICABILITY.—The amendments made by subsections (a) and (b) shall take effect on the date of the enactment of this Act and shall apply upon the earlier of—

(1) the date of the nomination by the President of an individual to serve in the position concerned, except that the individual serving in such position as of the date of the enactment of this Act may continue to perform such duties after such date of nomination and until the individual appointed to such position, by and with the advice and consent of the Senate, assumes the duties of such position; or

(2) the date of the cessation of the performance of the duties of such position by the individual performing such duties as of the date of the enactment of this Act.

SEC. 445. CLARIFICATION OF NATIONAL SECURITY MISSIONS OF NATIONAL GEOSPATIAL-INTELLIGENCE AGENCY FOR ANALYSIS AND DISSEMINATION OF CERTAIN INTELLIGENCE INFORMATION.

Section 442(a) of title 10, United States Code, is amended—

(1) by redesignating paragraph (2) as paragraph (3);

(2) by inserting after paragraph (1) the following new paragraph (2):

"(2)(A) As directed by the Director of National Intelligence, the National Geospatial-Intelligence Agency shall also develop a system to facilitate the analysis, dissemination, and incorporation of likenesses, videos, and presentations produced by ground-based platforms, including handheld or clandestine photography taken by or on behalf of human intelligence collection organizations or available as open-source information, into the National System for Geospatial Intelligence.

"(B) The authority provided by this paragraph does not include authority for the National Geospatial-Intelligence Agency to manage tasking of handheld or clandestine photography taken by or on behalf of human intelligence collection organizations."; and

(3) in paragraph (3), as so redesignated, by striking "paragraph (1)" and inserting "paragraphs (1) and (2)".

SEC. 446. SECURITY CLEARANCES IN THE NATIONAL GEOSPATIAL-INTELLIGENCE AGENCY.

The Secretary of Defense shall, during the period beginning on the date of the enactment of this Act and ending on December 31, 2008, delegate to the Director of the National Geospatial-Intelligence Agency personnel security authority with respect to the National Geospatial-Intelligence Agency (including authority relating to the use of contractor personnel in investigations and adjudications for security clearances) that is identical to the personnel security authority of the Director of the National Security Agency with respect to the National Security Agency.

Subtitle D—Other Elements

SEC. 451. CLARIFICATION OF INCLUSION OF COAST GUARD AND DRUG ENFORCEMENT ADMINISTRATION AS ELEMENTS OF THE INTELLIGENCE COMMUNITY.

Section 3(4) of the National Security Act of 1947 (50 U.S.C. 401a(4)) is amended—

(1) in subparagraph (H)—

(A) by inserting "the Coast Guard," after "the Marine Corps,"; and

(B) by inserting "the Drug Enforcement Administration," after "the Federal Bureau of Investigation,"; and

(2) in subparagraph (K), by striking ", including the Office of Intelligence of the Coast Guard".

TITLE V—OTHER MATTERS

Subtitle A—General Intelligence Matters

SEC. 501. EXTENSION OF NATIONAL COMMISSION FOR THE REVIEW OF THE RESEARCH AND DEVELOPMENT PROGRAMS OF THE UNITED STATES INTELLIGENCE COMMUNITY.

(a) EXTENSION.—

(1) IN GENERAL.—Subsection (a) of section 1007 of the Intelligence Authorization Act for Fiscal Year 2003 (Public Law 107–306; 116 Stat. 2442) is amended by striking "September 1, 2004" and inserting "December 31, 2008".

(2) EFFECTIVE DATE.—Subject to paragraph (3), the amendment made by paragraph (1) shall take effect as if included in the enactment of such section 1007.

(3) COMMISSION MEMBERSHIP.—

(A) IN GENERAL.—The membership of the National Commission for the Review of the Research and Development Programs of the United States Intelligence Community established under subsection (a) of section 1002 of such Act (Public Law 107–306; 116 Stat. 2438) (referred to in this section as the "Commission") shall be considered vacant and new members shall be appointed in accordance with such section 1002, as amended by subparagraph (B).

(B) TECHNICAL AMENDMENT.—Paragraph (1) of subsection (b) of such section 1002 is amended by striking "The Deputy Director of Central Intelligence for Community Management." and inserting "The Principal Deputy Director of National Intelligence.".

(b) FUNDING.—

(1) IN GENERAL.—Of the amounts authorized to be appropriated by this Act for the Intelligence Community Management Account, the Director of National Intelligence shall make $2,000,000 available to the Commission to carry out title X of the Intelligence Authorization Act for Fiscal Year 2003 (Public Law 107–306; 116 Stat. 2437).

(2) AVAILABILITY.—Amounts made available to the Commission pursuant to paragraph (1) shall remain available until expended.

SEC. 502. REPORT ON INTELLIGENCE ACTIVITIES.

Not later than 120 days after the date of the enactment of this Act, the Director of National Intelligence shall submit to the congressional intelligence committees a report describing authorizations, if any, granted during the 10-year period ending on the date of the enactment of this Act to engage in intelligence activities related to the overthrow of a democratically elected government.

SEC. 503. AERIAL RECONNAISSANCE PLATFORMS.

Section 133(b) of the John Warner National Defense Authorization Act for Fiscal Year 2007 (Public Law 109-364; 120 Stat. 2112) is amended—

(1) in paragraph (1)—

(A) by striking "After fiscal year 2007" and inserting "For each fiscal year after fiscal year 2007"; and

(B) by inserting ", in that fiscal year," after "Secretary of Defense"; and

(2) in paragraph (2)—

(A) by inserting "in a fiscal year" after "Department of Defense"; and

(B) by inserting "in that fiscal year" after "Congress".

Subtitle B—Technical Amendments

SEC. 511. TECHNICAL AMENDMENTS TO TITLE 10, UNITED STATES CODE, ARISING FROM ENACTMENT OF THE INTELLIGENCE REFORM AND TERRORISM PREVENTION ACT OF 2004.

(a) REFERENCES TO HEAD OF INTELLIGENCE COMMUNITY.—Title 10, United States Code, is amended by striking "Director of Central Intelligence" each place it appears and inserting "Director of National Intelligence" in the following:

(1) Section 193(d)(2).

(2) Section 193(e).

(3) Section 201(a).

(4) Section 201(b)(1).

(5) Section 201(c)(1).

(6) Section 425(a).

(7) Section 431(b)(1).

(8) Section 441(c).

(9) Section 441(d).

(10) Section 443(d).

(11) Section 2273(b)(1).

(12) Section 2723(a).

(b) CLERICAL AMENDMENTS.—Such title is further amended by striking "DIRECTOR OF CENTRAL INTELLIGENCE" each place it appears and inserting "DIRECTOR OF NATIONAL INTELLIGENCE" in the following:

(1) Section 441(c).

(2) Section 443(d).

(c) REFERENCE TO HEAD OF CENTRAL INTELLIGENCE AGENCY.—Section 444 of such title is amended by striking "Director of Central Intelligence" each place it appears and inserting "Director of the Central Intelligence Agency".

SEC. 512. TECHNICAL AMENDMENT TO THE CENTRAL INTELLIGENCE AGENCY ACT OF 1949.

Section 5(a)(1) of the Central Intelligence Agency Act of 1949 (50 U.S.C. 403f(a)(1)) is amended by striking "authorized under paragraphs (2) and (3) of section 102(a), subsections (c)(7) and (d) of section 103, subsections (a) and (g) of section 104, and section 303 of the National Security Act of 1947 (50 U.S.C. 403(a)(2), (3), 403–3(c)(7), (d), 403–4(a), (g), and 405)" and inserting "authorized under section 104A of the National Security Act of 1947 (50 U.S.C. 403–4a).".

SEC. 513. TECHNICAL AMENDMENTS RELATING TO THE MULTIYEAR NATIONAL INTELLIGENCE PROGRAM.

(a) IN GENERAL.—Subsection (a) of section 1403 of the National Defense Authorization Act for Fiscal Year 1991 (50 U.S.C. 404b) is amended—

(1) in the heading, by striking "FOREIGN"; and

(2) by striking "foreign" each place it appears.

(b) RESPONSIBILITY OF DIRECTOR OF NATIONAL INTELLIGENCE.—That section is further amended—

(1) in subsections (a) and (c), by striking "Director of Central Intelligence" and inserting "Director of National Intelligence"; and

(2) in subsection (b), by inserting "of National Intelligence" after "Director".

(c) CONFORMING AMENDMENT.—The heading of that section is amended to read as follows:

"SEC. 1403. MULTIYEAR NATIONAL INTELLIGENCE PROGRAM.".

SEC. 514. TECHNICAL CLARIFICATION OF CERTAIN REFERENCES TO JOINT MILITARY INTELLIGENCE PROGRAM AND TACTICAL INTELLIGENCE AND RELATED ACTIVITIES.

Section 102A of the National Security Act of 1947 (50 U.S.C. 403–1) is amended—

(1) in subsection (c)(3)(A), by striking "annual budgets for the Joint Military Intelligence Program and for Tactical Intelligence and Related Activities" and inserting "annual budget for the Military Intelligence Program or any successor program or programs"; and

(2) in subsection (d)(1)(B), by striking "Joint Military Intelligence Program" and inserting "Military Intelligence Program or any successor program or programs".

SEC. 515. TECHNICAL AMENDMENTS TO THE NATIONAL SECURITY ACT OF 1947.

The National Security Act of 1947 (50 U.S.C. 401 et seq.) is amended as follows:

(1) In section 102A (50 U.S.C. 403–1)—

(A) in subsection (d)—

(i) in paragraph (3), by striking "subparagraph (A)" in the matter preceding subparagraph (A) and inserting "paragraph (1)(A)";

(ii) in paragraph (5)(A), by striking "or personnel" in the matter preceding clause (i); and

(iii) in paragraph (5)(B), by striking "or agency involved" in the second sentence and inserting "involved or the Director of the Central Intelligence Agency (in the case of the Central Intelligence Agency)";

(B) in subsection (l)(2)(B), by striking "section" and inserting "paragraph"; and

(C) in subsection (n), by inserting "AND OTHER" after "ACQUISITION".

(2) In section 119(c)(2)(B) (50 U.S.C. 404o(c)(2)(B)), by striking "subsection (h)" and inserting "subsection (i)".

(3) In section 705(e)(2)(D)(i) (50 U.S.C. 432c(e)(2)(D)(i)), by striking "responsible" and inserting "responsive".

SEC. 516. TECHNICAL AMENDMENTS TO THE INTELLIGENCE REFORM AND TERRORISM PREVENTION ACT OF 2004.

(a) AMENDMENTS TO NATIONAL SECURITY INTELLIGENCE REFORM ACT OF 2004.—The National Security Intelligence Reform Act of 2004 (title I of Public Law 108–458; 118 Stat. 3643) is amended as follows:

(1) In section 1016(e)(10)(B) (6 U.S.C. 485(e)(10)(B)), by striking "Attorney General" the second place it appears and inserting "Department of Justice".

(2) In section 1071(e), by striking "(1)".

(3) In section 1072(b), in the subsection heading by inserting "AGENCY" after "INTELLIGENCE".

(b) OTHER AMENDMENTS TO INTELLIGENCE REFORM AND TERRORISM PREVENTION ACT OF 2004.—The Intelligence Reform and Terrorism Prevention Act of 2004 (Public Law 108–458; 118 Stat. 3638) is amended as follows:

(1) In section 2001 (28 U.S.C. 532 note)—

(A) in subsection (c)(1), by inserting "of" before "an institutional culture";

(B) in subsection (e)(2), by striking "the National Intelligence Director in a manner consistent with section 112(e)" and inserting "the Director of National Intelligence in a manner consistent with applicable law"; and

(C) in subsection (f), by striking "shall," in the matter preceding paragraph (1) and inserting "shall".

(2) In section 2006 (28 U.S.C. 509 note)—

(A) in paragraph (2), by striking "the Federal" and inserting "Federal"; and

(B) in paragraph (3), by striking "the specific" and inserting "specific".

SEC. 517. TECHNICAL AMENDMENTS TO THE EXECUTIVE SCHEDULE.

(a) EXECUTIVE SCHEDULE LEVEL II.—Section 5313 of title 5, United States Code, is amended by striking the item relating to the Director of Central Intelligence and inserting the following new item:

"Director of the Central Intelligence Agency.".

(b) EXECUTIVE SCHEDULE LEVEL III.—Section 5314 of title 5, United States Code, is amended by striking the item relating to the Deputy Directors of Central Intelligence and inserting the following new item:

"Deputy Director of the Central Intelligence Agency.".

(c) EXECUTIVE SCHEDULE LEVEL IV.—Section 5315 of title 5, United States Code, is amended by striking the item relating to the General Counsel of the Office of the National Intelligence Director and inserting the following new item:

"General Counsel of the Office of the Director of National Intelligence.".

Speaker of the House of Representatives.

Vice President of the United States and
President of the Senate.

DOCUMENT NO. 10

INTELLIGENCE AUTHORIZATION ACT FOR FISCAL YEAR 2008(H.R. 2082)—VETO MESSAGE FROM THE PRESIDENT OF THE UNITED STATES (H. DOC. NO. 110-100)

Congressional Record (House)

March 10, 2008

The SPEAKER pro tempore laid before the House the following veto message from the President of the United States:

To the House of Representatives:

I am returning herewith without my approval H.R. 2082, the ``Intelligence Authorization Act for Fiscal Year 2008." The bill would impede the United States Government's efforts to protect the American people effectively from terrorist attacks and other threats because it imposes several unnecessary and unacceptable burdens on our Intelligence Community.

Section 444 of the bill would impose additional Senate confirmation requirements on two national security positions—the Director of the National Security Agency and the Director of the National Reconnaissance Office. The National Commission on Terrorist Attacks Upon the United States (9/11 Commission) observed that the effectiveness of the Intelligence Community suffers due to delays in the confirmation process; section 444 would only aggravate those serious problems. Senior intelligence officials need to assume their duties and responsibilities as quickly as possible to address the pressing requirements of national security. Instead of addressing the 9/11 Commission's concern, the bill would subject two additional vital positions to a more protracted process of Senate confirmation. Apart from causing such potentially harmful delays, this unwarranted requirement for Senate confirmation would also risk injecting political pressure into these positions of technical expertise and public trust.

Section 413 would create a new Inspector General for the Intelligence Community. This new office is duplicative and unnecessary. Each intelligence community component already has an Inspector General, and the Inspector General of the Office of the Director of National Intelligence has been vested with all the legal powers of any inspector general to carry out investigations on matters under the jurisdiction of the Director of National Intelligence. There is no reason to commit taxpayer resources to an additional inspector general with competing jurisdiction over the same intelligence elements. Creating duplicative inspectors general, who may have inconsistent views on the handling of particular matters, has the potential to create conflicts and impede the Intelligence Community from efficiently resolving issues and carrying out its core mission. In addition, the creation of a new inspector general would add yet another position in the Intelligence Community subject to Senate confirmation, contrary to the 9/11 Commission's recommendations.

Section 327 of the bill would harm our national security by requiring any element of the Intelligence Community to use only the interrogation methods authorized in the Army Field Manual on Interrogations. It is vitally important that the Central Intelligence Agency (CIA) be allowed to maintain a separate and classified interrogation program. The Army Field Manual is directed at guiding the actions of nearly three million active duty and reserve military personnel in connection with the detention of lawful combatants during the course of traditional armed conflicts, but terrorists often are trained specifically to resist techniques prescribed in publicly available military regulations such as the Manual. The CIA's ability to conduct a separate and specialized interrogation program for terrorists who possess the most critical information in the War on Terror has helped the United States prevent a number of attacks, including plots to fly passenger airplanes into the Library Tower in Los Angeles and into Heathrow Airport or buildings in downtown London. While details of the current CIA program are classified, the Attorney General has reviewed it and determined that it is lawful under existing domestic and international law, including Common Article 3 of the Geneva Conventions. I remain committed to an intelligence-gathering program that complies with our legal obligations and our basic values as a people. The United States opposes torture, and I remain committed to following international and domestic law regarding the humane treatment of people in its custody, including the ``Detainee Treatment Act of 2005."

My disagreement over section 327 is not over any particular interrogation technique; for instance, it is not over waterboarding, which is not part of the current CIA program. Rather, my concern is the need to maintain a separate CIA program that will shield from disclosure to al Qaeda and other terrorists the interrogation techniques they may face upon capture. In accordance with a clear purpose of the ``Military Commissions Act of 2006," my veto is intended to allow the continuation of a separate and classified CIA interrogation program that the Department of Justice has determined is lawful and that operates according to rules distinct from the more general rules applicable to the Department of Defense. While I will continue to work with the Congress on the implementation of laws passed in this area in recent years, I cannot sign into law a bill that would prevent me, and future Presidents, from authorizing the CIA to conduct a separate, lawful intelligence program, and from taking all lawful actions necessary to protect Americans from attack.

Other provisions of the bill purport to require the executive branch to submit information to the Congress that may be constitutionally protected from disclosure, including information the disclosure of which could impair foreign relations, the national security, the deliberative processes of the Executive, or the performance of the Executive's constitutional duties. Section 326, for example, would require that the executive branch report, on a very short deadline and in accordance with a rigid set of specific statutory requirements, the details of highly classified interrogation techniques and the confidential legal advice concerning them. The executive branch voluntarily has provided much of this information to appropriate Members of Congress, demonstrating that questions concerning access to such information are best addressed through the customary practices and arrangements between the executive and legislative branches on such matters, rather than through the enactment of legislation.

In addition, section 406 would require a consolidated inventory of Special Access Programs (SAPs) to be submitted to the Congress. Special Access Programs concern the most sensitive information maintained by the Government, and SAP materials are maintained separately precisely to avoid the existence of one document that can serve as a roadmap to our Nation's most vital information. The executive branch must be permitted to present this information in a manner that does not jeopardize national security. The executive branch will continue to keep the Congress appropriately informed of the matters to which the provisions relate in accordance with the accommodation principles the Constitution contemplates and the executive and legislative branches have long and successfully used to address information sharing on matters of national security.

George W. Bush.
The White House, March 8, 2008.

The SPEAKER pro tempore. The objections of the President will be spread at large upon the Journal, and the veto message and the bill will be printed as a House document.

Mr. LOEBSACK. Madam Speaker, I ask unanimous consent that further consideration of the veto message and the bill be postponed until Tuesday, March 11, 2008.

The SPEAKER pro tempore. Is there objection to the request of the gentleman from Iowa?

There was no objection.

J. INTELLIGENCE ESTIMATES FOR CONGRESS

INTELLIGENCE ESTIMATES: HOW USEFUL TO CONGRESS?

CRS Report for Congress

December 14, 2007

Commentary

The final document provided in this volume, *Intelligence Estimates: How Useful to Congress?*, provides an interesting discussion of the pros and cons of Congress's increased appetite for such assessments. In this report the Congressional Research Service (CRS) questions the actual utility of national Intelligence Estimates (NIE) to Congress. The report acknowledges Congress's ever-increasing interest in NIEs, as the U.S. government's formal intelligence assessments of various critical issues affecting U.S. national security. However, the CRS report prudently cautions that formulation of an NIE is time-consuming and not an exact science. The report also reminds us that any NIE is only as good as the information upon which it is based.

The CRS report also points out that, in many cases, NIEs are produced by the Intelligence Community (IC) without taking into full consideration various diplomatic, economic, military, or legislative initiatives to address the problem under study. Therefore, Congress should be reluctant to legislate based on an NIE, without informing itself of what other agencies of government are doing to address the issues raised therein. The report realistically concludes, nonetheless, that Congress will continue to rely heavily on NIEs.

Still, the CRS believes Congress may find other presentations of national intelligence to be more useful, such as intelligence assessments or briefings prepared in a less structured way and within shorter time periods. Such intelligence exchanges may be more timely and encourage useful dialogue. The CRS report correctly observes that the recently created Office of the Director of National Intelligence (DNI) provides a central resource from which the analytical capabilities of all intelligence agencies can be accessed.

The CRS reasonably concludes that a combination of NIEs on some topics, supplemented by more limited assessments to provide ongoing dialogues with intelligence analysts, may provide the most effective support to the legislative process. The CRS report states that NIEs best serve Congress when they provide thorough assessments of perplexing international issues, present the different perspectives of a number of analysts, and provide a sober assessment of the reliability of the underlying data. In summary, the CRS report quite appropriately concludes that an NIE is a key element of the national security decision-making process but that this report does not always serve well as the sole basis for legislative discussion.

DOCUMENT NO. 11

INTELLIGENCE ESTIMATES: HOW USEFUL TO CONGRESS?

CRS Report
RL33733

December 14, 2007

Richard A. Best Jr.
Specialist in National Defense
Foreign Affairs, Defense, and Trade Division

Summary

National Intelligence Estimates (NIEs) are often of considerable interest to many Members of Congress. They represent the most formal assessment of a given issue by the U.S. Intelligence Community and address issues of major national security importance which may require congressional action. The intelligence process, however, is not an exact science and, on occasion, NIEs have proved unreliable because they were based on insufficient evidence or contained faulty analysis. This was demonstrated in the NIE produced in 2002 on Iraqi Weapons of Mass Destruction, parts of which were significantly inaccurate. NIEs can provide insights into the likely effects of certain policy approaches, but they are not usually made to take into account the details of planned U.S. diplomatic, economic, military, or legislative initiatives.

In the past, Congress was not a principal consumer of NIEs but now appears increasingly interested in obtaining NIEs on crucial security issues despite or perhaps because of the experience with the 2002 Iraq NIE. The FY2007 Defense Authorization Act (P.L. 109-364, section 1213) specifically requested a comprehensive NIE on Iran. In February 2007 the Intelligence Community also released an NIE on *Prospects for Iraq's Stability* in response to a congressional request.

In early December 2007 the Director of National Intelligence released the Key Judgments of a National Intelligence Estimate, *Iran: Nuclear Intentions and Capabilities*. The new NIE judged "with high confidence that in fall 2003,

Tehran halted its nuclear weapons program." Even though the NIE did recognize that "with moderate-to-high confidence that Tehran at a minimum is keeping open the option to develop nuclear weapons," this dramatic release of the Key Judgments on Iran heightened interest in the NIE process and its relevance to policymaking. Some observers assert, however, that public discussion on specific NIEs may not adequately reflect the process by which they are prepared or their inherent limitations.

This report will be updated when new information becomes available.

Background: The Intelligence Community's Most Authoritative Products

National Intelligence Estimates (NIEs) represent the highest and most formal level of strategic analysis by the U.S. Intelligence Community. They are by definition forward-looking; as one participant in the estimative process has written, "Estimates are not predictions of the future. They are considered judgments as to the likely course of events regarding an issue of importance to the nation. Sometimes, more than one outcome may be estimated."[1] NIEs focus on foreign developments; they are not net assessments that directly compare U.S. and foreign capabilities and plans.

The responsibility for producing NIEs rests on the National Intelligence Council (NIC), an entity within the Office of the Director of National Intelligence (DNI).[2] The NIC consists of senior analysts from the Intelligence Community and substantive experts from the public and private sector. After a decision is made to prepare an NIE, terms of reference (TORs) that define the major issues and drafting responsibilities are circulated to relevant intelligence agencies. One or more analysts, either from the ODNI or an intelligence agency, is asked to prepare a draft NIE. The draft estimates is then coordinated by senior officials of all intelligence agencies in a process that can be quite lengthy. Thereafter, NIEs are formally considered by the heads of relevant intelligence agencies and the DNI. The National Security Act requires that NIEs include, "whenever the Council considers appropriate, alternate views held by elements of the intelligence community."[3]

[1] Mark M. Lowenthal, *Intelligence: From Secrets to Policy* (Washington, DC: CQ Press, 2000), p. 88.

[2] For background on the NIC and the National Intelligence Officers, see [http://www.dni.gov/nic/NIC_home.html]. The NIC was established by Director of Central Intelligence (DCI) Stansfield Turner in 1979; a statutory basis was included in the Intelligence Authorization Act for FY1993 (P.L. 102-496, 106 Stat. 3191). Though composed of analysts from various government agencies and the public and private sector, the NIC has always depended heavily on CIA analysts for research and drafting NIEs. The NIC originally reported to the DCI in his role as head of the Intelligence Community, but the Intelligence Reform and Terrorism Prevention Act of 2004 (P.L. 108-458) transferred the NIC to the newly created Office of the DNI. Many, if not most, current NIOs are not CIA career analysts and some observers believe that CIA's preeminent analytical role has diminished. Nevertheless, CIA has the broadest analytical coverage of any agency and the largest number of analysts and is likely to be heavily involved in the preparation of future NIEs.

[3] 50 U.S.C. 403-3(b)(2)(A).

Thus they may contain text, or "footnotes," that pose alternative views from the judgments in the NIE. The conclusions of NIEs, however, are understood to reflect the official position of the DNI.[4] Once approved, the NIE is forwarded to the President, senior policymakers, and the two congressional intelligence committees.

In drafting NIEs, analysts marshal evidence from all sources available to the Intelligence Community–human intelligence, signals intelligence, overhead surveillance, and others including the exploitation of open sources (foreign media and, increasingly, websites). The lengthy drafting and coordination process includes participation by agency analysts and occasionally outside experts with varying perspectives. At their best, NIEs provide a careful assessment of an international situation based on extensive collection and careful analysis that provides policymakers with insights into the opportunities and risks that the United States will face.

In general, NIEs on topics that involve sensitive collection or analysis of trends that are largely unknown to outside experts are the most valuable. On the other hand, NIEs addressing broad topics as the future of democracy in the Middle East or the likely evolution of China in the next 20 years may not necessarily yield more accurate conclusions or more perceptive insights than the work of leading academic experts. Some observers argue that intelligence estimates that deal with such topics inevitably suffer from the absence of scrutiny by the wide and disparate community of scholars that challenges and debates conclusions of scholarly works in the open literature and ultimately has an important influence on public opinion. Most NIEs, on the other hand, describe the environment in which national security policy choices will likely be made in the foreseeable future, with analysis incorporating information that is not available to the general public.

At a minimum, NIEs require that differences among analysts be confronted and described. This is an important contribution as policymakers need to know what is known by the Intelligence Community and what remains unknown and what conclusions drawn by the government's most experienced analysts.

Historically, some NIEs have been essential to national security policymaking. During the Cold War, NIEs on Soviet strategic forces provided an agreed-upon set of figures that were an integral part of plans for U.S. force structures and negotiations of a series of arms control treaties.[5] U.S. policymaking,

[4] Yet according to Robert Gates, then Deputy Director of Central Intelligence, writing in 1987: "More than once, the late Director [of Central Intelligence] William Casey (and probably his predecessors) approved an estimate with which he disagreed personally, and separately conveyed his personal view to policymakers." Robert Gates, "The CIA and American Foreign Policy," *Foreign Affairs*, Winter 1987/1988, p. 227.

[5] In an oft-reported comment in 1967 President Lyndon Johnson stated, "I wouldn't want to be quoted on this but we've spent 35 or 40 billion dollars on the space program. And if nothing else had come

however, occasionally is based on directives by Presidents or senior officials that have not been coordinated throughout the executive branch or with Congress. Some policy makers assume that their own long experience and extensive personal contacts gives them better insights than even the most senior intelligence officials. In considering major new initiatives, there can be an obsessive concern with the potential for leaks that limits discussion to a very small circle of advisers and excludes much of the Intelligence Community which is independent of political appointees.

There are other inherent limitations to the NIE process. NIEs are often prepared on broad issues that may involve not just foreign states or international groups but also the influence of U.S. policy or the interplay of U.S. with foreign actors. Although some NIEs will address the implications of several broad policy options, detailed treatments of U.S. plans have traditionally been defined as beyond the cognizance of intelligence agencies. In many cases, other agencies will have little inclination to share sensitive planning with the substantial number of intelligence analysts involved in the preparation of NIEs. In other cases, U.S. plans will depend more on future initiatives such as legislation that intelligence analysts would be unable to predict with accuracy.

Intelligence agencies are committed—by statute[6] and as a matter of professional integrity—to prepare analyses that are unbiased and nonpartisan. At times the bureaucratic process that produces NIEs can shape the conclusions in ways that reflect agency perspectives; this can be the case, for instance, when intelligence judgments about threat environments have significant implication for U.S. military force structure. Moreover, if NIEs are tied too closely and too publicly to public debates there is a concern that intelligence agencies will either be inclined to emphasize evidence supporting an Administration's preferred policy options or avoid controversial issues.[7]

---

out of it except the knowledge we've gained from space photography, it would be worth 10 times what the whole program has cost. Because tonight we know how many missiles the enemy has and, it turned out, our guesses were way off. We were doing things we didn't need to do. We were building things we didn't need to build. We were harboring fears we didn't need to harbor." Quoted in *Eye in the Sky: the Story of the Corona Spy Satellites*, ed. by Dwayne A. Day, John M. Logsdon, and Brian Latell (Washington: Smithsonian Institution Press, 1998), p. 1. NIEs on the Soviet capabilities have been declassified and published in *Intentions and Capabilities: Estimates on Soviet Strategic Forces, 1950-1983*, ed. by Donald P. Steury (Washington: Center for the Study of Intelligence, 1996).

[6] 50 U.S.C. 403-3(a)(2).

[7] When an Administration is in the process of choosing a policy option there can also be a temptation for intelligence analysts to become advocates; Robert Gates claims that "Far from kowtowing to policymakers, there is sometimes a strong impulse on the part of intelligence officers to show that a policy or decision is misguided or wrong, to poke an analytical finger in the policy eye. Policymakers know this and understandably resent it. To protect the independence of the analyst while keeping such impulses in check is one of the toughest jobs of intelligence agency managers." "The CIA and Foreign Policy," p. 221.

Furthermore, it has been argued that NIEs are not necessarily the most important contribution of intelligence agencies, which produce thousands of assessments of varying complexity in a given year. A 9/11 Commission staff statement noted: "Some officials, including Deputy DCI [Director of Central Intelligence] John McLaughlin, are skeptical about the importance of comprehensive estimates. McLaughlin has been in charge of the estimate process. He told us such estimates are time-consuming to prepare. Judgments are watered down in negotiations. Conclusions may duplicate those already circulated in more specific papers."[8] A review of intelligence on Iraq by senior intelligence officials undertaken for the then-DCI in mid-2004 noted:

> NIEs rarely represent new analysis or bring to bear more expertise than already exists in analytic offices; indeed, drafters of NIEs are usually the same analysts from whose work the NIE is drawn. Little independent knowledge or informed outside opinion is incorporated in estimative products. The preparation of an NIE therefore consists primarily of compiling judgments from previous products and debating points of disagreement. . . .
>
> The fundamental question is whether National Intelligence Estimates add value to the existing body of analytic work. Historically, with few exceptions, NIEs have not carried great weight in policy deliberations although customers have often used them to promote their own agendas.[9]

Congress as a Consumer of NIEs

Pursuant to the National Security Act, NIEs are prepared "for the Government," not just executive branch officials.[10] Accordingly, NIEs are forwarded to the two congressional intelligence agencies (the Senate Select Committee on Intelligence (SSCI) and the House Permanent Select Committee on Intelligence (HPSCI))—and, on occasion, other congressional

---

[8] National Commission on Terrorist Attacks Upon the United States [the 9/11 Commission], *The Performance of the Intelligence Community*, Staff Statement No. 11, p.5. The drafters of the staff statement noted, however, that other officials "stress the importance of such estimates as a process that surfaces and clarifies disagreements. Through coordination and vetting views, the Community comes to collective understanding of the nature of the threat it faces–what is known, unknown, and a discussion of how to close these gaps." Ibid.

[9] Central Intelligence Agency, "Intelligence and Analysis on Iraq: Issues for the Intelligence Community;" July 29, 2004. (The document was the third in a series of reports by the Kerr Group (Richard Kerr, Thomas Wolfe, Rebecca Donegan, and Aris Pappas) to support an internal evaluation of intelligence analysis associated with the war on Iraq. It is available on the CIA website at [https://www.cia.gov/csi/studies/vol49no3/html_files/ Collection_Analysis_Iraq_5.htm].) Some observers believe that the Intelligence Community's greatest contribution may lie in the area of specialized studies or short-term reports that are based on information that only intelligence agencies have acquired and that needs to be analyzed and disseminated within a relatively short time frame. Such analytical products do not, in most cases, provide the basis for an entirely new policy but can have an important influence on the development of policy (or military campaigns). They can contribute invaluable new information and analysis that will shape the policymaking process.

[10] 50 U.S.C. 403-3(b)(2)(A).

committees.[11] Use of NIEs by committees will vary. The two intelligence committees oversee the activities of all intelligence agencies, including their analytical efforts, and thus they review NIEs on a continuing basis. Other committees—especially the armed services and international relations committees—may, along with the intelligence committees, be especially interested in NIEs that deal with issues that directly affect upcoming U.S. foreign and military decisions.

Although usually NIEs have been produced at the request of executive branch officials and have been used primarily by executive branch policy makers, NIEs have at times been the subject of considerable congressional interest.[12] Congress has from time to time informally requested NIEs (as was the case with the NIE on Iraqi WMDs produced in 2002, as discussed below), but the House intelligence authorization bill (H.R. 2082) for the current fiscal year included a provision (section 407) mandating an NIE on global climate change. The Administration has resisted this provision:

> This section sets a harmful precedent. The production of intelligence products on topics of interest to the Executive Branch or Congress should be left to cooperative relationships and established dialogue and should not be reflected in law, particularly in a manner that impinges on the flexibility of IC [Intelligence Community] professionals to approach a task in the most appropriate manner.[13]

Subsequently, the conference report on H.R. 2082 omitted the statutory requirement for an NIE, but noted that the DNI had stated that an assessment on the effects of global climate change was being prepared and the "conferees expect that the national intelligence assessment will be transmitted to Congress in a timely manner."[14]

Congress included a requirement for an NIE on Iran in the FY2007 Defense Authorization Act (P.L. 109-364, section 1213) to be submitted in classified form. The statute also stated that, "Consistent with the protection of intelligence sources and methods, an unclassified summary of the key judgments of the National Intelligence Estimate should be submitted." The Key Judgments of NIE on *Iran: Nuclear Intentions and Capabilities* were released

---

[11] L. Britt Snider, "Sharing Secrets with Lawmakers: Congress as a User of Intelligence," Central Intelligence Agency, Center for the Study of Intelligence, February 1997, p. 24. Snider's monograph although published in 1997 remains the most authoritative analysis of the use of intelligence by the Congress.

[12] For a discussion of extended controversy in 1959 over estimates of Soviet missiles, see David M. Barrett, *The CIA & Congress: the Untold Story from Truman to Kennedy* (Lawrence, KS: University Press of Kansas, 2005), pp. 323-330. In another instance in 1980 Senator Moynihan discussed press disclosures of NIEs regarding an NIE dealing with the strategic balance between the United States and the Soviet Union. *Congressional Record*, May 15, 1980, pp. 11371-11372.

[13] U.S., Office of Management and Budget, *Statement of Administration Policy: H.R. 2082–Intelligence Authorization Act for Fiscal Year 2008*, May 9, 2007.

[14] U.S. Congress, House of Representatives, *Intelligence Authorization Act for Fiscal Year 2008: Conference Report*, H.Rept. 110-478, December 6, 2007, p. 100.

in early December 2007 apparently without prior transmittal to Congress. The accompanying statement by Principal Deputy DNI Donald Kerr stated, without reference to the statute: "The decision to release an unclassified version of the Key Judgments of the NIE was made when it was determined that doing so was in the interest of our nation's security."[15]

Some observers suggest that NIEs could better support congressional deliberations if they were the subject of further hearings by relevant committees. More extensive hearings by relevant committees would provide opportunities for Members to assess the validity of the information on which the NIEs were based and the extent of support for conclusions reached by the drafters of the NIE although there would inevitably be concerns about enlarging the number of persons exposed to highly sensitive intelligence, especially detailed discussion of intelligence sources and methods. Other observers caution, in addition, that making sensitive NIEs the subjects of congressional hearings, especially when an important vote is approaching, could focus media attention on intelligence judgments that are only part of a complex decision-making process. There is a concern that hearings have the potential to undermine the statutory mandate that national intelligence be objective and "independent of political considerations.[16]" It is also possible that the mechanics of an NIE might be misinterpreted, especially the ways in which main and alternate views are set forth and that debate could result in "cherry picking" views that are congenial to one position or another.

NIE production schedules could also be more closely coordinated with the Legislative Branch to ensure that the Intelligence Community addresses major topics on which Congress expects to consider legislation. On the other hand, some observers argue that Congress might draw up lists of NIEs that would overly tax limited analytical resources and infringe on the President's authority to direct the work of the Intelligence Community.

The influence of intelligence assessments on congressional debates offers cautionary lessons. In late 1990, intelligence assessments (albeit not an NIE) concluded that Operation Desert Storm (that became the Persian Gulf War of 1991) would last at least six months and cause many casualties.

> Largely on the basis of these dire predictions several Senators on the SSCI—including its chairman, David L. Boren of Oklahoma—as well as the Armed

---

[15] Statement by the Principal Deputy Director of National Intelligence, Dr. Donald M. Kerr, December 3, 2007. The previous month DNI McConnell had indicated that unclassified key judgments of the Iran NIE would not be released. He explained: "I don't want to have a situation where the young analysts are writing something because they know it's going to be a public debate, or political debate. They should be writing it to call it as it is. I believe that we will be better off in our community if we can do that at a classified level." Remarks by Director of National Intelligence Admiral Michael McConnell at the AIS Journalism Conference, November 13, 2007, Federal News Service Transcript.

[16] 50 U.S.C. 403-3(a)(2).

> Services Committee Chairman, Sam Nunn of Georgia, ultimately voted against the resolution authorizing the President to send troops to the Gulf. Later, when it turned out that coalition forces achieved immediate air superiority and the ground war ended in a matter of days with relatively few American casualties, the Senators who had voted in the negative were understandably upset. Some had lost considerable political support in their home states as a result of their votes. Senator Nunn later said the vote not only had hurt his credibility as chairman of the SASC [Senate Armed Services Committee] but also had removed any thoughts he might have had about running for President, knowing that his vote would have been a "major debating point" in any election campaign. After all, they were Senators supposedly "in the know" and yet appeared to have egregiously misread the situation. Most felt "sandbagged" by the Intelligence Community.[17]

A former staffer was quoted as saying that "the real problem for the committee was that it was never given "blue team" information [information on U.S. military capabilities]. It was never advised, for example, that stealth aircraft were to be used. It was never provided an assessment of our forces versus theirs."[18]

The 2002 NIE on Iraqi WMD

Intelligence analysis is inherently an intellectual activity that requires knowledge, judgment, and a degree of intuition. These qualities are usually not quantifiable nor can they be simply mandated. Erroneous estimates can occur and have occurred in recent years. The history of the Iraq NIE prepared in 2002, *Iraq's Continuing Programs for Weapons of Mass Destruction*, is instructive in this regard. The fact that Iraq had had WMD in the past and had previously used them both against Iran and regime opponents within Iraq was well known. That Iraq had violated agreements made after the conclusion of Desert Storm in 1991 and expelled international inspectors in 1998 was also incontestable. It was also evident that Saddam Hussein's regime had demonstrated no eagerness to comply with more recent mandates of the U.N. and to cooperate with U.N. inspectors.

Because, however, much of the public debate focused on Iraq's then-current WMD capabilities, the leadership of the Senate Intelligence Committee asked for an NIE "on the status of Iraq's programs to develop weapons of mass destruction and delivery system, the status of the Iraqi military forces, including their readiness and willingness to fight, the effects a U.S.-led attack on Iraq would have on its neighbors, and Saddam Hussein's likely response to a U.S. military campaign designed to effect regime change

---

[17] Snider, "Sharing Secrets with Lawmakers," p. 49. Arguably, a full-scale NIE may have been more reliable.

[18] Quoted in ibid., p. 50.

in Iraq."[19] The NIE was requested on an immediate basis. Operating under intense pressure, the NIE was drafted and made available to Congress four weeks later, on October 1, 2002.[20] An unclassified White Paper, containing many of the NIE's judgments, was issued shortly thereafter.[21]

In large measure the NIE reinforced judgments that had previously been made in earlier intelligence products. The NIE maintained:

> Iraq has continued its weapons of mass destruction (WMD) programs in defiance of U.N. resolutions and restrictions. Baghdad has chemical and biological weapons as well as missiles with ranges in excess of U.N. restrictions; if left unchecked, it will probably have a nuclear weapon during this decade.
>
> Baghdad hides large portions of Iraq's WMD efforts. Revelations after the Gulf war starkly demonstrate the extensive efforts undertaken by Iraq to deny information.[22]

There was a consensus of all agencies that the Iraqis were determined to reconstitute their WMD programs and had made some progress in this effort. This judgment was pervasive among intelligence analysts in this country and abroad (indeed even some senior Iraqi military leaders believed Iraq had WMDs). In setting forth the evidence for WMD reconstitution, however, the NIE relied on evidence and analysis that was subsequently determined to be deficient. To a large extent the judgment that Iraq had begun reconstituting its nuclear capabilities depended on information regarding aluminum tubes that most, but not all, agencies judged to be designed for a uranium enrichment effort. There was a fairly wide agreement that Saddam Hussein planned to reconstitute the WMD programs once Iraq got out from under the sanctions regime.

In retrospect, few would deny that Saddam Hussein had not relinquished his ultimate goal of having viable WMD capabilities and his failure to comply with U.N. obligations regarding inspections, but it is clear that the Intelligence Community did not adequately flag the inherent uncertainties of the evidence supporting Iraq's WMD capabilities in mid-2002.[23]

---

19 S.Rept. 108-301, p. 12.

20 A summary was later made public in July 2003; at [http://www.dni.gov/nic/special_keyjudgements.html].

21 The White Paper is available at [https://www.cia.gov/cia/reports/iraq_wmd/Iraq_Oct_2002.pdf].

22 Director of Central Intelligence, *Iraq's Weapons of Mass Destruction Programs*, October 2002, p. 1.

23 Significantly, the NIE did not offer a contrarian case that Saddam Hussein did not have an active WMD program underway and was bluffing. As far as is known, no one in the Intelligence Community made the assessment that Iraq had only minimal WMD capabilities. Apparently no one asked the question posed by Joseph Nye, a former chairman of the National Intelligence Council: "What would it take for this estimate to be dramatically wrong? What could cause a radically different outcome?" Nye noted: "Experts often resist this exercise. Since they know their country or region and have already presented all the plausible scenarios, why waste any effort on scenarios that are by definition highly unlikely? The answer is that such questions help to alert the policymakers to low-probability but high-impact contingencies against which they might plan. It also informs intelligence

Intelligence agencies had provided copious information about Iraqi WMD programs, but ultimately did not reach accurate conclusions. In part, this failure resulted from the difficulty of the target, but it is apparent in retrospect that intelligence officials provided Congress with an over-generalized estimate that relied heavily on widely-accepted judgments (a tendency that has been described as "cognitive bias"), highly limited collection from human sources (and some of this reporting was wrong), and did not offer a better sense of the ambiguities and limitations of the available evidence. In particular, in this view, the Intelligence Community conveyed a sense of dynamism in regard to Iraqi WMD programs that was not justified by evidence available.

This NIE has been much debated. The Senate Intelligence Committee has reported two extensive, and highly critical, assessments of the NIE.[24] In 2004 the Committee concluded that:

> Most of the major key judgments in the Intelligence Community's October 2002 National Intelligence Estimate (NIE), *Iraq's Continuing Programs for Weapons of Mass Destruction*, either overstated, or were not supported by, the underlying intelligence reporting. A series of failures, particularly in analytic trade craft, led to the mischaracterization of the intelligence.[25]

Subsequently, the Commission on the Capabilities of the United States Regarding Weapons of Mass Destruction, headed by Laurence Silberman and former Senator Charles Robb also devoted attention to the NIE's shortcomings.[26]

After the collapse of the Saddam Hussein regime, the Iraq Survey Team, composed of experts from various U.S. agencies looked at all evidence available on the ground in Iraq and did not find evidence that Iraq had an active WMD effort. They did agree that there was a likelihood of reconstitution once sanctions were lifted. The Iraq Survey Team concluded that Saddam Hussein saw many benefits to an ongoing WMD program but was primarily concerned with seeing sanctions lifted. The Team concluded that Saddam Hussein viewed Iran as Iraq's principal enemy in the region and that he believed WMD were necessary to counter Iran.[27]

---

agencies about obscure indicators about which they should be collecting information." Joseph S. Nye, Jr., "Peering into the Future," *Foreign Affairs*, July-August 1994, p. 89.

24 U.S. Congress, 108th Congress, 2d session, Senate, Select Committee on Intelligence, *U.S. Intelligence Community's Prewar Intelligence Assessments on Iraq*, S.Rept. 108-301, July 9, 2004; 109th Congress, 2d session, *Postwar Findings About Iraq's WMD Programs and Links to Terrorism and How They Compare with Prewar Assessments*, September 8, 2006.

25 S.Rept. 108-301, p. 14.

26 See the report of the Commission on the Intelligence Capabilities of the United States Regarding Weapons of Mass Destruction, March 31, 2005.

27 See *Comprehensive Report of the Special Advisor to the DCI on Iraq's WMD with Addendums*, September 2004, Vol. I, pp. 1, 29.

An important question is the extent to which the faulty NIE influenced the congressional vote on the legislation that was enacted as the Authorization for Use of Military Force against Iraq (P.L. 107-243). The NIE made firm judgments about Iraq's *continuing* WMD programs, its links to terrorists, etc., and these judgments were reflected in the legislation.[28]

P.L. 107-243 did not, however, focus solely on WMD; it emphasized a long pattern of Iraqi violations of U.N. resolutions and its "brutal repression of its civilian population thereby threatening international peace and security in the regions." It also cited Iraq's support of terrorist organizations that "threaten the lives and security of United States citizens."[29] A problem for the Intelligence Community was the heavy emphasis on WMD programs in the public debate prior to congressional consideration of the resolution that tended to obscure other factors that were not dependent on technical analyses of highly limited evidence.[30]

NIE on Trends in Global Terrorism, 2006

Also instructive is the more recent NIE, *Trends in Global Terrorism: Implications for the United States*, prepared in April 2006 with the key judgments officially released in September 2006[31] after several accounts had appeared in the media. The NIE's Key Judgments reflected the Intelligence Community's conclusion that the global jihadist movement "is spreading and adapting to counterterrorism efforts." The jihadists, the NIE concluded, "will use improvised explosive devices and suicide attacks focused primarily on soft targets to implement their asymmetric warfare strategy, and that they will attempt to conduct sustained terrorist attacks in urban environments." Much public commentary on the NIE was directed towards its conclusions that the "Iraq conflict has become the 'cause celebre' for

[28] One clause of P.L. 107-243 argued that Iraq "remains in material and unacceptable breach of its international obligations by, among other things, continuing to possess and develop a significant chemical and biological weapons capability, actively seeking a nuclear weapons capability, and supporting and harboring terrorist organizations." Another clause stated: "Whereas Iraq's demonstrated capability and willingness to use weapons of mass destruction, the risk that the current Iraqi regime will either employ those weapons to launch a surprise attack against the United States or its Armed Forces or provide them to international terrorists who would do so, and the extreme magnitude of harm that would result to the United States and its citizens from such an attack, combine to justify action by the United States to defend itself."

[29] In addition to WMD concerns, there has been ongoing controversy on the planning for stabilizing Iraq once Saddam Hussein's military had been overcome and the regime removed; intelligence officials have maintained that estimates of the difficulties involved in this effort were accurate and were detailed prior to the commencement of hostilities. See "Intelligence and Analysis on Iraq," p. 2; also, Paul R. Pillar, "Intelligence, Policy, and the War in Iraq," *Foreign Affairs*, March/April 2006.

[30] See CRS Report RS21696, *U.S. Intelligence and Policymaking: the Iraq Experience*, by Richard A. Best Jr.

[31] Office of the Director of National Intelligence, "Declassified Key Judgments of the National Intelligence Estimate 'Trends in Global Terrorism: Implications for the United States' dated April 2006," [http://odni.gov/press_releases/Declassified_ NIE_Key_Judgments.pdf].

jihadists, breeding a deep resentment of U.S. involvement in the Muslim world and cultivating supporters for the global jihadist movement."

The detailed analysis that supported these conclusions has not been made public, but it worth noting that the NIE does give some generalized attention to policy approaches for the United States and its allies that could affect the future of jihadist terrorism.[32] The NIE referred to the possibility of "greater pluralism and more responsive political systems in Muslim majority nations," and the possibility that jihadists in Iraq will be perceived as having failed. It maintains that countering jihadists will require "coordinated multilateral efforts that go well beyond operations to capture or kill terrorist leaders."[33]

These brief references hardly exhaust the factors that will affect trends in global terrorism over the next decade. The NIE did not apparently address the question that has been the focus of much outside academic analysis—the overall religious and philosophical challenge by radical Islam to Western values. Arguably, a dialogue between Western intellectuals and Islamic leaders could be part of the equation.

The conclusions of this NIE may suggest a number of possible responses. Although NIEs can lay out in general terms the possible ramifications of different options, some observers believe that neither the drafters of the NIE nor the Intelligence Community as a whole should be viewed as best placed to propose alternative approaches for U.S. policy makers. Intelligence analysts can provide tentative assessments of the potential effect of various U.S. initiatives, but, according to this perspective, the full range of options will have to be developed elsewhere. Ultimately, policies are frequently based not only on an appreciation of the international environment and the threat, but also on the capabilities of the United States and its allies and budgetary and political constraints that they face. These latter factors are not the responsibilities of intelligence analysts.

NIE on Prospects for Iraq's Stability, January 2007

Responding to another congressional request, the Office of the Director of National Intelligence forwarded an NIE entitled *Prospects for Iraq's Stability: A Challenging Road Ahead* in January 2007 with unclassified key judgments released to the public.[34] The Key Judgments were accompanied by several pages of text describing the NIE process and an explanation of estimative language. Changes implemented subsequent to the Intelligence Reform

[32] The NIE notes "vulnerabilities in the jihadist movement have emerged that, if fully exposed and exploited, could begin to slow the spread of the movement."
[33] Ibid.
[34] See [http://odni.gov/press_releases/20070202_release.pdf].

Act of 2004 were noted, specifically new procedures to integrate formal reviews of source reporting and technical judgements and the application of more rigorous standards. The document notes that Agency heads are now required to submit "formal assessments that highlight the strengths, weaknesses, and overall credibility of their sources used in developing the critical judgments of the NIE." In addition, a textbox is to be included in future NIEs to explain the meaning of terms such as "we judge" or "we assess" and the differences between high, moderate, and low confidence in various judgments. The use of such terms has occasionally been a source of confusion when they had come to have accepted meanings among analysts that were not well understood by policymakers.

Written at a time of intense congressional concern about the future of Iraq and in response to a congressional request, the NIE's Key Judgments included a finding that the overall security situation in Iraq will continue to deteriorate unless serious efforts are made to reverse existing conditions. The NIE reviewed the various challenges facing the Iraqis–mutually antagonistic ethnic communities, the weakness of Iraqi Security Forces, and the extremist groups such as Al Qaeda that act as "accelerators" of the intersectarian struggle. The NIE maintained that "Coalition capabilities, including force levels, resources, and operations, remain an essential stabilizing element in Iraq." Looking at the regional environment, the NIE noted that although some of Iraq's neighbors provide support that "clearly intensifies the conflict in Iraq," the involvement of outside actors "is not likely to be a major driver of violence or the prospects for stability because of the self-sustaining character of Iraq's internal sectarian dynamics." Undoubtedly, the classified NIE provides the evidentiary background of these judgments and a discussion of the extent of the Intelligence Community's confidence in the NIE's conclusions.

NIE on Iranian Nuclear Intentions and Capabilities

On December 3, 2007 the Office of the Director of National Intelligence released unclassified Key Judgments of a NIE prepared in November 2007, *Iran: Nuclear Intentions and Capabilities*.[35] Donald Kerr, the Principal Deputy DNI stated in a covering memorandum that numerous statements based on a 2005 assessment[36] had been made on the record. "Since our understanding

[35] Available at [http://www.dni.gov/press_releases/20071203_release.pdf].

[36] On January 18, 2007, then-DNI John Negroponte testified to the House Permanent Select Committee on Intelligence: "Our assessment is that Tehran is determined to develop nuclear weapons. It is continuing to pursue uranium enrichment and has shown more interest in protracting negotiations than reaching an acceptable diplomatic solution." Transcript, Hearing of the House Permanent Select Committee on Intelligence Annual Threat Assessment, [http://odni.gov/testimonies/20070118_transcript.pdf].

of Iran's capabilities has changed, we felt it was important to release this information to ensure that an accurate presentation is available."[37]

The Key Judgments of the 2007 NIE state that "We judge with high confidence that in fall 2003, Tehran halted its nuclear weapons program; we also assess with moderate-to-high confidence that Tehran at a minimum is keeping open the option to develop nuclear weapons." The NIE assessed that the program was "was halted primarily in response to international pressure" and argued that this assessment"suggests that Iran may be more vulnerable to influence on the issue than we judged previously."[38]

The dramatic shift in analytical conclusions received extensive attention from the media and Members of Congress given Iranian policies in the region, Iranian President Ahamdinejad's campaign against Israel's legitimacy, and the efforts of the U.S. and European allies to impose sanctions on Iran until it complies with United Nations Security Council demands that it cease uranium enrichment. A factor in the background may have been media reports that a U.S. strike against Iranian nuclear sites had been under consideration.[39] The NIE's Key Judgments did not indicate that Iran had ceased its nuclear efforts but, in the view of some observers, it undermined the urgency of the Administration's efforts.

Few would argue that the conclusions drawn by the NIE should not have been brought to the attention of policymakers in the Executive Branch and Congress, but a number of observers have argued that the Key Judgments overemphasized the importance of the nuclear weapon design and weaponization work at the expense of ongoing uranium conversion and enrichment efforts that would be essential to achieving nuclear weapons capabilities. Dennis Ross, a retired diplomat with long experience in the Middle East, noted: "While nothing has changed, the NIE has created a new story line."[40] According to Ross, the NIE will unwisely focus public attention on nuclear weapons *per se* rather than Iran's larger nuclear effort. He writes:

> Weaponizing is not the issue, developing fissionable materials is. Because, compared with producing fissionable material, which makes up the core of nuclear bombs, weaponizing it is neither particularly difficult nor expensive.[41]

Former Secretary of State Henry Kissinger argued: "we could be witnessing not a halt of the Iranian weapons program—as the NIE asserts—but a

[37] Statement by the Principal DNI, December 3, 2007.

[38] For further discussion of U.S. policy towards Iran, see CRS Report RL32048, *Iran: U.S.Concerns and Policy Responses.*

[39] See, for instance, Tim Shipman, "Will he Bomb . . . or Is He Bluffing? George Bush Has Ramped Up the Rhetoric Against Iran. Is he Serious?", *Sunday Telegraph (London)*, September 2, 2007, p. 15.

[40] Dennis Ross, "The Can't-Win Kids," *The New Republic*, December 11, 2007.

[41] Ibid.

subtle, ultimately more dangerous, version of it that will phase in the warhead when fissile material production has matured."[42]

A focus of the Key Judgments was the assessment Iran ended its nuclear program "in fall 2003"..."primarily in response to international pressure." Observers have noted that the Key Judgments did not indicate whether such "international pressure" included the collapse of Saddam Hussein's regime in April 2003. It is plausible that Iranian officials, like the U.S. Intelligence Community, may have believed that Iraq had WMD capabilities and, when that turned out to be not the case, made a decision that its own nuclear program was no longer necessary. The released Key Judgments do not, however, address this issue.

The NIE's Key Judgments also suggest that "some combination of threats of intensified international scrutiny and pressures, along with opportunities for Iran to achieve its security, prestige, and goals for regional influence in other ways, might–if perceived by Iran's leaders as credible—prompt Tehran to extent the current halt to its nuclear weapons program." This judgment is based on an unacknowledged assumption being that Iran's goals can be accommodated by other countries, including the U.S., if they are pursued without an active WMD program. This crucial issue also is not addressed in the released Key Judgments.

To what extent the release of the Key Judgments of the NIE has changed the "story line" of U.S. policy remains uncertain. Observers suggest that intelligence analysis with all its inevitable uncertainties and ambiguities seldom yields a watertight argument for a new policy. Policy builds upon the factual base that intelligence analysis provides but it is also built upon assessments of our own national interests that are beyond the mandate of the Intelligence Community. Recognizing that any Iranian success in testing a nuclear weapon in the near future would seriously undermine confidence in its core capabilities, the Intelligence Community has presented important evidence about current Iranian nuclear efforts. These facts do not change U.S. interests, but only how they are pursued and how they are explained to the public. Although the "story line" may have to be adjusted, the realities of U.S. interests and the failure of the Iranian regime to abide by its treaty commitments remain.

Conclusion: Useful Products if Limitations Appreciated

Congress is and will continue to be an important consumer of national intelligence, but there are concerns that heavy emphasis on mandating NIEs may not assist the legislative process to the extent that some anticipate.

[42] Henry A. Kissinger, "Misleading the Iran Report," *Washington Post*, December 13, 2007, p. A35.

NIEs can provide the Intelligence Community's best evidence and analysis on major issues of national security and can highlight areas where information is lacking, but they usually require lengthy preparation and coordination before they can be disseminated. The example of the NIE on Iraqi WMD suggests that compressing the production schedule can be counterproductive. Moreover, conclusions of NIEs may not be informed by knowledge of initiatives planned or underway by others in the executive or legislative branches. A more public role for NIEs in debates on national security policy issues could obscure their inherent limitations and distort the discussion of the policy issues.

In some cases, Congress may find intelligence assessments or briefings prepared in a less structured way and within tighter time constraints better serve its legislative needs than formal NIEs. The creation of the Office of the DNI provides a focal point from which the analytical capabilities of all intelligence agencies can be brought to bear on given issues, even ones that are narrowly focused. It is considered likely that a combination of NIEs on some topics, supplemented by more limited assessments supported by an ongoing dialogue with intelligence analysts, may provide the most effective support to the legislative process.

NIEs are only one element of the national security decision-making process. They can outline the effects of various policy approaches in general terms, but it is unlikely that they will become the vehicles for detailed consideration of options that depend on the interrelationships of executive branch and congressional decision making. NIEs will arguably be most useful when they provide a thorough assessment of a given international situation, laying out different perspectives among analysts, and providing a realistic indication of the limitations of the evidence available

SUBJECT INDEX

Doc/Pg

Counterterrorism

Cuba

Cyber Security

Department of Homeland Security

Doc/Pg

Inter-Agency Cooperation

International Cooperation

Iran

Iraq

Islam

Lebanon

Doc/Pg

Legislation – Federal

Middle East

National Security – Threats to

9/11 Commission

North Korea

Nuclear Terrorism

www.ingramcontent.com/pod-product-compliance
Ingram Content Group UK Ltd.
Pitfield, Milton Keynes, MK11 3LW, UK
UKHW051224160926
475595UK00022B/161

9 780195 381016